# Succession, Wills and Probate

## Third edition

*Succession, Wills and Probate* is an ideal textbook for those taking an undergraduate course in this surprisingly vibrant subject, and also provides a clear and comprehensive introduction for professionals. Against an account of the main social and political themes of succession law, the book gives detailed explanations of core topics such as alternatives to wills and the making, altering and revocation of wills. It also explains personal representatives and how they should deal with a deceased person's estate and interpret and implement the will. Gifts may fail, estates may be insolvent or a person may die intestate, without a will at all. Increasingly relatives and others seek to challenge the will, for example on the grounds of the testator's capacity or under the law of family provision.

This third edition is edited, updated and revised to take account of new legislation and case law across all the relevant issues, including a new final chapter dealing with the potentially contentious issues that are becoming more central to professional work in the field of succession.

**Caroline Sawyer** is admitted in England and Wales as a solicitor, and as a Barrister and Solicitor of the High Court of New Zealand, where she practises in Wellington.

**Miriam Spero** is a Solicitor at Stafford Young Jones where she specialises in private client work. She is a member of the Society of Trust and Estates Practitioners and Solicitors for the Elderly.

Routledge
Taylor & Francis Group

LONDON AND NEW YORK

Third edition published 2015
by Routledge
2 Park Square, Milton Park, Abingdon, Oxon OX14 4RN

and by Routledge
711 Third Avenue, New York, NY 10017

*Routledge is an imprint of the Taylor & Francis Group, an informa business*

© 2015 Caroline Sawyer and Miriam Spero

First edition published by Cavendish 1995
Second edition published by Cavendish 1998

*British Library Cataloguing in Publication Data*
A catalogue record for this book is available from the British Library

*Library of Congress Cataloging-in-Publication Data*
Sawyer, Caroline, author.
Succession, wills and probate / Caroline Sawyer, Miriam Spero. – Third edition.
    pages cm
    1. Inheritance and succession–Great Britain. 2. Estate planning–Great Britain. 3. Probate law and practice–Great Britain. I. Spero, Miriam, author. II. Title.
    KD1518.S39 2015
    346.4105'2–dc23                                                2014048753

ISBN: 978-0-415-72052-6 (hbk)
ISBN: 978-0-415-72051-9 (pbk)
ISBN: 978-1-315-70738-9 (ebk)

Typeset in Joanna
by Wearset Ltd, Boldon, Tyne and Wear

MIX
Paper from
responsible sources
FSC® C013604

Printed and bound in Great Britain by CPI Group (UK) Ltd, Croydon, CR0 4YY

# Outline Contents

# Detailed Contents

# List of Figures

# Preface

Despite the growth in recent years of litigation over wills, whether disputing the testator's capacity to make the will or arguing about its contents, the subject of succession is still not appreciated for the lively arena that it is. The law has to find a solution for the fundamental problem of the acquisition of individual wealth – you cannot take it with you when you go – and succession law is the substance and the mechanism for dealing with that.

The game of succession law plays out against a background of the big social issues. One could prohibit inheritance of wealth entirely: that would clearly have major social effects. The law of England and Wales is towards the other end of the spectrum, with no compulsory gifts on death to family members, as is often the case in other countries. But testamentary freedom is limited by potential claims against the estate by family members or dependants who were not reasonably provided for, not to mention the claims of Her Majesty's Revenue and Customs. And the definition of eligible family members has moved with the rapid social changes of recent years, but still remains contentious.

For the individual, ownership of property represents success, security and power. On death, a person is forced to give everything away; the recipients of gifts may be able to pay off debts and live more comfortably, or they may be able to buy life-changing chances such as education or take potentially profitable business risks. The power to change people's lives is literally within the gift of the will-maker, and they may wish to extend the power that goes with their property beyond the grave. One relative may be favoured over another, or cut out entirely; gifts may be conditional on certain actions. Trusts may be set up so the deceased can direct the use of their property, and influence or control their friends and relations, for many years after their death.

The machinery of wills is just as intriguing. There must be ways of interpreting and implementing the testator's words when the question will arise only once they are dead and cannot be asked. Gifts may have been left to people who cannot be identified or found, or who have died. It may be unclear whether a partner is the one they had at the date of the will or the one they were with when they died. Children used to mean those of a marriage, but now potentially includes those who would previously have been considered entirely unrelated, but leaving a list of names risks further births and the testator's death before the will is changed. And the formalities of will-making protect against fraud, but may produce mistakes that need resolution.

The stories of succession case law are no less interesting than other areas of law, and some are true entertainment. Anyone who is interested in families, or in property and tax, or mental capacity – or just how to state your wishes clearly – will find much to amuse in this subject. In the midst of death, all human life is there.

# Table of Cases

# Table of Statutes

# Table of Statutory Instruments

# Chapter 1

# History

The history of any legal topic explains its structure as well as its odder phrases and references. In the common law system especially, laws deal with changing whatever came before, and so are easier to understand when one has some idea what that was. Succession law deals with the big issues of property and death, and those bring deeply-rooted social and cultural assumptions whose traces may persist in the law long after the conditions that shaped them, as well as resulting legal rules, have changed entirely.

## 1.1  Why study the history of succession law?

Who gets someone's property when they die is not a new question, and the issues in succession law today all have roots in the depths of history. Just as with institutions such as government or education, the study of the history of the law may provide explanations of how particular principles arose. Once the roots of the current law are clear, that law itself may become more apparently logical – or at least explicable.

## 1.2  Underlying issues remain the same: the old solutions may be the best ones

Live issues in succession today include, for example, the division of the deceased's property on intestacy (dying without a will), something which has been governed by rules since the first laws of this country were made in Anglo-Saxon times, and also the use of the law to override a testator's will and restrict his testamentary freedom.[1] The effects of the family provision legislation of today, which enable a claim to be made against the estate of a relative who did not leave much to the claimant, may look very like the reintroduction of the ancient principles whereby a person could dispose of only of a part of his personal property as he wished; the extension of the rules of family provision to the estates of intestates by the Intestates' Estates Act of 1952 echoes the proclamations of King Canute, who in the late eleventh century proclaimed that on intestacy property should be 'distributed very justly to the wife and children and relations, to everyone according to the degree that belongs to him'.[2]

---

1  Dorothy Whitelock, ed. and trans., *Anglo-Saxon Wills* (Cambridge University Press 1920/2011); Michael M Sheehan, *The Will in Medieval England: From the Conversion of the Anglo-Saxons to the End of the Thirteenth Century* (Vol. 6, Pontifical Institute of Mediaeval Studies 1963).
2  'Canute, King of the English Inheritance in Case of Intestacy, c.1016–1035' in Benjamin Thorpe, ed., *Ancient Laws and Institutes of England* (Eyre & Spottiswoode 1840).

## 1.3 Some things are gone forever

Some things have their roots in ideas that go back perhaps before the Norman Conquest of 1066.[3] Some things, on the other hand, have changed considerably. The rules of inheritance of land and personalty (property other than land) have been aligned. The rise of commerce and the increasing use of credit brought about changes in the role of a deceased person's personal representatives and their obligations to deal with his debts as well as his property. The principle of gender distinction has steadily been removed. These basic changes are most unlikely to be reversed.

## 1.4 Land and personalty

Historically, the division between land and personalty was fundamental. The inheritance of each has a separate history: they devolved under different rules of intestacy in England until 1926, and indeed the difference persisted in the Scottish law of intestacy until 1964.[4] Generally, it is said that the common law dealt with the devolution of land, and the ecclesiastical courts had jurisdiction over personalty; it has been suggested that the roots of the division do, however, lie further back, in Germanic laws which show the same dichotomy. The law governing the devolution of land was itself divided; various strands of law might combine to act differently on different parcels of land so that they did not all devolve alike, but varied in accordance with the tenure of the land, the prevailing customary law and the nature of the deceased's family relationships.

## 1.5 Land

Before the Norman Conquest of 1066, land was in most parts of England divided equally amongst the sons on the father's death. It was not permissible for a father to give more of his land to one son than another. In theory this did not stop him giving property outside the family, but rules grew up to prevent this. In the years following the Conquest, after a brief period during which realty was devisable by will and despite the reputed statement of William the Conqueror that 'I will that every child be his father's heir',[5] the rule of primogeniture ('the first-born') began to hold sway. This held that the eldest son took all his father's land to the exclusion of any younger brothers (and, of course, all sisters). The Anglo-Saxon rules determining who took a division of the inheritance were replaced by new rules for determining who the heir was who would inherit realty. The right to inherit never ascended lineally – parents could not inherit – but descended to the issue (children and remoter direct descendants) of the last person seised of the land.[6] Male issue had priority over female issue, and where there was more than one male, the eldest took alone, though females took together. Thus, if there was a son, or an eldest son, he took all his father's real property. The landowner's ancestor was represented by his lineal descendants; if this line failed, there was procedure for ascertaining the collateral heir.[7]

Once the demand of maintaining equality amongst the sons had gone, the reason for restricting alienation went too, so that by 1200 land had become freely alienable during a man's lifetime. There were also more lenient rules governing the passing of land that had been purchased rather than inherited. By the thirteenth century, the courts were resisting attempts to disguise

---

3 Brian Dowrick and Meryl Thomas, 'The Origin of Legitim in English Law: A reappraisal' (2014) 1 Journal on European History of Law 85.

4 Administration of Estates Act 1925; Succession (Scotland) Act 1964 (note that this book does not deal with the law of Scotland, which is very different from that of England and Wales discussed here).

5 Writ of William I in favour of the City of London, 1066. Note that 'heir' is a term of art; for more, see 11.2.3.

6 'Seisin' meant the type of possession that, until the twenty-first century, underlay the claim to legal title to land.

7 Linda Tollerton, *Wills and Will-Making in Anglo-Saxon England* (York Medieval Press 2011).

heirs as purchasers in order to avoid the rules against the alienation of land. It was not until the Inheritance Act of 1833, however, that ascendants as well as descendants were allowed to inherit. That Act replaced the old rules for ascertaining the heir with a simpler system, based on descendants, parents, siblings and their issue, grandparents and lastly the siblings of parents and more remote collaterals. The roots of the 1925 legislation, with its emphasis on the exclusion of inalienable interests in land, can be clearly seen in the history of the devolution of land.

## 1.6 Personalty

It was traditional for the personal property of a man who left a widow and children to be divided into three (or two, where the deceased left only a widow or only children), with his widow and children taking their parts and the remaining 'dead's part' being for him to distribute as he wished. This custom of the dead's part may even originate in the pagan custom of burying part – often a third – of the deceased's property with him to smooth his way in the underworld; reinterpreted under Christianity, this way of ensuring the safety of the soul of the deceased became construed as the making of charitable gifts on death.

By the thirteenth century, the church had assumed jurisdiction over the inheritance of chattels, and the making of a will expressing charitable gifts was regarded as an important religious duty almost equivalent to making a final confession of sins. There were customary rules as to the division of the chattels, a common scheme being the 'tripartite division' mentioned above, which persisted in London, Wales and Yorkshire until as late as the eighteenth century, and is perhaps echoed in the twentieth century judge-made 'rule' for the distribution of property between husband and wife on divorce.[8] The 'dead man's part' might be considered the origin of testamentary freedom, which has a more limited history than is sometimes supposed.[9]

## 1.7 Wills

Wills of a sort were made in the Anglo-Saxon period, but they were irrevocable and, probably, not ambulatory. Thus, once the testator had by his 'last words' made a will, he could not retract it and was probably also obliged to carry it out immediately, rather than retaining the property until death. He might, however, make a so-called 'post-obit gift', or an immediate gift of personalty but with the retention of the use of the chattels until death. Wills of land were not usually possible at all; in any case, it was considered proper for land to devolve in accordance with the customary rules of inheritance. Gradually, wills in writing evolved, stating what the testator considered would be his last words when the time came; the church did not insist on any formalities, given that the potential for technical defects could only open the way to sinful intestacies.[10]

After the Norman Conquest, the Anglo-Saxon forms of written wills disappeared, though the 'last words' remained. A century and a half later, however, a new form of written will appeared, owing much to the rediscovery of Roman law at the dawn of the Middle Ages. The ecclesiastical courts favoured testation rights in respect of both land and personalty, and would recognise and enforce wills of either, but the common law courts of the king did not accept devises of land; this devolved in accordance with a system which protected the rights of the feudal barons.[11]

---

8  See *Wachtel v Wachtel* (1972) and Lord Denning's explanation of the 'one-third' rule.
9  Henry Swinburne and Sarah Jennings Churchill, *A Treatise of Last Testaments and Wills* (BiblioBazaar first published 1813, reprint 2010).
10  Harold J Berman, *Law and Revolution: The Formation of the Western Legal Tradition* (Harvard University Press 1983) 234.
11  Miriam Anderson and Esther Arroyo i Amayuelas, eds, *The Law of Succession: Testamentary Freedom: European Perspectives* (Europa Law Publishing 2011).

The common law courts began to oust the jurisdiction of the ecclesiastical courts in respect of land, save in certain parts of the country where particular privileges operated, for example Kent and the City of London.[12]

## 1.8 Uses

In the centuries following the Norman Conquest, 'uses' developed to avoid the difficulties with the Crown's refusal to accept devises of land. Uses were a device by which the landowner passed the legal ownership of his land to grantees, retaining the use of the land during his lifetime and giving directions by will as to the use of it thereafter, thus bypassing the control of the common law courts over the inheritance of land. These directions would be enforced after his death by the Court of Chancery, until the Statute of Uses 1535 abolished uses altogether. This proved very unpopular, and was one of the sources of the uprising known as the 'Pilgrimage of Grace',[13] and in 1540 the Statute of Wills allowed certain forms of land tenures to be devised; in 1542 the scope of the Statute was widened by an Act Concerning the Explanation of Wills, and a further development of 1660 meant that estates in fee simple could be devised without restriction.[14]

## 1.9 Formalities

The Statute of Wills 1540 brought in a requirement of writing, but only for wills of land. The formalities were made stricter by the Statute of Frauds of 1677, which required wills of land to be signed by the testator and witnessed by three credible witnesses. A beneficiary under the will was not a credible witness and could therefore cause the will to fail if he attested – the current position, where a witness-beneficiary's gift, rather than the will, fails dates from 1752.[15] Nuncupative (oral) wills of personalty, unless the estate was worth no more than £30, had to be made in the testator's last illness in the house where he had lived for the previous ten days, witnessed by three witnesses and committed to writing within six days unless proved within six months.

The requirements as to formalities varied with the nature of the property disposed of in the will, and were not always easily understood. This was one of the principal reasons for the passing of the Wills Act of 1837, which, with various amendments, remains in force today. It still reflects the exclusion from the provisions relating to formalities for soldiers and sailors which existed in the earlier legislation.

## 1.10 Married women: dower and curtesy

After 1660, when a man became fully able to devise his real property, that freedom was nevertheless restricted by his wife's right of dower. This gave her one-third of his freehold property. However, by the Dower Act of 1833, the husband was enabled to defeat the right of dower by alienation or by declaring in a deed or a will that he overrode the right. A married woman could not devise realty, and could dispose of her personalty only with the continuing consent of her husband and in certain other limited circumstances; the restrictions on her under the Statute of

---

12  David Hughes Parry, *The Law of Succession Testate and Intestate* (Sweet and Maxwell 1972).
13  EW Ives, 'The Genesis of the Statute of Uses' (1967) 82 English Historical Review 325.
14  Lord Hardwicke's Wills Act 1752.
15  Tenures Abolition Act 1660.

Frauds 1677 were continued under the Wills Act 1837 and not removed until the Married Women's Property Acts of 1881 and 1893. The Acts also gave the wife a right to defeat her husband's right of curtesy, which was his equivalent of dower; his entitlement was to a life interest in all her real property, subject to certain conditions.

## 1.11 Executors

The church, which encouraged charitable giving, viewed the appointment of an executor as a religious duty almost as important as the making of the will itself. The history of the executor, who carries through the terms of a will, began with the role of the person to whom the testator gave his 'dead's part' for distribution. In the absence of an executor, the heir at common law could obtain the deceased's property without any obligation to make charitable gifts; the church would have to rely on its powers of persuasion over him. From the thirteenth century, the ecclesiastical courts had jurisdiction over the validity of wills and required the testator's will to be proved immediately on his death. The courts acted in the person of the bishop, or 'ordinary', to whom the property of an intestate also passed.

## 1.12 Intestacy

The traditional division of property amongst a deceased's family customarily applied on intestacy, but was subject to competing claims from the church and the king. Intestacy is first mentioned under King Canute, in laws which appear to uphold the customary distribution of the intestate's property amongst his widow and children. William the Conqueror appears to have confirmed that the king would not lay claim to the chattels of an intestate, though there is doubt as to whether this promise was adhered to. The intestate's property was often regarded as forfeit. By the time of Magna Carta (1215), however, the barons had given up their claim to the property of the intestate and it was distributed amongst the deceased's family by the church. The ecclesiastical courts thus oversaw the distribution of personalty on intestacy as well as succession to personalty by will.

## 1.13 Administrators

By a law of 1285, the same obligation was imposed on the ordinary in respect of an intestate's debts as on an executor for the debts of a testator.[16] Problems arose, however, where the estate of an intestate was administered by his family, for example, rather than the ordinary, who merely oversaw the administration. Creditors had no way of enforcing payment of the deceased's debts against the family members. In 1357, the ordinary became obliged to appoint administrators and they were in turn obliged to deal with the debts of the estate. The administrators were also empowered to sue on behalf of the intestate's estate. However, the common law courts so obstructed the overseeing of the administration by the church that eventually there was no enforceable obligation on the administrators to make a proper distribution once the debts had been met, until Parliament endeavoured to remedy the situation by the Statute of Distributions of 1670.

The Statute of Distributions prescribed the distribution of the personality of an intestate, setting out a different scheme of ascertaining the entitled beneficiaries from that operating for

---

16 Earl Finbar Murphy, 'Early Forms of Probate and Administration: Some Evidence Concerning Their Modern Significance' (1959) 3 American Journal of Legal History 125.

realty. The heir could be included in the list of next of kin, who took a share unless the deceased left both widow and children. In that case, the widow took one-third and the children two-thirds; if the deceased left only children, they took the whole estate; and if a widow only, then she took half, with the other half going to the next of kin. The medieval London rule of hotchpots was incorporated into the Statute of Distributions and its remains were buried only at the end of the twentieth century.

## 1.14 Lay courts

The Court of Probate was established in 1857. It was a lay court to which the jurisdiction over probate and administration was transferred from the ecclesiastical courts. In the 1870s, the Supreme Court of Judicature Acts transferred jurisdiction over all testamentary matters to the Probate, Divorce and Admiralty Division of the High Court. A century later, this was abolished, when the High Court was re-established with its three divisions of Queen's Bench, Chancery and Family. The Family Division retains jurisdiction over probate matters; contentious matters of construction are assigned to the Chancery Division.

## 1.15 Conflicts of laws, international and regional law and the global context

Although succession law is generally an aspect of a country's property law, a deceased person may have cross-border links that raise questions about which country's law should be applied to the devolution of certain property or how the estate overall should be dealt with. In an increasingly global age, where many people also have considerable personal wealth, such questions about the conflict of laws are becoming more common. The Hague Convention on the Law Applicable to the Estates of Deceased Persons of 1989 was passed to determine what law is applicable (rather than to deal with any formalities or substantive rights). It relies on the country of nationality or habitual residence of the deceased, or with which they had a notably close relationship, or which they had designated. States have shown little interest in this Convention.

Wealthy persons have, however, continued to cross boundaries with their money and to die leaving disputes behind them. If the deceased has used cross-border matters to head off a tax inspectorate during their lifetime, those are likely to complicate attempts to unravel their affairs. Unravelling any single matter, requiring as it does to be done in the context of the deceased's whole estate, is likely to be enmeshed by its own enquiries. The estate of the late Boris Berezovsky, for example, inherited his disputes with Aeroflot, and large sums were claimed in the continuing litigation, but the solvency of the estate was disputed, contributing to a lack of certainty or clarity as to what steps to take and who should take them.[17] The wealthy increasingly use offshore trusts in tax havens to avoid unwanted interference with testamentary freedoms as well as taxation, and the legacy of the British export of legal systems, as well as the number of wealthy people living in Britain, means that those cases may form part of the UK's jurisprudence.[18]

The European Convention on Human Rights, however, has begun to be used in the context of probate matters. Contested issues include the status of children to be included in inheritance provisions and the speed at which the legal system enables or requires probate to be granted and administered.

---

17  *Aeroflot v Berezovsky* (2013).
18  See for example *Schmidt v Rosewood Trust Limited* (Isle of Man) (2003).

## 1.16  Summary of Chapter 1

### History

All societies with even the most rudimentary form of individual property must have some way for their members' property to be dealt with when they die. That involves questions about the nature of individual property and the nature of the claims of different persons on that property. The rules of any society – its laws and customs – will prescribe when and how far a person can control his property, and sometimes, with it, other people, from beyond the grave.

Many systems do not allow testamentary freedom. Often in ancient societies the deceased's property was automatically divided amongst his family, subject to a certain amount which was reserved for spiritual purposes. For example, in certain ancient cultures it was buried with him, or under Christianity in Europe it was supposed to be left for charitable purposes. With the beginnings of the separation of church and state the part left to charity became the part a person could leave as he wished. In many systems of law the ability to leave your property as you wish is still curtailed by law, particularly by the demand that parts of it are divided amongst the family. In England, however, in theory there are no such demands, though this is much more recent than many people think.

The devolution of property was historically different according to whether it was land or personal property that was being dealt with. The systems were, in broad terms, governed and administered by the Crown and church respectively. The administration of the deceased's personal estate was originally carried out by the church, but it passed gradually into the hands of the deceased's family, being overseen at first by the church and then by the lay court.

The system of making wills and setting out what the deceased wanted to happen to his property evolved from the Anglo-Saxon spoken word to the formalities laid down by the Statute of Frauds of 1677, which required a will, in most circumstances, to be in writing. However, the formalities required for wills differed according to the type of property involved until they were unified under the Wills Act 1837, which remains the basis for the current law. All restrictions on testamentary freedom were gradually removed by the end of the nineteenth century, when such freedom did exist until it was limited by the introduction of family provision legislation just before the Second World War.

## 📖 1.17  Further reading

### Books

Miriam Anderson and Esther Arroyo i Amayuelas, eds, *The Law of Succession: Testamentary Freedom: European Perspectives* (Europa Law Publishing 2011).

Harold J Berman, *Law and Revolution: the Formation of the Western Legal Tradition* (Harvard University Press 1983).

Linda Tollerton, *Wills and Will-Making in Anglo-Saxon England* (York Medieval Press 2011).

### Journal articles

EW Ives, 'The Genesis of the Statute of Uses' (1967) 82 English Historical Review 325.

Earl Finbar Murphy, 'Early Forms of Probate and Administration: Some Evidence Concerning Their Modern Significance' (1959) 3 American Journal of Legal History 125.

# Chapter 2

# Will Substitutes

There are good reasons for not wanting to leave all your property by will. An important reason for not doing so, for many people, is the tax implications. Inheritance Tax is charged on the total value of the property the deceased owned at the moment before their death, with certain exemptions, so keeping the property until then, given that the deceased cannot take it with them, often means giving at least part of it to HM Revenue and Customs.

There are various ways in which a person may pass on their property without leaving it by will.[1] The obvious method is give it away during lifetime; this, if done sufficiently long before death, may have tax advantages. Death may effect a gift arrangement only partly completed during the deceased's lifetime. Property held on a beneficial joint tenancy will pass automatically to the other joint tenant or tenants; for the deceased's interest under a beneficial joint tenancy to pass under their will or intestacy to someone other than the other joint tenant or tenants, the joint tenancy must have been severed by one of the various methods available during the lifetime of the deceased, as it cannot be severed by will. A person may make a 'deathbed gift' of property or they may nominate it to another during their lifetime or deal with it through pension or life assurance arrangements. They may also contract to leave their property by will; such a contract may be enforceable. Sometimes, a person may succeed by virtue of statute to a social right, such as the right to continue a council tenancy, by virtue of their personal relationship to the deceased.

## 2.1 Lifetime gifts

Lifetime gifts differ from gifts on death not merely because that they are made whilst the donor is still alive. The transfer of ownership requires different formalities when it is made *inter vivos* (between living persons) from when it is made by means of a will. A gift of a chattel is made *inter vivos* by physical delivery of the chattel with the intention of making a gift. A gift of land *inter vivos* must generally be made by deed to be effective at law,[2] and for the requirements for registration to be complied with.

### 2.1.1 Capacity and intention

The transferor must have the appropriate capacity and intention to make the gift, and the degree or extent of understanding required is relative to the circumstances of the particular transaction. In *Re Beaney* (1978) the transferor in question was the mother of three children, namely Valerie, Peter and Gillian. The mother became ill and Valerie returned home to look

---

1 John H Langbein, 'The Nonprobate Revolution and the Future of the Law of Succession' (1984) 97 Harvard Law Review 1108.
2 S 52 Law of Property Act 1925.

after her. She looked after her mother for two years before the mother executed a deed making over her house to her. A fortnight later, the mother was admitted to a hospital for the mentally ill, where she eventually died intestate about a year later. The gift of the house was challenged in the courts by Peter and Gillian, and the court held that the mother had not had the necessary capacity to make the gift, so it fell into her estate and was shared between the three children equally.

## 2.1.2 Undue influence and lifetime gifts

If a person has used undue influence to obtain a gift from another that will negate the gift. The undue influence may be actual or presumed. A presumption of undue influence may arise in certain situations, which will give rise to a resulting trust in favour of the donor where there might otherwise have appeared to be a gift. This situation may arise 'where two persons stand in such a relation that ... confidence is necessarily reposed by one, and the influence which naturally grows out of that confidence is possessed by the one, and this confidence is abused...'[3] for example, a lawyer and client[4] or parent and child.[5]

In such a situation, the recipient cannot be allowed to retain their advantage. In *Allcard v Skinner* (1887), a nun had left her personal fortune to her convent. She had been under a duty of obedience to her Mother Superior, and in the circumstances of the case the court held that the Mother Superior had had undue influence over her. That finding of undue influence would have negated the gift had the claimant not left it so long before bringing her claim that the court also held her claim barred by the equitable doctrine of laches. The point in this case that there need be no deliberate attempt to abuse the personal relationship later came to the fore in the series of cases heard by the House of Lords in the judgment in *Royal Bank of Scotland Plc v Etridge (No 2)* (2001). Those cases concerned however the granting of security over jointly owned property to secure the debts of only one party, and focused on the making of the mortgage contracts and the third-party lenders' obligations.

Undue influence may arise in respect of a lifetime gift even where there is no presumption, if it can be shown by evidence. In *Re Craig, Meneces v Middleton* (1971), where a man of gentle disposition in his eighties took on a secretary of somewhat stronger character and gave her £28,000 of his estate of £40,000 during his last five years of life, the court found that the gifts had been the result of her undue influence over him and set them aside.

Undue influence is, however, something quite specific, and different from showing that a person's liking for their donee is (at least in the eyes of the disappointed relatives) unaccountable. In *In the Estate of Brocklehurst* (1978), the Court of Appeal considered the grant by an autocratic landowner of a 99-year lease to a small garage proprietor with whom he had been on good terms. The grant was made after the date of the landowner's last will, made when he was 87 years old, and some six months before his death. The court held that the gift might be eccentric, but that a person of sound mind is entitled to make eccentric gifts, and it did not find that there had been any undue influence. Lord Bridges said:

> The court should take full account of all that is known of the donor's character and attitudes. There is no warrant for the adoption of an objective test of motivation by putting a hypothetical ordinary man in place of the donor and asking how he would have been expected to act.

---

3 Per Lord Chelmsford LC in *Tate v Williamson* (1886).
4 *Willis v Barron* (1902).
5 *Roberts and Another v Pascal* (2009).

There is no presumption of undue influence in respect of gifts by will, but undue influence may be found on the facts (see 4.8).

### 2.1.3 Presumption of advancement

The presumption of advancement meant that certain transactions were to be considered gifts rather than giving rise to a resulting trust in favour of the donor if they were between certain categories of persons. These included, in particular, gifts from husband to wife (but not wife to husband), or father (but not mother) to child. The presumption of advancement from husband to wife but not the other way about was decried in *Pettitt v Pettitt* (1970), a constructive trust case where the husband claimed an interest in the wife's property, but applied in *Harwood v Harwood* (1991), a more directly matrimonial matter, in order to explain the decision of the court in that case. *Shephard v Cartwright* (1955) was about fathers and children: a father bought shares in the names of his children in 1929. During the 1930s, he sold them, and put the proceeds into the children's bank accounts. He subsequently withdrew the money and did not account for it. It was held by the court that he could not rebut the presumption of advancement of a gift by a father to his children. Lord Denning in *Falconer v Falconer* (1970) described the presumption of advancement as having 'no place, or, at any rate, very little place, in our law today', but its eventual abolition still gave rise to considerable academic criticism.[6]

Section 199 of the Equality Act 2010 abolished the presumption of advancement but the abolition does not apply to anything done before the section came in to force or anything done pursuant to any obligation incurred before it came into force on 1 October 2010.

## 2.2 Formalities

The formalities required to make a lifetime gift are very different from those required for a gift by will.

### 2.2.1 Delivery of personalty

A gift of most forms of personal property may be, and usually is, effected by delivery of the property. Where, however, some symbol of the property is given – for example, the key to a box – that will suffice. This rule appears to originate in practical considerations. The court in *Chaplin v Rogers* (1800) said:

> When goods are ponderous, and incapable ... of being handed over from one to another, there need not be an actual delivery; but it may be done by that which is tantamount, such the delivery of the key ... or by delivery of other indicia of property.

It appears, however, that whether or not property is capable of physical delivery, symbolic delivery will suffice, but that there must be some unequivocal delivery. The claim of a bankrupt's wife in *Re Cole* (1963) to the furniture she had been told was now hers failed because the Court of Appeal held the property still belonged to her husband. He had not made a deed nor sold the furniture to her, and when they were living together in the house it could not be said that the furniture had been delivered to her. The rules for *inter vivos* gifts could be compared to those for the making of *donationes mortis causa* (see 2.6).

---

6 Kelvin Low 'Presumption of Advancement: A Renaissance?' (2007) 123 Law Quarterly Review 347; Glister 'Section 199 of the Equality Act 2010: How Not to Abolish the Presumption of Advancement' (2010) 73 Modern Law Review 807.

## 2.2.2 Transfer of particular kinds of personalty
Certain sorts of personal property need to be dealt with in accordance with particular rules.

## 2.2.3 Cheques
Cheques must have gone through the bank account of the person who drew the cheque before the gift can be said to be complete. In *Re Swinburne* (1926), the Court of Appeal, categorising a cheque as an order for the delivery of money, held that it did not constitute an assignment of the money in the hands of the banker but only an authorisation for the cheque-holder to obtain the money from the bank.

## 2.2.4 Stocks and shares
Securities are usually transferred by using a form of stock transfer prescribed by statute. The usual stock transfer form requires a signature only, the Stock Transfer Act 1963 stating specifically at s 1(2) that a stock transfer need not be attested. Section 770(1) of the Companies Act 2006 sets out that

> A company may not register a transfer of shares in or debentures of the company unless,
> (a)  a proper instrument of transfer has been delivered to it, or
> (b)  the transfer –
>     (i)  is an exempt transfer within the Stock Transfer Act 1982 (c 41), or
>     (ii)  is in accordance with regulations under Chapter 2 of this Part.

Therefore, depending on the type of security, the transfer is therefore not complete until the transferee has sent both the signed transfer form and the share certificate to the company and the transaction has been registered.

## 2.2.5 Transfer of equitable interests
A transfer of an equitable interest is governed by s 53(1)(c) of the Law of Property Act 1925, which states that a disposition of an existing equitable interest must be in writing. The rationale behind this is that otherwise, if oral transactions were allowed, trustees could not be sure who was the real beneficiary. The only situation in which this does not apply is where the trust is a bare trust; the rationale for the requirement is irrelevant where the beneficiary can control the legal interest as well as the beneficial interest.[7]

## 2.2.6 Creation and disposition of equitable interests in land
Dealings with equitable interests in land are governed by s 53(1) of the Law of Property Act 1925. This states that dealings with equitable interests in real property must be in writing and signed, or made by will. It is expressly stated in s 53(2) that this rule does not affect the creation or operation of resulting, implied or constructive trusts.

## 2.2.7 Transfer of a legal estate or interest in land
A deed is generally required to deal with a legal estate or legal interest in real property (s 52 of the Law of Property Act 1925). The formalities required for deeds have changed a good deal over

---

7  *Vandervell v Inland Revenue Commissioners* (1967).

time, even though they may appear to be the essence of legal transactions. Before 1926, the making of a deed called for the deed to be in writing on paper or parchment, sealed by each of the parties and then delivered. The 1925 legislation added the requirement that the deed be signed. 'Signed, sealed and delivered' became a well-known phrase, but the Law of Property (Miscellaneous Provisions) Act 1989 s 1 implemented the recommendations of the Law Commission in its Working Paper No 93 *Transfers of Land: Formalities for Deeds and Escrows* by abolishing the need for sealing, and requiring the intention to make a deed to be apparent from its face. The phrase 'signed as a deed' therefore replaced both the recitation of 'signed, sealed and delivered' and the sticky red discs to which the seal had been reduced (save for companies). Attestation (witnessing), which was compulsory in registered conveyancing and common practice for all deeds, also became compulsory, though only one signature is usually required.

## 2.2.8 Gifts not properly made

The general rule is that where the gift is not properly made, it will not be perfected in equity because equity will not assist a volunteer. However, in certain situations, death itself may finally effect a gift (see *donationes mortis causa* at 2.6 and the rule in *Strong v Bird* (1874) at 2.7).

# 2.3 Nominations

A person may make a written nomination of certain types of investments which operates only at their death even though it is not a will. The nomination directs the person holding the relevant funds on his behalf to pay the funds to a named person on their death.

The original scheme was intended to avoid the need for those with little property to incur the expense of making a will. As the court in *Eccles Provident Industrial Co-operative Society Ltd v Griffiths* (1912) explained, it worked by giving the nominee a right to claim the relevant money from, in that case, the society, if the nominator died without having revoked the nomination.

Nominations may be non-statutory, which will usually mean those operating under pension schemes, or they may be statutory. Statutory nominations may be of sums not exceeding £5,000 payable by friendly societies or trade unions.[8] It is no longer (since 1 May 1981) possible to make unlimited nominations of National Savings.

## 2.3.1 Ambulatory in nature

A statutory nomination is ambulatory, like a will. The nominator may therefore deal with the property as they like during their lifetime; unlike a gift, a nomination can be rescinded. If the nominee predeceases the nominator then the nomination will fail.

Where nominations are required to be executed in the same manner as a will, they have been held to be testamentary; the designation of nominations as testamentary has also allowed the courts to apply the doctrine of lapse (see 10.6) where the nominee dies before the nominator. In *Re Barnes* (1940), the court held that 'this nomination has all the elements of a testamentary disposition and is, therefore, governed, so far as the question of lapse is concerned, by the ordinary rule in regard to a testamentary disposition'. So far as the formalities are concerned, in *Pearman v Charlton* (1928), the nomination failed when it was discovered that the person signing as 'witness' to the nominator's signature had not actually seen him sign.

---

8  Administration of Estates (Small Payments) Act 1965, ss 2, 6.

## 2.3.2 Differences between nominations and wills

A nomination is unlike a will in three ways:

(a)  first, a statutory nomination can be made by a person over 16. A formal will, however, requires a person to have reached the age of majority (18);

(b)  second, the formalities required differ. Provision is made in each statute for what is required for each kind of nomination; non-statutory nominations were discussed in the *Danish Bacon* case (see 2.3.3);

(c)  third, to revoke the nomination, the nominator will have to comply with the formalities laid down in the relevant statute, as a nomination cannot be revoked by a will or codicil. This last point can often be overlooked when the nominator later forgets that they have made the nomination.

However, the property the beneficiaries receive will still be taxable as part of the estate of the deceased. In *Kempe and Others v Inland Revenue* (2004) the deceased's employer had insured his life for US$380,000 and he had nominated beneficiaries well before his death. The beneficiaries claimed that the property had in effect left the deceased on his nominating them as his beneficiaries, but this argument failed. The deceased could have changed his nomination at any time, so it remained his property for tax purposes. The benefit was not the type of unenforceable gratuity or death benefit that is exempt from taxation. Since the default position was that the benefit would fall into his estate if he made no nomination, the benefit formed part of his taxable estate on death.

## 2.3.3 The case against execution

If a nomination is executed like a will, it can be admitted to probate provided that it is also proved that the person executing it intended it to take effect only at their death. A statutory nomination, however, takes effect under the relevant statute, which will provide for the necessary formalities. It was argued in *Re Danish Bacon Co Ltd Staff Pension Fund Trusts* (1971) that a non-statutory nomination should be ineffective unless executed and witnessed like a will, because it was essentially testamentary. The court held, however, that although the nomination had certain testamentary characteristics, it was not a testamentary disposition as such and did not require execution in accordance with the Wills Act 1837. The court regarded it as a contractual arrangement outside the deceased's estate and not as a disposition by the deceased.

The deceased in *Baird v Baird* (1990) had worked for an oil company which provided a contributory pension scheme for its employees, certain benefits of which could be passed to others if he was still in the company's employment when he died. The deceased nominated his brother by signing the company's form. Five years later, he married, and two years after that he died. His widow claimed that the benefit should go to her, but the company claimed it should go to the brother. The widow eventually appealed to the Privy Council on the grounds that the benefit was an ambulatory disposition valid only if it was executed with the formalities required for a will. The court held that the power under a contributory pension scheme to appoint a non-assignable 'death-in-employment' benefit subject to the prior approval of the trustees of the scheme was in essence no different from any other power of appointment and did not dispose of any property, and therefore did not have to be executed as if it were a will.

## 2.4 Life insurance

Life insurance benefits may pass outside the estate if the policy has been taken out for the benefit of other persons. If nothing is done to direct the proceeds of a policy, those proceeds will fall into the estate of the deceased and pass in accordance with their will or intestacy, and may therefore be subject to inheritance tax. As, however, they are never going to be of any practical use to them, the deceased will usually ensure they pass directly to the ultimate recipient. If a man directs that the policy proceeds should be held for his spouse or his children, then a trust in their favour will arise under s 11 of the Married Women's Property Act 1882. The policyholder may also divest him- or herself of the benefit under the policy by making a declaration of trust or by assigning the legal and beneficial interest to the insurance company who will then pay to the intended beneficiary on death. This can be a very tax-efficient way of providing for dependants, since the gift thus made does not fall to be calculated with the rest of the estate for inheritance tax purposes; although the premiums paid will qualify for assessment to lifetime inheritance tax, they will usually be exempt under the provision allowing for normal gifts out of excess income or fall within the annual personal allowances.

## 2.5 Contracts to make a will or leave property by will

A person may contract to make a will. If the testator then makes a will as anticipated by the other party to the contract, there is no difficulty, but there is no guarantee for the other party that it will remain valid until the death of the testator. It may be revoked by the testator deliberately, or by operation of law.

Alternatively, they may make a contract to pass their property to someone on their death. There is no guarantee that the testator will retain the property which is the subject of the contract in their ownership until death so that it falls to the estate and can pass to the other contracting party.

### 2.5.1 Requirements for establishing a contract or estoppel interest

A contract to make, or leave property in, a will is valid if it complies with the usual requirements of a contract. A contract not to revoke a gift in an existing will is similarly valid. The validity of the contract does not necessarily mean that it can be enforced.

Note, however, the converse situation, where an arrangement that is not valid as a contract may still be enforceable. This is particularly the case with proprietary estoppel, which frequently arises in succession cases. People may enter into arrangements about land which are not sufficiently formally made to operate as contracts, usually for lack of any writing.[9] The cases are often about farms – classically, a claimant is told they will inherit the farm if they work on it for little or no pay. When the owner dies without leaving the farm to the claimant, the property is worth suing for. The details of proprietary estoppel are an essential element of the study of land law and the law of equity, rather than central to this book, but claims to property by estoppel are relatively common in practice.

### 2.5.2 Effect of the contract on the making of wills or gifts by will

The existence of a valid contract or estoppel does not mean that the testator can be forced to make a will with the necessary provisions. Nor does it mean that the testator, if they make the will, cannot revoke it, if they so wish. The testator retains full testamentary freedom in that they

---

9 Since 1989, writing has been an essential element of a contract for the sale or other disposition of land (s 2 Law of Property (Miscellaneous Provisions) Act 1989, replacing s 40 Law of Property Act 1925, which made oral contracts valid but unenforceable by action unless evidenced in writing or where partly performed).

may still make their will in whatever terms they requires and they may freely revoke their will whenever they wish. The existence of the contract also has no effect on the general provisions for the revocation of wills by operation of law on marriage or civil partnership.[10]

### 2.5.3 Breach: making a will or gifts by will

If the testator has contracted simply to make a will, the contract will be fulfilled by the making of the will, although the testator will not be prevented from revoking the will afterwards.

If a testator has contracted to leave property by will and they breach that contract by leaving the property elsewhere, a remedy may be obtained for the breach. This was established in the early case of *Hammersley v De Biel* (1845), where a father covenanted to his proposed son-in-law that he would settle £10,000 on his daughter, on the basis of which the marriage took place. The father left no such gift in his will, however, and the House of Lords affirmed that in such a situation 'a Court of Equity will take care that he is not disappointed, and will give effect' to the contract.

### 2.5.4 Breach by marriage

Where the will the testator contracted to make is revoked by their marriage, however, there will be no breach of contract because, as was confirmed in *Re Marsland* (1939), public policy does not allow constraints on marriage. A purported prohibition on automatic revocation by marriage is considered to operate in restraint of marriage and thus to be void on grounds of public policy.

It was established in *Robinson v Ommanney* (1883), however, that the fact that a contract may be breached by marriage, and that a breach of this kind would not be recognised as such by the law because of the rules against restraint on marriage, does not mean that the contract is therefore invalid of itself. The court will look to see why the contract was apparently breached before deciding whether or not to remedy the breach. See also 7.2.11.

### 2.5.5 Breach by *inter vivos* alienation or insolvency

If, however, a testator alienates the property during their lifetime, in breach of contract, the contractor may sue immediately for damages for the breach, subject probably to a reduction for the possibility of dying before the testator. This construction does not square with the line of English authority which suggests that benefits passing by will in fulfilment of a contract may fail by the doctrine of lapse, but it is suggested, particularly from American authorities, that the doctrine does not apply to contracts to leave property by will.

If the testator's estate turns out to be insolvent, the contractor will not have any advantage over other creditors merely because of the breach of contract. In *Graham v Wickham* (1863), it was argued that the claimant should be paid out of the assets applicable to legacies; the court held that what had been created was a specialty debt.

### 2.5.6 Contract to leave estate or part of estate

Any contract or valid arrangement to leave the whole or a specified share of an estate to the contractor relates to the extent of the estate at death. Thus, if the testator who has made an agreement in those terms disposes of all their property during their lifetime, there will be no breach.

---

10 Wills Act 1837 ss 18 and 18B as amended.

### 2.5.7 Contract to leave specific property

However, if a contract concerns specific property, the situation is different. In *Synge v Synge* (1894), a man had persuaded a woman to marry him by telling her (in a letter) that he would leave her a life interest in his house if she did so. After she had married him, he contracted to sell the house elsewhere, and she immediately became entitled to proceed against him for damages for breach of contract.

### 2.5.8 Enforceability of contracts

Whether and how the contract can be enforced depends on whether what the contracting party is trying to enforce is the making of a will or the passing of property. The former is unenforceable, whereas the latter may be dealt with by the court. Thus, a court will not oblige a testator who has contracted to leave a person their house to make a will in those terms, but it may either enforce a claim by that person against the estate for the house if the testator does not make the gift of it by will, or award that person damages if the testator alienates the property during their lifetime.

### 2.5.9 Effect on contract property of claims against the estate

If a valid contract is established, it was held in the Privy Council case of *Schaefer v Schuhmann* (1972) (see 15.35) that the property so contracted to be left is not available for distribution on a claim under the family provision legislation. However, if the court finds that the deceased entered the contract in order to defeat any application under the family provision legislation the court may decrease the effect of the contract or cancel it entirely.[11]

The effect of a successful proprietary estoppel claim changed under the Land Registration Act 2002. By s 116 of that Act, proprietary estoppel gave rise not, as before (probably), to an inchoate equity, but to a proprietary interest. This was the case notwithstanding that the interest retains an inchoate element – whereas often a claim is satisfied by the awarding of whatever had been effectively promised, that is not always the case, and it may be satisfied with some lesser interest or with money.[12] There is therefore a proprietary interest whose proprietary nature is certain but the extent of which is uncertain. However, usually a person is awarded their expectation, and it can, eventually, be registered on the Land Register. After that it will be certain and near-unassailable.

Those dealing with estates, especially estates with farms in, should take potential proprietary estoppel claims very seriously.

## 2.6 *Donationes mortis causa*

*Donatio mortis causa* is a Latin phrase meaning 'a gift because of death'. The plural of *donatio* is *donationes*. They are sometimes called 'deathbed gifts', although that may be misleading as the donor does not have to be quite on their deathbed. Although the gift is made by the testator during their lifetime, it differs from an ordinary lifetime gift in that it is made in expectation of an imminent death and operates only if that death comes to pass. *Donationes mortis causa* are, however, unlike gifts by will because, although they are dependent on death and operate only at death, anyone, not just a person entitled to make a privileged will (see 6.5), may make a *donatio mortis causa* without the need for writing or the other formalities required for wills.

---

11  Inheritance (Provision for Family and Dependants) Act 1975 (see Chapter 15).
12  Elizabeth Cooke, 'Estoppel and the Protection of Expectations' (1997) 17 Legal Studies 258.

## 2.6.1  Origins of the *donatio mortis causa*

The phrase is Latin and the concept comes from Roman law. In Roman law, a gift was not originally treated as a way of acquiring property so much as a reason for requiring its delivery; it was the delivery itself which transferred the ownership. When under the Emperor Justinian the law was extensively codified, however, 'donatio' was treated as a mode of acquisition which passed ownership, divided into '*donationes inter vivos*' and '*donationes mortis causa*'. A *donatio mortis causa* was revocable at any time before death, unlike a *donatio inter vivos*, which could not be revoked. Unlike a legacy, however, a *donatio mortis causa* required no formalities and involved immediate possession. The *donatio mortis causa* of modem English law is a direct descendant of the Roman *donatio*, and 'dominion' (see 2.6.9), a descendant of the Roman concept of *dominium*.

Donationes mortis causa appeared in English law at the beginning of the eighteenth century, following the introduction by the Statute of Frauds of 1677 of the requirement for writing in the making of wills. In *Hedges v Hedges* (1708), the court defined a valid gift of this kind as one which a man makes when he believes he is in his last illness and fears he will die before he has a chance to make a proper will. He then 'gives with his own hand his goods to his friends about him: this, if he dies, shall operate as a legacy; but if he recovers, then does the property thereof revert to him'.

Two centuries later, however, the nature of a *donatio mortis causa* was still giving rise to conceptual difficulties. The court in *Re Beaumont* (1902) thought it neither fish nor fowl, calling it 'of an amphibious nature neither entirely *inter vivos* nor testamentary'. The difficulty lies in that the gift is not an *inter vivos* gift, because it is dependent on the death of the donor, but neither is it testamentary; not only can the gift be made without the need for the usual formalities required for gifts by will, but 'if the donor dies the title becomes absolute and not under but as against his executor'. Into the twenty-first century, *donationes mortis causa* remain live, but still uncertain, especially so far as gifts of land are concerned.

## 2.6.2  Essentials of a *donatio mortis causa*

To be valid as a *donatio mortis causa*, the gift must be made:

(a)   in contemplation of death; and
(b)   conditionally on death; and
(c)   by parting with dominion over the gift.

## 2.6.3  In contemplation of death

Donationes mortis causa, under Roman law, were essentially a way of avoiding the formalities required for the making of wills. The Roman *donatio mortis causa* did not have to be made in contemplation of death; this has been described as a 'peculiar requirement' and 'home-grown English law'.[13]

The death that must be contemplated is not the eventual death that will come to everyone but an imminent death, that is, 'not the possibility of death at some time or other, but death within the near future – what may be called impending death for some reason or other'.[14]

In the case of *Vallée v Birchwood* (2013) the deceased died intestate. His daughter, Cheryl Vallée, had been adopted by family friends and was living in France, but she still kept in touch with her Home Counties-based father. She visited him in July 2006 saying she would see him

---

13  Roger Kerridge, *Parry & Kerridge: The Law of Succession* (12th edition, Sweet & Maxwell 2009) 119.
14  Per Farwell, J in *Re Craven* (1937).

before Christmas. He handed her the key to his house and the title deeds to his unregistered house saying he would not make it until Christmas and that he wanted her to have his house; he was quite unwell and coughing, but did not mention any medical diagnosis. He died on 11 December 2006 without seeing Cheryl again. She claimed the house had been given to her by *donatio mortis causa*. The Court of Appeal found that the gift, made in contemplation of death within four months of the death, could be judged to be 'impending', although in prior cases the gift had always shortly preceded death.[15] This analysis was confirmed in *King v Dubry and Others* (2014).

The ordinary risks of life are however not sufficient to give rise to a *donatio mortis causa*: for example, undertaking ordinary commercial air travel is not sufficient grounds on which to infer the contemplation of imminent death.[16]

### 2.6.4 Mistake as to cause of death

If a gift purporting to be a *donatio mortis causa* is made in contemplation of a fairly imminent death from one cause and death subsequently results from another, the *donatio mortis causa* may still be valid. In *Wilkes v Allington* (1931), the donor had cancer and believed he would soon die from it. He made a *donatio mortis causa* in contemplation of that death. However, a month later he died of pneumonia which developed after he caught a chill on a bus journey. The court held the *donatio mortis causa* valid nevertheless.

### 2.6.5 Mistaken belief in imminent death

It is probable that a donor who genuinely but mistakenly believes they are in danger of imminent death can make a valid *donatio mortis causa*. Clearly, the *donatio* will not take effect unless the donor's parting with dominion over the property is followed by their death. There is no reason of logic why death from a cause the donor did not expect should render a *donatio* invalid where the cause of death they did expect could not have materialised, when, as in *Wilkes v Allington* (1931), it does not affect the validity of the *donatio* if the expected cause of death could have materialised but did not do so. However, an authority on the point is still awaited.

### 2.6.6 Death by suicide

There is no recent English case on the validity of a *donatio mortis causa* where the donor's contemplated or actual death occurs by suicide. Suicide was illegal until it was decriminalised by the Suicide Act 1961. No one was ever convicted of suicide, obviously. However, it remained an offence, as did attempting suicide.

The cases on *donationes mortis causa* and suicide predate the legalisation of suicide. The court in the Irish case of *Agnew v Belfast Banking Co* (1896) was explicit in its refusal to find a *donatio* valid when the death contemplated was one by suicide and therefore 'so purely voluntary as to be criminal in its origin'. The decision in that case was followed without analysis or discussion in the English case of *Re Dudman* (1925), but that again predates the 1961 Act. In another Irish case, *Mills v Shields and Kelly* (1948), the deceased had given property as a *donatio mortis causa* to a priest in contemplation of an imminent death from illness. On the way to Dublin for treatment, he left the train and killed himself. The *donatio mortis causa* was held valid by the court. The Chief Registrar of Friendly Societies has held valid a gift made in contemplation of suicide since the 1961 Act.[17]

---

15  The deceased in *Sen v Headley* (1990) died three days after passing dominion over the property.
16  *Thompson v Mechan* (1958).
17  *Report of the Chief Registrar of Friendly Societies* (Registry of Friendly Societies 1965) 13–14.

### 2.6.7 Conditional on death

The gift is revocable until death. Thus, if the donor finds they were mistaken about their imminent death, they can have the property back. Moreover, the *donatio* is always ineffective if the donee dies before the donor. The courts have been willing to infer the conditionality of a gift, which might otherwise appear to be expressed in absolute and immediate terms, from the circumstances of the case. In *Sen v Headley* (1991), the donor said 'the house is yours, Margaret'. In *Gardner v Parker* (1818) two days before his death, the seriously ill donor gave the donee a bond for £1,800 and said, 'There, take that and keep it' before dying two days later. In *Woodard v Woodard* (1995) the donor said 'you can keep the keys, I won't be driving it any more'. The court inferred that these gifts were intended to be conditional on the donor's death and therefore held them to be valid *donations mortis causa*.

The intention to make an immediate gift *inter vivos*, or the intention to make a gift by will, invalidates a gift as a *donatio mortis causa*, because the intention to do either of these things is incompatible with the necessary intention required for making a valid *donatio mortis causa*.

In *Edwards v Jones* (1836), the assignee of a bond signed a memorandum, not under seal (i.e. not by deed), some five days before her death. This memorandum was indorsed on a bond purporting to be an assignment bond, without consideration. It was delivered to the donee but the language of the assignment was held to exclude the possibility of treating the attempted gift as a *donatio mortis causa*. It was therefore held to be an incomplete gift which equity would not perfect because there was no consideration.

### 2.6.8 Knowledge not fear of death

There have been suggestions that there can be no *donatio mortis causa* where the donor does not so much fear an imminent death as know that it is inevitable. Such an argument was raised in *Re Lillingston* (1952) (2.6.14), where it was suggested that donor, from her references to 'when I am gone' knew that she could not recover from her last heart attack. The argument is that a person who knows they are about to die cannot sensibly be found to have made a gift carrying a condition that it will be returned if they recover, since they know they will not recover. The court in *Re Lillingston*, however, despite her words 'keep the key; it is now yours', construed the donor's words to mean that she would require the return of her property, both jewellery and keys, if she were to recover.

This point was, however, successfully argued in the case of *Lord Advocate v M'Court* (1893). The court was asked to construe a gift made by a donor who knew he was terminally ill. It held that the donor who knew he would not recover could not make a *donatio mortis causa* because the conditional element of the gift was lacking. However, it is submitted that this is one of those cases in which the court's view of the law may have been influenced by the preferred outcome of the case. At the time of this case, tax was payable on gifts passing on death, including *donationes mortis causa*, but not on lifetime gifts. The decision that it was a lifetime gift relieved the estate of a potential tax burden.

### 2.6.9 Parting with dominion

Parting with dominion is a difficult concept, long established in case law but not defined. It is more than mere physical possession but less than outright ownership. It 'lies somewhere in between title on the one hand and de facto possession on the other hand, and can best be defined as the right to possess or control the subject matter of the gift'.[18] For the requirements of a *donatio*

---

18  Andrew Borkowski, *Deathbed Gifts: The Law of Donatio Mortis Causa* (Blackstone Press 1999) 79.

*mortis causa* to be satisfied, there must be not only a parting with the goods – delivery of them to the donee – but also an intention existing at the time of delivery to part with control of them. Only once the two requirements of delivery and transfer of control have coincided will there be a parting with dominion sufficient to establish a *donatio mortis causa*.

In *Reddel v Dobree* (1839), however, the donor was ill when he gave a locked cash box to the donee telling her that the box had money in for her but that, while he lived, the donor wanted to see the box every three months. At his death, the donee was to go to the donor's son to get the key to the box. The court held that there was no valid *donatio mortis causa* because the donor had retained control over the property and had not parted with dominion it to the donee. It was demonstrated in *Cain v Moon* (1896), however, that the delivery and the intention to part with control over the gift do not need to occur together, provided they are both present before the donor dies. In that case, the deceased had asked her mother to take possession of a deposit note, not with the intention of giving it to her, but merely for the purposes of safe keeping. When she fell ill, her mother still had the deposit note, and she said 'the bank note is yours if I die'. The earlier physical delivery of the deposit note, taken together with the later intention to part with control over it conditionally upon the donor's expected death, was held to be sufficient parting with dominion to establish a valid *donatio mortis causa*.

It follows that the donor must deliver the property to the donee during his lifetime. The donor in *Bunn v Markham* (1816) believed he was dying and directed that the words 'For Mrs and Miss C' be written on sealed parcels containing money and securities. The donor then declared that the parcels were to be kept in his locked iron chest until his death, following which they were to be delivered to the addressees. This clearly was not an *inter vivos* gift since the purported donor had retained the property during his lifetime. It did not fulfil the requirements for a gift by will. However, it also failed to fulfil the requirements for a *donatio mortis causa*, since the donor had not delivered the property with the intention of parting with dominion.

In *Treasury Solicitor v Lewis* (1900), the purported donee said that the elderly Mrs Dash had given him all her property subject to his settling her affairs, seeing about her funeral and making certain gifts to charity. She delivered to him a deposit note and share certificate saying, 'Take charge of them. If I get better you will bring them back; if not, you will know what to do with them'. Later she told him where he would find gold and notes, but she gave no further directions. The court held that she had reserved dominion over the property during her life and therefore there was no *donatio mortis causa*. Nevertheless, in the more recent case of *Woodard v Woodard* (1995), the son already had the use of his terminally ill father's car when the father said he could keep the keys. The Court of Appeal held that the father's intention had been to make a *donatio mortis causa* of the car and that there was no need for him to take back the car first in order to make it. The specific background facts of this case may mean, however, that it will be readily distinguished, probably over the issue of duplicate keys or because an order against the son would have been of little practical effect as he would have been unable to satisfy it (see 2.6.12).

## 2.6.10 Parting with dominion does not necessarily mean giving a beneficial interest to the donee

A donor may part with dominion over the property they give to the donee even though there is a trust imposed on the donee in respect of the property. Thus, in *Hills v Hills* (1841), the donee took the property on the basis that he would meet the expenses of the donor's forthcoming funeral, and this was held to be a valid *donatio mortis causa*.

## 2.6.11  Agents of the parties

The delivery may be made by the use of agents, but they must be the agents of the relevant parties. This means that it will be sufficient for the donor to deliver to the donee's agent. It is not sufficient for the donor to deliver only to their own agent, even with instructions that the property be passed to the donee, because that is not equivalent to delivery to the donee.

## 2.6.12  Parting with dominion over the means of obtaining physical possession of the property

If the property is a chattel, it has long been settled that the chattel itself or else the means of obtaining it can be delivered. In *Re Craven* (1937), the donor's delivery of the keys to a box containing the gift was held to be sufficient delivery of the gift itself. Those were, however, the only keys. In *Trimmer v Danby* (1856), however, the donor's attempted gift to his housekeeper failed as a *donatio mortis causa*. He put ten Austrian bonds in a box and wrote a note indicating that 'the first five numbers of those Austrian bonds belong to and are Hannah Danby's property'. He then delivered the keys to the box to her. However, it was held that he had not parted with dominion over the property because the housekeeper, being the servant of the donor, was presumed to be the agent of the donor, and he was held not to have parted with dominion over the property by giving her the keys. The question of whether there might be a spare set of keys was raised in *Woodard v Woodard* (1995) (2.6.9), but not pursued. In that case, which Dillon LJ described as 'about the most sterile appeal that I have ever come across', the son had in any case sold the car on and spent the proceeds, and both sides were legally aided. Finding against him would have achieved nothing.

The issue of gifts of land presents further difficulties, including that of passing dominion. In *Re Wasserberg* (1915), it was held that it was not necessary for absolute dominion to be given up as long as the donor suffered some deprivation of power to deal with the subject matter, which parting with the title deeds to unregistered land does (see 2.6.24). It was argued by the appellant that the donor could have made physical alterations to the building after the gift but the judge found this wholly unrealistic in light of the donor's poor health. Retention of possession of the property was found to be consistent with a gift that took effect in the future. That unregistered land itself may be the subject of a *donatio mortis causa* was confirmed in *Sen v Headley* (1991). In that case, the donor handed over the only keys to the box with the deeds in it within days of his death, and did not return to the property. In *Vallée v Birchwood* (2013) the donor continued to live in the property having given a set of keys and the deeds to the donee. It was found that the delivery of the deeds sufficed: the circumstances meant it was necessary for the donor to stay in the house.

## 2.6.13  Parting with total dominion over the means...

In *Sen v Headley* (1991) (2.6.22), the court heard a claim by the deceased's housekeeper that the deceased had given her his house by *donatio mortis causa* by delivering to her the keys to the box of deeds to the property and the keys to the cupboard where the box was stored. She already had keys for the house. However, the housekeeper made no claim that the deceased had also given her the contents of the house by the same means, because he had kept a separate set of keys to the property

## 2.6.14  ...or over the means to obtaining the means

In *Re Lillingston* (1952), the donor gave the donee a parcel of jewellery and the keys to a trunk. She told the donee that the trunk contained the key to her safe deposit at Harrods, which in turn contained the key to her city safe deposit. She said she wished the donee to have the jewellery in the safe deposit as well, which the donee could go and get 'when I am gone'. The donee put the parcel of jewellery in the trunk and the donor then said 'keep the key: it is now yours'. The court held that there had been a valid *donatio mortis causa* of all the jewellery in both safes as well as the trunk.

### 2.6.15 Subject matter of the gift

The law of succession usually changes only slowly, but there has, in recent years (in the context of the antiquity of this doctrine), been a great change in the law relating to *donationes mortis causa* of real property. It used to be thought that the requirement for delivery, although much hedged about in the cases of such property as building society accounts (see 2.6.17), could not be effected even symbolically in the case of land, but this is no longer true (see 2.6.23).

### 2.6.16 Choses in action

Many items which are the subjects of *donationes mortis causa* are assets which are not really capable of delivery, but *donationes mortis causa*, as has been mentioned above, are an anomalous form of gift and the usual rules for the passing of title do not apply to them in the same way as to normal gifts. Some choses in action are clearly capable of delivery, for example, banknotes, or bearer securities such as cheques payable to 'the bearer' (these are less common now that most cheque books are automatically issued crossed 'account payee'). Bills of exchange, cheques and promissory notes payable to the donor have been held capable of passing by *donatio mortis causa* even though unendorsed and not capable of passing by delivery.

The deceased in *Re Mead* (1880) had held a banker's deposit note for £2,700. He had filled in a form requiring seven days' notice in order to give £500 of this to his wife, but died before the seven days were up. He had also signed a note saying 'pay self or bearer £500' and given this to his wife, as well as two bills of exchange payable to himself, not indorsed by him and falling due after his death. It was held that the orders not payable until after death could not form the subject matter of a *donatio mortis causa*.

In *Clement v Cheesman* (1884), the donor had given his son a cheque payable to the donor or to order. The court, applying the case of *Veal v Veal* (1859), held that it operated as a promissory note or a bill of exchange and that therefore it had passed by *donatio mortis causa*. *Veal v Veal* appears to be the origin of the present law on *donationes mortis causa* of choses in action.

### 2.6.17 Essential indicia of title

A chose in action which is not capable of delivery may become the subject of a *donatio mortis causa*, provided the 'essential indicia or evidence of title, possession or production of which entitles the possessor to the money or property purported to be given'[19] is delivered to the donee.

The definition of the essential indicia of title which are needed for a chose in action to pass by *donatio mortis causa* is taken from the judgment in *Birch v Treasury Solicitor* (1951). In that case, the donee handed over various post office and bank account books, intending the money to pass in the event of her contemplated death. The Court of Appeal held this amounted to a transfer sufficient to pass the money in the bank accounts by *donatio mortis causa*.

---

19  *Birch v Treasury Solicitor* (1951).

## 2.6.18  Need for *indicium* of title to be essential

The only accounts which may be transferred in this way are those which require the possession or production of a passbook. Obviously, the mere possession of a passbook does not entitle a person to the contents of the account in the normal way; a person finding a passbook in the street does not thus obtain entitlement to take the money from the account (though the principle that the thief of a chattel has a legal title to it remains good too). The delivery by the donor of the passbook is simply the way in which they may fulfil the requirements of a *donatio mortis causa* for an account which otherwise cannot be 'delivered'.

Most accounts, however, cannot be delivered at all, even for the purposes of *donationes mortis causa*. They do not have passbooks that must be produced in order for money to be taken out. Many accounts nowadays are Internet-only and have no indicia of title. The money in those accounts, it would appear, cannot be the subject matter of a *donatio mortis causa*.

## 2.6.19  Cheques made out to the donor

Cheques and promissory notes do not operate quite like most personal property. The donor of a lifetime gift of this kind of property (that is, a person making a gift of a cheque made out to himself by someone else) would have to endorse it in order to make the gift valid; this would mean signing the cheque to indicate that the money should be paid to someone else. Most cheques are now, however, routinely endorsed 'account payee only', which means that they cannot be signed over by the payee. However, where the cheque was drawn by someone other than the donor it can, however, probably still form the subject matter of a valid *donatio mortis causa* because the donor could have used it to enforce by action the debt it represents.

## 2.6.20  Cheques drawn by the donor

Where, however, a cheque is drawn by the donor himself, it is not enforceable as a *donatio mortis causa*. A cheque does not constitute entitlement to property of the sum drawn on it but is an order to the drawer's bank to pay that sum. The judgment in *Re Beaumont* (1902) made it clear that the order to the bank represented by the cheque is revoked by the donor's death, so the rule corresponds with that for lifetime gifts.

## 2.6.21  Real property: development of the *donatio mortis causa*

The origins and concept of the *donatio mortis causa* mean that it operates differently from most of the law of property, and contains perhaps unexpected areas of uncertainty. Until (in succession terms) very recently, it was thought that land generally could not pass by *donatio mortis causa*, although it had been held by the House of Lords that a mortgage could. The House of Lords in *Duffield v Elwes* (1827) held that a mortgage could be the subject of a *donatio mortis causa* by delivery of the mortgage deed. What passed was held to be the debt; the mortgage, being the security for the loan, then passed with it in a manner analogous to that of other securities and choses in action. The House of Lords went on to declare in that case that land as such could not be the subject of a *donatio mortis causa*.

## 2.6.22  *Sen v Headley* (1990) (High Court) – the last of the old rule[20]

Mummery J at first instance in *Sen v Headley* (1990) followed the accepted rule that land cannot pass by *donatio mortis causa*. The plaintiff, Mrs Sen, had remained a close friend of the deceased after

---

20  Described by William Moffett, counsel for the defendant in the Court of Appeal in *Vallée v Birchwood* (2013), as 'undoubtedly the most significant DMC case in the last 50 years, and arguably since the earliest authorities of the 18th century': *Deathbed Gifts in Rude Health: The Recent Case of Vallée v Birchwood* (Radcliffe Chambers 2013).

living with him for many years, and had visited him in hospital during what they both knew to be his final illness. He had given her the keys to his house, of which there were duplicates, and to a locked box, which had no other key and which contained the title deeds to the property. It was not in dispute that the deceased had given Mrs Sen the keys in contemplation of death and with the intention that the property should pass to her only after his death. The question was whether the title deeds could be regarded as the essential indicia of title necessary for property incapable of delivery to pass by *donatio mortis causa*; Mummery J held that this construction of a *donatio* could not be applied to land.

### 2.6.23 *Sen v Headley* (1991) (Court of Appeal)

However, Mrs Sen appealed and won. The Court of Appeal in *Sen v Headley* (1991) held that the whole system of *donationes mortis causa* was an anomaly, and that the different rules relating to the *inter vivos* transfer of land did not justify making exceptions from the rule that were themselves anomalous. An exception for land was anomalous because the same rules ought to apply to it as to choses in action and mortgages. The court found that it was insufficient to suggest that the requirements of the Law of Property Act 1925 meant that land could not pass by *donatio*, because those formalities represented the same kind of obstacle, albeit a larger one, as the obstacles to the transmission by *donatio* of choses in action and mortgages.

The Court of Appeal did not consider itself bound by the statement of the House of Lords in *Duffield v Elwes* (2.6.21), because that had been *obiter*. It stated that if the point under consideration had been the subject of decision, then it would have 'loyally followed it', but 'we cannot decide a case in 1991 as the House of Lords would have decided it, but did not decide it, in 1827'.

### 2.6.24 *Donationes mortis causa* of unregistered and registered land

Both *Sen v Headley* (1991) and *Vallée v Birchwood* (2013) (2.6.3) concerned unregistered land. Title to unregistered land is proved by production of the deeds to the land; the deceased had passed dominion over the deeds to the claimant. There is no decision as yet on whether the extension of the potential for *donationes mortis causa* to unregistered land covers registered land as well.

Although in theory the introduction of the system of registration of title was originally a conveyancing matter and was said not to be intended to alter the substantive law, it is clear that the increased operation of the registered system has led to substantive differences in the law relating to the two systems. However, if the *donationes mortis causa* principle extended to choses in action, despite the particular rules which apply to their transfer, and to mortgages and unregistered land, there originally seemed no reason why a court could not extend them to registered land as well. A *donatio mortis causa* is an exception to the rules about the passing of property, and the Court of Appeal said in *Sen v Headley*:

> A *donatio mortis causa* of land is neither more nor less anomalous than any other. Every such gift is a circumvention of the Wills Act 1837. Why should the additional statutory formalities for the creation and transmission of interests in land be regarded as some larger obstacle? The only step which has to be taken is to extend the application of the implied or constructive trust arising on the donor's death from the conditional to the absolute estate.

However, the passing of dominion – an essential element of the *donatio mortis causa* – in the decided cases on unregistered title involved passing dominion over the title deeds. Title deeds are used in unregistered conveyancing, where the transfer of title is accomplished by making a deed that conveys the transferor's title, and showing that title by producing the deed that transferred the title to the transferor and so on backwards to a 'good root of title', which now means one at least 15 years old.[21] Once title is registered, the title deeds are redundant. The nearest equivalent to deeds in the case of registered land was the Land Certificate, but this was not really analogous as the title to the land was properly to be found in the current records of the Land Registry, of which the Land Certificate was an official copy, referring to its own specific date on which it had been compared with the Register. The Register itself was where title resided. Moreover, when the Land Registration Act 2002 came into force in 2003, the Land Certificate ceased to be a document of title at all, and it has been doubted whether there can now ever be a *donatio mortis causa* of registered land.[22]

## 2.7 Imperfect gifts/incompletely constituted trusts

Equity will not assist a volunteer, nor will it perfect an imperfect gift; however, the rule in *Strong v Bird* (1874) may assist someone who has been the object of an ineffective attempt at the making of a gift. It might also be possible to save an ineffective attempt to make a *donatio mortis causa* by use of the rule, although the intention required to make a lifetime gift and that required to make a *donatio mortis causa* are arguably too different from each other.

### 2.7.1 The rule in *Strong v Bird* (1874)

The rule in *Strong v Bird* (1874) comes into operation where the donor had the necessary intention to make the gift but did not pass the title to the property, and on their subsequent death the purported donee becomes their executor. Because the executor has the legal title to the property in the estate, their appointment to that office will effectively perfect the gift. (The potential for this might be one reason why a person would be keen to take a grant. (see 12.4).)

The case of *Strong v Bird* concerned the forgiving of a debt. Mr Bird was the step-son of the deceased. The step-mother was living in his house and paying him for board when Mr Bird borrowed a large sum from her, which it was agreed should be repaid as a deduction of £100 from her next 11 quarterly payments for board. After two quarters of deductions, the step-mother forgave the debt expressly but not under seal or for consideration and thus not at law.

The step-mother died appointing Mr Bird as her executor. His debt was thus owed to her estate at law, but he was executor and could not sue himself. Thus, at common law, Mr Bird was no longer liable for the debt, and equity would not compel payment of it because the step-mother had intended to forgive it.

### 2.7.2 Imperfect gifts of property

The operation of the rule in *Strong v Bird* was extended to an imperfect gift of property. In *In Re Stewart* (1908), Neville J commented that

> where a testator has expressed the intention of making a gift of personal estate belonging to him to one who upon his death becomes his executor, the intention continuing unchanged, the executor is entitled to hold the property for his own benefit.

---

21  S 52 Law of Property Act 1925; s 23 Law of Property Act 1969.
22  N Roberts 'Donationes Mortis Causa in a Dematerialised World' (2013) 2 Conveyancer and Property Lawyer 113.

He held that the vesting of the property in the executor completed the imperfect gift and that the testator's continuing intention to make the gift prevailed over the gifts in the will, once the legal estate was vested in the executor.

However, in Re Freeland (1952) an imperfect gift of a car which was not delivered to the purported donee failed. The deceased had told one of her executrices that she intended to give her the car; she then lent it to a third party, which the Court of Appeal held was fatal to the claim that she had intended to make an immediate gift, even though the purported donee had consented to the loan.

Re Stewart was followed in Re James (1935), where the court, in upholding an imperfect gift of a house, stated that the rule applied to administrators as well as executors. Although this point was followed in Re Gonin (1977), where a daughter who had cared for her parents understood that she was to be given her mother's house when they died, the court doubted that it was correct. The mother died intestate and the daughter took out letters of administration of her estate, claiming this perfected the imperfect gift to her. The court disagreed strongly with the authority of Re James in respect of administrators and described the principle that a person taking the legal estate by operation of law, rather than under the deceased's will, should thereby be able to perfect an imperfect gift as 'in the nature of a lottery', doubting that equity was 'so undiscriminating'. In Re Ralli (1964), however, Buckley J said:

> In my judgment the circumstance that the plaintiff holds the fund because he was appointed trustee of the will is irrelevant. He is at law the owner of the fund. The question is: For whom ... does he hold the fund in equity?

The settlor had covenanted to transfer property to trustees, but failed to transfer her future interest of some property which had not vested at her death. However, as she was found to be the trustee of the future interest once she had declared the trust, the beneficiaries could enforce against her personal representatives.

## 2.7.3 Incompletely constituted trusts

The area of gifts only partially made also requires consideration of the cases on incompletely constituted trusts. These often involve the transfer of company shares; see 2.2.4 for the formalities.

In Milroy v Lord (1862), a settlor purported to transfer certain bank shares to trustees on trust for the plaintiff. The legal transfer required entry in the bank's books. The intended trustee held the share certificates as well as a power of attorney from the settlor which would have enabled the trustee to apply to the bank for completion of the transfer. However, under the terms of the power the trustee could only act as agent for the settlor. No entry in the bank's books had been made at the time of the settlor's death, and the court held, first, that the trust was not completely constituted and that the shares belonged therefore both in law and in equity to the settlor's estate, and, second, that it could not be said that the settlor had put it out of his power to recall the gift as the terms of the power of attorney equated the trustee with the settlor.

This case was applied in the case of Richards v Delbridge (1874), where the attempting donor had tried to make over a lease of a business property together with the stock-in-trade by writing and signing on the deed. Because the gift was not made by deed it was ineffective, and the court, applying Milroy v Lord, declined to treat it as a declaration of trust, as this had not been intended by the would-be donor. Regarding it as such would amount to converting an imperfect gift into a perfect trust, and equity coming to the assistance of a volunteer.

In Re Rose (1952) the deceased had executed a share transfer but the legal title could not pass until entry had been made in the company register, which could be refused at the discretion of the directors. The transfer was executed in March 1943 and the entry was made in June 1943.

The transferor died in 1947. The court held, for the purpose of estate duty computation, that the beneficial interest had left the deceased in March 1943, since from that date it lay within the power of the transferee to apply for registration. *Milroy v Lord* was distinguished on the ground that the power of attorney in that case was limited as described above. The court held that the deceased was in the position of a trustee of the legal title in the shares for the transferees. It distinguished the position of the transferee as regards the company from that of the transferee as regards the transferor. In *Milroy v Lord*, though the transfer form had been fully completed and the transfer and certificate delivered to him, the transferee had no rights as against the company until he was placed on the register; in *Re Rose*, the transferee became the beneficial owner because the transferor had done everything necessary to transfer his legal and beneficial interest in the shares. The case of *Re Rose* may be contrasted with, for example, that of *Re Fry* (1946), where the facts were similar but the transfer required Treasury consent because of the operation of exchange controls on foreign shares such as those concerned in that case.

## 2.8 Joint tenancies

If land is owned by more than one person, at law it must be held on a joint tenancy.[23] Severance of a joint tenancy of land at law is impossible. Personalty may still be owned jointly both at law and in equity, and both personalty and land may be owned on a tenancy in common, or in shares, in equity.

If any property is jointly owned by two people in equity, then the beneficial interest in it will pass on the death of one joint owner to the other. This is called the 'right of survivorship' or the *jus accrescendi*. It is very common for a matrimonial home to be owned jointly in equity as well as at law, but it can be the case with any property. If the beneficial interest is to be left to someone other than the other joint owner (or owners) at law, it must be severed before death (see 2.8.4–7).

### 2.8.1 Creation of a joint tenancy

The joint tenancy will come into existence where property is conveyed or bequeathed to two or more persons and there are no words to show that they are to take separate and distinct shares and there is no presumption of a tenancy in common.

### 2.8.2 Joint tenancy at law and in equity

Since the Law of Property Act 1925, all co-owners of land must be joint tenants at law, whether they are joint tenants or tenants in common in equity.

There are three requirements for a joint tenancy to exist in equity:

(a) the four unities must be observed;
(b) there must be no words of severance;
(c) it must not be one of the instances where equity presumes a tenancy in common.

---

23  S 1 Law of Property Act 1925.

### 2.8.3 The four unities

The four unities are as follows:

(a)  Possession:
     Each co-owner has the right to the enjoyment or possession of the whole of the property.
     This also applies where there is a tenancy in common.
(b)  Interest:
     The nature and duration of each co-owner's interest must be the same.
(c)  Title:
     Each co-owner must derive their title from the same instrument as all the others.
(d)  Vesting:
     Each joint tenant's interest should vest at the same time as the others' interest.

## 2.8.4 Words of severance

Words of severance include 'in equal shares', 'equally', 'between', 'amongst' – all words which show that each co-owner is to take a distinct share in the property. If there are no words of severance in the relevant instrument and the four unities are satisfied, then the presumption of a joint tenancy will arise unless equity presumes otherwise.

## 2.8.5 Equitable presumption of tenancy in common

Equity presumes a tenancy in common in three situations:

(a)  Purchase of partnership property:
     It is presumed that the holding of business property is inconsistent with the right of survivorship, which is more appropriate to family situations.
(b)  Joint mortgagees of land:
     Where money is lent by two or more persons on a mortgage, the mortgage is held by them as tenants in common.
(c)  Purchase money provided in unequal shares:
     Co-owners who provide purchase money in unequal shares are presumed to hold the property as beneficial tenants in common in the same proportion to their contributions. If there is, however, a declaration of trust stating that the beneficial interests are to be held jointly, that will rebut the presumption. (This principle is rarely applied in practice, however, where the joint tenants are spouses.)[24]

## 2.8.6 The effect of severance: tenancy in common

Where there is a tenancy in common, the co-owners have a right to a distinct share in the property but it is not physically divided between them. Tenants in common are said to hold the property in undivided shares. Such a share does not accrue automatically to any other legal joint tenants. A tenant in common's share on death devolves to their personal representatives and then, if it is not needed to meet debts or expenses, to the beneficiary entitled under the will or by intestacy.

It is not easy to tell whether or not a beneficial joint tenancy of a house is subsisting, because it is not necessarily indicated on the Land Register. Because severance is so easy to effect (see 2.8.8), and nothing but a little effort is lost in purporting to sever when it is unnecessary, a

---

24  See *Stack v Dowden* (2007) for further analysis.

notice of severance should be served when there is doubt as to whether a desired equitable tenancy in common already exists. It was confirmed in *Kecskemeti v Rubens Rabin & Co* (1902) that a solicitor who fails to advise a client of the effects of the right of survivorship on property held on a joint tenancy will be liable to an intended beneficiary who is thereby disappointed. In the more recent case of *Carr-Glynn v Frearson* (1998), a solicitor who failed to prepare a notice of severance was also liable, even though the client was uncertain as to the basis on which she owned her house and had said that she would check the title deeds herself.

Joint tenancies of bank or building society accounts are also popular. In the case of a joint tenancy, two or more persons hold the property as if they were one person, and each of them is entitled to the whole of the property.

### 2.8.7 Methods of severance of a joint tenancy

A joint tenancy is easily severed, by notice to the other party or parties, or by other method such as the homicide of one joint tenant by another, a variety of written or informal operations (see 10.10 and *Williams v Hensman* (1861)), but it cannot be severed by will. Thus, if a beneficial joint owner purports to leave their 'share' of the jointly owned matrimonial home to someone in their will, the gift will simply be ineffective.

In respect of severance occasioned by the bankruptcy of one joint tenant, it was confirmed in *Re Dennis* (1995) that severance occurs on the act of bankruptcy, not on the later adjudication of bankruptcy itself.

## 2.9 Secret and half-secret trusts

Where property is transferred by will to someone who has previously agreed to hold that property on trust for a third party, equity will enforce that trust, which operates outside the will and therefore does not conflict with the rule that wills must be in writing (s 9 of the Wills Act 1837).[25] A fully secret trust is one where the gift is apparently outright, but the recipients know they are actually trustees; a half-secret trust is apparent from the face of the will, but the terms of it are not. In both cases, the trust must satisfy the rules as to certainty. Clearly, however, there may be difficulties of evidence in establishing the existence of the trust.

A case in point was that of *Rawstron v Freud* (2014), where the painter Lucian Freud died leaving residue of £42,000,000 after payment of legacies and IHT, given to his solicitor and one of his daughters jointly. They later said they held it on a secret trust. Another of his children (of whom he had 'at least 14'), Paul, said the trust was a half-secret trust, and so failed because, he claimed, Lucian had not told the trustees about the trust until after the will was executed. Had Paul succeeded, he would have had a share of the estate on intestacy. However, the trustees said it was a fully secret trust, which they would not prove (bring into the probate process) as that would mean it was no longer secret as the testator had wished, and in any event they had known all about it before the will was made, so it would not have failed as a half-secret trust either. The court found it to be worded as a fully secret trust, replacing an earlier half-secret trust that was worded differently.

## 2.10 Statutory succession

A person may have a right to succeed to a residential or agricultural tenancy held by the deceased: such rights are limited to those created by the relevant statute (for example, Pt IV of the

---

25 See *Re Snowden (deceased)* (1979).

Agricultural Holdings Act 1986).[26] Right of this kind, on death as in life, are effectively vindicable rights to use property which is in the ownership of someone else. They can be so adverse to the property owner that they change the nature of the property, and certainly historically interests so adverse to a property owner would not have been created without the owner's express involvement and ability to charge for the transfer of those rights should they wish. Rights to use another's property based in social reasons – the human need for shelter and subsistence, or the need for most people to work in order to live – proliferated in the later twentieth century, with the growth of welfare states. They were created by statute rather than developing out of legal precedent, and flew against the trajectory of traditional property rules. The ideas behind new property rights have retreated somewhat in the decades since, along with the rights themselves, which are often in a state of flux.[27] Succession law reflects not only the existence of such rights but their questionable status as property.

Austin v Southwark (2008, 2009) concerned an attempt to succeed to a council tenancy. Where such council tenancies subsist at a tenant's death, they may pass automatically by virtue of statute to the deceased's spouse or a member of the deceased's family who has lived there for 12 months. However, the brother's tenancy had been terminated for non-payment of rent and a possession order had been obtained but not enforced, so although he remained at the flat, it was as a 'tolerated trespasser'. He fell ill and, after the appellant had moved in to care for him, died. The appellant then sought to make a posthumous application for a 'Lazarus' order, reviving the tenancy, as his brother's personal representative,[28] in order to succeed to the tenancy as the deceased's relative. However, it had been held earlier by the Court of Appeal in another case that the right to apply for a Lazarus order died with the original tenant. The appellant argued separately on the bases of his brother's right, or legitimate expectation of a tenancy; Article 1 of the First Protocol to the ECHR; and his own status as personal representative. He was unsuccessful, for both substantive and procedural reasons. The Court of Appeal dismissed his appeal, having considered particularly closely Parliament's intentions as evinced by the provisions of the Housing and Regeneration Act 2008. This, although it was not in force, would strengthen the rights of tolerated trespassers to have a new tenancy. However, the Court of Appeal took the view that: 'If, however, a tolerated trespasser dies, there will at the moment of his death be no secure tenancy to which these succession rights apply.'

## 2.11 Summary of Chapter 2

### 2.11.1 Will Substitutes

There are ways of disposing of property other than leaving it by will on death.

Lifetime gifts are an obvious solution; the formalities for making a successful lifetime gift are different from those for making a gift by will. All gifts by will are made in the same way, whereas the formalities for lifetime gift differ depending on the type of property. The lifetime donor must have sufficient mental capacity to make the gift. A presumption of undue influence will be raised if the relationship with the donee falls into certain categories. If the gift is not successfully made, the property will remain with the donor and fall into their estate on death if not otherwise disposed of in the meantime.

Certain property, for example under a pension scheme, may be nominated during lifetime to be paid out to a named person on death; this is not the same as leaving it by will. The

---

26  See *Fitzpatrick v Sterling HA* (1998).
27  Charles A Reich, 'The New Property' (1964) 73 Yale Law Journal 733; 'The New Property After 25 Years' (1989) 24 University of San Francisco Law Review 223.
28  S 85(2) Housing Act 1985.

necessary formalities are those which apply to the particular form of nomination, not those which apply under the Wills Act 1837.

One may provide for others by taking out a life insurance policy on one's own life. The premiums on the policy will not usually give rise to any charge to tax and the proceeds, if in trust for the donee, will not form part of the insured's estate for tax purposes after their death. Because the policy is comparatively worthless during the insured's life, the emotional difficulty of parting with property during one's life does not arise.

Contracts to leave property by will are valid if they fulfil the usual conditions for contracts, but enforcing them may be difficult. A person cannot be obliged to make a will or to make one in any particular terms; nor can they be prevented from revoking a will once it has been made. If the contract is not carefully phrased, just making the will may fulfil it, and revoking it will not give rise to any cause of action. However, if a contract is breached then that will give rise to an action for damages against the estate. But if a contract is breached when a will is revoked by marriage, the law will not remedy that breach, because to recognise it would constitute a restraint on marriage and would thus be against public policy.

A *donatio mortis causa* is a particular form of gift which the donor makes in contemplation of a particular and imminent death, conditionally on that death, and parts with dominion over the property to the donee during their lifetime. All these conditions must be fulfilled for there to be a valid *donatio*. If the donor then does not die, the property reverts to him or her. Parting with dominion usually means handing the property over, but where it is property incapable of being handed over then passing the essential *indicia* of title – for example, a building society passbook – is sufficient. It is now possible to pass land by *donatio mortis causa* by parting with dominion over the title deeds.

There is a general rule that equity will not assist a volunteer, so that if a person unsuccessfully attempts to make a gift, the donee cannot appeal to equity to perfect the gift. However, the rule in *Strong v Bird* is an apparent exception to this. It says that where the person who obtains the legal title to the deceased's property by virtue of being their personal representative after death also has the equitable claim on the property, the gift is thus perfected. This may be compared with the rules concerning incompletely constituted trusts. Equity will perfect a gift incompletely made only if the settlor or donor had so put the property out of their own control that they had become the trustee of the property.

If the deceased held property on a joint tenancy then it will automatically pass to any surviving joint tenant(s) at their death. Leaving a share of a joint tenancy by will is not possible; the joint tenancy must be severed before death. Once this is done, the property held by a person as tenant in common will pass in accordance with their will or intestacy.

Certain relatives of tenants of land may be entitled by statute to succeed to their tenancies and it should not be forgotten that equity will recognise a secret trust, where it can be proved.

## 📖 2.12 Further reading

Elizabeth Cooke, 'Estoppel and the Protection of Expectations' (1997) 17 Legal Studies 258.

Jamie Glister, 'Section 199 of the Equality Act 2010: How Not to Abolish the Presumption of Advancement' (2010) 73 Modern Law Review 807.

Kelvin Low, 'Presumption of Advancement: A Renaissance?' (2007) 123 Law Quarterly Review 347.

Charles A Reich, 'The New Property' (1964) 73 Yale Law Journal 733.

Charles A Reich, 'The New Property After 25 Years' (1989) 24 University of San Francisco Law Review 223.

N Roberts, '*Donationes mortis causa* in a dematerialised world' (2013) 2 Conveyancer and Property Lawyer 113.

# Chapter 3

# Nature and Characteristics of a Will

The testator's will, in the sense of the means of making their testamentary dispositions, is the document or documents in which they have expressed what they wish and intend to become of their property at their death. It should embody their will in the sense of their volition. If the testator has not had a will, in the sense of a volition, to make testamentary gifts of their property, then even if they make and execute a document which states on the face of it that it is the testator's will and which complies with all the formalities laid down by statute, the lack of intention to make a will means that the document does not operate as such.

The will, to be valid, must comply with all the necessary formalities: for most people, those mean a written document. It must be intended to take effect at the testator's death, disposing of their property or making other appointments. If it complies with all the requirements of formality and makes testamentary dispositions, it will be the testator's will even if it does not describe itself as such and the testator would not have said in terms that they were making a will. As elsewhere in the law, where an arrangement may be a lease if it fulfils the conditions for a lease and even if it does not describe itself as such, it is the substance, not the label, that is important.

## 3.1 Meaning of 'will'

Anything which is propounded (brought into the probate process) as the testator's will must have all the necessary characteristics of a will and also comply with the formalities. If both these general conditions are satisfied, then the will is valid; whether or not it describes itself specifically as a 'will' is not important.

A will that has been proved is a public document. This may seem less odd following the opening of the Land Register in 1990, but nevertheless, given the much more personal matters involved, could be considered to raise issues of privacy.[1]

### 3.1.1 Will is ambulatory

A will is ambulatory. This means that it is of no effect until the testator dies. The will may be changed at any time up until death. A declaration by a testator in their will that it is irrevocable is of no effect. The testator may revoke the will, including the clause stating that the will cannot be revoked, if they wish. The beneficiary named in the will obtains no interest or rights until the testator's death.

Before 1926, wills were not ambulatory as regards real property. This meant that the real property to which a will could refer was fixed at the date the will was made. If the testator made a gift of 'all my real property', it would not include any real property acquired after the date of the will. Moreover, the formalities for realty and personalty were different before the Wills Act of

---

1 Joseph Jaconelli, 'Wills as Public Documents: Privacy and Property Rights' (2012) 71 Cambridge Law Journal 147.

1837. This is no longer the case; the same formalities now apply to real and personal property, so far as wills are concerned. This might be compared to the provisions for passing property *inter vivos* (between living persons), when common law and statute lay down different requirements for the passing of land and personalty (see 2.2). The Wills Act 1837 is still in force; although it has been variously amended, the essence of a will has remained the same throughout.

### 3.1.2 How many documents?

Although the word 'will' is usually thought of as meaning – and is usually used to mean – a single document in which the testator sets out their intended testamentary dispositions, it is important to remember that, properly speaking, the testator's will is the embodiment of all their testamentary dispositions as whole in a form the law recognises as valid after their death. Thus, the testator has, strictly speaking, only one will, but it may be made up of many testamentary documents. The Privy Council considered this question in *Douglas-Menzies v Umphelby* (1908), saying:

> It is the aggregate or the net result that constitutes his will, or, in other words, the expression of his testamentary wishes. The law, on a man's death, finds out what are the instruments which express his last will.... In this sense, it is inaccurate to speak of a man leaving two wills; he does leave, and can leave, but one will.

## 3.2 Intention to make a will

Although a will may, in the appropriate circumstances, be found in various and perhaps unexpected forms, no one can ever make a will accidentally. It is one of the indispensable requirements of a valid will, of whatever kind, that the testator should have *animus testandi* (the intention of making a will) when the will is executed. Lack of testamentary intention renders a purported will invalid. The question of intention should not arise with a professionally-drawn will; the testator will have consulted their solicitor specifically to have a will drawn and there can be no doubt as to what they intended. Home-made wills, however, may be in the form of a letter, so that the true intention of the writer has to be inferred after their death from the words they use, and the privileged (or informal) wills of soldiers and sailors may be made orally (see Chapter 6), so that even establishing what was said, let alone the intention behind it, can present difficulties. Nevertheless, the intention to make a testamentary disposition must be established if the will, or codicil, is to be admitted to probate. The personal representatives must also give effect to the wishes contained in a valid will; they have no entitlement to carry out wishes expressed in a way which does not amount to a will just because they sincerely believe they represent the deceased's intention.

The case of *Corbett v Newey* (1996), confirmed that testamentary intention must coincide with the execution of the will. In the case the deceased, Miss Tresawna, had owned two farms which were occupied by relatives and which she had originally intended to leave to them by will, with the residue of her estate to the same persons equally. She then decided to make *inter vivos* gifts of the farms to their occupiers and leave the residue to two great-nephews, and instructed her solicitors accordingly. The will was ready in September, before the deeds of gift of the farms, and Miss Tresawna, realising that if she died having made the will but not the deeds, the farms would pass to the great-nephews, executed but did not date the will. She and her solicitor were under the incorrect impression that the will would become valid only when dated; however, a date is not a formal requirement (see 5.19). In December, the *inter vivos* gifts were made and Miss Tresawna dated her will. After her death, her niece claimed that the will was invalid because, when she executed it in September, Miss Tresawna had no immediate testamentary intention. In the first instance she lost, as the court found the will made in September valid as a conditional will. The Court of Appeal, however, found for the niece on the basis that the will was not conditional on the face of it and no extrinsic evidence was admissible to make it so; therefore, the question was simply whether it had been duly executed with testamentary intention and, clearly, it had not.

### 3.2.1 Presumption of intention

It is questionable how far proof of the necessary intention or *animus testandi* is required, or whether it will be presumed if the document appears to be intended to operate as a will. Certainly, however, any such presumption is subject, like any presumption, to being rebutted by evidence, as it was in *Corbett v Newey* (1996) (see 3.2). In *Nichols v Nichols* (1814), the deceased was a solicitor who, after a meal at which alcohol was drunk and the verbosity of lawyers criticised, made a document reading: 'I leave my property between my children; I hope they will be virtuous and independent; that they will worship God, and not black coats.' He wrote out his purported will with little apparent care and left it with his friend who later attested the signature (the formalities for attestation have since changed). There was evidence that the deceased died believing that he had no will and stating that his property would devolve quite satisfactorily on intestacy; the court accepted that the purported will had been a demonstration of how brief the deceased could make a will – it was based on the will of his friend, but much shorter – and perhaps even a joke. The will therefore failed for want of testamentary intention. Note that the state of mind of a testator is also relevant to their revocation of a will.

### 3.2.2 Document not made of testator's free volition

The testator may appear to have made a will freely and of their own volition, but appearances may be misleading. Even if the document contains dispositions which are exactly what the testator could be expected to make, it may be shown that the testator was pushed into making the document itself through the undue influence of another person, or that they did not know of the contents of the document and approve them before they executed the document. The details of other circumstances in which a will which is properly executed may yet fail for want of satisfaction of other mental requirements are dealt with in Chapter 4.

## 3.3 Conditional wills

A will may be conditional on certain events. For instance, it may be made expressly to take effect only if the testator should die on a particular voyage. If they survived the voyage, the will would then be of no effect. This is what occurred in *In the Goods of Robinson* (1870), where the will was expressed to be made 'in case anything should happen to me during the remainder of the voyage from here to Sicily and back to London'. He survived that voyage but died without making another will. The court held that the will was valid only if he died on the voyage specified. Similarly, in *Folds v Abrahart* (2003), a will made on the basis 'if we should die together' was held to be a conditional will and so invalid when the relevant parties did not die together.

Whether the will is conditional in such a way depends on the wording in each case; the precise meaning of the words used by the testator is a recurrent theme in the cases about wills. By the time the question arises, it is inevitably too late to ask the one person whose answer might be most useful. If the testator's intention was to make a conditional will, it will have to be established what the conditions were and whether or not they have been satisfied. Thus, resort may have to be had to a court as the final arbiter of not only what words mean but also of what a testator meant when they used them. In In the Goods of Spratt (1897), a soldier on campaign who expressed himself as writing to his sister because

> the chances are in favour of more of us being killed and as I may not have another opportunity of saying what I wish to be done with any little money I may possess in case of an accident, I wish to make everything I possess over to you

He was held to have shown the necessary intention to make an unconditional will.

## 3.4 Testator may do other things by will than dispose of property

As well as doing what one would conventionally think of as the purpose of a will, namely disposing of their property, a testator may do other things by will. They may appoint testamentary guardians, though the formalities for this are less strict since s 5 of the Children Act 1989 came into force in 1991. Appointments of guardians for children may now be made in ordinary writing.

A testator may also exercise powers of appointment by will – note that if they do so in another document which fulfils all the requirements of a will, including that it should take effect only on death, then the court may admit that document to probate too.

### 3.4.1 Testator may not dispose of his or her body by will

Testators may not, however, dispose of their own bodies by will, though attempts to do so are regularly made. The entitlement to possession of the body resides in the executors, and personal representatives generally have the primary duty of disposing of it in accordance with regulations about public health. Funeral arrangements are generally made amongst family in accordance with their religious beliefs or of lack of them, and the right to make those arrangements is not generally a subject of legal dispute, albeit since the deceased wishes are likely to be represented through the same people, any such dispute is unlikely to surface for practical reasons.

Generally a person will have said what sort of funeral they want and the family will respect those wishes, but not as a matter of legal obligation. Personal representatives do not have any rights of ownership in the body: private property in humans or parts of them is not generally recognised in English law. No doubt it often appears effective for testators to make directions as to the disposal of their bodies by will, as they do with their property, but such directions are effective only insofar as their executors choose to abide by them. In any event, the funeral will inevitably take place before probate is granted, and generally before the provisions of the will are addressed; it is usually felt to be decent to see off the bodily remains of the deceased before dealing with claims on their property. (For the avoidance of doubt, formal will-readings are found in movies, but not in real life.) It can thus be an extremely bad idea to rely on putting one's wishes as to the disposal of one's body only into one's will. The grieving relatives will undoubtedly return from the crematorium to find, too late, that the deceased wished to leave their body to medical science.

### 3.4.2 Organ donation

As with funeral arrangements, if a person wishes their organs to be available for medical transplants, they should make sure that their relatives are aware of that. Dealings with dead bodies and parts of them (as well as some issues relating to the tissue of living persons) are now governed by the Human Tissue Act 2004. This emphasises the importance of consent, whilst also making it easier to be sure of having sufficient consent. Schedule 1 to the Act sets out the purposes for which bodies may be used with the 'appropriate' consent, which is to be obtained from a ranked list of persons: these purposes include organ donation for transplantation. The list of those who can consent is based on a widening circle of family relationships, and so resembles the list of those entitled on intestacy under r 22 of the Non-Contentious Probate Rules (NCPR), but with the addition of step-parents and 'friends of long standing'. Moreover there are broad provisions for passing over anyone in the list. For wider, more public purposes, the deceased's own consent is required, as where the body is to be used for clinical audit or health education or training. Whilst the Act emphasises the primacy of the wishes of the deceased, it remains unlikely that doctors would in practice take organs for transplantation against the wishes of the remaining family, however clear it was that the deceased wanted to donate them.

The immediate political impetus for the Act was a series of media scandals over retention of children's body parts by doctors without the consent or indeed knowledge of their parents; the fundamental ethical question had been at issue since widespread transplantation became possible, and need exceeded availability. The Parliamentary Under Secretary of State for Health said in the House of Commons in 1991:

> We must accept that nobody has a right to anybody else's organs. If something untoward happens, our organs may be of value to someone else but that should be the result of an altruistic decision about how we want our bodies to be used when we die. It should not be as a result of a right of the recipient.... It is the responsibility of the living whose organs may be of use to someone else; it is not anyone else's job to claim the organs.[2]

The treatment and use of body parts clearly operates outside the law of property, which is the area into which the topics of wills and succession most obviously fall. There are nevertheless similarities in the underlying issues, especially how personal autonomy to be exercised after the person's death should be weighed against the moral claims of those who may live on. Although this is a political and ethical, rather than legal, question, the law does have to take a stance. Medical organisations in Britain tend to favour 'opt-out' provisions, by which doctors may take a person's organs on their death to use for transplants unless the person has registered an objection, but the current law in Britain remains 'opt-in', so that a positive form of consent, as defined by the 2004 Act, is necessary.

## 3.5 When is a will valid?

The most important date is the date of death. A will is valid to pass any property the deceased has at their death if it was made with the necessary mental capacity and intention and is executed in accordance with formalities laid down by the Wills Act 1837. The same applies to a codicil, which is a document amending a will but otherwise fulfilling all the same functions and conditions.

---

2  Stephen Dorrell. HC Deb 28 March 1991, vol 188, col 1140.

## 3.5.1 Presumption of will where document fulfils requirements

Although a will usually does describe itself as such, it is not necessary for it to do so. Lord Penzance in *Cock v Cooke* (1866) said:

> It is undoubted law that whatever may be the form of a duly executed instrument, if the person executing it intends that it shall not take effect until after his death, and it is dependent upon his death for its vigour and effect, it is testamentary.

If a document appears to be testamentary, a presumption will arise that the deceased intended it to take effect only at their death. This presumption may arise if the document complies with the formalities prescribed by the Wills Act 1837.

In *Re Morgan* (1866), the deceased had executed during his lifetime three deeds of gift conveying property to trustees for the benefit of his children. Each deed of gift contained a clause directing that it was not to take effect until after his death. The court looked at all the deeds and held that, taking them all together, they contained the deceased's will. They had been signed and witnessed in accordance with the formalities required for wills and they made dispositions which were to take effect on death. The court therefore granted probate of the deeds of gift as the deceased's will. In *Miles v Foden* (1890), the testatrix had executed a power of appointment over property by making revocable deeds which would take effect on her death. The court held that the deeds fulfilled all the requirements of a will and therefore admitted them to probate. In a much more recent case, that of *Re Berger* (1989), the court granted probate of a Jewish religious will as an English will because it was shown that the testator had fulfilled all the mental and formal requirements for an English will and had intended the document to take effect in all essential ways just as he would have done had he intended it as an English will. The religious will contained provisions also found in a purported earlier English will which had been found invalid; finding the religious will valid as an English will thus save the effects of those provisions.

## 3.5.2 Requirements

The court in *Re Berger* (1989) (3.5.1) held that, to be a valid provable will, an instrument must:

(a)   make a revocable disposition of the testator's property;
(b)   be in accordance with the formalities laid down in the Wills Act 1837;
(c)   be intended to take effect on death.

However, the testator need not have intended the document and its contents to be admissible to probate as an English will or even have addressed their mind to that point.

# 3.6 Provisions must be certain to be valid

For a will to be valid, the testator must not only have intended to make a will and have executed it with whatever formalities are necessary, but must also have made provisions which do not fall foul of the law – for example, contravening the rule against perpetuities. In particular, the gifts must be sufficiently certain.

## 3.6.1 Delegation of testamentary powers

It is a principle that testators may not delegate their testamentary power. This means that they may not pass it on to others on the basis that those others are entitled not to the property itself but to choose who will take it. The basis of this was expressed by Lord Haldane in the cases of *Houston v Burns* (1918) and *AG v National Provincial and Union Bank of England* (1924). In the former, he said:

> A testator can defeat the claim of those entitled by law in the absence of a valid will to succeed to the beneficial interest in his estate only if he has made a complete disposition of that beneficial interest. He cannot leave it to another person to make such a disposition for him unless he has passed the beneficial interest to that person to dispose of as his own.

More succinctly, in the later case he said: 'a man cannot disinherit his heir by giving away his property unless he really gives it away.'

### 3.6.2 Powers of appointment

The prohibition on the delegation of testamentary powers may appear to be somewhat contradicted by the possibility that a power of appointment may be conferred on, for instance, the trustees of a will. The testator in *Re Park* (1932) gave his residuary estate in trust, the income to be paid to such person (other than his sister Jane) or charitable institution as his sister Jane should direct in writing. The court referred to the principle that a testator may confer a general or a special power on any person by will and held that this was an 'intermediate' power and thus valid. The testatrix in *Re Carville* (1937), however, left £100 to each of her executors, with the residue to be disposed of 'as my executors shall think fit'. The court held that the disposition relating to the residue gave powers to the executors which were too wide and held that the residue went on intestacy because the gift failed. The essence of the rule is that a power given to trustees to appoint beneficiaries will be valid if the testator draws the class of beneficiaries from whom they may choose. This includes a class subject to a 'hybrid' power, like that in *Re Park*, where certain named individuals may be excluded.

### 3.6.3 Gifts to charity

The rule about the delegation of testamentary powers does not apply in the case of gifts to charities, since charity is considered to be a whole. However, if a gift infringes the rule against delegation and is not truly, but only potentially, charitable, it will not be saved. In *Chichester Diocesan Fund and Board of Finance v Simpson* (1944), the testator had directed his executors to apply his residuary estate for such 'charitable or benevolent' objects in England as they might in their absolute discretion select. The House of Lords held that the gift failed for uncertainty because it was not confined to charitable objects. Lord Simonds said:

> It is a cardinal rule ... that a man may not delegate his testamentary power. To him the law gives the right to dispose of his estate in favour of ascertained or ascertainable persons. He does not exercise the right if in effect he empowers his executors to say what persons or objects are to be his beneficiaries. To this salutary rule there is a single exception. A testator may validly leave it to his executors to determine what charitable objects shall benefit, so long as charitable and no other objects may benefit.

Where, however, the gift was not truly and exclusively charitable, that exception could not apply.

### 3.6.4 Other jurisdictions

It is worth noting that English law is particularly relaxed about the principle of delegation of testamentary power, and has always been happy for the same rules of certainty to apply in wills as in *inter vivos* trusts – broadly, that there is no need to be able to provide a complete list of beneficiaries, but that it is enough that, in any individual case, you can say whether or not the person is included (*McPhail v Doulton* (1970); *Re Beatty's Will Trusts* (1990)). The situation has been different, for example, in Australia. Several types of powers of appointment were rejected by Fullagan J in the case of *Tatham v Huxtable* (1950), including the 'hybrid' type of appointment mentioned in *Re Park* (3.6.2), where the choice amongst a class is restricted in respect of certain named individuals. It was also held in *Re Lutheran Church of Australia* (1970) that a power of appointment in favour of a range of beneficiaries consisting of one object would fail, and in *Re Nevil Shute Norway* (1963), that a power given for trustees to encroach on a gift to another beneficiary was likewise invalid – though it might have been valid in substance if drafted differently. But there has been much criticism of the rule, for example the statement of Thomas J in *Re Blyth* (1997) that: 'It is difficult to see why a person should not be able to dispose of property by will in the same way as he or she may dispose of it in his or her lifetime.' The trajectory appears to be towards the English analysis: in New South Wales, the rule in *Tatham v Huxtable* was removed by legislation in 2006.[3]

### 3.6.5 Certainty or delegation?

In the English jurisdiction, the principle that there should be no delegation of testamentary power has become indistinguishable in practice from the principle that gifts must be certain if they are not to be void for uncertainty, and any court asked to make a decision on the former point would probably be referred mostly to decisions on the latter.

## 3.7 Contents of wills

This book is not concerned with how to draft a will, but it is often useful to consider the outline of a basic will at the outset in order to see what shape it takes and how the clauses of the will fit together. Knowing what structure a will should have often makes it easier to see how problems and ambiguities have arisen. The essential structure of a will is what is contained on a printed will form of the sort obtainable in non-specialist shops such as newsagents, but in the individual situation of each testator it is likely that several clauses may require particular consideration and explanation if the clause is to be drafted to suit that testator precisely. A large part of the art of giving appropriate legal advice in matters of succession (as in other matters) consists in identifying potential difficulties or potential outcomes. However, how much an individual needs specialist advice depends not only on their assets and responsibilities but also on how those will change before they next update their will. The frequency of home-made wills is likely to increase as lawyering is increasingly deprofessionalised. Disputes over wills, however, will probably continue to require and attract specialist legal input.

---

3  Succession Act 2006 (New South Wales, Australia).

### 3.7.1 How a will is usually set out

Most professionally-drawn wills much resemble each other, at least in structure, the usual form being a logical order even if each firm of solicitors or even each individual solicitor has a particular way of dealing with each item. The basic parts of the structure might be categorised as follows:

(a) Setting the scene
- testator's name and address
- recitation that this is a will

(b) Preliminaries
- revocation of previous wills
- appointment of executors and trustees

(c) Dispositions – giving away the property
- provisions for payments of debts and expenses
- particular gifts to individuals
- provision as to from where legacies should be paid
- gifts of what remains (residue)
- substitutional gifts in case certain gifts fail

(d) Administrative powers for executors and trustees in addition to their powers under statute

(e) Execution
- testimonium (recitation that the testator signs to validate their will)
- attestation clause (reciting the presence of the testator and witnesses on signature by the testator)
- signatures of testator and witnesses

### 3.7.2 Example of will

A form of will might look like this:

This is the last will of me John Bonaparte of 13 Napoleon Street Bethnal Green

1. I revoke all testamentary dispositions previously made by me
2. I appoint my wife Josephine Bonaparte of 13 Napoleon Street Bethnal Green and Peter Alexander solicitor of 24 Moscow Avenue Chiswick to be the executors and trustees of this my will and I declare that the expression 'my trustees' used in this my will or in any codicil hereto shall mean the executors or trustees for the time being of this my will
3. I give the following specific legacies free of inheritance tax:
   (a) To my wife Josephine Bonaparte my yacht *Warfarer*
   (b) To my grandson Jasper Palmerston my collection of the novels of Charles Dickens bound in leather
4. I give the following pecuniary legacies free of inheritance tax:
   (a) To Ann Marengo-Brown the sum of £30,000 (thirty thousand pounds)
   (b) To Ethel Wellington-Smith the sum of £25,000 (twenty-five thousand pounds)
5. I give the whole residue of my estate (out of which shall be paid my funeral and testamentary expenses my debts and legacies and all inheritance tax payable in respect of the property passing under this will or arising on my death in respect of any gift made by me in my lifetime) to my trustees on trust:
   (a) For my wife Josephine Bonaparte absolutely if she survives me for the period of one calendar month and subject thereto
   (b) for such of my children living at my death as attain the age of twenty-one years and if more than one in equal shares but if any child of mine dies before attaining a vested

interest but leaving a child or children alive at or born after my own death who attain the age of twenty-one such child or children shall take absolutely and if more than one in equal shares such whole or part of the trust fund as that child of mine would have taken had such child lived to attain a vested interest

(c) In the event of the failure of the trusts hereinbefore declared my trustees shall hold the trust fund for The Old War Horse Charity absolutely (registered charity No . . .)

6. I declare that if under this will any money shall become payable to a beneficiary under the age of eighteen years then the receipt of the parent or guardian of such-beneficiary shall be a sufficient discharge to my trustees

7. My trustees shall have the following powers in addition to their powers under the general law:

(a) To exercise the power contained in s 31 of the Trustee Act 1925 in relation to any contingent gifts hereinbefore declared but as if the words 'the trustees may in their absolute discretion think fit' had been substituted for 'may in all the circumstances be reasonable' in paragraph (i) of subsection (1) and as if the proviso at the end of sub-section (1) had been omitted

(b) To exercise the power of advancement contained in s 32 of the Trustee Act 1925 but as if proviso (a) to subsection (1) were omitted provided that whenever s 71 of the Inheritance Tax Act 1984 or any enactment amending or replacing the same applies or would apply in respect of the whole or any part of the trust fund the said power shall not be capable of being exercised in any way which whether such exercise were carried out or were possible would prevent the said section from applying as aforesaid except and insofar as one or more 'beneficiaries' as defined in subsection (1)(a) of the said section would if such section ceased to apply become entitled to or to an interest in possession in the advanced part of the trust fund[4]

(c) To invest trust money and transpose investments with unrestricted freedom in their choice of investment as if they were absolutely entitled and to purchase retain maintain or improve a freehold or leasehold house or other dwelling in any part of the world including any for use by my beneficiaries as a dwelling-house

(d) All the powers of a beneficial owner including power to borrow on the security of all or any part of my estate or otherwise and for any purpose

8. Any executor or trustee of this my will who is a solicitor or other professional may charge and be paid all usual fees for work done by him or his firm in proving my will and carrying out its trusts including work outside the usual course of his profession which he could or should have done personally had he not been a professional person

9. In the execution of the trusts and powers hereof or of any statutory power my trustees shall not be liable for any loss in respect of any property for the time being comprised in the trust fund arising by reason of any improper investment made in good faith or for the negligence or fraud of any agent employed in good faith by any of the trustees or by reason of any mistake or omission made in good faith by a trustee or by reason of any other matter save individual fraud or wrongdoing by the trustee who is sought to be made liable

AS WITNESS my hand this first day of October 2014
SIGNED by the testator John
Bonaparte in our joint
presence and then by us in his ⎤ _____   _____
⎭

---

4 Clauses 7 (a) and (b): this is a common expansion of trustee powers expanding the powers under the 1925 Trustee Act. In 2014 statute was updated to take account of legal practice by virtue of the Inheritance and Trustees Powers Act 2014: the text here is the default statutory position before that Act. These clauses will therefore be found in wills made before October 2014.

The recital at the top of the document makes it easy to see what the document is but is not a technical requirement.

**(1)** Revocation clause

The revocation clause revokes all previous dispositions by will or codicil. Revocation may occur by other means, as discussed in Chapter 7, but revocation of all previous dispositions when making a will is standard, and good, practice. Revocation clauses are included in will forms, though their operation is sometimes misunderstood.

**(2)** Appointment of executors and trustees

Executors and trustees are appointed in the next clause. Here, two persons are appointed, which is usual except when there is a sole beneficiary of full age. Testators often appoint substitute executors in the event the other testators cannot act. The appointment of executors is dealt with in Chapter 12. Personal representatives are the people who take the place of the deceased and deal with their property after death.[5]

The executors will carry out the terms of the will, getting in the money and property belonging to the estate, paying the debts of the estate and the expenses involved in the administration and distributing the remaining property in accordance with the terms of the will and the general law. Executors and trustees should be people the testator trusts to deal with the estate efficiently and, especially if they are given any discretion, they should be people whom the testator trusts to know what he or she would have wanted. They should be people in whom the testator has complete confidence, even if they are expected to hand the paperwork over to a solicitor, and they should be able to work together. If there is property in the estate that will not vest in the appropriate beneficiary immediately – where there is a contingent gift (for example, one dependent on the beneficiary attaining a certain age), or where someone does not have an absolute interest (for instance, where a life interest arises), then trustees will be needed to administer the property involved.

**(3)–(4)** Dispositive provisions

Only at this point does a will in its usual structure begin the dispositive provisions – so called because they involve the disposal of the testator's property which many people think of as being the sole aim of a will.

The first dispositive provisions are usually specific gifts – gifts of a particular piece of property. These are usually followed by pecuniary and general legacies, which are gifts of money or of items which are not special parts of the testator's estate. The order in which these are mentioned in a will is not technically important because it is the type of gift which governs how it will be classified, not where it appears in the document. How each sort of gift is classified can be very important when it comes to deciding whether a legatee will get all of their gift. The distinctions between the different sorts of gifts are dealt with in Chapter 10.

**(5)** Dealing with failure

Different things happen to different sorts of legacies and their subject matter when they fail. There are some standard ways of dealing with the practical effects of failure of gifts, one of which is to provide an alternative should the original beneficiary not survive for a certain period. This 'survivorship clause' deals with the situation where the testator's chosen beneficiary would not be able to enjoy the property because the two died at the same, or almost the same, time. For more on what happens when two people die together, see references to *commorientes*.

---

5 These are called executors if there is a will dealing with the estate and administrators if the deceased dies intestate. Where there is a will which deals with only part of the estate, the personal representatives will take a grant of administration with will annexed.

The dispositive provisions should always include a 'gift over' of residue, even in the simplest of wills, or even where it appears that a testator has made sufficient substitutional provisions to deal with a major family disaster. The well-drawn will should always deal with the total catastrophe situation in which the testator's nearest and dearest are all wiped out and he or she too dies before updating the will further. If there is no provision by will to dispose of a deceased's property, they are said to be intestate, and the general law governs where their property goes (see Chapter 9). If the deceased dies intestate they will have lost the opportunity of choosing what becomes of their property and of maximising tax advantages and making the administration of their estate easier and more efficient. If only part of the testator's property is not disposed of by will, the deceased is said to be partially intestate, so the general law deals with the undisposed part of their property. A gift over to charity will solve such difficulties since gifts to charity will never fail (provided they are exclusively charitable). It is helpful, but not vital, to include a charity's registered number, which can readily be obtained from the charity itself. If there is difficulty in obtaining a number, it may be the case that the organisation is not, in fact, a charity. Universities are frequently exempt charities and do not have charity numbers although they have charitable status.

**(6)–(9)** Administrative powers

Specifying who is to deal with the estate and the beneficiaries to whom they are to pass the assets is not enough; the general law does not provide adequate powers for personal representatives and trustees to deal efficiently with a testator's property, especially where there are potential difficulties such as trusts for minor children or where property – for example a business – cannot simply be held in an inert state before being passed to a beneficiary of full age and able therefore to give a good receipt.

The possibility of having administrative clauses giving such powers is a very important reason for having a will. Powers which are commonly needed are those of investment, appropriation without consent, carrying on of any business and the power to take a receipt from a child under 18 or their parent or guardian. Why such clauses are needed can be seen in Chapter 13. Whilst the effects of the Trusts of Land and Appointment of Trustees Act 1996 and the Trustee Act 2000 may make some common trust powers redundant, especial care should be taken where a trust may turn out not to contain land.

Execution

The will ends with the 'testimonium' – a recitation that the testator signs to execute their will, leaving no room for doubt about the matter – and an attestation clause and the signatures of the testator and witnesses. Though the inclusion of the clause itself is not necessary as a technical matter, it makes the paperwork easier. The testimonium and attestation clause will give rise to a presumption that the testator had testamentary intention and that the will was properly attested. Precedents can be found for attestation clauses that confirm, for example, appropriate attestation; by a blind testator. The formalities for signing and witnessing are dealt with in Chapter 5 thorough knowledge of the formalities for wills is fundamental to the study and practice of this area of the law.

## 3.7.3 Any other matters

This is by no means an exhaustive outline of what may be found in a fairly ordinary will. Testators may wish to make (unenforceable and perhaps unhelpful) statements about how they wish their bodies to be disposed of, or may wish to set up more complex trusts or to make provisions about how the will should be treated in relation to other wills which deal with foreign property. They may need to impose other powers or to make their provisions dependent on the precise operation of the Inheritance Tax regulations. They may appoint guardians for minor children. Nevertheless, professionally-drawn wills follow the same basic structure, which reflects the essential matters that arise when a person dies and their affairs need to be wound up.

# 3.8 Summary of Chapter 3

## 3.8.1 Nature and Characteristics of a Will

The testator's will is the expression of their wishes of what will become of their property at death, made in a way the law recognises as enforceable. A will is of no effect until the testator's death and may be revoked at any time before then.

The testator must have the mental capacity to make the will and must also have testamentary intention. However, these will usually be presumed. A document which fulfils all the requirements for a will may be admitted to probate whether or not it describes itself as a will and whether or not the testator thought they were making a will as such. A will may be expressly conditional on certain events or may be found to have been conditional.

The testator must make their gifts sufficiently certain, because otherwise they will fail. Testamentary power – such as the ability to give away property – may not be delegated. The will should also make provision for where the testator's property should go if their original choice of gifts fails; for example, if a beneficiary predeceases them. Otherwise, the rules of intestacy will apply and the testator will have lost the opportunity of deciding where the property will go.

A professionally-drawn will in particular may do many things as well as dispose of property. It will appoint executors to deal with the administration of the estate and will usually give them powers over and above those given by the general law. That applies particularly where there is a fund which continues to need to be administered after the winding up of the estate itself. In that case, the testator will generally appoint trustees and give them a wide discretion to administer the fund. In relation to estates arising after 1996, personal representatives and trustees have wide powers under the general law where the estate includes land.

There is no property in the body of the deceased, but wishes as to its disposal – whether funeral arrangements or organ donation – will normally be carried out. People should, however, make those wishes clear to family or friends before death, or at least readily accessible and obvious on death. There is unlikely to be any comeback if the deceased's wishes are not adhered to, as those who would try to enforce any such wishes are likely to be those family members whose wishes have taken precedence.

# Chapter 4

# Capacity to Make a Will

The issue of testamentary capacity, or the mental capabilities needed to be able to make a valid will, has become a focus for contested cases. More and more frequently, disappointed family members in particular question the ability of their deceased relatives to make a valid will, often asserting that when they left their property to someone else, that was the result of their mental deterioration and not their true will. There is nowadays a wide appreciation of degenerative diseases such as Alzheimer's, which may progressively destroy a person's mental capacity. The underlying issue, however, is not new. Owning property and deciding what to do with it is so fundamental to a person's individual rights that any test of capacity to deal with property has implications for basic freedoms; restrictions must be kept to a minimum. Undoubtedly, though, a person may be deluded in ways that do mean their transactions are not really their true will, or they may be deliberately subjected to external pressures that produce the same effect. Succession law has long had to deal with these issues, and has evolved its own tests and rules. Doctors may be invited to record an opinion on the mental capacity of someone making a will, if it may be queried later, and it is good practice to obtain a medical report if that is the situation, but the legal issues that need to be satisfied are quite specific, and defining where the borderline of capacity lies depends on the law, not on medical opinion.

## 4.1  Need for testamentary capacity, free will and knowledge and approval

A person may make a valid will under English law provided that (save in the case of privileged wills) they are over the age of majority and they comply with the prescribed formalities and (in all cases) provided that the necessary mental elements are present. The testator must have the mental capacity to make a will and they must not be unduly influenced by any other person. The will must be truly the testator's — that is, they must know and approve of all parts of it that are to be admitted to probate. This last point can give rise to difficulties where the testator knew and approved of the words in the will but was mistaken as to their meaning. The documentary will should give expression to the testator's true 'will' about what should become of their property. Mummery LJ expressed this in *Hawes v Burgess* (2013):

> The basic legal requirement for validity are that people are mentally capable of understanding what they are doing when they make their will and that what is in the will truly reflects what they freely wish to be done with their estate on their death.

### 4.1.1  Age
Section 7 of the Wills Act 1837 provides that no will made by a minor shall be valid. When the 1837 Act was originally passed, that meant a person under 21. However, the recommendations made in 1967 by the Latey Committee on the Age of Majority that the age of majority be lowered

to 18 were implemented by the Family Law Reform Act 1969. Thus, with effect from January 1970 the age of majority has been 18.

The provisions of s 7 are part of the formalities from which soldiers and sailors are excluded (see the subject of privileged wills, at 6.5). Soldiers and sailors have always been able to make wills informally provided they come within the meaning of s 11 of the 1837 Act.

The attitude of the legislature to when a child becomes an adult varies depending on the topic under consideration. A person who is under the age for making a will may not own realty but may still marry, for instance. In New Zealand the rule is mitigated by a provision allowing a person to make a will under the age of majority if they have married, are in a civil union or a de facto relationship, or if they are at least 16 and have satisfied the family court that they understand the effect of making a will. The age for making a will is however generally the age of 'majority' or when a person becomes entitled to the most fundamental attributes of the adult citizen, such as the right to vote or to own a legal estate in land.

The Latey Committee in the 1960s felt that the age of majority needed lowering from 21 in respect of the making of wills because young adults often had responsibilities, including families of their own, which they needed to be able to make arrangements for in case of their death. The emphasis of the committee's reasoning was on the practical arrangements for the deceased's property rather than any consideration of the right of a person of the age of 18 to deal with their own affairs in full.

### 4.1.2 Other ways to challenge a will

The capacity to make a will is usually thought of in terms of mental capacity, or sometimes knowledge and approval. As contentious probate actions have become more frequent, often both these points are argued together by disappointed beneficiaries trying to overturn the will (see Chapter 16). However, since family provision legislation was introduced in 1938 it is no longer necessary for disappointed relatives to prove that the testator was mentally incapable as the court may provide for them anyway by overriding the valid dispositions of the testator (see Chapter 15).

### 4.1.3 Other ways to make a will

It has also been possible since the amendment of the Mental Health Act 1959 by the Administration of Justice Act 1969, now superseded by the Mental Capacity Act 2005, for the Court of Protection to make a will for a person who has become mentally incapable. For more on this point, see the subject of statutory wills (see 6.7).

### 4.1.4 Courts will define testamentary capacity on a legal basis

A testator must have the requisite mental capacity to make a will in order for it to be valid. A will may therefore be challenged on the basis that the testator lacked capacity, and as people live longer with more debilitating conditions, those challenges become more frequent.[1] If there is a dispute over whether the testator had the necessary mental capacity the court will consider the case on its own facts. This means that the standard of mental capacity will depend on a legal definition of mental incapacity, not a medical one, although medical evidence may be crucial to the

---

1 KI Shulman, CA Cohen and I Hull 'Psychiatric Issues in Retrospective Challenges of Testamentary Capacity' (2005) 20 International Journal of Geriatric Psychiatry 63.

court's decision. The courts were for a long time bound to apply the principles discernible from previous decisions, many of which were reached in the nineteenth century. Those principles are now overlain by the Mental Capacity Act 2005.

The 2005 Act brought in statutory provisions, building on a statement of overarching principles in s 1. It is presumed that a person has capacity unless the contrary is established on the balance of probabilities and a person is not to be treated as unable to make a decision unless all practical steps have been taken to help them do so without success. A person cannot be treated as being unable to make a decision just because they make an unwise one.

The test of capacity is specific both to the particular decision and to the time it is being made. A person may be capable of making a decision one day and not the next, or at a particular time of day but not all the time. All acts and decisions under the 2005 Act must be done in the person's best interests, and regard must always be had to whether something to be achieved on the person's behalf can be done in a way that is less restrictive of their rights and freedom of action.

Section 2 of the Act says that people lack capacity to make a particular decision if at the material time they are unable to make a decision for themselves in relation to the matter because of an impairment of, or a disturbance in, the function of the mind or brain, whether it is a permanent or temporary disturbance. Section 3 says that a person is considered unable to make a decision if they cannot understand and/or retain the relevant information, and/or cannot use or weigh that information as part of the process of making the decision, and/or cannot communicate the decision. A person is not considered unable to make the decision if the information can only be retained for a short period, but they should be able to consider the reasonably foreseeable consequences of failing to make a decision or making it in a certain way.

The previous case law remains, however, highly relevant to how it will be established that a person has testamentary capacity, which is not the same as other tests of capacity.

## 4.2 Assessing testamentary capacity

What has to be decided is whether, at the time of making the will, the testator had the necessary mental capacity. In theory testamentary capacity has to be proved by the propounder of the will in every case in which a grant is sought; in practice, unless something arises to disturb the position, it will be presumed. Sir JL Knight-Bruce VC in *Waters v Waters* (1848) said:

> The questions will be these: whether ... the testator had a mind undiseased at the time and of sufficient memory and understanding to know *generally* the state of his property ... if he is disposing of his property, he ought to know generally the state of his property and what it consists of, and he ought to have knowledge, memory and understanding of his relations in life.

A testator's capacity does not have to be perfect. They may be unable to handle their own day-to-day affairs and yet capable of making a will. In the case of *Simon v Byford and Others* (2014), it was held that the testatrix's failure to remember why she had made a previous will in the terms she had did not mean she lacked capacity. Lord Lewison cited Erskine J in *Harwood v Baker* (1840), saying: '"...a Testator ... [must] ... have *capacity to comprehend* the extent of his property, and the nature of the claims of others, whom by his will he is excluding from all participation in that property." (Emphasis added)'. He went on illustrate his point:

> Once I knew the dates of all the Kings and Queens of England, and the formula for Hooke's law; and was 'capable' of remembering them. Now I would have to look them up. The judge's

important finding was not that Mrs Simon had forgotten the terms of and reasons for her earlier will. It was that she was capable of accessing and understanding the information; but chose not to … once reminded of claims on her bounty she was able to make decisions about them.

## 4.2.1 Court's test of mental capacity: *Banks v Goodfellow* (1870)

The essential test of mental capacity that a court will apply in assessing whether or not a testator was capable of making a will was stated by Cockburn CJ in *Banks v Goodfellow* (1870) (for the facts, see 4.3.9). He said:

> It is essential … that a testator shall understand the nature of the act and its effects; shall understand the extent of the property of which he is disposing; shall be able to comprehend and appreciate the claims to which he ought to give effect; and, with a view to the latter object, that no disorder of the mind shall poison his affections, pervert his sense of right, or prevent the exercise of his natural faculties – that no insane delusion shall influence his will in disposing of his property and bring about a disposal of it which, if the mind had been sound, would not have been made.

In a talk in October 2012, Denzil Lush, the senior judge at the Court of Protection, noted that various decisions and articles had questioned the appropriateness of the *Banks v Goodfellow* test in the current day, and especially after the Mental Capacity Act 2005. Contrasting the concerns of law and of medicine, however, he pointed out that although psychiatry has advanced considerably, and John Banks would nowadays 'be treated by powerful anti-epileptic drugs for his succession of fits, instead of having a blister of mustard and muslin or vinegar and brown paper applied to his head', nevertheless *Banks v Goodfellow* is not concerned with psychiatry. He observed that the Mental Capacity Act complements rather than supersedes the case.

> The Act requires that someone should be able to understand, retain, and use and weigh the information relevant to the particular decision they are making at a particular time.
>
> What *Banks v Goodfellow* does is summarise – in simple and succinct terms – the information that is relevant to the decision of making a will.
>
> Essentially, this information has been the same since time immemorial and, unless there is some major evolutionary change in human nature itself, it will continue to be the relevant information evermore.[2]

The requirements for testamentary capacity have always been a specifically legal matter. Sir J Hannen in *Boughton v Knight* (1873) thought, in explaining what state the testator should have been in, that

> sound mind covers the whole subject, but emphasis is laid upon two particular functions of the mind, which must be sound in order to create a capacity for making a will; there must be a memory to recall the several persons who may be fitting objects of the testator's bounty, and an understanding to comprehend their relationship to himself and their claims upon him.

---

2 Lush www.step.org/banks-v-goodfellow-1870.

## 4.2.2 Issues of proof when capacity is questioned

Where a question arises as to whether a person had the mental capacity to make a will at the relevant time, the burden of proof of testamentary capacity lies on the person propounding the will.
This was confirmed in *Barry v Butlin* (1838), where an elderly man executed a will at the house of
his attorney. The attorney had prepared the will, under which he took one-quarter of the estate.
The will excluded the testator's son and other family members. There was much to excite the
suspicion of the court (see 4.9.5 on preparation of the will by a beneficiary) but the court heard
evidence from the witnesses, whom it found good, and found that there were no suspicious circumstances, and it held that the will was valid. It confirmed, however, that the *onus probandi*
(burden of proof) lies in every case upon the propounder of a will to satisfy the court that it is
the last will of a free and capable testator.

## 4.2.3 Presumptions and rebuttals

There are, however, traditionally two presumptions which are liable to be rebutted by evidence
produced by one party or another:

(a)     a will which looks rational on the face of it is so (*omnia praesumuntur rite esse acta* − everything
        is presumed to be okay which looks okay), and
(b)     any serious mental illness from which the testator suffered for a period prior to execution
        of the will was continuing at the time of execution and negated the testator's testamentary
        capacity.

It is doubtful that the presumption relating to continuing mental states still has much weight in
light of s 1(2) of the MCA 2005 which specifically provides that a person is assumed to have
capacity unless it is established they do not.

## 4.2.4 Presumption of capacity from rationality on the face of the will

If the will is rational on its face, making reasonable dispositions, the presumption of capacity may
arise, but it is by no means conclusive. The testatrix's will in *Cartwright v Cartwright* (1793) was
clear and rational, but she had been declared insane six months before making it and remained so
until death, so her will failed. The testator in *Harwood v Baker* (1840) made gifts to his wife to the
exclusion of the rest of his family; his will was held to be invalid, although those dispositions
might appear to be, in themselves, rational.

## 4.2.5 Irrational will raises no presumption of capacity

Bizarre provisions are not conclusive proof that the will is irrational on its face. Section 1(4) of
the MCA 2005 sets out that a person is not to be treated as lacking capacity simply because they
make an unwise decision. Mr Justice Hedley in *A, B & C v X, Y & Z* (2012) affirmed that

> it is important ... to bear in mind that an eccentric disposition of property is not in itself evid-
> ence of incapacity by reason of S1(4), but it is the whole picture that needs to be looked at as
> described by the Lord Chief Justice [in *Banks v Goodfellow*].[3]

---

3  Para 34.

A fine line exists, therefore, between unusual provisions of a will which do not give rise to concern about the capacity of the testator, and other (possibly quite similar) provisions, the effects of which do establish that the will is irrational on its face.

If the will is, however, irrational on its face, for example, if the testator states that they make the will in their capacity as King of Ruritania, or, sometimes, even if they leave their estate for the payment of the National Debt (as Sir Joseph Jekyll, a former Master of the Rolls, did; the court found this as rational as attempting to stop the middle arch of Blackfriars Bridge with a full-bottomed wig and concluded that the testator lacked testamentary capacity), then that presumption may not arise. Note that it is not the case that a presumption of no capacity arises as such – it was always the business of the propounder to prove capacity; so the starting point is that there is no presumption as to whether the testator was mentally capable and, in the absence of any presumption or evidence of capacity, the will fails.

### 4.2.6 Shifting the burden of proof

The evidential burden of proof may move from one party to the other during the case, as Lord Brougham observed in *Waring v Waring* (1848). In that case, the deceased was a widow who died without issue, leaving considerable real and personal property. She had made a will in 1834 and later was found 'lunatic by inquisition' (a phrase used under the law that preceded the Mental Health Acts). The question for Lord Brougham was whether she had had testamentary capacity in 1834. He said:

> The burden of the proof often shifts about in the process of the cause, accordingly as the successive steps of the inquiry, by leading to inferences decisive, until rebutted, casts on one or the other party the necessity of protecting himself from such inferences; nor can anything be less profitable as a guide to our ultimate judgment, than the assertion which all parties are so ready to put forward in their behalf severally, that, in the question under consideration, the proof is on the opposing side.

He commented on the way it is easily presumed that a testator was of sound and disposing mind. He said that the propounder of a will must prove the testator's capacity:

> But very slight proof of this, where the *factum* is regular, will suffice; they who impeach the instrument must produce their proofs, should, ... the party propounding choose to rest satisfied with his *prima facie* case, after an issue tendered against him.

If the slight proof necessary for a rational will is produced, 'the proof has shifted to the impugner; but his case may easily shift it back again'. But, as Mr Justice Hedley said, in *A, B & C v X, Y & Z* (2012) said

> it is important ... to bear in mind that an eccentric disposition of property is not in itself evidence of incapacity by reason of S1(4), but it is the whole picture that needs to be looked at, as described by the Lord Chief Justice [in *Banks v Goodfellow*].

### 4.2.7 Presumption displaced by evidence that testator was not rational

The example given by Lord Brougham of a situation in which grave suspicion as to the testator's mental capacity would arise at the outset of a case, was that in which the testator was shown to have made his will in a lunatic asylum. In that case (which he said he had known to happen), 'the burden of proving, and very satisfactorily proving, the testator's sanity would be so dearly on the propounding party, that no further proof would be required to impugn it'.

## 4.3 Testamentary and general capacity

The capacity to make a will is not necessarily the same as the capacity to do other things.

### 4.3.1 Type and degree of capacity

The mental capacity required to make a will is not the same as, for instance, the mental capacity required to contract a valid marriage. In *Re Park* (1953), a wealthy man whose wife had died made a will in favour of his step-nephew. Later he suffered a stroke from which he never really recovered. Medical evidence showed that he was sometimes lucid and sometimes confused. He then married one morning, made a fairly complex will in the afternoon in favour of his new wife and died that evening. The step-nephew argued that the marriage and the will were both invalid by reason of the testator's mental incapacity. The court of first instance held that 'a lesser degree of capacity is required to marry than to make a will'; the marriage was valid, but the testator did not have the mental capacity to make the second will. The Court of Appeal disagreed with the remarks of the court below about the capacity required respectively to conclude a marriage and to make a will, finding it better to say that the would-be testator lacked the capacity only to make a complicated will. It agreed, however, that he had the capacity to marry. The first will having been revoked by the valid marriage and the complicated second will being invalid, the testator's property passed on intestacy to the new wife.

In *A, B & C v X, Y & Z* (2012), a case which postdates the Mental Capacity Act 2005, the court looked at X's capacity to get married, make a will and a lasting power of attorney, to manage his affairs and to litigate. In 2008 X, a successful businessman, lost his wife of 56 years, was diagnosed with dementia and made a Lasting Power of Attorney in favour of his children, with whom he had a good relationship and who assisted him in managing his affairs. In 2010 Z was then employed as X's full-time carer; within four months X decided he wanted to marry Z. The judge found no ulterior motives on either side, but hostilities broke out amongst Z and X's children, A, B and C. Mr Justice Hedley found that X had enough capacity to marry – the bar for marriage is set low. He then went on to say

> I have concluded that I cannot make a general declaration that X lacks testamentary capacity, but that needs to be strongly qualified. There will undoubtedly be times when he does lack testamentary capacity. There will be many times when he does not do so. The times when he does lack such capacity are likely to become more frequent. It follows that, in my judgment, any will now made by X, if unaccompanied by contemporary medical evidence asserting capacity, may be seriously open to challenge.

He found the same applied to the creation of the Lasting Power of Attorney. He considered the time frames of taking a decision to make a will or appoint attorneys under a Lasting Power of Attorney as opposed to the ongoing need to manage affairs or to litigate, and found X incapable of managing his affairs or litigating.

### 4.3.2 Is mental incapacity the same as testamentary incapacity?

Once the court has assessed the testator's state of mind, it will have to decide whether it thinks that state of mind constitutes one of testamentary incapacity or not. The court in *Mudway v Croft*

(1843) said that eccentricity in one person may be mental incapacity in another; the eccentric behaviour must be tested against the whole life and habits of the testator.

It is not relevant how the testator came to be mentally impaired.

### 4.3.3 Delusions which deprive a testator of testamentary capacity

If the testator suffered delusions, they invalidate the will if they satisfy certain conditions. The definition for these purposes of a delusion which deprives the testator of testamentary capacity is one which:

(a)    no rational person could hold and which reasoning with them cannot eradicate from their mind; and

(b)    which is capable of influencing the provisions of their will.

In *Kostic v Chaplin* (2007), the testator had made a new will leaving everything to the Conservative Party, while affected by delusions which gave him a violent antipathy towards the more obvious beneficiary, for whom he had formerly felt affection. Finding the will invalid, the court raised, but ultimately did not answer, the question of whether it had to be shown, in order for the will to be valid, that the delusions did not in fact exercise any influence on the dispositions in the will, or whether it also had to be shown that the delusions were not likely to influence the dispositions in the will, an issue which the judge pointed out had remained undecided since *Banks v Goodfellow*.

### 4.3.4 Showing general mental incapacity is not conclusive

A testator may be, for other purposes, substantially mentally incapable without lacking testamentary capacity. Thus, although a person who is challenging the will on the grounds that the testator lacked testamentary capacity will be greatly assisted by being able to show that the testator was, for general purposes, not sane, they will not have made out a conclusive case. (What they will have done is put the propounder of the will in the position of having actively to prove the testator's capacity to make the will; there will no longer be any presumption of capacity.)

### 4.3.5 Not conclusive in respect of a particular will

Even if a testator's general incapacity is shown to be such that it would necessarily negate testamentary capacity, it may be possible to show that the will was made during a lucid interval. It may also be possible to show that even a high level of general incapacity may not have impinged on testamentary capacity.

### 4.3.6 Lucid intervals

In *Chambers and Yatman v Queen's Proctor* (1840), the testator had been suffering insane delusions for the three days previous to the execution of the will. Two days after the making of the will, the delusions returned and the testator killed himself. However, the court was satisfied that the deceased had been in a lucid interval when he made the will and it held the will to be valid.

The provisions which allow the Court of Protection to make a statutory will for a person who has become mentally incapable (see 6.7) do so by attributing to the testator a notional interval of lucidity.

## 4.3.7 Delusions must relate to the provisions of the will

In many cases, any delusions the deceased can be shown to have had will be highly relevant to their testamentary capacity, because they will often concern members of their family – exactly those who might have expected to benefit from the will. The person wishing to allege lack of capacity is commonly a disappointed relative who, because of a family relationship with the deceased, would benefit more from the application of the intestacy rules or, sometimes, from an earlier will being valid. The challenge to the will in *Dew v Clark* (1826) came from the testator's daughter. Her father had not provided for her in his will, which did not necessarily of itself raise any presumption of lack of capacity. However, the court heard that he had had an irrational aversion to her, believing her to be evil, though the court found as a matter of fact that she was 'charming and religious'. In the circumstances, the court found his aversion insane; he was found to be a lunatic by inquisition (an old procedure for establishing general mental incapacity) somewhat after the making of the will. His lack of capacity had influenced the provisions in his will and the court therefore found that he lacked testamentary capacity and that the will was invalid.

The testatrix in *In the Estate of Walker* (1912) was obsessionally insane, but took an intelligent interest in her affairs. When not under delusions, she made a will which was admitted to probate, the three doctors who witnessed it having certified that she was capable.

In the more recent case of *The Estate of Julie Spalding (deceased)* (2014), the testatrix was cared for for ten years by her nephew, the claimant. She promised him that, in return for caring for her (he left his job and was at her beck and call), she would leave her bungalow to him in her will In 2004–2005, however, she suffered a significant change in personality and became convinced that her nephew was not to be trusted. She subsequently made wills favouring her window cleaner, who had cared for her in the last years of her life. She died in September 2008. The nephew claimed that Mrs Spalding's later wills were invalid for want of capacity. The Chancery Division held that, for the purpose of the exclusion of the nephew in favour of the window cleaner, Mrs Spalding's paranoid personality disorder and her paraphrenia constituted testamentary incapacity, so the nephew's claim succeeded.

Situations can arise, however, which are very unclear, and in which it is difficult to draw a distinction between, say, a very strong aversion to a relative and an irrational and deluded one. Today, a person who a century ago might have sought to invalidate the will on the grounds of mental capacity might well be advised to seek relief under the family provision legislation, where a person should be able to feel more certain at the outset of establishing a good case and winning the action or obtaining a settlement.

## 4.3.8 What has to be proved

The case of *Re Nightingale* (1974) shows the difficult questions that can arise where the court is asked to infer the testator's state of mind from the provisions on the face of the will and the information available to it about the circumstances surrounding the making of the will. In that case, the testator was a widower in his last illness. He had made a will benefiting his son, but shortly afterwards made another cutting out his son, based on his belief that his son's treatment of him in the crises of his illness constituted attempts to kill him – the son had on two occasions pushed him back on his hospital pillow when he was struggling to breathe after a lung operation. There was no evidence of any general incapacity on the part of the testator, but clearly there was some reason, which the court had to hear about, why the testator had made the particular provisions he did. The view was that the provisions of the later will would be reasonable only if the testator was right in believing that his son had tried to kill him. The court held that, in order to establish that the testator had capacity to make the later will, its propounders had to establish in this case that the son had tried to murder the testator. This they could not do, so the later will was declared invalid and the son proved the earlier will.

### 4.3.9 Irrational and insane delusions do not equate with testamentary incapacity

Irrational delusions which do not affect the provisions of the will do not affect testamentary capacity. A testator may, therefore, be insane for many purposes but still capable of making a will. The testator in *Banks v Goodfellow* (1870) (4.2.1) suffered from delusions throughout his life and had spent a short period in an asylum. He managed his own affairs and he could cope with daily life, but he believed that he was haunted by evil spirits. In particular, he believed that he was persecuted by a man called Featherstone Alexander who was in fact dead. He made a will in favour of his niece. After his death in 1865, the will was challenged by another relative, who would have been entitled on his intestacy. It was admitted that the testator was generally capable in his everyday life, so it was a question of fact whether the testator had lacked testamentary capacity at the time of making the will in favour of the niece. The court held that he had had testamentary capacity and the niece would take.

## 4.4 Supervening mental incapacity

If the testator has testamentary capacity when they execute the will then that is sufficient.[4] This has been affirmed by the time- and decision-specific test of capacity set out in the Mental Capacity Act 2005. If the testator subsequently becomes incapable, that does not affect the will. Once they have lost the capacity to make a will, the only way in which any previous testamentary dispositions they have made (or failed to make, since the same applies to their intestacy) can be changed is by the making of a will for them by the Court of Protection under the provisions of the MCA 2005 (see 6.7).

### 4.4.1 Loss of capacity between instructions and execution – the rule in *Parker v Felgate*

There is, however, a possibility of saving a will where it can be shown that the testator, although lacking testamentary capacity to give instructions for a will at the time when they executed the will, had still had capacity when the instructions were actually given. It may be that later, even though they no longer had the capacity to give instructions, the testator did still have the capacity to understand that they was executing a will for which they had given instructions earlier. If the testator instructed a solicitor to prepare a will when they still had capacity, and, the solicitor having prepared the will in accordance with the instructions, the testator loses their testamentary capacity but knows on the later execution of the will that they executing their will for which they had earlier given instructions, that suffices to establish testamentary capacity. In *Parker v Felgate* (1883), the testatrix gave instructions for a new will and then went into a coma. When the will came to be executed, the testatrix realised that she was signing her will, but no longer had any real recollection of what it contained. It was held that the will was valid and could be admitted to probate. *Parker v Felgate* has since been confirmed in *Clancy v Clancy* (2003), in which the testatrix was not elderly but on medication when the solicitor attended the hospital to execute her will, and also in *Perrins v Holland* (2009), where there was a gap of 18 months between the multiple sclerosis patient giving instructions and signing his will. It was apparently referred to by Lord Lewison in *Simon v Byford* (2013), when he said:

---

4  Billinghurst v Vickers (formerly Leonard) (1810).

Testamentary capacity includes the ability to make choices, whereas knowledge and approval requires no more than the ability to understand and approve choices that have already been made. That is why knowledge and approval can be found even in a case in which the testator lacks testamentary capacity at the date when the will is executed.

### 4.4.2 Rationale for the rule in *Parker v Felgate*

The rule in *Parker v Felgate* appears to be a somewhat irregular creation of courts particularly anxious to save certain wills. It may, of course, be particularly helpful given that people often make their wills when they realise that they are terminally ill, and the situation may therefore arise comparatively frequently that, by the time the will is formally prepared, their condition has deteriorated further and they have arguably lost the capacity to deal with the provisions in the will even though they still have the capacity to execute it.

### 4.4.3 When the rule in *Parker v Felgate* will not apply

The rule in *Parker v Felgate* will not be available to save a will where the testator had not given their instructions to the solicitor direct, but had done so through an intermediary. This is a situation which the court always regards as raising doubts about the accuracy of the transmission of the testator's instructions (see *Battan Singh v Amirchand* (1948) at 4.9.9).

The rule will also be applied only to cases where the testator still had the necessary capacity to understand the execution of the will at the relevant time. In *Re Flynn* (1982), the capacity was questionable and the rule did not save the will.

## 4.5 An alternative approach?

The court may, however, take a different approach to the question of what to do with the will of a person alleged to be mentally disordered. The testator in *In the Estate of Bohrmann* (1938) made a will which included gifts to certain English charities. Later, he developed a delusion that he was being persecuted by the London County Council. After this delusion had set in, he executed a codicil by which he declared, inter alia, that the relevant clause of his will should be read as if the words 'United States of America' were substituted for the word 'England'. The court upheld the codicil with the exception of that part of it.

This is the only instance of a court holding that a testator had the capacity to make part, but not all, of a will or codicil. The alternative reasoning, namely that it rested on the practice of deleting parts of instruments not brought to the knowledge and approval of the testator, is doubted, given the facts of the case and the surrounding circumstances. It is suggested that the particular decision in this case is unlikely to be followed.

## 4.6 The infirm client

If there appears at the time of execution of a will to be a possibility that queries may arise later about the testator's mental capacity, arrangements should be made for a medical practitioner to confirm in writing the testator's capacity and understanding.

It was the witnessing doctors that saved the wills of the arguably insane testatrix in *In the Estate of Walker* (1912) (see 4.3.7). The practice has developed more recently. In *Kenward v Adams* (1975), the court referred to a 'golden rule':

> In the case of an aged testator or a testator who has suffered a serious illness, there is one golden rule which should always be observed, however straightforward matters may appear, and however difficult or tactless it may be to suggest that precautions be taken: the making of a will by such a testator ought to be witnessed or approved by a medical practitioner who satisfies himself of the capacity and understanding of the testator, and records and preserves his examination and finding

These recommendations were confirmed in *Hoff v Atherton* (2003) and *Scammell v Farmer* (2008), but this still does not mean that a doctor's certificate is required as a matter of routine. May LJ said on the one hand in *Sharp v Adam* (2005) that: 'The golden rule is a rule of solicitors' good practice, not a rule of law giving conclusive status to evidence obtained in compliance with the rule,' and on the other hand Norris J confirmed in *Cattermole v Prisk* (2006) that non-compliance does not mean that a will is invalid, though practitioners are at risk of criticism if they do not judge the situation correctly and obtain an expert confirmation where one is needed. The judge in *Hill v Fellowes Solicitors* (2011), a professional negligence claim against solicitors in respect of an *inter vivos* transaction, said there is 'plainly no duty upon solicitors in general to obtain medical evidence on every occasion upon which they are instructed by an elderly client just in case they lack capacity'.

The decision is ultimately a legal one, but may be based on any available expert medical evidence. In *Caton v Goddard* (2007), the court held that, on the balance of probabilities, the evidence produced by a medical expert commissioned after the death was to be preferred to the evidence of the solicitor who had attended the testatrix and drafted the will. In *Key v Key* (2010) evidence was given by two medical experts; the claimant's expert had the advantage of carrying out an assessment of the deceased during his lifetime which outweighed what would have been the greater weight attributed to the defendant's more experienced expert who had not examined the testator. In that latter case, addressing the extreme the judge noted

> a significant element of responsibility for this tragic state of affairs lies with Mr Cadge [the solicitor]. Contrary to the clearest guidance, in well known cases, academic texts and from the Law Society, Mr Cadge accepted instructions for the preparation of the 2006 Will, from an 89-year-old testator whose wife of 65 years standing had been dead for only a week without taking any proper steps to satisfy himself of Mr Key's testamentary capacity, and without even making an attendance note of his meeting with Mr Key and Mary, at which the instructions were taken. Mr Cadge's failure to comply with what has come to be well known in the profession as the Golden Rule has greatly increased the difficulties to which this dispute has given rise and aggravated the depths of mistrust into which his client's children have subsequently fallen.

However, in *Wharton v Bancroft and Others* (2011) the terminally ill testator made a will on his deathbed. The will was made in the morning, in anticipation of marriage to his long-term partner, and disinheriting his daughters. He then married, and died the next day. Norris J noted at paragraph 110 in his judgment that

> A solicitor so placed [i.e. at a death bed] cannot simply conjure up a medical attendant. He must obtain his client's consent to the attendance of and examination by a doctor. He must procure the attendance of a doctor (preferably the testator's own) who is willing to accept the instruction. He must make arrangement for any relevant payment (securing his client's agreement). I do not think [the solicitor] is to be criticised for deciding to make his own assessment (accepted as correct) and to get on with the job of drawing a will in contemplation of marriage so that Mr Wharton could marry. I certainly do not think that 'the golden rule' has in the present case anything to do with the ease with which I may infer coercion. The simple fact is that Mr Wharton was a terminally ill but capable testator.

The solicitor in this instance had made a careful and contemporaneous five and a half page file note knowing that a challenge might ensue.

In *Burgess v Hawes* (2013), an experienced lawyer had formed the opinion, from meeting her, that the testatrix understood what she was doing. When the will was challenged, the Court of Appeal upheld the trial judge's finding of a lack of knowledge and approval but not his finding of lack of capacity. Mummery LJ said that in this situation, the will should only be set aside on the clearest evidence of lack of testamentary capacity. He said that a court should be cautious about acting on the basis of evidence from a medical expert after the event, particularly where the expert has neither met nor medically examined the client. The court did not consider the 'golden rule' and there was no evidence the solicitor had considered the testator's capacity to make a will as such. *Burgess v Hawes* has been followed in a number of other recent cases, including *Greaves v Stolkin* (2013), where the solicitor who took Mr Stolkin's instructions for the will had asked him questions to assess his capacity. In the case of *Re Ashkettle (deceased)* (2103), the deputy judge suggested however that the principle did 'not go so far as to suggest that, in every case, the evidence of an experienced and independent solicitor will, without more, be conclusive'. The solicitor's view must be shown to be based on a 'proper assessment and accurate information or it is worthless', and the terms of the will itself might also suggest that the solicitor's assessment was unsound.

The UK Practice Committee of the Society of Trust and Estate Practitioners led some discussion on the 'Exceptions to the Golden Rule'.[5] In it they note that 'the fact that an expert did not see the deceased cannot automatically reduce the value of their evidence'. They point out that medical diagnoses are often based on investigations such as blood tests, CT scans and biopsies, and that pathologists' reports are not dismissed because the pathologist has not seen the patient. Most interestingly, they pointed out that: 'No reported case seems to have considered the research ... which shows how a "good social front" can mislead someone who is not medically trained into thinking that a would-be testator has capacity'; the research was mentioned in *Greaves v Stolkin*, 'but the judge apparently thought it was irrelevant to the facts'.

## 4.7 Judges or doctors?

The question of capacity to perform particular legal transactions still remains a legal, rather than medical, decision, as was confirmed in *Richmond v Richmond* (1914). In *Key v Key* (2010), Briggs J said 'The issue as to testamentary capacity is, from first to last, for the decision of the Court. It is not to be delegated to experts, however eminent.' Capacity is ultimately to be determined by a lawyer – not a doctor, because it rests in large part on the nature of the legal transaction. In *Gibbons v Wright* (1954), the court said:

> The mental capacity required by the law in respect of any instrument is relative to the particular transaction which is being effected by the instrument, and may be described as the capacity to understand the nature of that transaction when it is explained

thus entailing different criteria of competence for different transactions.

Where a practitioner arranges for an examination, they should ensure that it is capable of testing the right issues.[6] The court may consider that the provisions of the will provide some

---

5   UK Practice Committee, www.step.org/exceptions-golden-rule#footnote3_l5e97ca.

6   R Jacoby and P Steer, 'How to Assess Capacity to Make a Will' (2007) 335 British Medical Journal 155; KM Kennedy, 'Testamentary Capacity: A Practical Guide to Assessment of Ability to Make a Valid Will' (2012) 19 Journal of Forensic and Legal Medicine 191.

evidence as to whether or not the testator had mental capacity, but this should not be relied upon. In *Re Beaney* (1978) (an *inter vivos* case – see 2.1.1), the solicitor had asked the client relevant questions, but as they were all answerable by 'yes or no' answers, the court was not convinced she had really understood, even though the relevant dispositions were in no way unusual.

Given this, as Sir JL Knight-Bruce VC said in *Waters v Waters* (1848) (see 4.2): 'There can be no doubt that an intelligent and honest medical man is the very best witness you could have to speak to the competency of a party as to making his will.' It has however been suggested that, although the heavy reliance of courts on medical evidence in this area, as in others, is understandable, such reliance may call into question to what extent the judge is making their own decision and to what extent it is being made by the doctor.

## 4.8 Undue influence

If there is shown to have been undue influence on the testator at the time of the making of the will, then it will not be valid, the undue influence having overcome the testator's own 'will', in the sense of volition. The sort of undue influence that counts for legal purposes is very strong. It is difficult to discharge the burden of proof of undue influence, since, though the standard of proof is the balance of probabilities, as is usual in civil proceedings, a finding of undue influence tends to impute some immoral action on the part of the influencer, an imputation which courts may be unwilling to find. Proudman J noted in *Nesbitt v Nicholson* (2013), in which it was alleged the testator's daughter exerted undue influence over him by making fraudulent calumnies about her brothers:

> The burden of proof rests on the person alleging undue influence or fraud. Although … undue influence can be found by the court drawing inferences from all the circumstances, the cogency and strength of the evidence required to prove fraud is heightened by the nature and seriousness of the allegation.

In the recent case of *Wharton v Bancroft and Others* (2011), Norris J set out the elements required to prove undue influence, the burden being on the person asserting it. That person must establish coercion of the testator's will: persuasion is not enough. The dividing line between persuasion and coercion depends on the testator's physical and mental condition when instructions for the will are given. It depends whether the testator was free and able to express their own wishes or felt compelled to express the wishes of another person. Undue influence is usually proved by witnesses' direct evidence, but may be inferred from other proven facts. Norris J described undue influence as

> a complex of facts involving the establishment (by proof or inference) of the opportunity to exercise influence, the actual exercise of influence, the actual exercise of influence in relation to the will, the demonstration that the influence was 'undue' (i.e. went beyond persuasion), and that the will before the court was brought about by these means.

Undue influence was not found in the case of *Hubbard v Scott* (2011), although Proudman J said she could understand why the claimants thought it might have done. The testator, Albert Wiseman, had left everything to his cleaner, Mrs Kruk. Mr Wiseman's sisters alleged that Mrs Kruk had subjected Mr Wiseman to undue influence and that he lacked testamentary capacity, but Proudman J said there was no evidence of either. She said Mr Wiseman had had no dependants and had seen little of his sisters in his later years, and he had been happy and showing no signs of frailty or coercion when he made his will, and he had been lonely, and fond of Mrs Kruk.

### 4.8.1 No presumption of undue influence in gifts by will

In the making of wills, unlike the situation with gifts or contracts, there is no presumption of undue influence whatever the relationship between the testator and the person alleged to have influenced them as this is precisely the area in which gifts to persons with a close relationship are regarded as normal, and not liable to excite any suspicion. It is also, of course, the situation in which testators may be particularly vulnerable – because they are likely to be elderly and particularly dependent on those around them.[7] Nevertheless, if there were any such presumption of undue influence, it would also mean a great number of wills having to be proved in a formal manner, which would be inconvenient and expensive.

An example of a more unusual relationship which did not give rise to a finding of undue influence is that of testatrix and priest which arose in *Parfitt v Lawless* (1872), which in the particular circumstances might be usefully compared with the *inter vivos* case of *Allcard v Skinner* (1887), discussed at 2.1.1, where the testatrix was a nun who left her property to the Mother Superior of her convent; undue influence was found. The testatrix in *Parfitt v Lawless* left all her property to a Roman Catholic priest who had spent much time with her and her husband and acted as chaplain to them during the last years of her life. The will was challenged on the grounds of his alleged undue influence, but it was held that there was no evidence of it and that the relationship did not raise any presumption of it which needed to be disproved before a jury (nowadays, this would be just a judge). Accordingly, the will was valid.

### 4.8.2 Reasons why undue influence is viewed differently *inter vivos* and on testation

Historically, *inter vivos* gifts were dealt with by the Court of Chancery and gifts on death by the ecclesiastical courts, so involving two different lines of thinking. The court in *Parfitt v Lawless* (1872) explicitly discussed the differences between the rules relating to undue influence in transactions *inter vivos* and on death. Lord Penzance said that *inter vivos* it is considered by the courts of equity that the natural influence which certain relationships involve is an undue influence, but

> [t]he law regarding wills is very different from this. The natural influence of the parent or guardian over the child, or the husband over the wife, or the attorney over the client, may lawfully be exerted to obtain a will or legacy, so long as the testator thoroughly understands what he is doing and is a free agent.... No amount of persuasion or advice, whether founded on feelings of regard or religious sentiment, would ... set aside this will, so long as the free volition of the testatrix to accept or reject that advice was not invaded.

### 4.8.3 Reasons why undue influence should be more readily found on testation?

It was suggested by the Justice Committee in 1971 that Parliament should act to bring in a statutory presumption of undue influence where an elderly testator was found to have made a will giving a substantial benefit to a person on whom they were physically dependent. To exclude from the presumption those who cared for elderly relatives (that is, the allegation of undue influence could still be made, but the presumption of undue influence would not arise automatically) the provision was to be limited to those who cared for the elderly person under the terms of a

---

7  J Manthorpe, K Samsi and J Rapaport 'Responding to the Financial Abuse of People with Dementia: A Qualitative Study of Safeguarding Experiences in England' (2012) 24 International Psychogeriatrics 1454.

contract. Thus it would include a carer in a residential home but exclude for instance a daughter who devoted her life, or even some of it, to her parents. The Justice Committee thought the presumption should apply where the testator was over the age of 60. However, Parliament has not shown the will to implement legislation of this kind. It has, however, brought in a distinction between those who care for someone under a commercial contract and those who do it for love in the context of family provision claims (see 15.26).

### 4.8.4 Undue influence or reasonable persuasion?

It is difficult to draw the line between the reasonable persuasion of a testator, which is quite permissible, and the sort of persuasion which goes so far as to be coercion. There is no need for there to have been any use or threat of force for undue influence to be shown. It is not easy to elucidate the principles which will be applied by a court in deciding which side of the line behaviour in any particular case may lie, but the words of Sir JP Wilde in *Hall v Hall* (1868) may be considered. He said that persuasion

> appeals to the affections or ties of kindred, to a sentiment of gratitude for past services, or pity for future destitution.... On the other hand, pressure of whatever character, whether acting on the fears or the hopes, if so exerted as to overpower the volition without convincing the judgment, is a species of restraint under which no valid will can be made.... In a word, a testator may be led but not driven; and his will must be the offspring of his own volition, and not the record of someone else's.

### 4.8.5 The record of someone else's mind

It was said in *Smith v Smith* (1866) that the question of undue influence is often mixed with that of the capacity of the person under pressure from the influencer to resist.

In *Moneypenny v Brown* (1711), the deceased had made his will on his deathbed, with his wife importuning him and guiding his hand in making his signature. The will was held to be invalid for her undue influence. In *Mynn v Robinson* (1828), a woman who was dying of cancer made a will nine days before her death appointing her husband sole executor and leaving him all her property. A few months earlier, she had made a completely different will. The court held that she had been under the marital authority and undue influence of her husband.

In the case of *Re Harden* (1959) the testatrix had developed an interest in spiritualism after her husband's death. In the course of pursuing that interest, she met a man who rapidly trained as a spiritualist medium and thereafter held seances with Mrs Harden during which he apparently relayed messages from beyond about what provisions should be inserted in her will. Mrs Harden made two wills under which the new medium took substantial benefits. The court was quick to find that there had been undue influence on his part; he had not only taken over her mind, but had set out to do so, and what he had done went beyond permissible persuasion.

## 4.9 Knowledge and approval

This area is a particularly live one. At a time when wills are more often challenged, an assertion of a lack of knowledge and approval may often be part of such a challenge along with an assertion that the testator lacked mental capacity. It is often seen together with a claim that the testator lacked testamentary capacity, if not other bases as well (see Chapter 16).

The testator must know and approve of the contents of their will at the time of execution,[8] unless the rule in *Parker v Felgate* can save the will on the grounds that, at the time of the execution, the testator knew they were executing a document for which they had earlier given instructions.

The rule in *Parker v Felgate* (see 4.4.1) was applied in the case of *In the Estate of Wallace* (1952). The testator was seriously ill when he wrote and signed a document headed 'Last wish', stating that he wished two named persons to have all his possessions. He then instructed a solicitor to prepare a will which gave effect to this document, the contents of which he knew and had approved. The testator executed the will without reading it or having it read to him on the day before he died. He knew, however, that he was executing a will for which he had given instructions. The court followed *Parker v Felgate* and held the will to be valid. The rule also saved a will and its tax implications in the case of *Singellos v Singellos* (2010), where Andrew Simmonds QC, despite his stated misgivings as a deputy judge, pursued a very interesting discussion of the application of the rule to *inter vivos* transactions, finding this was possible.

## 4.9.1 Presumption of knowledge and approval where capacity is not in issue

The Court of Appeal in *Perrins v Holland* (2009) held that there is a distinction to be drawn between testamentary capacity and knowledge and approval. Knowledge and approval does not require anything more than the ability to understand and approve choices and instructions that have already been given. Full testamentary capacity is not necessary for knowledge and approval.

It was thought that if the will had been read over to the capable testator when it was executed or the contents brought to their attention and they duly executed it this was conclusive proof that they knew and approved of it.[9] Recent case law has suggested that there is a rebuttable presumption of knowledge and approval once the propounder of the will has discharged the burden of proof that the testator had mental capacity. If someone wishes to challenge the will, they have the evidential burden of rebutting that presumption. If they succeed, the burden of proving the will will pass back to the person propounding it. For an example, see *Singellos v Singellos* (2010).

In the case of *Gill v Woodall* (2010), Mrs Gill was married to a domineering husband. Instructions were given to a solicitor to prepare draft wills disinheriting their daughter and making the RSPCA their sole beneficiary. These drafts were sent to their farm for approval. The couple then attended the solicitor's office to execute the wills. It was argued that the fact that the will had been duly executed after being prepared by a solicitor and read over to the testatrix raised a very strong presumption that she knew and approved the will. However Mrs Gill suffered from anxiety disorders and agoraphobia and two highly qualified expert witnesses agreed that the testatrix's 'fairly extreme' condition 'very severely affected her understanding', but in a way that 'would not even have been appreciated by most doctors, let alone a solicitor reading a draft will to her, especially if he had not met her before'. The will was therefore invalid for want of knowledge and approval. Note however that in this case Lord Neuberger did emphasise in his ruling 'that the facts of this case are quite exceptional, and that we are differing from the Judge on an unusual basis' and that the presumption will normally apply.

A testator can have knowledge and approval of only part of their will, for example where wording is inserted by someone other than the testator after execution. In *Fuller v Strum* (2001), Chadwich LJ affirmed that in this situation a judge admitting the document to probate is bound to require that the parts they are not satisfied the testator knew and approved must be struck out.

---

8  *Guardhouse v Blackburn* (1866).
9  *Re Morris, Lloyds Bank Ltd v Peake* (1971).

The court has the power to omit words which were inserted and has jurisdiction to rectify wills under s 20 of the Administration of Justice Act 1982 (see 4.11.11).

### 4.9.2 No presumption of knowledge and approval where testator is blind, deaf and dumb or illiterate

There will be no presumption of knowledge and approval if the testator was blind, deaf and dumb[10] or illiterate,[11] unless the attestation clause of the will is so worded as to constitute prima facie evidence for the probate registry that the testator did know and approve the contents of the will. If the testator is blind, it must be shown that the will was read over to them in the presence of the witnesses or that the testator was otherwise acquainted with its contents.[12]

### 4.9.3 Reading the will out to the testator is not conclusive

There used to be a rule, set out in Atter v Atkinson (1869), that the testator was conclusively taken to have known and approved of the will, save in the case of fraud, if they had read it or had it read over to them. That is no longer the case, but evidence of it, albeit no longer conclusive, is of course weighty. It did not dispel the suspicions of the court in Re Ticehurst (1973), however. The testatrix, though elderly, was fully alert when she changed her will and left three houses to relatives rather than, as previously, to her tenants. The will was prepared by a solicitor after correspondence with the testatrix, but that correspondence had to be conducted by the testatrix through an amanuensis because her eyesight was very poor; the amanuensis was the wife of one of the testatrix's nephews. The nephew was also one of the relatives who benefited under the new will. The court's suspicions were raised by such close involvement of someone so near to the donee with the preparation of the will, and although it was shown that the will had been read out to the testatrix before she executed it, the court found on the facts that those suspicions had not been allayed and the will failed. Franks v Sinclair (2006) is a more recent case with a similar outcome, where knowledge and approval could not be presumed just because the will was read out to the testatrix just before execution. David Richards J considered what the testatrix knew – that she was signing a will that had been read over to her – but also how clear the import of the individual provisions of that will would have been to her, and declined to find that she knew and approved of the will in question.

### 4.9.4 Other circumstances in which there is no presumption of knowledge and approval

The presumption of knowledge and approval will also fail to arise where the will has been signed by someone else on the testator's behalf, although again a prima facie case may be raised by an appropriate attestation clause. There may also be other suspicious circumstances which will raise queries and mean that the testator's knowledge and approval has to be proved. Those suspicious circumstances include where there is a substantial gift to the person who prepared the will, especially if they are the main beneficiary, or where instructions for the will were conveyed through an intermediary. In Cowderoy v Cranfield (2011) it was confirmed that once the court's suspicions have been excited by such circumstances, positive evidence of knowledge and approval will be required.

---

10  Re Owston (1862).
11  Musson v Lee (2000).
12  Fincham v Edwards (1842).

## 4.9.5 Preparation of the will by a beneficiary

Where the will has been prepared by someone who receives a substantial benefit under it and those circumstances are brought to the attention of a court, the court will consider that there are suspicious circumstances which may rebut, or prevent from arising, any presumption of the testator's knowledge and approval of the contents of their will. This was stated in *Barry v Butlin* (1838), where the court said 'if a party writes or prepares a will under which he takes a benefit, that is a circumstance that ought really to excite the suspicion of the court'. It was confirmed in *Fulton v Andrew* (1875) that such a state of affairs will arouse the court's suspicions and put a heavy burden of proving that knowledge and approval on the person propounding the will.

In *Harmes v Hinkson* (1946) (a Privy Council case from Canada), a dying man had his will drawn up by the principal beneficiary. It was subsequently disputed by the next of kin on the grounds that the testator lacked mental capacity, had no knowledge and approval and suffered undue influence from the principal beneficiary. The court was, however, satisfied that the will represented the free intention of the testator and it was upheld.

## 4.9.6 Benefit to solicitor who prepares the will

There is no particular provision of law that prevents a solicitor who draws up a will from obtaining a benefit under it in a way that does not apply to anyone else. Solicitors are, of course, generally more likely than other people to draw up wills, and it does happen that their clients do wish to give them something over and above their professional fees. They are nevertheless also in a position to exert inappropriate power over the testator, perhaps even unwittingly.[13]

The most celebrated case, on knowledge and approval, is that of *Wintle v Nye* (1959). The defendant was a solicitor (since he eventually lost, this may in part explain the popularity of the case). He had been concerned with an elderly testatrix who had recently lost her brother and who wanted to make a will. Mr Nye, the solicitor, and the testatrix had a long series of interviews. The first draft of the will made Mr Nye and the bank the executors, with the estate going to charity. In the second draft, Mr Nye was the sole executor; there were legacies to charity and some annuities, and the residue to Mr Nye. The testatrix executed the second draft, and subsequently made codicils which reduced the amounts of the annuities, thus increasing the residue. On the death of the testatrix, her friend Colonel Wintle, after a physical attack on Mr Nye, bought a small interest under the will from one of the beneficiaries and, thus armed with *locus standi*, started court proceedings against him.

The court, too, was unhappy to hear about a will substantially benefiting the person who had prepared it, though it was not concerned that Mr Nye was a solicitor on principle. Mr Nye's explanation of the large gift to him was that the testatrix wanted to benefit her sister Mildred, but she was a Roman Catholic and the testatrix had not wanted the property to end up with the church. Thus, Mr Nye was to hold the money and gradually pay it over to Mildred. The court did not find this completely convincing. The matter went to the House of Lords, which found that the court's suspicions were not dispelled and that all the gifts in the will to Mr Nye should fail. It said, in the words of Parke B in *Barry v Butlin* (1838) (see 4.2.2 and 4.9.5), that the court must be 'vigilant and jealous' where a will had been prepared by someone who benefited substantially by it, and that such a person trying to show that a will had the knowledge and approval of the testator has a very heavy burden to discharge.

---

13 Roger Kerridge 'Wills Made in Suspicious Circumstances: The Problem of the Vulnerable Testator' (2000) 59 Cambridge Law Journal 310.

### 4.9.7 Solicitors' professional rules relating to benefits under wills they draft

However, the position of a solicitor is also governed by the solicitors' rules of professional conduct. Breach of those rules is a serious matter for the solicitor and can lead to disciplinary proceedings, as it did in the case of *Re A Solicitor* (1975). Any solicitor is required to ensure that the client is treated fairly, and in relation to gifts in wills the Solicitors Regulation Authority says the solicitor must ensure that if the gift is significant or disproportionate, the client obtains independent advice. The Law Society suggests that any gift over £500 is likely to be considered significant, and anything worth more than 1 per cent of the client's current estimated net estate or which might become valuable later, or which is not justified by the relationship between the solicitor and the client would also be significant. It also counsels attention where the client, if the solicitor declines a gift, makes a gift to someone close to the solicitor or to a charity the solicitor supports but with which the client has no connection.

### 4.9.8 Benefit of close relative

The same suspicions arise where the benefit is not for the person who prepared the will but for a close relative of that person. There is no presumption of knowledge and approval and the propounder of the will has a heavy burden to discharge in showing that the testator did know and approve the contents of the will. This situation arose in *Thomas v Jones* (1928), where the testatrix appointed her solicitor as executor of her will and made substantial gifts to his daughter; the will failed. In *Tyrrell v Painton* (1894), the testatrix was ill when she made a will in favour of her cousin, the plaintiff. Two days later, the defendant's son brought to her another will, prepared by himself and in favour of his father. The testatrix executed this will in the presence of the son and a young friend of his. No one else was present and the existence of the will was kept secret until the testatrix died a fortnight later. The Court of Appeal held that the circumstances raised a well-grounded suspicion and that the defendant had failed to remove that suspicion and to prove affirmatively that the testatrix knew and approved of the contents of the will in favour of the defendant.

### 4.9.9 Instructions through an intermediary

The testator may give instructions to their solicitor for the preparation of their will through an intermediary. This will however raise a query in the mind of the court as to the reliability of the provisions in the will and whether the testator truly knew and approved of them. The test in a situation such as this is quite strict. The testator in *Battan Singh v Amirchand* (1948) had made a series of wills, all of which benefited his nephews, until the last, which he made in the last stages of terminal illness. The testator stated that he had no relatives, and left all his property to two creditors. The will failed partly because, the nephews being still alive, the testator did not appear to know what he was doing when he stated that he had no relatives, but partly because the will was prepared through an intermediary, raising suspicion in the mind of the court. The House of Lords said that

> the opportunities for error in transmission and of misunderstanding and of deception in such a situation are obvious, and the court ought to be strictly satisfied that there is no ground for suspicion, and that the instructions given to the intermediary were unambiguous and clearly understood, faithfully reported by him and rightly apprehended by the solicitor.

The involvement of the intermediary in *Re Ticehurst* (1973) (4.9.3) also raised suspicions in a case which was perhaps less clear-cut, which were not dispelled by the evidence before the court about the precise circumstances in which the will was prepared and executed.

## 4.10 Lack of knowledge and approval or some other issue?

The facts on which a claim of lack of knowledge and approval might be based can also lend themselves to alternative interpretations, such as forgery or undue influence.

### 4.10.1 Lack of knowledge and approval or forgery?

In *Re Rowinska dec'd, Wyniczenko v Plucinska-Surowka* (2006) Deputy Judge Behrens rejected, on the balance of probability, an allegation of forgery. There was a real possibility that the will was forged, but the judge held, in the light of the suspicious circumstances surrounding the will, that the propounder had not shown that the testatrix had known and approved its contents. The deceased had come to England in the 1960s and died in 2002 aged 87 leaving an estate worth about £750,000. In 1993 she executed a professionally-drawn will leaving money to Polish Roman Catholic charities and bequests to relatives in Poland. Seven weeks before her death, when she was frail and terminally ill, she made a new will leaving everything to someone she had met in 1996, who befriended her after installing her satellite television. Expert handwriting evidence showed there was a possibility that the 2002 will was forged but, on the balance of probabilities, there was sufficient doubt for the forgery claim to fail. But the circumstances of the case raised a suspicion in the mind of the court that the testatrix might not have known and approved the contents. Because the claimant seeking probate had prepared the will under which he took the benefit of the estate, he had the burden of satisfying the court that on the balance of probabilities this was true as well. The claimant was not able to prove this and the will was not admitted to probate.[14]

### 4.10.2 Lack of knowledge and approval or undue influence?

Where a person seeks to challenge a will on the basis that the testator was persuaded into making and executing it by someone else, as a matter of practicalities they are far more likely to succeed if the case is presented as one of a lack of knowledge and approval rather than one of undue influence. This is because a finding of lack of knowledge and approval, even where it arises because of the involvement of another person, in no way reflects on the morality of the conduct of that other person, whereas a finding of undue influence involves some condemnation of what the other person has done and the courts are for that reason very unwilling to reach such a conclusion. The distaste with which the courts regard charges of fraud and undue influence was apparent from the judgment of Harman J in *Re Fuld* (1965), who expressed the hope that cases would, after *Wintle v Nye* (1959), be pleaded on the basis of lack of knowledge and approval.[15]

## 4.11 Mistake

The testator may have been mistaken about their will in various ways. They may have been mistaken as to the contents of it, so that it says something which, if they had considered it more carefully, they would not have included in the will at all, or it may contain some words which they mistakenly considered to embody what they wanted whereas their meaning and effect, in

---

14  See also *Bodh v Bodh* (2007).
15  Lee Mason, 'Undue Influence and Testamentary Dispositions: An Equitable Jurisdiction in Probate Law?' (2011) 75 Conveyancer and Property Lawyer 115; Roger Kerridge 'Undue Influence and Testamentary Dispositions: A Response' (2012) 76 Conveyancer and Property Lawyer 129.

law, is quite different. They may also have been completely mistaken about the document they was executing, so that it was not their will at all.

There are three possible remedies available where there has been a mistake:

(a)    The court has always had power to omit words from probate (but not to add words).[16]
(b)    In the case of testators who die on or after 1 January 1983, the Administration of Justice Act 1982, s 20 has conferred additional power on the court (in specified circumstances) to rectify defective wills.[17]
(c)    Omissions or errors in wills can sometimes be remedied by a court as a matter of construction.

### 4.11.1  Mistake about the whole document

If the testator was mistaken about the whole document, because it was not their will and the document is something completely different from what the supposed testator expected, it is usual to say that they were mistaken about the whole document, and that therefore it is not admissible to probate as their will. It might also be said, again, that the testator does not have the necessary knowledge and approval of the document. *Marley v Rawlings* (2014) (see 4.11.12), gives an example of a situation in which a person might be said to be mistaken as to the whole document.

### 4.11.2  Mistake about the document or lack of testamentary intention?

The situation where someone is in error about the will should be distinguished from that of the person who never intends the document as their will; in that case, the supposed testator lacks testamentary intention and the document is, for that reason, not their will. Mistake arises where the testator intends to make a will, but the document they execute does not have the wording or the effect they expected.

### 4.11.3  Mistake as to legal effect of words

Where there has been a mistake as to the legal effect of words used in a will, those words will still be admitted to probate. It makes no difference whether the mistake arose through the wrong advice of a solicitor or a lay person (a surprising number of people take legal advice from lay persons) as to the effect of the words used. This touches on matters of construction; where a testator uses technical language, it is construed technically, even if they have clearly done so in error because they do not understand what it means (see 11.2.3). The court will look at the words used and whether or not the testator knew and approved of the words; if it is satisfied that the testator knew and approved of the words, it will then go on to establish their meaning. In taking that first decision as to whether or not the testator knew and approved of the words, it will not examine whether they understood their technical meaning.

In the 2013 case of *Kell v Jones* the solicitor drafting the will included a number of charities in the class of residuary beneficiaries that the testator had not wanted to include. The solicitor had given careful thought to the wording of the clause, erroneously thinking he had achieved the

---

16  Before the Administration of Justice Act 1982 it was not possible to rectify a will unless fraud could be proved.
17  Roger Kerridge and AHR Brierley 'Mistakes in Wills: Rectify and Be Damned' (2003) 62 Cambridge Law Journal 750.

intended result. The testator then duly signed the will having knowledge and approval of its contents. The court could do nothing to correct this error.[18]

In *Collins v Elstone* (1893), the testatrix was making a home-made will dealing with an insurance policy. She was wrongly advised as to the effect of the printed revocation clause, being told that it would revoke her earlier will only as regarded the policy. The court nevertheless admitted the words of general revocation to probate, because the testatrix had intended those words to remain in the will. She knew and approved of the words, even though they did not have the legal effect she expected. The previous will was therefore revoked.

Problems over revocation clauses also occurred in *Re Howard* (1944) and *Re Phelan* (1972). In the former case, the would-be testator executed two wills on the same day, both of which contained revocation clauses. The wills were irreconcilable and the court held them invalid, save that they showed sufficient intention to revoke a previous will, leaving the deceased intestate.

## 4.11.4 Proper construction of the will may overcome the problem

In the later case of *Re Phelan*, however, the court was able to construe the wills so as to avoid the problem. The testator executed a home-made will in favour of his landlady and her husband. He had three holdings in unit trusts and conceived (wrongly) the idea that they each had to be disposed of by further, separate wills. He executed three more wills in favour of the landlady and her husband, each one on a pre-printed will form. He did not delete the printed revocation clause on any of the forms, all of which he executed on the same day. The court was faced with four will documents, of which only the last would be valid, as each one would have revoked any that came before it. As they were all executed on the same day, however, there was no way of telling which was the last. The court managed to admit all four wills to probate, with the revocation clause deleted from the last three on the grounds that the testator did not know and approve of it.

## 4.11.5 Two types of mistake identified

The difference between the mistaken inclusion of the revocation clauses in *Collins v Elstone* and *Re Phelan* might be said to be that in the latter case the testator did not address his mind to the words used at all and so could be said not really to know and approve the words themselves, whereas in the former the testatrix addressed her mind directly to the relevant words but came to the wrong conclusion about them. As to the difference between *Re Howard* and *Re Phelan*, the court was able to construe the wills together in the latter to make sense of all of them, whereas in *Re Howard* this was impossible since they were inconsistent.

## 4.11.6 Mistake as to the contents of the will

Testators can manage to make mistakes in their wills, especially as to the legal effect of the words they use (and more particularly where those words come from printed will forms) without the assistance of solicitors. In the case of clerical errors, however, the involvement of a solicitor is perhaps more likely to produce a mistake. In *Re Horrocks* (1939), the testator's solicitor, drafting the words of the gift of residue, used the words 'charitable or benevolent' rather than 'charitable and benevolent'. The argument that it was a typing error failed because the two phrases had different meanings and change would affect the meaning of the rest of the will. 'The insertion of words would run counter to the provisions of the Wills Act' stated Greene MR.

---

18  This case was heard after the Administration of Justice Act 1982. If the wording had merely been part of the solicitor's standard will precedent and he had included it without thought, rectification might have been possible under s 20.

### 4.11.7 Dealing with clerical error

A typing error or error of a drafter may mean that words are inserted into a document without the knowledge and approval of the testator. They can then be omitted from probate for that reason, provided that the meaning of the rest of the will is not affected. What can be classed as a clerical error has recently been significantly widened in the case of *Marley v Rawlings* (2014) (see 4.11.12).

### 4.11.8 Omission of words of which the testator did not know and approve

Until the Administration of Justice Act 1982, the court could not insert words into a will. The omission of words which the testator intended to be in the will and without which the will's meaning is changed from that which the testator intended, however, operates differently. In *Re Morris* (1970), the testatrix made various gifts by will and then intended to revoke by codicil certain clauses of the will, namely clauses 3 and 7(iv) – both of which favoured her housekeeper which were to be replaced by clause 2 in the codicil, the remaining sub-clauses of 7 were legacies to other parties. The (iv) was omitted from the codicil, so it appeared to revoke clauses 3 and also 7, both in their entirety. The court held that it could not insert the (iv) but it could omit the 7, so the revocation read 'clauses 2 and'. The testatrix's intentions were clear to Latey J from the extrinsic evidence brought to his notice, but he could not admit that evidence because it would be admissible only in the case of a latent ambiguity, not a patent one, as here.

### 4.11.9 Lack of power to insert words

The lack of a power to rectify by inserting words was also regretted by the court in *Re Reynette-James* (1975), where the typographical omission of a clause meant that a share of the estate devolved as capital to the testatrix's son instead of his receiving the income as she had wished. 'Any document other than a will could be rectified by inserting the words which the secretary omitted, but in this respect the court is enslaved by the Wills Act 1837' complained the court.

### 4.11.10 Law Reform Committee 19th Report

The case of *Re Morris* (4.11.8) prompted much comment. In 1973, the Law Reform Committee published its findings on proposals to change the powers of the court of construction so as to allow it to rectify a will to accord with the testator's intentions. It recommended that the court should have the power to insert words to achieve this, and also that the evidence admissible to the court of the intentions of the testator should not be restricted either by reference to the giving of instructions for the will or by time. It did not, however, suggest any solution to the problem which arises when the testator is reasonably felt to have intended something different from what they have said but has known what words were used and approved them, that is, where they have been mistaken as to the meaning the courts would put on the words or the effects they have in law.

### 4.11.11 Rectification and the Administration of Justice Act 1982, s 20

The recommendations of the Law Reform Committee as to powers of rectification were accepted and put into effect in s 20 of the Administration of Justice Act 1982. This allowed the court to rectify a will so as to carry out the testator's intentions if the difficulty was caused by either a clerical error or a failure to understand instructions. In such circumstances, the court may add words to the will as well as omit them.

In *Wordingham v Royal Exchange Trust Co* (1992), the problem was an error in the recording of the testatrix's intentions. She had made a will in 1975 exercising a power of appointment of income from her father's estate to the plaintiff. In 1979 she redrafted her provisions and made a new will. Unfortunately, when she did the same in 1989, the exercise of the power of appointment was inadvertently omitted. The court held, however, that such an 'inadvertent error made in the process of recording' the testatrix's intentions could be rectified under s 20(1)(a) of the Administration of Justice Act 1982 by the insertion of the missing clause.

The court in *Re Segelman* (1996) had to consider a similar question. The testator had executed the final draft of a fairly complex will which contained a class gift, namely a 21-year trust to the poor and needy members of the testator's family. The solicitor was told he would be provided with a list of names to include in a schedule, and on his own initiative he drafted a proviso to cl 11(a), which provided that if any of the persons named in the schedule died during the testator's lifetime or within 21 years of his death, 'then such issue shall stand in the place of such person and shall be eligible to benefit' under the trust. The testator's secretary subsequently provided the solicitor with the schedule of six named members of the testator's extended family and the 'issue' (who were not named) of five of them. The solicitor did not re-evaluate the need for the proviso to cl 11(a) in the light of the wording of the second schedule and the unnamed issue were unable to take whilst their parent was alive. The court was asked to find that the proviso which had been included in error. Chadwick J held that: 'the probability that a will which a testator has executed in circumstances of some formality reflects his intentions is usually of such weight that convincing evidence to the contrary is necessary.' However, in this case the burden was quite easily discharged, given the difficulty of construction the proviso presented, the judge saying: 'It is artificial to assume that a testator must know what he is doing if he uses language, the effect of which cannot be ascertained without a decision of the court.' The inclusion of the proviso was a clerical error within the meaning of s 20(1)(a) of the Administration of Justice Act 1982, and was thus capable of rectification by the court.

## 4.11.12 Mistake about the whole document, or mistake about part of it? The widening of clerical error

Cases of mistake about a whole document have in the past been decided in opposite ways on very similar facts in England and elsewhere. In the English case of *Re Meyer* (1908), two sisters instructed their solicitor to prepare wills in similar terms save for the names in each. Unfortunately, they then executed each other's documents, so that the references made in them to the other sister by name made no sense because they appeared to refer to themselves. The court refused to make any grant of probate, on the basis that the supposed testatrix did not know and approve the contents of the document. On similar facts, however, the New Zealand court in *Guardian Trust & Executors v Inwood* (1946) and the Canadian court in *Re Brander* (1952) admitted the documents to probate as wills by the expedient of omitting the names, those being the parts which the testatrices did not know and approve, leaving the references to 'my sister', with which the wills still made sense. The court in *Inwood* held that 'the testatrix did really know and approve of the effective provisions' which were the principal part of the document she executed. However, in the 2014 case of *Marley v Rawlings* the testator signed his wife's will in error. She predeceased him and the substitute gifts were identical in both wills. The Supreme Court ruled that the 'wife's will' which he had signed was his will and the estate passed under the will and not intestacy.

That recent Supreme Court case of *Marley v Rawlings* (2014) was a case about a whole document that has significantly expanded the scope of what is meant by clerical error. In 1999 Mr and Mrs Rawlings made mirror wills leaving their estates to each other and on the second death to their informally adopted son Mr Marley, disinheriting their own two sons. Mrs Rawlings died in

2003 but probate was not needed for her estate. It was only on Mr Rawlings' death in 2006 that it was discovered that they had signed each other's will. Mr Marley applied for solemn form probate and rectification of the document signed by Mr Rawlings.

At first instance Proudman J found that the document did not comply with s 9 of the Wills Act 1837 as the document was his wife's will and not his and therefore not signed by the correct testator and Mr Rawlings did not intend to give effect to the document he signed. It was therefore not a will that could be rectified under s 20. Proudman J found that, even if there had been a will for the purposes of s 20, the court would not have been able to carry out rectification as the mistake made by the solicitor – giving the wrong will to each party to sign – could not properly be characterised as a clerical error. It was not a mistyping, erroneous copy and paste or slip of the pen. The Court of Appeal regretfully upheld this ruling.

The Supreme Court however came to a different conclusion. It found the document to be formally valid, with Mr Rawlings signing the document he intended to be his will in the presence of witnesses who signed in turn. 'The fact that it is pretty clear from the provisions which it contains that a will may well face problems in terms of interpretation or even validity does not mean it cannot satisfy the formality requirements' [in s 9 of the Wills Act 1837][19] and even if the document had not been a valid will s 20 could still be invoked as the reference in s 20 to a will means 'any document which is on its face bona fide intended to be a will ... or a document which once it is rectified is a valid will'.[20] This means that the courts could admit apparently invalid wills to probate on the grounds that any defects could be addressed by construction or rectification.

Lord Neuberger found that

> the expression 'clerical error' can have a narrow meaning, which would be limited to mistakes involved in copying or writing out a document, and would not include a mistake of the type that occurred in this case.... However, the expression is not one with a precise or well-established, let alone a technical, meaning. The expression also can carry a wider meaning, namely a mistake arising out of office work of a relatively routine nature, such as preparing, filing, sending, organising the execution of, a document (save, possibly, to the extent that the activity involves some special expertise). Those are activities which are properly to be described as 'clerical', and a mistake in connection with those activities, such as wrongly filing a document or putting the wrong document in an envelope, can properly be called 'a clerical error'.[21]

This is has significantly widened the scope of what can be rectified, and it has been suggested that the decision in *Marley v Rawlings* not only shows the law of wills catching up with the law of contract but also has implications for the law of construction of wills more generally.[22]

However, rectification is not available where the intentionally selected words do not achieve the testator's intended outcome. In *Brooke v Purton* (2014), the testator wished to leave legacies to non-exempt beneficiaries and a discretionary nil-rate band trust of shares subject to Business Property Relief and cash to his children. The solicitor erroneously and without considering the implications used a precedent based on the residue going to a spouse and therefore being exempt from Inheritance Tax (see 14.4.3). This resulted in the nil-rate band being used up by the legacies, and a nil-rate band trust with no assets. The court found that the solicitor had used precedent

---

19 Para 58.
20 Paras 65–66.
21 Para 75.
22 Hugh Cumber and Charlotte Kynaston, 'Where There's a Will There's a Way: *Marley v Rawlings*' (2014) 25 King's Law Journal 137; Robert Ham, 'Thy Will Be Done: Construction and Rectification of Wills in the Supreme Court' (2014) 20 Trusts & Trustees 966.

wording without realising the implications and that this was a rectifiable clerical error. In *Kell v Jones* (2013), however, the court dismissed the claim for rectification as, although the will as drafted did not correctly reflect the testator's intentions, the error was not a clerical error or a failure to understand the testator's instructions for the solicitor had given the clause careful consideration and mistakenly, yet adamantly, believed it achieved the desired outcome.

For more on applications for rectification and what to do where the will is wrong, see Chapter 16.

## 4.12 Summary of Chapter 4

### 4.12.1 Capacity to Make a Will

As well as complying with the formalities for making a will, the testator must be shown to have had testamentary capacity. Unless they are entitled to make a privileged will, they must be over 18. For any kind of will, privileged or formal, the testator must be shown to have had mental capacity.

Testamentary capacity is not the same as general mental capacity and the test is legal rather than medical. However, mental capacity is generally presumed unless there is some medical indication of incapacity. Even then, testamentary capacity may be found for example during a lucid interval. The Mental Health Act 2005 places emphasis on respecting the autonomy even of a patient under the Act. More capacity is needed to make a complicated will than a simple one; the mental capacity required to make a simple will is less than that required to marry.

Testamentary capacity must generally be present at the time of execution of the will. However, where a testator with capacity has previously given instructions for a will and then loses full testamentary capacity, the will may be saved under the rule in *Parker v Felgate* if the testator understood, at execution, that they were executing a will for which they had previously given instructions.

The contents of the will must also reflect the free volition of the testator. There is no presumption of undue influence in respect of gifts by will, but it may be shown on the facts. However, this is a heavy burden to discharge.

The testator must know and approve the contents of the will. Wills or clauses they did not know and approve of will be excluded from probate. Reading over the will to the testator before execution raises a presumption of knowledge and approval.

The preparation of a will by a beneficiary or by a close relative of the beneficiary raises suspicion, as does the conveying of instructions through an intermediary. Solicitors are also subject to professional rules about taking benefits under wills they have drafted.

If the testator was mistaken about a part of the document they executed, that part may be omitted from probate if they did not know and approve of it. A mistake about the whole document may mean a lack of testamentary intention and so no will at all. Mistake as to the legal meaning of words known of and approved cannot be cured, though since 1982, it has been possible to add words as well as omit them under s 20 AJA 1982 if there was a clerical error or a failure to understand the testator's instructions.

## 4.13 Further reading

Hugh Cumber and Charlotte Kynaston, 'Where There's a Will There's a Way: *Marley v Rawlings*' (2014) 25 King's Law Journal 137.

Robert Ham, 'Thy Will Be Done: Construction and Rectification of Wills in The Supreme Court' (2014) 20 Trusts & Trustees 966.

Roger Kerridge, 'Wills Made in Suspicious Circumstances: the Problem of the Vulnerable Testator' (2000) 59 The Cambridge Law Journal 310.

Roger Kerridge, 'Undue Influence and Testamentary Dispositions: A Response' (2012) 76 Conveyancer and Property Lawyer 129.

Roger Kerridge and AHR Brierley, 'Mistakes in Wills: Rectify and Be Damned' (2003) 62 The Cambridge Law Journal 750.

Lee Mason, 'Undue Influence and Testamentary Dispositions: An Equitable Jurisdiction in Probate Law?' (2011) 75 Conveyancer and Property Lawyer 115.

# Chapter 5

# Formalities for the Execution of Wills

If people can leave instructions about the disposition of their property after their death, clearly at the point where those instructions are dealt with they cannot be asked about any queries that arise. This gives rise to problems both of construction – how the words testators have used are to be interpreted – and of being sure that the will documents truly represent the testamentary wishes and intentions of the deceased. Testators cannot be asked to confirm that the will is definitely their own, rather than forged, or that it was a considered opinion rather than something written in the heat of anger. The purpose of the prescription of formalities is to provide a safeguard against forgery and undue influence, and it also protects against dispositions in the heat of the moment.

## 5.1 Background to the current provisions as to formalities

That a will must be attested by two witnesses is one of the better-known provisions of the law. Historically, however, the need for attestation varied according to the amount and nature of property in the estate. By the early nineteenth century, the multiplicity of provisions was felt to be not only anachronistic but also unnecessary and positively harmful. There was even then a general belief, mentioned by the Real Property Commissioners in making an enquiry in the early nineteenth century, that a will which required attestation called for only two witnesses, although this was insufficient if the will purported to dispose of freehold realty. The varied provisions and the widespread failure to understand them (and, worse, the failure to appreciate that they were not understood) meant that testators could and did make wills which were valid as to some of their dispositions and invalid as to others, which created grave difficulties. When the Real Property Commissioners presented their Fourth Report in 1833, they recommended that there be only one set of provisions for the attestation of wills, whatever the nature or quantity of property they disposed of. They justified this not only by the importance of the execution of wills being easily and generally understood but also by pointing out that the purpose of formalities is to prevent forgery and fraud, the danger of which is the same whatever the nature of the property dealt with by the will. The resulting legislation was the Wills Act of 1837. Though it has been amended, most of its provisions remain in force. Compared to some other jurisdictions, England and Wales still insists on relatively strict compliance with the old idea of writing, signed and witnessed. There are no provisions for recognising wills that are not duly executed as such, and no current plans to bring in dematerialisation so as to allow wills to be made electronically.[1]

---

1 Gerry W Beyer and Claire Hargrove, 'Digital Wills: Has the Time Come for Wills to Join the Digital Revolution?' (2007) 33 Ohio Northern University Law Review 865.

### 5.1.1 Purpose of the formalities

The idea is that the formalities of the Wills Act 1837 make it difficult to forge a will or to pressurise the testator into making any particular provisions, because of its requirement that two people who are not beneficiaries of the will witness its signature. The very unwieldiness of the formalities makes it less likely that a testator would be able to make a valid will in the heat of the moment which they might later regret.

### 5.1.2 Problems with formalities

Of course, the disadvantage of having formal requirements is that they may in many cases mean that a will fails because it falls foul of those requirements, when in fact it was a true representation of the testator's testamentary intentions and, in that sense, a genuine will. This is a particular risk with those wills which are made without the benefit of legal advice, a situation in which the testator's estate and disappointed beneficiaries are also unable to seek redress for negligence.

### 5.1.3 A possible solution?

Other jurisdictions have provisions in their laws which allow courts to validate a will that does not comply with all the formal requirements if it largely complies with them and the court is satisfied that the will is a genuine representation of the testator's intentions and was intended by them to be their will. This is usually called the doctrine of 'substantial compliance'.[2] A provision often cited as setting out the way such a doctrine should operate in law is that of s 12(2) of the Wills Act 1936–1975 of South Australia. This provides that a document purporting to embody the testamentary intentions of a deceased person shall, notwithstanding that it has not been executed with the formalities required elsewhere in the Act, be deemed to be a will of the deceased person if the Supreme Court, upon application for probate, is satisfied that there can be no reasonable doubt that the deceased intended the document to constitute their will. New Zealand passed a similar provision at s 14 of the Wills Act 2007, allowing the High Court to declare valid a will that does not comply with the formalities specified in s 11 of that Act (broadly similar to s 9 Wills Act 1837) if it is satisfied that the document expresses the deceased's testamentary intentions. The court may take into account the document itself and evidence about how it was executed, as well as evidence about statements made by the deceased and evidence of their testamentary intentions. Such provisions are felt by some to enable justice and common sense, but by others to encourage uncertainty, litigation and even opportunism.

The Law Reform Committee, in its 22nd Report *The Making and Revocation of Wills*, invited consideration of whether a 'general dispensing power' should be given to the court to allow probate of a will which it was satisfied was genuine even where it was technically invalid, but this phenomenon has not been brought into English law.

### 5.1.4 Problems with this solution

There are, however, potential objections to the inclusion of such provisions within the law. One is that the formalities do serve a purpose. Such formalities as the requirement for the 'publication' of a will (the testator stating that it is their will) and for the signature to be at the end of the will, which caused some undoubtedly genuine wills to fail without apparently giving any real advantage, have been abolished. The provisions for signature and attestation which remain

---

2  John H Langbein, 'Substantial Compliance with the Wills Act' (1975) 88 Harvard Law Review 489; JG Miller, 'Substantial Compliance and the Execution of Wills' (1987) 36 International and Comparative Law Quarterly 559.

arguably do provide protection against forgery and undue influence. Another potential difficulty is that where rules are not hard and fast, uncertainty is raised as to whether something is valid or not which can be resolved only by litigation. In the context of the declaring valid of a defectively executed will, it is not even the case that the litigation can be settled without going to court, because it is precisely a declaration of the court that is required.

Legislators are very unwilling to pass any laws which might lead to uncertainty as to how the law applies to any given situation, because of the increased risk of litigation. There may also be an objection of principle in giving the final decision on whether a will is valid or not to a court. It is not an uncommon view that the courts have too much discretionary power in general, and also that their involvement in people's daily lives should be kept to a minimum.

## 5.1.5 Stricter formalities in other types of jurisdictions

Some other, continental, jurisdictions, operating under civil rather than common law, have formalities which might be described as stricter rather than more lax. They require that a will be notarised, which means that there is a necessary involvement of a professional, in order to be valid: see 5.1.7.

## 5.1.6 Law Reform Committee 22nd Report *The Making and Revocation of Wills*

In 1980, the Law Reform Committee presented its 22nd Report, which discussed certain specific difficulties with the formalities as they then stood. It referred in particular to the case of *Re Colling* (1972), where a will which was plainly 'genuine' – that is it represented the testator's true intentions – failed for want of compliance with the requirement for the simultaneous presence of two witnesses. It had also transpired that when the Probate Registry investigated home-made wills on which a printed attestation clause had been left to refer to the testator as 'him/her' it found that it appeared commonplace for that requirement to be breached, though normally the Probate Registry would not make sufficient enquiries ever to find that out. It seemed likely that this requirement was regularly breached without consequence. The committee queried whether there was a need for the requirement for the presence of witnesses at the time of the testator's own signature (there is no such requirement in Scotland).

The Law Reform Committee's 22nd Report also encompassed some other ideas. It suggested the possibility that nuncupative (oral) will, which are otherwise valid only if made by a privileged testator (see 6.1), might be valid for small estates. This had indeed been the position after the Statute of Frauds 1677, one of the exceptions to the requirement for writing being in respect of estates under £30. It also considered the suggestions that English law might bring in provisions relating to notarial wills and holographic wills.

## 5.1.7 Notarial wills

Some legal systems make attestation by a notary compulsory, the testator either having the notary draw up the will or else making a formal declaration that the document to be notarised is their will. The Law Reform Committee did not think it would change the current system much unless it were compulsory, since the problems now tend to arise where someone has attempted to deal with their own will without the assistance of a legal professional. They were not keen to see such provisions introduced compulsorily, and indeed the Law Commission in its 1966 Working Paper *Should English Wills be Registrable?* had said that

> although we are very conscious of the risks run by the testators who are not well advised, we apprehend that public opinion would not tolerate any change in the law which would compel testators to have resort to a solicitor.

There would also be some difficulties in aligning the English system with the continental notarial system stemming from the difference between solicitors and notaries; most English solicitors are not qualified as notaries and do not have their powers.

To become a notary in England and Wales is time-consuming and very expensive. Qualification is overseen by the Faculty Office of the Church of England, the powers of the Master of the Faculties having been confirmed by the Courts and Legal Services Act 1990 and the Legal Services Act 2007. Notaries may belong to the representative bodies, namely the Notaries Society or the Society of Scrivener Notaries, but these are not part of the Church of England, nor are notaries associated with the Church other than the connection through the jurisdiction of the Archbishop of Canterbury over the notarial profession.

Issues of notarisation may arise when dealing with foreign documents. Differences in practices led to the Hague Convention Abolishing the Requirement for Legalisation for Foreign Public Documents 1961, known as the Apostille Convention, to which all European Union countries (as well as others) are currently party. This deals with the certification of documents from signatory states so as to make them valid in other signatory states. An international certificate of this kind is known as an 'apostille', and this Convention is usually called the Apostille Convention or the Apostille Treaty. The Hague Conference on Private International Law, which made the Convention, specifies the authority in each country that is competent to affix an apostille. In England, this is the Foreign and Commonwealth Office in Milton Keynes. The apostille itself is a stamp or form with certain information to be put on the document, filled in and notarised. It should be noted that the apostille merely certifies the signature and stamp, rather than attesting to anything about the content of the document.

## 5.1.8 Holographic wills

A holographic will is one made by the testator in their own handwriting. These are valid in some jurisdictions without the need for attestation, on the grounds that, being handwritten, they are proof against forgery anyway. They do, however, have their own problems – a letter may contain terms which look like those of a will, but the question of whether the letter was made with testamentary intention may arise much more easily than with a more formal will, and already arises under English law in the similar situation of privileged wills. In jurisdictions which do have more informal provisions for holographic wills, the question of testamentary intention may fall to be decided by a court.[3]

In the Canadian province of Ontario, for example, holographic wills are permitted by the Succession Law Reform Act (RSO 1990), s 6, which says that: 'A testator may make a valid will wholly by his own handwriting and signature, without formalities, and without the presence attestation or signature of a witness.' The Canadian courts have, however, had to adjudicate in order to establish testamentary intention. They have evolved the requirement of a 'deliberate, fixed and final expression' of the testator's wishes for the disposal of their property at death. In *Bennett v Gray* (1958), however, the court had to consider letters of instruction written to the solicitor Mr Dysart from the purported testatrix Mary Gray; it held that, in their context, the letters expressed no testamentary intention as such and that therefore they were not valid as a will. In *Canada Permanent Trust Co v Bowman* (1962) the testator's words 'I would like Laura to have this property...' were, however, considered sufficient.

Canadian statute requires the holographic will to be made fully in the testator's handwriting, but Scottish law, which also admits holographic wills, allows for the adoption of a typewritten

---

3  Stephen Clowney, 'In Their Own Hand: An Analysis of Holographic Wills and Homemade Willmaking' (2008–2009) 43 Real Property, Trust and Estate Law Journal 27.

will provided the words of adoption are themselves handwritten (save in the case of an ill testator who always used a typewriter and who was allowed to type their own words of adoption).[4] Where adoption of a typewritten will as holograph is allowed, there is the further question over whether it is prudent to allow the holographic will in principle at all, as it becomes much easier to forge.

English law has no particular provisions relating to holographic wills.

### 5.1.9 Administration of Justice Act 1982

The Administration of Justice Act 1982 made certain provisions relating to the formalities required for wills. First, s 17 of the 1982 Act allowed the testator to sign anywhere on the will so that their signature would still be valid, provided that it appeared that they intended by their signature to give effect to the will. Previously it needed to be signed at the end. Second, it provided that witnesses could acknowledge their previous signatures. This meant that the acknowledgment by a witness of their previous signature has the same effect as their actual signature, so if one or both witnesses sign the will, the testator makes or acknowledges his or her signature in their simultaneous presence, and each witness either attests and signs the will or acknowledges their previous signature in the presence of the testator, the execution will be valid. If *Re Colling* (1972) (see 5.5.3) had been decided under the new rules following the implementation of the 1982 Act, it would have had the opposite conclusion. The Act applies to those testators who die after 1982.

The 1982 Act also made provisions as to deposit and registration of wills: see 5.20.

## 5.2 Current provisions as to formalities

Section 7 of the Wills Act 1837 provides that no will made by a minor shall be valid; at the time of the original Act, that meant a person under 21 but, since the coming into force of the Family Law Reform Act 1969 in 1970, it means a person under 18.

The provisions which have to be formally complied with for a will to be valid are contained in s 9 of the Wills Act 1837, as amended by the Wills Act Amendment Act 1852 and by the AJA 1982 for those dying after 1982. Section 9 applies to all English internal wills except privileged wills and statutory wills. Privileged wills are those which are made by soldiers or seamen and which do not have to comply with the formalities under s 9; they are sometimes called informal wills. Statutory wills are those made for the mentally incapable under the provisions of the Mental Capacity Act 2005. (These should not be confused with the Statutory Will Forms originally prescribed by the Lord Chancellor in 1925, which consist of a number of provisions which can be incorporated by express reference into any will; these have been very little used.) For details of these, see 6.7.

### 5.2.1 Wills Act 1837, s 9

Section 9 of the Wills Act 1837 should be considered in close detail. Each part of it has been subject to interpretation in cases decided under the Act, but in considering whether or not any particular will is valid, usually more than one part of the section is involved.

---

4  *McBeath's Trustees v McBeath* (1935).

## 5.2.2 How the formalities operate in practice

It is important, as a matter of practice, to bear in mind that, although all the formalities must have been complied with for a will to be valid, it is only in a very few cases that any enquiry is made specifically about whether the requirements were complied with, provided that the will on the face of it appears to have been properly made. The principle operating is usually expressed in Latin as *omnia praesumuntur rite esse acta* – everything which looks okay is presumed to be okay. Note, however, that this is only a presumption, and where there is evidence before a court that the appearance of compliance with the rules was misleading, the court will not overlook that evidence, but will find the presumption rebutted. In *In the Estate of Bercovitz* (1962), the court was invited to apply the maxim after it had heard that the particular signature the witnesses had attested had not been the one that would have been valid; the court declined to ignore that evidence in order to save the will and it was held invalid. The person contesting a will, as shown in the majority of recent cases, must show strong evidence to rebut the presumption of due execution (see 5.16.2).

Where no questions arise about the validity of a will, it is dealt with under the Non-Contentious Probate Rules, currently those of 1987 but under review at the time of writing, which set out precisely how a probate registry should deal with an application for probate in an ordinary case. To have a full enquiry about every will would take a great deal of time and therefore be extremely expensive, and it would very probably serve little purpose, since there is no difficulty with most wills.

In saying this, however, one might bear in mind the experience of the Probate Registry as reported in the Law Reform Committee's 22nd Report *The Making and Revocation of Wills* (see 5.1.6). The Registry began raising queries about the attestation of home-made wills and found that a high proportion of them had not been properly witnessed and therefore were not valid. No doubt this had always been the case, but they had not previously enquired. This discovery tends to suggest that the formalities may not be serving the purpose they are supposed to, or at least not very efficiently, if only because they are not being complied with and, perhaps, most of the time no one notices.

## 5.3 The formalities – s 9 itself

Section 9 of the Wills Act 1837, as amended, lays down that:

> No will shall be valid unless:
> (a)  it is in writing, and signed by the testator, or by some other person in his presence and by his direction; and
> (b)  it appears that the testator intended by his signature to give effect to the will; and
> (c)  signature is made or acknowledged by the testator in the presence of two or more witnesses present at the same time; and
> (d)  each witness either:
>     (i)  attests and signs the will; or
>     (ii)  acknowledges his signature, in the presence of the testator (but not necessarily in the presence of any other witness)
>     but no form of attestation shall be necessary.

Each of these provisions will be considered in turn.

## 5.4 In writing

The will must be in writing, but the interpretation given to that statutory requirement has been very wide. There is no difference in the English jurisdiction between the formalities prescribed for handwritten wills and those prescribed for other wills, as there is, for example, in Scotland. The will may be typed or handwritten or printed, or any combination of the same.

The cases show that the interpretation of 'in writing' is wide as to both the vital aspects of writing, namely the materials used and the language. Most wills are, obviously, typed or printed in English on paper, but the law allows for other methods.

### 5.4.1 Materials

In *Re Barnes* (1926), the court held valid a will which had been written on an egg-shell. No doubt the same would apply today, although it is possible that queries might be raised in the mind of the probate registrar about the testator's mental capacity. Clearly, where someone does not use ordinary paper for their will, it will be administratively more difficult to deal with. Egg-shells do not photocopy easily. However, the Non-Contentious Probate Rules, which govern the administrative side of proving a will, provide specifically for the difficulties created when people use non-standard materials – which might include an unusual size of paper. Rule 11 of the 1987 NCPR allows the court to require an engrossment (a fair copy, typed or printed) for the purposes of record, and provides how it should be set out.

Pencil may be used to write the whole will. If, however, there is writing in ink as well, it is generally stated on the basis of the decision in *In the Goods of Adams* (1872) that it will be assumed that the pencil writing was a draft only unless there is evidence to the contrary. However, in that case, which concerned a will written on a printed form, the pencil words were plainly written in draft, as they were partly obscured by other writing, and the will read sensibly if they were excluded and only the ink words included.

### 5.4.2 Language

There is also a very wide range of language that may be used. In *Whiting v Turner* (1903), a will written in French was held valid. The use of a code was also held not to invalidate a will in the case of *Kell v Charmer* (1856), where the deceased was a jeweller whose codes were those used in a jeweller's business and could be deciphered by reference to extrinsic evidence as to his business practices.

## 5.5 Signed by the testator

Anyone executing their will under the guidance of their solicitor will be asked to sign the will using their normal signature, or, sometimes, to sign with their full name. The courts have, however, had to look at various cases of somewhat less regular versions of signatures and to decide what the essential elements of a valid signature are.

### 5.5.1 What is a signature?

The decisions have elicited the principle that a testator may make any kind of mark which is intended to be their signature and it will be valid for the purposes of execution of the will. This has involved some decisions which may appear to be stretching the meaning of 'signature' to its limits. In *In the Goods of Savory* (1851), initials were a valid signature. A stamped signature was held to be valid in In the Goods of Jenkins (1863). An illiterate person may sign by means of a mark; this may be their usual signature and will be valid as such. The 'signature' of the testator in In the Estate of Finn (1935) was not so much a thumb-mark as 'merely a blot' as his thumb slipped and made a smudge. Nevertheless, it was held to be a valid signature, because the testator had intended it as such.

The testator's signature, whilst usually in their own name, may be in a form which is not their usual name or any name at all, provided that it was intended as their signature. In Re Cook (1960), the testatrix signed her will 'your loving mother'; this was held to be a valid signature for the purposes of executing the will. The court reviewed many cases on what constituted a signature, especially those of Baker v Dening (1838), where the court had in mind the provisions of the Statute of Frauds of 1677, which provided that the making of a mark was sufficient signature for a will of realty, and Hindmarsh v Charlton (1861), where the court had said that a signature was 'either the name or some mark which is intended to represent the name'. It concluded that the testatrix had meant 'your loving mother' as her signature.

### 5.5.2 Signature must be complete

However, the signature must be exactly what the testator intended, and in particular it must be complete. The testatrix in In the Goods of Chalcraft (1948) began to sign her codicil, but could not complete the signature because of her physical state. All she managed to write was 'E. Chal' before she became too weak to continue. It was held that 'E. Chal' was sufficient because, in the circumstances, it was intended by her as the whole of her signature.

### 5.5.3 Completeness as a matter of intention

The principle that a wide interpretation will be given to what constitutes a valid signature provided that it is what the testator intended as their signature was reinforced by the decision in Re Colling (1972). The testator was signing his will while ill in hospital. One of the witnesses was a fellow patient and one was a nurse. The nurse was called away while the testator's signature was still incomplete, and then returned afterwards and signed as a witness. The will was held not to have been validly attested. The partial signature at which the witnesses had both been present did not count as a valid signature for execution, because it was not all the testator intended.

## 5.6 Signature on the testator's behalf

Someone else may sign on behalf of the testator, provided that the signature is made in the presence of the testator and by their direction. This means they must be physically present and directly requesting that the other person sign on their behalf at the time of the signature. If either of these conditions is not satisfied, the signature will not be valid. In Smith v Harris (1845), it was confirmed that the person signing on the testator's behalf may be one of the attesting witnesses. The person signing for the testator may sign their own name rather than that of the testator, as was held in In the Goods of Clark (1839).

However, in the recent case of Barrett v Bem and Others (2012), the Court of Appeal found that

> the court should not find that a will has been signed by a third party at the direction of the testator unless there is positive and discernible communication (which may be verbal or non-verbal) by the testator that he wishes the will to be signed on his behalf by the third party [and that] there must be more than passive acquiescence in someone else's actions.

The testator was gravely ill and physically incapable of signing without assistance, but the court held that assistance had to be clearly and unambiguously given for the resulting signature to count as a valid signature of the testator. Direction could not be given by negative conduct.

## 5.7 Signature of the whole will

The whole will needs to be regarded as having been executed. The testator may leave various different documents – wills and codicils – which must each be properly executed if they are to be valid. However, it is not necessary to execute each page of a will. If only the last page of the will is executed, any other pages ought to be attached to it at the time of execution (or incorporated by reference; see 5.19.4). The question of how firmly they had to be attached has been addressed by the courts. The court in *Lewis v Lewis* (1908) held that, in the absence of proper securing at the time of execution, the pages being pressed together by the testator's finger and thumb will suffice. In *In the Estate of Little* (1960), the testator's pressing the pages together on a table with his hand was also considered sufficient.

In an Irish case, *In the Goods of Tiernan* (1942), and a case under the Northern Irish jurisdiction, *Sterling v Bruce* (1973), it sufficed that all the parts of a will which were shown to have been in the same room at the time of execution, even though they were not attached to each other physically. This rule might be followed in a similar English case.

The testator in *Wood v Smith* (1992) (see 5.8.3) 'signed' his will before writing out the dispositive provisions. He clearly intended his name in the heading 'My will by Percy Winterbone' to be his signature, as he said he had already signed the will at the top, and the Court of Appeal agreed that, as he had written the will as one action, the testator had effectively signed it (though he was found lacking in testamentary capacity so the will failed anyway). The distinction between writing all the will as one action and writing the signature substantially in advance was considered by the court in *Re White, Barker v Gribble* (1990).

### 5.7.1 Signature at the bottom of the will?

Under the original provisions of the Wills Act 1837, a will had to be signed at its foot or end. This led to some unsatisfactory decisions. In *Smee v Bryer* (1848), for example, the testatrix signed on the following page because there was less than an inch left at the bottom of the last page of her will. It was held that missing this space meant her will was invalid.

### 5.7.2 Amendments to the original rules

The testator's signature originally had to be at the very bottom of the will but this was amended by the Wills Act Amendment Act 1852 so that the signature could be somewhere about the end. This applied even if there was a blank space between the end of the will, and the signature could even be on a separate page from the text of the will. It could also be in or under the attestation clause and signatures of the witnesses. The essential element of signing at the end to prevent fraudulent insertion of anything further (*Re Stalman* (1931)) remained, however. It trapped the testator in *In the Estate of Bercovitz* (1962) (5.2.2), who had failed to have the signature at the bottom of his will properly witnessed and found that the signature at the top, which the witnesses had seen, would not do.

The Administration of Justice Act 1982 provided that the testator could sign anywhere on the will and the signature would still be valid, provided that the testator intended by it to give effect to the will and provided that the will complied with all the other necessary formalities. This applies to testators dying after 1982. There are, therefore, no longer any current rules relating specifically to where on the will the testator has to place their signature.

However, over-confidence in the re-amended provision almost trapped the testator in *Wood v Smith* (1992) (5.7, and see 5.8.3), who signed his will at the top – before writing the rest of its provisions. In such a case, one should note that the upholding of a will after a contested court case may be a pyrrhic victory; its gifts may have been rendered irrelevant by legal costs.

# 5.8 Intention to give effect to the will by the signature

Note the difference between intending to give effect to the will by the signature and having testamentary intention; the latter means that the testator intended the document to operate as their will, whereas the former means that they intended that the document should, by them writing their signature on it and the other necessary formalities being completed, be executed so as to comply with the rules as to validity of wills (see the case of *Marley v Rawlings* (2014) at 4.11 for a discussion on the distinction).

## 5.8.1 Signing something other than the will

In *Re Mann* (1942), the testatrix signed not the paper on which the provisions of her will were written but the envelope into which that paper was put. She wrote on the envelope 'Last Will and Testament of JC Mann' and then signed the envelope and had her signature duly witnessed. The court found that the paper with the provisions of the will on it together with the envelope which was duly executed constituted her will and that it was therefore valid.

In *In the Estate of Bean* (1944), however, the deceased again did not sign his will, but put it in an envelope. On this he wrote his name and address. The court found that this writing was intended not as a signature of the will but for the purpose of identifying the contents and that therefore the will was invalid for lack of a signature. Similarly, the testatrix in *Re Beadle* (1974) was held to have signed an envelope in order to identify its contents, rather than with the intention of giving effect to her will, when she wrote on the front of it 'My last will and testament, EA Beadle, to Charley and Maisy' and had those two friends write 'We certify that the contents of this letter was written in the presence of ourselves' on the back and then sign. The testatrix had believed the will was already properly executed, because she had signed the contents of the envelope, but only Charley witnessed her signature and so the document was not properly executed.

## 5.8.2 Establishing the intention

The intention to give effect to the will must, according to the 1852 Act, be apparent from the face of the will. However, s 21 of the Administration of Justice Act 1982 may be available in dubious cases (see 11.11). That section applies, inter alia, where the language used in any part of the will is ambiguous on the face of it, and it allows the introduction of extrinsic evidence (evidence from outside the will), including evidence of the testator's intention, to be admitted to assist in the interpretation of the will.

## 5.8.3 Time of the intention

*Wood v Smith* (1992) (5.7), a case about a home-made will, established that the testator may sign their will before it is written and their signature may still be valid for the purposes of execution. The testator had made a holographic (handwritten) will which he began 'My will by Percy Winterbone'; after writing out the provisions underneath, he asked two other persons to sign as witnesses, assuring them that he had already signed at the top of the document and that he could sign anywhere on the will. It was held in the Chancery Division that the testator could not have intended, at the point when he signed, to give effect to a will as, there being no dispositive provisions (those relating to how his property was to be disposed of), there was no will to which effect could be intended to be given. The Court of Appeal, however, regarding the writing out of the will and its execution as one operation, held the will validly executed (but note that it ultimately failed by reason of the testator's lack of mental capacity). It doubted however that if the will had not been completed on the one occasion it would have come to the same conclusion.

## 5.9 Signature or acknowledgment in the presence of witnesses

The signature of the testator must be either made or acknowledged by the testator in the presence of two witnesses present at the same time. This provision often appears to cause much difficulty, but in reality falls into two separate areas. First, if the testator does not write their signature in the witnesses' presence as one would expect, it must be established whether what they do do constitutes acknowledgment for the purposes of the formalities. Second, it must be clear that both the witnesses were present when the testator's signature is made or acknowledged by the testator, whether or not they are both then present while they are each signing.

The Statute of Frauds of 1677 did not require the three witnesses demanded for a will of freehold realty to be present at the same time. In *Ellis v Smith* (1754), the court held good a will witnessed separately by the three witnesses, but was reluctant. Willes CJ said:

> I think the cases admitting the attestation at three different times have gone too far ... I have known one man swear that he did not see the testator sign and the other two swear that he signed it before the three ... an inlet is made for great frauds and impositions. But when they attest it *simul et semel* [together and at the same time] they are a check on each other and prevent such frauds.

The courts were supported in their belief that the separate presence of witnesses could lead to fraud by the Ecclesiastical Commission in its General Report of 1832 and the Real Property Commissioners in their Fourth Report of 1833. The present requirement for them to be present together was therefore enacted in the Wills Act of 1837. Lord Brougham in *Casement v Fulton* (1845) described it as 'a most wholesome addition' to the law, saying that 'if one witness may be present one day and another a different day, perhaps at an interval of years, how can we say that both attest the same fact...?' This judgment reflected that the witnesses were to attest not only the making of the signature but the mental capacity of the testator to make the will.

## 5.10 Acknowledgment of signature

A signature may be validated later by acknowledgment. It can be elicited from the case law that three conditions must be satisfied for an acknowledgment to be valid:

(a)     the will must have been signed before the acknowledgment;
(b)     the signature must be visible at the time of the acknowledgment;
(c)     the signature must have been acknowledged by words or conduct.

If the will has not already been signed when the testator makes an acknowledgment, there is clearly nothing for them to acknowledge.

The second requirement above has been established by case law, but again it would be diffi-cult to read a requirement for the acknowledgment of a signature to be witnessed as sensibly countenancing a situation in which the witness does not have the means of seeing for himself that the signature exists. In *Re Groffman* (1969), only one of the testator's two proposed witnesses was present when he produced the will and showed the signature on it. It was held that, as the will had not been produced to the second witness so that the signature was visible to him, that signature had therefore not been acknowledged to both witnesses, and the will failed for lack of due execution.

The courts have evolved a very wide interpretation of the physical meaning of acknowledg-ment mentioned in the third point above. Not only are no particular words of acknowledgment required, but words are not necessarily needed at all. In the early case of *Keigwin v Keigwin* (1843), it was said that it was sufficient if it clearly appeared that the testatrix's signature was existent on the will when she produced it to the witnesses and was seen by the witnesses when they sub-scribed the will at her request. This was applied in *Daintree v Butcher* (1888), where the testatrix showed a witness a codicil, saying she had something requiring two witnesses. The second witness then came into the room and it was clear that someone had requested them to sign and that the testatrix's signature was present when they both signed. Although they did not know that the document was a testamentary paper, the will was held validly attested. Because the signature was so placed that they could see it, whether they actually did see it or not, her request that they witness her signature amounted to an acknowledgment of it. In *In the Goods of Davies* (1850), the testator's acknowledgment of his signature by gestures was held to be sufficient for the purposes of due execution.

Note that since the Administration of Justice Act 1982, witnesses may also acknowledge their signatures (see 5.14.1).

## 5.11 Presence

The essence of a person being in another's presence, in the context of wills, is that they are visible to the other person.

### 5.11.1 Simultaneous presence of testator and both witnesses on testator's signature

The witnesses have to be present both at the same time while the testator makes their signature, or else the testator must acknowledge their signature in the witnesses' simultaneous presence. Therefore, when concentrating on the question of whether a will has been validly executed, the question of the validity of the testator's signature requires it to be established, that both witnesses were present at the moment when the testator either wrote their signature or else when they acknowledged that it was their signature, by whatever method. This would mean that, in either case, the testator and the testator's signature were visible to them, though whether they looked carefully or not will not be examined since the cases show that to be present means, in the context of the simultaneous presence of testators and witnesses, being in the line of sight of the other person.

### 5.11.2 Old cases – presence and the line of sight

The old cases often involved careful consideration of whether it was physically possible for the testator and witnesses to have seen each other had they looked. In *Shires v Glascock* (1688), the court considered the purpose of the Statute of Frauds: 'The Statute required attesting in his presence, to prevent obtruding another will in place of the true one. It is enough if the testator might see, it is not necessary that he should actually see them signing.'

In *Casson v Dade* (1781), the testatrix had signed her will and was outside in her carriage when the witnesses in her attorney's office made their signatures. However, the court accepted on the facts that she could have seen them through the windows and so they were in her presence; the attestation was therefore held to be valid. The later case of *Norton v Bazett* (1856) looked at witnesses signing in the next room to the testator (the report includes a site plan). The court commented that, 'where the witnesses subscribe in a different room to that in which the testator is, they must be shown to have subscribed in a position visible to the testator' or the court is unable to find a constructive presence.

### 5.11.3 Later cases – lack of attendance
The more usual problem situation arose in *Wyatt v Berry* (1893), where, the first witness having signed, the second came in and was told by the testator, 'It is a bit of ordering of my affairs.' He signed, as requested, what was clearly a genuine will, but it failed for lack of simultaneous presence. Something similar occurred in *Re Davies* (1951), where the testator made his mark in the presence of one witness, who was writing his signature when the second witness came into the room. The testator acknowledged his mark to the second witness, who then signed. The will was held invalid because the testator should have signed or acknowledged in the presence of both witnesses at the same time. (Note that the possible solutions to this situation have widened since the Administration of Justice Act 1982 allowed for acknowledgment by witnesses as well as testators.)

### 5.11.4 Lack of attention?
A slightly more interesting case on 'presence' was that of *Brown v Skirrow* (1902) where the testatrix had her will witnessed during business hours by two shop assistants. It was held that the will must fail because the second assistant would have been unable to see even had he looked up; as it was, he was paying no attention. It is submitted, however, that the requirement for some mental 'presence of mind' as well as a physical presence is unlikely to cause difficulties save in the most unusual circumstances.

## 5.12 Simultaneous presence of testator and each witness on that witness' signature
Whilst the witnesses need not sign in the presence of each other, they must sign, or acknowledge, in the presence of the testator. The validity of acknowledgment arises from the Administration of Justice Act 1982. The difference between the requirement for the witnesses both to be present when the testator signs or acknowledges and the requirement for the testator – but not necessarily the other witness – to be present when a witness signs, is a frequent cause of some confusion. It demonstrates why it is the usual practice for solicitors to insist that all three, testator and two witnesses, remain together in the same room and each sign in the presence of both of the others, and the presence of the testator and both witnesses throughout the procedure is usually recorded in the attestation clause. This avoids any unnecessary error, even if it goes further than what the law strictly requires, and it makes it more likely that the witnesses will be able to recall the details necessary to show due execution. The requirements of the law would, for example, be satisfied by the situation in which the testator, having signed their will previously, acknowledges their signature to both witnesses in their joint presence and then remains in

the room while one witness leaves and the other signs, and then the other returns and signs the will after the first witness has left.

## 5.13  Acknowledgment of signature by a witness

The validity of an acknowledgment by a witness of their signature was one of the changes to s 9 of the Wills Act 1837 brought in by s 17 of the Administration of Justice Act 1982, in accordance with a recommendation made by the Law Reform Committee in its 22nd Report *The Making and Revocation of Wills*.

## 5.14  What the witnesses need to know

The witnesses do not need to know that the document is a will, still less to read it and be aware of its contents. What they are really witnessing is not the will but the testator's signature. In practice, however, although it is unusual for witnesses to be invited to read a will, a solicitor dealing with one will tell them what sort of document is being executed; most testators proceeding without the benefit of a solicitor will do the same. One of the functions of a witness is to be available after the testator's death so they can be asked about the circumstances of the execution of the will. If they did not know that they were attesting a will, they are much less likely to be able to remember the occasion at all, still less the details of what occurred.

What the witnesses do have to know is that the testator is making their signature. The witnesses must therefore be aware that the testator is writing and they must, to accord with the rules, be present together throughout the making of the signature. In *Smith v Smith* (1866), the attestation clause was handwritten. The testatrix held blotting paper over her signature while the witnesses signed. It was held that where the testatrix signed the will in the presence of the attesting witnesses, who saw her writing, then the attestation was good even though they did not see her signature and it was not acknowledged by her (though where the signature was covered by blotting paper in the case of *Re Gunstan* (1882), the will failed for that reason). A testatrix may also acknowledge her signature as, since the coming into force of the Administration of Justice Act 1982, may the witnesses.

### 5.14.1  *Couser v Couser* (1996)

*Couser v Couser* (1996) is an unusual case turning on the acknowledgment of a signature by a witness. The late Mr Couser, when in his seventies, had made a home-made will with clear dispositions, to which it appears, however, that his son, John, objected. John sought to have the grant of probate made to his step-mother revoked on the basis that the will had not been properly executed and was therefore invalid. He claimed that the deceased's signature had not been acknowledged in the presence of two or more witnesses present at the same time, and further, or alternatively, that the witness did not subscribe the will after the deceased acknowledged his signature on it. The court's view was that where there was nothing amiss on the face of the will, the burden of establishing that it had not been properly executed was a heavy one, and that John had failed to discharge it. Mr Couser had signed the will first, acknowledging the signature in the presence of both witnesses. The first witness then signed. However, she mistakenly believed that the will, which Mr Couser had drawn up himself on a printed form, would not be valid and she was some ten feet away on the other side of the room, protesting that the execution in progress was invalid, when the second witness signed. The court considered the old cases on testators' presence and remarked that what was important was not that a person had been looking but that they were able to see what was going on. It held that the testator and witnesses had all been present in the same room and were discussing the will when it was executed, that the necessary signatures and acknowledgments were made and that the will was therefore valid.

# 5.15 Capacity to be a witness

Almost anyone may be a witness, though clearly some persons will be more appropriate than others. Section 14 of the Wills Act 1837 specifically provides that if a witness turns out to have been incompetent to be admitted as a witness at the time of execution or at any time thereafter, the will will not be invalid for that reason. However, it is clearly best to choose as witnesses persons who are likely to be both available to give, and capable of giving, evidence of the circumstances of the attestation. Therefore, they should be, if possible, reasonably competent adults who are not too much older than the testator and in reasonable health, and therefore not too likely to predecease.

## 5.15.1 Blind witnesses

In *Re Gibson* (1949), the court held that a blind person was incapable of being a witness to a will because it could not be signed in their 'presence' and they could not be a 'witness' to the visible act of signing for the purposes of s 9. However, the court did leave open the possibility of a blind witness to a will written and signed in braille if the testator acknowledged their signature to the witness.

## 5.15.2 Compare blind testators

This is different from the situation for a blind testator – clearly if the testator's position were the same as for witnesses, it would be difficult or impossible for a blind person to make a will, which would be unacceptable (see attestation clauses at 5.16.1). The testator, however, merely signs the will, which is equally possible for a blind testator; they are, according to *Re Piercy* (1845), attributed with notional vision as far as the witnesses being in the testator's presence is concerned. The witnesses' role is to witness the testator's signature, so if they cannot see the signature itself, they cannot perform their essential function.

## 5.15.3 Witnesses' evidence as to due execution

If a witness is called, after the testator's death and on an attempt to prove the will, to give evidence as to the circumstances of the execution, they do so as a witness of the court. Where a witness is called in most proceedings, the party calling them may not cross-examine them; only the opposing party may do that. The effect of the witness being a witness of the court is that representatives of any party may cross-examine them. If no witness is available to give evidence as to the due execution of the will, the court may take evidence from other persons, as for instance in *Re Phibbs* (1917), where the will, after the testator's death, was lost in the post on the way to the testator's solicitor in Dublin. However, the two persons who had posted the will had read it before doing so and were able to give sufficient evidence as to its apparent execution to satisfy the court (fortunately, as one of them was the principal beneficiary).

An attesting witness who is a beneficiary or the spouse or civil partner of a beneficiary usually loses any gift under the will (see s 15 of the Wills Act 1837 at 10.8), but will still be a valid witness and may give evidence as to its execution.

### 5.15.4 Signatures of witnesses

The witnesses must attest and sign the will, or else acknowledge their signatures, in the presence of the testator. They do not, however, have to be in the presence of each other, even though they must both be present when the testator themselves signs or acknowledges. Thus the re-amended provision might not assist in a situation like that in *Bercovitz* (at 5.2.2, 5.7.2 and 5.15.5).

### 5.15.5 Which signature?

If there is more than one signature by the testator, the signature the witnesses see must be the operative one. The testator in *In the Estate of Bercovitz* (1962) signed his will at the top and also at the bottom. The witnesses saw the top signature but not the bottom one, which was covered by blotting paper. The will was held to be invalid due to lack of due execution, since at that time (before s 17 of the Administration of Justice Act 1982 re-amended s 9 of the Wills Act) the testator's signature had to be somewhere around the bottom of the will, as provided by s 9 of the Wills Act 1837 after the amendments of the Wills Amendment Act 1852. The testator's signature which was at the bottom of the will had not been properly witnessed because the witnesses had not seen it.

The operative signature since the further amendment to s 9 of the Wills Act 1837 by s 17 of the Administration of Justice Act 1982 is the one by which it appears that the testator intended to give effect to the will.

### 5.15.6 Witnesses' state of mind

The witnesses must intend by their signatures to attest the due execution of the will by the testator. This requirement was particularly useful before the comparatively recent amendments to the law relating to the taking of benefits under the will by superfluous witnesses made by the Wills Act 1968. Three people witnessed the testator's signature in *In the Goods of Sharman* (1869), two attesting and one signing as residuary legatee. The third signature was excluded from probate.

### 5.15.7 Witnesses' signatures

As with testators, the witnesses may sign by means other than their names (see 5.5). Where one of the witnesses who attested the testator's signature used a description of himself rather than his name, it was held that because he intended the description to operate as his signature, then it did so. He signed as 'Servant to Mr Sperling'; the court on considering the will of Mr Sperling (*In the Goods of Sperling* (1863)) found that sufficient signature for valid attestation.

### 5.15.8 Witnesses must sign by their own hands

However, the witness must sign him- or herself, even if their own hand is guided by another witness or a third person. There is no provision which allows for the signature of another person on the witness' behalf, whether in their presence and at their direction or not. This would be unnecessary in the case of a witness where it is not in the case of a testator; one can find another witness, but testators are not interchangeable.

### 5.15.9 Place of witness' signature

The witnesses' signatures may be anywhere on the will, so long as they intended them to attest the testator's operative signature and so long as they are on the same paper or paper physically attached to the paper on which the will appears. Obviously it will be clearer, and may save potential queries, if the signatures of the witnesses are just by the testator's signature, so that it appears clearly from the face of the will that the persons making the signatures will have had in mind the purpose of their signatures and thus their intention to attest will be quite apparent.

## 5.16 Attestation clause

Although the witnesses do not have to be in the presence of each other when they sign, it is usual for that to be the case, and likewise, although the Act states that no attestation clause is necessary, one is usual. The former procedure may not make any difference at all, or may be done to make it very easy for any witnesses asked years later what went on at the execution and who was in whose presence to remember that everyone was present all the time. The latter practice, of appending an attestation clause reciting the way in which the will was executed, has a definite reason behind it, as it raises a presumption of due execution.

### 5.16.1 Example of an attestation clause

Precise forms of attestation clause differ from solicitor to solicitor. In essence they recite that the terms of s 9 of the Wills Act 1837 were complied with. For example, the clause may read:

> Signed as her last will by the above named testatrix in our joint presence and then by us in hers

or:

> Signed by the testator in the joint presence of both of us together who at his request and in his presence have hereunto subscribed our names as witnesses

An attestation clause may be worded so as to raise the appropriate presumption of knowledge and approval in the case of a testator who is unable to read the will over or sign for himself. Examples of such clauses may be found in precedent books.

### 5.16.2 Purpose of an attestation clause

The granting of probate of a will is usually a fairly simple procedure. Provided that everything is in order, it can be done through the post, with the only required evidence being an affidavit by the proposed personal representatives (people who will administer the estate) which is made in a prescribed form – indeed on a form, since the oath is so similar in each case that printed forms are available which require only details to be filled in. The rules by which probate is granted in simple cases are set out in the Non-Contentious Probate Rules, currently those of 1987, of which r 12 relates to attestation clauses.

Only in the case of there being no attestation clause, or a defective clause, is the probate registrar obliged to require the due execution of the will to be established by affidavit evidence before granting common form (simple non-contentious) probate, because the attestation clause will raise a strong presumption that the will was executed as stated in the clause. It is particularly important to have an attestation clause where witnesses cannot give evidence of due execution after the death of the testator, if, for example, they are both dead themselves or cannot be found. But, in any case, no one administering an estate would wish to have the extra expense and paperwork involved in establishing due execution in any case when such problems can so simply be avoided.

*Harris v Knight* (1890) concerned a will without an attestation clause. The witnesses could not be called to give evidence as they had both died. In that case, the court fell back on the presumption *omnia praesumuntur rite esse acta* in order to find that, there being nothing else amiss, the will could be presumed to have been duly executed.

The case of *Re Sherrington* (2005) concerned the will of a successful solicitor who had disinherited his first wife and the three children of that marriage in favour of his second wife, by a will drafted by his step-daughter, who was not a lawyer but worked in his firm in an administrative capacity. The case turned on whether the will had been duly executed, and as well as examining the cogency of the witnesses' evidence, the court referred to the strength of the presumption:

> it is crystal clear that the strongest evidence is necessary to rebut the presumption of due execution, where the will is regular on its face and contains an attestation clause, as this Will does, stating that it was signed in the presence of both witnesses.

The first wife and family were ultimately unsuccessful. The Court of Appeal quoted from this case with approval and at length in the subsequent case of *Kentfield v Wright* (2010).

The case of *Channon v Perkins* (2005) concerned the particularly perplexing issue of whether or not a will could be proved when the two witnesses accepted that their signatures on the will were indeed their signatures but denied having any recollection of having acted as witnesses. At first instance it was held that the evidence of the two purported witnesses was sufficiently strong to rebut the presumption of due execution. The Court of Appeal overturned that ruling, saying again that the strongest evidence is required to rebut formal and apparently correct execution, recited in an attestation clause. (It was, moreover, not asserted that the witnesses' signatures were not genuine.) If a will on its face complied with s 9 of the Wills Act 1837 and represented the testator's wishes, it would take a good reason for the court to hold that the will had been improperly executed based on only extraneous evidence.

## 5.17 Beneficiary as witness

Section 15 of the Wills Act 1837 provides that, if a witness is also a beneficiary (or the spouse or civil partner of a beneficiary (see 5.17.5)), they will lose their benefit under the will. It now also provides that this rule will not apply if the beneficiary-witness in question can somehow be excluded as a witness without affecting the validity of the will; this essentially means that if a witness has a benefit under the will, they may still keep it if there were in fact at least three witnesses, so that the exclusion of the one who is also a beneficiary still leaves sufficient witnesses to validate the will.

If a gift fails because of contravention of s 15, that section will be applied after the gifts under the will have been ascertained, not before. In *Aplin v Stone* (1904), the testator gave his property to his wife for her life, with remainder to his two daughters Harriet and Ellen. The will was witnessed by Ellen's husband. The court held that, rather than Ellen's share going automatically to Harriet, it went on intestacy.

In *Barrett v Bem and Others* (2012) the will was signed at the deceased's direction by his sister Anne, who was the sole beneficiary. The method of signature was rejected (see 5.6), and, endorsing finding of the judge at first instance, Lewinson LJ in the Court of Appeal said:

> I echo the judge's view that it is plainly undesirable that beneficiaries should be permitted to execute a will in their own favour in any capacity; and that Parliament should consider changing the law to ensure that this cannot happen in the future.

### 5.17.1 Solicitors' charging clauses

There is also a separate rule, not confined to s 15 of the Wills Act 1837, which prohibits executors and trustees from obtaining any benefit from their office without specific authority to do so. In most cases, solicitors would not take on the job of executor or trustee if they could not charge for their work. Where a lay executor is appointed they may instruct a solicitor to deal with the estate and do exactly the same work that a solicitor-executor would do, but in that case the legal fees are expenses of the administration and therefore payable from the estate. The Trustee Act 2000 provides a significant exception to the basic general rule.

Before s 28 of the Trustee Act 2000, if there was a charging clause in the will allowing a solicitor to charge for their work in executing the will and administering the estate, they could not witness the will: any charges they made would constitute a benefit under the will and a conflict would arise with s 15 Wills Act 1837 (see 5.17.2). Sections 28 and 35 Trustee Act 2000 provide that remuneration is not a gift and the entitlement to remuneration will not be invalid if the professional (as those allowed to charge for probate work may now include accountants: see 12.4, 12.12.23) acts as witness to the will: the professional's fees will be treated as administration expenses. Under s 29, a professional executor may receive reasonable remuneration without a charging clause provided the other personal representatives agree in writing to the professional being remunerated in principle. Explicit provisions in the will override s 29.

### 5.17.2 Section 15 before the Wills Act 1968 amendments (*Re Bravda* (1968))

The change in the rules, allowing supernumerary witnesses to be excluded as witnesses in order to save gifts to them, was brought about by the case of *Re Bravda* (1968). This was an extremely sad tale of how the application of strict rules designed to prevent fraud on the testator defeated his intentions completely. Mr Bravda had been married twice when he died. He had purported to make a will in favour of the two daughters of his first marriage, Sarah and Rachel, but that will was contested after his death by his second wife, from whom he was judicially separated and who had previously accepted a lump sum in settlement of her future maintenance claims. The purported will was a home-made item drawn up by Mr Bravda himself. It was executed in the presence of two neighbours whom Mr Bravda sent out for specifically for the purpose of executing the will, saying of them 'he can be a witness' and 'she can be the other witness', which was accepted as indicating that he knew the will required witnessing by two independent persons. However, after they had signed their names and added their addresses, Mr Bravda asked Sarah and Rachel to sign 'to make it stronger', and they did so, under the word 'witnessed', though they did not put their addresses.

### 5.17.3 Strictness of the pre-1968 rules

The courts had often striven to save gifts which might have fallen foul of s 15. In *Gurney v Gurney* (1855), the court had held that where the beneficiaries under the original will had witnessed codicils, the gifts were not lost because for the purposes of s 15 the will and codicil would be treated as two separate documents. This goes against the idea that a testator leaves but one will, even if in several documents, but it saved the gifts to the intended beneficiaries. In *In the Estate of Crannis* (1978), the testatrix made a will in 1948 leaving everything to her sister, who was also her executrix. In 1958, she made a codicil with a gift over to her niece should the sister predecease. In 1960, the sister did die, and in 1962 the testatrix made a new will leaving all her property to the niece and appointing her executrix. The will was witnessed by the niece's husband.

The court held that the 1962 will would be read together with that of 1948 and the codicil of 1958 to save the gift to the niece.

In *Re Bravda*, the daughters sought to propound the will with the omission of their signatures, and at first instance Cairns J allowed them to do so, saying he was satisfied that the signatures of the daughters had been appended not to indicate that they were witnesses but to please their father. This was an argument essentially to show that the witnesses had not signed the will with the necessary intention to attest to the due execution of the will, by showing that there was some other reason. The widow appealed to the Court of Appeal, relying on the signatures and the description of them within the document as 'witnesses'.

The Court of Appeal disagreed with Cairns J, saying that it was clear on the facts that the daughters were witnesses and that this invalidated their claims under the will. Although no one had suggested to the court that, where two witnesses had validly attested, any others could simply be excluded if necessary to save a gift, the court brought the subject up itself, saying that the words of the Wills Act were too dear and that it was too late after 130 years to put a new construction on the 'well-known words' of the relevant section.

## 5.17.4 Consequences of *Re Bravda* – the Wills Act 1968 amendments to s 15 of the Wills Act 1837

The court in *Re Bravda* regarded the effects of its decision as 'monstrously unfair to the testator and his daughters'. Nevertheless, the signatures of the daughters under the word 'witnessed' had raised a presumption that they were indeed witnesses which they had not been able to rebut. The lack of their addresses did not assist. The court therefore allowed the widow's appeal, but recommended that the Wills Act 1837 should be amended. As a direct result of this case, the Wills Act 1968 was passed, and with astonishing speed. Section 1 of the 1968 Act amended s 15 of the Wills Act 1837 to read that any superfluous witnesses may be ignored. Thus, the sisters would have taken, given that without their signatures the will was still duly attested. Unfortunately, for them it was too late.

However, if a situation arises where there are three witnesses of whom two are also beneficiaries, then the gifts to them cannot be saved by using the rule separately in each case. In that situation, both witness-beneficiaries lose their gifts.

## 5.17.5 Spouse or civil partner of a witness as beneficiary

The same rules about a witness losing a benefit under a will apply to benefits to a spouse or civil partner of a witness. If there is a gift in a will to the spouse or civil partner of a witness, the gift will be lost unless the witness can be excluded under the amended s 15 of the Wills Act 1837.

Persons who are beneficiaries under the will and who marry or form a civil partnership with a witness after the execution of the will are not caught by these rules and may still take the benefit under the will whether or not the spouse-witness or civil partner-witness is supernumerary (see 10.8 and, for more, Chapter 16).

## 5.18 Date

It is not essential to include the date on the will, but it is sensible. The omission of the date does not of itself render the will invalid, because the date is not one of the required formalities (see *Corbett v Newey* (1996) at 3.2). However, if the will is not dated it may make it very difficult to establish whether it is valid or has been revoked, in whole or in part. A testator may make or have made other wills, and probably each will will have a general revocation clause revoking all previous wills. The wills may, alternatively, deal with the same property, so that the provisions of later wills override those of earlier wills. If any of the wills is not dated, it will be difficult to establish which of them or which provisions in any of them are valid. It may also be difficult to establish what a particular provision means if it makes a specific gift of a particular item of property, because the will speaks of the subject matter of a specific gift at the date of execution of the will; if it is difficult or impossible to establish that date, it may likewise be difficult or impossible to establish whether the gift is valid or not. Moreover, if the date of the will is uncertain there may also be problems in ascertaining the relevant beneficiaries (see 11.19-11.21).

## 5.19 Doctrine of incorporation by reference

The basic rule is that if a document is not properly executed in accordance with the formalities laid down by the Wills Act 1837, it will not be, or form part of, the testator's will. However, if it complies with the rules relating to the doctrine of incorporation by reference, a document which has not been duly executed by the testator may be incorporated into a will which has been so executed.

For the doctrine of incorporation by reference to apply, three conditions must be satisfied:

(a)     the document must already be in existence when the will is executed;
(b)     the will must expressly refer to the document to be incorporated as being in existence;
(c)     the document must be identified clearly in the will.

In *Palin v Ponting* (1930), it was held that 'see other side for completion' written on a page of the will was sufficient to incorporate the later page by reference (when it would otherwise have failed as wills then had to be signed at or about the bottom).

Many professional will-drafters incorporate The Society of Trust and Estate Practitioners Standard and Special Provisions into their documents. These are administrative provisions for the will and any trust that arises and are commonly incorporated by the inclusion of words such as: 'The Standard Provisions and all of the Special Provisions of the Society of Trust and Estate Practitioners (2nd Edition) shall apply.'

### 5.19.1 Document must already be in existence

The document must already be in existence when the will is executed; this rule was stated in *Singleton v Tomlinson* (1878). It is for the person who is alleging that the document has been incorporated to prove this; it will not be presumed. If, however, the document is not in existence when the will is made, but comes into existence subsequently and the will is later republished or confirmed (see 8.2) that is sufficient to comply with this rule. The relevant date for the execution of the will becomes that of the execution of the codicil, so that where the document to be incorporated is in existence by that date, it is deemed to comply with the rule in *Singleton v Tomlinson*. A document referred to in the will but expressly excluded will not be incorporated.

### 5.19.2 The will must expressly refer to the document as being already in existence

The will must expressly refer to the document as being in existence. References to existing documents which, however, include the possibility of substitution by non-existent documents will be invalid. If a will erroneously refers to a document as being in existence, and that document comes into existence before republication of the will, it will thus be incorporated. If the reference in the will is not, however, clearly a reference to a document that is already in existence, the fact of the document's existence at the time of republication or confirmation will not save it. All that republication of the will does is shift the relevant date; it does not remove the requirement for a definite reference to the document as already existing.

The testatrix in *Re Smart* (1902) directed her trustees to give certain articles 'to such of my friends as I may designate in a book or memorandum that will be found with this will'. The memorandum did not exist at the time of execution of the will and so could not be incorporated because it did not comply with the first rule for the doctrine of incorporation by reference to work. The testatrix later made the memorandum; this of itself made no difference to its validity and incorporation in the will. She then republished the will by codicil. This shifted the operative date to that of the execution of the codicil. However, the gifts still failed, because the reference was not worded in terms of a document which already existed.

A similar reason caused the failure of a substantial gift to the College in *University College of North Wales v Taylor* (1908), where the testator directed the income from the gift to be used for scholarships in accordance with 'any memorandum found with my papers'. It was held that here was insufficient reference to a document that was in existence; this could equally have been a reference to documents made after the date of the will. The gift therefore failed. Note that the difficulty is not that the relevant document did not exist at the time of the execution of the will – it might well have done – but that the will did not sufficiently refer to it as doing so. A similar problem arose in *Re Jones* (1942), where the testator referred to the terms of a deed of trust bearing the same date as the will but left open the possibility that it might be substituted with another at a later date; that possibility meant that the incorporation failed to operate.

### 5.19.3 Document must be identified in the will

The document to be incorporated must be identified in the will. In *Croker v Marquis of Hertford* (1844), the court described identification as of the very essence of incorporation. If the identification is too vague, it will be invalid, and, however clear it is as to what the testator meant, if there is no actual reference to the document, it and its contents will not, or should not, be incorporated. However, the decisions on this point do show that a court may interpret this requirement quite widely.

In *Re Saxton* (1939), the testator left, separately from his will, lists of names which began with the statement that the testator intended them to benefit from his estate. The court managed to hold that a reference in the lists that he wished to leave 'the following amounts' corresponded sufficiently to the reference in his will that he wished to leave legacies to 'the following persons'. This decision appears perhaps to have been an attempt by the court more to save apparently genuine gifts than to apply the law as such. The testatrix in *Re Mardon* (1944) referred to the document to be incorporated as 'the schedule hereto'; this too was held to be sufficient.

### 5.19.4 Effects of incorporation

An incorporated document is admissible to probate and operates as part of the will. This means it will form part of the probate documents which are a matter of public record. The doctrine of incorporation by reference is therefore of no use to someone who wishes to keep their affairs secret.

It is generally very unusual for a document incorporated by reference not to be included in the application to prove a will, but this may happen for example where the document is too large and inconvenient. Such exceptional circumstances did occur in *Re Balme* (1897), where the testator validly incorporated a large library catalogue. A more common situation is where the document being incorporated contains standard forms or clauses which are cited in a published document which has been previously lodged with the senior district judge and accepted by him or her as sufficient lodgment.[5] An example of this is the Society of Trust and Estate Practitioners Standard Provisions. Note that even a document which is not included in the probate is a valid testamentary document and must be construed with the will as such.

### 5.19.5 Republication or incorporation?

The possibility is discussed in Chapter 8 of a will being republished (or, in more modern terms, confirmed) by codicil, so that the operative date for any references to existing documents is shifted to that of the later codicil. There is, however, a different situation in which a codicil may validate gifts in an earlier will; rather than republishing a valid will containing an ineffective incorporation, thus making the attempted incorporation in that will valid, it may incorporate the will as a document so that the provisions of the earlier will, which may have been wholly invalid, become valid provisions under the codicil. The testatrix in *In the Goods of Heathcote* (1881) had made just such an invalid will. Later she duly executed a codicil describing itself as 'a codicil to the last will and testament of me ...'. It was shown that she had made no other will. The court held that the invalid will was sufficiently described in the codicil and would be incorporated and admitted to probate.

## 5.20 Safekeeping a will: deposit and registration

Wills do not have to be deposited or registered in England and Wales. They are fully valid once they are executed. If lay testators then just put them in a drawer they are, however, then somewhat vulnerable to being mislaid or accidentally destroyed, or even not to being discoverable by the executors if they have not been told where to look. The Law Society's publications for the profession regularly include advertisements for missing wills.

The Public Trustee may hold a will for safe keeping, if appointed a trustee under it, and in New Zealand, the Public Trustee there was found by the Law Commission to be frequently used as a depository for the safekeeping of wills. A registry set up in British Columbia in 1945 to record particulars of wills was also much used; this, though voluntary, was free. In the Netherlands, however, compulsory registration and deposit of wills was brought in in 1918, which was apparently completely successful in preventing disputes about the authenticity or date of Dutch wills.

The Law Commission in its 1966 Working Paper *Should English Wills be Registrable?* expressed grave concern that 'although an English will is a document of the greatest importance, the law does little to protect it from the very real danger ... that it will be suppressed or simply overlooked after the death'. Because of the lack of registration, it found much time and money was spent ensuring that when a grant of representation is taken out, it is taken out in respect of the last valid will or correctly on intestacy; nevertheless, the Law Commission found that about 100 grants were revoked each year, most because of the subsequent discovery of a further will. But extra requirements for the validity of wills would bring with it extra expense and inconvenience

---

5  *Practice Direction* [1995] 1 FLR 766.

to testators, and the consequential difficulties might mean that some would-be testators would fail to complete a valid will. So far, there is no compulsory deposit of wills in England or Wales.

A will may be kept securely by a bank, but should not be kept in a bank deposit box: after the death the executors will require probate in order to get access to the box, but they will not be able to get probate without the will. It has however long been the case that solicitors who draw wills usually offer to keep them in their deeds room (a secure place such as a fireproof basement) for no cost. This is generally safe and easily found, and there is recourse to the solicitor's insurance should the will still be mislaid. A solicitor will often generally store a will written by someone else, but may charge for that. If a solicitor ceases business, the Law Society will see that their matters are taken over by someone else and will assist in tracing where to find those matters. Will-writing services may store wills free or for a fee, but tend to have less secure provisions and less insurance, and are likely to have less continuity arrangement.

Provisions for deposit were contained in s 91 of the Court of Probate Act 1857 and re-enacted by s 172 of the Supreme Court of Judicature (Consolidation) Act 1925 and s 126 of the Senior Courts Act 1981. The High Court provided 'safe and convenient repositories for the custody of the wills of living persons' on the executors attending personally at a probate registry to be sworn and on payment of a fee. These provisions, governed by the Wills (Deposit for Safe Custody) Regulations 1978, were hardly used at all. They were replaced by provisions in ss 23 and 24 of the Administration of Justice Act 1982, with a view to allowing the UK to ratify the Council of Europe Convention on the Establishment of a Scheme of Registration of Wills 1972; there are appropriate transfer provisions for wills already deposited. In compliance with Article 6 of the Registration Convention, a will may be registered at the request of the testator. A testator may request that an authorised person, such as a notary, register the will in other Contracting States, and the Principal Registry of the Family Division will assist in registration in other jurisdictions.[6] Wills can be deposited with the Probate Service for £20. Only the testator can access the will during his or her lifetime; the executor can most easily obtain it by producing the certificate that the Registry will have given the testator when it was deposited.

## 5.21 Summary of Chapter 5

### 5.21.1 Formalities for the Execution of Wills

The purpose of formalities is to ensure that the will is truly the one the testator intended to make – that it is not a forgery nor something made in the heat of the moment. Formalities achieve their object largely by making the process of executing a valid will more awkward, and thus they also catch out many people who are attempting to make a genuine will but who fail to observe a particular requirement. Some jurisdictions allow a court to investigate in those circumstances, and to find that a will should be proved despite failing to comply with the formalities. In England however there is no such provision, though the formalities are less strict than they were.

The formalities are laid down in s 9 of the Wills Act 1837, which states that a will must be in writing and signed by the testator or by some other person in the testator's presence and by the testator's direction. It must appear that the testator intended, by their signature, to give effect to the will. The signature must be made or acknowledged by the testator in the presence of two or more witnesses present at the same time, who must either attest and sign the will or acknowledge their signatures in the presence of the testator. However, it does not matter whether

---

6  Michael Brandon, 'UK Accession to the Convention on the Establishment of a Scheme of Registration of Wills and of the Convention Providing a Uniform Law on the Form of an International Will' (1983) 32 International and Comparative Law Quarterly 742.

the other witness is present when each does this. No form of attestation is necessary, but one will raise a presumption of due execution.

Writing is interpreted widely, both as to materials and as to language. A signature is any complete mark the testator intended to be their signature. The whole will must be signed and the witnesses must attest the operative signature. Acknowledgment, like writing or signing, is interpreted widely. It may be effected by words or gestures. There is no formal requirement for the will to be dated, but it is usual and helpful.

The old cases show that being present means being in the line of sight, so that the witnesses could have seen the testator had they looked. The witnesses must know and be able to see that the testator is signing, but they do not need to know that he or she is signing a will, or to read the will. It follows that a blind person may not be a witness.

A beneficiary who is also a witness loses their gift under s 15 of the Wills Act 1837, as does their spouse or civil partner. Such a gift may be saved if there are more than two witnesses, and professional executors may still take their appropriate administration charges.

A document which has not been executed may nevertheless be incorporated by reference into the will and admitted to probate if it is in existence when the will is executed and is clearly identified and referred to in the will. A will may be formally deposited but usually is not.

## 📖 5.22 Further reading

Gerry W Beyer and Claire Hargrove, 'Digital Wills: Has the Time Come for Wills to Join the Digital Revolution?' (2007) 33 Ohio Northern University Law Review 865.

Michael Brandon, 'UK Accession to the Convention on the Establishment of a Scheme of Registration of Wills and of the Convention Providing a Uniform Law on the Form of an International Will' (1983) 32 International and Comparative Law Quarterly 742.

Stephen Clowney, 'In Their Own Hand: An Analysis of Holographic Wills and Homemade Willmaking' (2008–2009) 43 Real Property, Trust and Estate Law Journal 27.

John H Langbein, 'Substantial Compliance with the Wills Act' (1975) 88 Harvard Law Review 489.

JG Miller, 'Substantial Compliance and the Execution of Wills' (1987) 36 International and Comparative Law Quarterly 559.

# Chapter 6

# Special Wills

There are certain kinds of wills that differ from the usual kind of wills in that they have different requirements as to the formalities for validity or operate differently from ordinary wills. These include wills made under the statutory provisions relating to the making of privileged wills – those made by soldiers and sailors, who are exempt from the usual formalities; international and foreign wills; joint and mutual wills, which are governed by particular principles of equity; statutory wills, made for those without capacity, and the current rules by which people may arrange in advance to transfer their decision-making to others if they do lose capacity before they die. Though these last are not wills, they are included here as they perform similar functions: they pass control over a person's property, even if not ownership, to someone else when that person's own capacity for control diminishes or ceases.

## 6.1 Privileged wills

Section 11 of the Wills Act 1837 provides that s 9 of the Wills Act 1837 relating to the formalities necessary for a will to be valid – due execution, for example – do not apply to 'any soldier being on actual military service, or any mariner or seaman being at sea'. These people may dispose of their estate without any formalities at all. Before the Statute of Frauds 1677 there had been no requirements as to formalities for dispositions of personalty by will, but that Statute introduced formal requirements for all but small personal estates which were, however, still not required in the case of privileged testators. Originally, s 11 of the 1837 Act was worded so as to cover only personalty, but the privilege was widened by the Wills (Soldiers and Sailors) Act 1918 to cover realty as well.

There is some debate as to whether privileged wills are anachronistic, or whether the reasons for them remain valid.[1]

### 6.1.1 No formalities required

A privileged will may be written or it may be oral; there is no requirement as to formalities, not even that a privileged will should be a document. It may be made by a person under the age of majority and it requires no attesting witnesses, so if someone does witness the will then, provided it is intended to be an informal will, they may still take a gift under the will. This appears analogous with the provision of the Wills Act 1968 relating to supernumerary witnesses, but predates it. The Wills Act 1968 only amended s 15 of the Wills Act 1837; the formalities of the 1837 Act have never applied to privileged testators.

The privileged testator in *Re Limond; Limond v Cunliffe* (1915) was a lieutenant whose regiment remained on the Indian frontier at the conclusion of the Waziristan operations in 1895, escorting

---

1 Andrew G Lang, 'Privileged Wills – A Dangerous Anachronism' (1984–1986) 8 University of Tasmania Law Review 166; Jack Lee Tsen-Ta, 'A Place for the Privileged Will' (1994) 15 Singapore Law Review 171.

a frontier delimiting party in the Tochi Valley. He was mortally wounded by a sniper and dictated a will to his brother-in-law, under which the brother-in-law was the residuary legatee, before dying the following day. The will, which concerned personalty only, was signed by the testator and attested by the brother-in-law and another witness. The court held that the testator was on actual military service when he made the will, so the will was privileged and the brother-in-law would not fall foul of s 15 of the Wills Act 1837 and could take under it.

## 6.1.2 Requirements for capacity and intention

On the other hand, the privileged testator still needs to have testamentary capacity and testamentary intention, so if either of these is lacking there can be no privileged will.

## 6.1.3 Soldier or sailor

The interpretation of who is a soldier or sailor is perhaps surprisingly wide. It has included nurses and typists as well as what one might think of as soldiers in the ordinary way of serving members of the armed forces ready to fight the enemy. The interpretation of whether someone is a privileged testator does not involve a construction of the words in the will so much as a construction of reality; the courts will usually lean to finding that a purported privileged will is valid, especially, it is sometimes felt, when they approve of the dispositions made.

## 6.1.4 Typist may be sailor

Sarah Hale was a typist on the *Lusitania*. She wrote to her mother, including some testamentary dispositions in her letter, from Southampton before she left on her last voyage. The letter was held to be admissible as a sailor's will under s 11 of the Wills Act 1837 (*Re Hale* (1915)).

## 6.1.5 Nurse may be soldier

The privileged testatrix in *In the Estate of Ada Stanley* (1916) was a nurse in the Territorial Force Nursing Service. She was mobilised for service and sent abroad in the First World War. During a period back in England in 1915, after receiving orders to re-embark for duty, she wrote to her niece, Ada Louise Stanley. The document was in the form of a letter, dated and signed but not witnessed. It began 'I give you full liberty to deal with my affairs' and set out how she wished her property to be disposed of in the event of her death. The testatrix died of dysentery in hospital in England in December 1915 after another tour of duty, leaving an estate of about £550. Ada Louise Stanley applied to the court for the document to be admitted to proof.

The court, considering the authority of *Re Hale* (6.1.4), held that Ada Stanley had been a soldier, and it granted probate of the will as a soldier's will.

## 6.1.6 Others who may be soldiers

The Air Force is included by dint of the Wills (Soldiers and Sailors) Act 1918.

According to Lord Denning in *Re Wingham deceased; Andrews v Wingham* (1949) (see 6.1.8), 'soldier' includes 'not only the fighting men but also those who serve in the Forces, doctors, nurses, chaplains, WRNS, ATS, and so forth'.

A member of the Women's Auxiliary Air Force also fell within the Act. The testatrix in *In the Estate of Rowson* (1944) was a squadron officer serving in England when she sent her solicitors written instructions for a formal will; on her death those instructions were treated as a privileged will.

### 6.1.7 Actual military service

Actual military service begins when a soldier receives orders and is mobilised. Merely being a soldier during peacetime is not enough, in theory, although in Re Colman (1958) a soldier was found to have been on actual military service in Germany in 1954.

### 6.1.8 Is actual military service the same as active military service?

The court in Re Wingham (deceased) (1949) was considering a purported privileged will made by the deceased whilst an officer training as a pilot at a camp training school in Saskatchewan in Canada during the Second World War. The deceased's father applied to the court on the basis that the deceased was not in a position to make a privileged will because, when he signed the document, he was not on 'actual military service'. He succeeded at first instance, but failed on appeal. The Court of Appeal addressed specifically the question of the meaning of 'actual military service', and whether this meant the same as 'active' military service. (It also discussed the equivalent phrase in Roman law, in expeditione, and concluded that it was relevant to a soldier on Hadrian's Wall or in the camp at Chester, but not to an airman in Saskatchewan who was only a day's flying from the enemy.)

The conclusion it came to was that the words 'actual' and 'active' were not interchangeable, and that a person was entitled to make a privileged will 'if at the time he is actually serving with the Armed Forces in connexion with military operations which are or have been taking place, or are believed to be imminent'. The will was therefore admitted to proof.

### 6.1.9 What is a war and is it necessary?

War need not have been declared as such, which is particularly relevant in any cases of soldiers who were serving in Northern Ireland during the troubles there. (There has been little evidence of any contested use of privileged wills in relation to British persons involved in the more recent conflicts in Iraq and Afghanistan.) In Re Jones (deceased) (1981), the deceased, David Jones, had died in Northern Ireland in 1978 'at a time of armed and clandestine insurrection against the government'. He was a member of armed forces deployed at the request of the civil authorities. He was shot and mortally wounded, and on the way to hospital said to two officers of his battalion: 'if I don't make it, make sure Anne gets all my stuff.' Anne was his fiancée. David Jones had made a previous valid will leaving everything to his mother. The mother contested the case claiming David was not entitled to make a privileged will. The registrar referred the matter to the High Court on the question of 'actual military service' and the meaning of 'war'.

### 6.1.10 Insurrection and disturbances may be war

In Re Jones (1981), the court held that, although hostilities between two sovereign governments would constitute a war, previous cases, especially the 1874 case of Re Tweedale, showed that the definition was wider. In that case, it was held that the suppression of insurrection or disturbances within the ambit of the area of government, but contrary to the ordinances of that government, was a matter of actual military service where the military were called out to suppress the disturbances. It was held that, where a question arose as to whether the deceased was on 'actual military service', the answer depended on the nature of the activities of the deceased and the unit or force to which they were attached, not on the character of the opposing operations. It was irrelevant that there was no formal state of war or that the enemy was not a uniformed force. It was also not relevant whether there was a foreign expedition or invasion or a local insurrection. The court therefore held that David Jones' oral declaration should be admitted to proof; therefore Anne's application succeeded. (Anne had by this time married someone else.) War has not been declared by Britain or her allies since 1941, but the breadth of this definition means that privileged wills can still be used in modern armed conflict.

## 6.1.11 Mercenaries and others?

The cases do however leave open the question of whether all persons involved in hostilities and insurrections may make privileged wills under English law. Certainly, in *Re Donaldson* (1840), the testator served not the Crown but the East India Company and was nevertheless held to be entitled to make a privileged will. A court sitting in 1840 may, however, have proceeded on an assumption that the East India Company was an extension of the Crown by other means, or at any rate that it was not incompatible with the British government. It is questionable whether, for example, a person on the opposing side to David Jones would have been allowed to make a privileged will, as a matter of public policy.

Langan J confirmed in *Re Servoz-Gavin (deceased), Ayling v Summers* (2009) that the privilege accorded to mariners and seamen is not restricted to those who were serving, or had been engaged to serve, on British-registered ships. Mr Servoz-Gavin was a radio operator who had received orders to join a Panamanian-registered ship bound for India. The court found that his statement to his cousin: 'If anything happens to me, if I snuff it, I want everything to go to Auntie Anne' was a privileged will. The court rejected an assertion that the military activity had to be in the British national interest, saying that no concept of 'national service' was to be found in s 11 of the Wills Act 1837 and it did not have to be introduced in order to make the section workable or rational. In relation to s 2 of the Wills (Soldiers and Sailors) Act 1918 the most that could be said was that it suggested that the parliamentary draughtsman might have believed that s 11 did not apply to members of foreign (armed) naval services.

## 6.1.12 Being at sea

The interpretation of the phrase 'being at sea' is at least as wide as that of 'soldier'. To see why a person who is not on board ship has been considered to be at sea, one should consider the reasons for making some testators privileged in the first place. They are persons who are both more likely than most to die – on the battlefield or the open seas – and less able than most to obtain the advice of a solicitor and to make their will in a formal fashion.

This was perhaps a little strained in the case of *Re M'Murdo* (1868); the deceased was held privileged because he was a mariner on HMS *Excellent*, which was permanently stationed in Portsmouth Harbour. The court found that he was a mariner in Her Majesty's Service and 'still he is subject to the restraints of the service, and might have no opportunity of making a will with the usual formalities if he was taken on board when no lawyer was at hand'.

The will of Clive Rapley, unattested and made when he was also a minor, was considered in *Re Rapley* (1983) and fell on the other side of the line. He had made the will when he was an apprentice on leave ashore and awaiting orders to join his ship, but he had not actually received the orders. The court discussed the purpose of s 11 of the Wills Act 1837, as clarified by s 1 of the Wills (Soldiers and Sailors) Act 1918 and held that mariners and seamen at sea were exempted from the provision of the Act because they were unlikely to have legal assistance available to them and because they were under a greater risk of death than most people. It held that the exemption did not apply to Mr Rapley because he had not, at the relevant time, yet received his orders to join ship. Therefore, when he died in a typhoon in the Pacific 20 years later, he was found to have died intestate.

### 6.1.13  At sea in Surrey and Hertfordshire

The scope of 'being at sea' covers situations that may at first seem implausible. Ian Newland, the testator in In the Goods of Newland (deceased) (1952), was 19 years old in 1944, when the age of majority was still 21. He was apprenticed in the Merchant Navy and joined a ship whose movements were difficult to ascertain because of security considerations – this was during the Second World War. However, he spent his leave in Surrey, a landlocked county, where he executed a will before going off to rejoin his ship. He remained in the service until October that year, dying in India in 1951. His will was referred to the court on the question of whether he was 'a seaman at sea' when he made the will, because only if it was a privileged will would it be valid, given that he had been a minor when he made it. The court held that he was indeed 'at sea' because the will had been drawn up in contemplation of the forthcoming voyage, when he was already under orders to rejoin his ship before a certain date.

Similarly, the privileged testator in Re Servoz-Gavin (deceased), Ayling v Summers (2009) (6.1.11), was in the equally landlocked county of Hertfordshire when he made his testamentary statements, but was preparing for his imminent voyage to India, and his statements were held to constitute a privileged will.

### 6.1.14  How long does the privilege last?

The privilege may continue after the end of hostilities if the soldier is part of an army of occupation. This is supported by the decision in Re Jones (1981) (6.1.9–10) that no current war as such is required to establish privilege.

### 6.1.15  How long does a privileged will last?

The limits of Roman law, which held that a soldier's privileged will ceased to operate a year after he was demobilised, do not apply.

The testator in Re Booth (1926) was a Colonel Booth, who in 1882 was stationed in Gibraltar as a paymaster in the 46th Regiment. The regiment had received orders to start for Egypt when the colonel made a document purporting to be a will but which was not executed in accordance with the formalities. Later, he gave the document to his wife, who kept it in a wooden chest in a locked closet in their home at Hawstead House. In 1916, Hawstead House burnt down. Colonel Booth died in 1924, aged 81, without having made any other will. The colonel's widow sought to propound the will as a privileged will, and was opposed by the heir at law and the statutory next of kin. They would have had entitlements to the colonel's realty and personalty on his intestacy under the pre-1926 rules. Their case was that the colonel was not on 'actual military service' at the time of making the will, so the lack of formalities rendered it invalid. They also brought evidence that he knew of the (probable) burning of the will and regarded the will as having thus been revoked, and that he had referred to the need to make another. They further sought to introduce, from Roman law, the principle that a privileged soldier's will ceases to have effect one year from the date the soldier was discharged from the army.

The court held that the colonel's actual military service began on receipt of the orders to proceed abroad for service in a campaign, so the will was a privileged will and therefore valid. It also held that the rule of Roman law that a soldier's will became invalid one year after his discharge was not part of English law, and that acquiescence in destruction of the will by fire did not amount to revocation. The will (which had not of course been physically in existence for the past ten years) was therefore admitted to probate, with the widow bringing evidence about its contents.

## 6.1.16 Testamentary intent

The testator must intend deliberately to give expression to their wishes as to what should happen if they were to die. The cases in this area show that there may be a difficulty in distinguishing the fine borderline between a statement which constitutes a privileged will and one which is merely a statement of what the purported testator believes to be the case.

The testator in In the Estate of Donner (1917) said, 'I want my mother to have everything', but it was held that this did not show testamentary intention but, on the facts, an approbation of what the deceased had believed would happen to his estate on his intestacy. Similarly, the privileged testator in In the Estate of Knibbs (1962) said, 'if anything ever happens to me, Iris will get anything I have got'. He was at the time a barman on the ship Arcadia travelling from England to Australia, engaged in a casual conversation about family matters with a colleague just before closing time. The court held that the words were not spoken as a record of his wishes as to the disposition of his property with the intention that they should be remembered and be acted on by the person to whom they were uttered, and so did not demonstrate the intention that the testator's words should take effect as his will. Accordingly, there was no will.

Re Stable (deceased) (1919) however demonstrates that, although it is necessary for the privileged testator to have testamentary intention, that is not the same as believing that they are making a will. In this case, a young man said to his fiancée, in the presence of a witness (who was useful to the court in being able to give evidence of what was said, but not required for compliance with any formality): 'If I stop a bullet everything of mine will be yours.' These words were admitted to probate as a privileged will, the court accepting explicitly that the testator does not need to think they are making a will (see, also, Re Berger (1989) at 3.5.2).

In In the Estate of Beech, Beech v Public Trustee (1923), Mr Beech, a soldier on actual military service, wrote two letters clearly referring to elaborate testamentary dispositions he had already made. The letters paraphrased the effect of the will inaccurately, so that it was to the advantage of those contending for the admission of the letters as a soldier's will to get them admitted to probate. The court held that what the soldier was doing was merely referring, albeit inaccurately, to what he had already done by his will, and that this was clear from the terms of the first letter and not so clear, but also to be inferred, from the terms of the second. What must be intended is that the words of the will should have effect at death.

## 6.1.17 Revocation of privileged wills

Marriage revokes a privileged will as it does any other (see 7.2). This was held by Shearman J in In the Estate of Wardrop (1917) on the basis of the wording of s 18 of the Wills Act 1837, which provides that 'every will ... shall be revoked by ... marriage'.

A privileged will which is not nuncupative (oral) may be revoked by destruction in the same way as a formal will; that is to say, if the testator destroys it with the intention of revoking it, that will be effective (see 7.3).

In In the Estate of Gossage (1921), a formal will was declared to have been revoked by informal writing declaring an intention to revoke. (For details of the facts of this case, see 7.7.) The decision dealt with whether a further testamentary instrument was needed when the testator had claimed to have 'cancelled' his written privileged will, but the written will document was found amongst his possessions after his death. It refers to there being no requirement 'for the revocation of a soldier's will that there should be the formalities necessary to revoke the will of a civilian', although when the case concerned the revocation of a formal will, the formalities would be required. The court held explicitly, however, that the informal or privileged writing by which the deceased assured his sister that he had revoked the will leaving his property to his fiancée would have revoked the will under the law pertaining before the Wills Act 1837; the court held that, when s 11 of that Act stated that privileged testators were exempt from the formalities of the Act, it meant that what had to be examined was whether the acts done would have had effect under the common law. The common law allowed a soldier to make or revoke his will without any formality.

The court said:

> no formalities are required for the execution of a soldier's will, but soldiers are allowed to dispose of their personal estate as they might have done before the Act – that is, as they might have done before the Statute of Frauds.... In the case of a civilian's will certain formalities are required; in that of a soldier's will no formalities at all are necessary, and therefore upon the interpretation of the Act no formalities are required to revoke a soldier's will.

It held that, 'the power of revocation is merely another aspect of the power of disposition'. Thus, if a testator is privileged, they may use that privilege to revoke previous wills as well as to make new ones without being subject to the requirements of the Wills Act 1837 as to the formalities.

## 6.2 Foreign wills

If a will is made in accordance with the law of a foreign country, it will nevertheless be valid under English law if it is executed in accordance with the requirements in the country where the testator was domiciled or habitually resident, or of which they were a national when they made the will or when they died. If the testator had immovable property, their will is also valid if it conforms to the requirements of the jurisdiction in which the immovable property is situated. The position is governed by the Wills Act 1963 which incorporated The 1961 Hague Convention on the Conflicts of Laws relating to the Form of Testamentary Dispositions[2] into English and Welsh law. The Act applies where the testator died from 1964 onwards, regardless of the date of execution of the will.

Section 2 of the 1963 Act allows for a liberal interpretation of whether or not a formality needs to be strictly complied with. If a requirement is one of form, it need be adhered to less strongly than if it is one of essence as to the validity of the will, such as testamentary capacity. A will may be formally valid but essentially invalid with the bequests being contrary to the law of the country concerned with the disposition of the property, for example the testator may have drafted the will contrary to applicable forced heirship rules when they in fact apply to their estate.

The rules of private international law provide that the law of inheritance in respect of movable property is governed by the law of the deceased's domicile (*lex domicilii*) at the date of their death, and that of their immovable property by the *lex situs* (the law of the country in which the immovable property is situated). This may come into play particularly where there is an intestacy or where the country concerned has restrictions on testamentary freedom. For example, an English person who buys a house in France is, to the extent of their immovable property in France, subject to the rules of French law as to how far they may leave their property by will. If the issue were to come before an English court, under these principles it would be referred back to France under the doctrine of renvoi. However, this position may be altered by the new European Succession Regulation.

The European Union Succession Regulation (EU) No 650/2012 should become effective from 17 August 2015 (as at the time of writing). It will not apply in the UK (or Ireland or Denmark), but will apply in all other EU member states. It will mean that, in those states, the

---

2 The Hague; 5 October 1961; Cmnd 1729.

deceased's estate will be governed by the law of the country in which they died habitually resident, even if that is not a EU country, unless the deceased chose to apply the law of their country of nationality instead (Art 21). That choice can be made by provision in the will; it still applies even if the deceased's nationality is non-European, or if they had more than one nationality (Art 22(1)). This would mean that British nationals who retire to France should be able to choose to have their houses there devolve in accordance with English law (which allows freedom of testation, subject to family provision claims (see Chapter 15)) ather than French law (which has forced heirship provisions by which part of the estate devolves by law to family members). The Regulation also makes provision for a European Certificate of Succession, which will perform a similar function to that of a grant of probate but will be issued by the authorities of the state in which the deceased died habitually resident and recognised by all participating states. Since the UK has not opted in to this Regulation, however, the British national mentioned above may need a grant of probate in England and Wales to deal with their property there.

Although there have been broader attempts at harmonising succession law Europe, some have thought this would be difficult or undesirable, since succession law is difficult to separate from national culture.[3] The Regulation does not govern tax. If the deceased was domiciled in the UK for IHT purposes, however, the estate must pay IHT on the worldwide estate, subject to any double-taxation treaty with the relevant country.

## 6.3 International wills

Sections 27 and 28 of the Administration of Justice Act 1982 included the form of will which would be acceptable in all countries which ratified the International Convention on International Wills of 1973.[4] These requirements are in addition to the provisions of English internal law.[5]

The Convention combines the formalities of signature and attestation required under English law with that of notarisation, as found elsewhere in the world. It requires that the will be made in numbered and signed pages and attested by two witnesses and either a solicitor or a notary public (see 5.1.7), who under this legislation is an authorised person who will issue a certificate as to the compliance with the formalities. Such a certificate is conclusive save where there is evidence that the formalities were not complied with.

A small but diverse range of countries, including the Holy See, Iran, Canada and Belgium, have signed the Convention. However, it is not in force in a number of the signatory countries, including the UK, which has not ratified it or brought it into force.

## 6.4 Joint wills

Where two or more persons execute the same document as the will of both of them, it will be a joint will. Joint wills are lawful but not usually appropriate. A joint will operates as the separate will of each testator, and either (or any) of the testators may revoke or vary the joint will so far as it applies to them. It does not matter whether the other person is still alive or whether they consent.

---

3 Paul Terner, 'Perspectives of a European Law of Succession' (2007) 14 Maastricht J Eur & Comp L 147; Alain-Laurent PG Verbeke and Yves-Henri Leleu, 'Harmonization of the Law of Succession in Europe', in Arthur S Hartkamp, Martijn W Hesselink, EH Hondius, Chantal Mak and C Edgar du Perron (eds), Towards a European Civil Code (Kluwer Law International, fourth revised and expanded edition 2010) 459–479.

4 Kurt H Nadelmann, 'The Formal Validity of Wills and the Washington Convention 1973 Providing the Form of an International Will' [1974] The American Journal of Comparative Law 365.

5 Keith FC Baker, 'International Wills for UK Citizens' (1985) 10 International Legal Practice 115.

If the joint will remains valid for another person after it is admitted to probate as the will of a joint testator who has died, it is retained by the probate registry. This can be inconvenient, but does not mean that the will cannot be revoked or amended by codicil by any surviving joint testator.

Joint wills are rare in practice and useful only insofar as they can effectively exercise a power given to two persons jointly to appoint by will. A joint will may also be a useful way of making a mutual will (see 6.5), although there is no necessary connection at all between the two. The fact of having two separate wills in one document may be confusing, however, or may lead to misunderstanding and dispute as to whether the joint will also represents the conceptually very different phenomenon of mutual wills.

## 6.5 Mutual wills

The doctrine of mutual wills is an equitable doctrine and the creation of the Court of Chancery. Mutual wills are those which are made on the basis that the mutual testators – for example, as is often the case, husband and wife – each leave their property, usually, to the other, on the condition that the second to die will necessarily then leave all their estate – including that of the first to die – to an agreed third party, for example, their child.

### 6.5.1 An irrevocable will?

A mutual will is perhaps the nearest thing that exists to an irrevocable will. No will is irrevocable in law, but in the case of a mutual will not only will the breach of the agreement be remediable in an action for breach of contract but also the property involved will be fixed by equity with a constructive trust in favour of the agreed beneficiaries who, if they can prove the existence of the mutual will, can obtain the same practical results in terms of property as if the will had not been revoked, even if they cannot prevent revocation of the will itself.[6]

The contractual element in mutual wills has not been much pursued, presumably because the loser, in event of a breach of the original agreement, would be a third party to the contract and, prior to the Contract (Rights of Third Parties) Act 1999, would have been unable to obtain a remedy for its breach, though on occasion there has been some creativity. In *Beswick v Beswick* (1968), an uncle transferred his business to his nephew in return for the nephew's promise to pay £5 per week to the uncle's widow after his death. The uncle died but the nephew did not pay. The widow brought an action against the nephew. The court held that she could not sue in her personal capacity, as she was not a party to the contract. However, as administratrix of the uncle's estate, she did have standing to sue, as the estate had suffered a loss by virtue of the nephew's breach. The loss to the estate being purely nominal, the estate could obtain only nominal damages. As this would be an inadequate remedy, the court granted specific performance of the contract, with the estate therefore bound to pass the £5 per week to the widow in her personal capacity. Whilst in the mutual wills situation there is unlikely to be a loss to the estate enabling any direct enforcement of the original arrangement, the mechanism of its operation similarly finds equity rescuing that arrangement, fixing the property with a constructive trust.

The Contracts (Rights of Third Parties) Act 1999 allows a person who is not a party to a contract between a promisor and promisee to enforce a term of the contract in their own right if a term of the contract expressly provides they may or the term purports to bestow a benefit on them. The third party can be identified by name, be a member of a class or answer to a particular

---

6  *Olins v Walters* (2008).

description and need not be in existence when the contract was entered into; and the remedies available to the person are as if they were a party to the contract. The Act would apply to beneficiaries under a mutual will but has not been argued in any reported mutual wills case to date.

## 6.5.2 When revocation may take place and be of practical effect

The leading case is that of *Dufour v Pereira* (1769). Lord Camden in that case defined a mutual will thus:

> A mutual will is a revocable act. It may be revoked by joint consent clearly. By one only, if he gives notice, I can admit. But to affirm that the survivor (who has deluded his partner into this will upon the faith and persuasion that he would perform his part) may legally recall his contract, either secretly during the joint lives, or after at his pleasure, I cannot allow. [7]

## 6.5.3 Requirements for mutual wills

Three things must be established for a court to find mutual wills:

(a) agreement between the two or more persons executing the wills who also make provision for each other;
(b) agreement that the survivor will be bound;
(c) occurrence of the binding event.

## 6.5.4 Separate or joint wills

The will documents can be separate or there can be a joint will, and the terms of mutual wills may vary widely. In *Re Green* (1951), the parties were a married couple, and the agreement was that they would each leave all their property to the other, and the survivor would then leave half his or her own estate to charity. The surviving husband took the wife's estate and then remarried, making a new will leaving most of his property to his new wife. The court held that he could deal only with the half of his property that was not fixed with the trusts arising under the mutual will.

## 6.5.5 Proof of mutual wills

The agreement to be bound normally means that the survivor has promised not to revoke their own mutual will. Although it is usual for mutual wills to be in similar terms, the fact that close parties such as a husband and wife have made wills in the same terms does not amount to proof that the wills are mutual wills. There must be evidence of the agreement that the second to die will not revoke the mutual will. In *Re Oldham* (1925), a husband died after making a will in favour of his wife in the same terms as hers in favour of him. She subsequently remarried and made a new will in favour of her new husband. The court looked at the correspondence between the parties and their solicitor but found no evidence that there had been an agreement not to revoke. In *Charles v Fraser* (2010), (6.5.5), it was held that for the doctrine of mutual wills to apply there had to essentially be a contract between the two testators that both wills would be irrevocable and remain unaltered. A common intention, expectation or desire was not sufficient. Just executing mirror or reciprocal wills did not imply any agreement either as to revocation or non-revocation.

---

7  Richard J Partridge, 'The Revocability of Mutual or Reciprocal Wills' (1929) 77 University of Pennsylvania Law Review 357.

In *Olins v Walters* (2008) the Court of Appeal held that wills do not have to say in terms that they are mutual wills. The fact that the husband and wife made almost identical wills and mirror image codicils by agreement was sufficient to infer that they had created effective mutual wills. Mummery LJ said however:

> As recent cases have shown this equitable doctrine dating from the 18th century ... continues to be a source of contention for the families of those who have invoked it. The likelihood is that in future even fewer people will opt for such an arrangement and even more will be warned against the risks involved.

Nevertheless, in the case of *Fry v Densham Smith* (2010) the Court of Appeal did not overturn a finding of mutual wills based on oral evidence alone, where the wife's will could not be found.

In *Re Goodchild (deceased)* (1997), parents had made wills in similar terms benefiting their son, Gary, but the father had remarried after the mother's death, and had made a new will which was much less beneficial to Gary. Gary sought to show that the wills were mutual wills and brought considerable evidence from family and friends to suggest that his parents had considered themselves bound by irrevocable mutual wills. However, the court preferred the evidence of the solicitor who had advised the parents. The court found that any obligations the parents had were moral only, and did not have the necessary force of contract. It held that the wills were ordinary, separate wills and, along with a failed appeal on the mutual wills point, Gary proceeded with a family provision. claim instead (see 15.21.5). But in *Charles v Fraser* (2010) the court found on the balance of probabilities there had been an agreement between two sisters when they made their wills that each would leave her estate to the other and that on the second death the balance of their joint estates would pass to the beneficiaries in the shares stipulated in their wills. They had promised each other, explicitly or implicitly, that the survivor's will would not be altered, so mutual wills were found.

## 6.5.6 When does the final beneficiary's interest vest?

In *Re Hagger* (1930), a joint mutual will was made by a married couple by which they left property to each other for life and thereafter upon trust for various persons. The question arose as to when the interests of the beneficiaries of the trust vested and whether that was on the death of the first to die or the death of the second. It was a relevant question in this case because one of the beneficiaries had died after the wife but before the husband. If she had taken a vested interest on the death of the wife, her interest under the trust would be an interest in remainder postponed to the life interest of the husband, and the property would fall into her estate on his death. If she were not to take a vested interest until the death of the husband, her interest would lapse because she predeceased him.

It was also relevant to consider whether the interest which vested at the date of death of the first to die was the beneficiary's interest in the estate of the first to die or whether, at that point, the beneficiary also obtained a vested interest in the estate of the second to die.

## 6.5.7 Does the trust arise on death of the first to die or when the second to die takes a benefit?

The court held that the beneficiary's share vested on the death of the wife in *Re Hagger* (6.5.6) and that it vested in all the property covered by the mutual wills, that is, including all the property of the second to die that was involved in the agreement between the mutual testators. Clauson J held that the arrangement became binding in equity on the survivor when the first of them died.

There remained, however, a question mark over what the binding event was and thus when it occurred. It was not clear whether the trust came into operation when the first testator died leaving his mutual will unrevoked and believing the agreement as to the mutual wills still stood, or whether it did not arise until, that first death having already occurred, the survivor accepted a benefit under the will. The latter appeared to be implied by the reasoning for the imposition of a trust in *Dufour v Pereira* (6.5.2). However, Clauson J in *Re Hagger* had held that the arrangement bit in equity on the death of the first to die 'even though the survivor did not signify his election to give effect to the will by taking benefits under it', but this remark was *obiter*, though the same had been said in *Gray v Perpetual Trustee Co* (1928) some two years before.

## 6.5.8 Survivor does not need to take any benefit for the doctrine of mutual wills to come into operation

The question of whether the survivor needed to take a benefit for the doctrine to operate appeared to have been settled by *Re Dale* (1993). In that case, the terms of the mutual wills made by a married couple were that their property was left to their son and daughter in equal shares. After the death of the husband, the widow revoked her will and made a new one leaving very little to the daughter. On a preliminary hearing, the court found that the doctrine of mutual wills could apply even where the second to die had not received any benefit under the will of the first to die. In that case, the first of the two possible interpretations mentioned above necessarily applied so that the mutual wills would come into operation in equity on the death of the first to die.

The view that the event upon which the enforceability of mutual wills arises is the death of the first mutual testator was confirmed and refined in the case of *Re Hobley (deceased)* (1997). In that case, Mr and Mrs Hobley had made mutual wills in 1975 benefiting each other with substitutional gifts to various others which would come into operation when the second spouse died. The fact that the wills were mutual wills when they were made was not apparently in issue. One of the gifts was a house in Leamington Spa which was to go eventually to a Mr Blythe. Mr Hobley then revoked that gift by codicil, leaving the house in Leamington Spa to fall into residue. When he died in 1980, all his property, including that house, passed to Mrs Hobley. In 1992, she executed a new will, entirely different from the 1975 will, under which Mr Blythe did not get the house in Leamington Spa; she died the following year. If the mutual wills were still valid, then the property would be fixed with a constructive trust for those nominated in Mrs Hobley's 1975 will. The court held, however, that the effect of Mr Hobley's codicil had been to make an amendment which, whilst minor, was sufficiently significant to make it impossible for the court to embark upon an assessment of whether or not it was unconscionable for Mrs Hobley to have left her property elsewhere than as agreed. In the circumstances, she had been discharged from her obligations, which were no longer enforceable in equity, and her 1992 will was effective.

More recently still, in the case of *The Thomas and Agnes Carvel Foundation v Carvel and Carvel Foundation, Inc* (2007), it was held that under the doctrine of mutual wills a trust arises on the death of the first of the two testators to die. The trust does not arise from the will of the survivor but from the agreement between the two testators not to revoke their wills. Where two people had agreed to make mutual wills on the basis they would be irrevocable, equity would enforce that agreement after the death of the first testator by means of a constructive trust, since it would no longer be possible for those people to rescind the arrangement and the survivor could not in conscience rescind it unilaterally.

### 6.5.9 Practical difficulties with the doctrine of mutual wills – dissipation of assets by the second to die

A considerable problem with the doctrine of mutual wills is that it does not necessarily impose any duty on the second to die to account for property received from the estate of the first to die. Thus, the interests of the intended beneficiaries may possibly be defeated by the survivor of mutual testators dissipating all the assets.[8]

### 6.5.10 Later acquisition of assets by the second to die

The converse of this is that the trust arising on the death of the first to die may include the after-acquired property of the second to die. For example, if the agreement is that each party will leave all their property to the other and thereafter to a specified third person, as is commonly the basis of the arrangement, the second party to die will never be able successfully to leave any of their property anywhere else, even if they outlive the first to die by many decades and amass an unforeseeably large fortune.

### 6.5.11 A solution to the problem?

In *Re Cleaver* (1981), dealing with the problem of dissipation of assets in particular, the court implied into the agreement between the parties certain provisions which were arguably not really there and for which the authority seemed doubtful. The mutual wills were made by a married couple, and after the death of the husband the wife, taking the husband's whole estate, revoked her mutual will and made a new one by which, instead of the estate going equally to the husband's three children on her death, went to only one of them. The court held that a constructive trust had arisen over all her property at the death of her husband, including that which she obtained from his estate, the terms of which were that it would be shared amongst the husband's three children on her death. It went on to say, however, that she could not make large voluntary dispositions from the property, although she could otherwise use the property as she wished for her own benefit. This solution has the advantage of being practical and perhaps embodying the intentions of the parties, but it is not entirely certain whether it accords with the authorities or where the borderline between acceptable and unacceptable lifetime dispositions lies.

### 6.5.12 Enforcement of mutual wills

If the three requirements for mutual wills are met, and there have been no invalidating alterations to either will during the parties' joint lifetime, the practical effects of the arrangement can be enforced against the survivor in equity and under the Contracts (Rights of Third Parties) Act 1999. The survivor cannot be prevented from revoking their mutual will, but they will be frustrated in equity and the property subject to the constructive trust may itself be bound by the terms of the mutual will.

## 6.6 Religious wills

Religion may govern more or less of an individual's way of life and death, and some religions set out the way in which an individual should leave his or her estate. English law has been

---

8 There has been some discussion in the US jurisdiction about how far this right extends: see Thomas Finch 'Joint and Mutual Wills and the Marital Deduction' (1960) 40 Marquette Law Review 209, footnote 47.

influenced in many ways by its Christian heritage, especially in the field of wills and probate where the ecclesiastical courts held control until very late in historical terms and their formulations have passed into the underlying structure of English law (see Chapter 1).[9] Individual wills were often drafted historically with many religious overtones, though these might be somewhat formulaic.[10] Particular Christian denominations may require adherents to make specific provisions in their wills – adherents of the Mormon church (Church of Jesus Christ of Latter Day Saints) are required to tithe, or give 10 per cent of their wealth to the church by will, for example.

In some societies, personal law, including succession, may depend on the individual's religious affiliation. But this is not the case in England, where a person not only has no obligation in the general law to follow any religion or its dictates or desires but is free – or constrained – to see their estate devolve according to ordinary English law even if they do. Nevertheless, the formulations of religious obligations in respect of wills may shape what individuals do, and are interesting in their own right, and both the contrasts and the intersections of the different ideas of inheritance are of interest. There are many different communities in England besides the Christian: aspects of just two examples will be considered here, and in the broadest of terms.[11]

Sharia (Islamic) law allows the Muslim testator to dispose of one-third of their estate to individuals or charities who are not their heirs under the rules of Sharia succession if they so choose. Without the other heirs' consent an individual heir cannot receive a share of this one-third as they must be treated equally. It is only possible to give more than this one-third to a non-heir if all the heirs consent. A portion of the remaining two-thirds is divided between primary heirs and residuary heirs. There are 12 primary heirs in total – four males and eight females. The male heirs are: father, grandfather (father's father and mother's father), uterine brother ([half] brother on mother's side), and husband. The female heirs are: wife, daughter, granddaughter, full sister, consanguine sister ([half] sister on father's side), uterine sister ([half] sister on mother's side), mother, and grandmother (father's mother and mother's mother). The residuary heirs are the sons and brothers of the full blood (both parents the same). If there are no residuary heirs, then the entire estate is shared amongst the primary heirs pro rata to their original entitlements. If there are no primary heirs and no residuary heirs, the estate goes to more distant relatives. If the testator has no family he or she can create an heir by naming a successor by contract or ratify kinship with another person.

Under a Sharia will male heirs in most cases receive twice the amount inherited by a female heir of the same class. Non-Muslims may not inherit at all, only Muslim marriages are recognised and a divorced spouse is no longer a Sharia heir, as the entitlement depends on a valid Muslim marriage existing at the date of death. The children of a deceased heir are not able to inherit and can only receive a testamentary gift from the free third. The Muslim testator can give away gifts in their lifetime to whomever they choose but not on their deathbed when they are classed as being dead already.

Jewish law also has forced heirship based on the principle that dead people have no rights over the property they owned while alive and therefore have no right to dictate what happens to their property after death. However, a number of Modern Orthodox rabbis take the position that secular wills are acceptable, based on the principle that the law where the testator resides applies.

The Jewish forced heirship laws are set out in the biblical book of Numbers.[12] If the deceased had sons they are the only heirs of their father's estate, with a first-born son receiving two shares

9  Ralph Houlbrooke, *Death, Religion and the Family in England 1480–1750* (Clarendon Press 1998).
10  JD Alsop, 'Religious Preambles in Early Modern English Wills as Formulae' (1989) 40 The Journal of Ecclesiastical History 19.
11  For more see Omar T Mohammedi 'Shariah-Compliant Wills: An Overview' (2011) 25 Probate and Property 58; Prakash A Shah 'In Pursuit of the Pagans: Muslim Law in the English Context' (2013) 45 Journal of Legal Pluralism and Unofficial Law 58.
12  Num. 27: 5–11.

and the other sons receiving one share. If there are no sons then daughters inherit. The deceased's wife receives a payment as set out in the couple's prenuptial agreement and she is supported out of her husband's estate until she claims this contractual sum of money or until she remarries. Unmarried daughters are supported by the estate until they are married. If there is no one in a priority class it may pass to their children.

There are various ways to avoid forced heirship, one of the most popular being estate-indebtedness by which the individual executes a promissory note to a non-heir.[13] The note provides for an obligation far in excess of the projected value of the estate and is payable a moment before the testator's death. This technique's effectiveness arises from the fact that the note would confer to the beneficiaries under Jewish law the option of either paying the debt from the estate or consenting to the terms of the testator's will.

A religious will may take effect as an English will if it satisfies the requirements for a will (see Chapters 2 and 3). This was the case in *Re Berger* (1989), where a testator's Jewish religious will recited gifts he had expected to be made by an earlier will made under general English law. The earlier English will was invalid, but because the Jewish will fulfilled the requirements of an English will, it could be admitted to probate and so save the gifts.

## 6.7 Statutory wills

Wills made under statute for a person who is mentally disordered are generally called statutory wills, though this is not a term of art and it will not be found in the legislation. The provisions do not have any necessary correlation with those for assessing whether or not a person had testamentary capacity at the time of making their will, but a person who is a patient within the meaning of the Mental Capacity Act 2005 will usually not have the mental capacity to make a will. Although deputies may be appointed to deal with the affairs of those without capacity, they do not have the power to make a will for the person concerned, though they may apply to the court for one to be made.

If there were no statutory provisions entitling a will to be made for a mentally incapacitated person, then the intestacy provisions would apply in the case of anyone who had never had the capacity to make a will, and in the case of someone who lost capacity, their dispositions would remain as they were when the capacity was lost. This could mean irremediable intestacy, or could involve a will which would become outdated with changing circumstances in the testator's life and family.

Statutory will applications have also arisen in the past when a 'carer' marries his or her less mentally capable charge, for example, in *Re Davey* (1981), where the patient, not expected to live long, was found to have undergone a clandestine marriage to a man who worked at the home where she lived. The marriage was voidable because of her lack of mental capacity, not void *ab initio*. A voidable marriage revokes earlier wills, as was held in *Re Roberts* (1978). The court therefore made a new will for the patient as a matter of urgency under the then-applicable legislation, the Mental Health Act 1983, so that she did not die intestate. Statutory wills are now governed by the Mental Capacity Act 2005, especially s 18.

### 6.7.1 The Office of the Public Guardian and the Court of Protection

The Office of the Public Guardian is responsible for implementing the Mental Capacity Act 2005 by administering powers of attorney, supervising deputies who manage the affairs of others and

---

13 K Eli Akhavan, 'Basic Principles of Estate Planning within the Context of Jewish Law' (2011) 25 Probate and Property 60.

investigating and acting on allegations of abuse by attorneys and deputies. It is an executive agency of the Ministry of Justice.

The Court of Protection is the court which under the Mental Capacity Act 2005 has jurisdiction over the property, financial affairs and personal welfare of people thought to lack mental capacity to make their own decisions. Amongst the matters which the Court of Protection hears are applications for statutory wills, disputes regarding Lasting Powers of Attorney and granting deputyships, by which individuals have responsibility for taking decisions for the incapacitated person.

## 6.7.2 The making of a statutory will

The current law is governed by the Mental Capacity Act 2005, which is important in assessing testamentary capacity (see Chapter 4). The power for the Court of Protection to make and execute a will for a patient, or person lacking capacity, is at s 18. The power to make a statutory will is available when adult persons are considered by the Court of Protection to be incapable of making a valid will for themselves. It is a power which arises under statute and did not exist before the Mental Health Act 1959 was amended by ss 17–19 of the Administration of Justice Act 1969 to include it. Earlier, the High Court had used its inherent jurisdiction to make settlements with life interests for incapable settlors, as, for example, in Re WJGL (1965). The power was then restated at s 96 of the Mental Health Act 1983, later replaced by the Mental Capacity Act 2005.

The statutory will may contain any provision which the patient could have made were they not mentally disordered. The Court of Protection will order the dispositions in the patient's will as it thinks proper, and an appeal may lie to the court if there is any dispute. Schedule 2 of the MCA 2005 deals with the detailed powers of the court, and paragraph 3(2) specifies the formalities. The statutory will must be signed by the person lacking capacity, acting through the authorised person, who should sign with both names. It must be witnessed by two witnesses present at the same time and attested and subscribed by those witnesses in the presence of the authorised person, and it must be sealed with the official seal of the court.

## 6.7.3 Best interests and autonomy

The overarching principle of the Mental Capacity Act 2005 is the person's best interests, but in the context of statutory wills this does not mean substituting someone else's judgment for that person's. The idea of substituted judgment had governed the law and practice before the 2005 Act.[14] In NT v FS (2013), Behrens J addressed the weight to be given to the mentally incapacitated person's own expressed wishes, in the light of the best interests principle. Taking into account someone's best interests is also not the same as enquiring what the person would have decided if they had had capacity, but it does include taking into account the person's own wishes and feelings, which are amongst the circumstances that s 4 of the Mental Capacity Act 2005 specifies must be taken into account.

In VAC v JAD and Others (2010), Hodge J had addressed the relevance of any earlier will the person had made, describing it as 'obviously a relevant written statement which falls to be taken into account by the Court', but suggested that if the person had clearly lacked capacity when making it, it should carry no weight at all. The issue had arisen in the context of the question as to whether a statutory will should be made at all. The person clearly lacked capacity, but DJ Ashton at an earlier hearing had said that her earlier will

---

14  Re D (J) (1982).

was made under the guidance and supervision of ... reputable local firm of solicitors.... It is
only the role of the Court of Protection to authorise a statutory will when there has been a
material change of circumstances or there is a vacuum.

He had said it was not the role of the Court of Protection to decide disputes about the validity of
wills, and that the finance deputy had no basis for applying for a statutory will to be made to
replace the existing will: the application amounted to asking the Court of Protection to adjudicate
in a family dispute over inheritance. When later the matter came before Hodge J for the making
of a statutory will to which everyone consented, he too was careful to protect the person's autonomy: 'the execution of a will for a protected person is a decision which must be made by the
Court itself, and cannot be entrusted to a deputy'.[15] The court would be guided by the principles
in the 2005 Act, even if it eventually approved the will in the terms put forward by the family.

Relevant circumstances are the person's past and present wishes, always a significant factor
to which the court had to pay close regard, their beliefs and values, and the views of third parties
as to what would be in their best interests. In Re M (2009) Munby J noted

there is no place in [the] process for any reference to judicial decisions under the earlier and
very different statutory scheme. The 2005 Act lays down no hierarchy as between the various
factors which have to be borne in mind, beyond the overarching principle that what is deter-
minative is the judicial evaluation of what is in [the person]'s best interests.

It may be in a person's best interests to be remembered well, for doing the right thing, but arguably a person will not be held responsible for whatever is in their statutory will, and in any case,
as the court in NT v FS (2013) said, usually someone will think a person has made mistakes. In Re
D (statutory will) (2012) it was held to be in the best interests of the testator to order the execution
of a statutory will, rather than leaving her estate to be eaten away by the costs of litigation after
her death, and her memory to be tainted by the bitterness of a contested probate dispute between
her children. However in Re J(C) (2012) Senior Judge Lush noted of the person in question:

JC has an appalling track record. He has spent his entire life doing precisely 'the wrong
thing' in his relationships with others and his malevolence is such that he would probably
relish the prospect of thwarting his children's designs on his estate and would rejoice at
being remembered by them with disaffection.

## 6.8 Loss of capacity: beyond statutory wills

The High Court's jurisdiction to take over managing the affairs of a person when they lose capacity was not confined to the making of statutory wills. It could take over the management of their
affairs generally, acting through the Court of Protection. The inherent jurisdiction of the High
Court to deal with the affairs of a person who has lost mental capacity has effectively been
replaced under statute. A person may foresee their loss of capacity and make a Lasting Power of
Attorney, by which they authorise another person to manage their property and finances or their
health decisions should they lose mental capacity (6.8.1–3). If they do not do this, a friend, relative or a professional may apply under the Mental Capacity Act 2005 to be their deputy once
they have lost the capacity to manage their own affairs. It is quite common for a property and
finance deputyship to be granted but it is very rare for the court to grant a health and welfare

---

15  S 20(3)(b) Mental Capacity Act 2005.

deputyship, as health-care professionals working together with family members are considered already to have sufficient powers under s 5 Mental Capacity Act 2005.[16] The Court of Protection may issue a range of orders apart from deputyship orders: for example, where the person who has lost capacity is a trustee. Applying to the Court of Protection for the necessary orders can be slow and cumbersome, and it is also expensive.

By the later twentieth century, the traditional operation of the Court of Protection had been widely found to be an inadequate process in many cases. The organisation of a person's day-to-day affairs by a state authority is liable to be cumbersome, slow and expensive. A private arrangement that maintains as much as possible of the individual's autonomy is more efficient, quicker and cheaper to operate.

A person who fears the loss of mental capacity in the future may now authorise someone to take over looking after their affairs, with those powers only coming into operation once they have lost capacity. This is a form of power of attorney which has been developed in very recent decades; it is not a will as such, but operates some similar functions to wills, and such powers are often made by those who are making wills and generally considering arranging their affairs for the end of their life. The making of a power of this kind in no way suggests that there is anything particularly amiss with the maker. The loss of mental capacity whilst the body remains functional is a risk we all carry.

## 6.8.1 Development of Lasting Powers of Attorney: Enduring Powers, living wills and advance directives

Until the 1980s, the affairs of a person who lost capacity could only be dealt with under the inherent jurisdiction of the High Court. The Chancery Division of the High Court would delegate its powers to the Court of Protection, which would use its powers to manage the person's affairs. There was however much concern at the slowness and expense of the process. In 1983, the Law Commission published its Report No 122 *The Incapacitated Principal*. This considered ordinary powers of attorney, by which a person gives someone else authority to deal with their property or part of it. These cease to operate when the principal, the person who gave the power, loses capacity, which in this situation is exactly when they are most needed. The Law Commission recommended the creation of a power of attorney that would operate after the loss of capacity. The Enduring Powers of Attorney Act 1985 brought that into practice from March 1986, allowing a person to appoint someone as attorney to manage their affairs, and for that power to continue after the loss of capacity. The Enduring Power came into effect when registered by the attorney, when the donor of the Power lost mental capacity; the donor was informed about the registration, so they could object if they wished. Organisations such as banks were obliged then to deal with the attorney in relation to the donor's affairs.

Enduring Powers were a successful idea as far as they went. People liked being able to avoid their affairs falling under the Court of Protection. The early cases established that the capacity needed to grant an Enduring Power of Attorney was very low, and lower than that needed to make an *inter vivos* gift of property. The reasoning for this was that the grantor was not disposing of their assets but bringing in someone to manage the property in the interests of the grantor, with fiduciary duties and ultimately under court supervision.[17] However, Enduring Powers of

---

16  In a Court of Protection Update to the Association of Public Authority Deputies on 8 May 2014, Senior Judge Lush calculates that over 95 per cent of applications to the Court of Protection relate to property and affairs matters, almost 95 per cent of applications to the court are uncontroversial and can be dealt with on the papers, without attendance, and only 1.4 per cent of deputies are health and welfare deputies.

17  *Re K; Re F (Enduring Powers of Attorney)* (1988).

Attorney covered only the private delegation of powers to manage property. They did not cover delegation of the power to make decisions about medical treatment, on which debate continued to be very live. In particular, as medical science was able to keep people bodily alive for longer, beyond when they could request or consent to the withdrawal of treatment, there were questions about whether court authority was needed in all cases where a person had lost the capacity to consent to medical treatment. Here public concern over lack of patient autonomy met the concerns of the medical profession that they might need to obtain court sanction or risk legal pursuit, though the latter would apply only where there was disagreement in the patient's family as to whether the doctors' actions were appropriate; nevertheless, there is often disagreement in families, so this presented a considerable risk. Amidst continuing public debate over 'Gillick competence' – the ability of children under the statutory age of 16 to consent to (but not refuse) medical treatment,[18] concerns rose over whether some form of 'living will' could be made at the other end of life, passing the power of consent to another. 'Advance directives' were made, but without any statutory backing. In the 1990s, the Law Commission and the Lord Chancellor's Department issued consultation papers and reports.[19] The eventual solution came in the Mental Capacity Act 2005, which also governs statutory wills for those already incapacitated (6.7).

## 6.8.2 Lasting Powers of Attorney under the Mental Capacity Act 2005

Lasting Powers of Attorney are governed by the Mental Capacity Act 2005. They operate whilst the person who made the document is still alive. They deal with the period of limited personal capacity which arises before, and is often related to, death. Nevertheless, it is helpful to consider them in the context of succession law and practice because they relate to the giving over of personal powers after the loss of capacity, though the living physical body subsists.

Lasting Powers of Attorney replaced Enduring Powers of Attorney, which only covered the donor's property and finance. One can no longer make an Enduring Power of Attorney since 2007 but existing Enduring Powers of Attorney are still valid. Like Enduring Powers of Attorney, Lasting Powers differ from a regular power of attorney because they remain in force if the donor loses capacity. An ordinary power of attorney, under the Powers of Attorney Act 1971, is a deed by which a person grants another authority to deal with their property during their lifetime; this ceases to be valid if the donor loses mental capacity, whereas a Lasting or Enduring Power will come into its own at that point.

There are two types of Lasting Powers of Attorney. One covers the donor's property and finance and the other covers health and welfare. The property and finance Lasting Power of Attorney can be used whilst the donor still has capacity, but the health and welfare one only if capacity to make a decision has been lost. The format of the Lasting Power of Attorney and the procedure by which it is created is prescribed by regulation. The donor's details are entered into the form, together with those of the donee attorneys and any replacement attorneys. A single attorney may be appointed, but if there is more than one then the donor must decide whether they can act alone or must act jointly. Binding restrictions may be placed on their powers, and for a property LPA the attorney must not be bankrupt. An appropriate professional or someone who has known the donor for at least as more than an acquaintance is required to certify that the donor comprehends the implications of making the Lasting Power of Attorney and that there is no undue

---

18  Gillick v West Norfolk and Wisbech AHA [1985] UKHL 7.
19  Law Commission Mentally Incapacitated Adults and Decision Making (Nos 119, 1991 and 128 and 129, 1993) Mentally Incapacitated Adults (1995); Lord Chancellor's Department (later the Department for Constitutional Affairs) Who Decides? (1997), Making Decisions (1999).

influence. A second certificate provider is then required or the contact details at least one person to be notified when the Lasting Power of Attorney is registered. The form needs to be executed in a specific order – donor, certificate provider(s) and then the attorneys sign to confirm they are happy to accept the role. The LPAs must be registered at the Office of the Public Guardian before they can be used. If the powers are abused by the attorney, action may be taken against them by the OPG, including prosecution.

## 6.8.3 Operation of Lasting Powers of Attorney

The Office of the Public Guardian is responsible for supervising attorneys and if abuse occurs they may refer matters to the Court of Protection to request the Lasting Power of Attorney be cancelled. In the case of *Re Buckley* (2013) the attorney had invested her aunt's money in a reptile breeding farm (in addition to helping herself to her aunt's savings). She was removed and soundly chastised by Senior Master Lush.

A further case, also before Senior Master Lush, was that of *In the matter of CS; Public Guardian v Marvin* (2014). It demonstrates the burden placed on attorneys and the practical issues that may arise in carrying out the duties of caring for an incapacitated person, as well as the interaction of the powers of the individual to specify who will manage their affairs with the powers of the court. The attorney was the son of the person concerned, under both finance and health powers. He had allowed the finances to be used by others, though broadly for the support of the family much as he thought his father would have continued to do had he retained capacity. He had left the practical health care to his mother, whose efforts to cope had excited some concerns. A request was made for the court to appoint a deputy in the attorney's place. However, the Public Guardian considered the battle between the family and the public authorities was not what the court had to decide on:

> it is not for the Public Guardian to say whether an act done or decision made by any person as a health and welfare attorney on behalf of an incapacitated person is in their best inter-ests or not. The Public Guardian's statutory duty is to investigate concerns about the actions of attorneys when they are brought to his attention.

Only if the court decided that Marvin was not acting properly as attorney would it then move to consider whether a deputy should be appointed.

The court found that the son had failed to understand and carry out his duties, but that he had not positively abused his position, and the right course as to his financial affairs was to appoint him as deputy jointly with a solicitor, who could advise him and ensure that all decisions were properly taken. The court adverted to the provisions of the 2005 Act that required the making of the least restrictive order possible, and to Resolution 1859 of the Parliamentary Assem-bly of the Council of Europe (25 January 2012), which required the respect of a patient's previously-expressed wishes in order to protect their human rights and dignity, as well as Article 12.4 of the United Nations Convention on the Rights of Persons with Disabilities, requir-ing actions tailored to individuals' circumstances. In relation to the health power, it had been held in *Re Harcourt* (2013) that revoking a Lasting Power was an interference with the donor's rights under Article 8 of the ECHR, the right to respect for one's private and family life. The court was satisfied that the donor lacked the capacity to revoke the Power himself. However, by the time of the hearing the local authority was satisfied that the son would oversee his father's health care appropriately, and the health Power was not revoked.

## 6.9 Summary of Chapter 6

### 6.9.1 Special Wills

Privileged wills are those made under s 11 of the Wills Act 1837, which provides that soldiers on actual military service or mariners or seamen being at sea are excused from the requirements for formalities laid down by the Wills Act itself, including requirements as to age. The interpretation of who is a soldier on actual military service or a sailor is remarkably wide, as is that of being at sea. There is no need for writing or witnesses. However, proof of testamentary intention is still required; sometimes there can be difficulty in establishing this, particularly with an oral will.

A will made under foreign law will be valid in England if it conforms to the requirements of the testator's country of habitual residence, domicile or nationality at death. Succession to movable property is governed by the law of the testator's domicile at death, but where immovable property is concerned it will be governed by the law of the country in which the immovable property is situated. European law will shortly allow persons habitually resident in participating states to choose either the local law or the law of their nationality.

The Administration of Justice Act 1982 sets out a form of will which is to be acceptable in all countries which ratify the International Convention on International Wills. However, as at the time of writing, these provisions were not in force.

Two or more persons may execute the same document as a will; this will be valid as a joint will. However, it operates as the separate will of each person and can be revoked by them as they wish.

Mutual wills are made on the basis that each mutual testator makes their will in the terms that they do in reliance on the other making their will in particular agreed terms. If this occurs, then when one mutual testator dies, it is too late for the other to change their mind about the agreement. Even if the second will is revoked, the provisions will operate in equity under a constructive trust. The survivor may use the assets in the trust, but it remains unclear how far they may dissipate them.

A statutory will may be made by the Court of Protection under the Mental Capacity Act 2005 for a person who is not mentally capable of making a will for himself. The overarching principle is that of the person's best interests, which is not the same as substituting the court's judgment.

A person who may lose capacity can, whilst they still have capacity, make a Lasting Power of Attorney to allow another person to deal with their property and finances, or health and welfare, during their lifetime once they become incapable, Lasting Powers of Attorney and living wills are not wills as such and the Wills Act 1837 does not apply to them.

## 6.10 Further reading

### Book

Alain-Laurent PG Verbeke and Yves-Henri Leleu, 'Harmonization of the Law of Succession in Europe', in Arthur S Hartkamp, Martijn W Hesselink, EH Hondius, Chantal Mak and C Edgar du Perron (eds), *Towards a European Civil Code* (Kluwer Law International, 4th revised and expanded edn 2010) 459–479.

### Journal articles

Keith FC Baker, 'International Wills for UK Citizens' (1985) 10 International Legal Practice 115.
Andrew G Lang, 'Privileged Wills – A Dangerous Anachronism' (1984–1986) 8 University of Tasmania Law Review 166.

Kurt H Nadelmann, 'The Formal Validity of Wills and the Washington Convention 1973 Providing the Form of an International Will' [1974] The American Journal of Comparative Law 365.

Richard J Partridge, 'The Revocability of Mutual or Reciprocal Wills' [1929] University of Pennsylvania Law Review 357.

Paul Terner, 'Perspectives of a European Law of Succession' (2007) 14 Maastricht Journal of European and Comparative Law 147.

Jack Lee Tsen-Ta, 'A Place for the Privileged Will' (1994) 15 Singapore Law Review 171.

# Chapter 7

# Revocation of Wills

Once a will is properly made, it will be valid until it is revoked or superseded. Just as with making a will, revoking one is a matter both of actions and state of mind, because a will is both a document and an expression of the testator's wishes; in the case of a privileged will, no document is necessary, so the mental element of making a will is more obvious. There are formalities and rules for revoking wills, as there are about making them.

## 7.1 A will is ambulatory

A will is ambulatory; it is of no effect until the testator's death. It can be revoked by the testator at any time, provided they have the capacity. That is part of the essential nature of a will. However, it is not as easy to revoke a will as some people think, and many attempts to do so have failed, for example, a client may email their solicitor asking for their will to be destroyed and this would not be a valid method of revocation. Equally, wills have been revoked without the testator having intended that they should be.

### 7.1.1 Ways of revoking a will

There are, in essence, four ways of revoking a will. All are governed by the Wills Act 1837, by s 18 in respect of marriage, s 18B in respect of civil partnership and by s 20 in respect of the other methods.

A will may be revoked by:

(a) marriage or civil partnership;
(b) destruction with intention to revoke;
(c) later will or codicil;
(d) duly executed writing declaring an intention to revoke.

Note that divorce or dissolution of a civil partnership does not revoke a will, though it may have an effect on some of the appointments and dispositions made (see 10.9).

### 7.1.2 Proof of revocation

If it is alleged, when a will that is otherwise valid comes to be proved, that it has been revoked, the legal burden of proving the revocation falls on the person alleging the revocation. There is no way in which a will may be revoked simply by becoming obsolete, so the making of a will cannot be regarded as a final act by anyone who countenances a change in their circumstances, whether in regard to the persons they intend to benefit under their will or in respect of what they have to leave them. If a man of 25 makes a will leaving everything (at that point, his bicycle and his savings of £25) to his best friend, and does not change the will before he dies at 50 having made millions, the best friend, with whom he has no doubt fallen out, will inherit the millions.

The testator will have the capacity to revoke a will provided they are over 18 and mentally capable; the mental capacity required to revoke a will is the same as is required to make one, with the proviso that this means the capacity to make a simple will rather than to make a complex one (see *Re Park* (1953) at 4.3.1). In *Hinton and Hayes v Leigh and Reeves* (2009) the testator suffering from terminal cancer had left his estate to his nieces with whom he had a close and affectionate relationship, excluding his adopted children with whom he had a poor relationship. Shortly before his death he revoked his will saying he wanted his money to devolve by intestacy to his adopted children. Letters showed that he was suffering confusion due to his illness, falsely remembering attacks which never happened. The court found the testator's change of mind was based on delusions caused by a mental disease 'poisoning his affections' and that therefore – in accordance with the fourth part of the test of mental capacity in *Banks v Goodfellow* (see 4.2.1, 4.3.9) – he lacked the appropriate capacity to revoke his will; the nieces inherited.

## 7.2 Marriage and formation of a civil partnership revokes a will

Section 18 of the Wills Act 1837 provides that, subject to certain exceptions, a will is revoked by the testator's marriage. The same applies if the testator enters a civil partnership, under s 18B of the Wills Act 1837.[1]

Note that it is not the case that the ending of the marriage, whether through death, divorce or annulment, restores the previous position as regards the parties' wills, though a marriage which was *void ab initio* (and thus may have been the subject of nullity proceedings) will have had no effect in the first place.

### 7.2.1 Automatic revocation of will

It is immaterial whether someone intends by their marriage or civil partnership to revoke their will; it happens automatically by operation of ss 18 and 18B of the 1837 Act. The Law Reform Committee's 22nd Report *The Making and Revocation of Wills*, published in 1980, considered the justifications for the continuance of the old rule regarding marriage revoking a will and the points against it. As justifications for the rule, they concluded that marriage remained as fundamental a change in a person's life as ever, and that most testators would wish their spouse and children to inherit on their death and so should not inadvertently leave their property elsewhere through a failure to make a new will after marrying. They also felt that most people are aware of the rule that marriage revokes wills, so they were unlikely to fall foul of that rule itself. Against the retention of the rule, they mentioned particularly the change in the situation of married women, so that their property no longer passed automatically to their husband on marriage; this had made them less in need of protection than before, as they would now have their own property. If they did not, they could claim under the wider family provision rules, as could children, though their claims under those rules were more limited. The rule that marriage revokes a will was, on balance, retained.

### 7.2.2 Other ways of protecting the new spouse?

Note that the situation in this jurisdiction differs from that in the USA, for example. The Uniform Probate Code implies a provision that, where a testator who had made a will before marriage fails to provide for their spouse by will after the marriage, the omitted spouse receives whatever they

---

1 This was inserted by the Civil Partnership Act 2004, s 71, Sch 4, Pt 1, paras 1, 2, 5 and came into force on 5 December 2005.

would have obtained on intestacy unless it appears from the will that the omission was deliberate or the testator provided for them otherwise and in lieu of a gift by will.[2] The 1990 Family Law Act of Ontario in Canada gives an entitlement under s 5, and s 6 of the Act provides that the spouse may take that entitlement instead of a gift under the deceased's will or their entitlement on intestacy, as they prefer.

### 7.2.3 Void marriage does not revoke a will

A void marriage, that is, one which the law does not recognise at all, does not revoke a will. The current grounds on which a marriage is void are set out in s 11 of the Matrimonial Causes Act 1973. The grounds for declaring a civil partnership void are set out in s 49 of the Civil Partnership Act 2004. The widowed testator in *Mette v Mette* (1859) married, or purported to marry, his late wife's half-sister; this relationship was then within the prohibited degrees of affinity and the marriage was thus void. The court held that it had not revoked the testator's will. In *Re Gray* (1963), a void marriage was held to make no difference to the parties' testamentary position, whereas a valid one did. In that case, the wife, not realising the marriage was void for the husband's bigamy, made a new will after the purported wedding. On the later death of the first wife of her 'husband', she contracted a valid marriage with him. She was held to have died intestate, because although it was clear she made her will in the belief that she was already married, the subsequent true marriage still revoked it. In *Warter v Warter* (1890), the testator had been the co-respondent in divorce proceedings; he went through a form of marriage with the respondent on 3 February 1880, after the decree absolute had been pronounced on 27 November 1879. That marriage was void because it took place within six months of the decree absolute, which at the time was not permissible. The testator executed a will on 6 February 1880 leaving all his property to his 'reputed wife'. On 2 April 1880 the couple went through another form of marriage. It was held that the will had been revoked by the second marriage, which was valid.

### 7.2.4 Voidable marriage does revoke a will

A voidable marriage, however, is one which is valid when contracted but subject to later annulment in court proceedings for the reasons set out in the Nullity Act 1971 (now in s 12 of the Matrimonial Causes Act 1973). A voidable marriage, being recognised in law when it takes place even if it is later annulled, does revoke a will even where the marriage is later annulled. The 1971 Act shifted the boundaries of void and voidable marriages, so that some situations which had fallen into one category under the system of canon law which previously obtained subsequently fell into the other. This included the situation where one party to a marriage did not consent to it, which had previously rendered the marriage void but which now merely renders it voidable. Thus such a marriage will now revoke a will, even if it is later the subject of a successful petition for nullity. The same applies for civil partnerships which are voidable under s 50 of the Civil Partnership Act 2004.

The case of *Re Roberts* (1978) turned on this point; the person who would have benefited under the pre-marriage will alleged that the testator's marriage had been void because he did not have the mental capacity to contract it. The Court of Appeal held, however, that such lack of capacity only made the marriage voidable, so that it would revoke a will. Once the will has been revoked by a valid marriage, the ending of that marriage, whether by annulment or divorce, does not alter the position that the voidable marriage was valid when contracted and revoked the will at that time.

---

2  Uniform Probate Code Pt 3, s 2.

The question of lack of consent to a marriage arises most frequently in respect of those who are unable to consent due to lack of capacity; after their marriage much or all of their property will necessarily pass to their new spouse in accordance with the rules of intestacy (see Chapter 9), as they may be incapable of making another will. Such a situation may be a cause of considerable concern and the occasion of an application to the court for a statutory will to be made under the Mental Capacity Act 2005 (see 6.7).

### 7.2.5 Exceptions to rule that marriage or civil partnership revokes a will

In certain limited circumstances, a will may not be revoked by the testator's marriage.

### 7.2.6 Will expressed to be made in contemplation of a marriage or the formation of a civil partnership

It is not uncommon for a person who is to be married or is entering a civil partnership to want to arrange matters such as their will before the big day, rather than having to think about it when they are embarking on, for example, their honeymoon safari.

With regards to marriage, the Law of Property Act 1925 dealt with this situation by amending s 18 of the Wills Act 1837 to allow that a will expressed to be made in contemplation of marriage should not be revoked by the solemnisation of the marriage contemplated. That provision is in s 177 of the 1925 Act and applies to wills made after 1925 and before 1983 only. For wills made after 1982, there was a further amendment to s 18 of the Wills Act 1837 made by s 18 of the Administration of Justice Act 1982, so the current provisions of the 1837 Act as amended relating to marriage apply to wills made after 1982. Section 71 of the Civil Partnership Act 2004 amended the Wills Act 1837 to include s 18B to allow that a will made in contemplation of a specific civil partnership should not be revoked by the partnership ceremony, and generally to equate the formation of a civil partnership with getting married.

### 7.2.7 Wills made after 1925 but before 1983

For s 177 of the Law of Property Act 1925 to operate, the will must be expressed to be made in contemplation of the particular marriage which later takes place. Thus, the express statement in the will should refer to particulars of the marriage in order to fulfil the requirements of the section. The testator in *Pilot v Gainfort* (1931) gave by will 'to Diana Featherstone Pilot my wife all my worldly goods'. At the time of making the will, he was living with Diana, but their marriage came later. The court held that the will was not, however, revoked by the marriage because it 'practically' expressed contemplation of the marriage.

This case can be usefully compared with that of *Sallis v Jones* (1936), where the testator's will ended with the words 'this will is made in contemplation of marriage' but the court held that it was, nevertheless, revoked by the marriage contracted by the testator a few months after making the will. The problem was that the testator, despite apparently using the statutory wording, had not made it clear that he was contemplating a particular marriage, but appeared to be contemplating marriage in general. In the former case of *Pilot v Gainfort*, however, the marriage in question, to Diana Featherstone, was clear.

### 7.2.8 Whole will must be involved

It appears from the cases that the whole will or all its dispositions must be expressed to be made in contemplation of the particular marriage in order to satisfy s 177 of the Law of Property Act

1925. The testator in In the Estate of Langston (1953) executed a new will after the death of his wife leaving all his property to 'my fiancée Maida Edith Beck'. It was held that this was sufficient to satisfy the requirements of s 177 of the 1925 Act. However, in Re Coleman (1975) the testator by his will made gifts to 'my fiancée'. Two months later, he married her, and a year after that he died. The court held that the will had been revoked by the marriage, because it construed s 177 as requiring the will as a whole to be expressed to be in contemplation of marriage. The problem was that the testator could not be said to have made the will itself, as opposed to the particular dispositions to his fiancée, in contemplation of his forthcoming marriage.

## 7.2.9 The Law Reform Committee and the Administration of Justice Act 1982

The Law Reform Committee mentioned the case of Re Coleman (1975) in particular in its 22nd Report, finding the requirement for reference to the whole will too strict. They accordingly recommended that the law be changed so that

> if a will or any part of a will is shown by its language to be intended to survive a particular marriage, the presumption should be that the whole will survives ... capable of being rebutted to the extent that the will shows affirmatively that any particular provisions were not intended to survive the contemplated marriage.

These recommendations were implemented by the Administration of Justice Act 1982.

## 7.2.10 Wills made after 1982

For wills made after 1982 with regards to marriage and after 2004 with regards to civil partnerships, the position appears therefore more relaxed. A will is not revoked if it appears from it, first, that at the time it was made the testator was expecting to be married to or enter a civil partnership with a particular person and second, that he or she intended that the will or any disposition in it should not be revoked by the union.[3]

It is not clear whether the wording of the re-amended s 18 of the Wills Act 1837 after 1982 includes every situation covered by the section as amended only by s 177 of the Law of Property Act 1925 – is every will made in contemplation of marriage also necessarily made in expectation of marriage? Megarry J in Re Coleman (1975) (7.2.8–9) thought so – probably. There are no cases exactly on the point, but it is suggested that if one arose, the courts would construe the later provisions as widening rather than merely altering the applicable law.

Court and Others v Despallieres (2010) is a recent case turning on revocation by civil partnership. It concerned the will of an Australian music executive, Peter Ikin, who had made a will in 2002 leaving most of his estate to his nephew, and then a new will on 7 August 2008 leaving everything to Mr Despallieres, with whom he entered into a civil partnership in October 2008. In November 2008 he died, and Mr Despallieres obtained a grant of letters of administration with the will annexed (because he was not appointed executor: see 12.15) based on a photocopy of the 2008 will, as the original was said to have been stolen. Clause 1 of the 2008 will revoked all former wills; cl 2 provided 'I ... DIRECT that this, my last Will and Testament shall not be revoked by neither subsequent marriage, Civil Union Partnership nor adoption'; cl 3 declared that he was domiciled in the United Kingdom and cl 4 gave Mr Despallieres 'the entirety of my estate as a sole beneficiary'. The claimants – the executors and principal beneficiary under the

---

3  S 18 (3) and (4) and s 18B (4) Wills Act 1837 as amended.

2002 will – brought proceedings, contending, inter alia, that the testator's 2002 will was his last valid will and not the 2008 will. They also contended that, even if genuine, the 2008 will had been revoked as a consequence of the formation of the civil partnership between Pete Ikin and the defendant by virtue of s 18B(1) of the 1837 Act. It was held that s 18B(3) of the 1837 Act required that it appear from the language of the will in question that the testator expected to form a civil partnership with a particular person and intended that the will should not be revoked by the formation of that civil partnership, and that clause 2 of the 2008 will did not satisfy that requirement. The clause was found to be merely a general statement that the will was intended to survive marriage, civil partnership or adoption and it did not show that the deceased had expected to form a civil partnership, let alone a civil partnership with a particular person; there was nothing in the will to indicate any connection between cl 2 and cl 4. Accordingly, the application was allowed and the grant to Mr Despallieres revoked.

## 7.2.11 Contracts and covenants not to revoke and revocation by marriage

The ending of a marriage/civil partnership does not revoke a will, although it may affect the appointments or dispositions in the will (see 10.9). Note also that a covenant or contract not to revoke a will is valid insofar as the covenant itself goes, but does not affect the testator's ability to revoke the will, including by marriage. If the testator does so, the covenantee may sue for damages, but they cannot enforce or have revived the old will by their action. In *Re Marsland* (1939), the testator had covenanted not to revoke his will but did so by marrying. The beneficiaries under the old will sued, but were unsuccessful because the court held the will had been revoked not by the testator himself but by operation of law (s 18 of the Wills Act 1837); construing the covenant as one not to remarry would have been against public policy, which protects marriage. On the other hand, a suggestion that a contract should be found invalid in itself because its breach by marriage would offend public policy was rejected in *Robinson v Ommanney* (1833).

## 7.2.12 Appointments by will

Section 18 of the original Wills Act 1837 provided that an appointment made by will is not revoked by the testator's subsequent marriage if

> the real or personal estate thereby appointed would not in default of such appointment pass
> to his or her heir, customary heir, executor, or administrator, or the person entitled as his or
> her next of kin under the statute of distributions.

This involved the awkward and complex question of who those people might be, applying the rules which were in effect before the legislation of 1925 came into force in 1926. If the exception does apply, it saves the appointment, but not the rest of the will, from revocation.

The Law Reform Committee considered this in its 22nd Report. It discussed the case of *Re Gilligan* (1950), where the court considered the principal purpose of the section. The Law Reform Committee concurred with the view of Pilcher J that the intention of the section was that the fund under appointment should devolve as on an intestacy if the testator's will were revoked. This would mean the widow would take her statutory share of the estate. They thought this rule should remain as it was by the Administration of Justice Act 1982 but that the language of the section should be modernised.

Thus, if the appointment is made in a will made after 1982 then the amended section provides that 'a disposition in exercise of a power of appointment shall take effect notwithstanding the testator's subsequent marriage unless the property so appointed would in default of appointment pass to his personal representatives'. Essentially this re-enacts the earlier provision but with reference not to the persons who would have been entitled under the pre-1926 rules but to the persons entitled to the testator's own estate on intestacy. A parallel provision applies to civil partnerships in s 18B (2) of the Wills Act 1837.

## 7.3 Destruction

Section 20 of the Wills Act 1837 provides that the whole or any part of a will or codicil is revoked 'by the burning, tearing, or otherwise destroying the same by the testator, or by some person in his presence and by his direction, with the intention of revoking the same'. Both those distinct elements – of physical destruction and of intention – must be fulfilled.

### 7.3.1 Destruction must be physical, not symbolic

The act of destruction of the will must be physical; cutting may be included in 'otherwise destroying', as was said in *Hobbs v Knight* (1838). The complete scratching out of the signatures of the testatrix and witnesses was also regarded as physical destruction within the meaning of the section in *Re Morton* (1887), but not in *In the Goods of Godfrey* (1893) where the signature was struck through but remained legible.

Destruction which is not physical but symbolic will not do. In *Cheese v Lovejoy* (1877), the testator tried to revoke his will by crossing through part of it, writing 'revoked' on the back and throwing it away. When, after his death, the will was produced by his maid, who had retrieved it from a heap of old papers, the court had to decide whether his revocation had been successful. There was no problem with the testator's intention. The difficulty was whether the acts of destruction performed by the testator were sufficient under the Act. The court held that they were not, and admitted the will to probate, saying 'all the destroying in the world without intention will not revoke a will, nor all the intention in the world without destroying; there must be the two'.

### 7.3.2 Destruction of a will does not revoke a codicil to that will

Note that the revocation of a will by destruction does not revoke a codicil to that will. In *In the Goods of Turner* (1872), the testator gave by codicil a legacy to be held under conditions stated in the will. The will itself was later revoked by destruction. It was held, however, that this did not revoke the gift by codicil.

### 7.3.3 Sufficient destruction

To revoke the will, the destruction need not be of the whole will, but it must be of enough of it so as to impair the entirety of the will. It is therefore enough to burn, tear off or cut out or completely obliterate the signatures of the witnesses or the testator, as in *Hobbs v Knight* (1838) (7.3.1).

What amounts to sufficient destruction is somewhat reminiscent of what amounts to a sufficient signature (see 5.5); in *Perkes v Perkes* (1820), the destruction of the will by the testator's tearing it into four pieces with a definite intention to revoke it was held not be sufficient to revoke the will, because the testator was then stopped, partly by the devisee, whose behaviour had caused him to try to revoke the will, apologising. The testator then fitted the pieces back together, saying 'it is a good job it is no worse'. The court held the tearing insufficient to revoke the will because it was not all the destruction that the testator had intended to carry out. Thus, the sufficiency of destruction, like the sufficiency of a signature, may be determined by measuring what the testator did against what they intended to do.

## 7.3.4 Destruction of part of the will

Where part of the will is destroyed, it may be shown that there was revocation of that part only. In In the Goods of Woodward (1871), the testator had made his will on seven sheets of paper, each one signed by him and his witnesses at the end. The first eight lines of the will had been torn off and there was no information as to what they had contained. There was no proof of an intention to revoke the whole will and it was admitted to probate in its incomplete state. In Re Everest (1975), the lower half of the front page of the will was cut away. There was, again, insufficient evidence to establish that the testator had intended to revoke the whole will. It was admitted to probate without the missing first part.

## 7.3.5 Destruction by another person than the testator

If another person is to carry out the act of destruction, it must be in the testator's presence and at their direction. Both these elements need to be observed. The testator in In the Estate of de Kremer (1965) telephoned his solicitor to say that he wished to make a new will, asking him to destroy the old one. The solicitor, in the absence of the testator, did so. The court held that the destruction of the will had not revoked it. It also said that the solicitor concerned had committed a 'considerable professional error'. The will could not be revoked in the testator's absence; he could revoke it himself by destruction, but the extension allowing the revocation of a person's will by destruction by someone other than the testator himself should be considered to be a provision, like that for the signing of a will by a person other than the testator, to be used only as a last resort where there is some good reason, such as physical incapacity, why the testator cannot perform the act himself. Even then, the requirement for the testator's presence must be taken very seriously.

In Re Dadds (1857), the testatrix had called for assistance in revoking her will as she was too ill to manage by herself. Unfortunately, her assistants took the will out to the kitchen in order to burn it; it was held that this was not done in her presence and therefore was not effective to revoke the will. In the light of the improbability that the intestacy rules will satisfy the particular desires of any person, it is far better for practical purposes always to revoke a will at the same time as making further provisions for the disposal of property on death and by the same document.

## 7.3.6 Intention to revoke

Accidental destruction will not revoke the will; nor will destroying it intentionally but without the intention of revoking it. The first of these concepts is easy to see, but the second can cause some practical difficulty. It arises not infrequently, however, where a person mistakenly believes that a will has been revoked already or is invalid for some other reason, and therefore destroys it without the intention of revoking it – so far as they know, it does not need revoking. This was what occurred in Giles v Warren (1872), where a testator destroyed a will under a mistaken belief that it was invalid; the will was not revoked by that destruction. Likewise, in Scott v Scott (1859), the will was destroyed in the mistaken belief that a later will was valid and so had already revoked it. The later will was however not valid, so the destroyed will was therefore not revoked by the destruction.

The testator's errors in these circumstances result in the earlier will being valid, albeit physically destroyed, and the later will in Scott being worthless. In Re Jones (1976), the court addressed directly the question of the testatrix's state of mind when destroying a will she believed to be invalid in any event. It held that a testator who tore up a will under the mistaken impression that it was of no effect

> may have merely torn it up, thinking that it was no longer worth the paper it was written upon … the right inference to draw was that he did not intend to revoke it at all; he was merely disposing of what he thought was rubbish.

A testator may have some intention of destroying their valid will but not the intention to revoke it. This occurred in In the Goods of Brassington (1902), where the testator had made a will leaving everything to his wife and appointing her sole executrix. He was always liable to become drunk and incapable and as time wore on he got worse until one day whilst particularly incapable he tore up his will. He subsequently tried to stick it back together and also told his doctor that he had torn up his will while he did not know what he was doing. It was held that the destruction had not revoked the will and it was admitted to probate.

The same applies where a will is destroyed accidentally, as occurred in the case of Gill v Gill (1909). The testator had got drunk and so annoyed his wife that she tore up his will in anger. The court subsequently held that there was no revocation because the destruction had not been at his direction, and acquiescence to the destruction did not equate with the necessary intention to revoke.

Acquiescing in destruction was also insufficient in Re Booth (1926) (see 7.7). The will was propounded by the deceased's widow, the court refusing to allow that the deceased's apparent acquiescence in its destruction amounted to that sufficient to revoke the will. If a will has been accidentally destroyed, just as where it has been lost, it is no longer available for revocation by destruction, as the destruction must take place in the limited circumstances allowed under the Act in order to revoke the will.

### 7.3.7 Destruction of parts and inferences of intention

If the testator destroys their signature on the will, this will raise an inference that they intended to revoke the whole will (as in Hobbs v Knight, 7.3.1), but destruction of a part of the will that is not vital to the validity of the rest of the will does not affect it. In In the Estate of Nunn (1936), the testator had cut a strip out of the middle of his will and stitched the rest back together again. The court held that only the strip removed had been revoked and the rest of the will remained valid. Where, however, a will makes no sense without the destroyed parts, it will probably be considered to have been revoked in its entirety. The testator in Leonard v Leonard (1902) had destroyed the first two sheets of a will which consisted of five sheets of paper. Without the first two sheets, the remaining three were practically unintelligible and made no sense as a will. The court held that the testator had intended the revocation of the whole will. It should not be thought that actions of this kind will never be met in the course of the practice of an ordinary solicitor. Practitioners are well aware that, if there is some bizarre action that can be committed, there is an unexpectedly strong likelihood that sooner or later one of their clients will commit it.

### 7.3.8 Presumptions

There are two rebuttable presumptions in respect of the destruction of wills. These are that a will in the testator's possession which is missing at their death is presumed to have been revoked by destruction, and that a will found mutilated is presumed to have been mutilated with the intention of revocation.

## 7.3.9 Will missing at death

If the will was last known to be in the testator's possession but cannot be found at their death, it is presumed that the testator destroyed it with the intention of revoking it.[4] How strong that presumption is, and thus how difficult to rebut, will depend on how safely the testator was known to keep the will. As with all presumptions, this one may be rebutted. Evidence may be rebutted as to a wide range of facts that will tend to show the testator did not intend to revoke their will. For instance, it may be shown that their possessions were stolen in a burglary or destroyed by enemy action in wartime.

In the Canadian case of *Lefebvre v Major* (1930), the presumption of destruction *animo revocandi* (with the intention to revoke) was rebutted by evidence that the testator had remained on good terms with his sister, whom his will benefited, that his things (very possibly including his will) had been burnt after his death and, according to the court, by evidence of 'the simple character of the man himself'. In *Rowe v Clarke* (2006), a grant of letters of administration was revoked after it was found that the testator had been somewhat disorganised or careless and that this probably accounted for the will not being found amongst his possessions. His mother had a copy of the will, under which his partner was the beneficiary, rather than the brother who had taken out the grant.

## 7.3.10 Proving a missing will

It should be remembered that the difficulty of proving a will that cannot be found does not have any direct bearing on whether or not it is valid and has to be proved. Where a will cannot be found but it is shown that it has not been revoked, it can be proved by evidence of its contents. It is often the case that the only person who can give useful evidence about what was in the will is the beneficiary as in *Re Phibbs* (1917) (see 5.15.3) which might at first seem to render their evidence insufficiently weighty. However, as with most matters connected with wills, and indeed most family matters, the only persons likely to have any relevant knowledge about a matter usually are the close family members who are directly affected.

In *Re Booth* (1926), evidence as to the contents of a lost will was given by the wife of Colonel Booth, whose privileged will reading: 'I leave everything to my wife absolutely. I hope she will have regard to my sister Mary' was believed to have been burnt some eight years before his death. Mrs Booth was able to give evidence to the court of the contents of that will sufficient for it to be admitted to proof and thus to disinherit the heir and next of kin who would have taken on his intestacy (see also 6.1.15).

In the case of *Sugden v Lord St Leonards* (1876), the handwritten will was not found, though many long codicils were. The will was proved in almost all its complexity on the evidence of the testator's daughter Charlotte who had often been required to read the will to her father. The testator had been Lord Chancellor, and the court accordingly found that 'Miss Sugden's position is exceptional; of her integrity there can be no doubt', although Hannen J was not entirely happy about the lack of evidence from a lawyer. He felt that would have been 'more satisfactory than the evidence of a non-professional person, above all the evidence of a lady'. The court also considered that a lawyer would have destroyed all of the codicils as well as the will itself. In *Re Webb* (1964) there was evidence that a will had been destroyed in an air raid on the testator's solicitor's office where the will had been situated, and this too rebutted the presumption.

A more recent case about a missing will, *Ferneley v Napier* (2010), involved a discussion of the nature and standard of proof required, especially where the assertion is in effect that there was a conspiracy to suppress a valid will. Considering comments in earlier cases that were aimed at

---

4 *Welch v Phillips* (1836).

proof by parol (oral) evidence only, Mann J confirmed that the requisite standard was the balance of probabilities, even where the allegations made were very serious and might entail facts that would constitute a criminal offence. As was confirmed in *Treasury Solicitor v Doveton and Trixilis Ltd* (2008), a case in which a grant of probate was revoked when the will was indeed found to have been forged, probate proceedings are, however, civil proceedings, and, albeit forgery is a strong allegation and therefore attracts a heavy burden of proof because such a serious act is unlikely, nevertheless the standard of proof is still the balance of probabilities.

### 7.3.11 Will found mutilated

If at the testator's death the will which was in their possession is found mutilated, the presumption, again rebuttable, is that the testator mutilated it with the intention of revoking it, in whole or in part.

### 7.3.12 Capacity and the presumption of revocation by destruction

Tearing or mutilation during a period of insanity will not revoke the will, because the testator must always have the capacity to revoke the will in order to carry it out successfully. Showing that the testator was insane when they had possession of the will which it is alleged was revoked by them will reverse the burden of proof which would otherwise have operated, because it will mean that the presumption that the testator revoked the will by destruction will not operate. If the testator was insane during any part of the period when they had possession of the will, it will be necessary for anyone alleging they had revoked the will by destruction during that period to prove that they were mentally capable when they carried out the destruction. For example, in *Re Sabatini* (1969), a 90-year-old testatrix tore up her will at a time when she had been suffering from mental illness. It was found she was acting irrationally and did not have mental capacity when she tore it up, so the will was therefore not revoked.

## 7.4 By later will or codicil

Section 20 of the Wills Act 1837 provides that the whole or any part of a will may be revoked by another duly executed will or codicil.

### 7.4.1 Express revocation

Most wills, including will forms from a newsagent's shop, contain a revocation clause revoking all previous wills; this is normally the first clause of the will and comes immediately after the preamble stating who the testator is and what they are doing. Many codicils revoke a specific clause or paragraph of a specific will. Once they are duly executed, they are effective to revoke the will or clause or paragraph to which they refer. No particular form of words is necessary, but the phrase 'this is my last will' does not revoke earlier wills. It was said in *Lowthorpe-Lutwidge v Lowthorpe-Lutwidge* (1935) that a great deal of evidence is required to show that a general revocation clause is ineffective for want of intention since it is presumed that the testator knew and approved of the contents of their will. On the other hand, it was said in *Marsh v Marsh* (1860) that a general revocation clause worded as to revocation of 'all former wills' leads to the inference that the deceased intended to leave a subsisting will. If it can be found that the intention to make the revocation effected by a clause was based on a condition which has not been satisfied, the revocation will be ineffective (see 7.6.2).

There has to be some clear statement of revocation. In *Re Hawkesley, Black v Tidy* (1934), the testatrix made a will in 1927 which she described as her last will. However, it did not expressly revoke earlier testamentary dispositions, and she had also made a will in 1922, to which she had added a codicil in 1925. The earlier will and the codicil thus remained valid, and the combined effects of the documents had to be considered.

The express revocation of all former wills may still cause dispute where the testator has property abroad and does not clearly specify that they intend to revoke wills relating to the foreign property as well. Such wills may indeed be needed to deal with the devolution of property on death in the other jurisdiction. One such case was *Lamothe v Lamothe* (2002), relating to the will of a Dominican citizen who had lived in England for over 30 years and had property in both countries. The question was whether a will dealing with her Dominican property and containing the usual sort of general revocation clause was indeed intended to revoke an earlier will dealing with her English property. Roger Wyand QC surveyed many cases in the area, and concluded that on the evidence Mrs Lamothe had been advised that the later will would revoke the earlier one and that she had intended that to happen; accordingly, it did.

## 7.4.2 Effect of words of revocation included by mistake

Where a testator includes in their will words of revocation which they do not in fact intend to operate, whether the words operate or not will depend on how far they were aware of the words being in the document, not on how far they were aware of their legal effect. Thus, in *Collins v Elstone* (1893), where the testatrix was unaware (having been wrongly advised) of the true legal effect of the revocation clause in her will, but was clearly aware that it was there, it was held to be valid and thus to revoke her previous dispositions. In *Re Phelan* (1972), however, the testator was held to have been insufficiently aware of the revocation clauses in his last testamentary documents, so they were excluded from probate, thus achieving the result he intended as to his dispositions. The basis of the decision, however, appears to have everything to do with the testator's knowledge and approval of the contents of his will and nothing to do with his intention, or otherwise, of revoking his will.

## 7.4.3 Revocation clauses and wills for other jurisdictions

It may be questionable how far a revocation clause operates if there are wills made by the same testator which refer to other jurisdictions (see *Lamothe* (2002), 7.4.1). Such questions arise more frequently now that more people lead cross-border lives and have property in more than one country. A testator may, however, make provision to deal with this problem. In *Re Wayland* (1951), the testator made a will dealing with his Belgian property under the provisions of Belgian law. Later, he made an English will which contained a general revocation clause but also declared 'this will is intended to deal only with my estate in England'. The court construed the revocation clause as dealing also only with his English wills and admitted the Belgian will to probate as well.

## 7.4.4 Inoperative revocation clauses

A revocation clause in a will does not operate if it is contained in a conditional will which is inoperative owing to the specified condition not being satisfied, or if it is itself subject to a condition which is not satisfied.

## 7.4.5 Implied revocation

If a later will contains provisions which are inconsistent with or merely repeat provisions in an earlier will, without that will or the provisions in it being expressly revoked, the earlier will is impliedly revoked insofar as that applies. The inconsistency does not revoke the earlier will as a whole. Taking a later provision rather than an earlier one when there is inconsistency between the two is a general rule of construction which was confirmed in *Birks v Birks* (1865). A court will read all the testamentary provisions together, since that is how they constitute the testator's 'will', and later provisions prevail over earlier ones with which they are inconsistent. If the inconsistency or repetition is partial, it will be a question of construction as to which provisions the testator intended to take effect at their death. In *Dempsey v Lawson* (1877) the testatrix had made a will in 1858 disposing of all her property and leaving the residue to Roman Catholic convents. In 1860 she made another, without revocation or residuary clauses. The court held that she had intended to replace the earlier will and the residuary beneficiaries under the earlier will received nothing.

More recently, the question arose – again in the cross-border context – in *Perdoni v Curati* (2011) whether an English will made in England was revoked by a later Italian will naming the deceased's wife as his *erede universal* (sole heir or universal heir). The wife in fact had predeceased, and the case was brought by the husband's sister, who would inherit on intestacy (in either jurisdiction), against the niece and nephew who would inherit the English estate if the earlier will remained valid. The Court of Appeal, with an eye to the judge's discussion of the dispute over the deceased's domicile, dismissed an appeal against a finding that the later will did not entirely revoke the earlier one, so the niece and nephew took the English estate.

## 7.4.6 Implied revocation by codicil

A common reason for making a codicil is to revoke gifts made in a will. If the codicil is clear, as well as properly made, then the revocation will be effective. If, however, it is not effective, the gift will still stand. In the situation where there is doubt about whether the codicil is sufficiently clear, there is an old case suggesting that the courts will incline to retain the provisions of the will intact. In *Hearle v Hicks* (1832), the testator left his copyhold house to his wife for her life. Later, he executed another will, leaving his freehold and copyhold land to his daughter for her life. The court held that the clear gift to the wife should stand and was not revoked by the more general gift in the subsequent codicil.

In *Re Wray* (1951), the testator appointed an executor and left him a legacy. The residue was left on the basis that, if the named beneficiary predeceased, the property should devolve as part of his estate. Later, the testator directed by codicil that his will should be read as though the name of the executor were omitted and that person was dead. It was held, however, that this did not mean that person was excluded from the life interest in the residue which he took as part of a gift under the will of the testator's residuary beneficiary.

## 7.4.7 Proof of revocation

If a will or codicil is revoked by a later will or codicil, that revocation takes effect immediately and continues whether or not the later will or codicil can be produced at the testator's death. However, it will be necessary to establish that the later document was duly executed and that its contents were such as expressly or impliedly to revoke the earlier document. Evidence such as a copy, or oral evidence, may be adduced to support this contention.

The situation can arise where a will or codicil is inadmissible to probate and yet it may still revoke an earlier will. In *Re Howard* (1944), the testator left his estate to his son by will. He later executed two wills on the same day. One was in favour of his wife and the other in favour of his son. Unfortunately, each of those two contained a revocation clause revoking all previous wills, and the court held that the two wills effectively revoked the earlier will, though neither could be admitted to probate as they were inconsistent and there was nothing to show which was executed first.

The decision in *Re Howard* may be compared with that in *Re Phelan* (1972). There, the testator had executed even more wills on the same day, and the court got round the problem by omitting the revocation clauses for want of knowledge and approval. In that case, however, the wills were not inconsistent with each other, whereas in *Re Howard* they were. In effect, in *Re Howard*, the court viewed the revocation clause as effective where the rest of the will was not, and in *Re Phelan* it viewed the wills as effective whereas the revocation clause was not. Note that the reasoning in *Re Phelan* was that the testator, on the facts, did not know and approve of the revocation clauses, so they were omitted; in *Re Howard*, admitting either will would have involved the court making some more positive finding about the testator's intentions.

## 7.5 Duly executed writing declaring an intention to revoke

Section 20 of the Wills Act 1837 provides that 'some writing declaring an intention to revoke' a will and executed in the same manner as a will revokes the will. The testator in *In the Goods of Durance* (1872) had written a letter to his brother which was attested by two witnesses. It directed his brother to obtain his will and burn it without reading it. The letter was held to constitute duly executed writing declaring an intention to revoke. The codicil of the testator in *In the Goods of Gosling* (1886) was obliterated, and at the foot of it was written 'We are witnesses to the erasure of the above.' It was signed by the testator and attested by two witnesses. This was held to be writing declaring an intention to revoke and effective, within the meaning of the section, to revoke the codicil. The testatrix in *Re Spracklan's Estate* (1938) had written a letter containing the words 'will you please destroy the will already made out'. The letter was duly attested and was addressed to the manager of the bank where her will was held. The court, on the question of whether this letter was effective to revoke the will, held that it had been revoked immediately on the execution of the letter.

## 7.6 Conditional revocation

The intention to revoke may be absolute or it may be conditional. If the intention to revoke is absolute, then it takes effect immediately once the formalities for revocation – destruction (with intention), later will or codicil or duly executed writing declaring an intention – are satisfied. If a will is revoked as a result of a misunderstanding of fact, it will be a question of construction whether the revocation was conditional on the fact being true (*In the Estate of Southerden* (1925) (7.6.6) – here the misunderstanding was of the nature of the intestacy rules).

### 7.6.1 Conditional intention

If there is conditional intention, revocation will not take place until the condition is fulfilled. Thus, if a testator has said, in a manner that complies with the formalities, that their will should be revoked only if they return from a certain voyage, then whether or not their will has been revoked will turn on the question of fact of whether or not they did return. Questions of law and of fact should be distinguished very clearly in this area; the law is clear that a will may be made subject to conditional revocation. Assuming it is clear what event constitutes the condition, then the question is always whether that event has in fact occurred.

### 7.6.2 Revocation conditional on validity of another will

Sometimes the condition makes revocation dependent upon the validity of another will or codicil. This sort of conditional revocation is referred to as dependent relative revocation, or conditional revocation. A will destroyed after it was believed a second will had replaced its provisions was held still to be valid in Re Middleton (1864) when the second will failed for want of due attestation. Where a first will was revoked with a general view to making a new one, however, in Re Jones (1976), the Court of Appeal held that the necessary conditional intention was lacking, as the first will had been destroyed with the intention of revoking it, the replacement will being a separate matter.

In this area, establishing whether or not the revocation was conditional often involves considering evidence about the circumstances in which the testator made the new will, because it would be unusual for the testator to make it clear that their old will (which they clearly consider to be in need of updating) is only revoked if their new one is valid. However, this involves stretching the principles of the law somewhat. Testators rarely give a thought to what would happen if their new will were invalid, since they tend not to countenance the possibility. They cannot therefore be said really to have an intention about the validity of their old will; though the courts will uphold an old will as not revoked because of the failure of the new will, finding that the testator's intention to revoke was conditional can involve inferring a great deal into the state of mind of the testator – effectively, predicting what the answer would have been to a certain question (would you have wanted to revoke your old will if the new one were not valid?) when no such question was asked of or occurred to the testator.

### 7.6.3 Revocation partial and conditional

In Re Finnemore (1992), the testator had made three successive wills leaving most of his estate to the same person each time but varying the beneficiaries of the remaining quarter of residue. The last two wills, both containing express general revocation clauses, were witnessed by the main beneficiary's husband, so she stood to lose her gifts under s 15 of the Wills Act 1837. The court found two good reasons to save the gift. First, it found that the revocation clause, construed distributively, applied to some provisions absolutely and conditionally to others. Second, as an alternative, it found that the doctrine of conditional revocation would apply so that the revocation of the first will was conditional upon the validity of the main gift in the last will. This might appear to be a court fitting its findings around facts which are apparent but with which the law does not easily deal well.

### 7.6.4 Conditional revocation by destruction

Where the (purported) revocation of the old will was by destruction, it will be a question of fact whether the intention was conditional. In In the Estate of Green (1962), however, the testator made a new will and then destroyed his old one. The new will failed for want of due execution. The court looked at the testator's intention when he destroyed his old will, and held that his intention to revoke it was absolute and the old will was revoked immediately on its destruction.

The Law Reform Committee expressed some concern in its 22nd Report that the doctrine of conditional revocation was being used against testators' intentions. However, in Re Jones (1976) (7.6.2), the court showed that it was alive to this possibility. The testatrix had formed the intention of making a new will benefiting a different set of relatives, and she destroyed her old one; evidence of a testatrix's intention to make a new will is not conclusive, however, as to her intention to make the revocation of the old will conditional. The court held that the testatrix's intention was to disinherit the person who would have taken under the original will and that it was irrelevant that its revocation resulted in an intestacy.

In respect of these decisions, note that the fact that the old will had been destroyed, whilst it might have made it difficult to prove the old will, did not affect that will's validity. A will may be valid even though it has been destroyed, if it was not destroyed with the necessary intention. If the revocation was really to have been effected by a revocation clause in a new will, it might well be that there was no intention to revoke by destruction, but that the testator was, as was said in Re Jones (1976), disposing of so much rubbish. In that case, if the new will containing the revocation clause were invalid, the old will would not be revoked and so would have to be proved, even if that were inconvenient or difficult given that it had been destroyed.

## 7.6.5 Conditional intention where there is mistaken belief of revival of an old will

If a will has been revoked by a later will, the subsequent revocation of that later will does not revive the first one. If, therefore, the destruction of the later will is intended to revoke it conditionally on the revival of the first will, the revocation of the second will will be ineffective.

In Powell v Powell (1866), the testator executed a will in 1864 revoking all his former wills. He destroyed it in 1865 with the express intention of substituting for it a will of 1862 which he held. The court found the revocation by destruction to be conditional on the validity of the 1862 will, which had been revoked by that of 1864 and which was not valid. Therefore, it was held that there had been no revocation by destruction of the will of 1865. Sir JP Wilde said:

> [T]he principle [is] that all acts by which a testator may physically destroy or mutilate a testamentary instrument are by their nature equivocal.... It is ... necessary in each case to study the act done by the light of the circumstances under which it occurred, and the declarations of the testator with which it may have been accompanied. For unless it be done with *animus revocandi*, it is no revocation.

The testator in Cossey v Cossey (1900) had executed a series of wills. In 1887, he left a legacy of £2,000 to his niece and then all the remainder to his wife. In 1897, he executed another will leaving his property to his wife for her life, with the remainder to his sister-in-law. In April 1899, he made a third will, revoking the second will of 1897, and benefiting his wife more than by the second will but less than by the first. In May 1899, he said to his wife, on their anniversary, that he wished to revoke the 1899 will and go by that of 1887. His servant tore up the 1889 will in his presence and at his direction. The purported revocation took place in the belief that the 1887 will would thereby be revived. This was wrong, and it was held that the revocation of the 1899 will was conditional on its being true. The purported revocation was therefore ineffective and the will of 1899 remained valid.

The same happened in the Canadian case of Re Janotta (1976). The testator was wrongly informed by his niece that the revocation of his second will, of which the terms were almost identical with his first, would revive the first will. The court held that the second will was revoked only in order to revive the first, and conditionally on that occurring. It therefore admitted the second will to probate because its revocation had been ineffective.

## 7.6.6 Intention conditional on certain devolution of property

Similarly, if a will is destroyed conditionally upon a particular devolution on intestacy which is not satisfied, or a substantial misunderstanding about the nature of the testator's estate, it will not be revoked. The testator in In the Estate of Southerden (1925) (7.6) had made a will giving all his property to his wife. Later he burnt it, on the understanding that his wife would be entitled to all his property under his intestacy. The court held that this was a revocation conditional on that particular devolution on intestacy, and since that did not occur the condition was not fulfilled and the revocation was ineffective. The testator in *Re Carey* (1977) revoked his will because he had nothing to leave and considered the will superfluous. However, he came into an inheritance. The court managed to hold that the revocation had been conditional on the testator having nothing to leave, and that therefore, in the light of his inheritance, it was ineffective.

### 7.6.7 Conditional express revocation

A revocation clause in a will or codicil may be subject to an express condition which, if the condition is not satisfied, will mean that the clause does not operate. This may be a far simpler situation, as where the testator manages to state clearly their position about the revocation being dependent on a certain, ascertainable event. However, a revocation clause may also be construed as being conditional because of something expressed in it even if the condition as such is not express.

### 7.6.8 Implying the circumstances for revocation

In *Campbell v French* (1797), the testator gave legacies to his sister's two grandchildren, who were living in America. Later, by a codicil, he revoked the legacies to the grandchildren, 'they being all dead'. In fact, they were not dead. The revocation was held to be conditional on their being dead and, therefore, ineffective. The testator in *In the Goods of Hope Brown* (1942) had a will prepared by solicitors by which he carefully disposed of all his property. Some years later he made a will for himself, properly executed but not well drafted. This later will contained a full revocation clause revoking all previous testamentary dispositions, and gave a life interest to the testator's wife, directing for the payment of pecuniary bequests free of duty (but making no such bequests) and directing his trustees to divide his property, after his wife's death, to after-mentioned beneficiaries who were not, in fact, mentioned. The court managed to find that the revocation clause was conditional on the testator concluding his later will, and the later will was admitted to probate without the revocation clause.

### 7.6.9 Conditional implied revocation

Implied revocation is what occurs when the testator makes a later gift of the same property of which they have disposed in an earlier will, without expressly revoking the earlier will or gift in it. It is a question of construction whether a gift is impliedly revoked by a gift of the same thing in a later will if that later gift subsequently fails. The question to be asked is, as with the revocation of a will, whether the revocation of the earlier gift was conditional on the later gift being effective.

The testatrix in *Re Robinson* (1930) gave her estate by will upon trust to pay an annuity to her son and after his death to divide her estate equally between her grandchildren who attained 21. By a later will, she gave her whole estate to her son absolutely, but the disposition was void because her son's wife was an attesting witness. The court found no intention to revoke the earlier will in any event, since the only indication of such an intention in the later will was the different, failed, disposition. The revocation of the earlier provision was therefore ineffective.

## 7.7 Revocation and privileged wills

Privileged wills – those made in circumstances where the testator is excused the need to comply with the formalities – are revocable in the same way as other wills, save that an oral (nuncupative) will cannot, of course, be revoked by destruction. They will be revoked if the testator makes a further will revoking them, whether that is a privileged will or not. Whether or not the testator can make a further privileged will depends on their situation at the time of making it. If they are not entitled to make a privileged will, they are not entitled to revoke a will without the formalities either.

The Court of Appeal considered the revocation of privileged wills in In the Estate of Gossage; Wood v Gossage (1921). (Note that the headnote to this short case is somewhat misleading.) The testator made a formally executed will in 1915, appointing his fiancée executrix and leaving her the residue of his estate after certain legacies. He then left with his regiment for South Africa, where he changed his mind and wrote to his fiancée asking her to give the will to his sister, which she did. In 1918, he wrote to his sister giving her instructions about the disposal of his property and saying, 'As regards the will, if you haven't already done so, I want you to burn it for I have already cancelled it': the sister accordingly burnt the will, but after the death of the testator later that year, a copy of it was found amongst his possessions. The fiancée sought a declaration that the will should be admitted to probate. The deceased's next of kin claimed that the letter to the sister was writing declaring an intention to revoke. The court of first instance agreed with the next of kin and the fiancée appealed to the Court of Appeal.

The Court of Appeal held that s 11 of the Wills Act 1837 meant that privileged wills were outside the formalities of that Act completely, and therefore they continued to be governed by the law which applied before the 1837 Act. Lord Sterndale MR commented:

> There can be no question as to the intention of the testator to revoke his bequest to the plaintiff.... Obviously it would be a great injustice if the plaintiff were to take the property, but I hope that that fact does not influence me to strain the Act of Parliament against her. It is said ... that there is no valid revocation here because by s 20 a soldier's will cannot be revoked, though it can be made without the formalities required.... This appears to me to be an absurd result, but, however absurd it is, effect must be given to it if that result arises from the Act. I do not think, however, that it requires any straining of the language of the Act of Parliament to arrive at an opposite conclusion. It is quite clear that, apart from the Wills Act, a soldier could at common law make or revoke his will without any formality.... If one reads ss 9 and 11 together, no formalities are required for the execution of a soldier's will, but soldiers are allowed to dispose of their personal estate as they might have done before the Act – that is, as they might have done before the Statute of Frauds.

Younger LJ said: 'it is not required for the revocation of a soldier's will that there should be the formalities necessary to revoke the will of a civilian. Nothing more is required by s 11.'

The question of the revocation of privileged wills was also addressed in Re Booth (1926), where the testator had made a privileged will when starting out for Egypt with his regiment in 1882. It was made in writing but would have been inadequately executed had the testator not been in a position to make a privileged will. After that war, he gave the document to his wife, who kept it in a wooden plate chest in a locked closet in their home at Hawstead House. In 1916, that house burnt down. Colonel Booth died in 1924, aged 81, without having made any other will. The widow sought to propound the will; the defendants made various objections. They brought evidence that he knew of the (probable) burning of the will and regarded the will as having thus been revoked. They showed that the colonel had referred to the need to make another will. The court held, however, that acquiescence in destruction of the will by fire did not amount to revocation. The defendants also suggested that there should be imported into English law the principle of Roman law that a privileged will was automatically revoked by operation of law one year from the end of the testator's privilege – for example, a year after a sailor returns home or a soldier ceases to be on actual military service. The court declined to accept these objections and held that the will was valid.

More recently the topic was discussed in *Re Servoz-Gavin (deceased)* (2009) (see 6.1.12). The deceased had made wills in 1985 and 1990, both of which lacked formalities and so would have to constitute privileged wills in order to be valid. The court doubted that the first will was properly a privileged will, but in any case the second was, and that impliedly revoked the earlier one if indeed that was valid.

## 7.8  Summary of Chapter 7

### 7.8.1 Revocation of Wills

A testator may, provided they have the necessary mental capacity, revoke a will at any time. The capacity required is the same as to make a simple will. The burden of proving that a will is valid is with the person alleging the validity; the burden of proving that a valid will has been revoked is with the person alleging revocation.

A will may be revoked in four ways:

(a)   marriage or civil partnership;
(b)   destruction with intention to revoke;
(c)   by later will or codicil;
(d)   by duly executed writing declaring an intention to revoke.

Marriage or the formation of a civil partnership revokes a will, including a privileged will, by operation of s 18 of the Wills Act 1837 as amended. A void marriage or civil partnership does not revoke a will, but a voidable one does. The position under the Wills Act 1837 was changed by s 177 of the Law of Property Act to provide that a will expressed to be made in contemplation of a particular marriage would not be revoked by that marriage. The Administration of Justice Act 1982 then provided that the will would not be revoked by the marriage if it appeared from the will that the testator was expecting the marriage and that they did not intend the revocation.

If destruction is to revoke a will in accordance with s 20 of the Wills Act 1837, then it must be physical destruction of all, or the vital parts, of the will, and it must be accompanied by the intention to revoke, which will not be available if the testator then lacks mental capacity. Accidental destruction does not revoke a will. A will known to have been in the testator's possession at death but which cannot be found will be presumed to have been destroyed by him or her with the intention of revocation, and a similar presumption applies where the will is found mutilated. However, presumptions as always are subject to rebuttal by evidence. The contents of a will which has been lost or destroyed but remains valid must be proved by whatever evidence is available.

The whole or part of a will may be revoked by another duly executed will or codicil. Later valid dispositions will impliedly revoke any earlier dispositions with which they are inconsistent. Revocation may be conditional on certain facts or, sometimes, on the validity of another will. This may be expressed by the testator or may be found by implication from the facts.

# Chapter 8

# Alteration, Republication and Revival

A person may want to change their will without revoking the whole thing. Although the best way to change or update a will is usually to make a new one, revoking the old one, this may be considered too cumbersome or expensive an operation. However, nothing in a will is valid unless it has been duly executed, so there are rules to tell whether alterations have been duly executed. A will may also be updated by a later document that is properly executed and refers to the will, or by re-executing the existing will, so the will then carries the date of the later execution. Revival is more like making a new will, using the words of one that has been revoked for the purposes of a newly-executed document. These processes are not often used, but an understanding of how they operate is vital when they are encountered.

## 8.1 Alteration

The basic rule is that alterations are not valid if they are made after execution – the words of the will are fixed at execution, and anything added afterwards will not have been executed and therefore cannot be admitted to probate. This is stated in s 21 of the Wills Act 1837, which provides that

> no obliteration, interlineation, or other alteration made in any will after the execution thereof shall be valid or have any effect, except so far as the words or effect of the will before such alteration shall not be apparent, unless such alteration shall be executed in like manner as hereinbefore is required for the execution of the will.

It is also clear, however, that this basic rule gives no guidance as to what should be done if a will is found, duly executed, but containing alterations – provisions crossed out with new provisions inserted. The new provisions will be valid if they were made before the will was executed; how is anyone to tell whether they were or not?

It may be noted, but as an exception only, that r 14(2) of the 1987 Non-Contentious Probate Rules allows a registrar to grant probate of a will including any unattested alterations without evidence that the alterations were made before execution, if the alteration appears to him or her to be 'of no practical importance'.

### 8.1.1 Alterations before execution

A finding as to whether an alteration was made before or after execution may begin with the application of presumptions. These presumptions are, as always, rebuttable; they will give a basis for a preliminary assumption, but if there is evidence to the contrary, that may overcome the presumption.

## 8.1.2 Time of alteration

The rebuttable presumption is that an unattested alteration (one which has not itself been executed) was made after the execution of the will or codicil it is contained in. In practice, small alterations are often made before execution – the testator, having approved the will, may only notice a misspelling of a beneficiary's name when he or she arrives at the solicitor's office to execute the will – but where substantial amendments have to be made, a professional adviser will have the will prepared afresh. If alterations are made before execution, it is the practice for the testator and witnesses to initial each alteration. It is then clear from the face of the will that the alteration existed before the will was executed. Extrinsic evidence, such as the statements of the witnesses, as to the circumstances of the execution, as well as the internal evidence of the contents of the will itself, may also be admitted in disputed cases.

## 8.1.3 Presumption of alteration after execution rebutted by internal evidence

There may also be other types of internal evidence which will rebut the presumption of alteration after execution. Where the will does not make sense without the alteration, it may therefore be found that the alteration was made before execution. In *Birch v Birch* (1848), the alterations consisted of filling in blanks which the draughtsman of the will had left for the amounts of legacies. It was held that the blanks had been filled in before execution. The alterations in *In the Goods of Cadge* (1868) consisted of interlineations in the same ink as the rest of the will. Without them, the will was unintelligible. It was held that they were made before execution and were therefore valid.

## 8.1.4 Due execution of alterations

If an alteration made after the will was executed is itself executed in accordance with the usual formalities for a will (as contained in s 9 of the Wills Act 1837), it will be valid. The alteration may be attested by the testator and witnesses signing by the alterations, usually in the margin, or by their adding a memorandum, itself attested, referring to the alterations.

## 8.1.5 What constitutes due execution of an alteration?

The cases on what constitutes due execution of an alteration show that the formalities must be adhered to strictly. In *Re Dewell* (1853), the testator inserted a small amendment after execution and acknowledged the document as his will, and the witnesses initialled the amendment. The execution of the amendment was accepted and the alteration admitted to probate. In *Re Shearn* (1880), however, the testatrix similarly discovered a small omission immediately after execution and inserted it by interlineation, acknowledging the document as her will to the two witnesses who then initialled in the margin near the interlineation. In that case, the court held that the alteration had not been duly executed because the testatrix had not signed it nor, before the witnesses signed, acknowledged her signature of the whole will as such to them.

## 8.1.6 'Not apparent' – revocation of part by obliteration

Alterations which make a part of the will 'not apparent' revoke that part of the will, provided that it can be shown that the testator intended by obliterating that part of the will to render it ineffective. As with revocation of a whole will by destruction, for revocation of part of a will by obliteration – since that is what this form of alteration amounts to – to be effective, there must be both the mental element of sufficient intention and the physical element of sufficient obliteration.

## 8.1.7 Examining the altered part – has it been made 'not apparent'?

Section 21 of the Wills Act 1837 foresees that some alterations may make part of the will not apparent, and provides that in those circumstances such a part will be revoked even if the alteration was not duly executed. This means not apparent on the face of the will itself.

Two related questions then arise – how far does the testator have to go to make the previous provision 'not apparent', and how far do the personal representatives and the court go in trying to establish whether the old provision is apparent or not?

Following the death of the testatrix in *Re Adams (deceased)* (1990), her will was found scribbled on, with the signatures of the witnesses and the testatrix heavily scored with a ball-point pen. It was shown that she had intended to revoke the will. The court held that making the signatures not apparent in this way was sufficient to revoke the will.

## 8.1.8 Investigating and deciding

The question must then arise of what methods may or should be used in trying to work out what was written before the alteration took place. The cases have established what methods may be used to try to decipher the altered part. Any 'natural means' of discovering what the words are will be admissible, which appears to include anything which does not involve interfering physically with the will or making another document. If the original wording can be deciphered by natural means, it will be valid.

The testator in *Ffinch v Combe* (1894) had attempted to obliterate some of the words in the will, after execution, by pasting slips of paper over them. It was held proper to try to read them by holding the paper up against the light framed with brown paper around the pasted-on slips. A decision on the same facts – indeed, the same will – in *In the Goods of Horsford* (1874) held that physically interfering with the will by removing the slips of paper was unacceptable.

For more on what happens when something has gone wrong and common form probate is unlikely to be appropriate, see also Chapter 16.

## 8.1.9 Borderline between natural means and other means

It is difficult to define where the borderline lies between natural means, which may be used to see whether words are 'not apparent', and other means, which may not. It might at first sight appear to be the doing of any acts that require any equipment. However, in *Ffinch v Combe* (1894) (8.1.8), the light from a window was used, but increased in effect by framing the will with brown paper, which itself might be considered an interference involving the use of equipment. The use of magnifying glasses was held to be permissible in *In the Goods of Brasier* (1899). An infra-red photograph showing the wording beneath a pasted-on strip of paper was, however, held inadmissible in *Re Itter* (1950) (8.1.12).

There is no case to say whether the functions of an infra-red machine might be considered in the same light, as it were, as those of a magnifying glass, if the court were invited to look at the image directly rather than on a second document.

Altering – as opposed to clarifying – what means could be used to establish whether or not words have been made 'not apparent' could, however, alter the burden on testators when making obliterations. If any method could be used to decipher obliterated words, rather than just 'natural means', then the likelihood of the testator being able to tell whether or not they had sufficiently obliterated words would diminish greatly. Perhaps the answer lies in an unspoken inference that testators have magnifying glasses, but not infra-red machines.

**Alterations**

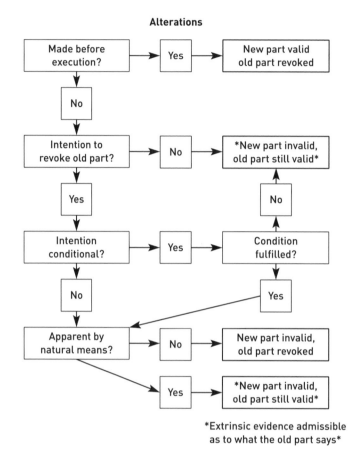

*Extrinsic evidence admissible
as to what the old part says*

## 8.1.10 Alteration without intention

As with the revocation of the whole of a will by destruction, it is necessary for both elements, the physical element of obliteration and the mental element of intention, to be present. Accidents do not suffice. If the obliteration was not deliberate, it will be necessary to establish what the provisions were so as to have them admitted to probate. This will also apply where the testator, though they had an intention that the obliteration should revoke the relevant part of the will, had only a conditional intention, and the condition was not satisfied.

## 8.1.11 Alteration with conditional intention

In the circumstances of both revocation of a will by destruction and revocation of part of a will by obliteration, the necessary physical acts may be accompanied only by a conditional intention. If there is no true intention to revoke, the revocation will not be valid. Thus, if conditional intention applies, and the condition on which the intention is based is not fulfilled, the word obliterated must be ascertained so that it can be admitted to probate.

## 8.1.12 Evidence

In these circumstances, a wide range of methods may be used to determine what the obliterated part said. The court is seeking not to decide whether the words on the will before the alteration are apparent or not – it may well be very clear that they are not apparent, just as it is very clear in the case of a will which has been burnt without being revoked that one cannot read what was in it – but to discover what the words were.

The question of whether the intention to revoke was conditional is one of fact. The admissible evidence of that also includes direct extrinsic evidence – direct evidence of the testator's intention which comes from outside the will – as to the testator's declarations of intention.

The testator in *In the Goods of McCabe* (1873) made a gift by will to his niece, believing the niece's mother to be dying. However, the mother recovered, and the testator substituted her as the beneficiary of the gift. The court admitted evidence of what the testator had declared to be his intention and it was held that the obliteration of the niece's name was conditional and her name was admitted to probate. This contrasts with *Townley v Watson* (1844) where an attempt to call the draughtsman of a will to give evidence as to what the words which had been obliterated were, failed. Sir H Jenner Fust said the construction which the courts had put on 'apparent' was 'apparent on inspection of the instrument itself'.

The testator in *In the Goods of Itter* (1950) attempted to substitute a different legacy for the one he had first made, though he did not attempt to change the legatee. The previous provisions could not be discovered except by the making of another document, in this case an infra-red photograph. That was unacceptable in the context of deciding whether the previous words were 'not apparent' and, since the infra-red photograph was not admitted, the words could not be deciphered and were indeed not apparent. The court held, however, that the intention to revoke the first legacy was conditional on the validity of the substituted legacy; the doctrine of conditional revocation applied. Extrinsic evidence such as the infra-red photograph was then admissible to discover what the previous words had been; the infra-red photograph was then admitted so the court could tell what words should be admitted to probate.

## 8.1.13 Deliberative and final alterations

Alterations before execution will not be valid if they are deliberative rather than final. There is a rebuttable presumption that pencil alterations are deliberative and ink ones final. In *Hawkes v Hawkes* (1828), it was said that each presumption is all the stronger if there are both pencil and ink alterations.

## 8.1.14 Alterations to privileged wills

There is a presumption that, if an alteration has been made to a privileged will, it was made while the testator was still able to make a privileged will. Such an alteration will therefore not be liable to fail for want of compliance with the formalities for execution laid down in s 9 of the Wills Act 1837.

# 8.2 Republication

'Publication' of a will originally meant a declaration by the testator, in the presence of witnesses, that the instrument produced to them was their will. The requirement that a will be published in this way in order to be valid was abolished by s 13 of the Wills Act 1837. It is still reflected, however, in the name of the doctrine of republication. When republication is talked about in practice, it may be called 'confirmation', reflecting the fact that the testator is making a later affirmation of the validity and contents of their will. Republication, or confirmation, occurs when a will is re-executed with the proper formalities. It may also be effected by codicil, and this is a fairly common occurrence.

Republication differs from revival (8.3) in that revival, if successful, brings back a revoked will or codicil, whereas republication confirms an unrevoked will or codicil.

There are two methods of republication:

(a)   re-execution with the proper formalities;
(b)   by a duly executed codicil containing some reference to the will or codicil to be republished.

## 8.2.1 Intention to republish

The testator must have intended to republish the will, but a very low standard of proof is required, so that it may appear more accurate to say that all that is required is a reference to the will and a court will then infer the intention. It has been found that merely referring to the codicil as being a codicil to a will identified by its date shows sufficient intention to republish the will. In *Re JC Taylor* (1888), a codicil which described itself as 'codicil to my will' was held to be sufficient to republish the will. A will is, however, commonly republished more emphatically by the testator making a codicil to a specified will, the new provisions being followed by some words such as 'in all other respects I confirm my said will'. In that situation, there is no room for doubt about the testator's intention.

It may be possible to show, by a codicil, that a testator was treating the will as unaltered. The testatrix in *Re Hay* (1904) struck out three legacies in a will, but the alteration by which she did this was unattested. Later, she made a codicil revoking only one of them. It was held that the other two legacies stood, as the testatrix's codicil was held to confirm her will without the alterations.

## 8.2.2 Effects of republication

Republication alters the date at which the will takes effect, so that it is no longer the original date of execution, but the date of republication. Before 1837, a will could not dispose of realty acquired after its own date, so a gift, for example, of 'all my real estate' would refer only to the real estate the testator had at the date of making the will. It was therefore necessary for a testator to update even the most generally worded of wills whenever they acquired any real property. If there had been no other developments of significance which justified making a new will, the desired effect could be achieved by simply republishing the will. The situation now is that, subject to contrary intention, the will speaks as to property from the date of death. Where a will is republished, that will validate a final alteration made after the previous execution but before the later one.

## 8.2.3 Time of alterations

Republication of an altered will by codicil will not, however, assist in validating the alterations in the will unless it can be shown that the alterations were made before the execution of the codicil. The presumption will still be that the alterations were made after execution. However, that presumption may of course be rebutted. The testator's will in *In the Goods of Heath* (1892) showed interlineations, but the court looked at the wording of the codicil and held that the interlineations in the will had been made before the codicil.

## 8.2.4 Date from which a republished will speaks

The general rule is that a will speaks from the date of the testator's death as to property and from its own date as to persons, save where there is contrary intention in the will (see 11.19–11.21). If a contrary intention is found so that a gift is held to be a specific gift of property which the testator had at the time of making the will, but which they no longer have at the date of death, the gift will fail by ademption (see 10.7).

Section 34 of the Wills Act 1837 deals with wills that are re-executed or revived as well as republished. It says that such a will is deemed for the purposes of the Wills Act to have been made at the time of its re-execution, revival or republication. A republished will operates, generally, as if it had been executed at the time of its republication.

This is, however, only a general rule, and will not be applied so as to defeat the testator's intentions. In *Re Moore* (1907), Barton J said:

> The authorities … lead me to the conclusion that the courts have always treated the principle that republication makes the will speak as if it had been re-executed at the date of the codicil not as a rigid formula or technical rule, but as a useful and flexible instrument for effectuating a testator's intentions, by ascertaining them down to the latest date at which they have been expressed.

## 8.2.5 No republication where change of date would defeat the testator's intention

As has been shown above, the intention to republish the will is readily inferred. In *Re Heath* (1949), however, a testator had executed a will containing a clause of a kind which it later became impossible validly to include, making a gift to his daughter with restrictions which could not be created after 1936. The relevant date was that of execution of the will. The court was asked to make a finding as to whether the testator had republished his will by his later codicil, because if he had then the clause would have been invalid. The court held that a finding that the original will had been republished would defeat the testator's intention and accordingly held that it had not.

## 8.2.6 Date of republication and objects of gifts

Generally, however, the effect of republishing the will is to make it speak from the date of republication. Persons referred to in it will be ascertained by reference to the date of republication, as, for example, in the case of *Re Hardyman* (1925), where the testatrix made a gift to her cousin's wife. The will was republished after the death of the wife who was alive at the time of the execution of the will, so at that time there was no specific person for it to refer to. Subsequently, the cousin remarried, and on the death of the testatrix it was held that the words used referred to the second wife, on the basis that, given there was no particular individual fulfilling that description at the date of republication, the reference must be taken to be any wife of the cousin.

Note, however, that by virtue of the provisions of s 1(7) of the Family Law Reform Act 1969, republication after 1969 does not mean that references to 'children' made before that date will change their effect as regards illegitimate children. Although the effect of s 15 of the 1969 Act was to include within the definition of 'children' all children, whether legitimate or illegitimate, unless a contrary intention appeared, s 1(7) specifically excludes from this any will or codicil executed before that Act came into force on 1 January 1970, even though the will or codicil was republished by codicil after that date.

### 8.2.7 Date of republication and subject matter of gifts

Where a will is republished by a codicil, the date from which it speaks is that of the codicil. In *Goonewardene v Goonewardene* (1931), the Privy Council considered a case from Ceylon (Sri Lanka) where a will had been republished by codicil and, if the relevant date for ascertaining gifts was that of the codicil, the wife would take money and property under a life interest determinable on marriage rather than absolutely. Lord Russell said:

> It is well settled in England that by virtue of s.34, English Wills Act, the effect of confirming a Will by codicil is to bring the Will down to the date of the codicil and to effect the same disposition of the testator's property as would have been effected if the testator had at the date of the codicil made a new will containing the same disposition as in the original will but with the alterations introduced by the codicil.

It is not clear whether republication can operate to save a specific gift which would otherwise fail by ademption. In *Re Galway* (1950), the testator had previously devised land, republishing the will after the Coal Act 1938 came into force, bringing with it a right to compensation for the assets nationalised under it. The nationalisation removed some of the testator's interests in his land from his estate, but the republication of the will was held not to pass the compensation for the gift itself, which had failed through ademption. In *Re Harvey* (1947), republication of the will after the asset had changed its legal nature saved the gift. The testator had made a will in 1912 which included an undivided share in land. By 1926, this had become personalty under s 35 of the Law of Property Act 1925 (between 1926 and 1997, land held on a statutory trust for sale, as arose in all cases of joint ownership, was liable to be regarded technically as subsisting in personalty, because of the operation of the doctrine of conversion; this was partially abolished by s 3 of the Trusts of Land and Appointment of Trustees Act 1996, so that these interests were then held as realty). A codicil of 1927 which merely confirmed the cancellation of an earlier will was held sufficient to republish the will and preclude ademption. This might be considered the converse of the decision in *Re Hardyman* (8.2.6).

### 8.2.8 Republication of will with general revocation clause – effect on codicils

If a will is republished which contains a general revocation clause, this does not operate to revoke any earlier codicil to that will, even though logically it might appear to do so because the will, now speaking from a date later than that of the codicil, revokes all previous testamentary dispositions. In *In the Goods of Rawlins* (1879), however, the court held that 'prima facie the re-execution of the will is a confirmation and not a revocation of the codicil, which became part of the instrument'.

### 8.2.9 Republication and s 15 of the Wills Act 1837

If a will contains a gift which is invalid because the will was witnessed by the donee or their spouse, the republication of that will by a codicil with other witnesses will validate the gift.

### 8.2.10 Republication – a trap for the solicitor?

It is clear from this that the implications of republishing a will are very great. Wills are frequently republished, however, by their confirmation in a codicil, and this is often done without careful examination – or even any examination – of whether the effect of their clauses will be altered by the change in date. There are no cases reported of actions for compensation by disappointed

beneficiaries who have lost out unexpectedly through the operation of the rules relating to republication where the courts have not applied their ingenuity to saving gifts. This does not, however,
mean, that there is no such case waiting to happen.

# 8.3 Revival

Section 22 of the Wills Act 1837 provides two ways for a will or codicil to be revived. Any part
of a will or codicil which has been revoked may be revived by the testator, provided that it still
exists and has not been destroyed. The methods available are:

(a)    re-execution with the proper formalities;
(b)    by a duly executed codicil showing an intention to revive the earlier document.

## 8.3.1 Revocation of a revoking document does not revive

If the first will is revoked by a second will, revocation of the second will does not revive the first
one. This was demonstrated in In the Goods of Hodgkinson (1893), where the testator had made a first
will giving all his property to his dear friend Jane. He later made a second will giving his realty to
his sister Emma. This impliedly revoked the first will so far as the gift in the first will consisted of
realty. The testator then revoked the second will by destruction. The Court of Appeal was asked
to decide whether the revocation of the second will to Emma had effectively revived the gift of
realty to Jane in the first will. It held that the testator's realty would pass on intestacy because the
revocation of the second will did not revive the part of the first will that had been impliedly
revoked.

## 8.3.2 Intention: no inference of an intention to revive

There is a greater burden of proof of intention to be satisfied for revival than for republication;
there must be much more than a mere reference to the will. The court will enquire into the testator's intention and will not infer it. The court in In the Goods of Steele (1868) was dealing with a
codicil; it was asked how much intention to revive must be shown in the codicil for the revival to
be effective. It held that the intention must

> appear on the face of the codicil, either by express words referring to a will as revoked and
> importing an intention to revive the same, or by a disposition of the testator's property incon-
> sistent with any other intention, or by some other expressions conveying to the mind of the
> court, with reasonable certainty, the existence of the intention in question.

The court in Marsh v Marsh (1860) held that an intention to revive must, since the Wills Act 1837,
appear from the codicil itself, and could not be established from any act dehors (outside) the
codicil such as merely tying the codicil to the revoked will, as in that case.

## 8.3.3 Admissibility of evidence

Extrinsic evidence may be admissible in construing a codicil. The testator in In the Goods of Davis
(1952) made a will giving all his property to one Ethel Phoebe Horsley, a lady who was not his
wife. A year later he married her, thus revoking the will. Subsequently, he wrote 'The herein
named Ethel Phoebe Horsley is now my lawful wedded wife' on the envelope containing the
will, signed what he had written and had it attested. Ethel's sister gave evidence that she had

pointed out to him that the marriage had revoked the will just before he made the writing. The court held that writing on the envelope amounted to a codicil showing the testator's intention to revive the will, declaring itself baffled as to what other intention the deceased could possibly have had except to revive the will.

### 8.3.4 Effects of revival

Section 34 of the Wills Act 1837 provides that a revived will is deemed for the purposes of the Act to have been made at the time of its revival. If there is a partial revocation of a will followed by a revocation of the whole will, a subsequent revival does not extend to the part first revoked unless an intention to the contrary can be shown. Note that revival may validate an attested alteration made before the revival, or may incorporate a document which came into existence after the first execution of the will or codicil but before the revival.

## 8.4 Summary of Chapter 8

### 8.4.1 Alteration, Republication and Revival

Alterations made after execution are not valid. The will should be proved as it was at the time of execution.

If, however intentional alterations made after execution have made the old words of the will not apparent by natural means, they will effectively have revoked those words.

Alterations made after execution which are not intentional will not be effective, and the same applies to alterations made with a conditional intention where the condition is not satisfied. Where such an alteration is made, then the old words remain valid and extrinsic evidence may be admitted to discover what they are.

It is presumed – subject to rebuttal – that alterations to privileged wills were made while the testator was still privileged.

A will which has been republished or revived is deemed by s 34 of the Wills Act 1837 to have been made at the time of its republication or revival.

A will which is valid may be republished by re-execution in accordance with the formalities or by being confirmed by a duly executed codicil referring to it. The result will be that the effective date of the original will becomes the date of republication, save in certain cases where that would defeat the testator's original intention. Alterations which can be shown to have been made before republication will therefore be validated even if they were made after the date of the original execution.

A will which has been revoked may be revived if s 22 of the Wills Act is complied with. It will not be revived by revocation of the document which revoked it, though the expectation that it will may make the second revocation conditional on a condition which is not satisfied. Revival will validate alterations made after the original execution in the same way as republication.

# Chapter 9

# Intestate Succession

A person who dies without leaving a valid will is said to be intestate; a person who leaves a valid will which fails to deal with all their property is said to be partially intestate. There are rules of law governing what happens to a person's property in either situation. Intestacy was an abomination to the Christian church in the centuries when English succession law was establishing itself;[1] the courts still strain to avoid any intestacy when interpreting wills (see Chapter 11).

Many people have particular ideas about what will happen if they die intestate, and sometimes fail to make a will for that reason. For example, they often have the impression that their spouse or civil partner, if they are married or in a civil partnership, will inherit everything they have when they die. This will not necessarily be the situation if they have a substantial estate – in some cases, that may just mean a family house – and also leave children. Despite this, anything up to two-thirds of people in England and Wales have no will, so the law is of considerable practical relevance.[2]

## 9.1 General structure of the intestacy rules

The rules of distribution on intestacy are supposed to give the intestate's family something akin to what the legislators believe the deceased would have left them had they made a will. Broadly, this has for some time meant that any surviving spouse gets the deceased's personal goods and a substantial sum of money; the next claim on the estate is that of the deceased's children, and some other less close relatives may be provided for. In recent decades the rules have moved towards a greater favouring of the surviving spouse, though this has not yet gone as far as the Law Commission would like.

### 9.1.1 Historical background to the intestacy rules

Historically there were different provisions for realty and personalty. Realty devolved onto heirs – a word with a technical but historical meaning; who the heirs were had to be ascertained by a complex system, subject to curtesy or dower for the widow or widower (see 1.10). Personalty was governed until 1890 by the Statute of Distributions 1670, which allowed provision for a widow or widower, issue and next of kin according to degree.

The history of the rules of intestacy demonstrates the historic differences in the ownership of property resulting from the different legal and social roles of husbands and wives, but those differences have now been abolished at least so far as the letter of the law is concerned. The original provision of the Law of Property Act 1922 was that the spouse would be entitled to the first £1,000 of the intestate's estate; this was designed to give him or her the whole estate in the

---

1 Charles Gross, 'The Medieval Law of Intestacy' (1904) 18 Harvard Law Review 120.
2 Law Commission Consultation Paper 191, 2009 *Intestacy and Family Provision on Death*, para 1.4.

majority – 98 per cent – of cases. The basic current provisions are still those laid down in the Administration of Estates Act 1925, although they have been amended and the spouse (or, now, civil partner's) entitlement increased by subsequent legislation. The previous distinctions between the devolution of personalty and realty have also been abolished and new categories of entitled persons have been set up.

The essential structure of the system of distribution set up in 1925 was for the first claim on the intestate's estate to be any surviving spouse, whose entitlement included the personal chattels of the deceased and then an additional sum – originally £1,000. If there were surviving children as well, the remainder of the estate was held as to half for the spouse for his or her lifetime and otherwise on the statutory trusts for the children. There were provisions for the claims of parents, siblings and other more distant relatives. This system was described by Lord Cairns as 'a will made by the legislature for the intestate' and based on the presumed intentions of the deceased. It has been suggested that the stirpital construction of gifts – that where grandchildren take in the place of their parents who have predeceased, they take a proportionate part of their parent's share, not so much per grandchild – is inconsistent with this presumption, as most people would divide their property according to the number of recipients.

One commentator has described the evolution of intestacy law in Scotland as well as England as having changed from a pre-twentieth-century family-based, dynastic model that preserved the estate for successive generations to a modern one focused on the interests of the spouse or civil partner, with current reforms abandoning the idea of the deceased's 'presumed intention' in favour of the outcome of public opinion surveys and whatever seems simple and administratively efficient.[3] Instead, she suggests that it should favour the most economically vulnerable, such as aged spouse or civil partners, minors and disabled adults. Others regard such public surveys as legitimately supporting provision on the model of the nuclear family, but with the inclusion in that definition of subsequent partners and cohabitants, whilst protecting the children of previous relationships, demonstrating shared ideas of commitment, dependency and support, and a sense of lineage.[4] The economic environment has also changed, and the rise in both house prices and home ownership mean that people are more likely to find the intestacy rules do not make the arrangement they would expect; nevertheless one-third of people in England and Wales still die intestate.[5]

## 9.1.2 The Morton Committee Report 1951 and the Intestates' Estates Act 1952

Intestacy law was substantially reviewed in 1951, after the Morton Committee reported on the state of the law of intestate succession. It made four basic recommendations:

(a)  an increase in the fixed entitlement for the spouse on intestacy;
(b)  a right for the spouse to retain the matrimonial home;
(c)  the avoidance of life interests in small estates;
(d)  the extension of the family provision legislation to totally intestate estates.

As a result, the Intestates' Estates Act 1952 was passed. The spouse's statutory legacy was increased, but s 49(1)(aa) of the Administration of Estates Act 1925, since repealed, was introduced to compensate for this. It required the spouse to bring into account benefits received under the will on a partial intestacy (see 9.10).

---

3  Fiona Burns, 'Surviving Spouse or Civil Partners, Surviving Children and the Reform of Total Intestacy Law in England and Scotland: Past, Present and Future' (2013) 33 Legal Studies 85.
4  Gillian Douglas, Hilary Diana Woodward, Alun Humphrey, Lisa Mills and Gareth Morrell, 'Enduring Love: Attitudes to Family and Inheritance Law in England and Wales' (2011) 38 Journal of Law and Society 245.
5  Law Commission, *Inheritance and Family Provision Claims on Death* (2011) para 1.3.

### 9.1.3 Law Commission Report No 187 (1989)

In 1989, the Law Commission made several suggestions for improving the system in its Report No 187 *Family Law: Distribution on Intestacy*. It recommended:

(a)     that a surviving spouse or civil partner should receive the whole estate;
(b)     that the hotchpot rules (see 9.5 and 9.8) should be abolished;
(c)     that a person should have to survive the deceased by 14 days in order to inherit from their estate on their intestacy.

The Law Commission thought that the administration of estates would be 'easier, cheaper and shorter' without the inconvenience of life interests, even if in some situations they answered a need for provision very well. The position of cohabitants was already causing concern as cohabitation was becoming commonplace and acknowledged, but cohabitants had no particular interests on intestacy. The Law Commission did not recommend that cohabitants should have any automatic rights, but it did suggest changes to the family provision rules (albeit this was outside their brief) to make it easier for them to bring a claim. Survivorship provisions were brought in separately in 1996 (see 9.2.5).

### 9.1.4 Law Commission Report No 331 (2011) and the Inheritance and Trustees' Powers Act 2014

In October 2009, the Law Commission issued a public consultation on *Intestacy and Family Provision Claims on Death*.[6] It took into account public attitude surveys and also the practices of other countries, and proposed keeping the spouse or civil partner's entitlement to the personal chattels, but simplifying the existing definition of them. They also proposed that the surviving spouse or civil partner should inherit the whole estate where there were no children or remoter descendants of the deceased. A proposal that the spouse or civil partner should also inherit everything even where there were children, however, provoked concern for the children of a deceased's earlier relationship where they had later remarried or entered into a civil partnership.

The Law Commission was particularly concerned about the lack of any automatic entitlement on intestacy for cohabitants where there was no formal marriage or civil partnership, however long they had been together and regardless of whether they had children together. Reform was suggested to bring English law on intestacy closer to the regime that already applied in fatal accident cases and also in other Commonwealth jurisdictions, recognising cohabitation after a certain period. They suggested that the test should be whether a couple had lived together continuously for five years or had a child together. Cohabitants were not to get the deceased's personal chattels but could choose items up to the value of their statutory sum. They also suggested that cohabitants of two to five years' standing should be entitled to half the amount a spouse or civil partner would get.

Other issues that concerned them were:

● the preference for parents over siblings and for full siblings (children of the same parents) over half-siblings (those sharing one parent but not the other)
● the loss of inheritance from their birth parents by children who were later adopted
● the fact that unmarried fathers could not inherit from deceased children
● who should pay the costs of tracing missing relatives.

---

6  Law Commission Consultation Paper No 191 (2009). A supplementary paper to this was issued in May 2011, looking at trustees' powers under ss 31 and 32 Trustee Act 1925 to deal with children's money held on the statutory trusts.

The final report was published in December 2011 and two parliamentary bills followed. One eventually became the Inheritance and Trustees' Powers Act 2014, which came into force on 1 October 2014 and affects deaths from that date. An Inheritance (Cohabitants) Bill related solely to cohabitants' claims, and has not yet, as at the time of writing, been passed. However, it would extend the spouse's or civil partner's statutory entitlement to cohabitants of five years' standing, the period being only two years if the couple have a child together who is living them at the deceased's death.

In relation to intestacy (it also covers family provision, for which see Chapter 15, and some trust powers), the 2014 Act therefore provided principally that where the deceased left no issue, the surviving spouse or civil partner would take the whole estate, but if there is issue, then after the personal chattels and the statutory legacy, the spouse or civil partner takes one-half of the balance of the estate absolutely – previously the spouse or civil partner had taken that half for life only, so receiving income or interest rather than the capital outright. The 2014 also amends the definition of 'personal chattels' in s 55(1)(x) of the Administration of Estates Act 1925.

## 9.2  Disadvantages of relying on the intestacy rules

Although the idea persists that the intestacy rules represent more or less what a testator would be expected to provide for by will, a person who appreciates their effects is very likely to want to make a will in order to avoid them. Apart from the dictation of who would receive the property in the estate, intestacy means the deceased has not chosen whom they wish to appoint to deal with their property when they die; in many cases the lack of express powers in relation to administering the estate can create practical difficulties. Although the situation is better since the ITPA 2014 as the powers of personal representatives and trustees are wider, it is also usually still preferable for the testator to be able to make administrative provisions by will.

As no one can be sure when they will die or how much property they will have when it happens, not making a will means a lack of control over their property, which may have unpredictable consequences. For example, the intestate may leave more property than is covered by the entitlement of a joint home-owner, and the house may have to be sold if the co-owner cannot raise enough to buy out the other interests. Intestate estates also attract liability to inheritance tax just as any other estate does, but by failing to make a will the deceased has lost the chance to organise their affairs so as to minimise the liability to tax.

### 9.2.1  Administering the estate

Where there is a valid will appointing executors, they take their authority from the will and so there are people to deal with the estate from the moment of the testator's death, but where the deceased died intestate there has to be some provision of law because no one has authority to deal with the estate until they are granted authority to administer it by the court.[7] The personal representatives in the case of an intestate estate are called administrators and they are required to deal with the estate in accordance with the rules of intestacy. They do not have a discretion to do what they think the deceased wanted; if the deceased did not want the intestacy rules to operate, he or she should have made a will. The rules cannot be varied: a Canadian testator attempted to exclude the rules by making a will stating that he did not wish his separated wife to benefit from his estate, but as he failed to make any alternative provisions in his will, she took under the intestacy rules anyway (*Re Snider* (1974)). An estate may be partially intestate where the will does not

---

7  Sometimes for example a bank will release a sum without a grant, especially if it is to be used to pay funeral expenses, but they do not have to. See Administration of Estates (Small Payments) Act 1965.

deal with all the deceased's property, though any well-drafted will should contain provisions that ensure every feasible eventuality is covered. To avoid intestacy in the event of complete disaster, it could be borne in mind that a gift over the charity will never fail.

On the death of an intestate, their property used to vest, by operation of law, in the President of the Family Division of the High Court pending a grant of letters of administration. The property remained legally vested in that person until the grant, and did not pass with his or her office. The Law Commission, in its Report No 184 *Property Law: Title on Death* (1989), recommended a change to this rule, and this was implemented by s 14 of the Law of Property (Miscellaneous Provisions) Act 1994, so that s 9 of the Administration of Estates Act 1925 now provides that the property of an intestate is vested in the Public Trustee until the grant of administration, when it passes to the administrators.

## 9.2.2 Statutory trusts – s 33 of the Administration of Estates Act 1925

Where person dies intestate as to any property, that property will eventually be held by their personal representatives under s 33 of the Administration of Estates Act 1925 on trust, with a power to sell. Note that particular rules were brought in under the Intestates' Estates Act 1952 relating to the house in which the intestate's spouse was living when the intestate died (not quite the same thing as a matrimonial home for the purposes of divorce matters). Schedule 2, para 4(1) says that whatever interest the intestate had in that house must not be sold without the resident spouse or civil partner's consent until 12 months have elapsed from the first grant of representation to the estate, unless there is no other way of finding the money to pay for the administration of the estate. However, this has not been a frequent problem.

## 9.2.3 Administrators and distribution of the estate

The administrators hold the proceeds of the sale to be distributed in accordance with the provisions of s 46 of the Administration of Estates Act 1925, after payment of funeral, testamentary and administration expenses, debts and other liabilities of the estate. Where there is a partial intestacy they also hold the fund subject to the legacies in the will. Therefore, in the usual way, no one, including the deceased's spouse or civil partner, can receive anything from the estate by operation of the intestacy rules unless all the payments under those categories have first been satisfied in full.

## 9.3 Entitlements on intestacy

Though the details of the entitlements can be quite complex, it is first of all useful to consider their basic shape. This has developed over time and has very recently been changed by the Inheritance and Trustees' Powers Act 2014, but the essential structure remains as described above – provision first of all for any surviving spouse or civil partner and then for any surviving children. After that a wider circle of relatives, including parents and siblings, may inherit. If there are none of those then the estate will go to the government, who will advertise the fact. An interesting illustration of what might occur in the last kind of case may be found in *Treasury Solicitor v Doveton and Trixilis* (2008), a well-crafted tale of the Treasury Solicitor's dogged pursuit of an interloper who saw such an advertisement indicating that the deceased had no family to inherit – or raise a dispute – and then 'found' a will in his favour.

### 9.3.1 Surviving spouse or civil partner – definition

The definition is the lawfully married spouse alive at the death, or the equivalent civil partner. Thus, this will not include a divorced spouse or a civil partner where the partnership has been formally ended, nor anyone whose marriage or civil partnership is null and void. Nor will it include a judicially separated spouse or civil partner; because although judicially separated spouses or civil partners are still technically married or in a civil partnership, their marriage or civil partnership not having been dissolved, they are excluded from entitlement by s 18(2) of the Matrimonial Causes Act 1973. Provisions of this kind about judicially separated spouses date from 1970, and the equivalent for civil partnerships since their inception. Note that when a spouse or civil partner ceases to be entitled under the intestacy rules differs from when they cease to be entitled to gifts or to take up an appointment as executor in a will, in that for gifts by will the disentitlement applies only where the marriage or civil partnership has been dissolved or annulled.[8]

It is for the surviving spouse or civil partner to prove a valid marriage or civil partnership, but if they can show that a lawful ceremony was apparently concluded, then it will be for anyone disputing that to disprove its validity. They may be able to do so by showing the marriage was void for bigamy, for example, as occurred in *Re Peete* (1952), where the purported widow's evidence of the death of her first husband was disputed and rejected. Where, however, the dispute related to a defect in the formalities of the marriage proceedings, it was not clear whether the standard of proof was 'beyond reasonable doubt' (*Mahadervan v Mahadervan* (1962)) or merely 'firm and clear' (*Re Taylor* (1961)).

Polygamous marriages cannot legally be made in Britain, but those lawfully concluded abroad may be recognised: the Matrimonial Proceedings (Polygamous Marriages) Act 1972 allowed the parties to polygamous marriages to seek ancillary relief (such as property orders) in the English courts even if the marriage itself was void, and in *Re Sehota, Kaur v Kaur* (1978) the spouse of a polygamous marriage was held to be entitled to apply under s 1(1)(a) of the Inheritance (Provision for Family and Dependants) Act 1975 as a spouse of the deceased.[9] *Re Sehota* was adverted to in the intestacy case of *The Official Solicitor to the Senior Courts v Yemoh and Others* (2010). Benjamin Yemoh had died in 1981, domiciled in Ghana but owning two properties in London as well as having money in English bank accounts. He was intestate, and letters of administration were granted in 1985 in relation to his English estate. In 1996 proceedings were issued for guidance on the question of the entitlements of the deceased's polygamous spouses and their children. Seven of the eight women claimed to be his wives were readily accepted as such as a matter of law, and it was held that they should share the spouse's statutory legacy amongst themselves in equal shares. As this case predated the 2014 change which made the spouse or civil partner's half-interest in the remainder of the estate absolute (see 9.4.2 and 9.4.4), there was also a question about the treatment of what was then a life interest. The court held that where a polygamous widow had died after the deceased intestate, the spouse or civil partner's life interest in half the remainder should be held by the surviving widows until the death of the last of them to die, when it would fall in for the children.

In the Australian case of *Re Morrison* (1945), the intestate's widow was also his cousin. It was held that she took her entitlements on intestacy in both capacities. This could not arise under English law, however, since where there is a surviving spouse or civil partner, all those who might inherit with her have always been within the prohibited degrees of affinity. However, it is theoretically possible for a person to obtain two entitlements under the English intestacy rules; for example, a widower whose deceased wife was also his adopted sister may take in both capacities.

---

8  Section 18 of the Wills Act 1837, as amended by the Administration of Justice Act 1982 and the Civil Partnership Act 2004.
9  TC Hartley, 'Polygamy and Social Policy' (1969) 32 Modern Law Review 155.

## 9.3.2 Cohabiting couples who are not married or in a civil partnership

Cohabitants who are not married or in a civil partnership have no rights under the intestacy rules. They may of course have property rights arising independently of the relationship: for example, they may be joint tenants in equity of a property they owned together with the deceased, in which case they will be entitled by virtue of the right of survivorship to the deceased's share of the property. They may also set up, as may a spouse or civil partner, a claim in equity based on their contributions to a property in the sole name of the deceased, such as a claim under a resulting trust. The Law Commission in its Report No 187 of 1989 (see 9.1.3) did not suggest broadening the category of those entitled under the intestacy rules to include unmarried cohabitants, although they did suggest they should be able to establish a claim under the Inheritance (Provision for Family and Dependants) Act 1975 more easily than they could under that statute as it then stood (see 15.3), but they have suggested it more recently.

In some other jurisdictions, the intestacy rules do provide for cohabitants who are not married or in a civil partnership to take under the intestacy of their partners. In British Columbia, there is a discretionary allowance for 'common law spouse or civil partners'. In Queensland, the spouse or civil partner takes all the estate on intestacy (a recommendation made by the Law Commission here which has been rejected by the government), and 'spouse or civil partner' includes a cohabitant of two years' standing or a person living with the deceased intestate at death who is a parent of the intestate's child; where there is both an established cohabitant within these rules and a lawfully married or in a civil partnership spouse or civil partner, they share the estate as to half each.

The Law Commission has persistently recommended the introduction of automatic rights for cohabitants, but this has not so far appeared in legislation. There is difficulty both in policy – finding a consensus on when cohabitants should obtain quasi-marital rights – and in definition, since it is much more difficult to see whether the facts of a situation constitute cohabitation than it is to produce a marriage or civil partnership certificate. Such rights were not included in the Inheritance and Trustees' Powers Act 2014, which brought in many reforms also recommended in the same, most recent, Law Commission study. However, a bill was introduced by Lord Lester in 2012 that would give cohabitants rights on intestacy, and this or something like it is likely to be reintroduced in future.

## 9.3.3 Survivorship: principles

It used not to matter how long the spouse or civil partner survived the deceased; even if it were only for a few minutes, the property of the first to die would pass on their death. Thus, if intestate spouses were involved in a road accident, one being killed instantly and the other being found alive but dying on the way to hospital, the spouse entitlement would pass from the estate of the one killed immediately and then, within minutes, into the estate of the second to die. Thus, much of a person's estate might pass to someone else's family, for example, to parents-in-law, instead of perhaps to the deceased's own parents as they would have wished. Taken in conjunction with the *commorientes* (dying together) principles, this had potential for injustice as well as distress.

## 9.3.4 *Commorientes:* rules for who died first where people appear to die together

Sometimes it is not possible to tell who died first. Such a situation is clearly likely to occur in particular where spouses or civil partners are involved, since what is required for this difficulty to arise is people who are beneficiaries of each other's estates and who die together; this is likely to happen to people who travel together in cars or aeroplanes, or take extended holidays in far-flung places, as people do when they retire.

Wherever it cannot be told who died first, the *commorientes* rule (dying together) is applied. The rule under s 184 of the Law of Property Act 1925 is that where two persons die in circumstances in which it cannot be told who died first, there will be a presumption that the elder did.

However, an exception to this rule applied where the people in question were spouses or civil partners and the elder of them died intestate. In those circumstances, s 46(3) of the Administration of Estates Act 1925 provided instead that it should be deemed that the younger spouse or civil partner did not survive the older intestate. This prevented the scenario envisaged above from occurring where the couple were properly *commorientes*.

If, however, there was evidence, as in the example above, that one did survive the other even by a short period, neither the *commorientes* rule nor its exception applied. That exception to the rule was ended by the omission of s 46(3) AEA 1925 after the ITPA 2014 came into force. Therefore the exception applies to deaths before 1 October 2014, but not to deaths after 30 September 2014.

### 9.3.5 Survivorship

Where a person is making a will, they will usually make any gift conditional on the beneficiary surviving them by a specified period, usually 28 days or a calendar month (see 10.6.9). This makes it more likely that the beneficiary will take the property and be able to enjoy it rather than, as would be the case should the two die in quick succession, perhaps as a result of the same accident, the property passing from one to the other and then directly to the other's family.

On intestacy, however, there was, until recently (in succession law terms), no such provision, and there was a particular risk that the law would operate unfairly. For example, a couple might die as a result of a road accident, the wife being killed outright and her husband dying later in hospital. If the wife were intestate a large amount, or all, of her property would pass to her husband; it might then pass under his will to his family, with nothing going to her family at all even though her husband was unable to enjoy the property himself as the intestacy provisions would intend. The Law Commission investigated, and recommended a statutory survivorship period of 14 days, in relation to spouse or civil partners only, feeling that any longer period could cause too great a delay in the administration of an estate. However, the situation was rectified by the insertion of a survivorship period of 28 days, in relation to spouse or civil partners only, as s 46(1)(2A) of the Administration of Estates Act 1925 by s 1 of the Law Reform (Succession) Act 1995. This relates to deaths on or after 1 January 1996.

## 9.4 Spouse or civil partner entitlement

The surviving spouse or civil partner is entitled first of all to the personal chattels, as defined by s 55(1)(x) of the Administration of Estates Act 1925, and then to a fixed net sum if they are not entitled to the whole estate.

A spouse or civil partner is not necessarily automatically entitled to the whole of the estate of the deceased. The entitlement to the whole estate for deaths before October 2014 arose only where there were no children and also, for larger estates, no other specified relatives. For deaths after September 2014, spouse or civil partner entitlement to the whole estate on intestacy will arise if the spouse or civil partner survives and there are no issue (children or remoter descendants).

## 9.4.1 Personal chattels – s 55(1)(x) of the Administration of Estates Act (AEA) 1925

The definition of personal chattels before the changes made by the ITPA 2014 had been much criticised. Personal chattels were

> carriages, horses, stable furniture and effects (not used for business purposes), motor cars and accessories (not used for business purposes), garden effects, domestic animals, plate, plated articles, linen, china, glass, books, pictures, prints, furniture, jewellery, articles of household or personal use or ornament, musical and scientific instruments and apparatus, wines, liquors and consumable stores, but do not include any chattels used at the death of the intestate for business purposes nor money or securities for money.

It was often unclear what it meant and therefore difficult for a personal representative to be sure whether a particular item fell within it. The statutory definition excluded chattels used for business purposes, money, or securities for money, but otherwise reference often had to be made to past cases which were not intestacy cases but which nevertheless involved the definition of personal chattels. The earlier cases may continue to influence the reading of the new section.

In *Re Collins* (1971), a reference in a will to 'personal effects' was regarded as analogous to one referring to 'personal chattels'; the court went on to hold that the definition included collections of coins and stamps and a motor car. In *Re Crispin* (1975), the question was whether 'furniture' in the definition of 'personal chattels' included clocks maintained as a collection: the Court of Appeal said that since clocks fell within the relevant definition, it did not matter what use they were put to. But in *Re White* (1916) motor cars were held not to come within the definition of 'carriages' in the list provided by the section, though they were within the more general definition of articles of personal use. It was not, and apparently still is not, clear whether items subject to hire purchase agreements were included. New Zealand legislation expressly does so, but this throws no light on the subject, since it may mean either that decisions in this country would follow that principle by analogy or, conversely, that it is necessary for there to be an express provision for them to be included.

A relevant consideration was, however, the user of the item. If it was used for business purposes, even in part, it would not be a personal chattel within the meaning of the section. In *Re Ogilby* (1942), the deceased intestate's herd of cattle did not fall within the definition of personal chattels because they were used for farming purposes, even though they were a total failure as a business venture because they were farmed at a loss. The category of 'horses' was, however, held in *Re Hutchinson* (1955) to include racehorses, given that their use by the deceased was recreational rather than for business purposes.

In *Re Reynolds Will Trusts* (1966), the court called the section a 'curious collection of terms', and the court in *Re Chaplin* (1950) employed some spoof Latin to express its opinion that the wording was 'an omnium gatherum…. The enumeration of specific articles in the definition is neither happy nor clear'.

The definition of 'personal chattels' was changed by s 3 ITPA 2014. It now covers all tangible movable property except money or securities for money and property the deceased used solely or mainly for business purposes or held solely as an investment. Where the term 'personal chattels' is used in a will, the old definition will apply if the relevant will or codicil was executed before October 2014, so it may apply to the estates of those who die much later. In the context of intestacy, by definition, the new definition will apply from that date.

## 9.4.2 Fixed net sum

As well as the personal chattels, the spouse or civil partner is entitled to either the whole estate – if the deceased left no issue – or, if there is issue, a fixed sum (also called the statutory legacy) of up to £250,000 plus half any remainder of the estate. For deaths before October 2014, if there was no issue but certain other relatives survived the deceased, the fixed sum was £450,000, and where a spouse or civil partner took a half-interest in a remainder, it was a life interest only. The rest of the estate went to the issue on the statutory trusts, or to the other relatives absolutely.

The figures for the fixed sums were historically updated by order of the Lord Chancellor from time to time, but in fact quite rarely, and they do carry interest. The sum can be used to 'buy' the matrimonial home (see 9.6). Sudden uprating of the statutory legacy figures (for example, the increase in December 1993 was from £75,000 to £125,000 where there was issue and £125,000 to £200,000 where there was none) was felt by the Law Commission to lead to unacceptable discrepancies in the intestacy provisions relating to deaths either side of the relevant date, and to be a further good reason for providing that the surviving spouse or civil partner should take the whole estate. Following the implementation of the ITPA 2014, the Lord Chancellor will have to set the fixed net sum within 21 days of publication of the Consumer Prices Index figures if they have risen more than 15 per cent, and in any case to make an order at least every five years. The fixed net sum, under current legislation, can only go up, not down, even if there is deflation rather than inflation.[10]

In *Re Collens (deceased)* (1986), the court had to consider the question of how a spouse's rights under English law interacted with her rights under foreign law. In that case, the deceased died intestate in 1966, domiciled in Trinidad and Tobago, leaving a widow and several children from a previous marriage. His estate consisted of property in Trinidad and Tobago and Barbados as well as property in the UK, some of which was immovable. The widow accepted $1,000,000 in satisfaction of her rights in the Trinidad and Tobago estate. She also obtained one-third of the rest of the estate under the law of the deceased's domicile, which governed succession to movable property. She then also claimed the statutory legacy of (then) £5,000 under s 46 of the AEA 1925 in respect of the English estate. The court held that even if under s 46 of the AEA 1925 the residuary estate of the intestate meant all his worldwide property, it could only regulate succession to the deceased's immovable property in England and could not charge assets where succession to them was regulated by foreign law. Therefore s 46 could not regulate succession to the deceased's movable property because it was regulated by the law of the deceased's domicile. Thus, the charge on the English immovable assets could not be said to have been satisfied out of the overseas assets of the deceased. The widow's benefits in Trinidad and Tobago were obtained by virtue of the intestacy laws of Trinidad and Tobago or the deed of compromise in the proceedings, and did not satisfy the charge on the English immovable property. Therefore, the widow was entitled to the statutory legacy under English law.

## 9.4.3 Remainder of the estate where there is a surviving spouse or civil partner

The surviving spouse or civil partner who does not inherit the whole estate will always have an entitlement to more from the estate than the personal chattels and the fixed net sum – provided there is more! – but the amount and mode of their inheritance depends on whether other relatives of the deceased survived him or her.

From October 2014, if the deceased is survived by a spouse or civil partner but no issue, the spouse or civil partner takes the whole estate; if they are survived by issue as well as a spouse or

---

10 These figures date from February 2009. For more see Law Commission 331 *Intestacy and Family Provision Claims on Death*, para 2.6.

civil partner, the spouse or civil partner gets the personal chattels and £250,000 (assuming there is that much in the estate), and half any remainder; the other half goes to the issue. Before October 2014, after the fixed net sum, the spouse or civil partner would only get a life interest in half of the rest of the estate, with the other half, and the remainder of the spouse's half after their death, going to the children absolutely on their attaining 18. Having a life interest meant being able to use the interest or income from the money, but having no entitlement to the capital. After September 2014, the spouse or civil partner's half-share became an absolute entitlement.

If the deceased died leaving a spouse or civil partner, but no issue, but also leaving certain other relatives, before October 2014, the spouse or civil partner would get the personal chattels and a fixed net sum of £450,000, and half the remainder. The other relatives – for these purposes, first, parents or if none then siblings or their issue – would before October 2014 have taken the interest not taken by the spouse. After September 2014, in this situation, where there is a surviving spouse or civil partner and no issue, then regardless of what other relatives survive, the spouse or civil partner takes the whole estate. The specified other relatives take the estate if there is no surviving spouse or civil partner and no issue. For the specified other relatives, see 9.8.

## 9.4.4 Capitalisation of life interest (deaths before October 2014)
In relation to deaths before October 2014, the surviving spouse or civil partner was entitled only to a life interest in half the remainder after the statutory legacy; the remainder of that half, and the other half absolutely, went to the issue. The spouse or civil partner could capitalise their entitlement if they wished, provided it was in possession, rather than have it as income for the rest of their life. (If he or she was under 18, they could not receive the capital until they reached that age.) The provision enabling the capitalisation was inserted into the Administration of Estates Act 1925 by the Intestates Estates Act 1952, so that it was s 47A of the AEA 1925; it was governed by the Intestate Succession (Interest and Capitalisation) Order 1977, as amended in 2008, which set out how the figure for the capital sum was to be calculated. This was in essence the same system that an insurance company would use, based on interest rates and a calculation of how long the person was expected to live according to actuarial tables which would take into account, for example, age and other considerations. The surviving spouse or civil partner had to elect for this procedure within 12 months from the first grant, unless the court extended that period. The procedure for doing this was laid down in the Act, and requires them to give notice in writing, which they could retract only with the consent of the personal representatives. If the spouse or civil partner was him- or herself the sole personal representative, the notice had to be given to the Principal Registrar of the Family Division. The costs involved in this came out of the estate.

These rules still apply to deaths before October 2014, but under the ITPA 2014 s 47A (along with s 49 (4)) was removed. This was because the spouse or civil partner's half-interest in the remainder after her statutory legacy became absolute rather than a life interest – that is, there is no longer a life interest to capitalise.

## 9.4.5 Entitlement where neither spouse/civil partner nor issue
If the deceased left neither spouse or civil partner nor issue, there is a circle of more distant relatives who are entitled on intestacy: parents; siblings; half-siblings; grandparents; aunts and uncles; half-aunts and half-uncles. Anyone in these categories can claim, and only if there is no one in the category above them will they obtain anything. Thus, if a person dies intestate without leaving a spouse or civil partner or issue, their parents will take. However, if they leave no parents, their brothers and sisters will take. If they have no parents or siblings either, then their half-siblings will take, but if there are none of those either, then one looks to grandparents, and so on.

### 9.4.6 Where no spouse/civil partner, issue or specified other relatives

If there is no one available in any of these categories, the estate will go to the Crown as *bona vacantia* (literally: empty goods – belonging to no one). It will be administered by the Treasury Solicitor, who will particularly consider making a grant from the estate to a cohabitant, carer or charity that supported the deceased at considerable expense. Note the case of *Re Robson (deceased); White v Matthys* (2014), where the court directed payments to the deceased's sons after an ineffective gift to the British National Party (see 10.10).

## 9.5 Property rights claims

Persons entitled under the intestacy rules may have property interests in property owned by or together with the deceased. Their interests on intestacy arising from the relationship with the deceased will then be in addition to those property claims.

### 9.5.1 Jointly owned property

Often, the property will be in the joint names of the deceased and their spouse or civil partner. They must be joint tenants at law; the question of the passing of the deceased's beneficial interest will depend on whether they were joint tenants or tenants in common in equity. If the spouse or civil partner were joint tenants in equity, then the deceased's interest passes to their spouse or civil partner by operation of the right of survivorship or *jus accrescendi* and it never falls into the estate. The spouse or civil partner therefore receives the deceased's interest in the house, as well as their full entitlement under the intestacy rules, if they and the deceased were joint tenants. Only if a house jointly owned at law by the spouses or civil partners is held by them as tenants in common in equity will there be any question at all about whether the surviving spouse or civil partner can effectively keep the matrimonial home. If the deceased and the surviving spouse or civil partner were tenants in common in equity, the survivor may have to make such financial sacrifices in terms of losing their statutory legacy or even taking on extra debt to buy the deceased's share of the house that keeping the house and family going could become unaffordable. Many widowed spouses or civil partners are in no position to raise cash by way of mortgage because they have insufficient earning capacity and years of working life remaining to obtain a mortgage, or perhaps because they have the care of children and cannot take paid work.

### 9.5.2 Resulting or implied trusts

Even where the property is in the deceased's sole name, it may be possible to show that the surviving spouse or civil partner has obtained an entitlement to a share in the property by virtue of their own contributions. The types of contributions the courts are willing to countenance as giving rise to an interest in property in such circumstances varies, but a close consideration of the principles of such constructive trusts will not be made here. However, direct payments towards the purchase price, or the mortgage, generally give the payer an interest in the property despite there being neither legal title in them nor any written evidence of any trust arrangement.[11]

---

11 See s 52(2) Law of Property Act 1925.

### 9.5.3 Proprietary estoppel

A person – whether spouse or civil partner, cohabitant or anyone else – may also be able to establish a property right to a share in land by virtue of proprietary estoppel. This is what happened in *Re Basham (deceased)* (1987), where the plaintiff was the deceased's step-daughter. The deceased had married the plaintiff's mother when the plaintiff was 15; she gave up hairdressing to help her step-father in various business ventures. Both she and her husband carried out work on a house belonging to the deceased which it had always been understood would be left to her as payment for all her work, and they were dissuaded from moving away from the area by the deceased on the promise of that gift of the house. The rest of the family also believed the plaintiff would be left the house. Unfortunately, the deceased failed to make a will to that effect. The plaintiff, as a step-daughter, had no entitlement under the intestacy rules, under which everything would go to two nieces of the deceased. She brought a claim based on proprietary estoppel and, on the basis of the evidence, succeeded.

Proprietary estoppel claims, in both probate cases and intestate estates, have increased in recent years. They are perhaps particularly likely in intestacy situations where the deceased has not arranged their affairs formally. A more recent example is *Thorner v Major* (2009), a House of Lords case in which a second cousin of the deceased had worked for 15 years on his farm on the understanding that he would leave it to him when he died. But the will giving him the farm was revoked by destruction and no further will was made, so the farm was to pass on intestacy to other people. The House of Lords held that the second cousin was entitled to claim the farm, discussing in particular what sort of assurance had to be made for a claim in proprietary estoppel to succeed.[12]

## 9.6 Matrimonial home

The intestacy rules give the spouse or civil partner no automatic entitlement to the matrimonial home as such. Believing that such an entitlement exists is another common error; a person who thought there was no need to make a will because they owned nothing much of value besides an interest in the family home might not have realised that, if they died intestate, the house might have to be sold to satisfy the entitlements of their various relatives under the intestacy rules. This problem has however been somewhat lessened by the changes made under the 2014 Act: see further 9.3.12.

The spouse or civil partner may however be entitled to the house, or a share in it, by virtue of their interests under normal property law, however, and so their entitlement on intestacy will be in addition to that, as above (9.5).

### 9.6.1 Appropriation of the matrimonial home

Under provisions in the Second Schedule to the Intestate Estates Act 1952, the surviving spouse or civil partner can require the personal representatives to appropriate the matrimonial home to him or her in satisfaction of any absolute interest in the intestacy. This means that the surviving spouse or civil partner can force the personal representatives to let them have the house in lieu of an interest of equivalent value, for example, the fixed net sum (statutory legacy). Absolute interests did not include the life interest which a spouse or civil partner obtained in half the residue where there were issue, relating to deaths before the ITPA 2014 came into force in October 2014, but that could be capitalised if the spouse or civil partner so elected (9.4.4).

---

12  Mark Pawlowski, 'The Promised Land' (2009) 153 Solicitors Journal 10.

The deceased's share in the matrimonial home may be worth more than the fixed net sum or other interests available to the surviving spouse or civil partner from the deceased's estate. In that case, the spouse or civil partner may have to pay 'equality money' making up the difference in value. In *Re Phelps (deceased)* (1979), the court held that a spouse may require the personal representatives to appropriate the matrimonial home partly in satisfaction of that spouse's absolute interest and partly in return for the payment of equality money. In a case where a surviving spouse or civil partner is trying to raise a sum to give by way of equality money in order to keep the matrimonial home, it can be particularly useful to establish that they have a property entitlement under trust rules, because that will reduce the sum of money they have to find by the amount to which they are held to be entitled.

There is a rule that any beneficiary of an estate may avoid (have declared invalid) the purchase of an asset from an estate by a personal representative. This would obviously be a risk in the situation where an intestate leaves a surviving spouse or civil partner who wishes to keep the matrimonial home but needs to pay equality money to do so, and where the estate exceeded the spouse or civil partner's entitlement so that others are also entitled. The spouse or civil partner would also be entitled to the grant of representation (see 12.17). There is therefore a limited exception to the rule, to deal with this situation, in the Second Schedule to the Intestates' Estates Act 1952.

Problems have arisen with the appropriation of the matrimonial home to the spouse or civil partner because the fixed net sum is valued at the date of the intestate's death (not that it has necessarily kept pace with inflation, especially south-eastern English house-price inflation), whereas the value of the house is taken at the date of appropriation. When house values were rising very quickly during the 1970s and the mid-1980s in particular, this meant that the surviving spouse or civil partner could find that, although at the date of the deceased's death they could have 'bought' their share of the matrimonial home with their fixed net sum, by the time the paperwork came to be dealt with, there was a huge shortfall. In *Robinson v Collins* (1975), the matrimonial home was valued at £4,200 at the date of death, but by the date of appropriation the value was £8,000. The sum the spouse or civil partner had to deal with was the latter. In a period when property prices are relatively stable, there is less practical difficulty with this provision, and, of course, when prices were falling a spouse or civil partner might have obtained an unexpected advantage. Its potential for causing unwarranted mischief for the surviving spouse or civil partner remains, however, and its existence was one of the reasons the Law Commission gave in its Report No 187 (made in 1989, after the property market explosion of the 1980s) (9.1.3) for recommending that the surviving spouse or civil partner of an intestate be entitled simply to the whole estate. That change was not even made by the ITPA 2014, the result of a later Law Commission consultation in the context of rapidly-rising house prices after the financial crisis of 2008: though the spouse or civil partner's entitlements were strengthened, the surviving spouse or civil partner will still inherit the whole estate only if there are no surviving issue or if the value of the estate falls below the fixed net sum.

## 9.7 Issue: definition

Issue means children or remoter direct descendants, for example, grandchildren or great-grandchildren. It does not include step-children or children of the family in the sense in which they are included in matrimonial proceedings; the Law Commission considered this question in its Report No 187 but felt that it would lead to uncertainty as to who was included in the definition and therefore to litigation and expense beyond any advantage it might bring.[13]

---

13  The broadened definition of 'child' in s 5(3) of the ITPA 2014 refers to family provision claims, not to who is entitled on intestacy.

The definition of issue does, however, include those who are adopted or legitimated (see, also, 11.17). Section 4 of the ITPA 2014 introduced a provision preserving the contingent interests of children who are adopted after the death of a parent (whether testate or intestate), which previously would have been terminated by the adoption before they fell in to possession.

Until the Family Law Reform Act 1969, illegitimate children had no claim on the intestacy of their parents. This reflects the historical primacy of the regulation of property interests in succession law, rather than the current greater focus on family justice and the support of family members.[14] However, in respect of deaths from 1970 onwards, s 14 of the 1969 Act provided that the child and its parents would stand in relation to each other in the same way as if the child were legitimate. This Act did not, however, affect relationships other than those between parents and children, so it gave an illegitimate child no claim for example on the intestacy of grandparents or siblings, and if an illegitimate child died intestate without parents, the estate would pass as *bona vacantia* to the Crown, even if they were close to their siblings or grandparents.

The Family Law Reform Act 1987 applied to the estates of those who died intestate after April 1988. The general purpose of the Act was to lessen the effects of illegitimacy (where a person's parents were not married to each other); that lessening has been a long and gradual process in the law generally. However, s 18 of the 1987 Act provided a rebuttable presumption that an unmarried father had not survived his child, so that he could not claim on the child's intestacy, and nor could anyone claim through him. That presumption is modified in relation to deaths since the coming into force of the ITPA 2014 where the father's paternity is formally recorded and registered.

In *The Official Solicitor to the Senior Courts v Yemoh and Others* (2010), the deceased intestate left seven or eight widows and a number of children still to be ascertained almost three decades after his death. (The polygamous widows were recognised because the deceased was domiciled in Ghana.) The court took a pragmatic approach to the schedule of children that had been prepared, saying it 'reasonably' identified the deceased's many children. Having been asked to confirm that illegitimate children inherited just as did legitimate ones, which since the deceased died after the coming into force of the Family Law Reform Act 1989 was the case, Mr Elleray QC also considered the wording of the Act when referring to the next generation. Had an illegitimate adult child of the deceased died during the deceased's lifetime leaving illegitimate grandchildren of the deceased, it would be unclear whether s 14(1) of the 1969 Act would allow those grandchildren to be entitled or whether it would have them disentitled because of their illegitimacy. However, in *Yemoh* no adult children had died leaving children, so there was no need to establish legitimacy in any event.

## 9.7.1 Statutory trusts

Where there are issue entitled on intestacy, they take 'on the statutory trusts'. This means that their entitlement is held in the way prescribed by statute until they attain an absolutely vested interest when they reach the age of majority. This was set at 21 until the Family Law Reform Act 1969 took effect in 1970, lowering the age to 18. The statutory trusts are set out in s 47 of the AEA 1925.

---

14 The ECtHR case of *Marckx v Belgium* (1979) dealt with the clash of the status of children under existing Belgian law and the human rights of 'illegitimate' and adopted children, who had a different and less advantageous status, including on intestacy.

### 9.7.2 Stirpital entitlement

Under the statutory trusts, the issue take *per stirpes* (s 47(1)(i)). This means that the intestate's estate is divided in proportion to the number of children they had, and where remoter issue are entitled, they take the share of the estate which falls to their branch. Remoter issue are entitled only where the person or persons through whom they claim have predeceased the intestate: a grandchild may claim from their grandparent's estate only if the relevant parent died before the grandparent. Therefore, if a widowed intestate died leaving three children, each with two children of their own, and one of the intestate's children had died before her, the two surviving children would take one-third of the estate and the two grandchildren whose relevant parent had died would take one-sixth each.

Note that if any child entitled on intestacy does not reach the age of 18, their entitlement fails. Thus, in the example illustrated here, if Diana died at 17, her share would be divided amongst the others entitled at Imelda's death *per stirpes*, so that Emily, Belinda and Charlotte would each take one-third of Diana's share.

Since the Estates of Deceased Persons (Forfeiture Rule and Law of Succession) Act 2011 came into force, amending s 46 of the Administration of Estates Act 1925 as well as s 33 of the Wills Act 1837, the children of those who have lost their entitlements on intestacy because they have killed the deceased will be entitled to take in their parent's place.

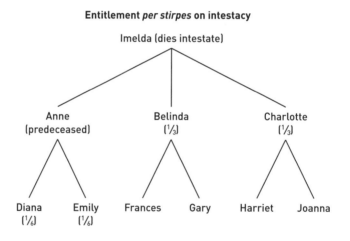

**Entitlement *per stirpes* on intestacy**

### 9.7.3 Main tenance and advancement

Where the deceased died before October 2014, the provisions of ss 31 and 32 of the Trustee Act 1925 as to maintenance and advancement apply to the entitlement of issue on intestacy (s 47(1)(ii) of the AEA 1925). This has meant that the amount of income and capital that could be applied before the relevant person became entitled has been somewhat limited. For deaths before 1 October 2014, s 31 provided, in brief, that the trustees could apply the income from the fund for the maintenance, education or benefit of the beneficiary child insofar as that was reasonable, and otherwise would accumulate it, and s 32 provided that up to one-half of a person's presumptive share of capital could be applied for the advancement or benefit of that person before they became entitled.

The limitations of these powers were discussed by the Law Commission and also by the Law Reform Committee. The Law Commission thought them too strict, since it is often when a child is young that money is most needed for him or her. The Law Reform Committee, on the other hand, considered the matter in its 23rd Report *The Powers and Duties of Trustees* (1982), and concluded that as the recipients of the money were persons only contingently entitled, the provisions were sufficient. Obviously, had the Law Commission's recommendations as to the surviving spouse or civil partner taking the whole estate been accepted and implemented, then where there was such a spouse or civil partner, the statutory trusts would not arise. However, where the spouse or civil partner had predeceased or the marriage had ended in divorce, or the relevant parties had never been married or been in a civil partnership, the statutory trusts could still apply. The Inheritance and Trustees' Powers Act 2014 also did not provide that a surviving spouse or civil partner would take the whole estate, and in any event there would still be statutory trusts where there was no spouse or civil partner even had it done so. However, the ITPA 2014 did amend s 31 so that in relation to deaths after September 2014 trustees could exercise their power as they 'think fit', and their powers under s 32 were extended so that all of a beneficiary's presumptive share could be advanced, rather than only half of it.

### 9.7.4 'Hotchpot' (death before 1996)

Children of the intestate – but not remoter descendants – entitled on an intestacy arising before 1996 have to set against their share of the intestate's estate the value (as at the date of the intestate's death) of certain benefits conferred on them by the intestate during his or her lifetime. Intestate estates can be very slow to be dealt with and some may remain to which this applies. Setting off of such benefits against an entitlement under the intestacy rules is called hotchpot.

### 9.7.5 Advancements

Giving an advancement is akin to setting someone up in business or assisting them in making their way in the world; marriage gifts probably seemed more easily to fit into the same category in 1925 than perhaps they do today. As well as applying to intestacies arising before 1996, the rules on what constitutes an advancement may be relevant in situations other than hotchpot. In *Taylor v Taylor* (1875), it was held that the payment of the admission fee to an Inn of Court for an intending barrister and the purchase of a mining plant for a son's business were advancements, but the payment of a fee to a special pleader for an intending barrister to read in chambers, payments made to a curate to assist him in his living expenses and payment of an army officer's debts did not constitute advancements. In *Re Hayward* (1957), nominations amounting to £507 in favour of a son aged 43 were held not to be *prima facie* an advancement for the purposes of hotchpot on intestacy, though it was thought that had the son been 20 years younger the answer might have been different.

### 9.7.6 Hotchpot and contrary intention

Section 47(1)(iii) of the AEA 1925 also said that the hotchpot rule was excluded by 'any contrary intention … expressed or appearing from circumstances of the case'. Therefore, an intestate's child who received a substantial sum from their parent during their life might well seek to establish that that parent still wanted them to have the same share of the estate as the other siblings. The onus of proving a contrary intention is on the person who asserts it, so if an intestate's child is saying that they should not have to bring an advancement into hotchpot, they have to show that the parent intended that that should not happen. In *Hardy v Shaw* (1976), Goff J said that the test of contrary intention was not objective; it was not what the intestate's intention would have been likely to be had they thought of everything. The court should look at all the circumstances of the case and decide whether, subjectively, they required an inference that the intestate's intention was that the gift should not be brought into hotchpot.

### 9.7.7 Accounting for advancements

The mathematical side of accounting for advancements is fairly simple, once it has been established what has to be brought into hotchpot in relation to an estate arising before 1996. The value of the advancements should be added to the distributable residue, so that if the five branches of issue were to share between them £47,000, but one of them had to account for an advancement worth £8,000, the sum to work with would be £55,000. That sum should then be divided by five, for each of the branches of issue, giving an entitlement of £11,000 per branch. The £8,000 is then deducted from the share of the child who has to account, so that they receive £3,000 and each of the four other branches receives £11,000, making a total of £47,000. Note however that where the advancement received exceeded the child's entitlement, they would not have to make any repayment into the estate, and the distributable residue should simply be divided amongst the others.

## 9.8 Other relatives

Where no spouse or civil partner or issue survives the intestate, certain specified 'other relatives' may inherit (see 9.4.2, 9.4.3, 9.4.6). The order of entitlement set out in s 46 of the Administration of Estates Act 1925, based on a widening circle of relationships, is as follows:

(a)    parents absolutely (if both then in equal shares);
(b)    brothers and sisters of the whole blood on the statutory trusts;
(c)    brothers and sisters of the half blood on the statutory trusts;
(d)    grandparents absolutely (if more than one in equal shares);
(e)    uncles and aunts of the whole blood on the statutory trusts;
(f)    uncles and aunts of the half blood on the statutory trusts;
(g)    *bona vacantia*.

Each category should be exhausted before the next applies, and persons in the same category are equally entitled. Thus, if there are no parents or brothers or sisters of the whole blood, but there are brother and sisters of the half blood and also grandparents, the grandparents will get nothing and the brothers and sisters of the half blood will split the money equally amongst themselves. Hotchpot never applied to these other relatives, and the relationships must be blood ones. Thus, the wife of a parent's brother is not an aunt for these purposes. If someone in one of these categories has predeceased, their children or remoter issue may take their share.

The Law Commission in 2009 consulted on amending these rules, especially as to whether a wider circle of relatives – second cousins as well as first cousins, for example – should be included, or the *bona vacantia* provisions replaced with a statutory gift to charity – but concluded that there was no need for change. In those examples, the inclusion of wider relatives could be administratively highly burdensome, and consultees expressed misgivings about prospective testators believing there was no longer any need to make charitable provisions by will, as well as the relatively-unappreciated existing powers and practice of the Treasury Solicitor of making discretionary gifts to those the deceased might have wished to benefit.

## 9.9 Failure of intestate benefits

An entitlement to an interest on intestacy may fail. Usually this will be because the beneficiary disclaims the benefit or there is some rearrangement of the estate by deed, varying the arrangement usually so as to minimise tax (see Chapter 10).

## 9.9.1 Disclaimer and Variation

A beneficiary entitled under the intestacy rules may disclaim their interest, just as anyone entitled under a will may do (see, also, the subject of disclaimer at 10.5). In *Re Scott* (1975), the deceased's brother and sister disclaimed their entitlements under both her will and the intestacy rules. The question then arose as to what would happen to their shares, namely whether they would go to the Crown as *bona vacantia* or would go to the persons entitled had the brother and sister predeceased rather than disclaiming. The court held that if a beneficiary disclaims their interest under both the deceased's will and the deceased's intestacy, the disclaimer will operate as though the brother and sister had predeceased the intestate, so the further next of kin would take the undisposed-of interest on the testatrix's partial intestacy. This position has been formalised by the effect of s 1(2) of the Estates of Deceased Persons (Forfeiture Rule and Law of Succession) Act 2011 in relation to claims that fail under s 46 of the Administration of Estates Act 1925 because the person who should inherit killed the deceased.

If there was a life interest with a contingent gift in remainder, the remainder would be accelerated if the life interest was disclaimed, save while the remainder remained contingent. Therefore, under the rules relating to deaths before October 2014, where a spouse or civil partner disclaimed their life interest, the issue did not have to wait until their surviving parent died to obtain their shares, but they did have to wait until they attained the age of 18, and their entitlements were still contingent on their attaining that age. For deaths after September 2014, a surviving spouse or civil partner takes an absolute interest rather than a life interest. Children's interests remain contingent on their attaining 18.

## 9.10 Partial intestacy

Where the estate is partially intestate – that is, there is a valid will which fails to deal with the whole estate – the position is governed by s 49 of the AEA 1925. Section 55(1)(vi) of the AEA 1925 provides that 'intestate' includes a person who leaves a will but dies intestate as to some beneficial interest in their real or personal estate. The general principle is that the same rules as those on a total intestacy apply, subject to the provisions of the will. This means such provisions as are operative, and not those relating to a gift which has failed and of which the subject matter is now undisposed; in that situation the provisions the testator has made directing how the gift is to be treated will be redundant and will not operate (*Re Thornber* (1937)). The operation of the rules in this section causes considerable problems, and many people would agree with the judge who called it 'as bad a piece of draughtsmanship as one could conceive, in many respects' (Danckwerts J in *Re Morton* (1887), referring, however, to s 49(1)(a)).

It is important to distinguish between residue and undisposed-of property. There may be a gift of residue which fails in part: for example, where a testator leaves a residuary gift to four people, one of whom predeceases the testator. Unless the wording of the will provides that the lapsed share should then be divided amongst the other three, or there is some other provision as to what should happen to it, it will be property undisposed-of by the will, and s 49 will come into operation.

## 9.10.1 Hotchpot on a partial intestacy (death before 1996)

On a partial intestacy, the deceased's spouse and issue used to have to account for benefits under the will as against their entitlements under the intestacy rules. The provisions under which the spouse or civil partner and issue of the deceased had to account were contained in s 49(1)(aa) (spouses) and (a) (issue, specifically excluding other persons). This was repealed for deaths after 1995 by the Law Reform (Succession) Act 1995, but still applies where the partial intestacy arises before 1996, like the provision on total intestacy that children – but not remoter issue – had to bring into account benefits received by them from the deceased during his or her lifetime, under the rule in s 47(1)(iii) (see 9.5). Intestate estates can be very slow to be dealt with and there may be some such early estates still unadministered.

The spouse caught by the pre-1996 rules must account for testamentary benefits against the entitlement to the statutory legacy; this does not affect their entitlement to the personal chattels, so if there are personal chattels undisposed-of by the will, the spouse will get them. The testamentary benefit should first be identified and valued. If it is a life interest, actuarial tables will have to be used to give a figure for the capital value of the future entitlement to income. The value of the testamentary benefit should then be subtracted from the value of the statutory legacy. This general principle arises from the case of Re Bowen-Buscarlet's Will Trusts (1971), which interpreted s 33(1) of the AEA 1925. That case contradicted, on the point of the time for payment of the statutory legacy, an earlier case, Re McKee (1931).

## 9.10.2 Payment of spouse or civil partner's statutory legacy

Section 33(1) of the AEA 1925 provides that on the death of a person intestate as to any real or personal estate, such estate shall be held by their personal representatives on trust with the power to sell. This can create a particular problem in the situation of a partial intestacy where there may also be an express trust under the provisions of the will.

In Re McKee (1931), the deceased had made a will leaving his residuary estate on trust for sale for his wife for life and then for those of his brothers and sisters who survived her. None of his brothers or sisters survived the wife, so there was a partial intestacy. The court held that s 33(1) of the AEA 1925 did not apply to an asset of the deceased's estate if the deceased had effectively disposed of some beneficial interest, for example, a life interest, in the whole of that asset by his will. Nor could s 33(1) apply to an asset held upon an express trust for sale imposed by the deceased's will, because the express trust for sale excluded the statutory trust for sale imposed by s 33(1); there cannot be two subsisting trusts for sale at the same time.

The effect was the intestacy should be treated as arising on the death of the wife, and that her estate should receive the statutory legacy and interest on it. The effect of this decision was to establish that a partial intestacy may arise some time after the death of the testator, on the death of a life tenant, and that the intestacy rules relating to the payment of the spouse or civil partner's statutory legacy will be applied at that time. It also established that s 33(1) will apply to an asset if the deceased dies wholly intestate as to that asset, or as to a share in that asset, if the will imposes no trust for sale on that asset. Where, however, there is an express trust for sale, that will effectively displace the statutory trust for sale; they cannot exist together. Section 49(1) operates as if the legislature had inserted at the end of every deceased's will an ultimate gift of any undisposed-of property or interest in property in favour of the persons beneficially entitled on intestacy, and it applies irrespective of whether s 33(1) imposes a statutory trust for sale.

Re McKee may come into its own again. It predates the provision in s 49(i)(aa) of the Administration of Estates Act 1925 relating to hotchpot on a partial intestacy (see 9.10.1). That provision was inserted by the Intestates' Estates Act 1952 and removed again by the Law Reform (Succession) Act 1995.

The deceased in Re Bowen-Buscarlet's Will Trusts (1971) left a widow and a married daughter. His will directed his trustees to hold his residuary estate for his widow for her life, but unfortunately failed to say what should happen thereafter. A partial intestacy therefore arose, bringing into operation the statutory rules. Had there been no daughter, the widow would have been entitled to the whole estate, subject to her own life interest; she could have merged the two interests and claimed the whole estate immediately. However, where there was issue, what the widow could claim under the then-operating intestacy rules was the fixed net sum or statutory legacy and a life interest in half the residue. Here, that claim had to be fitted in with the widow's claims under the will. The question was how the residuary estate should be held, since the life interest under the intestacy rules failed because the widow could not enjoy it after her own death when her life interest under the will would end. The Court of Appeal held that, under the will, the estate was held on trust for the widow during her life and thereafter under the intestacy rules. Under the intestacy rules, subject to the payment to the widow of the statutory legacy and interest thereon, the estate was held on trust for the daughter absolutely, because of her absolute entitlement under the statutory trusts for the deceased's issue. The widow was entitled to immediate payment of the statutory legacy with interest, because her interests under the two sets of terms merged (rejecting the Court of Appeal on that point in *Re McKee*). It has been generally felt that the decision in *Re Bowen-Buscarlet* is the preferable one. *Re Bowen-Buscarlet* was followed in an Australian case, *Re Wade* (1980), but in that case the court went further. Reasoning that the intestacy was supposed to occur on the termination of the widow's life interest, it said that she did not have to account for the value of that life interest.

## 9.10.3 Issue – s 49(1)(a) of the AEA 1925 (hotchpot – death before 1996)

In relation to estates arising before 1996, s 49(1)(a) of the AEA 1925 says that the provisions of s 47 as to bringing property into account shall apply to beneficial interests acquired by issue under the will. It specifically excludes beneficial interests so acquired by other persons. Section 47(1)(iii) involves *inter vivos* advancements being brought into account by an intestate's child. Clearly a contrast, if not confusion, arises, because of the different references to 'issue' and 'children'. In particular, there is the practical question of exactly what benefit has to be brought into account, in the situation, for example, where the testator gives a life interest to their daughter, with remainder to her issue.

The deceased in *Re Young* (1951) left his residuary estate to his wife for life and directed that thereafter it was to be divided into seven parts. A one-seventh part was to go to each of five of his six children, and another seventh on trust to apply the income or capital at the discretion of the trustees for the maintenance of his sixth child and his children during his life, and after his death on trust for those children absolutely. The deceased made no provision as to what would happen to the remaining seventh share after his widow's death, so the intestacy rules came into play. The first five children had to bring their one-seventh shares into account against their entitlement on intestacy; the question was how much the sixth child, whose interest in his one-seventh share was only a life interest, had to account for. The court held that the relevant value was the whole capital value, rejecting the argument that only the very limited interest of that child in that one-seventh share was liable to be brought into hotchpot. Harman J construed s 49(1)(a) as if it referred to accounting for benefits being done not by individual beneficiaries but by branches of the family; as though accounting, as well as entitlement, were based on a *per stirpes* rules. He said that 'issue' in s 49(1)(a) must mean children or remoter issue and 'any member of the family belonging to a certain branch must bring in everything that has been taken or acquired under the will by that branch'.

That decision, as well as the awkward wording of the section itself, has been heavily criticised. Dankwerts J in *Re Morton* (1956) commented that 'to value the interest as being equivalent to a gift of capital in a case where a person takes no more than a life interest seems to me contrary to fairness, common sense and everything else'. The decision in *Re Young* was followed in *Re Grover* (1970), where a child had to account for his testamentary life interest at its capital value, but the judgment of Harman J was criticised. Pennycuick J thought the section contained 'great difficulties of language' and that Harman J's statement was 'in extremely wide terms'. He suggested an alternative construction, under which the testator's descendants accounted for beneficial interests they themselves received under the will as against their own entitlements on intestacy, but not for interests received by other members of their branch of the family.

Note that, for deaths after 1995, this provision has been repealed by the Law Reform (Succession) Act 1995.

## 9.11 Summary of Chapter 9

### 9.11.1 Intestate Succession

If a person dies without leaving a valid will they are said to be intestate. If someone leaves a valid will which does not deal with all their property they are said to be partially intestate. In both cases, the law provides rules as to the administration and disposition of their estate, which are set out in the Administration of Estates Act 1925. The entitlements (s 46) are based on family relationships. A spouse or civil partner must survive the intestate by 28 days in order to inherit. Directions by a testator in a valid will that the intestacy rules should not operate are ineffective. The only way to exclude them is to make valid alternative provisions.

The property is fixed with a statutory trust by s 33 of the Administration of Estates Act 1925, but there are directions to the personal representatives as to what property they should sell or keep after settling debts.

Where the estate goes is governed by s 46 AEA 1925. If the testator left a spouse or civil partner but no issue, they will take the whole estate. If there is a spouse or civil partner and also issue, the spouse or civil partner will first have the deceased's personal chattels and the statutory legacy, which is now £250,000, plus half any remainder of the estate. If there is neither spouse or civil partner nor issue, but certain specified other relatives, the estate will go to those other relatives. There is a list of such relatives (parents; siblings; half-siblings; grandparents; aunts and uncles; half-aunts and half-uncles), and each category is entitled to take the full estate if there are members of it, before the next category is considered for entitlement. The surviving spouse or civil partner is not entitled to the family home as such, but if they can afford to buy it from the estate then they may compel the estate to sell it to them (s 47A of the AEA 1925). If there is no one in any of these categories, the estate goes to the Crown.

Issue means children or remoter direct descendants, who become entitled to their inheritance at 18. They will have the intestate's estate subject to the entitlement of any surviving spouse or civil partner. If an intestate's own child dies before attaining their inheritance, that child's descendants share out that inheritance amongst themselves. If the children are minors, how their entitlements are managed until they attain their majority at 18 is governed by the usual statutory rules set out principally in the Trustee Act 1925.

Cohabitants who were neither married to nor in a civil partnership with the deceased are not included in the definition of spouse or civil partner and step-children are not included in the definition of issue. However, 'issue' does include adopted and illegitimate children.

The complex 'hotchpot' provisions no longer apply, save where an estate arising before 1996 is concerned.

## 9.12 Further reading

Fiona Burns, 'Surviving Spouse or Civil Partners, Surviving Children and the Reform of Total Intestacy Law in England and Scotland: Past, Present and Future' (2013) 33 Legal Studies 85.

Gillian Douglas, Hilary Diana Woodward, Alun Humphrey, Lisa Mills and Gareth Morrell, 'Enduring Love: Attitudes to Family and Inheritance Law in England and Wales' (2011) 38 Journal of Law and Society 245.

Charles Gross, 'The Medieval Law of Intestacy' (1904) 18 Harvard Law Review 120.

TC Hartley, 'Polygamy and Social Policy' (1969) 32 Modern Law Review 155.

J Roger Kerridge, 'Reform of the Law of Succession: The Need for Change, Not Piecemeal Tink-
ering' (2007) 71 The Conveyancer 47.

Mark Pawlowski, 'The Promised Land' (2009) 153 Solicitors Journal 10.

# Chapter 10

# The Classification and Failure of Gifts

Gifts by will fall into different categories. There is generally nothing to be gained by describing the category of the gift, as it depends on its nature. The category that a gift falls into can be important if there is not enough in the estate to satisfy all the gifts, because some types have priority. It is also important because there are rules about when different types of gift fail to operate even if there is plenty in the estate. Gifts may also fail for other reasons, such as divorce or where the beneficiary has killed the testator. The rules as to classification and failure of gifts are often of practical importance in working out the prospective meaning of wording in a will, and so in drafting, and especially in ascertaining how to administer an estate.

## 10.1 Classification of gifts

Gifts may be specific, general, demonstrative or residuary. The classification of legacies gives rise to the most frequent difficulties and the most important consequences. How a legacy is treated in various circumstances depends on what category it falls into, so it is necessary to be able to distinguish them.

### 10.1.1 Specific legacies

A specific legacy is the gift of a particular piece of the testator's personal property. The will is construed to ascertain whether the testator intended the piece of property to pass to the beneficiary in *specie*, that is, whether they intended the particular item itself to pass. If a court has to construe whether or not a particular gift is a specific gift, it will usually lean against finding that it is and will prefer to find that it is a general gift. This is because specific legacies are liable to fail by ademption (see 10.7), although they hold a more privileged position than general legacies where the estate is insufficient to meet all the gifts in the will (see abatement at 10.12).

A specific legacy may be indicated by the use of the word 'my' when the gift is being described, though if the testator describes the gift as a general gift, it will not be found to be specific (*Re Compton* (1914)). In *Bothamley v Sherson* (1875), the testator made a gift of 'all my shares or stock in the Midland Railway Company'. This was held to be a specific legacy, the court defining a specific legacy as 'what has been sometimes called a severed or distinguished part' of the testator's estate. Two gifts of shares in a private family company were held to be specific bequests without the use of the possessive pronoun in *Re Rose* (1949).

In the early case of *Innes v Johnson* (1799), the testator left his sister the interest on a £300 bond for her life and thereafter left her daughter the interest due on the bond and the capital. The testator left various bonds, but it was held that this was a specific gift of the one of that value. In *Re Wedmore* (1907), the testator in his will forgave his children all their unsecured debts to him. Two of his sons owed him such debts. It was held that the forgiveness of them was a specific legacy.

## 10.1.2 General legacies

A general legacy does not refer to any particular piece of the testator's estate. Gifts of stocks and shares are usually general gifts, although they may be made specific if the testator describes them as 'my' shares in the particular company. In *Re Willcocks* (1921), the testatrix made a gift of £948 3s 11d Queensland 32% stock. She died owning exactly that sum of that kind of stock, but the court held that the gift was nevertheless a general legacy (compare *Re Rose* at 10.1.1).

A gift of a piece of property which the testator does not own, if it is a general gift, will be fulfilled by the personal representatives purchasing the property for the beneficiary from the funds in the estate. For example, if Nick's aunt had been a keen sailor but died without owning any yacht at the date of her death, the effect of a gift to him of 'my yacht' would be completely different from that of a gift of 'a yacht'. In the former case, the gift would be a specific gift, and where it is no longer in the testatrix's estate it would fail by ademption, because she left Nick a particular item which is not available. However, in the latter case, she will have left him a yacht – no particular yacht – and the personal representatives will buy him one, provided his aunt left enough money to cover the purchase.

## 10.1.3 Demonstrative legacies

Demonstrative legacies are legacies which the testator directs to be satisfied out of a specified fund or pool of property. The classic example of the demonstrative legacy is a sum of money to be paid out of a particular bank account.

Demonstrative legacies operate as specific legacies unless they fail because the specific property is not available. Insofar as the specific property to answer the gift is lacking, they operate like general legacies. In *Re O'Connor* (1970), the testator had directed that a gift be satisfied only out of specified property. The court held that this could not be a demonstrative legacy, because it was an essential characteristic of a demonstrative legacy that it operated as a general legacy if the fund was insufficient. In *Re Webster* (1937), the testator gave a legacy of a sum to be paid out of his share in the family business. This was held to be a demonstrative legacy. Therefore when it was found that the deceased's share in the business was worth less than the gift, there was no failure for that reason. The beneficiary was entitled to have the sum paid out of the testator's general estate instead.

In *Walford v Walford* (1912), the testator gave to his sister 'the sum of £1,000 to be paid out of the estate and effects inherited by me from my mother'. This included a gift in remainder subject to the life interest of his father, who died seven years later. The House of Lords held that the legacy was demonstrative and it was irrelevant that it was to be paid from a sum to be received later.

## 10.1.4 Pecuniary legacies

The phrase 'pecuniary legacy' can cause difficulties, because it refers to different things depending on the context in which it is used. It is primarily a gift of money, which may be specific, general or demonstrative. A pecuniary gift of the money in the testator's piggy bank may be construed as a specific gift, and will then fail if there is nothing there. A general pecuniary gift is a sum of money; a demonstrative one is directed to be paid from a particular fund. It was said in *Re O'Connor* (1948) that the term 'pecuniary legacy' is insufficient; it must be ascertained whether the particular gift is specific, demonstrative or general.

However, where the mechanics of the administration of the estate are concerned, the expression is defined at s 55(1)(ix) of the AEA 1925 to include a general legacy, an annuity, any tax payable on a gift which the testator has directed to be paid free of tax and any part of a demonstrative legacy that cannot be discharged out of specified property.

## 10.1.5 Annuities

An annuity is a form of pecuniary legacy; the word is not specific to legacies, and the annuity is the usual or at least traditional form, for example, of a pension. It was however described by the court in *Re Earl of Berkeley* (1968) as 'a series of legacies payable at intervals'. It may be specific (in which case it is liable to fail by ademption), general or demonstrative, depending on the construction of the will. An annuity is payable from the date of the testator's death unless they state otherwise. The personal representatives will usually appropriate (see 13.10) certain assets to make reasonably certain of the payment of the annuity, or may purchase an annuity from the estate. If the testator has directed for the purchase of an annuity, the annuitant may take the purchase price instead.

Annuities used to be the classic form of the pension, and often used provided there was enough capital to buy one in the first place. They do, however, depend on the stability and credibility of the financial system, and are not as much the obvious choice as they used to be. Moreover, as credit and debt and current cash flow become urgent considerations at the national level, it is proposed that prospective pensioners be allowed to take their pension 'pots' without the previous obligation to use them to buy an annuity. This apparently abstruse point may be the visible part of a larger issue about how older or younger generations support each other.

## 10.1.6 Devises

A devise is the gift by will of real property. Devises are usually specific – 'my freehold house at 24 Acacia Avenue', for example. It used to be the case that only a specific devise would function, because wills were not ambulatory as to real property and could not operate to pass realty acquired by the testator after the date of the will. Now, however, devises may be general, as with a gift of 'all my freehold property', for instance, and may also be residuary – 'my house at 24 Acacia Avenue to Anne and all the rest of my land to Belinda'.

## 10.1.7 Residuary gifts

Every properly drafted will should have a provision for the application of residue, preferably one which foresees all reasonably possible events of failure such as divorce or predecease. The residuary gift includes whatever remains after all the debts and liabilities have been cleared and the legacies and devises paid out. Residuary gifts may be divided, for example, as to realty and personalty, or shared out between beneficiaries. If there is no residuary gift, or such residuary gift as there is fails, there will be property undisposed-of by the will and the rules of partial intestacy will apply. An ultimate gift of residue to charity, should all other gifts fail – even if the testator has no intention that this gift should mean anything, is the surest way of avoiding such a partial intestacy, since once a general charitable intention is evinced, the gift will not fail.

Sometimes, it may be unclear whether a gift is residuary or specific. This may need to be ascertained so that the personal representatives know what the proper distribution of the estate will be. The testator in *Re Green* (1880) left a leasehold pub with directions for it to be sold. He gave a legacy to a beneficiary of the rents and profits until sale and of the proceeds of sale, and left the residue and other residuary real and personal estate to his two daughters. The court held that all the gifts to the daughters were residuary. In *Re Wilson* (1966), the testatrix gave pecuniary legacies and then left 'all my real estate and the residue of my personal estate' to her daughter. The personal estate was insufficient to pay the pecuniary legacies, so the question was whether the gift of 'all my real estate' was residuary or specific. (If the latter, it would take precedence over the pecuniary legacies.) The court held that the gift was residuary.

## 10.2 Different effects

It may be necessary to be able to distinguish what class of legacy is being dealt with because, as shown in *Re Wilson* (10.1.7), different rules apply to the different categories.

### 10.2.1 Ademption

If the property mentioned in a specific legacy or a specific devise is not part of the testator's estate at their death, the gift is adeemed. This means that the legatee or devisee will receive neither the property itself nor anything representing it, for example, the proceeds of sale of a house left to them in the testator's will but in fact sold before the testator's death. General and demonstrative legacies do not fail by ademption (see 10.7).

### 10.2.2 Abatement

This relates to the payment of the liabilities of the estate. Part 11 of the First Schedule to the Administration of Estates Act 1925 regulates where the burden of the liabilities will fall. Specific gifts rank behind general gifts in the statutory order of application of property to the discharge of liabilities and gifts in the same class abate at the same rate. This means that if there are both specific and general gifts, the general gifts will be used first to pay debts. A testator may vary the statutory order by their will.

For more on this, see 10.12 on failure of gifts and 13.13–15 on the incidence of debts and legacies.

### 10.2.3 Income and interest

Specific legacies and devises carry with them their own income or profits accruing from the testator's death, whereas general or demonstrative legacies carry interest at a fixed rate and only from the date at which they become payable (generally from the end of the 'executor's year', as was the case with the interest on the demonstrative legacy in *Walford v Walford* (1912) (10.1.3)). The details of the rules as to payment of interest and the exceptions to the rules are numerous and complex.

### 10.2.4 Expenses

There are also different rules about where the expenses of the different parts of the estate fall. Expenses incurred by the personal representatives in preserving specific gifts must be reimbursed by the relevant beneficiary. The court in *Re Rooke* (1933) said it could not see on what principle a beneficiary should get the income and profits from a specific gift if he or she were not liable for the expenses. Expenses incurred in preserving the subject matter of general or demonstrative legacies are payable out of the estate as part of the costs of administration.

## 10.3 Failure of gifts

Even if a will is valid, individual gifts made in it may fail.

There are several reasons why a gift made in a will may fail:

- the beneficiary disclaims;
- the beneficiary predeceases the testator (lapse);
- a specific gift is adeemed;
- the beneficiary or their spouse or civil partner witnesses the will (s 15 of the Wills Act 1837);
- a gift to the testator's spouse or civil partner fails following divorce or annulment of the marriage or ending of the civil partnership (s 18A and B of the Wills Act 1837);
- by reason of public policy or because it promotes an illegal purpose;
- the gift is contrary to the principle of inalienability;
- abatement or insolvency;
- uncertainty;
- the gift is contingent on a condition which is not satisfied or it is forfeit under a 'no-contest' clause;
- the gift was made as a result of fraud on the testator.

Some of these reasons for failure may also apply on intestacy, for example, disclaimer, forfeiture or lapse.

## 10.4 Effect of failure

The subject matter of a gift which fails in any well-drawn will either falls into residue and forms part of the gift to the testator's residuary beneficiary or passes to the person the testator has specified as the substitutional beneficiary. If there is no residuary beneficiary and no substitutional gift or other arrangement (see 10.5), the property will pass on intestacy. The property will also pass on intestacy if there is a residuary beneficiary but the testator has shown an intention that the subject matter of the gift should be excluded from their residuary bequest in any event. If the gift which fails was a life interest, then the interest in remainder will be accelerated.

## 10.5 Disclaimer and variation: choice by the beneficiary

Generally speaking, any beneficiary may disclaim a gift by will or an entitlement on intestacy. This includes a beneficiary who is a company or an unincorporated association. Abbot CJ in *Townson v Tickell* (1819) said, 'The law certainly is not so absurd as to force a man to take an estate against his will.' The position with gifts under a will has been clear for a very long time. The beneficiaries under the deceased's intestacy may also disclaim. In *Re Scott* (1975), the two siblings of the deceased took under the intestacy rules on the deceased's partial intestacy. They both disclaimed, the court being asked to decide whether, as a result, the property disclaimed would pass to the Crown as *bona vacantia* or to the persons who would have been next of kin but for the two siblings; it held that it would pass to the next of kin.

The usual context is, however, where a beneficiary agrees to pass their interest to someone else in the context of a general rearrangement of the gifts in a will (or the default gifts on intestacy) so as to make it more tax-efficient and minimise the liability to IHT (See 10.5.3, 14.11 and

---

1  *Russell v IRC* (1988).

16.4.2). This is routinely done, and HMRC will accept variations made within two years of death. Variations that go wrong or are delayed are a frequent source of further applications such as applications for rectification (see Chapter 16).[1]

### 10.5.1 The act of disclaiming and variation

Disclaimers and variations are often made by deed, but that need not be the case.

Disclaimer can be effected by simple writing or even by conduct. It may be done at any time provided the beneficiary has not accepted the gift or derived any benefit from it; the disclaimer may then be retracted if no one has placed any reliance on it, whether other beneficiaries or the personal representatives. Once the disclaimer has been made it will be read back to the date of death.

Variations for tax purposes are usually made by deed, but will be effective for HMRC provided they are in writing and signed by all the relevant parties. Only one variation may be made for any property; anything further would have to be done, if possible, by way of rectification (see 16.4); a disclaimer may be withdrawn after it is made provided no one has relied on it to their detriment.[2] Where beneficiaries were to take jointly, both would have to disclaim to release the gift entirely, but one joint beneficiary may release their interest to the other unilaterally.[3] Disclaiming a gift does not give the person a right to redirect where it should go – it will be as though the person had predeceased, and subsequent interests, whether by will or on intestacy, will be accelerated.[4]

### 10.5.2 Reasons for disclaiming and varying provisions in a will

There are various reasons for disclaiming:

(a)    gift brings with it obligations the beneficiary does not want to fulfil;
(b)    personal unwillingness to accept testator's gift;
(c)    tax.

Of these, the last, at least, is certainly not uncommon. However, disclaimer and variation of benefits by will may be motivated by generosity or a feeling that the testator has been unfair.

In *Crowden v Aldridge* (1993), it was held that a document signed by the 16 beneficiaries of an estate confirming their agreement to the variation of the estate was enforceable even where the form of agreement had not been executed as a deed (that being the usual form) and some of the beneficiaries changed their minds after signing. The deceased had left his housekeeper £100, and it was agreed amongst the family that this was insufficient and that she should have £5,000 and the bungalow in which she lived. The last four beneficiaries to sign the memorandum of agreement then suggested that the housekeeper should take only a life interest in the bungalow and declined to proceed on the original basis. The court held, however, that the original signed agreement was enforceable.

### 10.5.3 Tax savings

A beneficiary may disclaim because the result of the disclaimer is a minimising of liability to tax, usually Inheritance Tax but sometimes also Capital Gains Tax.[5] This is usually seen in the form of

---

2   *Re Cranstoun* (1949).
3   *Re Schar* (1950).
4   *Re Stratton's Disclaimer* (1958).
5   Inheritance Tax (IHT) is paid on the value transferred out of the deceased's estate to non-exempt donees (exempt donees are spouses or civil partners and charity). Capital Gains Tax is generally less relevant in administering estates because it is charged on the difference between the value at death and that on transfer.

all the beneficiaries effectively rearranging the provisions of the testator's will or intestacy between them; this can be done whenever the relevant beneficiaries are all of full age and all consent to the rearrangement. HMRC will accept a deed of variation made within two years of death as effective for tax purposes, provided notice is given to it within six months (though if there is a prior disclaimer, rather than a variation, notice is not required). It will read the provisions back to the date of death by virtue of s 142(1) of the Inheritance Tax Act 1984 and s 62(6) of the Taxation of Chargeable Gains Act 1992. Deeds of variation may also be used in the same way on intestacy, so as to vary the statutory provisions to result in a tax saving. This is the process sometimes known as 'post-death tax planning' (see 14.20).

## 10.5.4 Personal feelings

The beneficiary may disclaim for any reason. Thus, if the beneficiary would feel embarrassed to take any sort of gift from the testator for personal reasons, they may disclaim. They need not give reasons.

## 10.5.5 Gift carries obligations which the beneficiary does not wish to fulfil

Some gifts come bearing obligations, either because of their nature – the freehold of a house subject to a long lease containing onerous landlord's covenants, perhaps – or because the testator has stated in their will that the gift can be taken only if the beneficiary fulfils certain conditions.

## 10.5.6 Partial disclaimer not possible

The person who finds the obligations which come with a gift cannot avoid them and still take the benefit by attributing the obligations to one part of the gift and taking the rest, unless a sufficient intention on the part of the testator for that to be possible can be found.[6]

## 10.5.7 Disclaimer of one of two or more separable gifts

A beneficiary may disclaim one gift and accept another provided the two are truly separable; otherwise, the doctrine of election may apply (see 11.13). In *Guthrie v Walrond* (1882), a gift of 'all my estate and effects in the Island of Mauritius' was held to be an indivisible gift, so that it could be disclaimed as a whole or not at all.

*Re Scott* (1975) (10.5) showed how a disclaimer may lead to a partial intestacy even where the will appears to provide for all eventualities, if there is no specific provision for a gift over of property otherwise undisposed-of. The testatrix left a gift of income to her brother and sister, to pass on the death of the second of them to those of her brother's children who attained 21 or, being female, married under that age. Thereafter, the fund went to two charities absolutely. The brother and sister disclaimed. The question was whether the income was accelerated, so that pending the birth of a child of the brother it went to the charities, or whether it should be accumulated for 21 years, or until the deaths of the brother and sister, and added to capital, or whether it should devolve on partial intestacy, or what should happen to it. The court held that it should devolve on partial intestacy, the gift to charity being contingent and therefore not liable to be accelerated, and the testatrix having evinced an intention against accumulation by disposing of life interests.

---

6  *Re Joel, Rogerson v Joel* (1943).

## 10.6 Lapse

The doctrine of lapse holds that a gift fails if the beneficiary predeceases the testator. This is because the will is of no effect until the testator dies. The same applies to gifts to a limited company or other corporate body which has been dissolved and also to gifts made by way of nomination rather than by will (see 2.3.1). The doctrine of lapse cannot be excluded by a provision in the will (Re Ladd (1932)), although a testator may make a substitutional gift to the beneficiary's personal representatives or to his or her children which is to take effect should the beneficiary predecease. There are also certain exceptions to the doctrine.

### 10.6.1 Joint tenants and tenants in common

The doctrine of lapse does not apply where there is a gift to joint tenants (not to tenants in common) or a class gift, since the subject matter of the gift will go to the other joint tenant(s) or the remaining members of the class. This is the reason for the phrase often seen in wills which leaves a certain gift 'to such of my children as survive me and if more than one in equal shares'. The phrase 'to such of my children as survive me' ensures that the effect of a child predeceasing will still be to pass his or her share into the pool to be divide amongst the others, but the use of the words 'in equal shares' ensures that the beneficiaries receive the gifts, as amongst themselves, as tenants in common.

### 10.6.2 Gifts to issue

The doctrine of lapse is altered by s 33 of the Wills Act 1837 as amended by s 19 of the Administration of Justice Act 1982. It was also held in Re Meredith (1924) that the statutory provisions do not operate if there is a contrary intention appearing in the will.

### 10.6.3 Section 33 of the Wills Act 1837

Section 33 of the 1837 Act states that a gift made by a testator's will to any of their issue, provided that the testator was survived by some issue and that the gift was one not determinable at or before the named beneficiary's death, would be effective as though the beneficiary had died immediately after the testator. This provision now includes deceased issue who are members of a class, so that where the gift is to the testator's children, the issue of a child who has predeceased may take their share.[7]

This rule was explored in the case of Ling v Ling (2002). The testator's wife had predeceased him, as had his son. The testator therefore left a daughter and a minor grandson, the son of his predeceased son. By his will he left the residue of his estate to his wife or, if she predeceased, any child of his living at his death who attained the age of 21, and if more than one as tenants in common. The court was asked whether this meant it was a gift to both the testator's children (in which case the grandson took the son's share under s 33) or only the surviving children (in which case the son's share lapsed as he was not a member of the class). The solicitor's drafting was criticised, but Etherton J considered that the subsequent change in the law (the will was drafted in 1961, before the law implied the substitutionary gift under the amended s 33) did not help with construing the testator's intention when the will was made. He found that s 33 was not about class gifts, but was designed to prevent the lapse of an individual gift, and that there was no indication that the testator had intended that his son's issue should be excluded from taking

---

7 For deaths after 1982: s 19 Administration of Justice Act 1982.

under the law. However, the grandson would have to satisfy the age requirement himself, even though his father had already satisfied it before he died.

Note that this only applies where the beneficiary who has predeceased is the deceased's issue. It does not apply to claims through other relatives.

### 10.6.4 Benefit *per stirpes*

The shares under s 33 are taken stirpitally, so that the benefit is divided not according to the absolute number of persons who will take a benefit, but according to the number of branches of the family. Thus, where there are two surviving children, and two have predeceased, one leaving two grandchildren of the testator and one leaving no grandchild but three great-grandchildren, there will be four branches of the family, one for each child of the original testator. Each of her two children will take a quarter-share. The two grandchildren will share their deceased parent's quarter-share, taking one-eighth each, and the three great-grandchildren will take one-twelfth each, making up the last quarter-share.

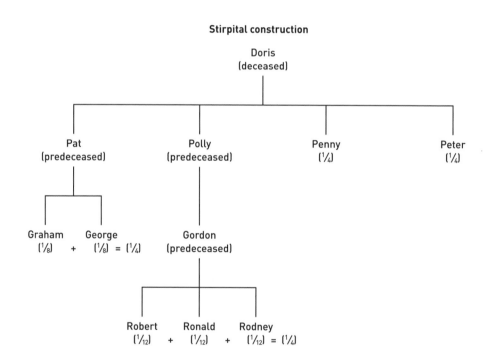

**Stirpital construction**

### 10.6.5 *Commorientes*

The presumption, introduced by s 184 of the Law of Property Act 1925, is that where two persons have died in circumstances in which it cannot be told which died first, the older died before the younger. Note that the persons do not have to die together – one may be lost at sea on a completely unspecifiable date whilst the other dies in hospital on land. Like all presumptions, it may be rebutted by evidence. Thus, if someone could be found who had seen the deceased sailor still alive at a time when his younger land-based colleague was known to be already dead, then the presumption would not operate. In that situation, survivorship may be found on evidence on the balance of probabilities (*Lamb v Lord Advocate* (1976)).

The question of when the presumption was applicable was discussed in detail in *Hickman v Peacey* (1945) by the House of Lords. In that case, five bodies were discovered in the remains of a house bombed during the Second World War. The deceased had left various gifts to each other; there was some suggestion that they had not all died together as their bodies were found in different places. However, the court cited Lord Cranworth LC in *Underwood v Wing* (1855), 'It cannot be assumed to be proved, or probable, or possible, that two human beings should cease to breathe at the same moment of time' and Lord Macmillan said that the question to be answered was a practical one 'Can you say for certain which of these two deceased persons died first?' If not, the presumption applied.

## 10.6.6 Purpose of *commorientes* rule

The presumption in s 184 of the Law of Property Act 1925 is designed to avoid the frustration of the testator's intentions by passing their property to someone who cannot enjoy it. However, the presumption itself may frustrate those intentions, in that it may operate in some cases to pass all the property of the elder to the younger, if that person is the sole beneficiary under the elder's will, though where they have died together, the younger will not have time to enjoy the property, which will immediately pass to his or her own beneficiaries under their will or intestacy.

## 10.6.7 Exception to the *commorientes* rule for spouses where the elder is intestate

As well as being particularly likely to leave property to each other, spouses and civil partners are likely to die together unexpectedly, say in a road accident. The presumption in s 184 of the Law of Property Act 1925 was excluded by s 46(3) of the Administration of Estates Act 1925 if the two persons being considered were spouses or civil partners and the older of them died intestate. The reason for a different provision for intestate spouses was that they are likely to die together and, before the application of a survivorship period of 28 days in cases of spouses' intestacy under the Law Reform (Succession) Act 1995, the result would be merely to pass all the property of both spouses to the family of only one of them.

The exception did not apply in cases where the older person was not intestate, even where the will contained no survivorship clause. In *Re Rowland* (1962), a married couple were lost at sea. The husband left a will without a survivorship clause, in favour of his wife. The existence of the will excluded the exception under s 46(3) of the AEA 1925 to the usual *commorientes* rule under s 184 of the LPA 1925. Therefore, that rule operated and, as he was older than his wife, he was presumed to have predeceased her, and his property passed to her and then, she being dead too; to those entitled to her estate. S 46(3) AEA 1925 is no longer in force, following ITPA 2014.

## 10.6.8 *Commorientes* rule operates without court discretion

Although the statutory presumption, and its exception for spouses, was designed to make the operation of the rules easier to deal with, its own existence and method of application does not bring with it any discretion for the court to decide when or whether to apply it. It was held in *Re Lindop* (1942) that although the statutory presumption under s 184 of the LPA 1925 may be rebuffed by evidence, there is no discretion given to the court to disregard it on the ground that it would be unfair or unjust to act upon it.

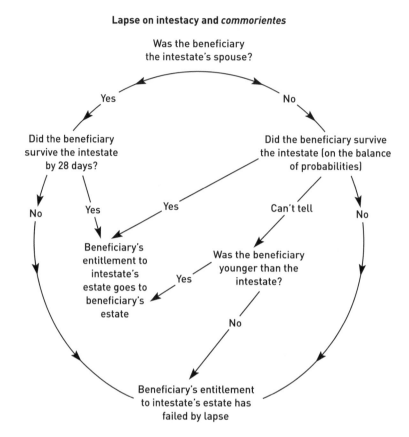

**Lapse on intestacy and *commorientes***

### 10.6.9 Survivorship clauses

It is usual to see a 'survivorship clause' in a will, which passes the property only if the beneficiary survives the testator by a certain period, usually about one month. Since 1995, there has been a statutory survivorship period of 28 days in cases of intestacy with respect to spouses. A survivorship clause provides a way of dealing with the practical question of how to avoid passing an estate to someone who dies in such rapid succession that they have no chance of enjoying the property, so that passing it to them would mean, effectively, passing it to whoever benefits under their will or intestacy. It also avoids the problem that arises where there is evidence that one person was still alive at the scene of a disaster, even if they died of their injuries shortly thereafter. Section 184 is not brought into operation where it is certain who died first.

A period of up to six months will allow for the tax advantages of avoiding two incidences of Inheritance Tax, which potentially comes into operation whenever a gift is made, but such a long period would risk delaying the administration of an estate. Whilst the appropriate length of a survivorship period ought to be considered in each case, in practice, a period of 28 days or one calendar month would be usual.

## 10.7 Ademption

Specific gifts may fail by ademption, though general and demonstrative legacies do not. In the early case of *Ashburner v Macguire* (1786), the testator's gift of 'my £1,000 East India Stock' was held to be a specific gift and therefore to have been adeemed because the testator had sold that stock during his lifetime. In *Gordon v Duff* (1861) the testator left 'the sum of £2,000 Long Annuities standing in my name in the books of the Bank of England'. At his death, he had only £300 worth. The testator's gift was held to be specific and, despite his leaving a great deal of other property, most of it was adeemed.

As courts lean towards finding gifts valid, they also lean in cases of doubt towards construing a gift as general rather than specific. In *Re Gage* (1934), the testator gave to his niece by will 'the sum of £1,150 War Loan 1929–47 stock and to MG the sum of £500 New South Wales Five per cent stock now standing in my name'. The court construed the gifts separately and held that the niece could take cash in the place of the gift of the War Loan.

If there is something in the wording of the will which shows the testator had a particular asset of theirs in mind at the time of making the will, and that wording cannot be construed as referring generally to articles of that type, the gift will, however, be a specific gift and liable to fail by ademption. The testator in *Oliver v Oliver* (1871) recited his entitlement to receive £5,602 Consols from his sister's estate and left part of that gift to his son. However, he received the Consols during his lifetime and sold them. The gift to the son was held to have failed by ademption.

A specific gift which speaks from the death of the testator (s 24 of the Wills Act 1837 provides that a will speaks from the date of death in respect of the estate comprised in it; see 11.20) will fail only if the gift does not form part of the testator's property at the date of their death.

Note that, for the purposes of ascertaining whether a specific gift has failed by ademption, there is something rather like a *commorientes* rule for the testator and their property. Where the two perish in the same disaster, the rule stated in *Durrant v Friend* (1852) holds that, in the absence of any evidence to the contrary, the property is assumed to have been destroyed before the testator died. This means that a gift of a car written off in a fatal road accident will be adeemed, rather than the beneficiary obtaining the proceeds of any insurance policy on it, as would have happened had it been destroyed after the testator's death.

### 10.7.1 Does the subject matter of the specific gift still exist?

It was held in *Re Slater* (1907), where the court was considering a gift of shares in a water company which had been taken over by a local water authority, that a specific gift will fail if the testator, at the time of their death, had no assets of the description given in their will. The court asked itself: 'where is the thing which is given? … it is no use trying to trace it unless … you find something which has been changed in name or form only, but which is substantially the same thing.' A specific gift will be adeemed where there has been a change in its subject matter, that is, the thing itself, but where there has merely been a change in name or form, there will be no ademption.

*Re Slater* was applied in *Re Kuypers* (1925), where 15 per cent shares had been reduced to 8 per cent shares and new shares issued in compensation. The tenant for life was held to have no right to the income from the new shares. The court said that the name of the old shares had been changed and they had lost some of their attractiveness, but they remained the same shares. Consequently, the tenant for life took them as they were.

*Re Slater* was also applied in the recent case of *Re Dorman* (1994). Edward Dorman died in 1985 leaving his widow the income from a trust, which she used for living expenses, paying the rest into a deposit account. The widow made a will giving the balance of her deposit account back to the trust. She also gave an Enduring Power of Attorney (see 6.8); her attorney, unaware of the terms of the will, transferred the money to a higher-paying account with the same bank. The court held that the gift was not adeemed, because the reference was essentially to the fund of money, the details of the account being for identification only. The change was not one of substance, as in *Re Kuypers*. The court also distinguished the Scottish case of *Re Ballantyne* (1941), where, on similar facts, the gift was adeemed, because in that case there had been a change of bank.

A situation that becomes more common as the underlying situation spreads is where a testator's property was managed before their death by a person who had been given authority to do that because of the testator's failing health. Items of a testator's property that are the subject of a specific gift in their will may have been disposed of by a person acting under, for example, an Enduring Power of Attorney or a Lasting Power of Attorney (see 6.8). Senior Judge Lush considered this in *Public Trustee v JM* (2014), saying: 'The law regarding ademption caused by an attorney is a minefield and over the last twenty years there have been a number of conflicting judgments in several Common Law jurisdictions.' He observed however that problems can be resolved by the making during the person's lifetime of a statutory will (see 6.7).

## 10.7.2 Changes in name or form do not lead to ademption

The change in name or form of the subject matter of the gift will not cause it to be adeemed, however, provided that it remains substantially the same property.

The testator in *Re Clifford* (1912) gave a specific gift of 23 of his shares in a certain company. After the will was made – but before the testator's death – the company changed its name and subdivided each share into four new shares of one-quarter the value each. The court held that the gift would not be adeemed, because the new shares were 'identical in all but name and form' to the old shares; the legatee therefore took 92 of the new shares in place of the original 23 old ones. The difference between this situation and that in *Re Kuypers* (10.7.1) is that, in the later case, the shares had been changed and not simply subdivided.

In *Re Leeming* (1912), the testator's gift was a specific legacy of 'my ten shares' in a named limited company. Between the making of the will and the death of the testator, the company was voluntarily liquidated. After reforms, a new company was created under the same name as the old one. The court looked at what the practical effects of these changes were, rather than at the dissolution of the company in which the testator had had his shares, and held that the specific legacy had not been adeemed. The beneficiary took the shares in the new company.

## 10.7.3 Ademption by operation of law

A gift will still be adeemed even if the subject matter has vanished from the testator's estate by operation of law, as happened under nationalisation. The question may then arise as to whether the original gift is replaced by whatever compensation the law offers for the property, or whether the gift is simply adeemed.

In *Re Galway* (1950), the testator made a gift of land. After the making of the will but before his death, the Coal Act 1938 was passed, nationalising the property rights in the coal so that they could not pass under the will, but providing for the payment of compensation. The question before the court was whether the beneficiary could take the compensation in place of the coal, or whether the compensation was separate personalty which would; in this case, fall into residue. It was held that in these circumstances, if there was no contrary intention in the will sufficient to pass the compensation on nationalisation instead of the property which had been nationalised, the specific gift of the nationalised property would fail by ademption. The compensation therefore went to the residuary legatee.

## 10.7.4 Ademption, the doctrine of conversion and the Trusts of Land and Appointment of Trustees Act 1996

Similar questions used to arise in respect of equitable interests in land. Testators may leave their realty to one person and their personalty to another. Before 1926, shares of land could be held at law, and after 1996, shares in land have been realty. However, in between, where land was held on trust, an automatic trust for sale arose by virtue of s 35 Law of Property Act 1925. This applied in all cases of co-ownership, and the doctrine of conversion meant that, because the land had in principle to be sold, in equity it was regarded as already sold (by virtue of the maxim 'equity regards as done that which ought to be done') and therefore personalty rather than land. Such gifts, even in pre-1926 wills if the testator died after 1925, failed unless saved by, for example, republication (Re Harvey (1947)). The courts were, however, generally uncomfortable with the operation of the doctrine of conversion in family, as opposed to commercial, situations: the idea that a married couple who jointly owned their matrimonial home should have an interest not in the house itself but only in the proceeds of its sale was described by Lord Wilberforce in Williams & Glyn's Bank v Boland (1980) as 'just a little unreal'. The doctrine of conversion was abolished for these purposes by s 3 of the Trusts of Land and Appointment of Trustees Act 1996, with effect from 1 January 1997.[8]

## 10.7.5 Specific gifts subject to a binding contract of sale

The position with property which is the subject of a specific gift and which the testator has contracted to sell (but of which they have not completed the sale) is rather complex. If the will is made first and then the contract entered into, the beneficiary may enjoy the property until the contract is completed, whereupon it is adeemed.

However, if the contract predates the will, the doctrine of conversion operates on the gift in the will itself, so that the beneficiary will receive the proceeds of sale.

In neither case can the beneficiary retain the property itself.

## 10.7.6 Options and the rule in *Lawes v Bennett*

The position with property over which the testator has granted an option to purchase to a third party is governed by the anomalous rule in Lawes v Bennett (1795). This deems the conversion to occur at the date of the option, so the gift operates from that point as one of the proceeds of sale. Nevertheless, on the exercise of the option, the gift is adeemed.

In Re Sweeting (1975), the testator died leaving properties subject to contracts of sale, which were held to be enforceable despite being conditional, since the widow had consented to the sales. The conditional contracts were treated as options under the rule in Lawes v Bennett, and therefore the gifts of the properties were adeemed on completion of the contracts. The rule did not, however, cover the situation in Pennington v Waine (2003), where pre-emption rights in private company shares were exercised after the testatrix's death. This would have extended the rule because the testatrix had done nothing herself that would trigger the option. The court declined to extend the rule that far. It distinguished this case from the earlier ones saying that in Lawes itself, and in cases following it, the options had been granted by the testators, who had therefore given control of the situation to the purchasers and therefore effected conversion (by which legally the property is regarded as though it were the proceeds of sale), but in the case of pre-emption rights, the decision on whether or not to go through with the transaction at all rests with the original owner.

---

8  MJ Prichard, 'Trusts for Sale: The Nature of the Beneficiary's Interest' (1971) 29 Cambridge Law Journal 44; Stephen Cretney, 'A Technical and Tricky Matter' (1971) 34 Modern Law Review 441.

### 10.7.7 Practical ways of dealing with the risk of ademption

The unavailability of property that is no longer in the testator's estate can cause grave disappointment. In the days when property was taken by the state rather than privatised, there was nothing to be done to reverse the effects of nationalisation on the will of any individual testator, and any testator who had not altered their will in respect of property which has been nationalised since the date of the will needed to make a new will to deal with the altered state of their property. Nationalisation is, however, no longer current. Similarly, whilst problems with the doctrine of conversion operating on real property should not have arisen when a will had been properly drawn, the doctrine itself was abolished in 1997.[9] A testator may ensure that their intention to make a gift will not be totally frustrated by the ademption of a specific gift, however, by making a substitutional gift, a course approved in *Mullins v Smith* (1860). Thus, the testator may, for example, leave their Steinway grand or such other piano as they have at the date of their death or if they have no piano then some other, general gift.

## 10.8 Witnessing of the will by beneficiary or beneficiary's spouse

By s 15 of the Wills Act 1837, any gift to an attesting witness or their spouse is void (see 5.17). Where, however, the attesting witness and the beneficiary marry after the date of attestation, the beneficiary will not lose the benefit by reason of the later marriage (*Thorpe v Beswick* (1881)).

### 10.8.1 Signature as other than attesting witness

Section 15 of the 1837 Act does not apply when that person signs the will otherwise than as an attesting witness. This occurred in *Kitcat v King* (1930), where a supernumerary witness signed to indicate approval of the contents of the will. Nor, since the Wills Act 1968, will it apply if there are still sufficient attesting witnesses if that person's signature is discounted (see 5.17 and the case of *Re Bravda* (1968)).

### 10.8.2 How a gift to an attesting witness may be saved

Gifts to the attesting witness on trust for someone else do not fail, nor do gifts to someone else on secret trust for the attesting witness. A gift made or confirmed by another will or codicil, if that is properly witnessed, may thus be validated.

This area of the law is still not as clear as it might be. The courts have found some latitude for interpretation in the wording of the statute.

### 10.8.3 Charging clauses

It is fairly common for a person to instruct their solicitor to prepare a will in which that solicitor or the solicitor's firm is appointed executor (see 12.12.2). Many lay executors would in any case pass their paperwork to a solicitor to deal with it; appointing the solicitor as executor enables the testator to choose who deals with their estate. The fees of a solicitor appointed by the executors, or by any other administrators of the estate, have always been payable as administration expenses of the estate, but where the solicitor is appointed by the will as executor, they may not make

---

9  Trusts of Land and Appointment of Trustees Act 1996, s 3.

what are effectively those same charges unless there is a direct provision in the will for them to do so.

An executor or trustee used not to be able to be paid for their services in dealing with the estate unless there was a specific provision to that effect in the will. This rule was confirmed in Re Orwell (1982), the case which concerned the estate of the writer George Orwell. In that case, however, the court declined to construe the charging clause for the trustees so as to exclude payment to the firm of literary agents of one of the executors.

It therefore became standard practice to include a 'charging clause' authorising such payment whenever solicitors were appointed as executors or trustees. It allowed them to charge the estate for their professional services in executing the will and administering the estate. Since the Trustee Act 2000, however, professionals have been able to charge for their work as executors, even if it is such that a layperson could have done it (see 12.12.3).

## 10.8.4 Attesting solicitors and charging clauses

The benefit of a charging clause was previously, however, a benefit under the will, so if the solicitor named as executor also witnessed the will, they would be prevented from charging under the charging clause. In Re Pooley (1888), the will was attested by a solicitor who was appointed executor under it. The will contained a charging clause. The court held that the payment the solicitor might obtain under the provisions of the charging clause was a benefit under the will, and because he had witnessed the will he could not therefore claim for his services. This, again changed with the Trustee Act 2000, so that attesting solicitors may also be paid as executors, as their fees are regarded as administration expenses rather than gifts.

## 10.8.5 Benefits to attesting witness confirmed by codicil attested by others

The case of Re Trotter (1899) also concerned a solicitor who witnessed a will appointing him executor and containing a charging clause. He later also attested a second codicil to the will. Nevertheless, the court held that he could take the benefit of the charging clause in the will under the first codicil which confirmed the will and which he had not attested himself. This resembles the saving found for supernumerary witnesses (see 5.17).

## 10.8.6 Gift to beneficiary as trustee

Re Ray (1936) is authority for the assertion that a beneficiary who takes as trustee, as opposed to being beneficially entitled to the gift, will not be deprived of the gift because they were also an attesting witness. In applying the decision in this case more widely, however, care must be taken with the precise facts. The testatrix was a nun and left her property by will to whomever should be the abbess of her convent at the date of her death, upon trust for the convent. The will was witnessed by two other nuns. When the testatrix died, one of the attesting nuns was the abbess of the convent. The court's decision rested not only the grounds that the attesting nun was not beneficially entitled to the gift but also on the grounds that a gift made to a person described by a formula referring to their station at the date of the testatrix death should not fail because that station was then filled by someone who had witnessed the will, if the testatrix could not have known at the time of making the will who would fill that station at the date of her death.

It is submitted that the second limb of this decision would not be sufficient alone where the witness was beneficially entitled and the sole point on which the case turned was the use of the formula to identify the beneficiary.

## 10.9  Dissolution or annulment of marriage or civil partnership

In historical terms, widespread divorce is a recent phenomenon. It has been suggested by sociologists that the duration of marriages has not in fact altered much over time; what has happened is that people's life expectancy used to be so much less that the number and pattern of divorces now mirrors the number and pattern of marriages which previously ended early through the death of one party; the broadening of practice into same-sex marriage is unlikely to change that general pattern. Since, however, laws are not, on the whole, created to deal with something which is not perceived to present a difficulty, the historical pattern of succession law addressed what happened when one spouse died; that was the likely outcome. It did not address what would happen on divorce, still less the breakdown of a civil partnership.

### 10.9.1  Section 18A of the Wills Act 1837, introduced by the Administration of Justice Act 1982

Section 18 of the Wills Act 1837 deals with the revocation of wills by marriage. Section 18A was added to the Wills Act 1837 by s 18(2) of the Administration of Justice Act 1982, originally amending the original section so as to provide that any gift by will to a spouse would lapse if the marriage were later dissolved or annulled by a court, unless a contrary intention appeared in the will. (The same now applies to the ending of a civil partnership, under s 18B, introduced by the Civil Partnership Act 2004.)

### 10.9.2  *Re Sinclair* (1985)

The deficiencies in this formulation rapidly became apparent in the case of *Re Sinclair* (1985). In that case, the testator made a will leaving his whole estate to his wife. There was a gift over to the Imperial Cancer Research Fund if she predeceased him or failed to survive him for one month. The marriage was dissolved and the testator died, but the former wife lived on. The Court of Appeal held that the gift to the Imperial Cancer Research Fund was effective in accordance with the terms of the will, namely only if the testator's former wife had indeed predeceased him or died within a month of his death. As neither of these things had happened, the estate passed under the rules relating to intestacy

### 10.9.3  Section 18A amended by Law Reform (Succession) Act 1995

The Law Commission's Report No 217 of 1993, *Effect of Divorce on Wills*, considered the effects of *Re Sinclair* (1985) (10.9.2). It recommended an amendment to s 18A so that a divorced spouse was treated as having predeceased. This was implemented in respect of estates arising after 1995 (that is, deaths on or after 1 January 1996, regardless of the date of the will, or of the divorce or annulment) by s 3 of the Law Reform (Succession) Act 1995. This applies where a will appoints a spouse as executor or trustee, or gives them a power of appointment, or if a gift is made to them by the will. If the marriage is later dissolved or annulled, the spouse is treated as having died on the date of the divorce or annulment unless a contrary intention is expressed in the will. This would have produced the correct result in *Re Sinclair*, had the testator died after 1995. Note, however, that the divorced spouse is not treated as having predeceased for all purposes, so, for example, a gift to a third party dependent on the spouse not predeceasing would still take effect. Care should also be taken if the substitutionary gift should be effective in other circumstances of failure of the original gift, such as disclaimer or death within the survivorship period; the current practice of specifying that the substitutionary gift should operate if the original gift fails for any reason may still be advisable, although in respect of gifts to third parties of which the operation really is dependent on the predecease of a spouse, extra care should be taken that the effect of the two spouses' wills is not to give an unintentional double gift to the third party because of the effect, for example, of a survivorship provision. Again, the same now applies in relation to former civil partners, following the introduction of civil partnerships under the Civil Partnership Act 2004.

### 10.9.4 Judicial separation

Note that judicial separation has no effect on gifts by will, though it does affect entitlement on intestacy (see 9.3.1).

## 10.10 Public policy and illegality

A gift may be held void as being in contravention of public policy, for instance if it is held that it tends to promote the ending of an existing marriage. A gift will likewise fail if it promotes an illegal purpose. The rules relating to this area are the same as those for *inter vivos* trusts. Thus, a gift to a wife provided she divorces her husband will be invalid. A gift which, though the same in practical effect, is phrased so as to provide for her in the event of her no longer being married (and thus no longer dependent on her husband) may well be valid.

A gift that was directly contrary to law, though perhaps at one remove from public policy as a more general phenomenon, was that in *Re Robson (deceased); White v Matthys* (2014). The testator was a divorced man who had lived in Spain for more than five years before his death. He left his Spanish estate to his sons and his non-Spanish estate (the bulk of his wealth) to the British National Party. The sons claimed that the gift to the BNP was unlawful because of the prohibition in the Political Parties Elections and Referendums Act 2000 on foreign donations, namely those from people who had not been on the electoral register in the preceding five years. They claimed the gift to the BNP failed and the non-Spanish estate would come to them on intestacy. Deputy Judge Richard Sheldon QC found that the gift was a prohibited donation within the meaning of the Act, and that the trust the BNP had set up to receive the money pursuant to a deed of variation did not save the gift either, since the proposed transaction still involved accepting the prohibited gift under the will. He held that the money went *bona vacantia* to the Crown. However, he directed that it then be paid to the sons.

### 10.10.1 A person may not profit from his or her own crime

A common reason for a gift by will or entitlement on intestacy being held void for reason of public policy is, however, the rule that a person may not profit from their own crime. In the context of succession, this is seen as the rule that a beneficiary who is guilty of the murder or manslaughter of the deceased may not take a benefit from the estate of the deceased. This applies whether the benefit comes through the will or the intestacy of the deceased, or under a nomination or *donatio mortis causa* or some form of trust including a joint tenancy (note however that homicide by one joint tenant of another joint tenant severs the joint tenancy).

### 10.10.2 The forfeiture rule

The forfeiture rule is the name given to that rule of public policy which states that a sane person who commits murder should not be allowed to benefit from the estate of their victim. How far the rule applies in the case of manslaughter is unclear. In *Re Giles* (1971), a woman who had killed her husband was found not guilty of murder but guilty of manslaughter by reason of diminished responsibility, and was sent to Broadmoor (a secure psychiatric unit). She sought her benefit from her husband's estate on the basis that she was not morally, only criminally, guilty of the killing, but the court held that the benefit was still forfeited. The forfeiture rule was held to apply in manslaughter cases such as Re K (1985) (10.10.7) and Land v Land (2006).[10] It was held however in Re H (1990) that the forfeiture rule did not apply in a manslaughter case because the verdict meant that the person had not been guilty of the necessary degree of deliberation and intention. It is a rule of public policy and not one arising under statute; the Forfeiture Act 1982 (10.10.5) did not create the forfeiture rule, but modified it by providing for relief from the effects of the rule.[11]

## 10.10.3 Homicide by the insane does not lead to forfeiture

If a person is not convicted of murder or manslaughter, the forfeiture rule does not come into operation. Thus, if they are found insane and not convicted for that reason, they may keep any benefits under the will or intestacy of the deceased.

## 10.10.4 Operation of the rule: family troubles

The rule was exemplified in the case of Dr Crippen, the murderer who tried to escape to America but was caught by the use of the transatlantic telegraph. He had murdered his intestate wife; before her estate was administered, he was executed for his crime. It was held that the forfeiture rule prevented her estate from passing to him. Therefore, the beneficiary of Crippen's will could not claim the estate of the murdered wife, because it had not passed to Crippen during his life and did not form part of his estate (Re Crippen (1911)). Whilst this might be a reasonable result, given that unfortunately homicides are so often committed within the family, more difficult cases can arise.

Where a gift fails under the forfeiture rule, it falls into residue like any other failed gift. In Re Callaway (1956), the testatrix, who was a widow, was murdered by her daughter. She had left her whole estate by will to that daughter, who was disentitled to her benefit under the will by operation of the forfeiture rule. All the deceased's property therefore should have passed under the intestacy rules, but the operation of those rules meant the convicted daughter would share the estate with the deceased's son. Her murder of the deceased also disentitled her to her share under the intestacy rules. The question arose as to where that share would go. The Crown claimed the daughter's half-share as bona vacantia. However, the court rejected this suggestion and awarded the whole estate to the son, as though the daughter had predeceased. In Land v Land (2006), the would-be claimant for relief from forfeiture was out of time and in the absence of discretion to extend time, the judge held that a claim could be made instead for family provision (see chapter 15). However, had it been held that, in the light of the 'tragic story' in this case, that the forfeiture rule did not apply, no such family provision application would have been needed.

---

10  Debate in the Court of Appeal in Dunbar v Plant (1998), a case concerning the survivor of a suicide pact, was inconclusive on the point.
11  There is an interesting provision in Scotland, under the Parricide Act 1594. This provides that where a person is convicted of the murder of their parent or grandparent, they and all their descendants are precluded from taking from the murdered person's estate. The idea of 'corruption of the blood' is thought to have arisen by analogy with the rules pertaining to treason (since abolished). The Act is so complex that it has never been successfully applied. In a near-miss case, Oliphant v Oliphant (1674), a man killed his mother but escaped from custody and so was never convicted of murder; therefore the Act did not apply.

A further issue arose in the cases of *Jones v Midland Bank Trust Co* (1997) and *Re DWS (deceased)* (2001). In *Jones v Midland Bank*, a mother had left her entire estate to her son or, if he predeceased her, to two nephews. The son killed the mother and was convicted of manslaughter, and in dealing with the question of where the son's lost inheritance would go, the Court of Appeal construed the wording of the will so that the gift to the nephews was dependent on the son's predecease; unfortunately the will clause did not contain the customary additional 'or if this gift should fail for any other reason'. In *Re DWS*, a son killed both his parents. They left brothers and sisters, and a grandson who was the son of the killer. The question was how the parents' estate should pass on their intestacy. The Court of Appeal held it passed to the victims' brothers and sisters, with a dissenting voice holding that it should go as *bona vacantia* to the Crown. It was felt that the latter in particular was an inappropriate result, especially given the emphasis elsewhere on the deceased's presumed intentions, and the effect of s 33 Wills Act 1837 as amended, which allowed the next generation to take what was originally intended for the parent, both in relation to forfeited interests and also in respect of interests disclaimed on intestacy. The Law Commission consulted[12] and as a result what the Society of Trusts and Estates Practitioners (perhaps a little snarkily) described as the 'snappily titled Estates of Deceased Persons (Forfeiture Rule and Law of Succession) Act 2011' was passed, which amended s 33A Wills Act 1837 and inserted a new s 46A into the Administration of Estates Act 1925. It also inserted new provisions into s 47 dealing with the estates of single parents who die under the age of 18. The powers of the court in relation to modifying the forfeiture rule will however not be affected. A by-product of this amendment is the confirmation that an interest on intestacy can be disclaimed, though that may remain unclear in relation to disclaimers before the amendments effected by the 2011 Act.

A commentator has questioned the application of the rule where the victim forgives the killer and makes or republishes a testamentary gift to them between the attack that kills them and their subsequent death.[13]

## 10.10.5 Forfeiture Act 1982

Note that statute is not what gives rise to the forfeiture rule itself; that is a creation of public policy. The forfeiture rule existed long before the 1982 Act, but before that Act there was no possibility of seeking relief from the effects of the rule. This Act is not what deprives the homicidal beneficiary of their gifts but is what may allow them to avoid the effects of the forfeiture rule and keep the gifts. (It would have been helpful if the Act had been called the Relief From Forfeiture Act.)

## 10.10.6 Provisions of the 1982 Act

Section 2 of the 1982 Act allows for the modification of the effects of the forfeiture rule in cases of manslaughter, though not murder. Anyone convicted of murder will still lose all benefit from the deceased's estate and the court has no power to grant them relief from the effects of the forfeiture rule.

Proceedings under the 1982 Act for modification of the forfeiture rule must be brought within three months of the conviction for manslaughter. If the court is satisfied that the justice of the case so requires, it can grant complete or partial relief from the effect of the forfeiture rule. The decision is in the court's discretion and it will have regard to the conduct of both the offender and the deceased and to any other material circumstances.

---

12  Law Commission *The Forfeiture Rule and the Law of Succession* (2005, Law Com No 295).
13  Andrew Simester, 'Unworthy but Forgiven Heirs' (1990) 10 Estates and Trusts Journal 217.

### 10.10.7 Development of the relief

In *Re K* (1985) a wife was convicted of the manslaughter of her husband on the grounds of diminished responsibility. He had been persistently and seriously violent towards her over a long period. She was sentenced to two years' probation for his manslaughter. On her application for modification of the forfeiture rule, the court allowed her to take his interest in their family home, which was jointly owned, and her benefits under his will: compare this with the result in the arguably similar case of *Re Giles* (1971) (10.10.2), before the 1982 Act.

In an Australian case on similar facts, *Public Trustee v Evans* (1985), in the New South Wales Supreme Court, Young J said that the exclusion from benefit rule was essentially judge-made and the courts should recognise that there may be good reasons for departing from it.

In *Jones v Roberts* (1995), the court considered a man's application for relief from the forfeiture of his interest in the estate of his father. He had been convicted of the manslaughter of both his parents on the basis of diminished responsibility because, although his actions were deliberate, he was found to be suffering from paranoid schizophrenia and to be deluded that his parents were persecuting him, though not to the extent that he was considered criminally insane (which would have meant acquittal). The court considered the pre-Forfeiture Act case of *Gray v Barr* (1971) in which it had been said that the forfeiture rule should apply, as a matter of public policy, in cases of deliberate, unlawful and intentional violence or threats of violence. Distinguishing *Re K* (1985), which has a different factual background, the court said that public policy in this respect had not moved on and that therefore relief from forfeiture should not encompass cases such as this, where there were 'deliberate and intentional acts of violence' resulting in death. The application for relief therefore failed.

### 10.10.8 Degrees of manslaughter

In a manslaughter case, therefore, the current position seems to be that, whilst murderers certainly cannot share in their victims' estates, those convicted of manslaughter may be regarded in one of three ways. First, their conduct may not only bring the forfeiture rule into play but also be so bad as to exclude relief; second, they may be regarded as having brought the forfeiture rule into play (for example, if the court regards all manslaughter cases as leading to forfeiture) but be successful in seeking relief; or third, their conduct in relation to the manslaughter may be regarded as not bringing the forfeiture rule into play in the first place (if the court entertains in principle the idea that not all manslaughter convictions lead to forfeiture).

## 10.11 Inalienability; perpetuities and accumulations

Whilst succession law as a whole is about how people can control their property after their death, the rule against perpetuities was designed to prevent their doing that for too long.[14] Although being able to control where your property goes after your death is considered a proper part of succession law, a greater imperative is the market idea that property in general should be alienable – it should be capable of being bought and sold. The perpetuity rule came into being in the seventeenth century to specify when marketability overcomes private control as a matter of principle, so an interest must either vest or take effect. In principle, the rule favours the freedom of future generations to operate a market in property, including such details as avoiding tax in the light of law changes, over the right of the 'dead hand' to exert control from beyond the grave.[15]

---

14  The rule against perpetuities forms an essential part of the plot of the film *Body Heat* (Lawrence Kasdan 1981).
15  Lewis M Simes, *Public Policy and the Dead Hand* (University of Michigan Press 1955); Ruth Deech, 'Lives in Being Revived' (1981) 97 Law Quarterly Review 593.

If a gift offends against the perpetuity rule, it will be void for that reason.[16] In *Ward v Van der Loeff* (1924), a codicil was held partly inoperative for perpetuity; Lord Haldane found this a good reason for awarding costs out of the estate since 'the difficulty has been entirely caused by the testator himself'. The tendency was, however, for courts to construe the terms of a will so that the rule against perpetuities was not offended, so as to save a gift that would otherwise be void. In *Re Vaux* (1939), an express limitation to whatever period fell within the law against perpetuities, without reference to lives in being as would have been required, was held sufficient. Careful construction of the settlement in *Re Drummond* (1988) saved the position where a contingent gift was not satisfied and there was no gift over.[17]

The basic common law rule was that interests must vest within a period not exceeding that of a 'life in being' plus 21 years, and interest could not accumulate beyond that period. A 'life in being' was someone who was alive at the date of the creation of the trust, which could include the settlor or testator.[18] At the time 21 years was the age of majority, so this preserved, for example, any gift to a testator's minor child that was contingent on their attaining legal adulthood.

The rule was the cause of difficulties for a long time, especially where it was found to apply to land interests outside the context of family wills from which it sprang.[19] As well as court attempts to alleviate its effects in individual cases, the rule itself has had two major statutory modifications. The common law rule originally required that if a gift might possibly offend against the rule, by commencing or vesting outside the perpetuity period, then the gift was void for that reason. The Perpetuities and Accumulations Act 1964 modified that rule so that the gift would be avoided only if vesting outside the perpetuity period actually happened. This became known as the 'wait and see' rule, because it meant that the validity of the interest might be determined only at the end of the perpetuity period.[20] The 1964 Act also allowed a fixed perpetuity period of 80 years to be employed, and provided that options would have a perpetuity period of 21 years.[21]

The current rules are those under the Perpetuities and Accumulations Act 2009, which governs all non-charitable trusts created on or after 6 April 2010. In relation to wills, the relevant date is the date of execution of the will or codicil.[22] The new perpetuity period is 125 years beginning on the date of the creation of the trust, unless a shorter period is specified by the trust instrument, and the 'wait and see' rule is broadened. The 2009 Act also allows trustees of a trust created under the old rules, where the perpetuity period is specified by reference to lives in being and those are difficult to ascertain, to apply to the court to have that replaced with a fixed perpetuity period of 100 years. For trusts created on or after 6 April 2010, there is no limit to the period for accumulation of income save the lifetime of the trust itself; again, unless the trust instrument specifies otherwise.

Whilst no doubt the new law is an improvement on the old, it is also certain that disputes will continue to arise under the older law: it is of the nature of wills and trusts that their problems can lie dormant or persist for protracted periods, and law reform can even complicate the issues in the individual case.[23]

---

16  The rule does not apply to charity: for an illustration of the practical implications of this see the discussion in *Cuppage, Attewell and Russell v Lawson, Chignell and Her Majesty's Attorney General* (2010).

17  Note that the headnote of this case is misleading.

18  A life is in being in the womb (*en ventre sa mère*) for the purposes of this rule.

19  See for example *Air Jamaica Limited v Joy Charlton and Others (Jamaica)* (1999), or for a more domestic example *Souglides v Tweedie* (2012), paras 27–30; the latter also demonstrates a variation on the 'peppercorn rent', namely consideration of 'one red rose'.

20  S 7 Perpetuities and Accumulations Act 1964.

21  Trusts and relevant interests created before 16 July 1964 still run under the preceding rules: consider for example *Wilson v Truelove* (2003).

22  It is not clear whether a codicil executed after 5 April will bring a will within the new rules. It is best to re-execute the will.

23  See for example *Wyndham v Egremont and Bridges* (2009), concerning Lord Egremont's 1969 Trust.

# 10.12 Insolvency and abatement

A gift may fail because there is insufficient property in the estate to satisfy it. This may be because the estate is insolvent, so that there is simply no property available from which the gift may be satisfied, or because the estate is insufficient to pay all the gifts in full, so that they abate, in which case a beneficiary may receive part of the gift. For the order of payment of debts in an insolvent estate, see 13.7.

## 10.12.1 Insolvency

The estate is insolvent if it cannot meet its debts and liabilities. Those payments are met first, and none of the beneficiaries has any claim on any property in the estate until they have been made in full. An estate is not insolvent if it can meet all its debts and liabilities, even if there is not enough in it to fulfil all the gifts made in the will.

## 10.12.2 Abatement

Where the estate can meet all its debts and liabilities in full, the personal representatives will then deal with any remaining property in it in accordance with the deceased's will or intestacy.

On intestacy, the rules are clear; the surviving spouse or civil partner, if any, has a first claim on the estate, and thereafter the division of any residue is prescribed amongst the deceased's family.

Where the deceased left a will, however, there may be various provisions of different kinds which the personal representatives cannot implement in full because there is insufficient in the estate to do so. The rules of abatement provide how the gifts should be dealt with when they cannot all be made in full.

## 10.12.3 Different rules depending on type of gift

Residue abates first, then general legacies and lastly specific and demonstrative legacies. Each class abates completely before the next class begins to abate, and gifts in the same class abate at the same rate, on the principle that 'equality is equity'.

In practical terms, this means that, after payment of debts and liabilities, all the specific and demonstrative legacies are paid out first in full if possible, and then if there is anything remaining it is used to pay general legacies. Only if those are all paid in full will there be any residue.

## 10.12.4 Inheritance Tax

Where a testator has specified that a specific gift which would otherwise bear its own tax should be paid free of tax, the tax that is payable on it is treated as a pecuniary legacy. Thus, a beneficiary may receive the specific gift in full but have to pay part of the tax on it because the deemed pecuniary legacy represented by the provision that the gift be free of tax has abated in the next class of gifts because of a lack of funds in the estate.

## 10.12.5 Subject to contrary intention in the will

The rules of abatement are subject to any contrary intention shown in the will. The testator may have indicated by the terms of their will that they wanted the gifts to be paid out in a particular order of priority. In *Sayer v Sayer* (1714), the testator directed that the pecuniary legacies given by his will should be taken out of the whole personalty. As there was insufficient in the estate to pay both the pecuniary legacies and the specific legacies in full, the question arose as to whether the direction meant that the pecuniary legacies would take precedence over the specific legacies. The court held that it did mean that, and the specific legacies abated.

How expression of a contrary intention works in practice is discussed further in 13.15. What is discussed here are the rules implied by law, which operate where there is no such contrary intention.

## 10.13 Dealing with uncertainty

It is a general provision of the law of property and trusts that a gift will be void if it is uncertain either as to its subject matter or as to its object (beneficiary). Uncertainty may render a gift void even where it appears certain on the face of it. The testator in Re Gray (1887) made a gift of company shares, which was a general legacy. However, the company had been wound up before the testator's death. The gift failed for uncertainty because the personal representatives could neither purchase the shares nor ascertain their value so as to satisfy the gift in money.

A court will lean to construing a gift as being certain, however, and may admit evidence to establish the identity of either the subject or the object. For more on this, see 11.4–10. Note, however, that so far as uncertainty of object is concerned, no charitable gift will ever fail for want of an object, because charity never fails. If the gift is clearly charitable, the court can direct which particular charities will receive it. In Re White (1893), the testator left a gift on trust for 'the following religious societies' without naming any. The court treated it as prima facie confined to charities and so it was held valid as a charitable gift even though the objects were not named and therefore, had it not been charitable, it would have failed for uncertainty of objects.

The courts have evolved rules to deal with common sorts of uncertainty. In Re Baden (no 2) (1972), Megaw LJ said the test of certainty of objects (beneficiaries) was satisfied if:

> as regards at least a substantial number ... it can be said with certainty that they fall within the trust; even though, as regards a substantial number of other persons, if they ever for some fanciful reason fell to be considered, the answer would have to be, not 'they are outside the trust', but 'it is not proven whether they are in or out'.

In Re Poulton; Smail v Litchfield (1987), however, the testatrix left property to a life tenant with the direction that she should on her death divide it 'among her own relatives according to her own discretion'. The life tenant left a share to her cousin for life and then to the cousin's children, who were not that original life tenant's statutory next of kin. The plaintiff claimed that this was not permissible given the rule of construction that 'relations' were the same as 'next of kin'. However, the court held that this rule existed purely to save gifts which would otherwise be void for uncertainty.

## 10.14 Non-compliance with condition

A gift by will may be subject to a condition. The condition may be a condition precedent or a condition subsequent, and it may be valid or void.

### 10.14.1 Condition precedent

A condition precedent is one which has to be satisfied before the event contingent upon it can take place. Thus, a gift might be conditional on the beneficiary attaining a certain age or giving a certain piece of their property to a third party (in which case it is unclear what sort of interest – whether in the property itself, or as a charge on it, or personally only against the beneficiary – the third party obtains in the property if the beneficiary obtains it without fulfilling the condition). Only when this had happened could the gift pass. In *Folds v Abrahart* (2003), the whole will was held to be conditional on the proviso that the testator and his wife should 'die together'. Since they did not, the claimant was granted letters of administration.

If the testator prescribes a period during which the condition must be satisfied, that will probably need to be adhered to precisely if the gift is not to fail, although there is some Commonwealth authority for the proposition that a court may extend the time limit laid down by a testator where the condition is largely fulfilled (*Re Bragg* (1977)).

If a condition precedent is void, the gift itself will fail.

### 10.14.2 Condition subsequent

In the case of a condition subsequent operating as a condition of defeasance, the beneficiary loses the gift if the condition is not satisfied. If a condition subsequent is void, the gift becomes unconditional. In the case where the condition of defeasance is ambiguous, evidence may be adduced.

In *Re Tepper* (1987), the testator made gifts conditional on the beneficiaries remaining in, and not marrying outside, the Jewish faith. The court held that, though the gift appeared to be void for uncertainty, the condition was one of defeasance rather than a condition precedent and accordingly evidence should be filed as to the meaning of the phrase 'the Jewish faith'.

If a condition subsequent is void, the gift will be absolute.

### 10.14.3 'No-contest' clauses

A 'no-contest' clause is one which provides that the interest of any beneficiary who contests the will shall, should they not win that case, be forfeit and subject to a gift over to someone else.[24] Along with clauses under which a beneficiary would forfeit a benefit should he or she marry, it is a traditional type of *in terrorem* clause; however, restraint of marriage is against public policy. 'No-contest' clauses, on the other hand, are well established, and are also encountered in *inter vivos* trusts, especially those which are established for tax reasons and thus with a particular focus on their operation, and often overseas. The beneficiary in *AN v Barclays Private Bank & Trust Company (Cayman) Limited and Others* (2007) asserted that the *in terrorem* clause was invalid on the grounds of uncertainty, repugnancy or public policy, also alleging wrongdoing on the part of the trustees and seeking their replacement. The court held that the circumstances in which the clause would operate had not yet arisen and she was not challenging the instrument itself. However, it considered that the instrument raised a 'conundrum' where it purported in effect to exclude the beneficiary's right to ensure due execution if it deprived her of her benefit should she impugn the trustees' decision-taking processes. In this it resembled the issue in the Court of Appeal case of *Adams v Adams* (1892), though there the challenge to the instrument was considered 'frivolous and vexatious'.

It remains to be seen whether this type of clause becomes more common and more controversial: there could be resistance if these clauses are perceived to be attempts to oust the jurisdiction of the courts over the proper administration of estates. There is also a long-standing question

---

24 *Evanturel v Evanturel* (1874).

as to whether in terrorem clauses are invalid if they do not come with a gift over.[25] Those cases show endeavours by the courts to avoid the effects of the clauses, and so may indicate the likely future treatment of 'no-contest' clauses. A legal change in California in 2010, for example, was aimed at making contesting 'no-contest' clauses easier, since otherwise they tended cause more, rather than less, litigation as would-be challengers sought preliminary declarations as to the likely effects of an action and whether or not it would be considered to be a 'contest'.

## 10.15 Fraud

If a beneficiary has committed a relevant fraud on the testator, that will disqualify them from taking a benefit under the will. The testator in *Wilkinson v Joughlin* (1866) believed himself to be married to the woman whom he named as 'my wife' when leaving her a benefit under his will. The court held, however, that she had deliberately misled him about her marital status – she was already married, and the marriage to the testator was void because of her bigamy – and that this amounted to fraud. She, therefore, did not take the benefit under the will of her 'husband'. In *Re Posner* (1953), the testator similarly left a gift to the person he called 'my wife' but to whom he was not legally married. However, in that case, there was no element of fraud and indeed neither party had realised that the marriage had not been valid. The 'wife' therefore took her benefit under the will of the testator.

## 10.16 Summary of Chapter 10

### 10.16.1 The Classification and Failure of Gifts

Gifts are classified in different ways. Legacies may be specific, demonstrative, general or residuary. How a legacy is classified may have important practical effects on whether or not a beneficiary receives the gift or whether it is used to pay the debts of the estate. A 'legacy' is a gift of personal property, whereas 'devise' refers to a gift of land.

(a) Specific gifts are gifts of a particular, severable part of the testator's property.
(b) General gifts do not refer to any particular part of the estate and if a testator makes a general gift of something that is in the estate, the personal representatives will have to buy that gift for the beneficiary.
(c) A demonstrative legacy is a gift out of a particular fund. Insofar as the fund exists, the gift is specific, but if the fund is insufficient to meet the gift, the rest of the gift operates as a general legacy.
(d) Residuary gifts are gifts of all the remainder of a particular kind of property or all the remainder of the estate after the specific, general and demonstrative gifts have been taken out.
(e) Pecuniary legacies are gifts of money, which may fall into various categories. Annuities are regarded as a series of pecuniary legacies, but are governed by particular rules as to their administration.

A beneficiary may disclaim a gift made to them. This may have an effect on what other beneficiaries receive, in that they will receive more or receive it sooner.

---

25  *Re Hanlon* (1933); *Re Dickson's Trust* (1850); *Leong v Lim Beng Chye* (1955). This discussion is more developed in North America: see Peter G Lawson, 'The Rule Against In Terrorem Clauses' [2005] Estates, Pensions and Trusts Journal 71.

If the beneficiary predeceases (dies before) the testator, their gift will lapse, subject to the provisions of s 33 of the Wills Act 1837, by which relate to gifts to predeceased children may go to remoter issue. The doctrine of lapse does not apply where there is a joint tenancy or a class gift.

Specific gifts fail by ademption (or 'are adeemed') where the specified property does not form part of the testator's estate at their death.

Where a beneficiary or their spouse has been an attesting witness to the will, the gift will fail under s 15 of the Wills Act 1837, subject to some saving provisions.

If a marriage or civil partnership is dissolved or annulled, then any gift to the former spouse or appointment of that person as executor will be treated as though that person had predeceased.

A gift will fail if it is contrary to public policy, especially if it falls foul of the forfeiture rule which says that a person who has been convicted of killing another may not benefit from the deceased's will or intestacy. However, in the case of manslaughter (but not murder) the beneficiary may apply to the court for relief from forfeiture under the Forfeiture Act 1982.

Where the estate is insolvent – there is insufficient in it to meet its debts and liabilities – the creditors will be paid in an order laid down by statute. Where the estate is solvent but there is insufficient to meet all the gifts, they will also be paid out in an order laid down by statute, according to their classification, unless the testator has specified otherwise in the will. Gifts within a class are paid out proportionately; they abate rateably within the class.

Gifts which contravene the rules against inalienability or perpetuities and accumulations will fail for that reason. Gifts also fail if they are insufficiently certain, do not comply with a valid condition or if they have been obtained by the fraud of the beneficiary.

## 📖 10.17 Further reading

### Book

Lewis M Simes, *Public Policy and the Dead Hand* (University of Michigan Press 1955).

### Journal articles

Stephen Cretney, 'A Technical and Tricky Matter' (1971) 34 Modern Law Review 441.
Ruth Deech, 'Lives in Being Revived' (1981) 97 Law Quarterly Review 593.
Peter G Lawson, 'The Rule Against *In Terrorem* Clauses' [2005] Estates, Pensions and Trusts Journal 71.
MJ Prichard, 'Trusts for Sale: The Nature of the Beneficiary's Interest' (1971) 29 Cambridge Law Journal 44.
Andrew Simester, 'Unworthy but Forgiven Heirs' (1990) 10 Estates and Trusts Journal 217.

# Chapter 11

# Construction of Wills

The construction of a will is the way its wording will be interpreted. Questions of knowledge and approval may dictate what parts of a will may have to be omitted from probate as invalid; questions of construction arise when considering what the import of the valid parts of the will may be. Construction deals with how the meaning of particular words and phrases will be established, and what will be done to resolve cases of ambiguity. No two persons use language the same way, and there is always the risk that what was perfectly clear to the testator may be rather less clear to their personal representatives or indeed to a court. Moreover, even if the personal representatives knew the testator well and are satisfied that, though the testator appeared to say one thing, they definitely meant another, it would not be a satisfactory state of affairs to allow them to interpret the testator's will in accordance with their own beliefs or their own agenda in a way that gave scope for their rewriting it. That would mean that the testator's family and friends, rather than the testator him- or herself, wrote the will.

## 11.1 General principles: rules of construction

There have to be rules which state how certain words are to be interpreted or what is to be done with particular kinds of ambiguity In the early case of *Jones v Westcomb* (1711), for example, the court had to decide how to deal with a will by which the testator devised a term of years (lease) to his wife for life and then the child *en ventre sa mère*,[1] with one-third of the gift to the wife if the child died before the age of 21, when the wife was not in fact pregnant – it held that the devise was good, though the contingency had never occurred. There may be cases in which the implementation of those rules does an injustice which is manifest to onlookers, but there are others where the rules will bring a resolution and allow the administration of an estate to proceed when otherwise the arguing could have continued indefinitely. Moreover, once the meaning that the law will attribute to words is clearly established, future testators and their advisers may be confident in the knowledge that, as far as the legal interpretation of their wills goes, they have said what they mean.

Again, the problem in this area as in others is that by the time the question arises it is too late for the testator to be asked to clarify their position. As so often, it is the general function of the law to provide rules to resolve difficulties and ambiguities.

### 11.1.1 Function of the rules of construction

The object of the rules of construction is to ascertain the testator's expressed intention. This should be clearly distinguished from simply attempting to ascertain the testator's actual intention.

---

1 'In the mother's womb' – children in gestation are generally considered to be included within the definition of existing children for the purposes of law in this area.

If that were the object, then the will document itself would be just one piece of evidence about something which is probably undiscoverable and certainly cannot be checked, namely the deceased's previous state of mind. The rules of construction are rules on how to construe the will itself, as the expression of the testator's intention. The testator must be taken to have meant what they said when they said it; however, many rules have to be followed in order to establish what, legally, the testator did mean. To go behind the words to the extent of passing over them as the fundamental expression of their testamentary wishes would be to deprive them of the ability to do exactly as they wished. In *Higgins v Dawson* (1902), Lord Shand said of a particular proposal to lead evidence that it was 'to supply a basis for inferring the intention of the testator and to take one away from the true construction of the will as showing that the testator intended something different from what he has said'; that is not the function of a court of construction and the evidence was not admitted.

Seeking to ascertain the testator's intentions after their death rather than dealing with their expressed intentions in their will would also contradict or at best render irrelevant the statutory requirement in s 9 of the Wills Act 1837 that the will be 'in writing'. The importance of what is written must be upheld, and the courts must not overstep the bounds of interpreting wills so as to allow themselves to go so far as writing them. Lord Simon LC said in *Perrin v Morgan* (1943) that:

> The fundamental rule in construing the language of a will is to put on the words used the meaning which, having regard to the terms of the will, the testator intended. The question is not, of course, what the testator meant to do when he made his will, but what the written words he uses mean in the particular case – what are the 'expressed intentions' of the testator.

Thus, if what the testator says is clear, then however unlikely it may seem, it must stand, and must not be interpreted to the extent that the court is not interpreting, but writing, the will. That would negate the idea of testamentary freedom and the property rights of testators.

## 11.1.2 Construction or re-construction?

There may sometimes be a temptation to stretch the rules of construction, no doubt so that the testator's real and true intention (as often discernible by their family and friends) may be honoured rather than what they appear to have said, without meaning it. There may often be a genuinely disappointed relative who truly believes that their great-uncle meant to benefit them by leaving them the Mercedes he had when he died, but if his will leaves the Mini he had when he made the will and which he no longer has, without any substitutional provision relating to the Mercedes or such other cars as great-uncle might have at his death, who is to say that the omission was not deliberate? Perhaps there had been a row which the great-nephew has not mentioned. It is too late to ask the testator personally.

The court of construction's function is not to improve upon what the testator has said, only to give effect to what is in the will itself, described by Jenkins LJ in *Re Bailey* (1951) as 'the dispositions actually made as appearing expressly or by necessary implication from the language of the will applied to the surrounding circumstances of the case'. Thus, in some situations a court will look at the circumstances around the case and take evidence as to what was said or done – but this is with a view to the proper interpretation of the will itself, not in order to see whether it could be improved upon. Rules as to when a court will look at evidence from outside the will – extrinsic evidence – have also evolved and are adhered to strictly. They do usually have a discernible logic.

### 11.1.3 How much latitude does the court have?

The court cannot interfere with what the will actually says, even if it appears arguable that that would achieve a 'better' result. The only way a court can alter the provisions of a will is under the Inheritance (Provision for Family and Dependants) Act 1975, and what it does then is not so much alter the provisions of the will as amend their effects – the will itself remains, but the implementation of its provisions is partly undone by the implementation of the subsequent court order. Nevertheless, a court may often have some latitude in its decision, being able to justify more than one construction of the will or, for example, being able to decide which of two meanings with nothing to choose between them constitutes the more probable representation of the testator's intention; in this area, as in others, there may often be a lingering doubt as to whether a court's view is based on the law or on the facts of the case.

In *Underwood v Wing* (1855), the testator's will gave his personalty on trust to William Wing for the testator's wife absolutely, but if she died in his lifetime on certain trusts (which failed), and subject to this to William Wing. The testator and his wife were lost at sea together and there was no evidence as to who died first. (Note that now the *commorientes* rule would be available: see 9.2 and 10.6). It was held that the gift to William Wing was dependent on the testator surviving his wife and the mere failure of the practical operation of the gift did not mean William Wing was entitled. But in a similarly difficult situation in *Re Whitrick* (1957), the court construed the testatrix's true intention to the opposite effect. She had left her estate to her husband or, if he died 'at the same time' as her, to three named beneficiaries. He predeceased her. The court construed 'at the same time' effectively to include 'or before' to save the gifts, as this appeared to be the testatrix's clear intention.

### 11.1.4 Practicalities of construction – where do you take the problem?

The construction of a will may well be a contentious point, and if it cannot be resolved it is possible to take the matter to a court for its decision. This may mean a full-scale court process. Where a matter becomes contentious, although it would normally go to the Family Division of the High Court for the question of the validity of the will to be dealt with, questions of construction usually go to the Chancery Division of the High Court.

The Chancery Division has historically been concerned with wills and those who practise in it, on both sides of the bench, have long experience of construing deeds of trust and settlements. The Chancery Division in particular is felt to be very lawyer-like in its approach, and some people (particularly those who find a decision has gone against them, perhaps) feel that it is too pedantic and too much biased towards the interpretation a lawyer would put on words rather than the meaning which to them appears obvious and which they feel should be recognised by the court.

### 11.1.5 Why different courts for different functions?

The system under which the courts deal with different questions about wills may appear to be one of those systems which, if you did not have them already, you might not invent.[2] The court to which one usually refers when talking about probate matters is the Family Division of the High Court, usually in its incarnation as a local District Probate Registry where it generally exercises its judicial function in a way that is essentially not judicial at all, but administrative. The Family Division is the renamed Probate, Divorce and Admiralty Division of the High Court,

---

2 Fiona Cownie and Anthony Bradney, 'Divided Justice, Different Voices: Inheritance and Family Provision' (2003) 23 Legal Studies 566.

which took its new title under the Administration of Justice Act 1970. By then it had already exercised its probate functions for a century under the organisation of the courts which took place under the Judicature Acts in the 1870s. That organisation assigned construction functions, however, to the Chancery Division.

## 11.1.6 The division of functions between courts

The present structure is at least clearer than what went before, although it reflects it. That was involved with the different jurisdictions of the ecclesiastical courts, the common law courts and the Court of Chancery. The ecclesiastical courts imported a great deal from Roman law. They retained jurisdiction over the *validity* of wills of personality for a very long time. The Court of Chancery, also importing many principles of Roman law, gradually managed to obtain jurisdiction over the *interpretation* of wills of personality. The courts of common law, which also brought in Roman law principles, tended to hold simply that realty devolved to the devisee named in the will or else to the heir upon intestacy; both they and the Court of Chancery would adjudicate on the *interpretation* of wills of realty.

The division of functions between courts is therefore largely historical; that is certainly its origin. It is possible moreover to observe a sense in the structure of the system. The Family Division is concerned with disputes about people and what they do, and so perhaps it is the right place for decisions about the validity of a will and, if the question comes up, exactly what form of the will is the right one to be accepted as valid. The Chancery Division has always been concerned with property and with the meaning of settlements and other disposals of property which are set out in disputable language, and so if a question of construction of any substance arises, it considers itself a more appropriate venue than the Family Division. However, in *In the Estate of Fawcett* (1941), the probate court held that where it was considering a question of validity, it had a limited jurisdiction to construe a will and a duty to exercise that jurisdiction to save costs.

## 11.1.7 Where do you find the rules?

There are various presumptions and rules which have evolved over the course of the centuries of case law, and there are statutory provisions. Some of these relate directly to the construction of wills: for example, those which set out what certain expressions will mean as a matter of law or which deal with the evidence a court may look at in a construction matter. Some of them are of more general application, for instance rules about the age of majority.

## 11.1.8 What will the court do?

The court will construe the will as a whole. Lord Halsbury in *Higgins v Dawson* (1902) (11.1.1) said:

> Where you are construing either a will or any other instrument ... you must look at the whole instrument to see the meaning of the whole instrument, and you cannot rely upon one particular passage in it to the exclusion of what is relevant to the explanation of the particular clause that you are expounding.

In *Re Macandrew* (1963), the testator's will of 1900 directed his trustees to hold his son W's share of the residue during his life on discretionary trusts for one or more of a class including W and his wife and issue if any. After W's death, the trustees were to pay the income to W's widow and then in trust for his children. The testator had then provided that 'if my said son W shall not leave a child or widow' then the fund should be held of trust for certain children of another son.

Where the testator left a widow but no children, the court construed the will as a whole and held that 'or widow' was superfluous as well as incongruous, so that the widow took her life interest and then the fund passed in trust for the children of the other named son.

The court will apply all the rules which have evolved from past cases as well as statutory rules of construction. It will also try to read the will so as to make it cover all the testator's property, rather than allowing its construction of the will to lead to an intestacy. Esher MR in *Re Harrison* (1885) justified this by suggesting that a testator who 'has executed a will in solemn form ... did not intend to make it a solemn farce ... to die intestate'. The principle was reiterated in *Ark v Kaur* (2010), where one element of the claim disputing the will was that it applied only to the deceased's Indian estate, meaning that the deceased would be intestate as to his English estate. It was confirmed that the court would lean against a construction that led to intestacy.

However, this can be done only where there are genuine alternative readings of the will. The court cannot step completely outside the boundaries of the law just to save a will from failing. Extrinsic evidence (evidence not found on the face of the will itself) may be admissible, and if that is the case then the court will use it. (For the circumstances in which extrinsic evidence is admissible, see 11.5.) In respect of the wills of testators who died after 1982, s 20 of the Administration of Justice Act 1982 allows for rectification where it can be established that there was a clerical error or a failure on the part of the testator's solicitor to understand their instructions; this involves (apparently) changing the wording of the will rather than simply construing it. It may, however, resolve similar difficulties.

## 11.1.9 What will the court not do?

The court will not readily read words into a will. In *Scale v Rawlins* (1892), the testator made a gift of three houses to his niece for her life. He provided that if she died leaving no children, the houses should go instead to his nephews. The House of Lords would not imply a provision that if, as occurred, the niece should die leaving children, they should take the gift. The testator's provisions were clear and, even if it also seemed clear they were not what he intended, they had to stand as they were. In some cases, however (see *Re Whitrick*, 11.1.3), it may be possible for the court to overcome such difficulties by construing the offending parts of the will in the light of the rest of the provisions and holding that, in the light of those other provisions, effectively something must be implied into the will for it to make sense as a whole.

There are procedures for resolving ambiguity by looking outside the will; there are none which allow an ambiguity which does not appear from the will to be created by the introduction of evidence from outside the will. If this were done, it would be tantamount to the court writing, rather than interpreting, the will, and would contradict the fundamental requirement that a will be in writing.

## 11.1.10 Rectification

If the testator dies after 1982, the court is empowered by s 20 of the Administration of Justice Act 1982 to rectify the will, including by inserting words into the will, in the cases of clerical error or a failure to understand instructions. If neither of those conditions is satisfied, s 20 does not apply. The provision does not assist where the testator has misunderstood the legal effects of their words, or where there is a lacuna in the will. It is thus not a method of construction proper, since that deals with the correct interpretation of the wording of the will, but it is a matter related to establishing the contents of the will, albeit on the facts of a case the borderline may not always be discernible and the two functions may operate together. For a discussion of how the two functions operate differently, see the judgment of Latey J in *Re Morris* (1970), predating the 1982 Act (see 11.6).

## 11.2 Basic presumption – words have their ordinary meaning

There is a presumption, set out in *Re Crawford* (1854), that ordinary words will be given their ordinary meaning; the same goes for ordinary phrases. This presumption can, however, be unhelpful where the ordinary word has more than one meaning and is thus ambiguous, or where the testator has used words which appear ordinary and unambiguous but which they are known to have used in a particular way that was out of the ordinary.

### 11.2.1 The 'dictionary principle'

A testator may supply their own dictionary – that is, give instructions as to the interpretation and meaning of the words they use. Thus, a testator who clearly says that he gives his house to his beloved may also state that, when he says his beloved, he means Susan Jones of 24 Acacia Avenue, and the instructions will be effective. A 'dictionary' may be implied. The testator in *Re Davidson* (1949) was held to have supplied his own definitions sufficiently by naming his step-son but referring to him as 'my son' and to one of the step-son's children as 'my granddaughter'. Therefore the step-son's children took a share of the residuary gift which the testator left to 'my grandchildren'.

It may not always be completely obvious where the borderline is between the courts holding that the testator was using words in a particular way supplying their own dictionary – and their finding that a word may be ignored. In *Pratt v Matthew* (1856), for example, the testator referred to 'my wife Caroline' where the purported marriage had not been valid and so Caroline was not the testator's wife, but the court discounted the word 'wife'. In the case of *Re Smalley* (1929) (11.2.2), however, the use of the word 'wife' in similar circumstances was found to be a particularly wide use of the word and valid for that reason.

### 11.2.2 Obvious and secondary meanings

In the absence of a dictionary supplied by the testator, where the obvious meaning of a word makes no sense, it may be shown that a secondary meaning of the word makes sense in context. However, this rule cannot always be used to cure poor writing on the part of the testator. The obvious meaning of words has to be shown to give a result which is essentially nonsensical before a court would agree to looking elsewhere than their obvious import for a meaning. In *Gilmoor v MacPhillamy* (1930), the Privy Council said:

> In order to justify a departure from the natural and ordinary meaning of any word or phrase there must be found in the instrument containing it a context which necessitates or justifies such a departure. It is not enough that the natural and ordinary meaning may produce results which to some minds appear capricious or fail to accord with a logical scheme of disposition.

The testator in *Re Smalley* (1929) left a gift to 'my wife Eliza Ann Smalley'. His wife was called Mary Ann. Although Eliza Ann with whom he lived was not his lawful wife, the court held that the testator was using the word 'wife' in a secondary meaning of 'reputed wife', and so he had validly left the gift to Eliza Ann.

### 11.2.3 Technical words

If the testator has used technical words, even if they might reasonably be felt to mean something different to the layman and therefore arguably to have a different 'obvious' meaning, they must be interpreted in their technical meaning. This is a great pitfall for the writer of a home-made will, especially one who feels that the document will be all the better if it contains legal-sounding language and expressions even if they are not certain of their precise meaning. The word 'heir', for example, has persisted in the popular vocabulary although it has no current application since the 1925 legislation. If it were to be used in a will, undoubtedly it would be found to refer to whoever would have fulfilled the category of 'heir' under the pre-1926 rules, something which few, if any, students or solicitors would know. The presumption that technical words will be given their technical meaning may, however, be rebutted in the same way as the presumption that ordinary words will be given their ordinary meaning.

## 11.3 Particular points

There are many particular rules of construction which have evolved to resolve particular kinds of ambiguity; some are encountered more often than others.

### 11.3.1 Construction *ejusdem generis*

*Ejusdem generis* is a Latin phrase which means 'of the same kind'. It is the name given to the rule which says that, when there is a list of words, they will be construed so that they all have the same scope of reference. Where some of the words have, on the face of them, a wider scope and some have a narrower scope, the wider ones will be limited by the narrower. It is not a rule which will be applied if there is any indication of a contrary intention. For example, the word 'effects' is a very wide word, capable of meaning personalty in general, and that is how it was construed in *Re Fitzpatrick* (1934), the gift being of 'my house and all my furniture and effects'. In *Re Miller* (1889), however, the word was used at the end of a list and, in that context, the court held that the words did not include share certificates and banknotes, because it held that this did not accord with the other items on a construction *ejusdem generis*.

### 11.3.2 Erroneous use of legal words – the do-it-yourself lawyer

The testatrix in *Re Cook* (1948) made a home-made will which made gifts of 'all my personal estate whatsoever' to certain named relatives. Her estate consisted mainly of real property. The court accepted that it was unlikely that she had meant her realty to devolve on intestacy, but that she had chosen to use a term of art and had been so clear in stating in legal terms that she was dealing only with her personalty that there was no room for construing the phrase otherwise than in its usual legal sense. 'Testators can make black mean white if they make the dictionary sufficiently clear,' said Harman J, 'but the testatrix has not done so.' In *Re Bailey* (1945), however, another testatrix who made a home-made will and made a similar, but less clear, error was luckier. She made gifts of realty and personalty to named persons, concluding with a gift to 'my residuary legatee'. The word 'legatee' is, of course, appropriate only to a person receiving personalty; a person receiving realty is a devisee and the general term covering both is 'beneficiary'. However, the court found that, in the context of the will, the word 'legatee' was used to mean 'beneficiary' and the gift to the 'residuary legatee' included real property.

### 11.3.3 Inconsistency

Where there is inconsistency between two provisions of the will, the later of two provisions will prevail if no other solution can be found. Usually, however, this 'rule of despair', as it was described in *Re Potter* (1944), can be avoided. If it is clear from the will itself both that there has been an error in the wording and what the correct version is, the correct provisions may be carried out. The courts may ignore part of a description of something if it turns out to be untrue in the light of the facts, or they may interpret the words which produce the difficulty not as an essential part of a description but as restricting the scope of the words which do apply on the facts. Sometimes, the legal basis for the decision as to what is 'correct' is less than clear or convincing, even if the result seems to be sensible; this might be felt to show the gap between what the law should do and what it does do, or perhaps the difficulty of formulating laws and principles of law which can be applied to produce sensible results in the right cases without leaving scope for each individual court to make up, on the hoof, what law and principles it will apply.

### 11.3.4 Problems with allowing courts latitude to arrive at 'sensible' decisions

There are two basic problems with allowing courts to do as they wish in any particular case. One is that it is often felt to be wrong in principle to allow judges to make the law – that is the job of Parliament. The other is that, if there is no set basis for decisions, they become very unpredictable. What is a sensible decision to one person (usually the person who benefits from it) may be the contrary to another (who loses out). Therefore, cases are less likely to be settled, or abandoned before they begin, by the parties' lawyers advising them that an offer is good or a case hopeless; this leads to a proliferation of litigation, which is be a bad thing.

## 11.4 Ambiguity

If the words of the will are ambiguous, the court may look at evidence from outside the will to assist with construing its meaning. Ambiguity may arise either on the face of the will – where a person looking at the will can see that there is an ambiguity – or in the light of the circumstances surrounding the testator and the provisions of the will. Different systems of law provided different rules for the admissibility of evidence depending on what the problem was which needed solving. In *Guardhouse v Blackburn* (1866), Sir JP Wilde said:

> I venture to think that the Ecclesiastical Courts created a difficulty (perpetually recurring) for themselves, when they attempted to adopt the well-known rules as to parol evidence and patent and latent ambiguities, existing in the courts of law and equity, to cases of probate to which such rules were not properly applicable.

Amendments to the common law position on the admissibility of extrinsic evidence were made by s 21 of the Administration of Justice Act 1982 (see 11.11).

### 11.4.1 How does the court decide in cases of ambiguity?

It may appear that it would be helpful to look at either or both of the will and other evidence, for example, statements of the testator's intention – evidence of these can be given by the persons who heard them where admissible.

### 11.4.2 The will itself

The grant is conclusive as to the words of the will, and a court of construction cannot admit evidence of what the deceased's original will contained that did not make it through probate in order to deal with any alleged errors. Nor can it do so in order to fill in blank spaces. The original will is, however, admissible to prove how its contents are set out – for example whether there are commas or indentations (*Re Steel* (1979)).

## 11.5 Extrinsic evidence

Extrinsic evidence is evidence which comes from outside the will. It may be direct or circumstantial. Direct evidence will refer to the provisions the testator intended to make by their will. Circumstantial evidence will not refer directly to testamentary provisions but will assist in ascertaining what they mean.

For example, where the testator has made a gift to 'my beloved daughter', that will be a latent ambiguity since it becomes clear that it is ambiguous only once one discovers he had three daughters. The testator may have said to other persons that he intended to benefit his daughter Beatrice; that is direct extrinsic evidence, which can be given to the court by those other persons. If the same testator always referred to his daughter Beatrice as his beloved, and never referred to any other daughter that way, evidence of that may be circumstantial evidence of the meaning of the words in his will.

### 11.5.1 Extrinsic evidence – existence of subject matter

Evidence from outside the will is always called extrinsic evidence. A court will always hear evidence as to whether the property in the will or the beneficiary who is to receive it exists: it would clearly be impossible for a court to make any helpful statement about the practical effects of a will if this were not the case.

### 11.5.2 Extrinsic evidence – patent and latent ambiguity

What kind of extrinsic evidence the court will admit as to the testator's intention depends on whether the ambiguity arises on the face of the will (patent ambiguity) or whether it is apparent only in the light of surrounding circumstances (latent ambiguity). Thus, if a person looking at the will, but knowing nothing about the testator, their property or their nearest and dearest would be able to see that the will was ambiguous, the ambiguity was held to be patent and the rules for dealing with ambiguity on the face of the will would apply. However, if the ambiguity was latent, and could be discovered only when there was an attempt to apply the provisions of the will to reality, then a different set of rules applied.

## 11.6 Patent ambiguity – pre-1983 rules

In respect of patent ambiguity where the testator died before 1983, direct extrinsic evidence would be admissible only where there was equivocation.

This was discussed by Latey J in Re Morris (1970), who was dealing with a will which required rectification but to which the reforms of 1982 obviously did not apply. The testatrix had stated in her codicil that she revoked cl 3 and 7 of her will, when it was clear from the instructions she had given her solicitor that she had intended to revoke not cl 7 in its entirety but cl 7(iv). Latey J, explaining that his options were either to pronounce against the whole instrument or to exclude part and admit the rest, went on to say:

> Of course, the ambiguity being a patent one, the court of construction will not be able to admit the external evidence which makes the testatrix's intentions as clear as crystal, or to have regard to the findings of fact in that regard in this action. One can only say that that is a situation which WS Gilbert would have found ripe, but is otherwise unattractive.

## 11.7  Latent ambiguity – pre-1983 rules

Where the language of any part of the will was shown to be ambiguous in the light of evidence other than that of the testator's intention, both direct and circumstantial evidence could be admitted to assist with the construction of the will.

## 11.8  Ambiguity after 1982

Since the Administration of Justice Act 1982 came into force, referring to testators dying after 1982, the situation has been governed by s 21 of that Act (see also 11.11), and both direct and circumstantial evidence is admissible whether the ambiguity is apparent on the face of the will or appears only when the provisions of the will are applied to reality.

### 11.8.1  What if the extrinsic evidence does not answer the questions?

In Re Williams (1985), however, the court was unassisted by evidence about what the testatrix had meant by her lists of those to whom she had intended to give gifts. It rejected the extrinsic evidence of a letter to her solicitor. The court held that where the construction of the language used was concerned, 'language' includes numerals as much as words or letters, but it was not decided whether it would include the division of legatees into three groups. Declining, however, to hold that the ambiguity was one of language in any event, it proceeded to construe the will without the aid of any helpful extrinsic evidence as giving equal gifts to each of the named beneficiaries.

## 11.9  Direct extrinsic evidence

Direct extrinsic evidence is admissible under the common law where there is equivocation or to rebut particular presumptions of equity.

### 11.9.1  Equivocation

Where there is equivocation – a description which applies to more than one person or thing – then direct extrinsic evidence of the testator's meaning is admissible. There is no equivocation where the testator's meaning can be ascertained by using the 'armchair principle' (see 11.10).

### 11.9.2  Equitable presumptions

Direct, extrinsic evidence of the testator's declaration of intention is also admissible to rebut certain equitable presumptions. Note that these equitable presumptions are not themselves rules of construction. They are presumptions that a legacy in a will satisfies certain other obligations.

The presumptions are:

(a)    that a legacy satisfies a debt;
(b)    that a legacy satisfies another legacy;
(c)    that a legacy satisfies a portion-debt.

### 11.9.3 Satisfaction of a debt

If the testator owed a debt and they leave a legacy which appears to refer to the debt, without saying that the creditor should have the legacy as well as being able to claim the debt from the estate, then equity may presume, if all the requirements are satisfied, that the testator intended the legacy to satisfy the debt. The testator must owe the debt before the date of the will (since they can hardly be presumed to have intended to satisfy a debt they did not have), and they must leave the creditor by will a legacy equal to or greater than the debt. The legacy must be of the same general nature as the debt and must also be as beneficial to the creditor as the debt.

### 11.9.4 Satisfaction of another legacy

The rule is that the legatee will take only one of two similar legacies in the same instrument. If, however, they are not similar – for example they are of different amounts or the subject matter is different, or the testator gives different reasons for giving them – then the legatee will take both. If the legacies are contained in different instruments, for example in a will and then in a codicil, then the legatee will take both. However, an exception to this latter rule was stated in *Hurst v Beach* (1821) so that when the testator has stated their reason for giving the gift and it is the same in both cases, only one legacy is payable. This presumption is, as always, subject to the contrary intention of the testator.

### 11.9.5 Satisfaction of a portion or portion-debt

A portion is a gift from the testator to a child of theirs, or someone whom they treat as a child, to establish that child permanently in life. The provision of a portion *inter vivos* will lead to the ademption of a subsequent legacy of a portion, which is the corollary of the rule that a portion-debt will be satisfied by a legacy; essentially, the child cannot take the gift of a portion twice.

The reason that the gift of one-third of a fund to a child of the testatrix in *Re Ashton, Ingram v Papillon* (1897) did not have to be brought into account against her subsequent share of the rest of the fund was that the donor, being the child's mother and not her father, was not considered to be in *loco parentis*, but that rule would surely not apply now. Cases have been largely about fathers and children, though the reason for the gift may have morphed from setting the child up in life to recognising the value of the care adult children have given to elderly testators. In *Kloosman v Aylen and Frost* (2013), a residuary estate was to be divided amongst three children, but the estranged son suggested that his two sisters should account for lifetime gifts of £100,000 to each of them by the testator on the sale of his house. The court found that the gifts were separate recognitions of the expenses incurred by the daughters in looking after their elderly father, and did not have the character of portions that had to be accounted for. A similar position was taken in *Casimir v Alexander* (2001), where the gift of a house was found to be just reward for a daughter's care of the deceased and his wife.

A slightly different motive was found in *Barraclough v Mell* (2005), where an executrix had to account for £20,000 given to her by her father towards her divorce settlement, as a portion, against her entitlement to a share in residue. However, the father (under persuasion from another potential beneficiary) had later stated that the £20,000 should be deducted from her share of residue under his will, and so it was. A slightly more unusual and complex face of this rule was *Phillips v Cameron and Others* (1999), where payment of a grandson's education fees under an Enduring Power of Attorney was counted against his father's presumptive share of the grandmother's estate.

# 11.10 Circumstantial extrinsic evidence – the armchair principle

The 'armchair principle' of construction allows for the admission of circumstantial extrinsic evidence where there is uncertainty or ambiguity in the will. In order to arrive at the correct intention of the testator, the construer places him- or herself 'so to speak, in the testator's armchair' (*Boyes v Cook* (1880)) and considers the circumstances by which they was surrounded when they made their will.

## 11.10.1 The armchair principle and the object of the gift

It is usually used to ascertain the identity of the object of the gift, that is, person to whom it is given. In *Charter v Charter* (1874), the testator had appointed 'my son, Forster Charter' as executor and left him his residuary estate. The testator had had a son of that name, who had died some years before the will was made, something of which he was obviously aware. Therefore, he could not have intended, in saying 'my son, Forster Charter', to mean that son. At the date of the will, he had two sons, William Forster Charter and Charles Charter. William obtained common form probate, and Charles successfully applied for the grant to be revoked, showing that, in the circumstances, the will really referred to himself. In *Thorn v Dickens* (1906), the court admitted evidence to show that the testator, whose will read simply 'All for mother', always called his wife 'mother'.

## 11.10.2 The armchair principle and the subject matter of the gift

The armchair principle may, however, also be used to ascertain the identity of the subject matter of the gift. In *Kell v Charmer* (1856) the testator left 'to my son William the sum of i.x.x. To my son Robert Charles the sum of o.x.x'. Evidence as to the system of symbols used by the testator in his jeweller's business was admitted to show that these symbols meant £100 and £200 respectively.

## 11.10.3 Limits of the armchair principle

The armchair principle does have it limits. Circumstantial evidence may clarify the meaning of ambiguous or uncertain words, but it may not give them a meaning which they are incapable of bearing. In *Higgins v Dawson* (1902) (see also 11.1.1 and 11.1.8), Lord Davey said:

> The testator may have been imperfectly acquainted with the use of legal language ... he may have used language the legal interpretation of which does not carry out the intentions that he had in his mind ... that fact should not induce the court to put a meaning on his words different from that which the court judicially determines to be the meaning which they bear.

Similarly, Nicholls J said in *Re Williams* (1985) (11.8.1):

> if, however liberal may be the approach of the court, the meaning is one which the word or phrase cannot bear, I do not see how in carrying out a process of ... interpretation ... the court can declare that meaning to be the meaning of the word or phrase. Such a conclusion, varying or contradicting the language used, would amount to rewriting part of the will.

## 11.10.4 Ambiguity must be present to be interpreted

Moreover there must be an ambiguity; the armchair principle cannot be used to create one, as that would, again, amount to ignoring the clear instructions in the written will. In *Higgins v Dawson* (1902) (see also 11.1.1, 11.1.8 and 11.10.3), again, Lord Shand said:

> In the class of cases in which you cannot tell exactly what is given or to whom it is given because of obscure or doubtful expressions ... you must have recourse to extrinsic evidence in order to ascertain his meaning. But here ... the will is in its expression and language ... unambiguous, and that being so, no proof in reference to the amount of the testator's estate at the date of the will can affect its construction.... Even if it could be shown that the intention of the testator was something different from the language of the will that intention would not prevail.

In *National Society for the Prevention of Cruelty to Children v Scottish National Society for the Prevention of Cruelty to Children* (1915), the testator gave legacies to various Scottish charities, and also one to 'the National Society for the Prevention of Cruelty to Children'. This was the exact name of an English charity, but there was evidence that the Scottish National Society had been brought to the testator's attention shortly before his death. There was no evidence as to his having paid any attention to the English charity at all. The House of Lords held, however, that there was no ambiguity which it needed to cure and the English society therefore took the gift. (Note, however, that such an error could now possibly be established as falling within the terms of s 20 of the Administration of Justice Act 1982 as a clerical error, so that the court could consider rectifying the will by adding in the word 'Scottish'.)

# 11.11 Section 21 of the Administration of Justice Act 1982

This section widened the areas in which extrinsic evidence is admissible. In respect of testators who die after 1982, direct and circumstantial extrinsic evidence of their intention is admissible to assist with the interpretation of the will in three situations:

(a)     Where any part of a will is meaningless, as, for example, were the gifts in *Kell v Charmer* (1856) (11.10.2). Note that the meaninglessness of a blank is not assisted with, however, as that cannot be 'interpreted'. Nor can this provision assist with a gift which is quite clear on its face, even if someone feels – or is – quite justified in claiming that it was meant to signify something completely different. This provision deals only with the situation where there is something in the will which is meaningless in itself.

(b)     Where the language of any part of a will is ambiguous on the face of it. Circumstantial extrinsic evidence only would be admissible before 1983; after 1982, direct extrinsic evidence is also admissible.

(c)     Where evidence other than evidence of the testator's intention shows that the language used in any part of a will is ambiguous in the light of surrounding circumstances. This provision may assist where the will appears to make sense on its face, but does not do so when it is applied to reality.

## 11.12  Decisions the courts have reached

In *Bristow v Bristow* (1842), the testatrix left a bequest of £800 to the four eldest children of her cousin George Bristow and £200 to the three remaining children of her uncle of the same name. Her cousin had seven children; her uncle had one child, but had had four grandchildren, of whom three remained: the court eventually decided that the £200 went to the three youngest children of the cousin. In *Re Rickit* (1853), the testator left a gift to his 'niece, the daughter' of his late sister Sarah. This was taken by his nephew, the son and only child of the testator's late sister Sarah Ann. In *Ellis v Bartrum* (1857), the testator left gifts of ten guineas to the surgeon and resident apothecary of the Southern Dispensary There were two surgeons and no apothecary, though there was a dispenser. The court held that the gift to the 'resident apothecary' went to the resident dispenser, although the two words are not interchangeable, and the effect of the will was that the three persons took ten guineas each.

A comparatively recent example of a court looking at all the circumstances and interpreting the will in a way that might appear to go against the words in it is *Re Fleming* (1974). In that case, the testator held a leasehold of a house in Hampstead and had left that leasehold, specifically referring to it as such, to the Hampstead Old People's Housing Trust. However, after the will was made, the testator had also acquired the freehold of the house, and he had not merged the two. It appeared, therefore, that the freehold fell into residue and it was accordingly claimed by the residuary beneficiaries. Whilst this interpretation might accord with the law on a very strict interpretation, the court nevertheless held that the freehold passed with the leasehold. It based this interpretation on a line of decisions in cases with similar facts, where the courts had held that such expressions as 'my leasehold house' referred to the whole of the testator's interest in the property, because the implications of saying 'leasehold' were not apparent at the time the will was made. At that time the word was merely a description of the testator's whole interest, not a limitation of any kind. In *Struthers v Struthers* (1857), the court had said that the gift of a lease of four houses passed the freehold which the testator subsequently acquired because 'the words were used to express the whole extent of property he might leave at his death, not anticipating that he should then be entitled to any greater interest': in *Saxton v Saxton* (1879), a gift of 'all my term and interest in the leasehold ... premises' also passed the later-acquired freehold because the court held there was 'nothing more clear than that this testator intended to give the house as a provision for his wife, and he intended by the words he used to give any interest he might have in that house'.

More recently again, the courts seem to have found it sufficient to construe the testator's intention in general terms. In *Hayward v Jackson, Re Bowles* (2003), the judge construing how an option granted in the will had to be exercised said: 'The starting point is that the object of the court in construing a will to discover the intention of the testator', and, referring to a case preceding the AJA 1982 (*Perrin v Morgan* (1943)), that: 'Decided cases on the meaning of words or phrases in other wills are of little assistance, unless they are decisions on a relevant rule or principle of law.'

## 11.13  The doctrine of election

There is a general principle that, in order to take a benefit under a will, a person must comply with all the provisions of the will as a whole. The doctrine of election was set out in full by Lord Cairnes in *Codrington v Codrington* (1875). It applies where a testator has given someone a gift by will and, at the same time, purported to give some property which belongs to that person to a third party. It may not be the case that the donee under the will can both keep their own property and take the gift made under the testator's will. The doctrine of election asks them to choose, or elect, whether to keep the gift under the will and pass on the property the testator purported to give, or to keep their own property and forgo the gift under the will. If they wish to have both, the doctrine of election says that they may do so only if they compensate the third party for the loss of the gift the testator purported to make to them by will.

The doctrine of election applies wherever the above situation arises and the testator has not expressed a contrary intention; there is no requirement for an actual intention that the doctrine should operate to be established. The basis of the doctrine is questionable, but the Court of Appeal has said that the view that it is a creature of equity is the correct one. This view says that equity imposes the election on the conscience of the donee, so that it will not allow them to take the gift to them without their complying with the condition, which equity imposes, of making the gift to the third party.

The view that the doctrine of election is a doctrine of equity was first clearly stated in *Re Mengel* (1962). The testator's gifts of property had to be construed in the light of the Danish law of community of property within marriage, which meant that some of the things he had purported to leave by will were not entirely his to give away. He had left all his personal and household goods to his wife, and the remainder on trust for his wife during her life. He had also left two specific gifts, subject to the gifts to his wife, of his books to his niece and his collection of etchings and mountain photographs to his nephew. It was held that the doctrine of election depended not on the testator's intention but on his having purported to dispose of property of which he could not validly dispose. His widow therefore had to elect for the books, etchings and photographs under the gift to her of personal and household goods, because the testator was purporting to give what was not his, but not under the gift of the remainder of his property.

## 11.14  Absolute or lifetime gifts?

By virtue of s 28 of the Wills Act 1837, unless a contrary intention appears in the will, a devise of real property without any words of limitation passes the fee simple or other existing whole interest which the testator has the power to dispose of. Note, however, how far the apparent expression of a contrary intention may be ignored; see the cases applied in *Re Fleming* (1974) (11.12). The same principle also applies to personal property.

## 11.15  The rule in *Lassence v Tierney*

The rule in *Lassence v Tierney* (1849), also called the rule in *Hancock v Watson*, states that if there is an absolute gift to a legatee, with trusts then imposed on that gift which fail, then the absolute gift will still stand. The question of whether there is an initial absolute gift is one of construction; the gift may be directly to the beneficiary or to trustees on trust for him.

In *Hancock v Watson* (1902), the testator left a residuary gift of personalty to his trustees, on trust for his wife for life and thereafter to be divided into portions. Two of these portions were left to one Susan Drake, but the testator then said 'it is my will and mind that the two fifth portions allotted to her shall remain in trust, and that she be entitled to take only the interest … of the shares so bequeathed to her during her natural life'. There were other trusts which were to come into operation after Susan Drake's death. Those other trusts failed, and the court, looking at the words 'I give' and 'allotted' which were used in the will in respect of the gift to Susan Drake, held that she should take the two portions absolutely.

## 11.16  Exercise of power of appointment by will

Section 27 of the Wills Act 1837 states that a general devise of the real estate of the testator includes any real estate which they have power to appoint in any manner they may think proper, unless a contrary intention appears in their will. This means, if the testator has any such power of appointment, that there is no need for the testator to state in their will that they are exercising the power. Although the operation of s 27 is excluded by any contrary intention in the testator's will, describing the property as 'my' property is not sufficient to establish a contrary intention. Section 27 applies only to general powers of appointment, not to special powers, nor to a hybrid power to appoint in favour of anyone save certain named persons (see, also, delegation of testamentary powers at 3.6).

## 11.17  Children

A testator may identify his or her beneficiaries by reference to their relationship to him- or herself or others, especially as 'children'. That term however may have a variety of meanings. It is not limited to minor children; we are all children of someone.

### 11.17.1  Adopted children

In respect of any testator who dies after 1975, an adopted child is treated by virtue of s 39 of the Adoption Act 1976 as the lawful child of its adopter(s) and not the child of its natural parents, subject to contrary indication. The adopted child also stands in the relationship of sibling to its adoptive parents' other children. The date of the adoption order is irrelevant, even if it comes after the testator's death.

If the gift in a will depends on the date of birth of the child, then, subject to contrary indication, an adopted child will be treated as having been born on the date of its adoption. Two children adopted on the same day will be treated as having been born on that day in the order of their age. References in the will to the age of the child are not affected, however, by these provisions (s 42(2)).

The development of the law traces a pattern of increasing acceptance of adoption. If the testator died before 1976, the adoption order must have been made before their death, which is no longer required. Where, however, the date of execution of the relevant will or codicil was also before April 1959, the adoption order has to have been made before that date (note the possible effects of republication however) but after 1949 in order for the child to take.

Note that s 69 of the Adoption and Children Act 2002 provides that adopted children retain interests vested in them before the adoption, and the Inheritance and Trustees' Powers Act 2014 now means that children who are adopted after the death of their parents do not lose their contingent inheritance from their birth parents.

### 11.17.2  Legitimation

Illegitimate children used to be regarded as filius nullius – nobody's child.[3] Although testators could always make gifts to illegitimate children by name, they were not always included in gifts given to the testator's children as such, and legitimacy legislation was not universally approved.[4] The

---

3  See for example Wilkie Collins' 1862 novel No Name.
4  Ginger Frost, '"Revolting to Humanity": Oversights, Limitations, and Complications of the English Legitimacy Act of 1926' (2011) 20 Women's History Review 31.

position before the Family Law Reform Act 1987 (11.7.3) could depend on the operation of the Legitimacy Act 1976. The Legitimacy Act 1976 states that, in respect of a testator dying after 1975, a legitimated person may take as though they had been born legitimate, subject to contrary indication. In respect of the children of void marriages, it mattered whether the child was born before or after the ceremony. In *Re Spence* (1989), it was held that a child born before the celebration of a void marriage would not be legitimated by that marriage.

From 1 April 1988, the position is governed by s 28 of the Family Law Reform Act 1987. Since that Act came into force, the situation has changed and the result in the *Re Spence* situation would now be different, because whether a child was illegitimate or not would be irrelevant.

## 11.17.3 Illegitimate children

At common law, references to 'children' were presumed to mean legitimate children only. By s 15 of the Family Law Reform Act 1969, however, in wills or codicils made after 1969 references to children were presumed (that is, the testator could exclude the presumption by making a gift explicitly to their legitimate children only) to include illegitimate children, and relationships traced through an illegitimate line were also included. However, this applied only where the illegitimate children, or those claiming through them, were to benefit. It did not allow, for example, a child's unmarried father to claim from that child's estate. Nor did it apply where reference was made, for instance, to a gift to someone 'if he dies without leaving children', which was still presumed to mean legitimate children only, subject to contrary indication.

Until the Family Law Reform Act 1969, illegitimate children also had no claim on the intestacy of their parents save in very limited circumstances. However, in respect of deaths from 1970 onwards, s 14 of the 1969 Act provided that the child and its parents would stand in relation to each other in the same way as if the child were legitimate. This Act did not, however, affect relationships other than those between parents and children, so it gave an illegitimate child no claim, for example, on the intestacy of grandparents or siblings, and if an illegitimate child died intestate without parents, its estate would pass as *bona vacantia* to the Crown, even if they were close to their siblings or grandparents.

The Family Law Reform Act 1987 applies to the estates of those who die intestate after April 1988. Section 19 of the Act means that, in the tracing of a child's relationships, it no longer matters whether the child's parents were married to each other or not.

The Family Law Reform Act 1987, s 19, also applies to wills or codicils made after 3 April 1988 and provides that references, whether express or implied, to any relationship between two persons are to be construed without regard to whether the father and mother of either of them, or of any person through whom the relationship is deduced, were married to each other at any time or not, subject to contrary intention.

For deaths on or after 1 October 2014, illegitimacy is also irrelevant where an unmarried father seeks to claim on the intestacy of his child.

## 11.17.4 AID and IVF – artificial insemination by donor and in vitro fertilisation

Children born after April 1988 as a result of artificial insemination by donor were regarded by virtue of s 27(1) of the Family Law Reform Act 1987 as the children of their mother and, subject to contrary proof, of the mother's husband if she is married. From August 1991, this includes children born as a result of in vitro fertilisation or egg donation.[5] They are regarded as the

---

5  S 28 Human Fertilisation and Embryology Act 1990.

children of the mother's husband, or the man with whom she obtained the treatment, unless it is shown he did not consent, to the exclusion of the donor.

### 11.17.5 Children of the family

The concept of 'children of the family' originally belonged to family law as such. Children who were not related by blood or marriage to the deceased had no standing to make a claim under the Inheritance (Provision for Family and Dependants) Act 1975 unless they could show that they came within the category of 'dependants' (see Chapter 15). This could mean, for example that a 'step-child' of unmarried partners had no standing to claim against the estate of the non-blood parent, even where the family had been together for decades and since the child's infancy. The Law Commission consulted on including such children in the scope of those with automatic standing under the 1975 Act and found that the response was generally favourable, although some people felt it could lead to inappropriate litigation as the term would of necessity be ambiguous.[6] Accordingly s 1(d) of the 1975 Act was amended by the Inheritance and Trustees' Powers Act 2014 to provide that a child who was treated as a child of the family by the deceased, in relation to a family where the deceased had the role of a parent, had standing. Moreover, it was confirmed that this would include families in which the deceased and the potential applicant were the only members.

## 11.18  Age of majority

The age of majority is the age at which a person ceases to be a 'minor' or 'infant' and becomes entitled to property as an adult of 'full age'. The age of majority is now 18, following s 1 of the Family Law Reform Act 1969, which came into force on 1 January 1970. Previously, it was 21. The date for ascertaining which age of majority is relevant is the date of execution of the will. A will executed before 1970 but republished after 1969 will not be treated as having been made after 1969 for these purposes.

## 11.19  Dates from which a will speaks

There are different rules for the dates on which property – the subject matter of the gift – and beneficiaries – the objects of the gift – are identified. Note that in relation to specifications of beneficiaries according to gender, where the person has changed gender, the devolution of property also depends on whether the will was made before or after the Gender Recognition Act 2004 came into force, namely 4 April 2005.[7]

## 11.20  Property and s 24 of the Wills Act 1837

Section 24 of the Wills Act 1837 states that a will speaks from the date of death as to property, subject to contrary intention. This includes the subject matter of specific gifts, unless that is described so as to show that the testator intended a particular object which was in existence at the

---

6  Law Commission Consultation Paper 191 (Responses) *Intestacy and Family Provision Claims on Death: Analysis of Consultation Responses*, December 2011.

7  S 15 of the Act provides 'The fact that a person's gender has become the acquired gender under this Act does not affect the disposal or devolution of property under a will or other instrument made before the appointed day' (i.e. the commencement of the Act).

date of the will. In that case, one not unusual with specific gifts, a contrary intention will be found which excludes s 24. If it is held that the testator intended a particular object which existed at the date of the will but does not exist at the s 24 date – immediately before the testator's death – then the gift will be a specific gift and will fail by ademption. It is therefore very important to know exactly when a gift will be found to be specific rather than general in this context. In *Re Sikes* (1927), for example, the testatrix made a gift of 'my piano'. She had a piano at the time, but before her death she sold that piano and bought another. The court held that the phrase 'my piano' made the gift a specific gift of the piano she had at the time of making the will, and that it therefore failed by ademption. It is suggested, however, that reported cases of this nature have been influenced by the fact that the replacement item has been so much more valuable than the one held at the time of making the will, and that where the item was more similar it might be found easier to suggest that the use of the word 'my' did not constitute evincing a contrary intention to passing whatever item was in the deceased's possession at the date of death. See for example *Re Gibson* (1866), where a gift of 'my one thousand North British Railway preference shares' was adeemed after the testator was shown to have sold those shares and bought a larger number of the same. This could however also have raised the question of whether shares are fungible, which might also explain why the judge in the case discussed the hypothetical replacement of a poor quality picture with a valuable one.

### 11.20.1 'Now' and contrary intention

The use by the testator of the words 'now' or 'at present' will be found ambiguous as to whether this means the date of the will or the date of death. As a matter of common sense, one might assume that the testator, at the time of making the will, meant, by 'now', that time of writing. As a matter of law, however (an entirely different matter), it may seem that s 24 implies the date of their death. The question then arises as to whether the use of the words 'now' or 'at present' by the testator constitute an intention contrary to that imported by s 24. The cases do not appear to give any clear guidance as to how 'now' or 'at present' will be construed. Some courts, for instance the court in *Willis v Willis* (1911), have chosen to regard the words as no more than additional description, which can be ignored if the situation changed between the making of the will and the date of death. Others, however, have construed 'now' as showing a contrary intention, for example, that in *Re Edwards* (1890), where the court was asked to decide how much of a property a beneficiary could claim where the gift was of 'my house and premises where I now reside'. At the time of making the will, the testator owned and resided in the whole property; by his death, he had let part of it. However, the court held that the beneficiary took the whole property; note, however, that this concerned realty in respect of which wills were not ambulatory before 1926 (see 3.1.1). It is submitted that there is no clear rule at all in this area, and that either course can be justified with reference to the cases. The matter will therefore be entirely in the lap of the individual judge.

### 11.20.2 Effect of republication

If the will is republished, it speaks from the date of republication (see Chapter 8). In *Re Reeves* (1928), the testator gave his daughter 'all my interest in my present lease'. The lease expired three years after the making of the will. The testator later took a further lease on the same property and then confirmed his will by codicil. The court (assuming that 'present' amounted to a contrary intention) held that the daughter was entitled to the new lease because the effect of the republication was to make the will speak as if it had been executed at the date of the codicil, and as the original lease was not specified in the will, as it would have been had it been described, for example, by reference to its dates, then the republication was effective to pass the subsequent lease.

## 11.21 Beneficiaries

A will speaks from its own date as to the object of a gift, subject to contrary intention in the will. (This is not altered by s 24 of the Wills Act 1837, which refers to real and personal property, i.e. the subject matter of the will, only.) It still may not be immediately clear whether a person is entitled to take under the will, because even where the person in the will is described by their situation in life and that situation is filled by someone at the testator's death, in the absence of a clear provision for the substitution of the situation by another person the description will be taken to refer to the particular individual who filled it at the date of the will. Thus, if that person has predeceased the testator, the gift will lapse. In *Re Whorwood* (1887), the testator gave to 'Lord Sherborne and his heirs my Oliver Cromwell cup'. The person who was Lord Sherborne at the date of the will predeceased the testator. The court held that the gift lapsed, even though the gift had been made explicitly 'for an heirloom', because that did not amount to a substitutional gift to Lord Sherborne's heir.

### 11.21.1 Contrary intention

The testator may show a contrary intention in their will, giving an alternative time for the ascertaining of the beneficiaries. In *Re Daniels* (1918), it was held that the testator's gift to 'the Lord Mayor of London for the time being' had sufficiently expressed a contrary intention by the words 'for the time being' so as to pass the gift to the person who was Lord Mayor at the time of death.

A contrary intention will be implied if the provision of the will would make no sense if the time for ascertaining the beneficiary were the date of the will; in *Radford v Willis* (1871) a gift to the 'husband' of an unmarried woman was construed as one to the man she subsequently married. Something similar occurred in *Re Hickman* (1948), but in that case the gift was to the wife of the testator's unmarried grandson. The wife he had at the date of the testator's death was his second; the first was still alive, the marriage having ended in divorce. It was held that once the first wife had fulfilled the description, she did not lose her gift by the divorce. In our present society, which is much more used to and tolerant of divorce, it might be, however, that the courts would seek to distinguish this case, were similar facts to arise.

### 11.21.2 Effect of republication

The testatrix in *Re Hardyman* (1925) gave a legacy 'in trust for my cousin his children and his wife'. At that time, the cousin was married, but that wife died not only before the testator but also before he republished his will by codicil. It was shown that the testator, at the date of republication, was aware of the death of the wife. The court held on that basis that the effect of the republication was to make the will refer to any woman the cousin might marry so the legacy did not lapse. Instead, the cousin's second wife took the interest originally intended for his first wife.

## 11.22 Class gifts

A class gift in the strict sense is one by which something is to be shared out, so that the size of the gift to each person depends on how many persons there are in the class (*Pearks v Moseley* (1880)). If it is established that a gift is a class gift, the class-closing rules will apply to govern the category of persons who fall within the class. If they did not, the class could remain open for a very long time, preventing the estate from being distributed, subject always to the provisions of the perpetuities rules (see 10.11).

### 11.22.1 Class gift proper and individual gifts to members of a class

If there is an individual gift to each member of a class, the class will close at the testator's death, just as it would in any other case of ascertaining the object of a gift. The difference between individual gifts to each member of a class and a class gift is the difference between '£1,000 to each of A's children' (of whom there are five) and '£5,000 to A's children' (as a class). Although the effect in each case is the same if A has five children, only the latter is a class gift in the strict sense. If one of the children predeceased, in the case of individual gifts then each of the remaining four children would still take their £1,000, but the £1,000 which would have gone to the other child will go elsewhere. In the case of the latter class gift, however, the £5,000 would be divided amongst the remaining four children, giving them £1,250 each.

### 11.22.2 Naming individuals

The mentioning of particular individuals by name is not fatal to a finding that a gift is a class gift. This was stated in *Kingsbury v Walter* (1901), where it was held that, on the proper construction of the will, the testator had intended the gift to take effect as a class gift. As well as importing the class-closing rules, such a finding can exclude the doctrine of lapse; therefore a reference to a person who had predeceased the testator will not entail the doctrine of lapse.

## 11.23 Class-closing rules

These apply where there is a class gift in the true sense. The personal representatives need to know that a class has closed in order to be sure that they can distribute the whole of the property to be shared out amongst the members of the class. They do not want to run the risk of a further class member appearing in the future wanting their share. Of course, closing the class early may exclude some persons whom the testator, had they been specifically asked, would have liked to include. On the other hand, it would not be in the general interest for the distribution to be delayed for a protracted period or even indefinitely.

### 11.23.1 Closing of a class entitled to an immediate gift

The basic rule, of when a class entitled to an immediate gift closes, is as set out in *Viner v Francis* (1789). In the case of an immediate class gift where each member takes a share at birth, the class closes at the testator's death if any member of the class is then in existence. Where, however, there is no member of the class in existence at the testator's death, then no class-closing rule applies and the class remains open indefinitely (*Shepherd v Ingram* (1764)).

### 11.23.2 Closing of a class entitled to a postponed gift

A gift may be immediate or postponed, for example, to vest after a prior life interest. In *Re Chartres* (1827), it was said that if there is a postponed class gift, the class will close when the postponement ends. If, however, there is no member of the class when the postponement ends, then, as with the situation where there is an entitlement to an immediate gift but no member of the class in existence at the testator's death, no class-closing rule will apply and the class will remain open indefinitely.

### 11.23.3 Closing of a class where there is a contingency imposed on the class members

Where there is a contingency imposed on each member of the class (for example, to the children of A who attain the age of 18) the relevant class-closing rule is the rule in *Andrews v Partington* (1871). This says that if the gift is an immediate one, the class will close as soon after the testator's gift as there is anyone who satisfies the contingency.

It was held in *Re Wernher, Lloyds Bank Ltd v Earl Mountbatten* (1961) that the rule in *Andrews v Partington* applies whenever a testator's words invite it. The use of words inviting the application of the rule will give rise to a presumption that the testator intended the will to be construed in accordance with it. In *Re Wernher*, there was a bequest of an aggregate fund to children as a class payable on their attainment of a given age or on marriage. The period of distribution was held to be the time when the first child was entitled to receive and children coming into being after that time were thus excluded.

If the gift is postponed, for example, by a preceding life interest, the class will close after the end of the postponement if any member of the class who was in existence after the testator's death has satisfied the contingency. If this does not happen immediately, the class will close when a class member does satisfy the contingency.

### 11.23.4 Difficult cases – gifts postponed to something which does not happen as expected

A particular problem arises if, as is not an unlikely combination, a gift is made to a person for their life and subsequently to others, and the life tenant disclaims. This is particularly likely to happen where the life tenant is the parent of the remaindermen and feels they do not need the life interest. The question arises as to when the class closes – at the date of disclaimer or the date of death?

If the former, then those children born after that date will be excluded by operation of the rules. It does not appear that this will necessarily accord with what the testator intended. If, however, the latter applies, then either the distribution of the property is held up, with complications arising as to how it is dealt with in the meantime, or the property is distributed, so that some may have to be returned to satisfy the claims of class members who appear later or those claims may go unfulfilled because the property has been dissipated and cannot be recovered.

### 11.23.5 Class closing at date of disclaimer (interpretation 1)

In *Re Davies* (1957), there was a gift for life with remainder to that beneficiary's issue; she had three children. The beneficiary disclaimed her life interest and the question before the court was whether the gift in remainder was accelerated and the class closed at that date, or whether it would close, as the testator would have expected, at the date of her death. Vaisey J held that the vested class gift in remainder was accelerated on disclaimer of a life interest and that it was not liable to be affected by the coming into existence of any future issue of the original beneficiary.

### 11.23.6 Class closing at date of death (interpretation 2)

On the other hand, in *Re Kebty-Fletcher* (1967), a gift on trust for X for life and after his death to his children was interpreted differently. In that case, the testator had left gifts to his nephews and nieces for their life and thereafter for the children of those beneficiaries at 21. One nephew had assigned and released his life interest by deed to the Public Trustee, on the basis that the original trusts remained. The question was whether the class closed in accordance with the rule in *Andrews v Partington*, as soon one of the nephew's children reached 21, or on his death.

Stamp J doubted the sense of *Re Davies* (11.23.5), and said he was content to treat it as applicable only to cases of acceleration. He did not accept that it could be applied to alter the composition of the class. He said:

> The release of a life interest in favour of children is one of the commonest features in the field of trusts and, so far as I am aware, it has never hitherto been suggested that such a release may have the dramatic effect now claimed of altering the membership of the class of children to take.

He held that the disposition of the life interest did not accelerate the interests of the nephew's children or alter the composition of the class. Discussing the rule in *Andrews v Partington*, he said:

> in my view ... that rule ought only to be applied where the testator ... must, or may, be taken to have intended a distribution at a moment of time which may be applied to the benefit of all the members of the class.

In *Re Harker's Will Trusts* (1969) too, Goff J held that the rule in *Andrews v Partington* did not apply. He held that the class of beneficiaries whose interest had been accelerated and brought into possession by the disclaimer of the preceding life interest remained open until the death of the person who disclaimed. Therefore, although those members of the class took an accelerated benefit, it remained liable to be diminished by further class members in the future.

*Re Harker's Will Trusts* (1969) provides a practical solution to the question of whether and how to distribute property where a life tenant has disclaimed but the class has not closed. In saying that the beneficiaries may receive an accelerated interest, rather than that the property must be preserved pending final ascertainment of exactly what that interest should be, it preserves the class of beneficiaries the testator intended to benefit but avoids the problem of what to do with the property in the trust pending the closing of the class. This leaves the way open, however, for difficulty or unfairness to later beneficiaries if the property should be dissipated before they become entitled.

## 11.23.7 Excluding the class-closing rules

It is possible to exclude the class-closing rules, but this must be done with care. It was held in *Re Tom's Settlement* (1987) that a settlor may supply their own 'closing date'. In that case, the court discussed the purpose of the class-closing rules. It said they were intended to resolve conflict between the testator's intentions to give a share of their estate to the members of a class whenever they were born and to give a share to a person as soon as they became entitled. However, where a testator had clearly specifically included a class-closing date, that could exclude the class-closing rules. References in the will to a specified date as 'the class-closing date' showed an intention that the class would remain open until that date, even if the application of the usual class-closing rules would have closed it earlier.

In *Re Edmondson's Will Trusts* (1972), it was held that the use of the phrase 'whenever born' was sufficiently emphatic to exclude the class-closing rules and equivalent to the phrase 'at whatever time they may be born'. In *Re Chapman's Settlement Trusts* (1978), it was held, confirming *Re Edmondson*, that the use in respect of children of a phrase such as 'now born or who shall be born hereafter' will not exclude the class-closing rules, because a phrase of that kind could simply refer to children born before the closing of the class.

## 11.24 Summary of Chapter 11

### 11.24.1 Construction of Wills

Construing a will means interpreting the meaning of the words used in it. Construction should not be stretched to rewriting the will: the dividing line is sometimes difficult to draw. Words are presumed to have their ordinary, everyday meaning. However, the testator may supply their own dictionary, providing an alternative meaning for any particular words they use. Technical words are given their technical meanings.

Ambiguity on the face of the will is said to be patent. Where ambiguity is apparent only when the words are applied to reality, it is said to be latent. The court will always admit extrinsic evidence – evidence other than just the will itself – about the property mentioned in the will. Direct extrinsic evidence refers to what provisions the testator intended to make by their will. Circumstantial extrinsic evidence assists in interpreting the words used.

Where the question is what the testator intended the words of the will to mean, the court may be allowed to admit extrinsic evidence. The rules governing this were widened by the Administration of Justice Act 1982. Before 1983, direct extrinsic evidence was admissible in the case of a patent ambiguity only where there was equivocation. In the case of a latent ambiguity, both direct and circumstantial evidence were admissible. After 1982, direct and circumstantial evidence are both admissible in cases of ambiguity whether it is patent or latent. Direct extrinsic evidence may be adduced to rebut the equitable presumptions of satisfaction of debts, portion-debts or legacies.

Admitting circumstantial extrinsic evidence means using the 'armchair principle' in order to see the meaning of the testator's words as they saw them him- or herself, where the words are obviously ambiguous. By s 21 of the Administration of Justice Act 1982, direct and circumstantial extrinsic evidence is admissible where any part of a will is meaningless, consists of patently ambiguous language or is shown to be ambiguous in the light of surrounding circumstances other than evidence of the testator's intention.

If a beneficiary is left a gift by a testator who also purports to leave part of that beneficiary's property to another person, the doctrine of election says that the beneficiary may not keep both items.

Gifts are assumed to be as absolute as the testator's interest in them unless they provide otherwise in the will. The rule in *Lassence v Tierney* holds that a gift to a person as trustee becomes absolute if the trusts fail.

A general gift to children will now include adopted, legitimated and illegitimate children, and many children born by artificial insemination by donor or by in vitro fertilisation, as well as legitimate children and children *en ventre sa mère*.

A will speaks from the date of death as to property, subject to contrary intention, in accordance with s 24 of the Wills Act 1837. However, it speaks from its own date as to beneficiaries, again subject to contrary intention.

A class gift is a gift to be shared out amongst a particular set of individuals, so that how much each receives depends on the number in the class. Rules specify when a class closes, so the funds may then be distributed. The class-closing rules may be excluded by careful drafting.

# Chapter 12

# Personal Representatives

Personal representatives are the people who administer the estate left by the deceased. They are sometimes described as stepping into the deceased person's shoes; they stand in relation to the property in the estate very much as he or she did when still alive, but many special rules apply to them. Personal representatives may be either executors or administrators, depending on whether or not they are appointed by the testator's will, but all personal representatives have essentially the same duties. Those duties are aimed at having them deal with everything in the testator's estate so as to wind it up with everyone concerned getting exactly what they should and nothing being left over. The duties involved in administering and winding up the estate are, in essence, to collect in the assets, pay the liabilities and, probably, then to distribute what remains. If there is property which then has to be retained on a continuing trust, the personal representatives should pass it to the trustees. Sometimes the personal representatives and the trustees are the same people, but with different formal roles.

## 12.1 Duties of the personal representatives

More specifically, the personal representatives must first ascertain what the assets and liabilities of the estate are, calculate the Inheritance Tax payable and accordingly pay it and obtain any grant of probate or letters of administration. They must then collect in the assets and pay the debts and liabilities in the estate, and fulfil any gifts made by will. The tax position must be confirmed and the expenses of the administration paid, and then estate accounts prepared confirming all assets received and payments made and showing the balance due as residue. The residue will then be transferred to beneficiaries direct or to their trustees.

It is also the duty of the personal representatives to see to the proper disposal of the body of the deceased. In *Buchanan v Milton* (1999), Hale LJ confirmed that there is no right of ownership in a dead body, but that there exists a common law duty to arrange for its proper disposal, falling primarily on the personal representatives. An executor may pursue obtaining possession of the body immediately, but an administrator may need to obtain a grant first (see 12.15–12.17).[1] If there is no personal representative, the duty will fall on the local council. *Ibuna and Tanoco v Arroyo and Dignity Funerals Ltd* (2012) was a dispute about the right to take possession of the body of a congressman from the Philippines, who was domiciled in the Philippines and resident both there and in California, but died whilst in England for medical treatment. The High Court confirmed that the primary duty of disposal of the body rested with the executor, who was not bound by the deceased's wishes but might have regard to them.

Sometimes personal representatives are appointed for limited and specific purposes, and those will limit their duties. For example, as well as a general personal representative to deal with their everyday affairs, an author might appoint a literary executor, whose job would be to deal

---

1  Dobson v North Tyneside Heath Authority (1997).

with the author's creative work, both financially – ensuring that the continuing income after the author's death is properly dealt with – but also to take decisions and, for example, sign contracts for future rights to use the material. Some literary executors have become well known for the way they have conducted their role: for example, Christopher Tolkien performed a strong editorial role that allowed the publication of uncompleted works by his father JRR Tolkien; Stephen Joyce's protection of his father James' work included threatening to sue the Irish government for a public reading from his father's book at a public celebration of the author's work in 2004; and Max Brod did not destroy Franz Kafka's work as instructed, but published it instead.

### 12.1.1 Executors or administrators?

In any properly drafted will, executors will be appointed to carry out the testator's wishes. The testator may thus choose whomever they like to be the executors, and they may also make provision for the substitution of someone else of their choosing if their first choice is unavailable. A trust corporation, for example a bank, may be appointed executor. The executor will, almost always, deal with the estate as the result of the testator appointing them expressly and personally to do so, although in a few exceptional situations, considered below, an executor may be appointed by other means.

If there is no one named as executor in the will who takes up the post (and none of the other, less usual, provisions apply), or there is no will at all, then the law provides who may deal with the estate. Such people, whose entitlement comes from general legal provisions rather than from those of a will, are called administrators. Executor and administrator are masculine terms: the feminines are executrix and administratrix (plurals: executrices and administratrices). Executors and administrators have the same essential duties, but there are some differences as to how they are carried out.

### 12.1.2 Specific differences between executors and administrators – when the power to deal with the estate is obtained

Executors obtain their power under the will. This means that, provided they are not disqualified as executors by reason of infancy, for example, or mental incapacity, the estate vests in them and they are entitled to deal with it as soon as the testator dies. Their power does not come from a grant of probate, though for certain operations a grant is needed, such as making title to land.

No one is forced to act as an executor or administrator, but because the office of executor is thrust upon the relevant person automatically on the death of the testator, any executor who does not wish to take on that office must take the positive step of renouncing probate. Administrators, however, have no authority until a grant is made to them – in the meantime, the property vests in the Public Trustee. An executor may begin litigation relating to the estate at any time after death, but at the point where they need to prove their title, they will have to produce a grant, since that is the means for doing so. An administrator, however, may not commence any action in their capacity as administrator until they hve had their grant of letters of administration. The administrator in *Mills v Anderson* (1984) settled a claim within court proceedings on behalf of the deceased's estate before obtaining his grant of letters of administration. The court held that the settlement was not binding because the administrator had no authority to make it.

### 12.1.3 Personal representatives and the deceased's court proceedings

Sometimes, a person's interest in taking a grant focuses not so much on winding up the deceased's affairs as on furthering some issue of their own. This was the case in *Wintle v Nye* (1959) (see 4.9.6), and might have been that of the creditors in *Aeroflot v Berezovsky* (2013) had they been successful in obtaining a grant (12.3.1). Another such case was *Austin v Southwark* (2008), which concerned the unsuccessful attempt by Mr Austin to succeed to his late brother's council tenancy, which had been ended during his lifetime because of non-payment of rent. Mr Austin wanted to apply for the tenancy to be effectively resurrected (a 'Lazarus order') (see 2.10), but first of all he had to find a right to apply. The judgment is particularly interesting for its consideration of Civil Procedure Rule 19.8.

CPR 19.8 allows an ongoing court action to continue where a party dies, with his personal representative stepping in on behalf of his estate. In *Austin*, Mr Austin wanted not to continue but to begin a claim for the Lazarus order, so his contention was that CPR 19.8 allowed him as personal representative to use his late brother's right to apply. Flaux J held that an interest in ongoing legal proceedings could qualify, but that the brother had no ongoing proceedings about his tenancy and CPR 19.8 did not give a personal representative any right to bring a claim as such:

> Upon his death Mr Alan Austin's right to apply for a Lazarus order ceased as did any right he had to possession of the premises as a matter of English law. There was nothing capable of being passed to his Estate.

The appellant had only 'a hope of recognition of the survival of an old property right, which it has not been possible to exercise since his brother's death.'

Mr Austin's only chance of postponing the possession date to after his brother's death was to find a way of applying to the court for the Lazarus order, and he took that issue to the Court of Appeal, saying that CPR 19.8(1)(b) meant he could make that claim. It says that 'Where a person who had an interest in a claim has died and that person has no personal representative the court may order— ... (b) a person to be appointed to represent the estate of the deceased.' The Court held that the relevant 'claim' was the claim to be able to apply for the order (not the application itself), and considered three contemporaneous House of Lords cases with claims of a similar nature. It favoured giving the Act 'a purposive and practical construction'. However, the authorities had found that:

> The right to apply for a postponement of an order for possession is not an interest in land capable of being inherited. Further, the right to apply under s 85 is a right given to the tenant ... a person who is qualified to succeed as a tenant under a secure tenancy ... only ... where there is a tenancy in existence.

For a person to succeed to a tenancy on death under the Act, the deceased must have died a secure tenant, not a tolerated trespasser.

## 12.2 Doctrine of relation back

By the doctrine of relation back, however, the letters of administration, once obtained, may in limited circumstances relate back to the death of the deceased. This doctrine enables an administrator to recover a loss to the deceased's estate from a wrongdoer who injured the estate in the time between the death and the grant of letters of administration. If there were no such provision, the administrator would be unable to bring the wrongdoer to account, since in general they can deal only with the estate after the date of the grant of representation to them. This doctrine does not enable an administrator to do anything before the grant, only to deal after the grant with certain matters which occurred before it.

## 12.3 What is a grant of representation?

A grant may be of probate, to an executor, or of letters of administration, to an administrator. (There are also variations on both themes, which are considered below.) The grant is confirmation of the executor's authority and title, and confers authority on the administrator. It is an officially sealed document obtained from a local probate registry, which is part of the Family Division of the High Court, in most cases without any need for anyone to attend the Registry or any court at all. The process is governed by the Non-Contentious Probate Rules, currently those of 1987. Non-contentious probate means where a grant is obtained without dispute, using an essentially administrative process. Probate claims that are disputed are called 'contentious probate' matters and the process is governed by Part 57 of the CPR.

Because a grant is needed to prove title in various circumstances, and it would be inconvenient and difficult to produce the original grant on every occasion when it is needed, the probate registry will for a small fee provide as many 'office copy' grants as are requested along with the original grant itself; these are sealed with the official seal and are used to prove title where necessary. For example, a grant or office copy grant will be needed where a personal representative wants to sell land from the estate, to prove that they are entitled to deal with the property.

### 12.3.1 What if no one takes out a grant?

The grant is issued to the personal representatives personally. If no one takes out a grant, and any executor there may be renounces probate, any dealings with the estate must be dealt with through the Family Division: note that family provision applications (see Chapter 15) can now be issued before a grant. Proceedings can be issued against the estate by issuing a writ or originating summons against the estate and applying to the court under s 2 of the Proceedings Against Estates Act 1970 for an order appointing someone to represent the estate in the proceedings, possibly the Official Solicitor.

This situation must be distinguished from that where the deceased is only believed, not proven, to be dead; in that situation, it will be extremely difficult to have any dealings with the estate at all, at any rate until his or her death can be legally presumed (see 16.1.2).

During the period before a grant is taken out in relation to the deceased's estate, anyone interested in the estate may, however, apply to the Chancery Division of the High Court for the appointment of a receiver to protect the assets of the estate. The executor in *Re Sutcliffe* (1942) carried on the deceased's solicitor's practice for three years after his death; a creditor successfully applied to the court for the appointment of a receiver. Creditors can apply for a grant themselves, but, as the discussion in *Aeroflot v Berezovsky* (2013) confirms, such an application may raise its own questions. In that case, there was a dispute as to what the assets in the estate were and whether it was solvent or insolvent. The creditors wanted to take a grant, which would also give them access as personal representatives to privileged information which it was not appropriate for them to have if the estate was not insolvent. The dispute over the grant itself was partly responsible for there being no personal representative in place: it was ordered that the late Mr Berezovsky's daughter would take a grant *ad colligenda bona* (12.26.1) to preserve the estate.

### 12.3.2 Resealing

A so-called 'colonial grant' may be resealed, normally without leave, on the application of the person to whom the grant was made or on their written authorisation. The 'colonies' referred to include territories in, for example, Canada. The detailed rules are contained in the Colonial Probates Act 1892 as extended by the Colonial Probates (Protected State and Mandated Territories)

Act 1927, and the territories to which these provisions apply are specified in the Colonial Probate Act Application Order 1965 (as amended).

### 12.3.3 Forthcoming revision of the Non-Contentious Probate Rules 1987

The current Non-Contentious Probate Rules date from 1987, when they replaced the previous Rules of 1954. Revision has been on foot since early 2009, when a working group was set up to consider how to implement the recommendations of an earlier Probate Review. The main criticism of the 1987 Rules was that they were 'far from user-friendly', as Sir Mark Potter, President of the Family Division said, and that they provided little guidance. They also did not fit well with the Civil Procedure Rules brought in in 1998.

Draft new Probate Rules (without the Non-Contentious title) were issued for consultation in 2013 with the expectation that they would be implemented in 2015, but on which at the time of writing there is no further news. The principal changes are to the language used and the order of the rules. The romance of the Latin will be changed to the familiarity of modern English:

caveat → objection
citation → notification
common form probate business → probate matters
grant ad colligenda bona defuncti → collection grant
nuncupative will → oral will

However, apparently the eternally confusing (to the layman) term 'office copy' will be retained: this means an official copy, so one that is sealed as an original, rather than a photocopy. The Rules will be re-ordered so as to begin with an introduction and the rules relating to the court, and then to follow the process of applying for a grant, ending with how records and appeals are dealt with. Witness statements will replace oaths and affirmations.

Some provision will be made to deal with a common current practice by which unregulated advisers deal with estates. They do this by taking a power of attorney from those entitled to a grant in order to deal with the probate registry. This practice may continue to be possible, or may be restricted to family members (however defined) and/or probate practitioners, or it may be ended.

## 12.4 Executors

Executors are those chosen by the testator to administer his or her will, though this general statement is subject to the qualifications set out below. They will usually be either family members, who perform the task for love and in the interests of seeing the estate properly administered, or professionals, such as a bank or other trust corporation, or solicitors or accountants, who will be paid for their work, either under a charging clause in the will or under the Trustee Act 2000 (see 12.12.3). Professional will-writers who are not practising solicitors or accountants are not currently authorised to administer estates, though they may (for a fee) advise lay executors as to the process for obtaining a grant and carrying out the administration without instructing (and paying) solicitors or accountants to deal with the work, or they may obtain a power of attorney from the executor to do the work. It is, however, entirely proper for executors and administrators to instruct solicitors or accountants in this way and to pay them out of the estate. The only advantage (professional fees apart) to come to an executor personally from their office as such will be, exceptionally, if the rule in *Strong v Bird* (1874) can perfect a gift to them from the deceased (see 2.7.1).

There is no prohibition on executors taking gifts from the will and, indeed, beneficiaries may often be the most appropriate executors. This is reflected in NCPR r 20, where the next choice for personal representative after the executor appointed in the will is the residuary beneficiary.

Executors are usually appointed expressly, but may be appointed in other ways.

### 12.4.1 Failure of appointment of executors

If the will itself is valid, the failure of any appointment of executors in it – or the failure to make any such appointment – does not invalidate it. What it does is activate the provisions for authorising persons to act as administrators with the will annexed (see 12.5 and 12.20.8); the will is annexed to the grant of letters of administration, and they must administer the estate in accordance with the terms of the will.

A failure to appoint executors who take a grant of probate does not render the estate intestate; that term refers to a failure to deal with property by will. An estate in which only some of the property is dealt with by will is said to be partially intestate, and the entitlement to the property in the estate will be the same whether the administration is carried out by executors or by administrators with the will annexed.

## 12.5 Express appointment

Express appointment occurs when the will contains a clause naming a particular person and stating that they are to be the executor. The reason for putting in the address and occupation of an executor is so they can be identified and found when the time comes; it is not a requirement of law but, as a practical act, is very sensible.

Express appointment enables the testator to appoint different executors for different parts of an estate or to deal with the estate only during a certain period. Obviously such provisions are very unusual where there is a small and ordinary estate. It may, however, be entirely appropriate to make such an appointment, especially where, for instance, an author wishes to appoint special people to deal with his or her literary works (see 12.1) but a family member to deal with their ordinary family matters, or a parent wishes to leave all their property to their child, appointing executors to deal with the estate until the child attains his or her majority.

### 12.5.1 Number of executors

Although it may be usual to appoint two persons as executors and trustees, as a matter of law any number of executors may be appointed. Even where a trust arises, one executor alone may be appointed. Where there is a sole beneficiary of full age, for example, where the testator leaves all their property to their spouse or civil partner, it is most appropriate for that person to be the sole executor.

Where many executors are appointed, however, probate will be granted to no more than four executors, in accordance with s 114(1) of the Supreme Court Act 1981. The executors will be chosen simply by reference to the first four named; probate will be granted to them with power reserved to the others, so that, for example, if the executors with the grant die, the others may more easily step in.

### 12.5.2 Conditional or substitutional appointment

The appointment of the executor may be conditional, but as always with anything in a will the condition should be clearly drafted. A condition may relate, for example, to the age of the executor; the appointment may be conditional on the executor having attained a certain age at the date of the testator's death.

A substitutional appointment may also be made, for example, where a particular person is appointed to the office of executor with a provision that another should take that office if the first one dies before the testator. Again, the drafting should be clear so that there is no doubt about the circumstances in which the substitution will operate. In this example, the substitutional executor would be appointed by the will only where the first died before the testator, so if the first one survived the testator by one day only, the appointment of the second would not be valid.

### 12.5.3 Reservation of powers and double probate

A person appointed as executor in a will does not have to take a grant of probate (see 12.13). Sometimes this may be, for example, where a grieving widow feels unable to cope with the paperwork of her deceased husband's estate. Such a person may have power reserved to them instead of renouncing completely. Other people take the grant and deal with the estate, possibly involving the person with power reserved to them as a consultee or decision-maker. She may prove the will later by applying for a grant of double probate. She will then join with the previous executors and will, for example, have to be included as a signatory of any necessary documentation.

## 12.6 Implied appointment

Executors may also be appointed by implication of the wording of the will.

### 12.6.1 Meaning of 'executor according to the tenor'

An executor whose appointment is not express but implied is called an executor according to the tenor. The tenor means the general tone of the will or the way it reads. If the wording of the will implies clearly that its terms should be carried out by a particular person in accordance with the usual duties of a personal representative, but does not expressly appoint them as 'executor', they may be held to be an executor according to the tenor. In a professionally drafted will, an executor will always be expressly and unambiguously appointed; an appointment which is less clear can lead to queries from the probate registry if not litigation, and thus obviously to delay and expense.

It is not the case that if a testator leaves all their property to one person, that person is impliedly the executor. It was confirmed in *Re Pryse* (1904) that a person who is the sole beneficiary, or the residuary beneficiary, will not be the implied executor for that reason. There must be something in the will which implies that the testator wanted the implied executor to carry out the terms of the will in an administrative capacity. Thus, it is possible for there to be an executor according to the tenor who is impliedly appointed to deal with the estate and pass all the benefit under the testator's will to another person, without retaining anything for him- or herself.

### 12.6.2 Examples of executors according to the tenor

The will must show the expectation that the person impliedly appointed will fulfil the essential duties of an executor. It was held in *In the Goods of Adamson* (1875) that the essential duties of an executor are to collect the assets of the deceased, to pay the funeral expenses and debts, to discharge the legacies and other gifts made by the will and to account for the residuary estate.

A particular example of what constitutes appointing a person to carry out these duties without quite expressly appointing them executor is the testatrix statement in In the Goods of Cook (1902) that she desired John Goodrick to pay all her just debts. Where the testator in In the Estate of Fawcett (1941) said: 'All else to be sold and proceeds after debts, etc., Barclays Bank will do this, to Emily Thompson', this was held impliedly to mean the bank was executor according to the tenor (though the action was essentially compromised and the bank renounced on the basis that Emily Thompson would take the grant instead).

Although it may be usual for a testator making express appointments to appoint the same persons as executors and trustees, this is not compulsory, and a person appointed as trustee by the will is not the executor solely for that reason. Where the testator in In the Goods of Punchard (1872) said: 'I wish PA Collins to act as trustee to this estate', it was held that Mr Collins was not the executor according to the tenor. This was because he was not required by the wording of the will to perform the essential functions of an executor, namely to pay debts or take on the general administration of the estate. The functions of personal representatives and trustees are not the same.

## 12.7 Settled land executors

Particular provisions apply to land settled under the Settled Land Act 1925 which remains settled after the death of a tenant for life. Note that, following the implementation of the Trusts of Land and Appointment of Trustees Act 1996, although no new strict settlements can be created after 1996, all strict settlements already created before that date (including settlements created by will where the testator died before the end of 1996) remain valid by virtue of s 2 of the 1996 Act until they come to an end.

### 12.7.1 Appointment of settled land trustees s 22 of the AEA 1925

It is unusual to see land settled under the Settled Land Act 1925 in practice, and therefore unusual to see settled land executors; although the standard form of application for a grant of probate still contains a reference to them, it is proposed that it will be removed when the Non-Contentious Probate Rules are updated (there was no timetable for the implementation of any new rules at the time of writing). However, where settled land trustees are found, they are governed by special provisions under s 22 of the Administration of Estates Act 1925. This states that a testator may appoint the Settled Land Act trustees as their special executors in regard to the settled land. If the testator does not appoint them expressly, then the section deems them to be appointed. This is the only statutory provision dealing with the deeming of an appointment as executor. Probate may be granted to such trustees specially limited to the settled land and the grant to the executors of the rest of the estate will specifically except the settled land.

What this means is that if the testator is entitled to settled land during their lifetime, and on their death the settlement continues, the law will appoint the trustees of the settlement to deal with the passing of that entitlement to the next person entitled under the trust, if the testator does not appoint them him- or herself. This does not affect the appointment of executors for the rest of the testator's estate.

### 12.7.2 Where there are no settled land trustees appointed – s 30 of the SLA 1925

If, however, the land is settled by will without the testator appointing settled land trustees, then s 30 of the Settled Land Act 1925 comes into operation. It is unusual to see a settlement under the Settled Land Act made deliberately. However, under the system of land trusts operating before the implementation of the Trusts of Land and Appointment of Trustees Act 1996, there were two separate ways, each with a different machinery, to create successive interests in land, which must subsist in equity, behind a trust, because they cannot exist at law (see s 1 of the Law of Property Act 1925). There would be a strict settlement wherever no trust for sale could be found; trusts for sale were implied by statute in cases of co-ownership but otherwise had to be express. Thus, where a testator left a life interest without expressly creating a trust for sale, a strict settlement would arise. This might be seen in, for example, a home-made will by which the testator left his property to his wife for her lifetime and thereafter to their children. The interaction of the accidental creation of strict settlements and their possibly somewhat unexpected consequences, especially the provision that a tenant for life under a strict settlement has the power to sell the property regardless of a settlor's attempts to fetter such a power, was one of the reasons for the passing of the 1996 Act.

Where a pre-1997 strict settlement is found to have been created by will, s 30(3) of the Settled Land Act provides that the personal representatives of the deceased settlor are deemed to be trustees of the settlement until other trustees are appointed. This would mean that if the settlement without expressly-appointed trustees arose under the terms of the testator's will, their personal representatives would become the settled land trustees and would continue to be those trustees even after the completion of the administration of the estate. On the subsequent death of the tenant for life, they would be his or her settled land executors.

### 12.7.3 Additional or special settled land executors

The trustees of a settlement under the Settled Land Act or any beneficiary of it may apply to the court for the appointment of an additional or special settled land executor.

## 12.8 Executors appointed under a power in the will

It is unusual for executors to be appointed under a power in the will rather than directly. The situation arises where the testator nominates, by their will, another person to make the appointment to the office of executor. The testator may specify the group of persons from whom the appointees are to be chosen or may specify persons who may not be appointed under the power, or they may leave the choice completely open to the nominated person. In the absence of any contrary provision by the testator, the nominated person may appoint him- or herself.

The testator may thus delegate the power to appoint executors. What the testator may not do is delegate the power to make the will itself. (If the testator tries to do this, the document they make and by which they purport to give that power will not itself be a will: see the subject of delegation of testamentary powers at 3.6.1.)

## 12.9 Executors appointed by the court

The court has power to appoint executors. This is very unusual, save perhaps in the case of a minority or life interest where there is only one personal representative to deal with the trust which then arises. The court's powers may arise in three alternative situations:

(a)    where there is a minority or life interest;
(b)    where a personal representative or beneficiary applies to the court for the appointment of a substituted personal representative; or

(c)    where the trustees or a beneficiary of settled land apply to the court for the appointment of additional or special settled land executors (see 12.7).

### 12.9.1 Minority or life interest

Where a minority or life interest arises, and there is only one personal representative to deal with the trust, the court may appoint one or more further personal representatives to act with that person. This does not apply, however, if the lone personal representative is a trust corporation, for example, a bank. The application to the court can be made by any person interested (in the technical sense of having an interest such as a life interest in the estate) or their guardian or Mental Health Act deputy.

### 12.9.2 Substituted personal representative

Anyone who is a personal representative or a beneficiary may apply to the court for an order appointing a substituted personal representative. The court's powers under s 50 of the Administration of Justice Act 1985 are wide (see 16.4.5). The substituted personal representative may be appointed to act with the existing representatives or instead of any or all of them. They will be an executor if acting with any other executor. Otherwise, if acting alone or with administrators, they will be an administrator.

## 12.10  Executor by representation – s 7 of the AEA 1925

An executor may obtain their power by virtue of the operation of the important provisions of s 7 of the Administration of Estates Act 1925. These provisions are usually called the 'chain of representation'. If there is more than one executor, then in the event of any of them dying, the other(s) will carry on. However, when the last one dies having already taken probate, then any executor of theirs will also be the executor of the first testator, provided they obtain probate of the second testator's will. That second executor cannot take on the office of the first executor's executor without also taking on the office of the original testator's personal representative, so if they do not want to deal with either, they must renounce both.

### 12.10.1  Chain of representation

This is how the 'chain of representation' works:

(a)    T is the testator;
(b)    X takes probate of T's will;
(c)    X is T's last or sole executor;
(d)    X dies without fully administering T's estate;
(e)    Y obtains probate of X's will;
(f)    Y is T's executor by representation.

All the conditions mentioned above must be fulfilled for the chain to function. If T or X fails to appoint an executor (for instance if either is intestate and for that reason has an administrator instead) or X or Y fails to take out probate, the chain will not operate. If the chain operates, Y becomes the executor by representation of T.

## 12.10.2 Recommendation for change

The Law Reform Committee in its 23rd Report *The Powers and Duties of Trustees* (1982) found the results of the operation of the chain of representation 'often unsatisfactory'. In particular, it was unhappy that a person could find him- or herself unable to get rid of the obligation to administer an estate with which they had no real connection without renouncing the estate for which they were really appointed as well. The Law Reform Committee recommended that the retirement of personal representatives should generally be allowed more easily than at present, and that the case of an executorship acquired through these rules was a good example of a situation where, provided there had been no intermeddling, such retirement should be allowed: see 16.4.5.

## 12.11 Executors *de son tort*

'Executors *de son tort*' are not, in general, executors or personal representatives as such. They are persons who have intermeddled with the estate – dealt with it without authority – and who have thus incurred the liability to be treated as though they were personal representatives and to be held responsible to creditors in particular, especially HM Revenue and Customs, in respect of whatever they have intermeddled with. The phrase is sometimes used somewhat metaphorically in non-succession cases, to mean someone who has intermeddled and become liable without its necessarily having been established that they are a constructive trustee.

### 12.11.1 Acts which do not make a person an executor *de son tort*

A person does not become an executor *de son tort* by carrying out acts of common humanity which are not connected with the essential functions of a personal representative. The distinction between acts which make a person an executor *de son tort* and those which do not is one of the nature of the acts, not their objective financial significance. Arranging for a funeral, for example, will not make a person executor *de son tort*, as was established in *Harrison v Rowley* (1798). Collecting assets and paying debts, as in *Re Stevens* (1898), will, however, render a person an executor *de son tort*, because those are the essential functions of an executor.

### 12.11.2 The personal representative as executor *de son tort*?

Occasionally, a personal representative who acts wrongly is referred to as an executor *de son tort*. If a person entitled to a grant acts prior to the grant, they can be cited to take a grant; this applies equally to an executor appointed by will, who takes their power from the will, though they can only prove their title to the property in the estate by means of a grant of probate. If the executor acts as such without taking out the grant, they may also be called an executor *de son tort*. Although the word tort has to do with wrongdoing, the executor *de son tort* need not necessarily have committed any acts wrong in themselves, and if subsequently they take out the grant of probate, an executor who has intermeddled as an executor *de son tort* will become an executor in the same way as if they had never been an executor *de son tort*. The same applies to an administrator who acts without authority before the grant but subsequently takes out a grant of letters of administration.

### 12.11.3 Executor *de son tort* who is entitled to a grant

The significance of a person intermeddling with an estate and becoming an executor *de son tort* depends on whether they are a person entitled to a grant to the estate or not. If they are, they can be cited to take a grant because the acts which made them an executor *de son tort* will constitute acceptance of the office of executor or administrator. This was the case with Mr Glew, the husband of the married couple appointed executors in the case of *In the Estate of Biggs* (1966). They were elderly persons in poor health. They both absolutely refused to take out a grant even though the husband had not only intermeddled with the estate but had also been specifically ordered by the court to take probate. The court could have imprisoned him for his disobedience of its order, but it was unwilling to do so – it appeared he would prefer going to prison to taking probate. (The court found another solution, considered at 12.12.1.)

### 12.11.4 Executor *de son tort* who is not entitled to a grant

If the intermeddler is not entitled to a grant, then, as was confirmed in *Re Davis* (1860), they cannot be compelled to take one out. The true personal representatives will be bound by their acts only if they involved paying over money or assets to a person who reasonably believed they had authority to act as personal representative, or if what they have done is something the personal representatives were bound to do anyway.

### 12.11.5 Liability of an executor *de son tort* – Inheritance Tax

The liability of the executor *de son tort* to account to beneficiaries and creditors of the estate as though they were an executor or administrator includes a liability as to the payment of Inheritance Tax, pursuant to ss 199 and 200 of the Inheritance Tax Act 1984, on anything with which they have intermeddled. Cases involving HMRC provide a fruitful source of examples of executors *de son tort*, because companies can become executors *de son tort* by dealing with the deceased's shareholdings. They can then be fixed with the obligation to pay the tax on the deceased's estate and comparatively easily located in order to oblige payment. It is stated in s 55(1)(ix) of the Administration of Estates Act 1925 that so far as liability to pay Estate Duty (now Inheritance Tax) is concerned, the term 'personal representatives' includes executors *de son tort*. They are helpfully defined in that subsection as persons who take possession of or intermeddle with the deceased's property without the authority of the personal representatives or of the court. It is the liability for tax which is often the cause of greatest concern to a person who finds him- or herself executor *de son tort*.

In *New York Breweries Co Ltd v Attorney General* (1899), the English company which registered the transfer of shares from the name of the deceased to his American executors was held to have made itself executor *de son tort* by doing so, and was therefore liable to pay the Estate Duty on the English estate of the deceased, who had died domiciled in America.

### 12.11.6 Extent of other liabilities of an executor *de son tort*

The executor *de son tort* does not have the personal representative's duty to get in and collect, and account for, all the assets of the estate. They are liable to account only for those items with which they deal. If the items are used to discharge liabilities in the same way that a personal representative should have done, the executor *de son tort* will be given credit for such payments by virtue of s 28 of the Administration of Estates Act 1925. Therefore, if they discharge only debts which would have been discharged anyway, or otherwise give the property where it should properly have been given, they will not incur any further liability. If they were a creditor of the estate, they may keep anything properly obtained by them in satisfaction of a contractual debt to them. This must be proper, however; if they have paid themselves out of turn and deprived a person with a prior claim of their rightful entitlement, they will be liable. They may also keep any expenses a personal representative could lawfully keep, such as the deceased's reasonable funeral expenses if they have paid them.

## 12.12 Who may be an executor

A testator may appoint anyone they wish as executor. Any person or trust corporation may be appointed. Whether and when they can act as such will, however, depend on the circumstances. A minor or a mentally incapacitated person may not act as an executor; if a minor is appointed, they can take probate at 18 but not before.

### 12.12.1 Who may be granted probate or letters of administration

Probate may be granted to a sole executor, or to any number as appointed, up to a maximum of four for any part of the estate. Two is the usual number for which a will drafter strives, save where there is a sole adult beneficiary who is also the executor. A court may pass over an executor 'by reason of any special circumstances', by virtue of its power under s 116 of the Supreme Court Act 1981. The executrix whose appointment was considered in In the Estate of S (1968) was serving a sentence of life imprisonment for the manslaughter of the testator, which the court felt made it quite impossible for her to act as executrix. Both of the two executors appointed by the testator in In the Estate of Biggs (1966) (12.11.3) refused to take probate, even though the husband had been cited to take out a grant. The court declined to use its powers to imprison an elderly man in poor health, who appeared more willing to go to prison than to comply with the court's order. There was also the thought that even had either or both of the couple taken probate, they would have done so under protest and probably carried on causing difficulties. The court used its powers under s 116 SCA 1981 and appointed an administratrix with the will annexed instead.

### 12.12.2 Appointing a firm of solicitors – the Horgan clause

It is fairly common for a firm of solicitors to be appointed to the office of executor, usually by a clause appointing the partners in the specified firm, or its successor, at the date of the testator's death, as executors. The testator may express the desire that a specific person act if they are available, or that only two partners act in the proving of the will, but such provisions will be precatory only (expressing an unenforceable wish). It was confirmed in Re Horgan (1971) that the appointment of a firm of solicitors in this way will be valid, and a clause which appoints a firm of solicitors is usually called a 'Horgan clause'. The usual formulation is to appoint the firm and to request that a particular person acts. Note, however, that there can be unexpected pitfalls: the will under which the solicitors in Gray v Richards Butler (2001) acted was later declared invalid, and they were not entitled to payment under it.

That common formulation caused problems when solicitors' firms became able to convert to limited liability partnerships. The partners in a firm might become members of the LLP and the LLP might succeed to and carry on the firm's business, but the operation would no longer fall within the wording of the Horgan clause. The probate registrars decided in 2003, at their annual conference, that grants would not be made in these circumstances. Re Rogers (2006) was a case brought and paid for by a variety of solicitors to ascertain what should then be done. If the court had followed the registrars' view, the people the testator thought he had validly appointed would have had to apply for a discretionary grant or, with the co-operation of the residuary beneficiaries, perhaps an attorney grant.[2] Either course would clearly cause expense. The application was treated as a matter of construction and Lightman J decided that the change effected by the firm becoming an LLP would be 'likely totally to escape' people giving instructions for their

---

2  S 116 of the Supreme Court Act 1981; NCPR r 31.

wills, 'unless given a lesson in the law which they may well not follow'. He went on to say that: 'Even if they do grasp the distinction, they are likely to regard it as a distinction without any relevant difference,' and held that where there was a Horgan clause appointing a particular firm, probate should be granted to profit-sharing members of the ensuing LLP, as well as advising that future wills should be drafted so as to make express and explicit provision on the point.

### 12.12.3 Appointing professionals rather than lay persons

It used to be the case that most lay executors passed the administration of the estate to solicitors for them to deal with; such expenses of the administration as payment of the solicitors' fees come out of the estate, not the executors' own pockets. However, more and more executors are doing the probate work themselves, and indeed if they are entitled to residue, they will benefit directly from the professional costs remaining in the estate. Appointing solicitors as executors in the will rather than leaving it to lay executors to pass on does however still effectively enable the testator to choose which firm is appointed where the estate is likely to be administered by a paid professional.

Until the Trustee Act 2000, solicitors were not entitled to charge for their services (though out-of-pocket expenses were always allowable, as for any executor) unless a clause allowing them to do so was included in the will. Note that even if they were authorised to charge for their professional services, that would not cover charging for services which were not professional (Re Chapple; Newton v Chapman (1884)), unless the charging clause also covered non-professional services. If the charging clause was left out, it was likely the solicitors would renounce probate (see 12.13). The same would apply to a trust corporation such as a bank where one was appointed, though the Public Trustee could always charge. An alternative way of paying executors, less used nowadays, could be to leave legacies to proving executors or those who accept office. Any such legacy would be presumed to be a conditional legacy, but any drafting of such a gift should be clear and explicit, especially as the presumption does not apply to residue.

In relation to deaths on or after 1 February 2001, s 20 of the Trustee Act 2000 has given a personal representative acting in a professional capacity an entitlement to receive reasonable remuneration if all the other personal representatives agree in writing that they may be remunerated. By s 28, a professional personal representative is to be treated as entitled to be paid even if a lay person could do the work. The payments are treated as remuneration for services, not as a gift, for the purposes of s 15 of the Wills Act 1837 (witnessing) and s 34(3) AEA 1925 (order of distribution).

In 2014, the Institute of Chartered Accountants in England and Wales was given statutory authority to license accountants to conduct non-contentious probate business as from 14 August 2014.[3]

## 12.13 Renouncing probate

Anyone appointed executor may accept or renounce probate before acting without giving any reason. This also applies to those deemed to have been appointed as special executors in relation to settled land. However, renunciation is a positive step and will not happen simply by the executor doing nothing. There are precedents to be found in the appropriate practice books for forms by which to renounce. The renunciation takes effect once the signed form is filed with the probate registry. Partial renunciation is not possible. Where an executor Y by taking out probate

---

3 The Legal Services Act 2007 (Licensing Authority) Order 2014: SI 2014/1925. Previously this had been the reserved business of solicitors, but para 15(1)(a) of Sch 10 to the Legal Services Act 2007 made it possible for the Lord Chancellor to authorise a body to become a licensing authority in relation to one or more activities which constitute one or more reserved legal activities.

of the will of X becomes the executor by representation of T, under s 7 of the Administration of Estates Act 1925, they may not renounce the executorship of T's will without renouncing that of X as well (see 12.10.1). Having renounced probate, an executor may retract their renunciation only with the leave of the court, which will be given only if the court thinks it in the interests of the estate. Having been wrongly advised and therefore renounced will not entitle an executor to retract their renunciation.[4]

## 12.14 Citation

If the executor neither accepts nor renounces probate, the court may issue a citation summoning the executor to make a formal decision one way or the other. Obviously, the court will not do, or be able to do, this automatically. There is no central authority overseeing the day-to-day administration of estates. Anyone who would, if the executor renounced, be entitled to letters of administration, may apply to the court for a citation to be issued.

### 12.14.1 If the executor intermeddles

Acceptance can be constituted not only by taking out probate but also by intermeddling, as in In the Estate of Biggs (1966) (12.11.3). Any executor who has intermeddled but does not then take out a grant of probate may be cited by anyone interested in the estate, who may alternatively ask for that executor to be passed over so that the grant may be issued to someone else. A citation could be used by a court to require an intermeddler who is entitled to take a grant to do so; it would then be contempt of court to refuse.

### 12.14.2 Failure to take out grant causing loss

If something is lost to the estate through the failure of an executor to take out probate, the decision in Re Stevens (1898) shows that the beneficiary cannot claim against them for that reason. Criticism was, however, made more recently in Sifri v Clough & Willis (2007) (see 16.2.5) that an interim form of grant had not been taken out to protect the assets in the estate pending resolution of disputes over the will, so this may be subject to change.

## 12.15 Administrators

The term 'administrator' applies to a personal representative appointed not by the testator but by virtue of the provisions in the Non-Contentious Probate Rules 1987, which are made under s 127 of the Supreme Court Act 1981. Administrators take a grant of letters of administration rather than of probate.

Obviously, if there is no will, no executor will have been appointed, but administrators are also appointed where there is a will but it does not name anyone who can or will act as executor. Such a person must, nevertheless, administer the estate in accordance with the terms of the will, and they will be granted 'letters of administration with will annexed' – the grant will have the will attached to it. There is no obligation on anyone to be an administrator if they do not wish to do so.

---

4  In the Goods of Gill (1873).

## 12.16  Order of priority where there is a will – NCPR r 20

The order of those who may take a grant where there is a will is regulated by r 20 of the Non-Contentious Probate Rules; the first is the executor, but the rest of the rule applies equally even if no executor was ever appointed. This list follows a pattern based on the entitlement to property in the estate.

The provisions of r 20 as to the order of priority of entitlement to a grant where there is a will are as follows:

(a)   the executor;

(b)   any residuary legatee or devisee holding in trust for any other person;

(c)   any other residuary legatee or devisee (including one for life) or where the residue is not wholly disposed of by the will, any person entitled to share in the undisposed-of residue under the intestacy rules;

(d)   the personal representative of any residuary legatee or devisee (but not one for life, or one holding in trust for any other person), or of any person entitled to share in any residue not disposed of by the will;

(e)   any other legatee or devisee (including one for life or one holding in trust for any other person) or any creditor of the deceased;

(f)   the personal representative of any other legatee or devisee (but not one for life or one holding in trust for any other person) or of any creditor of the deceased.

### 12.16.1  Operation of NCPR r 20

After the executor him- or herself, the person most nearly carrying out those functions is a trustee of the residuary estate; such a person is accordingly the next in line to take out a grant where no executor is available. If there is no trust of residue, then the person who takes residue him- or herself has the closest function to that of executor and is accordingly the most appropriate person to deal with the estate as a whole.

### 12.16.2  Resolving a dispute as to who will take a grant

If persons entitled in the same degree cannot decide who should take the grant, the court may decide. The general rule according to which it will make its decision is that the best person to deal with the claims of the beneficiaries and creditors will take the grant, although in practice this means proving that another potential applicant is not of the right character to take the grant.

If there is a dispute as to who of the persons entitled in the same class should take a grant, the court will in appropriate cases apply r 27(5) NCPR. This states that a grant should go to a living person in preference to the personal representative of a deceased person, and to a person of full age in preference to a guardian of a minor.

## 12.17  Order of priority where there is no will NCPR r 22

There is a very different rule of entitlement where there is no will at all and the deceased died wholly intestate. The structure of the provisions of r 22 is based on family relationships. Entitlement to a grant under this rule also depends on a beneficial entitlement to property under the intestacy rules, which, again, are based on the same family relationships. The rules of entitlement to a grant of letters of administration on intestacy are as follows:

(a)     Provided they have a beneficial interest under the intestacy rules:
- the surviving husband or wife;
- the children of the deceased and the issue of any deceased child who died before the deceased;
- the father and mother of the deceased;
- brothers and sisters of the whole blood and the issue of any deceased brother or sister of the whole blood who died before the deceased;
- brothers and sisters of the half blood and the issue of any deceased brother or sister of the half blood who died before the deceased;
- grandparents;
- uncles and aunts of the whole blood and the issue of any deceased uncle or aunt of the whole blood who died before the deceased;
- uncles and aunts of the half blood and the issue of any deceased uncle or aunt of the half blood who died before the deceased.

(b)     In default of any person having a beneficial interest in the estate, the Treasury Solicitor (or solicitor for the Duchies of Lancaster or Cornwall, depending on the residence of the deceased) if they claim *bona vacantia* on behalf of the Crown.

(c)     If all prior persons entitled to a grant have been cleared off, a creditor of the deceased, or the personal representative of such creditor, or any person who may have a beneficial interest in the event of an accretion to the estate.

Again, if persons entitled in the same degree cannot decide who shall take a grant, the court may decide.

## 12.18  Clearing off

Where a person wishes to apply for a grant but they do not come at the top of the list of those entitled to one, they must establish that those with a prior entitlement to the grant can be passed over. 'Clearing off' is the process of getting rid of someone with prior entitlement. Thus, anyone applying for a grant of administration in relation to the estate of an intestate ('simple' administration) must establish that everyone entitled with priority has either renounced their right to administration or has been cited to accept or refuse a grant of administration.

## 12.19  Form of grants of representation

Grants are the form of court order issued to personal representatives giving them authority to deal with an estate. They are technically court orders, but acquiring a grant does not usually involve attending any court and nor does it usually involve anyone exercising any fully judicial function. If every grant had to be ordered individually by even a junior form of judge in court, there would need to be a huge number of courts of probate sitting many hours each week. In practice almost all applications for grants are dealt with not judicially but, in reality, administratively, by clerks. They will deal with all non-contentious or 'common form' business, as defined in s 128 of the Supreme Court Act 1981, which is dealt with by the Family Division of the High Court in the form usually of the local District Probate Registry of the executors' solicitors. Contentious, or 'solemn form' business is generally assigned to the Chancery Division, to be begun by writ, though actions over smaller estates may be brought in the county court.

### 12.19.1 Need for a grant – Administration of Estates (Small Payments) Act 1965

It may not be necessary to obtain a grant before being able to use certain funds in an estate. The Administration of Estates (Small Payments) Act 1965 provides a list of assets, including National Savings, building society accounts and arrears of salary or superannuation benefits due to state employees, which may be paid over without the need to produce a grant. The limit is £5,000 (which is also the limit below which no fee is payable for a grant of probate).

The fact that the authority concerned has power to make such payments does not, however, mean that it can be compelled to do so, and it may have its own particular regulations about when it will make payment.

Conversely, some bodies, including large financial institutions, allow payments of substantially higher value without a grant. They generally have their own forms and procedures. It is always worth asking.

In some estates, the only substantive assets may be covered by provisions of this kind and there may be no need for a grant at all. However, a grant will be needed if land or shares are to be dealt with, as it will be required to show the personal representatives' title to deal with the property.

### 12.19.2 What is admissible to probate?

A will is admissible to probate if it appoints executors, even if they renounce, or if it contains a disposition of property within the jurisdiction. Thus a will which only appoints a guardian for a child or only revokes a previous will without making further dispositions is not admissible to proof unless the court exercises its discretion. It must be remembered, however, that in every case it is necessary for the will to satisfy all the criteria for validity, both as to the state of mind of the testator when they made the will and, save as to formalities and age in the case of a privileged will, as to compliance with the formalities in the Wills Act 1837 (see chapters 3 and 4).

The court's powers of discretion are wide, and they will be exercised if the court sees fit. Although in theory the court has no jurisdiction at all over property outside England and Wales, it may issue a grant in respect of a will dealing exclusively with such property, though the application for the grant must include a recital of the reason for seeking a grant in such circumstances. In Re Wayland (1951), the court admitted to probate a will which dealt exclusively with property outside the jurisdiction, namely the deceased's Belgian will, in order to clarify the effect of a revocation clause in the deceased's English will (see 7.4.3).

## 12.20 Obtaining a grant

If a grant is needed, which will generally be the case in an estate of any appreciable size, the application should be made in the post to the local probate registry. No grant may be issued within seven days of death where there is a will, or 14 days in the case of administration on intestacy.[5] There is a very informative website at www.gov.uk/wills-probate-inheritance/overview.

---

5  NCPR r 6.

## 12.20.1 Papers to be submitted

Executors may obtain a grant of probate themselves or may use a solicitor. Where there is IHT owing on the estate (see Chapter 14), it has to be declared to HMRC on the relevant form and usually paid and the receipt from HMRC sent in to the probate registry with the application for the grant. For dealing with having to pay the IHT before the assets of the estate are available, see 20.20.4. There are different HMRC forms to be used depending on whether tax is payable or reliefs and exemptions claimed.

The probate application form is PA1 and should be submitted to the local probate registry with the IHT form, an official copy of the deceased's death certificate, the original will and codicils plus three copies, and the application fee. There is no fee if the estate is under £5,000; otherwise, for personal applicants the fee is £215 and for applications submitted by solicitors it is £155. Official copies of the grant cost 50p each. Because this is part of a court process, evidence must be given on oath: the executor seeking a grant has to swear that what is in the application is true, exhibiting the will. This can be done for a small fee before any solicitor or free at the local probate registry.

## 12.20.2 Contents of the oath form

The oath form deals with the details of the deceased and of their death, and the details of the person applying for a grant. It asks them to explain what their entitlement to the grant is – for example, that they are the executor appointed by the will or the surviving spouse of the intestate, and to swear or affirm that they will duly administer the estate according to law.

## 12.20.3 Personal representatives liable for Inheritance Tax (IHT)

The personal representatives are liable under s 200(1) of the Inheritance Tax Act (IHTA) 1984 for the IHT payable on:

(a) any property which was not immediately before the deceased's death comprised in a settlement; and

(b) any land in the UK which immediately before the deceased's death was comprised in a settlement and which devolves upon or vests in the personal representatives.

However, the personal representative is only liable for tax to the extent they receive (or should have received but for their own neglect or default) the property as personal representative (s 204(1)).

## 12.20.4 Generally no grant until IHT paid

In principle, no grant of probate or administration will be issued unless the probate registry is satisfied that any Inheritance Tax due on the estate has been paid. There are obvious administrative advantages in not enabling anyone to get their hands on the estate until after HMRC has been satisfied; it could be considerably more awkward to enforce payment later, but if a person has to pay the tax in order to get the grant of probate, they will have a strong push to do so. Thus, although the probate forms for a small estate may be very simple, for a substantial estate, even where the dispositions are simple, considerable paperwork may be required with respect to tax.

## 12.20.5 Outline of IHT forms for a grant

The amount of Inheritance Tax payable and the complexity of the paperwork will depend on the amount in the estate (see Chapter 14). The threshold for Inheritance Tax is currently £325,000 (from 2009), the sum under that being known as the 'nil-rate band' and there are various exemptions and reliefs. Once the tax is payable, the rate is 40 per cent unless a relief for charitable donations applies. Since October 2007 it has been possible for the first partner in a marriage or civil partnership to transfer their unused IHT nil-rate band to the surviving spouse so that the nil-rate band on the death of the second partner is up to £650,000. The Finance Act 2012 introduced Sch 1A into the Inheritance Tax Act 1984. This allows a 36 per cent tax rate on the deceased's taxable estate if 10 per cent of the estate above the nil-rate band is left to charity. These rules are quite complex.

Gifts to spouses and charities are exempt and do not form part of the nil-rate band. Gifts made seven years before death will be exempt, but those made within seven years of death will be subject to a tapering rate of IHT. £3,000 may however be given away per year, rolled over for a maximum of one year, plus an unlimited number of small gifts of up to £250 per year, without attracting IHT. There are also exemptions and reliefs for wedding and civil partnership gifts and the inheritance of certain forms of landed business.

Where the deceased lives in England and Wales, as well as the relevant probate application Form PA1 a Form IHT205 will be needed if the estate is an excepted estate (no IHT payable), or Form IHT 207 if they lived abroad and their assets in the UK were under £150,000. Form IHT217 is used to claim a transfer of unused nil-rate band between spouses. Where IHT is payable or the estate is not an excepted estate, Form IHT 400 should be used, and Form IHT 422 to obtain an IHT reference number and paying slip. There are other forms to deal with trusts, or, for example, corrections to accounts.

The IHT on the estate should be paid within six months from the end of the month of the death. After that, interest begins to run.

## 12.20.6 Paying the IHT

The personal representatives must deliver any HMRC account within 12 months from the end of the month of death, or, if later, three months from the date when they first acted. Interest is payable on tax unpaid after six months from the end of the month of death; thus, to avoid paying interest, the personal representative have to have submitted the account and paid the tax by then.

There is clear potential for a practical difficulty here. One of the purposes for which the property in the estate may be needed is for the payment of the IHT on the estate, but the tax has to be paid before the property can be obtained and used for any purpose. The IHT may be paid in instalments where this is the case, or another solution to this paradoxical situation which is often adopted is for the personal representatives to pay the IHT by means of a loan to the estate from a beneficiary who stands to gain from the estate and has some cash available. The consequent speeding-up of the probate process is a considerable encouragement to such a beneficiary. Alternatively, a commercial loan may be sought from a bank, since an estate which has enough in it to require the payment of IHT will be sufficient to service and repay a commercial loan. On occasion, HMRC may agree to the grant being issued in effect on credit, with the IHT paid later.

A further potential for practical difficulty is that the value of the estate may be difficult to ascertain. A provisional estimate may be submitted if necessary, with an undertaking to deliver a better account later. If a mistake in valuation is discovered, a corrective account must be delivered within six months.

### 12.20.7 Common minor problems in seeking probate

The fact that there are problems with some particular aspect of the application for the grant will not necessarily lead to a court hearing. It is comparatively common for a will to be found in a poor state and for an 'affidavit of plight and condition' to be submitted with the application for probate to explain how this came about, avoiding any need to investigate questions of destruction, for example. Affidavits are also fairly frequently required where the testator has attached something to the will, for example, a note to their solicitor confirming that they have obeyed all instructions (including the one not to attach anything to the will). Otherwise the probate registry may raise queries about what the document was and why it was attached.

### 12.20.8 Obtaining a grant of letters of administration

The process of obtaining letters of administration is broadly similar to that of obtaining probate. Where there is a will to be annexed to the grant, whether or not it covers all the property in the estate, it will be referred to on the oath form; where the deceased died wholly intestate, that fact will be referred to. The applicant for the grant will have to recite their entitlement to the grant by reference to r 22, rather than r 20, of the NCPR in the case of intestacy.

## 12.21 Caveats – NCPR r 44

A caveat records someone's objections to the issuing of a grant. The entering of a caveat will prevent the sealing of a grant until the caveator's objections have been dealt with. The caveat is a notice as specified by r 44 of the Non-Contentious Probate Rules 1987 sent to the Family Division of the High Court; the applicant for the grant will be told about it and may then issue a warning to the caveator, who should then state their contrary interest to that of the applicant, or else issue a summons for directions if they have no such contrary interest. Otherwise, the caveat expires after six months if it is not extended.

## 12.22 Omissions from probate

There may be some reason why even a will, or part of a will, which has been properly executed and is otherwise valid will not be admitted to probate. This will apply where there is fraud or forgery, or where the testator did not know and approve of the will or part omitted. The relevant parts will not be included in the probate because the testator did not fulfil the necessary conditions as to state of mind and *animus testandi* (intention to make a will) in relation to those parts of the will.

It is not permissible for documents which are valid to be omitted from probate even by the agreement of all the beneficiaries. If the beneficiaries agree to vary the provisions of the will, they must negotiate from the starting point of the gifts in the will; the agreed variation can then be effected, formally, once the will has been proved. A variation or disclaimer can then be read back into the will for tax purposes (see 10.5 and 14.20). Even where a document's validity is doubtful and it is agreed by all parties that it is not valid, it should be propounded by the executor. This was held by the court in *Re Watts* (1837), where the testator was a proven lunatic (in the terms of the time); the court nevertheless refused to grant letters of administration on the basis of the agreement of almost all the persons involved that the will should be ignored. It was not up to them to decide that the will not valid, or up to anyone to decide that it would be ignored.

## 12.23 Revocation of grants

The court has power not only to make but also to revoke grants, although the particular circumstances in which a grant may be revoked are not specified by statute. The power to revoke grants is contained in s 121 of the Supreme Court Act 1981. A grant may be revoked for various reasons, but it will usually be either because it was wrongly made in the first place or because of subsequent events.

### 12.23.1 Grant wrongly made

Where the grant is wrongly made, then this has usually been caused by the applicant for the grant having made a false statement. That may, however, have been inadvertent.

### 12.23.2 Wrong statements by applicants

The deceased may prove not to have been dead after all. The application for revocation of the grant in the case of In the Goods of Napier (1809) was made to the, court by the 'deceased' who had not, after all, died on the field of battle. He had been left there for dead by his fellow-soldiers and the applicant for the original grant had been quite unaware that he was still alive.

The applicant may have made some false claim as to their relationship to the deceased, so that once the truth was known it was apparent that the grant should not have been made to that person. The applicant in In the Goods of Moore (1845) claimed to be the widow of the deceased, but it turned out that she had not actually been married to him. The grant to the deceased's relative in Re Bergman's Goods (1842) was revoked when it was discovered that he was illegitimate and therefore not entitled to the grant for that reason; the law today in respect of illegitimacy is different. A more recent case, Shephard v Wheeler (2000), concerned a grant made to someone who claimed to be a chartered accountant and a creditor of the estate without revealing that he was bankrupt and had been struck off as an accountant.

### 12.23.3 Contravention of procedure

Grants have been revoked where a caveator was not given notice before the making of the grant, as in Trimlestown v Trimlestown (1830), and where persons entitled in priority to the grantee were not cited and cleared off before the grant was made, in Ravenscroft v Ravenscroft (1671).

### 12.23.4 Other matters discovered later

It may become clear after a grant has been made that it should not have been because the will of which probate was granted, for example, later turns out not to have been valid because it was forged, or the testator was still alive.[6] Less dramatically, a will may be found after a grant of letters of administration has been made, or a later will found after a grant of probate. A codicil may be found appointing different executors, or the grantee may turn out to be an infant. It may also transpire that the deceased had remarried after making the will which was proved, so that it was revoked, as occurred in Priestman v Thomas (1884). In Rowe v Clarke (2006), a grant of administration was revoked where the deceased's brother had asserted that the disappearance of the original will, which had been in the possession of the deceased, meant that it was presumed to

---

6 Re Napier (1809). See also the story of the will of which the first defendant in Treasury Solicitor v Doveton and Trixilis (2008) was granted probate, and which he was found to have been forged.

have been destroyed with the intention of revoking it. However the claimant, the deceased's partner, showed that the deceased had sent a copy to his (the partner's) mother and successfully rebutted any such presumption, asserting that the brother had himself destroyed the original will, with which the deceased had been very careless, so the court thought it possible the deceased had destroyed or lost it accidentally.[7]

## 12.23.5 Subsequent events

Where a grantee becomes incapable and there are other grantees, the original grant will be revoked and a fresh grant made to the other(s). If, however, there are no other grantees, the grant will not be revoked; rather a grant of letters of administration *de bonis non* (see 12.26.2) for the use and benefit of the grantee will be made. This occurred, for example, in the case of In the Goods of Galbraith (1951), where, six years after the original grant to two executors, both were too physically and mentally infirm to act. The court made a grant *de bonis non* with will annexed. A grantee may be relieved of their duties by the court under s 50 of the Administration of Justice Act 1985. Advanced age and ill health might be a good reason for this. See also the removal and retirement of personal representatives at 12.31.

The court may revoke a grant where it becomes apparent that the grantee will not carry out the administration properly. Where the grantee disappears before administration is completed, the court may decide to make a fresh grant on the grounds that the first one has turned out to be 'abortive or inefficient', as occurred in the case of In the Goods of Loveday (1900). In that case, the deceased's widow obtained a grant of letters of administration and later disappeared without carrying out the administration of the estate.

A grant may be revoked because the grantee has committed a breach of duty. Not every breach will be considered serious enough to warrant revocation, however, and the standard of breach required may appear quite high. In In the Estate of Cope (1954), the administrators of the estate submitted estate duty accounts which turned out to be inaccurate in that certain assets were omitted and a disputed debt (owed by the deceased to one of the administrators) was included. The court thought there might be a case for ordering the administrators to account to the court for their administration but did not think the breach warranted revocation of the grant. In Re Flynn (1982), however, the estate had appeared insolvent until further property fell into it. The court refused to strike out an action to revoke the grant on the basis of delay, as the delay was not unreasonable in the light of the previous apparent futility of such an application. It appeared, however, that the court would be unwilling to strike out any such action before a hearing save if it were frivolous, vexatious or otherwise an abuse of the process of the court.

## 12.24 Powers of amendment

The court also has power to amend a grant under r 41 of the Non-Contentious Probate Rules. This applies only where the amendment is not of any great substance.

## 12.24.1 Will proved in solemn form

Most wills are proved in common form. There are no court proceedings in the sense that is usually meant, but an application on paper to the probate registry for a grant, supported by affidavits as necessary. Most of the narrative above concerns common form probate. Where, however, there is

---

7 For the operation of this presumption see also *D'Eye v Avery* [2001]; *Chana v Chana* (2001); *Wren v Wren* (2007).

a major dispute (the entering of a caveat or the issuing of a citation does not of itself take the matter out of the realm of 'non-contentious' business) about the validity of a will, there may be court proceedings in which the court makes a final order as to the validity of the will.[8] This then becomes *res judicata* (a matter about which the court has adjudicated) and that question cannot be reopened save in exceptional circumstances: for example, the finding of a later will or proof of fraud. In *Re Barraclough* (1965), for instance, there was a claim that the deceased had lacked testamentary capacity; the plaintiff, on losing her legal aid certificate, compromised the claim and was later prevented by the *res judicata* rule from re-opening the question in further court proceedings.

## 12.25  Effect of revocation

Clearly where someone's authority to deal with an estate is revoked, that could have serious and far-reaching consequences. There is a set of rules protecting persons who have dealt with a personal representative whose authority to deal with the property in the deceased's estate is later revoked.

### 12.25.1  Protection for persons who have dealt with former personal representatives

A person who has purchased property from the former personal representative is protected by various statutory provisions, in particular s 204(1) of the Law of Property Act 1925 and s 37 of the Administration of Estates Act 1925.

### 12.25.2  Revoked court orders – s 204(1) of the LPA 1925

A purchaser will be protected by the provisions of s 204(1) of the Law of Property Act 1925, which states that any person acting under a court order whilst that order is in force will be specifically protected if the order is subsequently revoked because of some irregularity. A grant is technically a court order. The section further states that its protection operates even for a person who was aware of the irregularity or impropriety. In *Re Bridgett & Hayes' Contract* (1928), land was settled on Emily Bridgett for life and after her death on trust for sale. She died in 1926, the estate being vested in her as tenant for life. John Jackson was the sole trustee of the settlement. Emily's executor, Thomas Bridgett, contracted to sell the land to a purchaser, who objected to his title on the ground that the legal estate was vested in Mr Jackson as Emily's special executor (see settled land executors, 12.7). The court held Thomas Bridgett could make a good title, because the settlement ended at Emily's death, and the legal title vested in Thomas Bridgett as from the grant of probate.

### 12.25.3  Conveyances and revoked grants – s 37 of the AEA 1925

Section 37 of the Administration of Estates Act 1925 states that a conveyance will be valid notwithstanding subsequent revocation of the grant. 'Conveyance' under this section includes most dispositions made by deed, including mortgages, leases and vesting instruments, provided the purchaser acquired the interest in good faith and for valuable consideration.

---

8  This means it becomes a contentious probate matter: see CPR 57.

### 12.25.4 Payments to or by the former personal representative – s 27(2) of the AEA 1925

Provided that any transaction has been carried out in good faith by the person seeking to rely on the subsection, s 27(2) of the AEA 1925 provides that the receipt of a former personal representative given whilst their grant was still in force is a good discharge. It also allows a personal representative to reimburse him- or herself for payments properly made by them in the administration of the estate whilst their grant was still in force.

### 12.25.5 Indemnity of former personal representative – s 27(1) of the AEA 1925

A personal representative who has acted in good faith during the subsistence of their grant of representation will be protected by s 27(1) of the Administration of Estates Act 1925. This provides that every person who makes a disposition under a representation shall be indemnified and protected in so doing, regardless of any defect or circumstances affecting the validity of the representation.

## 12.26 Special and limited grants

The grant of representation will usually authorise the grantee to deal with all the deceased's property and wind up the estate. However, this is not always the case.

### 12.26.1 Special grants

There are certain situations in which the court will make a grant limited to the carrying out of a particular purpose which cannot wait for the appointment of personal representatives under a full grant. This will apply where there are assets in the estate which need to be collected in speedily or where legal proceedings need to be dealt with. The first is a grant *ad colligenda bona defuncti* (for the collection of the goods of the deceased), and the second may be a grant *pendente lite* or a grant *ad litem* (pending suit or during litigation). The former confers rights over the assets in the estate whereas the latter merely confers the right to represent the estate in proceedings, for example, as in the case of *Re Knight* (1939), where the Official Solicitor took out a grant *ad litem* so that a claimant could start proceedings against the estate for personal injuries under the Law Reform (Miscellaneous Provisions) Act 1934. Nowadays, however, the Proceedings Against Estates Act 1970 could be used (see 12.3.1).

A grant with limited powers may be made where it is necessary to avoid damage to the estate caused by, for example, a dispute as to who should take a grant of probate. David Richards J in *Ghafoor v Cliff* (2006) described it as: 'a useful, sometimes vital, power enabling urgent steps to be taken at a time when it is not yet practicable to obtain a full grant of probate or administration'. In *Sifri v Clough and Willis* (2007), a side issue that arose from the central probate dispute (see 16.2.5) was that premium bonds were not cashed in on time and appropriate high-interest investments were not made. Although these losses were not attributed to the fault of the solicitors, there was an element of criticism of them in not having applied for a grant to safeguard the position. A grant *ad colligenda bona* was however sought and made in the case of *Aeroflot v Berezovsky* (2013) to the deceased's daughter, amidst arguments about whether or not the estate was solvent and the suggestion that the creditors, were they given a grant, would use it to get behind the deceased's legal privilege, which would pass to his personal representatives.

### 12.26.2 Limited grants

A grant of limited probate will be made where the executors are not to deal with all the testator's property or are not to carry on dealing with it indefinitely. Section 113 of the Supreme Court Act 1981 provides that the court may make limited grants as it sees fit. There are narrower provisions relating to insolvent estates.

Limitations as to property commonly apply where there is a grant limited to settled property where the settlement continues after the testator's death (if it does not, the property ceases to be settled property), where the testator has appointed particular executors to deal with a specified part of their estate, for example, literary executors (12.1 and 12.5), or where the administrator, having taken out a previous grant, fails to complete the administration of the estate, perhaps by dying without an executor taking on the first estate by a chain of representation. This last form of limited grant is called a grant *de bonis non administratis* (grant of the goods which were not administered); where the personal representative had become a trustee, his or her own personal representatives would have the power under s 36 of the Trustee Act 1925 to appoint a new trustee, and no grant would be needed.

If a grant limited as to property is to be made, the grant relating to the rest of the estate will be made stated to be a grant *save and except* the property to which the limited grant relates; if the limited grant has already been made, the grant relating to the rest of the estate is called a grant *caeterorum* (of the other things).

Limitations as to time arise in various circumstances, although the only one commonly met in practice is where the will appoints a minor as executor. By s 118 of the Supreme Court Act 1981, a minor is prevented from taking a grant until they reach their majority. There may be a grant of administration *durante minore aetate* (during minority) grant. The grant will be specified to last until the minor attains their majority. It will be made to the person entitled to the residuary estate if the minor has no interest in the estate but is appointed sole executor (NCPR r 32(1)), or otherwise to the minor's parent(s) or guardian unless the district judge or registrar appoints another person to act alone or jointly under his or her overriding discretion (NCPR r 32(2)). It may then only be renounced on the minor's behalf by order of the registrar. The only limit to the grantee's rights and liabilities is the minor's minority.

Other grants limited as to time are grants of administration during mental incapacity, administration *pendente lite* and administration *durante absentia* (in absence). A grant of administration *pendente lite* may be made where there is a dispute about the validity of the will or the right to administer the estate. It will be made only if the court thinks it necessary and 'proper in all the circumstances', to someone unconnected with the action, for example an accountant, who can do nothing with the estate save with leave of the court. A grant *durante absentia* may be sought where the personal representative remains out of the jurisdiction; the court may issue the grant to any person interested in the estate, including a creditor. Where there is known to be a valid will in existence which cannot be found, it is also possible for the court to make a grant 'till the will be found', as was done in the case of *Re Wright* (1893).

## 12.27 Other grants

Other particular types of grants may be appropriate in certain circumstances.

### 12.27.1 Double probate, cessate grants, attorneys and settled land

Where one executor, having given notice to the others, obtains a grant to act alone, that grant will state that there is power reserved to the others should they wish to apply for a grant later. If they do so, the result will be 'double probate'; the first grant is not recalled.

A cessate grant is one which is issued following the expiry of a period of administration under a previous grant. In this it differs technically from a grant *de bonis non administratis*, since in theory it is a renewal of the whole grant rather than a new grant dealing only with the remaining property. However, the practical effect is the same.

A person's attorney may take a grant on their behalf, which will be revoked if the principal calls for his or her own grant or, alternatively, dies.

The particular rules relating to the appointment of settled land executors are discussed at 12.7. Where there is settled land, they will take a separate grant in their separate capacity limited to the settled land, and the grant relating to the rest of the deceased's estate will be save and except the settled land.

## 12.28 The duties of personal representatives and trustees

The personal representatives' duties are not the same as those of the trustees, though both are in a fiduciary position so they must act in good faith, putting the interests of the estate before their own and taking no profit from their position (save where specifically authorised). Personal representatives must act for the benefit of the estate as a whole, but trustees owe their duty to the beneficiaries as individuals (*Re Hayes* (1971)).

Personal representatives and trustees have different powers and duties under the general law. Trustees will be needed if there is any property which will not be distributed immediately, for example where it is held pending the fulfilment of a condition such as the beneficiary attaining a certain age, or where any recipient will not get an absolute title to the property, for instance a life interest under a trust for sale.

### 12.28.1 Personal representatives who are also trustees

Although it is usual to appoint the same persons as trustees as are appointed executors, their functions are different and it is possible to appoint different persons. The reason they are often the same is that the elements which make a testator choose a person to be their executor – the testator trusts them to deal honestly and efficiently with their property – are the same elements that would make him or her choose them as their trustees.

The personal representatives will also become trustees where the nature of the estate calls for them – because a trust arises – but no trustees have been expressly appointed. This is certainly the case where there is a trust created under a will and the testator has failed to appoint trustees, but the situation may be more difficult where the trust arises on an intestacy.

## 12.29 Personal representatives and trustees: different rules and roles

The personal representative's function is to wind up the estate and distribute the assets appropriately. The personal representative retains this function for life, so that even where an estate has apparently been finally wound up, if something further accrues to the estate or proceedings are commenced against it, they are bound to deal with it, whereas the function of the trustee is to hold the title to the property pending the end of the trust.

### 12.29.1 Acting jointly

Personal representatives may act severally – each one by him- or herself – including in the giving of receipts, whereas the authority of trustees is joint and they must act unanimously unless given authority by the will to do otherwise. The situation when personal representatives deal with land is somewhat different. The rule that one personal representative could bind all of their colleagues to convey land by entering into a contract to do so (see *Fountain Forestry Ltd v Edwards* (1975)) was altered by s 16 of the Law of Property (Miscellaneous Provisions) Act 1994, amending s 2(2) of the Administration of Estates Act 1925 as from 1 July 1995. All personal representatives must now concur in both the contract and (as before the 1994 Act) the conveyance for them to be valid. Practitioners should beware of the situation where, on the death of a legal joint tenant, the beneficial ownership is, or may be, held on a tenancy in common; the deceased's personal representatives will need to concur in any contract.

### 12.29.2 Overreaching

Where there is only one personal representative, they can overreach equitable interests on the sale of property from the estate (s 2 Law of Property Act 1925). Where, however, the person selling the property from the estate is a trustee, they cannot overreach equitable interests if they are acting alone (save in the case of a trust corporation, under s 27(2) of the LPA 1925 and s 18(1) of the SLA 1925). However, where there is a sole trustee, another can be appointed for the purposes of conveying the property and overreaching any beneficial interests.

### 12.29.3 Appointment of new persons to act

Where the sole or last personal representative is still acting as such when they die and the administration of the estate remains incomplete, someone else will have to take out a further grant of representation to the estate. Where, however, the person is a trustee, a new trustee of the existing trust can be appointed by the personal representatives of the last surviving trustee, under the powers in s 36 of the Trustee Act 1925. If a new trustee is required whilst there are trustees still in office, they can appoint one of themselves under powers in the same section.

### 12.29.4 Ceasing to act

Retirement is difficult for a personal representative once they have taken out a grant, and the appointment of additional representatives is equally difficult unless they are a sole personal representative and the estate is one which calls for two (where there is a minority interest, for example; see 12.9). Under s 36 of the Trustee Act 1925, however, a trustee has the power to appoint additional or substitutional trustees.

On the death of a sole personal representative without completing the administration of the estate, then either the chain of representation under s 7 of the Administration of Estates Act 1925 (see 12.10) will operate or an application will have to be made by the person entitled for a grant *de bonis non administratis*. The trust property of a trustee devolves on their personal representatives.

### 12.29.5 Limitation

There are different limitation periods relating to the time during which an action against personal representatives and trustees may be brought, save where there is fraud or the personal representative or trustee keeps the relevant property him- or herself, when there is no limitation period. An action must be brought against a trustee within the usual period of six years of the cause of action accruing, whereas in the case of a personal representative the relevant period for actions in respect of personalty (save interest on legacies) is 12 years.

### 12.29.6 Personal representative who has become trustee

Where a personal representative has become a trustee, the rules relating to trustees apply to him or her. In *George Attenborough & Son v Solomon* (1913), one of the testator's two sons who were appointed personal representatives sold valuable items of silver plate ten years after the testator's death. It was held that the preparation of the residuary account showed that all the debts and legacies had been paid before the purported sale and that the personal representatives had become trustees by the time of the sale. Therefore the one son could not act alone, and the transaction was invalid.

### 12.29.7 Law Reform Committee 23rd Report *The Powers and Duties of Trustees*

The Law Reform Committee in its 23rd Report *The Powers and Duties of Trustees* (1982) recommended that the rules for personal representatives should be aligned with those for trustees, so they could no longer act alone, though in practice they could have power delegated to them by co-personal representatives. The powers of personal representatives and trustees were brought closer by the Trusts of Land and Appointment of Trustees Act 1996, but are still far from fully aligned.

## 12.30 When does a personal representative become a trustee?

Personal representatives are supposed to wind up the deceased's estate; trustees hold property and administer it in accordance with the terms of the trust, until the trust comes to an end. Where the two roles are performed by the same persons, it may be difficult to tell when the transition occurs.

### 12.30.1 Under a will

It is not unusual to find the same persons appointed as executors (personal representatives) and trustees in a will. In *Re Grosvenor* (1916), it was held that once personal representatives have indicated by an assent that the subject matter of a specific gift is not required to meet debts and expenses, they hold that asset on trust for the beneficiary.

The situation is less clear so far as residue is concerned. In *Harvell v Foster* (1954) (12.30.5), the Court of Appeal held that personal representatives remain liable as such in respect of residuary property until it is vested in the entitled beneficiary, which may be delayed considerably where that beneficiary is a minor at the testator's death. The decision in *Re Yerburgh* (1928) (12.30.4), however, left open the possibility that personal representatives become trustees once their essential functions of collecting the assets and paying the debts, expenses and legacies are complete and the residue has been ascertained. Although *Re Yerburgh* was an intestacy case, it would seem logical for the rules to be the same in both situations.

### 12.30.2 Particular problems on intestacy

An administrator who has not paid the funeral and testamentary expenses, debts and legacies (if any), cannot be said have duly administered the estate according to law – this wording is part of the promise an administrator makes on oath when they apply to the court for a grant authorising them to deal with the estate in the first place. If, however, they have done all those things and then received the money to be held in a continuing trust, the question is whether they have automatically become a trustee or whether they are still an administrator.

### 12.30.3 Pre-1926 – administration completed, administratrix becomes trustee

The deceased intestate in *Re Ponder* (1921) left a widow and two infant sons. The widow obtained letters of administration, paid the expenses and debts, and invested her sons' shares of the personal property in her own name. Sargant J held that she had become a trustee and the Public Trustee could therefore be appointed to be a trustee jointly with her. Had she still been a personal representative, the court would have had no such power.

### 12.30.4 Post-1926 – the old rules apply, but is a vesting assent needed?

It is not entirely clear whether it is now necessary for a personal representative to make an assent to him- or herself, vesting property in him- or herself as trustee, in order to make the transition of status. However, the practice seems gradually to have developed away from the pre-1926 procedure and the need to make an assent may now be universally accepted. It may be that the need for a written assent in the case of land is consistent with the way that land is dealt with generally, and that the practice appears usual and has also spread to personalty.

In *Re Yerburgh* (1928), the deceased died intestate in 1926, just after the major legislative changes of the previous year came into force. He left a widow and two infant children. His administrators wound up the estate save for the continuing trusts. They were unsure how to proceed thereafter and applied to the court for directions, because the new law did not make it clear. Romer J said that s 33 of the Administration of Estates Act 1925 had imposed certain duties on legal personal representatives, and when the estate had been fully administered in accordance with those duties, they became trustees on the basis that the old law applied and determined the time at which they ceased to be legal personal representatives and became trustees for sale. He held that at that point the personal representatives ought to make a vesting assent to themselves under s 36 of the Administration of Estates Act 1925. Unfortunately, it was not clear from Romer J's judgment whether he meant the making of the assent was desirable (as evidence of the automatic change in status) or essential (to effect it), although obviously if he meant the latter, that could have greatly assisted in solving the problems about when and whether, in any particular case, the personal representatives become trustees. The old law, however, as can be seen from *Re Ponder* (12.30.3), did not require an assent.

### 12.30.5 Doubts cast on *Ponder* and *Yerburgh*? The position where the deceased dies testate

The decision in *Harvell v Foster* (1954), however, departed from those in *Re Ponder* and *Re Yerburgh*. The testator appointed his daughter sole executrix and gave her all his estate, but she was a minor at his death and a grant of administration was made to her husband. He entered into an administration bond (these have now been replaced by guarantees) with two solicitors as sureties. The solicitors acted for the husband in the administration of the estate paid over the balance to him. He decamped with most of the money and failed to pay to the daughter when she reached full age. The Court of Appeal, reversing the decision in the court below, held that the two solicitors were liable to the daughter for the missing money. It based its decisions partly on the wording of the administration bond, and partly on the limited nature of the husband's grant. Evershed LJ said that a personal representative's duties included retaining residue in trust where it could not be distributed immediately because the intended beneficiary was an infant. The court disagreed with the implication in Re Ponder that the offices of personal representative and trustee were mutually exclusive. Unfortunately, the court did not explain precisely when, in that case, it considered that a personal representative does become a trustee.

## 12.30.6 A robust approach

Dankwerts J in Re Cockburn (1957) had no doubt about the matter at all. He held that personal representatives, whether executors or administrators, became trustees automatically once they had completed the administration in due course. Thereafter they held the property for the beneficiaries under the terms of the will or on intestacy, and were bound to carry out the duties of trustees. Unfortunately, again, his explanation of how his reasoning related to that of Harvell v Foster was not entirely satisfactory or helpful, because he dismissed the suggestion that there was any substantive contradiction between that case and the decision in Re Ponder.

## 12.30.7 The problem identified – but not entirely solved?

Some of the problems have arisen because of the possibilities of alternative readings of the words of the statute. This problem was identified and discussed in Re King's Will Trusts; Assheton v Boyne (1964). The testatrix in this case had appointed executors and trustees and made specific devises upon trust. After two executors had taken probate, one of them died, and the other appointed a further trustee of the will. The other original executor then died, and his executor became executor by representation of the will of the original testator. He appointed the plaintiff to be a trustee of the will and then he too died. No one had ever made a written assent to the vesting of the legal estate of the land in accordance with s 36 of the Administration of Estates Act 1925. The question was whether the plaintiff held the legal estate in the land, as trustee of the will, or whether it was held by the defendant, the executor by representation. Pennycuick J held that the legal estate in the land still vested in the executor by representation of the original testator, rejecting the argument that, prior to the appointment of the other further executor, the legal estate had become vested in the second of the original executors.

He discussed the construction of s 36(4) of the Administration of Estates Act 1925, which falls into two parts.

The first part of that subsection states that an assent to the vesting of a legal estate must be in writing, signed by the personal representative and naming the person in whose favour it is given. This will operate to vest the relevant legal estate in the named person. The judge held that this laid down a rule applicable to any assent to the vesting of a legal estate, including an assent by a personal representative in their own favour.

The second part of s 36(4) says that 'an assent not in writing or not in favour of a named person shall not be effectual to pass a legal estate'. The judge held that this set out the consequences if this rule were disregarded, and it did not create an exception to that rule. He held that the appointment of new trustees by deed did not lead to the implied vesting of the legal estate in them, because for that to happen, the person making the appointment by deed had him- or herself to hold the property as trustee.

Academic writers criticised the decision in this case, but the courts followed it in Re Edwards (1981). Although the Law Commission considered the question, it reported in its Report No 184 in 1989 (Property Law: Title on Death) that solicitors reported little problem in practice in dealing with assents. The implications of the decision in Re King's Will Trusts being quite well known, the practice had become to make a written assent in any event, thus avoiding potential difficulties. The requirement for a written assent was accepted by the Court of Appeal in the relatively recent case of *Jemma Trust Company Ltd v Kippax Beaumont Lewis* (2005) when it was considering whether solicitors had been negligent in failing to ensure that an assent had been made at the most efficient time from a tax-planning point of view.[9]

## 12.31 Removal and retirement of personal representatives

The court may, where there are special circumstances, pass over someone in appointing a personal representative under the powers conferred on it by s 116 of the Supreme Court Act 1981. Once the personal representative has been appointed, however, the powers to remove them are much more limited, even where they actively desire to retire. There was no power at all until the passing of the Administration of Justice Act 1985 (see 16.4.5). Section 50 of this Act implemented the recommendation of the Law Reform Committee who, in their 23rd Report, said the court should be allowed the discretion to accede to the application by, or on behalf of, a personal representative or beneficiary for a personal representative to be removed or replaced.

## 12.32 Summary of Chapter 12

### 12.32.1 Personal Representatives

Personal representatives administer the deceased's estate in accordance with the law. They may be either executors, appointed expressly or impliedly in a valid will, or administrators, who can apply for a grant of representation if they fall within the rules laid down under the law. If there is a valid will but no executors, an administrator will have to implement the will. There are different rules for settled land executors and for executors by chain of representation under s 7 of the Administration of Estates Act 1925.

Executors take their power from the will and so technically do not need a grant to deal with the property in the estate, but they do need the grant to prove their title to property. Administrators have no power to act before a grant is made to them. A person who intermeddles with the estate (deals with the property in it when they have no authority to do so) is called an executor *de son tort* and is liable to the estate like a personal representative in respect of the property they have dealt with.

Anyone may be appointed executor but a person who is incapable by reason of mental incapacity may not act, and a person who is under 18 cannot act until they reach their majority. A grant of probate will be issued only up to a maximum of four individuals. A trust corporation such as a bank may also be appointed. An executor may renounce without reason if they do not wish to act.

The Non-Contentious Probate Rules lay down who takes a grant where there is or is not a will. Insofar as there is a valid will, it must be administered. Rule 20 specifies who take a grant if there is a will; Rule 22 deals with the situation where there is an intestacy. The latter rule, like the entitlement to property itself on intestacy, is structured around family relationships. Who takes out the grant does not affect the entitlements themselves.

The Administration of Estates (Small Payments) Act 1965 says that certain assets may be paid over without a grant. To obtain a grant, the personal representatives must calculate the value of

---

9  Para 119.

the estate and pay any Inheritance Tax on it. There are ways round the cash flow problems this may cause.

A person who objects to a grant may enter a caveat. No grant will be issued until the caveator has had a chance to present their objections. Grants of probate may be revoked if they were wrongly made or a grantee becomes incapable or does not carry out their functions. Grants may also be amended. There are statutory protections for purchasers from personal representatives, so they get good title.

Special grants and limited grants are available where the usual grant cannot be waited for or the personal representatives are not dealing with all the property in the estate for the total duration of the administration.

Personal representatives administer and wind up the estate. Trustees administer a continuing trust. A vesting assent is generally needed to transfer the property into the trust.

# Chapter 13

# Administration of Estates

The task of the personal representatives is to collect in the assets of the estate, pay the debts, liabilities and legacies and distribute the residue. The process of doing this is the administration of the estate. Administration may be very simple, as where the estate is solvent, the debts and assets are easily ascertained and how the estate should be disposed of is clear and uncontentious. There are, however, many complications that may arise, and there are not always very clear or satisfactory answers to the question of how to deal with them.

## 13.1 What is in the estate?

At common law, only personalty devolved upon the personal representatives, and realty went directly to the devisee by will or the heir on intestacy. The position as to realty altered in the late nineteenth century and is now governed by s 1 of the Administration of Estates Act 1925. The estate now comprises all the deceased's personalty and all realty in which the deceased was entitled to an interest not ceasing on their death. Examples of interests ceasing on death are an interest under a joint tenancy or a life interest.

The estate should be valued as at the date of death. However, valuation is, on occasion, as much an art as a science, and it is involved with questions of liability to pay tax (see Chapter 14).

### 13.1.1 Assets available to meet debts and liabilities

The assets of the estate available for the payment of debts and liabilities are defined in s 32(1) of the Administration of Estates Act 1925 as any property the deceased owned, to the extent of their beneficial interest, property subject to a general power exercised by the deceased by will and entailed property disposed of by the deceased under s 176 of the Law of Property Act 1925.

### 13.1.2 Other assets available

Other assets may, however, fall into the estate of the deceased, and they are included in the assets available. The commonest of these will be income arising in the estate after the date of death. Property appointed by will may also be available, as may the subject matter of a *donatio mortis causa*[1] if there is nothing else to satisfy the debts of the estate, in addition to nominated property, and property for which an option to purchase is given in the will.[2]

---

1 *Re Korvine* (1921).
2 *Re Eve* (1956).

### 13.1.3 Property not available

Property subject to a special power is not available, and neither is property the deceased held under a trust but in which they did not have the beneficial interest. This latter point is of great practical use; it was held in *Re Webb* (1941) that the proceeds of a life policy, on which the deceased had paid the premiums but which he had written in trust for his son, did not form part of his estate; the proceeds are also therefore not liable to IHT. Some property may be unavailable to the personal representatives as a matter of practicality, such as foreign land.

One of the amendments made to the law by the Administration of Justice Act 1982, in this case by s 19, was to the way gifts were saved by s 33 of the Wills Act 1837. Section 33 of the Wills Act 1837 provides that a gift to issue of the testator will be saved where that issue, though predeceased, leaves issue of their own; before 1983, such gifts were first of all available as assets of the estate of the predeceased issue to satisfy any unmet debts and liabilities before passing to the beneficiaries. After 1982, however, they passed straight to the beneficiaries, thus bypassing the estate of the predeceased and avoiding the liability to satisfy his or her debts.

## 13.2 What has to come out of the estate and when?

It is important to know the order in which funds are applied because there may be insufficient assets in the estate to meet all the liabilities. The personal representatives must pay the funeral expenses, the administration expenses, the debts of the estate at the date of the deceased's death and debts of the estate arising thereafter, in that order of priority. Thus, if the deceased died insolvent, owing large sums of money when all that is in the estate is enough to pay the funeral bill, the personal representatives must pay that before they look at settling the liabilities to creditors at all. The personal representatives may make only reasonable payments for funeral expenses; though 'reasonable' is interpreted broadly in the case where the deceased was wealthy, in the case of an insolvent estate only an amount to cover necessary expenses will be allowed.

The assets must be applied first to the obligations incurred by the deceased during their lifetime, before being used to settle obligations incurred by the personal representatives after the death. It may seem unfortunate, in the light of this, that liability to Inheritance Tax (IHT) arises under s 4(1) of the Inheritance Tax Act 1984 on the deceased's deemed disposal of all his or her property immediately before death. However, the personal representatives will in any case have had to pay any IHT on the estate in order to obtain the grant.

### 13.2.1 Other action at the personal representatives' discretion

Personal representatives have a power to settle or abandon debts and claims, provided they do so in good faith. They may also seek a termination of any contract not automatically frustrated by death.

### 13.2.2 The executor's year: times for payment, and interest

The personal representatives' duty is usually said to be to deal with the administration within a year, so that during the so-called 'executor's year' they cannot be called upon to make payments,[3] and payments made within that year will not usually incur interest whatever the will may provide. Interest is generally only payable from the anniversary of death (or the date when

---

3  S 44 Administration of Estates Act 1925.

the contingency takes effect if applicable) until payment of the legacy, though where the testator leaves a minor child, or where there is a legacy satisfying a debt which itself carries interest or which is charged on land, it may be payable during the year itself. The personal representatives should, however, always deal with the estate and make payments 'with due diligence', the import of which may vary from case to case according to the circumstances.[4] Sometimes delay will be justifiable, and in that situation the personal representative will not be liable for loss caused by it.

## 13.3 Dealing with the assets and liabilities

The personal representatives must collect in the assets and meet all the debts and liabilities before distributing the estate to the beneficiaries.

Some amendments to how personal representatives deal with land were made by the Law of Property (Miscellaneous Provisions) Act 1994, which allows registration of land charges in unregistered conveyancing to be made against the name of the deceased rather than the personal representatives. It also allows service of notices as it were on the deceased where the server had no reason to believe they had died and, where the server did know of the death, allows service on the personal representatives of the deceased at their last known address.

### 13.3.1 Ascertaining the debts and liabilities before distribution

The basic rule is that the personal representatives are liable to pay all the debts which the assets of the estate will cover, save those which are statute-barred (though they have an exceptional discretion to pay these). This remains the same even where they have distributed the assets to the beneficiaries on the assumption that no more debts can be discovered, unless they have complied with the obligations set out by statute for personal representatives and trustees to obtain protection against such later claims.

### 13.3.2 Protection against later claims – s 27 of the Trustee Act 1925

The personal representatives can obtain protection against later claims by unknown creditors and beneficiaries by complying with the provisions of s 27 of the Trustee Act 1925. The personal representatives should place advertisements requiring any person interested in the estate to send them particulars of their claim on the estate within the time specified in the notice; this must be at least two months. The advertisements required are placed as a matter of course by practitioners in this area in every administration except when the personal representatives and the beneficiaries are the same people. The personal representatives must give notice of their intended distribution in the London Gazette and, where there is any land in the estate, in the newspaper in circulation in the area where the land is; for personal property the London Gazette alone is enough. If there is some difficulty or query the personal representative should apply to the court for directions as to what notices should be placed: for example, perhaps in the appropriate trade journal if the deceased carried on a business. Once the two months (or greater specified period) have expired, the personal representatives may distribute the estate on the basis of the claims of which they have actual or constructive notice.

---

4 *Re Tankard, Tankard v Midland Bank Executor and Trustee Co Ltd* (1942).

In *Re Aldhous; Noble v Treasury Solicitor* (1955), the testator died partially intestate. The executors advertised in accordance with s 27 of the Trustee Act 1925, but no claims were received and they passed the estate to the Treasury Solicitor as *bona vacantia*. When the next of kin turned up later making demands, the executors were protected against them by having complied with the provisions of s 27. As s 27 notices do not, however, protect the personal representatives from family provision claims (see Chapter 15) or claims arising from rectification (see 16.4), they should place them six months after the grant.

### 13.3.3  Directions of the court

Personal representatives may also solve problems and protect themselves by seeking the direction of the court. In the case of *Re Gess* (1942), the deceased died intestate in 1939 domiciled by choice in England, though he was originally from Poland. His administrators were unable to advertise for creditors in Poland because of the outbreak of the Second World War. The only known debts amounted to £1,092 10s which the court ordered should be paid to the Custodian of Enemy Property, and the remaining estate could then be distributed to beneficiaries without advertisements.

## 13.4  Ascertaining the beneficiaries

Where there is a will, usually the beneficiaries will be named; frequently, they will be family members and the personal representatives will know who they are and where to find them.

### 13.4.1  Benjamin orders and authority from the court to distribute

Sometimes, a personal representative will be aware of the existence of a beneficiary – for example, one who is named in a will – but will not know how to find them. In most cases, the executors of a will or members of the deceased's family can provide all the necessary information, but sometimes neither that nor the expedient of advertising in newspapers or even employing someone to trace the beneficiary is successful.

It may transpire that, to the best of anyone's knowledge, a named beneficiary is dead, though this cannot be proved. This occurred in the case of *Re Benjamin* (1902), where the deceased left a gift to his son, who had last been heard of some while previously on the return journey from France. The personal representatives made enquiries and advertised for the son, to no avail. Eventually, they applied to the court and obtained an order allowing them to distribute the estate as though that beneficiary had predeceased. The court will require evidence that the fullest enquiries have been made before granting such an order.

However, it was said in *Re Green's Will Trust* (1985) that 'the true view is that a *Re Benjamin* order does not vary or destroy a beneficial interest. It merely enables trust property to be distributed in accordance with the practical probabilities'. Thus, if the deceased's son had turned up after the court order, awkward readjustments would have been necessary.

Another situation that may arise is, for example, that in *Re Pettifor* (1966) where the personal representative sought authority from the court to distribute the estate on the basis that a woman of 70 would not have another child. Pennycuick J criticised such applications as of no practical use and a waste of time, but in *Figg v Clarke (Inspector of Taxes)* (1997), it was suggested that if such a problem arose, seeking the court's authority to distribute, rather than a court distribution, was appropriate.

### 13.4.2 Alternatives to a Benjamin order where the existence of a beneficiary is known

A potentially slow and expensive application for a Benjamin order is not the only option. An indemnity can be sought from the other beneficiaries, promising to reimburse any money they obtain on the basis that the missing person is dead, should they turn out to have been alive; this cannot work if a beneficiary is a minor. Alternatively, the personal representatives could insure against the unexpected return of the missing beneficiary: they would have to make full disclosure, but the premium would normally be allowed as an estate expense.[5] Under s 22 of the Limitation Act 1980, a beneficiary has 12 years to claim personal estate, so the money could be put into a reserve fund, to be distributed to the other beneficiaries after that period if it was still unclaimed. As a last resort, they could pay the money into court under s 63 of the Trustee Act 1925, but that could mean the beneficiaries never see it.

## 13.5 Dealing with an estate pending distribution

The personal representatives have wide powers to collect in the deceased's assets and to hold them pending distribution of the estate. Their powers in respect of the way in which they may deal with the property within the estate once they have it are, however, limited, unless the testator has widened them in their will.

### 13.5.1 Powers to collect in the estate

The personal representatives will probably obtain possession of most or all of the deceased's estate by virtue of their office. Where this is not the case, usually the person who does have possession will hand the property over on the personal representative's request and on their production of evidence of authority, usually the grant of representation. If, however, a request does not succeed, the personal representatives may sue under their general power to do so in order to recover assets. They may also commence court proceedings to recover liabilities to the deceased's estate or to pursue a tort claim on the estate's behalf, in order to maximise the assets.

### 13.5.2 Court actions as assets (or liabilities) of the estate

The common law rule is that the right to sue dies with the claimant. However, this was altered by the Law Reform (Miscellaneous Provisions) Act 1934 so that most causes of action survive an individual's death, whether or not the proceedings had actually commenced during the deceased's lifetime, though no awards of exemplary damages may be obtained.

In *Rickless v United Artists* (1987), the court held that the estate of the actor Peter Sellers included his right under s 2 of the Dramatic and Musical Performers' Protection Act 1958 to consent to the reproduction of his performances. The performances of Jimi Hendrix were asserted by interested parties to be beyond the protection of s 180(1) of the Copyright Designs and Patents Act 1988 because he had died, but the court in *Experience Hendrix LLC v Purple Haze Records Ltd* (2007) disagreed, especially as s 192(2) implied the opposite, and that interpretation would have left the UK in breach of the international TRIPS agreement that amended the effect of the CDPA 1988.[6] The court held that Mr Hendrix's rights could be vindicated by his personal representatives.

---

5   *Re Evans, Evans v Westcombe* (1999).
6   The TRIPS Agreement (Agreement on Trade-Related Aspects of Intellectual Property Rights) is Annex 1C of the Marrakesh Agreement Establishing the World Trade Organization (1994).

Actions in defamation, however, are expressly excluded from s 1(1) of the 1934 Act and do not therefore survive death – hence the outpouring of journalists at the death of the newspaper proprietor Robert Maxwell; neither he nor his estate was in any position to take any action about it. In *Smith v Dha* (2013), the claimant in a libel action died after the hearing, judgment having been reserved. Davies J, after considering Civil Procedure Rule 40, held that the action had abated on the date of his death so that no judgment would be given.

### 13.5.3 Fatal Accidents Act actions

Actions under the Fatal Accidents Act 1976 are usually brought by the personal representatives for the benefit of the deceased's relatives, as opposed to the situation with other actions where they are brought for the benefit of the estate. Of course, the personal representatives, the beneficiaries and the deceased's relatives are often drawn from the same group of persons. Fatal Accidents Act claims are for the loss of dependency or for bereavement. Loss of dependency claims can be very large, representing years of a breadwinner's wages; bereavement claims are for a fixed sum, currently £12,980 per deceased person (from 1 April 2013), claimable by a limited range of relatives roughly equivalent to those entitled on intestacy.

## 13.6 Is the estate solvent?

If there is sufficient in the estate to meet the funeral and administration expenses and pay all debts and liabilities in full, the estate is solvent. All these payments must be made before any gift in the testator's will or entitlement under their intestacy is considered. The creditors in a solvent estate will be paid in full before the legacies are paid and the assets distributed.

### 13.6.1 Dealing with the debts

Just because an estate is solvent does not mean that the beneficiaries will all be paid in full what they expect to receive. It may be that the testator has left legacies amounting to more than remains in the estate after payment of all the liabilities, or the beneficiary may be expecting to receive a house whereas that house was subject to a heavy mortgage liability – what occurs in these circumstances will be discussed in more detail later.

## 13.7 What if the estate is insolvent?

The personal representatives may still administer an insolvent estate (where the insolvency does not present a problem in fact or law), or, alternatively, an administration order can be obtained from the Chancery Division (where there are likely to be difficulties in the administration as the personal representatives are acting under order of the court and are so protected) or an insolvency administration order may be issued in which case the estate is administered by a trustee in bankruptcy (where a bankruptcy order has been made against the estate).

The Insolvency Act 2000 introduced a new s 421A into the Insolvency Act 1986 which allows joint property to be taken in to account when an insolvency administration order has been made against the deceased's estate, following a petition presented within five years of the deceased's death. Such an order, if granted, might mean that a surviving spouse would be asked to give up the deceased's notional share of the joint home, as the legislation provides that the creditors' interests outweigh all others save in exceptional circumstances.

The priority of debts in an insolvent estate is governed by the Insolvency Act 1986 and the Administration of Insolvent Estates of Deceased Persons Order 1986. The reasonable funeral, testamentary and administration expenses have priority over the preferential debts and thereafter payments are to be made as they are in respect of the distribution of the property of a living person who has declared bankrupt. The testator cannot alter that order by the terms of their will. The only situation in which it does not apply is where the debt is secured; for example, a debt secured by way of mortgage on a house will be met in full from the value of the house, provided that value is sufficient to cover the debt. Any debt remaining thereafter ('negative equity') will be unsecured.

### 13.7.1 Payment of debts in an insolvent estate

The order of priority for insolvent estates is set out in s 4 of the Administration of Insolvent Estates of Deceased Persons Order 1986. In respect of unsecured debts, it is as follows:

(a)     Specially preferred debts:[7] money, held by the deceased in certain official capacities in connection with friendly societies[8] or military duties.[9]
(b)     Preferred debts: arrears in state and occupational pension contributions and money owed to employees in respect of salaries and accrued holiday pay (up to specified limits).[10]
(c)     Ordinary debts: almost anything which is not in any other category.
(d)     Interest on any debts in the previous categories.
(e)     Deferred debts including loans from the deceased's spouse.

Each class must be exhausted before payments are made under the next. Failure to observe the proper order, or to distribute equally within the same class, will render a personal representative liable personally to pay any debts superior to those they have paid, provided they had notice of them, or to make good the unequal distribution, save where they had no reason to believe the estate was insolvent when they made a payment.[11]

## 13.8 Managing the property in the estate

Personal representatives have a range of powers to manage the estate, many of which are statutory. These powers mainly derive from the Administration of Estates Act 1925, the Trustee Acts of 1925 and 2000, the Trusts of Land and Appointment of Trustees Act 1996, the Trustee Delegation Act 1999 and the Inheritance and Trustees' Powers Act 2014. These statutory powers apply whether the deceased died intestate or testate and are frequently widened in professionally-drawn wills.

The Trusts of Land and Appointment of Trustees Act 1996 ('TLATA 1996') defines a 'trust of land' as any trust of property which consists of, or includes, land. Trustees of land have all the powers of a beneficial owner, subject, of course, to the provisions of the individual trust and to the trustees' general fiduciary duties. Personal representatives have by s 18 of TLATA 1996 the same powers as trustees of land, though with modifications as to consents, consultation and court applications in cases of dispute.

---

7   Sch 6 Insolvency Act 1986.
8   *Re Eilbeck* (1910).
9   Where the deceased was subject to military law, money or property in the deceased's possession which is subject to s 2 of the Regimental Debts Act 1893.
10  Before s 251 of the Enterprise Act came into force on 15 September 2003, this category included Crown Preference categories such as debts to the Inland Revenue and Customs and Excise, and social security contributions.
11  S 10(2) of the Administration of Estates Act 1971.

The amendments made to trustees' powers by the 1996 Act represented a radical change from the law applying before 1997. That gave trustees only very limited powers, though the Law Reform Committee had long since recommended, in its 23rd Report *The Powers and Duties of Trustees* (1982), that they should be widened, not least because they so restricted trustees as to make them unable to deal with property in accordance with the general scheme of the Trustee Act 1925, which emphasises the standards expected of an ordinary prudent man of business. The partial abolition of the doctrine of conversion by s 3(1) of TLATA 1996 does not apply where the trust was created by the will of someone who died before 1997 (see 10.7.4).

The Trustee Act 2000 conferred on trustees and personal representatives newer and wider powers of investment as if they were the absolute owner. It cured the deficiency in the 1996 Act by extending broadened powers to all trustees, including those of personalty only. A trust of land from which all the land is sold ceases to be a trust of land; if land is bought into a trust of personalty, that becomes a trust of land. Trustees can now purchase a legal estate in land in England and Wales, delegate investment and investment-holding powers, and charge property. All kinds of investments, apart from equitable interests in land, are now authorised. The Act imposes an excludable statutory duty of care.

## 13.8.1 Powers to insure

Before the Trustee Act 2000, where trustees' powers were not widened by the trust instrument, they had a very limited power to insure under s 19 of the Trustee Act 1925. Section 34 of the Trustee Act 2000 gave personal representatives the power to insure any building or other insurable property against any risk for the full replacement value and to pay the premium out of income or capital. In the context of the trustees' general duty of care imposed by s 1 of the 2000 Act, that power might be considered a duty.

## 13.8.2 Powers to carry on the deceased's business

The personal representatives' powers to carry on the deceased's business are very limited, and if a person wishes his or her business to be dealt with by them he or she should put some specific provision in their will. Explicit powers are needed specifically because they are not implied, and they should be full and clear, because the cases show that the courts take a very restrictive view of what is authorised in practice by a direction simply to carry on the testator's business. In M'Neillie v Acton (1853), the court held that such a direction did not authorise the personal representative to have recourse to any assets other than the capital already in the business to carry it on, so that a security given over property in the estate for that purpose was invalid against the beneficiaries. The personal representatives' powers are limited to carrying on the business with a view to selling it as a going concern.

## 13.8.3 Pros and cons of carrying on the business

A business is, of course, worth far more as a going concern, with all its goodwill, than it is if it has been allowed to collapse and lose all its trade. A personal representative is, however, personally liable to those they deal with if they carry on the deceased's business. This was described by the court in Re Garland (1804) as 'very hard', but the court pointed out that no one is obliged to take on such liability. 'He becomes liable, as personally responsible, to the extent of all his own property.... But he places himself in that situation by his own choice.' He or she is, however, entitled to indemnify him- or herself from the estate.

### 13.8.4 How long can a sale of the business be postponed?

If there is no specific power to carry on a business, then the personal representatives should do so only with a view to its proper disposal, which one would expect to be contemplated within the 'executor's year'. If there is no express authority, the testator will be taken to have impliedly given the authority to run the business if they have given the personal representatives a power to postpone the sale of the business. The testator in *Re Crowther* (1895) left his estate on trust for sale and gave his trustees power to postpone such sale and conversion 'for such period as to them shall seem expedient'. At the time of his death, he had two businesses, one of which he ran alone as sole proprietor and the other which he ran in partnership with his son, who was one of the trustees of the will. Twenty-two years later, the trustees were still running both businesses, not with a view to their sale but for the benefit of his widow, who was the life tenant under the deceased's will. The question before the court was whether the trustees had authority to carry on both the businesses in this way under their power to postpone sale. In this case, the court held that the power to postpone the sale of a business involved a power of continuing the business in the meantime.

### 13.8.5 Effect of carrying on the business without authority

In *Dowse v Gorton* (1891), it was held that personal representatives not only have authority to carry on a business with a view to selling it as a going concern, but may also claim indemnity from both beneficiaries and creditors, provided they are carrying on the business with a view to the proper realisation of the estate. However, if the business is carried on under an authority in a will but not with a view to proper realisation, indemnity may only be claimed against beneficiaries and not against creditors. This may, however, not be the case with a particular creditor if he or she has assented to the carrying on of the business.

### 13.8.6 Creditors' acquiescence in unauthorised carrying on of business

Where, however, a creditor has not assented to the carrying on of the business, and the business has been carried on but not with a view to proper realisation, as occurred in *Re Oxley* (1914), the creditor of the estate may treat the continuance of the business as improper. They are then entitled to be paid out of the value of the assets which existed at the death of the deceased, and the personal representative has no right to be indemnified in priority to them. Assenting to the carrying on of the business has to be more than just knowing about it and doing nothing to stop it. The court in *Re Oxley* held that, for a personal representative to succeed in asserting that a creditor had assented to the carrying on of the business, it was necessary to show an active affirmative assent. The court held that mere standing by with knowledge and doing nothing was not sufficient. The application in this case was made by persons who had become creditors of the estate in the course of business carried on by the personal representatives. They were seeking a declaration that they had priority over those creditors who had allowed the personal representatives to carry on unauthorised business transactions; the court refused their application.

## 13.9 Assents

When the property in the estate vests in the person entitled, the assent of the personal representatives is required. At common law, an assent need not be in writing. It can be made expressly, even though not in writing, by a few informal words spoken by the executor.[12] However, under

---

12  *Barnard v Pumfrett* (1841).

statute an assent by a personal representative to the vesting of a legal estate in land in another person, in whatever capacity – beneficially or as trustee or personal representative of another deceased person – is governed by s 36(4) of the Administration of Estates Act 1925, which says that:

> ...an assent to the vesting of a legal estate shall be in writing, signed by the personal representative, and shall name the person in whose favour it is given and shall operate to vest in that person the legal estate to which it relates; and an assent not in writing or not in favour of a named person shall not be effectual to pass a legal estate.

Note that a vesting assent is one of the forms of conveyance listed in s 52(2) of the Law of Property Act 1925 which are effective to pass a legal estate in land despite not being a deed. Where covenants are necessary the assent must be by deed.

It has long been unclear whether the provisions of s 36(4) of the Administration of Estates Act 1925 mean a personal representative needs to assent to the vesting of a legal estate in land in him- or herself, in whatever capacity.[13] In *Re King's Will Trusts* (1964), Pennycuick J held that the same rule applied to an assent by a personal representative to the vesting of a legal estate in land in him- or herself (whether beneficially, as trustee, or as personal representative of another deceased) as to an assent by them in favour of another person. Whether or not that decision is questionable, on the basis that it rests on an interpretation of s 36(4), the signed written assent by the personal representative in their own favour is still highly desirable, as documentary evidence of the title to the legal estate. Indeed the Law Commission, investigating the point, found that it was the usual practice to make such an assent, solicitors having generally absorbed the implications of *Re King's Will Trusts*.

However, in the later case of *Re Edwards Will Trusts* (1982), a woman who owned real property died intestate, leaving her husband solely entitled. Her husband obtained letters of administration and occupied the property for 20 years before dying without at any time making an assent in writing in his own favour. It was held that the husband had by his conduct assented to the vesting of the equitable interest in himself, so that it passed to his executors.

Section 36(6) of the Administration of Estates Act 1925 provides some protection for a purchaser (or mortgagee or lessee) of a legal estate in land in good faith for money or money's worth. A person purchasing from a personal representative should check the grant to see whether a previous assent or conveyance to trustees or beneficiaries has been made and a notice of this appended to the grant – the trustees or beneficiary can require this to be done. If, however, it has not been done, s 36(6) provides that a statement in writing by the personal representative that they have not given or made an assent or conveyance in respect of the legal estate shall be sufficient evidence of that in favour of the purchaser. In practice, the conveying personal representative will insert such a statement in a conveyance of unregistered land. Unfortunately, it was held in *Re Duce and Boots Cash Chemists (Southern) Ltd's Contract* (1937) that such a statement may be sufficient, but it is not conclusive.[14]

Other assets can be transferred by the appropriate form of transfer – for example shares are transferred using stock transfer forms. For physical assets, the specific legatee, unless the will has provided otherwise, will bear the cost of storing, insuring and transporting the item.

---

13  EC Ryder, 'Re King's Will Trusts: A Reassessment' (1976) 29 Current Legal Problems 60.
14  Joel Nitikman, 'The Forgotten Law of Assent' (2012) 18 Trusts & Trustees 672.

## 13.10 Appropriation

Section 41 of the Administration of Estates Act 1925 gives personal representatives wide powers to appropriate assets in satisfaction of beneficial interests arising out of a will or intestacy. It applies whenever the deceased died and to any part of the estate.

The personal representative may exercise the power as they think just and reasonable, according the rights of those interested in the estate. The assets are valued at the date of appropriation, not at the date of death. In times of fluctuating house prices in particular, this can have harsh results. The value of the house in *Re Collins* (1975), for example, was £4,200 at the death in 1972 and £8,000 when the court heard the case in 1974.

There are two principal consequences of a personal representative exercising the right:

(a) the beneficiary's interest transfers to the appropriated assets, so if they increase or decrease in value, the beneficiary bears that;[15]
(b) the appropriation clears the other assets for distribution.

The consent of the beneficiary is, however, required:

(a) from a beneficiary absolutely entitled;
(b) from the trustee (not being the personal representative) or the person entitled for the time being to the income of any settled legacy, share or interest.

The personal representatives must have regard to the rights of anyone who is not consenting, though they will be bound by an appropriation duly made. Consent maybe given for an infant by its parents or guardian or by the court.

The power in s 41 is not prejudiced by any other powers of appropriation conferred by law or under the deceased's will. It is quite common to see a provision in a will allowing appropriation but without the consents required by s 41, as this can make the administration easier.

The power of appropriation is a fiduciary one. The self-dealing rule applies to personal representatives as it applies to trustees. Section 41 makes no reference to a personal representative appropriating to him- or herself. However, a personal representative may not make an appropriation in their own favour in satisfaction of a pecuniary legacy to him- or herself, unless the assets appropriated were cash or the equivalent to cash. In *Kane v Radley-Kane* (1998) the deceased's widow and sole personal representative was left a legacy of £125,000. Without obtaining any consents, she appropriated to herself shares in Shiredean Ltd, an unquoted company, which had been valued for estate purposes at £50,000. The estate overall was valued at £93,000. The shares were subsequently sold for £1,100,000. The widow's actions were found on the application of the deceased's children, who could have benefited had the shares been sold at that price by the estate, as impermissible self-dealing, in breach of fiduciary duty.

## 13.11 Does a beneficiary have a proprietary interest?

The position of the beneficiary is not entirely clear-cut; the legal title to property devolves on the personal representatives, but it is less easy to say what becomes of the beneficial interest. It cannot be said, for example, that the beneficial interest in the deceased's house has passed to you just because the deceased left it to you in their will; it may be mortgaged to the hilt, without any

---

15 *Ballard v Marsden* (1880).

other provision for the satisfaction of the secured debt, or the estate may be insolvent, so that in reality the deceased had nothing to leave you. Unfortunately, in those circumstances, although you will know the deceased probably intended well towards you, you will not obtain any interest in anything of any practical value.

## 13.11.1 Beneficiary's interest in an unadministered estate
A beneficiary does, however, clearly have some interest in the estate. What needs to be established is when and how that arises, and what its nature is. The basic questions considered here are not exhaustive: for the more complex issues that arise when the beneficiaries wish to go against third parties, see *Hayim v Citibank* (1987) and *Roberts v Gill* (2010).[16]

## 13.11.2 No interest in residue until it is ascertained
In *Dr Barnardo's Homes v Commissioners of the Income Tax Acts* (1921), which concerned a gift of residuary estate, the court held that the legatee of a share of residue has no interest in any of the property of the testator until the residue has been ascertained. The same was held in *Lord Sudeley v Attorney General* (1897), which concerned a gift of a share of the residuary real and personal estate. The beneficiary claimed a share of mortgages in New Zealand, but the court held that the entitlement was to a share of the estate once ascertained, not to anything in it in particular.

In *Commissioner of Stamp Duties (Queensland) v Livingston* (1965), the question was important because the beneficiary, although she survived her husband (or her gift would have lapsed), died before his estate had been administered. The question was not whether her interest could be passed on to her estate; that clearly could happen, as she had survived the deceased and there was no provision preventing it – an example of such provision might have been a condition that she survive the deceased by a certain length of time which she had failed to fulfil. The question was whether, at the time of her death, she already had a proprietary interest in her share of the property in the deceased's estate. If she did, taxes would have been payable. The Privy Council, hearing the matter on appeal from the High Court of Australia, said that, as a general rule, a beneficiary under a will or intestacy has no legal or equitable proprietary interest in the unadministered assets of the deceased's estate. The entire ownership of the unadministered assets is in the deceased's personal representatives. It was said that whatever property comes to a personal representative by virtue of their office comes to them 'in full ownership without distinction between legal and equitable interests. The whole property [is] his'.

The case of *Eastbourne Mutual Building Society v Hastings Corporation* (1965) concerned the interest of a widower solely entitled to the estate, being the next of kin on intestacy where the estate was quite small. The date at which he acquired his interest was relevant because the house was to be compulsorily purchased by the council, who would pay compensation at the full market value if it was occupied by the person who acquired it or a member of the family of that person who was also entitled to an interest in the house. The level of compensation otherwise would take no account of the buildings on the land, but pay the value of the site only. The widower carried on living in the house but never took out any grant of representation or had the title to the house transferred to himself. The question for the court was whether he nevertheless had an interest in it, and unfortunately for the mortgagee, who was the interested party, the court held that he did not.

---

16  Meryl Thomas and Simon Cooper, 'The Nature of the Beneficiary's Interest and the Role of the Personal Representative in the Administration and Distribution of an Estate' (1995) 17 Liverpool Law Review 69.

*Commissioner for Stamp Duties v Livingston* was affirmed by the court in *Marshall v Kerr* (1995), where Lord Templeman also cited Buckley J's judgment in *Leigh's Will Trust* (1970) with approval (see 13.11.4):

(1) The entire ownership of the property comprised in the estate of a deceased person which remains unadministered is in the deceased's legal personal representative for the purposes of administration without any differentiation between legal and equitable interests;

(2) No legatee or person entitled upon the intestacy of the deceased has any propriety interest in any particular asset comprised in the unadministered estate of the deceased;

(3) Each such legatee or person so entitled is entitled to a chose in action, viz. a right to require the deceased's estate to be duly administered, whereby he can protect those rights to which he hopes to become entitled in possession in the course of the administration of the deceased's estate;

(4) Each such legatee or person so entitled has a transmissible interest in the estate, not-withstanding that it remains unadministered. This transmissible or disposable interest can, I think, only consist of the chose in action in question with such rights and interests as it carried in gremio.... If a person entitled to such a chose in action can transmit or assign it, such transmission or assignment must carry with it the right to receive the fruits of the chose in action when they mature.

The view that there is no proprietary entitlement and therefore no tax is payable was confirmed again in *Pope (deceased)* (2012). Mr Pope was working as a geologist in Angola when he was abducted by rebels and eventually presumed dead. His parents received sums from Equitable Life under an insurance policy, plus interest as an 'Extra Payment', before Mr Pope's death was legally accepted. Interpreting the relevant legislation to find that no tax was payable under statute, the Tribunal said:

Because Jason Pope's estate was unadministered (and not even in the course of administration) at the time when the Extra Payment was made by Equitable, no person entitled under his assumed intestacy will have had any sufficient entitlement to the death benefit and the Extra Payment to make him or her 'entitled to the income in respect of which the tax is directed by the Income Tax Acts to be charged'.

As to the parents, who received the payments: 'The most they had were potential choses in action to require the "estate" to be duly administered.'

## 13.11.3 Interest in specific bequest at death

However, in *Inland Revenue Commissioners v Hawley* (1928), it was said that a beneficiary entitled under a specific bequest or devise took an equitable interest in the subject matter of the gift at the death of the testator, and this was confirmed in *Re K (deceased)* (1985). This did not assist the son living in the testator's bungalow in *Barclay v Barclay* (1970), however, because the testator had expressly directed that it be sold and the proceeds divided between his five sons and daughters-in-law. The son refused to move out and the daughter-in-law who took the grant brought possession proceedings against him. The Court of Appeal held that she should succeed, but Lord Denning MR also said that an equitable interest in property itself could arise under the will if it were appropriately worded. This last may be questionable.

## 13.11.4 Ensuring of due administration is a chose in action of the beneficiary

It was held in *Re Leigh's Wills Trusts* (1970) that the ensuring of due administration is a chose in action of the beneficiary. This means they are entitled to bring an action about the administration of the estate and, insofar as that entitlement constitutes property, it is the property of the beneficiary. This entitlement was what led Colonel Wintle to acquire part of the testatrix's estate in *Wintle v Nye* (1959) (see 4.9.7); he wished to be in a position to take Mr Nye, the solicitor, to court.

In *Re Leigh's Will Trusts*, the testatrix had made a specific gift in her will to Frederick Durbridge of 'all shares which I hold and any other interest … which I may have' in a sheet metal company. The deceased had never had any such shares or interest, but at her death she was the sole administratrix and sole beneficiary of the unadministered estate of her husband, who had died intestate owning some shares in, and a debt due from, the company. The court held that the specific gift to Mr Durbridge took effect by the testatrix having transmitted to her executors her chose in action of the right to ensure due administration. As sole beneficiary, the testatrix had a right to require the new administrator to administer the husband's estate in any manner she or her executors might require, consistent with the rights of anyone else against the estate. The specific gift in the will imposed a duty on the executors to exercise this right so as to ensure so far as possible that the shares and the debt became available to satisfy the specific gift.

# 13.12  Apportionments

There are, or were, rules designed to ensure that all beneficiaries are treated fairly, namely the rules of equitable and legal apportionment: the rule in *Howe v Dartmouth* (1802), the rule in *Earl of Chesterfield's Trusts* (1883) and the rule in *Allhusen v Whittell* (1867). These are extremely awkward to apply in practice, involving somewhat complex calculations. In professionally drafted wills where they might have applied, they were expressly excluded and to most professionals' relief under the Trusts (Capital and Income) Act 2013 these rules of equitable and legal apportionment no longer apply to new trusts created or arising on or after 1 October 2013 – except in the unlikely event of a contrary indication in the instrument itself.

The rules of apportionment are briefly outlined here principally so that why they needed to be excluded and disapplied may be fully appreciated.

## 13.12.1  Rule in *Howe v Dartmouth* (1802)

The rule in *Howe v Dartmouth* (1802) is the duty to maintain equality between beneficiaries entitled in succession to unspecified personalty under a will. The duty is to convert certain property (wasting assets, unauthorised investments and reversionary interests) into authorised investments.

## 13.12.2  Rule in *Earl of Chesterfield's Trusts* (1883)

The rule in *Earl of Chesterfield's Trusts* (1883) is the duty to divide the sum realised on the falling into possession of a reversionary interest between capital and income so that the tenant for life receives a sum representing what they would have received had the reversionary interest been sold within the executor's year, calculated on a figure which would have grown to the sum realised if invested at the testator's death at 4 per cent compound interest.

### 13.12.3 Rule in *Allhusen v Whittell* (1867)

The rule in *Allhusen v Whittell* (1867) is the duty to ensure that when distributions are made and debts are paid, some of the cost is charged to income so that the life tenant does not take the income from those parts of the estate that should have been applied to the payment of debts and legacies.

### 13.12.4 Legal apportionment

Section 2 of the Apportionment Act 1870 requires calculations to be apportioned from day to day.

## 13.13 The incidence of debts and legacies

In the course of administering the estate, the personal representatives will have to pay debts, expenses and liabilities and also, if there are any, general legacies. The question will arise as to what funds should be used to pay the debts and legacies. Any properly drafted will should make valid provision as to what assets are to be used to pay the debts and legacies, but if it does not, then the position as to debts is governed by statute. The position as to legacies is, however, less clear.

It is important that payments of both debts and legacies are made out of the correct part of the estate because of the impact of such payments on the size of the remaining parts of the estate, to which different beneficiaries may be entitled.

## 13.14 The incidence of debts, expenses and liabilities

In default of valid provision by the testator ousting the statutory provisions, the incidence of debts is governed by the Administration of Estates Act 1925 (AEA 1925).

### 13.14.1 Order of payment of debts out of the solvent estate s 34(3) of the AEA 1925 and Part II of the First Schedule

Section 34(3) of the AEA 1925 applies where the estate is solvent (see 13.7 for insolvent estates). It says that assets should be used to pay funeral, testamentary and administration expenses, debts and liabilities in the order specified in Part II of the First Schedule to that Act. It also states that this order may be varied by the will of the deceased.

The Act contains other provisions as to the incidence of debts, such as those in s 35 which relate to secured debts. Note that where a beneficiary takes a gift by will which is made expressly subject to their payment of any debt, the statutory provisions do not apply to that arrangement.

### 13.14.2 Part II of the First Schedule – the 'statutory order'

Part II of the First Schedule to the AEA 1925 sets out the order of application of assets where the estate is solvent, and reads as follows:

- Property of the deceased undisposed of by will, subject to the retention thereout of a fund sufficient to meet any pecuniary legacies.
- Property of the deceased not specifically devised or bequeathed but included (either by a specific or general description) in a residuary gift, subject to the retention out of such property of a fund sufficient to meet any pecuniary legacies, so far as not provided for as aforesaid.

- Property of the deceased specifically appropriated or devised or bequeathed (either by a specific or general description) for the payment of debts.
- Property of the deceased charged with, or devised or bequeathed (either by a specific or general description) subject to a charge for the payment of debts.
- The fund, if any, retained to meet pecuniary legacies.
- Property specifically devised or bequeathed, rateably according to value.
- Property appointed by will under a general power, including the statutory power to dispose of entailed interests, rateably according to value.
- The following provisions shall also apply:
  (a)  The order of application may be varied by the will of the deceased.
  (b)  ... [this part repealed].

The categories referred to have been subject to some considerable case law, for much of which see 10.1. The cases also show that there are other problems with the application of the statutory order. Its ambiguities are capable of resolution in various ways. Unfortunately, the courts have not chosen to follow only one of the routes available to solve the ambiguities, which would have clarified the meaning of the Act or at least clarified how it had to be interpreted, but have oscillated between the options open to them.

# 13.15  Problems with the First Schedule

There are sufficient problems with the operation of the First Schedule for them to fall into particular areas.

## 13.15.1  Variation of the statutory order by the terms of the will

Paragraph 8 of the statutory order provides that the order itself may be varied by the terms of the will, but it is often questionable whether the terms of the will are clear enough to make an effective variation. Wills usually provide for payment out of general residue but it may not be clear when the assets out of which the debts should be paid are to be identified. Undisposed-of property and general residue are not necessarily the same thing. If the will simply directs for payment out of residue (a commonly-seen provision), and a gift of a share of the residue has failed, it may not be clear whether payment should be made out of the lapsed share or out of residue as a whole. If it is made out of the lapsed share first of all, the person who would take the lapsed share of residue under the rules of intestacy bears all the payments. If, however, it is made out of the residue before it is divided into shares, all the shares of residue bear the burden equally. (Section 35 makes its own stipulations for the variation of its provision by will, but they refer only to the secured debts to which that section applies: see 13.16.)

The question often arises as to whether the testator has used words in their will which are sufficient to vary the statutory order.

## 13.15.2  'Subject to the payment of my ... expenses ... and debts'

In *Re Harland-Peck* (1941), the testatrix left the residue of her estate 'subject to the payment of my funeral and testamentary expenses ... and debts' to A and B in equal shares. B's share lapsed, because he predeceased. The question was whether the provision in the will was sufficient to vary the statutory order. If it did not, the debts would be paid out of the lapsed share; if it did, they would be paid equally from both shares of residue. The Court of Appeal held that the words did vary the statutory order, so the debts were paid equally from A's share as well as B's lapsed share.

*Re Harland-Peck* (1941)

If the statutory order applied ...

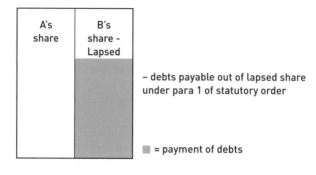

– debts payable out of lapsed share under para 1 of statutory order

■ = payment of debts

... but the will varied it.

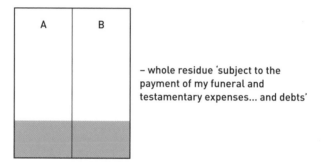

– whole residue 'subject to the payment of my funeral and testamentary expenses... and debts'

## 13.15.3 Direction for payment out of residue as a whole

The case of *Re Kempthorne* (1930) resembled *Re Harland-Peck*; the testator left his residue to his brothers and sisters after payment of debts and legacies. Two of his sisters had predeceased. If the statutory order applied, their shares would be used to pay the debts. At first instance, the court held that the statutory order did apply, but the Court of Appeal reversed that decision and held that it did not. It held that the testator had clearly provided that the residue should be divided into shares 'after' the payment of debts.

## 13.15.4 Direction for payment from one source exonerates other

A rule had been established under the case law preceding 1926 that a testator who wished to shift the burden of debts away from personalty and onto realty had to show a definite intention to exonerate the personalty. Later cases echoed the same understanding of what was required to alter the usual order of payment, although after 1925 the distinction between realty and personalty did not apply. In *Re Meldrum* (1952), the testator by his will gave Annie Meldrum a pecuniary legacy and also gave her the contents of a deposit account 'after … legacies debts funeral and other expenses have been liquidated'. The residue would have been primarily liable for the debts and expenses, under para 2 of the statutory order, as it would come before the deposit account which fell within para 4, unless the terms of the will had varied that order. The court held that the direction for the payment of debts and funeral and other expenses out of the deposit account necessarily involved an intention to exonerate the residue.

Upjohn J in *Re Meldrum* did not lay down any particular rules for the interpretation of whether the terms of a will are sufficient to vary the statutory order. He said it was 'essentially a matter of construction of the will in each case whether the provisions of the schedule apply, or whether they have been varied by the terms of the will'.

### 13.15.5 Clear intention to exonerate other funds

In *Re Gordon* (1940), the testatrix had made a specific gift and given a pecuniary legacy, being the balance of a sum after the payment of debts. She had not provided for the residue. The court held that the direction did not displace the statutory order, because no intention to exonerate residue was shown. Therefore, the debts were paid out of residue in accordance with the statutory order rather than out of the pecuniary legacy, despite the wording of the will.

### 13.15.6 Direction for the payment of debts and expenses 'as soon as possible'

The testator in *Re Lamb* (1929) left directions for his executors to pay his debts and expenses 'as soon as possible'. He left the residue equally between four persons. One of them predeceased, so his share lapsed and was undisposed-of by the will. The court held that the statutory order applied; the testator had not varied it because he had not specified the fund or property from which the debts should be paid.

### 13.15.7 Assets not referred to in the schedule

Some assets which may arise in an estate are not referred to in the schedule. Although in most estates there will not be any such assets, clearly difficulty may arise if there are any, and the principle that statute, if it governs something such as the application of assets, should be clear and should be applicable to all eventualities is further offended by the omissions. The assets not referred to include money paid into the estate if the grantee of an option over property in the estate exercises that option, and property which is subject to a general power of appointment.

In *Re Eve* (1956), the testator left an option to one of the beneficiaries, which entitled him to purchase certain shares from the estate at less than market value. The question was whether the shares should be applied as specific gifts; if there is a shortfall of funds, specific gifts have priority. The court found that it was not a specific gift of the shares, but that if the money paid for the shares would render the estate capable of meeting its debts and liabilities, then the personal representatives should use the money for that rather than selling the shares to meet that beneficiary's share of the liabilities, and the property subject to the option should be the last to be available for the payment of debts. This would appear to have been a helpful compromise in the circumstances of the case, avoiding bringing the shares within para 6 of the statutory order.

The schedule is also silent as to the subject matter of *donationes mortis causa*.

## 13.16 Debts charged on specific property – s 35

Until the later part of the nineteenth century, a beneficiary who inherited realty could usually have any mortgage debt paid out of the deceased's general personalty. Now, however, s 35 of the AEA 1925 says that where any interest in property that belonged to the deceased is charged with a debt, and the deceased has not signified a contrary intention by any document, that interest is primarily liable to bear the charge. It also provides specifically that a contrary intention is not deemed to be signified by a general direction for the payment of debts out of the testator's personalty or out of their residuary real estate or residuary real and personal estate, or by a charge of debts on any such estate, unless the testator signifies their intention further, by words which refer either expressly or by necessary implication to the particular charge itself.

The usual situation to which this section will apply is that of a mortgaged house or similar property, as was the case in *Ross v Perrin-Hughes* (2004). The testator's home-made will contained a gift to his fiancée: 'I leave devise and bequeath my apartment and contents thereof to my friend Irene Perrin-Hughes.' The residue was left to Ms Perrin-Hughes and the testator's brothers. The testator owned a leasehold maisonette in a building of which he also owned the whole freehold reversion. These had been bought on an endowment mortgage, and shortly before his death he had agreed an increase in the monthly premiums because the insurance company had advised that otherwise there would be a shortfall in paying off the mortgage. The executor sought directions as to whether the gift to Ms Perrin-Hughes bore the mortgage debt, and the court held that s 35 should be construed expansively. It found that the taking out of the endowment policy and its assignment to the mortgagee, and especially the agreed increase in premiums, was evidence of a sufficient counter-intention to mean that the mortgage should be discharged out of the policy proceeds, which were not part of the estate, so the fiancée took the property free of mortgage.

However, it may also apply to more unusual situations, such as a vendor's lien for unpaid purchase money, a limited company's lien over its own shares or a charging order made by the court.

The section also provides that every part of the charged interest should bear a proportionate part of the charge on the whole, in accordance with its value. This means that if a beneficiary takes only a share of the charged property, they do so subject to a proportionate share of the charge. If the beneficiaries of the other shares do not take them and pay their share of the charged debt, their shares of the debt will not (as between beneficiaries) come out of the value of the charged interest, but will fall to be paid by the estate, into which the uncharged value of the interest will also fall.

The property is only 'primarily' liable; this section does not confine a creditor whose loan is secured to looking to the mortgaged property for satisfaction of the debt. That point is particularly important in the case of 'negative equity' – where the property on which a debt is secured is of a lower value than the debt, for example where a house worth £300,000 is subject to a mortgage debt of £350,000. The £350,000 was a debt owed by the testator and the creditor may look to his estate as a whole to satisfy it, just as the deceased was liable for the whole debt when he was alive.

A charge in the sense meant by s 35 of the 1925 Act is a formal charge of the kind represented by a house mortgage to a building society. The section does not apply when the relationship between the debt and the property, though close and perhaps completely intertwined, falls short of a mortgage or formal charge.

Note that there is no obligation on a mortgagee (for example, a building society) to continue loan arrangements made by and with the deceased. It is not necessarily the case that a person who inherits a mortgaged house can keep it so long as they keep up the mortgage payments. If they cannot afford to pay off the loan secured on the house immediately, they will have to have the mortgagee agree to make the loan to them instead of the deceased – that is, they will have to remortgage it themselves with the same, or another, lender. However, in many cases the deceased will turn out to have had life assurance which will specifically repay the secured debt, as in *Ross v Perrin-Hughes*.

## 13.17  Marshalling

A creditor of the estate will not lose their claim because of the result of the rules as to the incidence of debts as between the beneficiaries. They may satisfy their claim out of any assets in the estate. Adjustments must then be made to reassert the proper position as between the beneficiaries so that the incidence rules finally prevail. Where a beneficiary's gift has been taken to pay a creditor, they may take in compensation the property which should, according to the rules of incidence of debts, have been used to pay the creditor. This process is called marshalling. A recent example of this occurred in *Petterson v Ross and Others* (2013), where the gift of a house was specified to be free of mortgage. When it was sold, however, the Woolwich Building Society discharged the mortgage out of the proceeds of sale. The beneficiary who was supposed to have received the property free of mortgage could therefore claim the mortgage money back as a liability of the estate.

## 13.18  The incidence of general or pecuniary legacies

Having established where the debts and liabilities of the estate must be paid from, the personal representative must also establish what property is to be used to meet any general, or pecuniary legacies.

### 13.18.1  The situation before 1926

Things were clear before the reforms of 1925, even if they were not ideal. Unless the testator altered the position by will, realty and the subject matter of specific legacies were exempt from the burden of general legacies and the general personal estate was liable *pari passu* (each part as much as another) for the legacies.

If the testator gave the residue of realty and personalty after payment of general legacies, then the rule in *Greville v Brown* (1859) meant that the legacies would be paid first out of the personalty, but that realty could be resorted to in order to meet the general legacies if the general personalty did not suffice. If the testator directed payment of the general legacies out of a mixed fund of realty and personalty, then the two parts of the fund were liable to be used for legacies in proportion to their values, in accordance with the rule in *Roberts v Walker* (1830).

### 13.18.2  The situation after 1925

There is no provision in the Administration of Estates Act 1925 as to what part of an estate legacies, as opposed to debts, should be paid from. In principle one would assume, therefore, that it was intended that the old law should still apply. However, given that the whole structure of the application of property was altered by the reforms of that year, the old law no longer fits well with the rest of the legal provisions. As well as the general alignment of rules about realty and personalty, there are particular parts of the new law which are very difficult to reconcile with the continuation of the old. It seems likely that the omission of any statutory provision as to the payment of legacies from the 1925 legislation was an oversight rather than deliberate.

There are two main areas of query. First, it is unclear how the rules in *Greville v Brown* and *Roberts v Walker* (13.8.2) operate when the testator dies partially intestate and s 33 of the Administration of Estates Act 1925 imposes a trust on the undisposed property. Second, there is potential for applying s 34(3) of the AEA 1925 and the statutory order, but it not clear whether this is appropriate. It is unclear whether s 34(3) includes legacies in any event, since it refers only to 'funeral and testamentary expenses, debts and liabilities'.

### 13.18.3 Legacies in a partial intestacy after 1923

Section 33 of the Administration of Estates Act 1925 deals with the administration of assets on a partial intestacy (in the case of a total intestacy, there will by definition be no general legacies). Section 33(1) provides that 'On the death of a person intestate as to any real or personal estate, that estate shall be held in trust by his personal representatives with the power to sell it'.

Section 33(2) provides:

The personal representatives shall pay out of –

(a)  the ready money of the deceased (so far as not disposed of by his will, if any); and

(b)  any net money arising from disposing of any other part of his estate (after payment of costs),

all such funeral, testamentary and administration expenses, debts and other liabilities as are properly payable thereout having regard to the rules of administration contained in this Part of this Act, and out of the residue of the said money the personal representative shall set aside a fund sufficient to provide for any pecuniary legacies bequeathed by the will (if any) of the deceased.

This makes undisposed money primarily liable for general legacies on a partial intestacy.

It may be the case that the earlier imposition of the statutory trust on all the property in the estate or the later specifications about the use of ready money and net money amount to an ousting of the rule in *Greville v Brown*, and that the persistent lack of distinction between realty and personalty means that that should be inferred. It would be in keeping with the general trend of the 1925 legislation. However, the statute does not say so.

### 13.18.4 Section 34(3) of the AEA 1925, the statutory order and general legacies

It is possible that legacies given by the will should be treated in the same way as the debts and liabilities referred to in s 34(3) of the Administration of Estates Act 1925 (see 13.14). However, it does not refer specifically to them. If they are not to be included, then the Act fails to make any provision for how assets are to be applied to pay legacies. In that case, the old law ought logically to apply, since it was not varied by the Act. This question will be of practical importance where the estate is wholly covered by the will if, as in *Re Thompson* (1936) (13.18.6), the legacies are payable out of residue but the residue is divided as to realty and personalty, and the personal representatives need to know which part of the gift will be depleted by the payment of the legacies.

The courts have had no fixed view on the fundamental question of whether s 34(3) of the AEA 1925, which refers only to debts and liabilities, includes legacies. They have oscillated between the view that the old rules as to the incidence of legacies still apply, as the AEA 1925 made no provision changing those rules, and the view that the incidence of legacies should be regarded as analogous to that of debts and therefore dealt with in the same way. It is even possible to find the same judge apparently holding different views on the law in different cases (see the decisions of Danckwerts J in *Re Beaumont* (1950) and *Re Martin* (1955) (13.18.6 and 13.18.7 respectively)).

### 13.18.5 Two funds of undisposed-of property

A further question may arise in relation to the payment of legacies out of a partially intestate estate where there are two separate funds of undisposed-of property, the first being property totally undisposed-of by the will and therefore covered by the statutory trust for sale under s 33

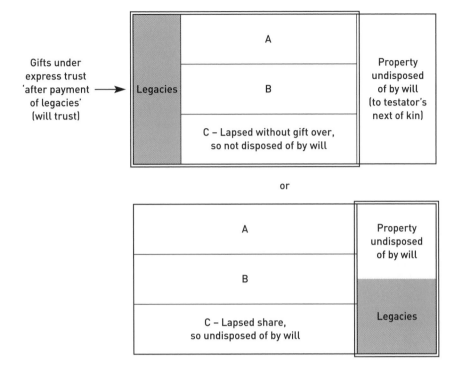

of the AEA 1925, and the second arising under a trust set up by the will, part of which does not, however, have a beneficiary. Although the statutory provisions can be varied by the will, it may not be entirely clear whether or not this has been done. If, for example, there is a will trust providing for the payment of legacies, with the residue of that property going to three beneficiaries, of whom one has predeceased without a gift over, the question will arise as to whether the shares of the beneficiaries under the trust should be ascertained before or after the payment out of legacies, or whether legacies should come out of the totally undisposed-of property, in accordance with s 33, rather than out of the property covered by the will trust.

## 13.18.6 Courts hold that s 34(3) has no effect on legacies...

Clauson J held in Re Thompson (1936) that the pre-1926 rules still applied to the incidence of general legacies. The testator gave general legacies and then left his residuary realty and personalty to charity. The court had to decide whether the legacies were payable rateably out of the residuary real and personal estate, or whether they were payable primarily out of residuary personalty in accordance with the rule in Greville v Brown. The court held that s 34(3) and the statutory order had not altered the old rules. Clauson J said,

> It is suggested that the effect of that provision is to alter the law.... The provision does not say so.... The provision is concerned with the way in which funeral testamentary and administration expenses, debts and liabilities are to be met. There is no indication there that there is any intention of altering the law...

in respect of general legacies. This is, in essence, the difficulty, since an alteration is implied by the change in other rules and by the general restructuring of administration, but yet nothing is stated, either as to whether the rules remain the same or whether they should be considered analogous to those for debts and expenses.

If this is correct it means that a pecuniary legacy fund should be retained out of the testator's undisposed-of property under para 1 of the statutory order only insofar as the undisposed-of property was liable to be applied to legacies under the old rules. The same would apply in respect of retaining a pecuniary legacy fund out of residue under para 2. This would entail reading the reference to a pecuniary legacy fund in paras 1 and 2 of the statutory order as restricting the fund to being retained only insofar as it would have been liable to meet pecuniary legacies under the old rules.

*Re Thompson* was applied by the court in *Re Anstead* (1943), where the testator left general legacies and made a gift of residue in trust. There was no direction as to what funds should be used to pay legacies, and the question was again whether the rule in *Greville v Brown* applied. The court held that the debts and expenses were payable out of the remaining residue after setting aside a pecuniary legacy fund under para 2 of the statutory order. This meant that the pecuniary legacy fund would become liable for the debts and expenses only under para 5, which entailed that the retention of the fund was in accordance with the old rules rather than rateably out of residuary personalty and realty.

*Re Thompson* was also applied in *Re Beaumont* (1950). The testatrix in that case gave pecuniary legacies free of duty and then left all her realty and personalty on trust for sale, after payment of

### *Re Thompson* (1936)

If s 34(3) of the AEA 1925 and the statutory
order had altered the old rules ...

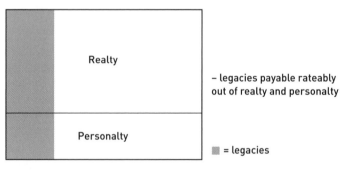

– legacies payable rateably
out of realty and personalty

■ = legacies

... but the rule in *Greville v Brown* still applied

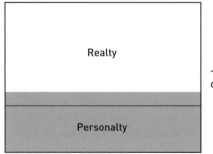

– legacies payable primarily
out of personalty

*Re Beaumont* (1950)

If s 34(3) and the statutory order applied ...

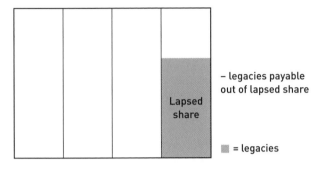

Lapsed
share

– legacies payable
out of lapsed share

= legacies

... but Danckwerts J held that the old order still applied

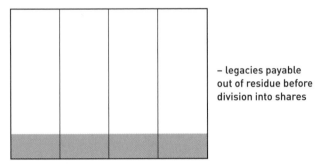

– legacies payable
out of residue before
division into shares

her expenses and debts, to be divided amongst four persons. One of the four predeceased, so that share lapsed and went as on intestacy, falling within para 1 of the statutory order. Danckwerts J said that s 34(3) 'has in effect made no provision with regard to such things as legacies ... the position of the legacies depends on the old law'. Under the old law, the legacies were payable out of the estate before it was divided, rather than being taken first of all out of the undisposed-of share as under para 1 of the statutory order.

## 13.18.7 ... courts hold that legacies are governed by s 34(3) and the statutory order

The alternative view holds that s 34(3) and the statutory order have altered the old rules as to the incidence of general legacies, so that a pecuniary legacy fund must be retained out of the testator's undisposed-of property under para 1 (and by analogy out of residue under para 2) of the statutory order, whether or not the property referred to in that paragraph would have been applicable to legacies before 1926.

In *Re Worthington* (1933), as in *Re Lamb*, the testatrix directed for the payment of debts and expenses (which are payable anyway) and legacies without specifying what property should be used to pay them. Her residuary estate was left to two persons, of whom one predeceased. If the pre-1926 rules applied, the incidence of the legacies was governed by the rule in *Greville v Brown*, and they were payable primarily out of the residuary personalty whether or not it went on intestacy, with residuary realty only liable in aid. The decision at first instance was the provisions of the AEA 1925 applied only insofar as the payment of debts was concerned, which were to be

**Re Worthington (1933)**

If the rule in *Greville v Brown* applied ...

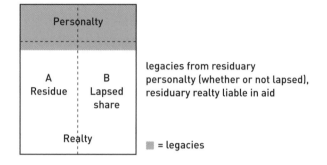

legacies from residuary
personalty (whether or not lapsed),
residuary realty liable in aid

■ = legacies

... but the court held the statutory order applied

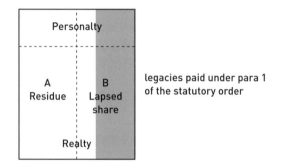

legacies paid under para 1
of the statutory order

taken from the lapsed share of residue. In respect of the legacies, the court of first instance held that the old law applied, and they were payable out of the estate before the ascertainment of the residue. The Court of Appeal, however, held that the legacies should be treated in the same way as the debts. The lapsed share of residue should be ascertained first and the legacies then paid out of it.

The court in *Re Midgley* (1955) followed *Re Worthington*. In *Re Midgley*, the testatrix gave pecuniary legacies and then left her residuary estate, after payment of debts and expenses, on trust to be divided amongst six persons. She later revoked one person's gift, which was undisposed-of at her death. Harman J held that para 1 of the statutory order required the legacies to be paid out of that one-sixth share, asking:

> What, then, is to be done with the fund which has been retained thereout?... The answer, it seems to me, is that it must be used to meet the pecuniary legacies, because it has been retained for that purpose. It is, if I may say so, a tortuous way of legislating.

The same view was taken by the court in *Re Martin* (1955), where the testator gave pecuniary legacies, and then left all his residuary personalty on trust, having revoked the gift of his realty, which was undisposed-of at his death. There was no express trust for sale of the undisposed-of realty, so s 33(1) and (2) applied to it. Danckwerts J held that the legacies were payable out of the realty pursuant to s 33(2), construing para 1 of the statutory order without regard to the pre-1926 rules which made legacies payable out of the general personal estate. This appears to contradict the view of the law he took five years earlier in *Re Beaumont* (1950) (13.18.6).

*Re Martin* (1955)

If the rule in *Greville v Brown* applied ...

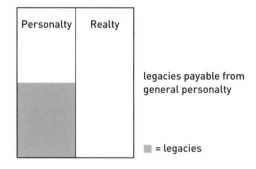

... but Danckwerts J held the old rules had
been altered by s 33(2) of the AEA 1925

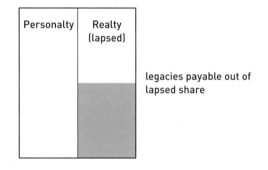

### 13.18.8 Legacies and debts

In *Re Wilson* (1967), the testatrix gave such generous pecuniary legacies that there was insufficient in the estate to meet them. Notwithstanding this, she left her realty and residuary personalty to her daughter. The personal representatives needed to know whether the realty should be used to endeavour to satisfy the pecuniary legacies. The court held, on the wording of the will, that the testatrix had not intended the realty to be depleted by the legacies. However, the pecuniary legacies would exhaust the personalty, so the question also arose as to what funds should be used to meet the debts. If they were paid out of the personalty, they would reduce still further the amount available for the legacies. The court held that the realty fell within para 2 of the First Schedule to the AEA 1925 as 'property ... included ... in a residuary gift' and that the debts should be paid out of the daughter's realty.

## 13.19 Liability of a personal representative

A personal representative may be liable in various ways. They will be liable to the estate and its beneficiaries if they do not deal with its assets properly and they may become liable to those who deal with the estate, such as landlords or parties to contracts. In some situations they may be liable only so far as the estate is liable, and able to indemnify him- or herself from the estate. In other cases, they will be personally liable.

### 13.19.1 *Devastavit*

*Devastavit* means 'he wasted it' – a breach of a personal representative's duty to preserve the assets of the estate and administer the estate properly and in accordance with the law which makes them liable for their failure. The personal representative is personally liable to beneficiaries and creditors of the estate for any loss caused by committing *devastavit*, whether they have used the assets for their own purposes, failed to administer them properly without, however, any improper intention, or failed to preserve the assets.

An example of the personal representative using the assets for their own purposes might be simply pocketing money, or could be something more complex. It need not involve anything that might be considered misappropriation for their own gain. A personal representative who improperly administered the estate without appropriating any gain to his own purposes was said to have committed *devastavit* in *Shelly's Case* (1693) when he incurred funeral expenses out of keeping with the estate.

### 13.19.2 Breach of trust

There is, however, a distinction between breach of duty as a personal representative and breach of duty as a trustee, though some acts may constitute both. Breach of trust is, however, usually wider, so an executor who makes a profit from their office which is unauthorised by will, without causing loss to the estate, is liable to the estate for breach of trust, but not in *devastavit* (see the case of *Kane v Radley-Kane* (1998), 13.10).

### 13.19.3 Funeral expenses

The personal representative, if they arrange the funeral in that capacity, is not liable for the funeral expenses to the extent that the assets in the estate meet the cost of a funeral in keeping with the deceased's position in life. If they request a funeral which is more expensive than the estate warrants, they are personally liable to the undertaker for the full cost and will not be able to recoup the excess cost, but only the cost of what the estate warranted and its assets can bear. If another person deals with the undertaker, they will be directly liable to the undertaker for the whole cost, though they are entitled to be indemnified from the estate to the same extent as the personal representative.

### 13.19.4 Liability to account

The personal representative has a liability in law to keep an inventory of the assets of the estate and to keep full and accurate accounts showing both receipts and payments. They are also obliged to exhibit them when the court requires: the standard wording of an oath for a grant of probate states: 'I will ... when required to do so by the court exhibit in the court a full inventory of the above estate and render an account of it to the court.' Equity provides remedies for many breaches of duty by a personal representative, including accounting.

### 13.19.5 Liability for co-personal representative

Generally there is no vicarious liability for the breaches of duty of a co-representative, though a personal representative must take care not to be led into involvement in bad deeds by a co-personal representative which will involve him or her in personal liability.

## 13.19.6 Limitation

Limitation is available to a personal representative as a defence in certain circumstances, the normal period being 12 years. However, it is no defence where the personal representative still holds the property in question, nor where they have committed fraud.

## 13.19.7 *Plene administravit*

*Plene administravit* means 'he has fully administered the estate'. It is a matter of procedure, and can be of great practical importance. Any personal representative who, having dealt with the estate and distributed it, finds an action being brought against them by a creditor who had a claim against the estate at the date of death should enter the plea, because if they do so they will be protected from personal liability in most cases.

If the personal representative fails to enter the plea they may find that they are liable for the full amount of judgment, even where the plea was available, as occurred in *Midland Bank v Green* (No 2) (1979). In that case, the son sued his father for breach of contract in respect of the option granted him on his property, which the father deliberately frustrated by selling the land to his wife with a clear land charges search, the son having failed to register his option. The father died in the course of the proceedings and the personal representative, having failed to plead *plene administravit*, was liable for the full amount of the judgment, which greatly exceeded the father's estate.

## 13.19.8 Relief from liability granted by court

The personal representative may be authorised to do certain things, including to be paid for administering the estate, by a clause in the will. Alternatively, they may seek authorisation from the beneficiaries, provided they are all of full age and agree.

If instead they seeks relief from the court from liability, however, the court may grant it if it sees fit in its discretion under s 61 of the Trustee Act 1925, the onus of proving honesty and reasonableness being on the personal representative. In *Re Rosenthal* (1972), for example, the court regarded the behaviour of a professional trustee who paid estate duty on a gift from residue when the donee of the gift should have paid it much as did the residuary beneficiary; it may have been honest, but it was not reasonable or excusable, and there was no order for relief from liability. In *Re Evans, Evans v Westcombe* (1999) the deceased died intestate in 1987. The administrator (his daughter) assumed the claimant (her brother) was no longer alive as she had not heard from him in 30 years. She obtained a missing beneficiary policy for half the value of the estate (£21,000) and the estate was distributed. In 1994 the brother reappeared and the policy paid out. The brother claimed lost interest since 1990 and took issue with the insurance premium of £525. The court held that taking out such a policy was sensible rather than delaying the distribution of the estate for years and that the payment of the premium was an allowable expense of administration and allowed relief under s 61. It should be noted that the fact a personal representative acts on legal advice does not automatically mean s 61 relief will be granted.

# 13.20 Rights of wrongfully deprived beneficiaries

Where a beneficiary has been wrongfully deprived of their benefit under the deceased's will or intestacy, they have first of all the right to pursue the personal representatives for the wrongful distribution. However, they may not be able to satisfy the beneficiary's claim.

The beneficiary will have two further avenues to pursue, against the person who received the property and against the property itself. They may use their right in equity to claim a refund personally from anyone to whom money or property has been wrongfully given, or they may trace the property itself, also in equity.

## 13.20.1 Refund

The beneficiary may claim a refund against the recipient if the personal representative made a wrongful payment and the beneficiary has exhausted all their remedies against the personal representative, either because the personal representative is insolvent or because they are protected from liability by having complied with the advertisements provisions of s 27 of the Trustee Act 1925 or by having obtained a Benjamin order before distributing the assets (see 13.4.1).

## 13.20.2 Tracing

A beneficiary may try to trace the money or property which has been wrongfully paid over. Tracing in equity goes further than in common law, but a claim in equity will not lie against a bona fide purchaser without notice of the wrongful payment. The beneficiary does not have to have exhausted their remedies against the personal representatives in order to trace, although if he or she has pursued them, then anything obtained from them must be set off against the property the beneficiary claims to trace.

## 13.20.3 Example – the Diplock estate

The principle of the equitable refund was used in the case of *Ministry of Health v Simpson* (1951). This was one of the cases, with *Chichester Diocesan Fund and Board of Finance v Simpson* (1944), which concerned the estate of Caleb Diplock, who left a substantial residuary estate to such 'charitable or benevolent' object as his executors selected. Only after some £200,000 had been distributed did the next of kin bring their challenge to the validity of the wording to create a charitable gift. The House of Lords held the gift not wholly charitable and therefore it failed. The next of kin could not obtain more than £15,000 from the executors, so, they claimed both a refund from the charities who had received the money and a right to trace the property. The latter claim did not succeed against the hospital which challenged the next of kin's claim, but the House of Lords held that the claim for a refund did. It held that, although the charity had notice of the wrongfulness of the payment, it had changed its position as a result of the gift, which it used it to commission a new building, so the remedy of tracing was unavailable. It was held the personal representatives had been under a mistake of law, not of fact, when they made the payment.[17]

# 13.21 Summary of Chapter 13

## 13.21.1 Administration of Estates

The administration of the estate is the process whereby the personal representatives collect in the assets of the estate and then meet the debts and liabilities and pay out the legacies and devises before distributing the residue, managing the estate as necessary in the meantime.

The funeral expenses come first, and then the administration expenses and the debts of the deceased at their death. Debts arising after death are next, followed by any specific gifts and then general gifts. Only after this can the residue be ascertained.

---

17 SJB and JACT, 'Administration. Payments by Executors under Mistake of Law. Limitation Act, 1939. Equitable Doctrine of Tracing. Re Diplock, Diplock v Wintle [1948] Ch. 465 (CA)' (1949) Cambridge Law Journal 260.

The personal representatives may be personally liable to those who suffer if they do not carry out the administration properly. There are however systems for them to protect themselves against the possibility of claims arising after they have distributed the estate, including advertising for creditors and dealing with any known but untraceable beneficiaries.

Where a personal representative passes land, this should be done by written assent under s 36 of the Administration of Estates Act 1925. A personal representative may also appropriate assets in satisfaction of gifts under s 41 of the AEA 1925.

The beneficiaries probably have no proprietary interest in the property in the estate, although they have the chose in action of the right to ensure due administration of the estate. A residuary beneficiary probably obtains an interest when the residue is ascertained, but not before. There is authority for saying that a specific beneficiary may obtain some form of equitable interest in the relevant property at death.

If the estate is insolvent and cannot even meet all its debts, they must be paid out in the order set out in s 34(1) of the Administration of Estates Act 1925. Debts charged on specific property are covered separately by s 35.

A personal representative may be liable in *devastavit* or breach of trust for failing properly to administer the estate, but if they have acted in good faith and reasonably they may seek relief from the court under s 61 of the Trustee Act 1925. A beneficiary who has lost out because the estate has not been properly administered may be able to go against the personal representatives, or may also have rights of action in equity against the recipient of the property or may be able to trace the money or property which has been paid over. This may also apply to the subject of a Benjamin order, where distribution is authorised without taking into account a known beneficiary who cannot be found, who turns up later and cannot pursue the personal representatives.

## 13.22 Further reading

Joel Nitikman, 'The Forgotten Law of Assent' (2012) 18 Trusts & Trustees 672.

SJB and JACT, 'Administration. Payments by Executors under Mistake of Law. Limitation Act, 1939. Equitable Doctrine of Tracing. Re Diplock, Diplock v Wintle [1948] Ch. 465 (CA)' (1949) Cambridge Law Journal 260.

Meryl Thomas and Simon Cooper, 'The Nature of the Beneficiary's Interest and the Role of the Personal Representative in the Administration and Distribution of an Estate' (1995) 17 Liverpool Law Review 69.

# Chapter 14

# Tax and Tax Planning

The subject of taxation is primarily relevant to the practice of wills and probate rather than to the substantive law of succession. However, it is an academic subject as well, both in itself and in what it reveals about the priorities held by the society that imposes it on its members.

Succession law is mainly concerned with the transmission of property; inevitably, it attracts questions of whether and how that property should be taxed. The imposition of tax on a person's wealth on death might be thought to be the obvious opportunity, since the deceased can no longer make use of their wealth and will be able neither to feel the effects of the tax nor to complain. As for the deprived beneficiaries, they are obtaining a windfall anyway. The very principle of taxation is, however, described by some contemporary theorists, for example Robert Nozick, as 'theft';[1] the idea of taxing transfers on death was specifically attacked by an economist, Barry Bracewell-Milnes, who said: 'death duties are a tax on seed corn', meaning they prevent investment across generations.[2] It should be noted however that Inheritance Tax (IHT) is in fact a gift tax, payable on lifetime gifts as well as on death. The principal method of avoiding it is to give property away sufficiently in advance of death for tax reliefs to apply; in this sense, it encourages the wealthy to give property away, rather than merely taxing it on death, so that the relatively low historical yield of IHT (something criticised by economists who advocate its abolition) might be seen as a mark of its success.

Some people believe that the inheritance of substantial wealth is wrong in principle because it gives certain individuals an unearned head start over others for which no amount of hard work can compensate, and so is destructive of fairness, social cohesion and democratic principles. Others believe that objections to inherited wealth run contrary to the natural concern of parents to provide for their children and are based on nothing more edifying than jealousy. In this area, those who support 'traditional family values' are usually those who are against taxation as an unjustifiable form of state interference and for the free disposition and inheritance of wealth; this may be contrasted with the situation in respect of family provision (see Chapter 15), where the minimisation of general taxation tends to call for state interference to enforce private moral obligations within the family if the deceased has failed to provide properly for their family after their death.

There is, however, little likelihood of Inheritance Tax, the principal tax dealt with in this chapter, being ended in Britain, and it remains particularly important to professionals such as solicitors and accountants who are involved in dealing with wills and succession.

---

1  Robert Nozick, *Anarchy, State and Utopia* (Basic Books 1974).
2  Barry Bracewell-Milnes, *Free Wills* (Adam Smith Institute 1995).

# 14.1 Principles of taxation in succession matters to be applied to minimise liability

The practical aspect of dealing with taxation in the context of wills is the minimisation of a liability to tax. To understand the principles of how the basic rules of taxation would apply in outline to the situation of a given estate, there is no need to perform precise mathematics. The requirement is to see where the tax liability would fall.

The vital difference between tax avoidance and tax evasion must be considered. The former is lawful whilst the latter is fraud. A general anti-abuse rule ('GAAR') was introduced by the 2013 Finance Act, which aimed to counteract abusive tax arrangements with relation to taxes including Income Tax, Capital Gains Tax and Inheritance Tax: abusive arrangements are defined essentially as those that are unreasonable. It should be remembered that other taxes than IHT may be involved (see *Vinton and Others v Fladgate and Another* (2010); and *Mason and Others v Mills & Reeve* (2012) (14.1.2)) and that tax regimes change so that wills may need updating for that reason.

The basic structure of IHT is simple. The estate pays 40 per cent on any value over the current allowance of the nil-rate band of £325,000. Transfers to a spouse or civil partner or to charity are exempt from IHT, and there are numerous reliefs. Lifetime transfers are in principle subject to IHT as well, but if the donor survives making the gift, the liability decreases over time and, if they live for seven years, disappears entirely.

## 14.1.1 Potential liability to be minimised in advance of death

Once the areas of tax liability have been established, the ways of reducing them should be apparent. With tax, the planning element is often vital, since many advantages cannot be achieved unless the testator begins early. None of us knows when we will die, so there is a constant need for anyone with any substance to their property to keep their tax situation in mind. Even those who have little or no property may come into some, perhaps unexpectedly. Just as a person should keep their will up to date in order to benefit the family and friends they consider appropriate in the event of their death, so they should keep their tax situation under review in order to take account of changes both in the property they own and in the law relating to taxation. For example, the change that allowed married couples to transfer their IHT allowance on death (the nil-rate band) meant that this was often the most useful way of minimising tax in married families, where previously the method used had been a discretionary trust consisting of the previous single nil-rate band. IHT, like other taxes, operates more by way of reliefs than by payment to the government, but the reliefs are subject to change, not always to the advantage of the potential taxpayer. Avoiding tax often involves giving away money and property: it is important not to focus so much on avoiding tax that one is left with too little to live on.

## 14.1.2 Structure and general rules change but slowly

The structure of the law of taxation does not normally change rapidly, so once that structure is understood it becomes easier to deal with any changes in the details. There are however occasional major changes, such as those of 2006 to the nil-rate band (the first tranche of non-exempt estate that is subject to tax at 0 per cent). A person making a will must always be advised of the tax liability their proposals may incur and ways of reducing it. This applies even to a person making a will with a non-specialist 'High Street' firm of solicitors, as it is by no means uncommon for there to be a potential liability to tax which could be minimised by sensible tax planning even in a modest estate which appears to consist mainly of an interest in an ordinary family house.

Failure to take tax liability into account may lead to a negligence action, but there is no general duty on solicitors to ensure that a client or estate pays as little tax as possible. IHT is payable primarily by the personal representatives, but also in certain situations by trustees or residuary beneficiaries. In *Daniels v Thompson* (2004), the Court of Appeal held that no liability to the estate in negligence would arise in relation to IHT, however, because the inadequate advice was given to the testator, who could never have paid the tax: that liability fell on her estate after her death. This decision has been much criticised. In *Rind v Theodore Goddard* (2008) it was suggested that it justified the beneficiaries claiming for the amount by which the advice reduced what they received from the estate. *Mason and Others v Mills & Reeve* (2012) was a more complex case, where the allegation was first of all that solicitors drafting a will negligently failed to advise the testator to delay selling shares until after an elective heart procedure, or just to advise fully. On his death, the transfer gave rise to IHT liability of about £1,000,000. Had he kept the shares, a combination of Business Property Relief and Capital Gains Tax uplift on death (see 14.4.4) would have saved a great deal of tax liability. The children's claim failed, including on appeal to the Court of Appeal, with Lloyd LJ in the High Court saying that he realised however that they would feel 'ill-served by the legal profession'. The solicitors were specialists, and they could have been clearer about the limitations of their advice, especially as some of the children were unsophisticated in tax matters, or could have suggested the clients took advice from accountants: these could all have produced a better result. But the court held that the solicitors' duty depended on all the circumstances: the heart procedure was not obviously risky, and it was not obvious what the deceased would have done had he not sold his shares as he did, so the solicitors were not liable to the beneficiaries.

### 14.1.3 The art of tax planning?

The art of tax planning, it has been said, is that of detaching the testator sufficiently from their property to satisfy HMRC that they have truly given it away, whilst retaining for the testator as much control over it as possible. The ownership of property brings with it power, and where a person is dealing with the making of a will they are dealing with their power over their family and friends, which they will usually want to retain as long as possible. This desire pulls against the desire, also usual, to let the tax man have as little of their property as possible, because the former demands the retention of control over the property and the latter demands the release of it.

The main concern in this chapter is with Inheritance Tax, but considerations of Capital Gains Tax and Income Tax may also arise in an estate. However, the former is interesting mostly because of the provisions which mean it generally does not arise, and the latter pertains mostly to continuing trusts, which are outside the scope of this book.

The discretionary trust can be an important element of tax (and other financial) planning. Because the trustees of the trust have discretion as to who gets the funds, even though they have to choose amongst a specified range of beneficiaries, none of the beneficiaries has an entitlement to the funds. The beneficiaries therefore do not have taxable property in the trust fund unless something taxable is given to them. The trustees can therefore give money where it attracts the least tax, or withhold it if giving it would simply mean the recipient lost welfare benefits to the extent they received trust money.

# 14.2 Tax avoidance, transfer of assets and paying for care

Note that avoidance of tax, however lawful, should not be allowed to become a fetish. It may be better to risk one's successors paying tax on their inheritance than to risk giving away so much property in pursuit of tax avoidance that there is not enough to provide for one's old age.

It can be very difficult to estimate what property a person needs to keep to ensure proper provision in old age. A major factor in this difficulty is that one cannot know how long one will live. Moreover, where a person is living off the income on a capital investment, they will be affected not only by changing interest rates, which can fluctuate somewhat unpredictably, but also by inflation, which may render capital permanently inadequate. Whilst inflation is currently low, interest rates have been extremely low for several years, affecting those who rely on the income from their savings. The aftermath of the Global Financial Crisis is still making financial investments look less than unassailable, raising questions about the stability of future such income. Residential property has recently been a very good investment especially in some parts of England, but it is not certain that anything, not even houses, is a completely safe investment for the future.

## 14.2.1 Maximising the use of capital for retirement

There are various ways of maximising the use of property and capital for one's retirement and old age, but specialist professional advice is usually required. In the past annuities were popular because they were favourably treated for tax purposes. This may change as pension law changes introduced in the 2014 budget come into force and annuity income declines.

Home equity releases, where an insurance company lends a property owner money under a mortgage arrangement and is repaid from the proceeds of sale after death, may be appropriate and may be favourable for Income Tax purposes, but should be treated with great caution. They are a way for income-poor but capital-rich people to access capital, but can prove expensive. Compound interest (interest on interest owed) means the debt increases rapidly and early redemption penalties can be very severe. There is little risk attached, however, to advising elderly clients on the increased personal allowances for Income Tax after the ages of 65 and 75, or advising them to elect to take any interest from building society or bank account in gross, preventing the need to reclaim tax deducted at source.

## 14.2.2 The cost of care

The biggest potential drain on an elderly person's finances is likely to be the cost of personal care as they grow more frail. Elderly people are no longer kept in NHS hospitals unless they require medical treatment as such. Once they require only general social care, they will be returned home. Some people can rely on family to look after them, but often paid care is needed. The cost of this is very high, often considerably more than the average salary, and capable of wiping out even a substantial inheritance.

An elderly person needing paid care may be able to obtain financial assistance from the local authority, but eligibility and how much they are expected to contribute themselves will depend on how much income and capital they have. Access to state provision of residential care has been means-tested ever since the inception of the welfare state under the National Assistance Act of 1948. Local authorities and the NHS were then allocated statutory responsibilities that have always been both overlapping and complementary. Most people nowadays will be expected to pay something towards the cost of their accommodation in a care home, using their income and capital, although they may receive an NHS contribution towards their nursing costs.

Those with savings of £23,250 in England, or £23,750 in Wales (as at the time of writing), have to pay all of the fees of the care home until their savings are depleted to below that limit. However, the definition of savings for this purpose does not include the surrender value of life insurance policies, personal injury damages held in trusts and personal items that have not been bought with the deliberate intent of avoiding paying care home fees. The value of the resident's own home may be ignored if the stay in care is temporary, or where it is still occupied by one of a range of family members: otherwise, the value of the property will be taken into account, meaning that the resident will have to pay for their local authority care.

### 14.2.3 Planning for the cost of care

People may try to put themselves below the £23,250/£23,750 limit by giving property or assets away, or selling them at an undervalue. Where a significant part of the motivation of such a transaction is found to have been an attempt to avoid care charges, the National Assistance (Assessment of Resources) Regulations 1992 allow the local authority to attribute the value of the assets to the resident as 'notional capital', leading to charges being made nevertheless, and if the transfer of the assets took place within six months before the resident sought care, the transaction may be undone. The basis on which a council can decide whether the resident really was unable to pay the care home charges was discussed in *Yule v South Lanarkshire* (2000), where it was held to be

> open to a local authority to reach a view as to the purpose of a transaction such as the present, without any specific finding as to the exact state of knowledge or intention of the applicant, so long as the primary facts are such as reasonably to lead to the inference that the purpose was at least in part that specified

and further in *Beeson v Dorset County Council* (2002) where an approach to the decision-making process more favourable to the resident was taken, and upheld in the Court of Appeal. The CRAG (the Department of Health's *Charging Guide for Residential Accommodation*) says:

> It would be unreasonable to decide that a resident had disposed of an asset in order to reduce his charge for accommodation when the disposal took place at a time when he was fit and healthy and could not have foreseen the need for a move to residential accommodation.

But in *Beeson*, it appeared that an elderly person's intention to die at home could be queried by council officials in any event.

## 14.3 The development of Inheritance Tax

Taxation of a person's capital wealth is of long standing. Taxation on death means the owner does not feel the pain of it directly, and it has always been possible to avoid. The main predecessor of Inheritance Tax, Estate Duty, was in force from 1894 to 1975. It was a charge made on wealth at death and as such was a narrow fiscal tax, easy to avoid by giving away all your property before you died. When the Liberal government first introduced it, they did so with the justification that 'nature gives man no power over his earthly goods beyond the term of his life' so that the state could legitimately claim to prescribe the conditions and limitations under which the power of the dead hand to dispose of property was exercised. In later years, the duty was widened to include gifts made immediately before death, and finally to include gifts made during the last seven years before dying and most lifetime trusts.

There were proposals to change the basis of the tax on the passing on of wealth: for example, by charging it on the basis not of what the deceased passed on but on the basis of what each beneficiary received, possibly with allowances where the beneficiary was closely related to the deceased, extending the exemptions from the spouse to other family members. This process is used in other countries, such as France and Spain, and it means they are an inheritance tax as such. But this was not implemented, despite the name of the current Act. The name of 'Inheritance Tax' may appear misplaced, as it is a tax on gifts, merely including – or consisting mostly of – gifts made on death.

The introduction of the more aptly-named Capital Transfer Tax in 1975 brought in a 'cradle to grave' gifts tax, to cure the perceived deficiencies of Estate Duty and to function as a means for the redistribution of wealth. Avoidance was to be eliminated by taxing all gifts. That principle was steadily eroded in the later 1970s, and a ten-year cumulation period was introduced in 1981. Margaret Thatcher's Conservative administration elected in 1979 had promised to repeal the tax.

Inheritance Tax (IHT) was brought into operation by the spring budget of 1986. The then Chancellor of the Exchequer described the old Capital Transfer Tax as two taxes, an inheritance tax and a lifetime gifts tax. He felt that the deterrence operating on lifetime giving had the effect of locking in assets, particularly the ownership of family businesses, often to the detriment of the businesses concerned and, accordingly, he proposed to abolish entirely the tax on lifetime gifts to individuals. Others interpreted the changes differently. They were described in the *Financial Times*, referring to the Chancellor of the Exchequer, Nigel Lawson, as 'some reasons for making a shabby handout to the very rich. Not only has he reverted to the old estate duty, he has falsified the label'.[3] Since Inheritance Tax under the current Act is not confined to inheritances as this is popularly understood, but applies to lifetime gifts as well, it has been described as 'a welding of certain Estate Duty rules onto the already battered corpse of CTT ... simply a mess'.[4]

### 14.3.1 The operation of Inheritance Tax today

Although it used to produce very little revenue, the yield of IHT has risen recently, especially with the rise in property prices in the south-east of England. Net receipts in 2012–2013 were £3.1 billion; in 2013–2014 they were £3.4 billion.[5] It is estimated that they will to continue by rise by nearly 11 per cent per year, to £5.8 billion by 2018–2019.[6] Currently, about 5 per cent of estates attract IHT; the OBR expect this to rise to nearly 10 per cent. IHT has, according to James Mirrlees of the Institute of Fiscal Studies, so 'many loopholes and opportunities for avoidance' that it is 'a somewhat half-hearted tax', unfair and difficult to defend.[7] Nevertheless, the impetus to make lifetime distributions could be seen as a justification for the tax by itself, enforcing redistribution, or encouraging economic activity.

## 14.4 Basic concepts

It is useful to approach the question of the different taxes applicable in the law and practice of wills by appreciating first of all the basic structure of the tax system, the most relevant part of which in this context relates to IHT. This is a tax on the wealth the deceased parted with at death,

---

3 Cedric Sandford, *Financial Times*, 26 March 1986.

4 Natalie Lee, *Revenue Law: Principles and Practices* (32nd edn, Bloomsbury 2014) 808.

5 National Statistics, 'Inheritance Tax: Analysis of Receipts', www.gov.uk/government/uploads/system/uploads/attachment_data/file/338949/140722Table12-1DUChecked.pdf, accessed 16 February 2015.

6 Office of Budget Responsibility, *Economic and Fiscal Outlook*, March 2014.

7 James Mirrlees, Stuart Adam, Tim Besley, Richard Blundell, Steve Bond, Robert Chote, Malcolm Gammie, Paul Johnson, Gareth Myles and James Poterba, 'The Mirrlees Review: Conclusions and Recommendations for Reform' (2011) 32 Fiscal Studies 33.

with additional provisions relating to gifts made in the seven years before death and the setting up of lifetime trusts. There are also some exemptions, principally for gifts to a spouse or charity and lifetime gifts.

### 14.4.1 Gratuitous intent

IHT is charged on the value transferred in any chargeable transfer[8] where there is gratuitous intent. 'Gratuitous intent' means the intention to benefit the recipient by making some form of gift to them. Therefore, a deliberate sale at an undervalue is included – if you sell your house worth £150,000 to your friend for £50,000, then assuming you were aware of the discrepancy you are making them a gift of £100,000. A bad bargain – where you unwittingly sell your house for much less than its real value – is not.[9] In those circumstances, you will have had no gratuitous intent and there will be nothing for the HMRC to charge IHT on.

### 14.4.2 Excluded property[10]

Some property is excluded from IHT, including property situated outside the UK or involving another foreign element such as beneficial ownership by a person who is not domiciled or resident in the UK.

### 14.4.3 Exempt transfers – in life and on death

Some transfers of value are not chargeable but are exempt from the tax. Transfers between spouses, gifts to charity, gifts for national or public benefit, gifts to qualifying political parties, gifts to housing associations, gifts of shares to employee trusts and gifts of heritage property are exempt. These are the only lifetime exemptions which are reflected in the exemptions available on death.

Business Property and Agricultural Relief may be available for transfers on life and death and may reduce the amount of tax chargeable but they do not exempt the gift from IHT (14.5.7–8).

### 14.4.4 The potentially exempt transfer[11]

The potentially exempt transfer or 'PET' is the main vehicle for encouraging lifetime giving. The concept applies, with certain exceptions, to gifts made by individuals (that is, real persons, not those who are merely legal persons such as companies) to individuals after 17 March 1986. Although the gifts are called 'potentially exempt', they might in practice be better called 'potentially chargeable', as the tax is not paid and then recouped, but is assumed not to be payable unless a later event makes it so. (For details of the operation of PETs, see 14.7.)

## 14.5 Lifetime IHT on death

The rules for IHT during lifetime and on death are intertwined, because of the rules relating to PETs and relevant property trusts, and so it is necessary to appreciate the structure of the former when dealing with the latter. Some gifts made during a deceased's lifetime will have to be

---

8   S 1 IHTA 1984.
9   S 10 IHTA 1984.
10  S 6 IHTA 1984.
11  S 3A IHTA 1984.

accounted for for IHT purposes at their death, unless the gifts can be shown to fall within one of the various exemptions.

## 14.5.1 Lifetime allowances
For lifetime gifts, the IHTA 1984 has a much wider range of exemptions and allowances. There is an array of allowances which apply during a person's lifetime but which are not available on death. However, they often affect the administration of an estate and therefore need to be considered by the succession lawyer. It should be noted that allowance rates have not changed since the IHTA came in to force on 1 January 1985!

## 14.5.2 Annual allowances per donor[12]
A taxpayer is allowed to make a gift of their annual lifetime allowance of £3,000 to one individual. This can be used as an allowance on a bigger gift and can be rolled over, if not used, for one year, so that a person who makes no gifts in one year may make £6,000 worth of gifts in the following year without their being chargeable to IHT. If, however, they leaves the making of gifts until the year after that, the first year's exemption, or whatever part of it remained unused and available, will fall out of the calculation.

## 14.5.3 Annual allowances per donee[13]
The donor can give £250 to as many people as they choose, save the person they gave the £3,000 in 14.5.2.

## 14.5.4 Normal expenditure out of the donor's excess income[14]
There is a provision that regular gifts out of income are not chargeable provided they do not reduce the donor's standard of living. This has a particular application in the area of succession law; it means that the premiums paid for a life assurance policy will not usually be chargeable to IHT and the policies themselves can be written in trust and used to pay IHT on the donor's death. It also means, of course, that a person with a larger regular income effectively has a larger tax allowance just because they are richer; however, they can make use of it only if they give their money away regularly. In *Bennett and Others v CIR* (1995), careful consideration was given to what is meant by normal expenditure. It was held to be expenditure as part of a settled pattern, although there is no fixed minimum time period – payments could be once a month or once a year, with some variation as to the amount and the donee. Where there is no formal expression that the gifts are out of excess income and intended to be regular the intention may be inferred from three or possibly even two payments.

## 14.5.5 Dispositions for maintenance of family[15]
There is an exemption for lifetime dispositions for the maintenance of a spouse or civil partner, child under 18 or in full-time education, a relative incapacitated due to old age or infirmity or the donor or the donor's spouse or civil partner's parent. These dispositions do not have to be

---

12  S 19 IHTA 1984.
13  S 20 IHTA 1984.
14  S 21 IHTA 1984.
15  S 11 IHTA 1984.

out of excess income or intended to be regular, unlike the requirements under s 21 IHTA 1984 (see 14.5.4). In the case of *McKelvey v HMRC* (2008), a woman who had cancer was financially supporting her sick mother. The daughter, having given her mother two of her properties worth £169,000 to be sold to pay for the mother's nursing care, died in 2003. HMRC viewed the full amount as a PET and liable to IHT because of the daughter's death shortly after the gift. The Special Commissioner did not agree with this. He found that it was likely the mother would survive five and a half years and have nursing costs of £21,000 per year, and hence £115,500 and a contingency of £25,000 fell under the exemption for maintenance of family members. It was the sum above that, here £28,500, that was a PET.

## 14.5.6 Marriage gifts[16]

Gifts on marriage are also exempt, although certain limits apply. These differ according to the donor's relationship with the couple. Close family relationships are the most advantageous. Parents may give £5,000, other relatives £2,500 and other persons £1,000 without a charge to IHT.

## 14.5.7 Business Property Relief

Business Property Relief ('BPR') is set out in ss 103–114 IHTA 1984 and applies to gifts of business property, both lifetime transfers and on death. In its practical use, it has complex provisions equivalent to those for PETs which may operate where the transferor dies within seven years of the transfer or the transferee sells the property on or uses it for ineligible purposes.

The rationale of the relief is that a functioning business should not have to be sold and possibly destroyed by having to be sold to pay the IHT on it. BPR began in 1975 and became much more generous after 1992; the relief claimed has risen sharply and may therefore be rethought soon. BPR can be claimed by sole traders, partnerships or limited companies, on relevant business property anywhere in the world. 'Relevant' business property is defined by s 105 IHTA very broadly, including interests in the business as well as its assets. The rate of relief differs according to the nature of the property, being 50 per cent for physical assets and 100 per cent for most forms of interests in the business. The property must have been held for two years before death or, in certain circumstances, can apply to property owned during the five years before the transfer and replaced by the property owned at death; a spouse or civil partner is deemed to have owned the business property for the time their spouse or civil partner owned it.[17]

The meaning of 'business' is not set out in the legislation and can include a profession or vocation, so long as it is carried out with the intention of making a gain. The relevant factors for ascertaining whether a business is being carried out for gain are set out in *Customs and Excise Comrs v Lord Fisher* (1981), covering the manner in which the business is run and profit pursued, and its objectives in supplying customers. Even investments such as stocks and shares used as assets by underwriters at Lloyd's of London insurance market are eligible for BPR as they are used by the underwriter in their business.[18] However, businesses which consist wholly or mainly of holding or 'dealing in securities, stocks or shares, land or buildings or making or holding investments' are specifically excluded by s 105(3) of IHTA 1984. BPR could mean a saving of £400,000 in IHT on a £1 million business, so there have been many disputes as to what comes within this exclusion, particularly in relation to furnished holiday lettings and caravan parks. In *HMRC v Pawson (Deceased)* (2013), for example, the Upper Tier Tax Tribunal decided that a furnished holiday

---

16  S 22 IHTA 1984.
17  S 106–108 IHTA 1984.
18  *Hardcastle (executors of Vernede, dec'd) v IRC* (2000).

letting business did not qualify for BPR as the owners did not run the business actively enough; there were insufficient ancillary services. In *Hall v IRC* (1997), a caravan park was not eligible for BPR as most of the income was mainly from rents and standing charges but in *Furness v IRC* (1999) the business made more money from sales of caravans than rents. The boundaries of BPR eligibility remain unclear and HMRC routinely treats such cases as problematic.

## 14.5.8 Agricultural Property Relief

Agricultural Property Relief ('APR') is the equivalent of BPR, but designed to prevent the need to sell a family farm. The relief under ss 115–124 IHTA 1984 reduces the amount of tax payable on a broad range of agricultural property anywhere in the EU. However, if agricultural buildings or houses are of a disproportionate size to the farm and so not ancillary to the farm, or are not used for agricultural purposes, they will be excluded.

Claims for APR run high and are often disputed by HMRC: they rose from £195 million in 2008/2009 to £370 million in 2012/2013. Disputes have included what is meant by a 'farmhouse' and what is a proportionately-sized building.[19] APR may reduce the tax payable by treating the land at its agricultural value. The house must be used in the business, which means the farm office should be in it. The relief will not exempt the estate from tax but may reduce the value in light of the agricultural value, being the 'value which would be the value of the property if the property were subject to a perpetual covenant prohibiting its use other than as agricultural property', which would be lower than land available for other purposes.[20]

In *Lloyds TSB (Antrobus Deceased) v Inland Revenue* (2002), Special Commissioner Brice considered Cookhill Priority in Alcester, Wiltshire, an old house with perhaps 125 acres of land which Miss Antrobus and her family had farmed for many decades. Dr Brice identified the test as whether Miss Antrobus' farmhouse was 'of a character appropriate to the property', which in turn was a test based on ordinary ideas of the appropriate size, content and layout of a farm, looking at the farm buildings and the area of farmland. Against the background of a discussion of the considerable history of the house and Miss Antrobus' accounts of her stock and crops, Dr Brice considered the layout and buildings of the property and concluded that 'the man or woman on the rural omnibus' and 'the educated rural layman' would regard the house as 'a farmhouse with a farm and definitely not a house with land'.

As with BPR, the rate of APR varies, here depending on the right to possession or whether the land is subject to tenancies. Availability of the relief depends on occupation of the land for agricultural purposes for a period between two and seven years before the transfer; spouses and civil partners are deemed to be included.[21] Where 100 per cent relief cannot be claimed, HMRC may allow relief at 50 per cent. Again as with BPR, there are complex provisions equivalent to PETs for IHT.

## 14.5.9 Chargeable lifetime transfers

A chargeable lifetime transfer will usually arise where an individual has established a trust. However, it can arise in other circumstances where a PET would not apply, such as where a grandparent pays school fees for a grandchild: the grandparent's estate decreases but the

---

19  IHTM 24052 – *Character appropriate: How are the factors to be balanced:*

   caseworkers should ask the parties to send in any photographs of the farmhouse that exist. The point of getting any available photographs is to see if the property passes the 'elephant test' that is, does it look like a farmhouse?

20  S 115(3) IHTA 1984.
21  S 120(1) IHTA 1984.

grandchild's assets do not increase. In such a case there may however be an exemption which applies, such as that for regular payments from excess income (see 14.5.4).

## 14.6  Exemptions on death

On death the exemptions are for gifts to spouse, charity, political parties or for the national or public benefit only. Thereafter the estate is chargeable. The estate below the nil-rate band, currently £325,000 (from 2009), is taxed at 0 per cent and the rest at 40 per cent. Some or all of the nil-rate band may be used up if any PETs or chargeable lifetime transfers have not fallen out of the donor's estate. This occurs when the deceased dies within seven years of making a lifetime gift or chargeable lifetime transfer.

## 14.7  Potentially exempt transfers (PETs) – s 3A(1) of the IHTA 1984

PETs were brought into force by the Finance Act 1986 and refer to lifetime gifts to individuals only. If a gift is a PET, no tax is payable at the time of the gift. If the donor manages to live for seven years after the date of the gift, the gift falls out of the calculations entirely. In between, there is a sliding scale relief so that if the donor lives for three years after the gift, the amount of tax payable is reduced by 20 per cent per year, until the full relief is reached at seven years. This relief is known as 'taper relief'.

### 14.7.1  PETs and personal representatives

PETs can present a great problem to personal representatives dealing with an estate. To assess the charge on the estate to Inheritance Tax, they need full details of all the PETS the deceased made during their last seven years (for payment accruing on his or her death) and the seven years before that (because of the potential debt to HMRC), of which they may or may not have kept accessible records.

Although the donee is primarily liable to pay the tax on the gift, if the tax remains unpaid a year after the testator's death, the HMRC may look to the personal representatives for payment of the outstanding sum. Personal representatives are personally liable for the payment of IHT, so getting the figures wrong, even if that is because of the deceased's failure to keep clear or detailed figures, can have deeply adverse consequences for them. The personal representatives have no statutory right of recovery against the donees, unlike in the case of gifts with reservation of benefits and lifetime transfers. In a letter to the Law Society in 1991 HMRC said that it would not normally pursue personal representatives for the 'PET' IHT if they had made full enquiries to discover the deceased's life transfers and done all they could to disclose these to HMRC and then obtained a certificate of discharge and distributed the estate before the relevant chargeable transfer came to light.[22]

### 14.7.2  Advantages of PETs: taper relief[23]

If the donor fails to survive the requisite seven years after making the PET it becomes chargeable to IHT. There is a sliding scale for the rate of tax payable. If the donor lives for three years after

---

22  The Law Society Gazette, 13 March 1991, 17.
23   S 7(4) IHTA 1984.

making the gift the tax reduces by 20 per cent per year to year 7. The effective rate of tax in year 3–4 is therefore 32 per cent, and it reduces each year. Often taper relief is of no benefit as the gifts made by the donor are below the nil-rate band.

PETs are therefore lifetime gifts that may potentially become free of tax. In times of higher inflation or when assets are rapidly increasing in value, they also had the considerable advantage of freezing the value of the asset chargeable to tax at the value at the date of the gift, rather than the date of death. Section 131 of the IHTA 1984 contains provisions for relief of the liability to tax if the subject matter of a PET has fallen in value by date of death.

# 14.8 Settlements for IHT

Settlements, or putting assets into a trust, have always been a way of avoiding tax or otherwise keeping those assets from falling into unwanted hands. Settlements for IHT purposes are defined in s 43(2) of the IHTA 1984. They may be settlements with interests in possession, where a beneficiary has an entitlement under the trust, or those without an interest in possession, namely discretionary trusts. Until recently, these were taxed differently.

## 14.8.1 Settlements and IHT before March 2006

Before 22 March 2006, notably different rules applied to interest-in-possession trusts, accumulation and maintenance settlements, and relevant property trusts.

Where a beneficiary had an interest in possession under a trust, creation of the trust, or a gift into the trust, was treated as a PET. If the settlor survived for seven years, no IHT would be payable. The beneficiary's own estate would be increased, however. Settlements by a settlor on him- or herself did not give rise to a change of entitlement and so were not taxable. If assets were put in to an interest-in-possession trust before 22 March 2006, it is not a relevant property trust provided no further assets are put in after that date. During the life of the trust there is no Inheritance Tax to pay as long as the asset stays in the trust and remains the 'interest' of the beneficiary, although it will fall into their estate on their death.

Accumulation and maintenance settlements (A&M trusts) were governed by s 71 of the IHTA 1984. A person under 25 had to be entitled to the income or capital; there could be no interests in possession; the income had to be applied only for the maintenance, education or benefit of a beneficiary, or else accumulated; and the trust had to last no more than 25 years unless all the beneficiaries were related as prescribed in the Act. A&M trusts could be discretionary, but if there was an overriding power to appoint to a person over the age of 25, it was not an A&M trust and did not have the tax advantages of one.

Relevant property trusts, including discretionary trusts, were subject to the 20 per cent lifetime rate when they were set up and, if the settlor died within seven years, became subject to further IHT.

## 14.8.2 Changes of 2006

In the Finance Act of 2006 the government introduced sweeping changes to the way settlements were to be taxed for IHT. Since 22 March 2006 both interest in possession and discretionary trusts are subject to IHT at the lifetime rate when they are set up. This is half the IHT rate, at 20 per cent, payable on assets above the available nil-rate band when they are transferred into the trust. If the settlor then dies within seven years, further IHT is payable.

### 14.8.3 Post-22 March 2006 settlements

The principal change, and it is a disadvantageous one to the taxpayer, to the tax implications of setting up a relevant property trust is that the settlor incurs an immediate IHT charge (if the value of the settlement exceeds their cumulative nil-rate band). Before 22 March 2006 the settlor would make a potentially exempt transfer (PET) on establishing an interest-in-possession trust or accumulation and maintenance settlement. A further drawback to the relevant property trust is that there are ongoing IHT charges throughout the life of the trust – when property leaves the trust and at ten-year anniversaries – although these charges are at reduced proportionate rates. Conversely, there are no charges on the death of a beneficiary.

The exceptions to the usual rules for relevant property trusts, besides pre-2006 trusts and some transitional arrangements, are where assets go into a trust under a will or intestacy, are set aside for a disabled person or bereaved minor, or put into trusts for persons aged 18–25.

### 14.8.4 Bereaved Minors Will Trust and 18–25 trusts

The Finance Act 2006 amended s 71 of the Inheritance Tax Act 1984. New trusts created for people under the age of 25 no longer enjoy the favourable IHT treatment of the old accumulation and maintenance trusts. Any lifetime trusts created for children will fall into the relevant property regime, unless the beneficiary is disabled.

The new s 71A established bereaved minor's trusts, which arise when a minor child inherits on the death of a parent and will become absolutely entitled to both capital and income at the age of 18. Whilst the child is under 18, the trustees have discretion over the accumulation of income and the application of funds for the minor's benefit. IHT is not charged on a bereaved minor's trust when property is transferred out of the trust, nor if the child were to die under the age of 18, nor when they becomes entitled to the trust capital at 18.

Section 71D established bereaved 18–25 trusts. These arise when a child under the age of 25 inherits on the death of a parent and will become absolutely entitled to both capital and income by the age of 25. The trust is not subject to IHT whilst the beneficiary is under 18. When the child reaches 18, the trust moves into the relevant property regime. Exit charges are applied on a proportionate scale when property is transferred out.

### 14.8.5 Settlements with an interest in possession

A beneficiary with an interest in possession is treated by virtue of s 49(1) of the IHTA 1984 as beneficially entitled to the property in which the interest subsists. They will be considered to have an interest in possession if they have an immediate right to use the property, for example to live in a house, or to receive the income arising from it, for example the rent paid for the house by the tenants. The lifetime creation of, or a gift into, a settlement of this kind is immediately chargeable and cannot be a PET. Moreover, the effects of giving someone a life interest in possession include the swelling of their estate, for IHT purposes, by the capital value of the gift. The creation of such a gift in a will or under an intestacy will be an immediate post death interest (see 14.8.6).

Thus, where a settlor creates a lifetime settlement under which a beneficiary is given a life interest in a house worth £400,000, the settlor makes an immediately chargeable gift of £400,000 and the beneficiary at once has the likelihood of dying with an estate substantially chargeable to IHT even if they are otherwise of very modest means.

Note, however, that under s 55(1) of the IHTA 1984 if the settlor settles the property on him- or herself for life, that particular part of the transaction does not give rise to a charge to tax. The charge to tax arises only where there is a change of interest in possession, so the same applies where a remainderman surrenders their interest to a life tenant.

## 14.8.6 Immediate post death interest

Since 22 March 2006, if a beneficiary acquires an interest in possession in a settlement arising on the settlor's death either under a will or an intestacy, the assets are not regarded as 'relevant property'. The beneficiary will continue to be treated according to the old rules for interest-in-possession trusts. This means that there is no charge to IHT on a ten-year anniversary, and there will be no IHT to pay as long as the asset stays in the trust and remains the 'interest' of the beneficiary. This is called an immediate post death interest. However, the asset may give rise to a charge to IHT on the death of the beneficiary, as part of their estate.

## 14.8.7 Trusts for disabled beneficiaries and Inheritance Tax[24]

A disabled trust is set up for someone with a mental or physical disability. These are one of the few trusts which are not relevant property and can be set up during a lifetime or on death. Under the original s 89 of the IHTA 1984 there was only one such trust: a discretionary trust. The Finance Act 2006 introduced s 89A, which allowed persons to settle property on themselves if they can show they have a condition which makes it likely they will eventually qualify under s 89. It also brought in s 89B, allowing a life interest disabled trust. In the case of a discretionary trust, there must be a named disabled beneficiary, and there are restrictions on funds that can be paid for the benefit of anybody else. Under new rules introduced in s 216 of the Finance Act 2013 from 17 July 2013, only 3 per cent of the trust fund or £3,000 in any given year, whichever is the lower, may be paid out of a discretionary trust for the benefit of someone other than the disabled beneficiaries, and life interest trusts have the same restrictions. In the case of a life interest trust, the life tenant needs to be the disabled person. There are no ten-yearly charges and exit charges do not apply if the asset stays in the trust and remains the 'interest' of the beneficiary. A disabled trust can be a PET if the settlor survives for seven years after making the transfer.

## 14.8.8 Settlements without an interest in possession – discretionary trusts

If no one has an immediate right to use or obtain income from the property in the settlement, as where all the payments out of the fund are made at the discretion of the trustees, it will be a settlement without an interest in possession. In *Pearson v Inland Revenue Commissioners* (1980), the trust fund was held for three adult beneficiaries, who were each to get one-third of the income unless the trustees exercised their power to accumulate the income or their power of appointment. The House of Lords, by a whisker, held that there was no interest in possession.

Discretionary trusts were once a good way of avoiding estate duty, but the system has been modified so that tax is chargeable. The fund is charged to tax at a rate that works out at 6 per cent every ten years, or more if the settlor dies within seven years of making the settlement. The settlor may fall foul of the rules relating to reservation of benefit unless they have been excluded from the trust for the seven years before death. Discretionary trusts may be used to maintain flexibility, controlling young and improvident beneficiaries, protecting beneficiaries against creditors, or protecting beneficiaries from care home fees and loss of means-tested benefits.

---

24  Ss 89, 89A and 89B IHTA 1984, as amended by the Finance Act 2006.

## 14.8.9 Appointment from a discretionary trust within two years of death[25]

Where a testator leaves any amount of property to trustees who have the widest possible class of beneficiaries amongst whom to exercise their powers of appointment, there will be no charge to tax on the making of distributions ('exit charge') within two years by virtue of s 144 of the IHTA 1984. The testator may leave the nil-rate band (see 14.8.10) or the whole of their estate this way, giving their trustees secret instructions which are not admissible to probate.

If appointed to a spouse or civil partner, the funds should not be appointed until at least three months after the creation of the trust, so that IHT can be reclaimed. There is an elephant trap in the wording of s 144: reading back into the will only happens if the event is one 'on which tax would be chargeable'. No IHT is chargeable on an absolute appointment in the first three months after death from a discretionary trust – the charge arises on full quarter years. In *Frankland v IRC* (1997), significant assets were appointed to the spouse within three months; the spouse exemption was not available. This problem does not arise where the appointment is of an immediate post death interest in favour of the spouse or civil partner.

## 14.8.10 Using the nil-rate band

Each estate has a nil-rate band of the first £325,000 in the estate, on which IHT is charged at 0 per cent. Since 2007, the nil-rate band has been transferable between spouses and civil partners, so a person's nil-rate band is not lost if they leave everything to their spouse, as they can leave the nil-rate band as well.

Before 2007, a very popular use of the discretionary trust by a married person was to pay the nil-rate band into it and leave the rest to the spouse, who could also be one of the beneficiaries under the discretionary trust, as a well as a trustee. This worked well in most estates, meaning no IHT was payable, because but the discretionary trust would mean that assets up to the value of the nil-rate band would not fall into the spouse's estate liable to IHT on her subsequent death (the accumulation of the assets in the estate of the second to die, and the consequent adverse tax implications, were known as 'bunching'). The spouse would also be able to use the assets in the nil-rate band if he or she needed them, but otherwise they could be used for other beneficiaries such as the testator's children. Gifts to the spouse during their lifetime did not attract tax, and the balance held for and paid out to the other beneficiaries after the surviving spouse's death were also not taxable if it was distributed within ten years. It would be particularly advantageous for the testator to leave their severed share in the matrimonial home into the discretionary trust; the surviving spouse could continue to occupy by virtue of his or her own joint interest in the house whilst retaining the advantages of the deceased's severed share. It meant that the testator did not leave the property outright to the next generation, protecting the surviving spouse's home from the children's bankruptcies, divorces and bad temper.

Discretionary trusts such as this are still used in wills for a variety of reasons, particularly if the couple are in a second marriage with children from a previous relationship, or one of the couple has been previously widowed and has an extra nil-rate band. There is, however, now no need to use a discretionary trust in this way if the sole reason is to not waste the first to die's nil-rate band. A discretionary trust can be cumbersome and expensive to run and many wish their spouse to have the property outright. Nevertheless, if there is still a risk of 'bunching', because the couple's estate is likely to be greater than two nil-rate bands on the death of the second to die, this may still be a useful avoidance technique.

---

25 S 144 IHTA 1984.

## 14.9 Gifts with a reservation[26]

A donor retaining a benefit in a 'gift' they have given away is treated for IHT purposes as still owning the gift, and as giving it away on their death. Such a benefit would arise, for example, where a house-owner settled their house on him- or herself for life with remainder to their children or gave the house to children whilst continuing to live there rent free. If there were no rules about gifts with reservations, this would be a good way of avoiding IHT on the value of your house without having to move.

In *Chick v Commissioner of Stamp Duties* (1958), Viscount Simonds said that where the donor had settled his property and then acquired some enjoyment of it which did not arise from an exchange related to the settlement, the question was not whether or not the non-exchange was advantageous to the donee. The relevant question was the exclusion of the donor.

For there to be a gift without a reservation of benefit the donor has to be excluded or virtually excluded from benefit of the gift property. HMRC gives some examples of what it will consider de minimis and so not to lead to liability to IHT: if you give away your library you can use it not more than five times a year; if you give away your house, you can stay in it in the absence of the donee for up to two weeks a year or for up to a month if the donee is in the property; and you can accept up to three lifts a month from someone you gave your car to.[27]

In *Buzzoni and Others v Revenue and Customs Comrs* (2013) Mrs Kamhi granted a rent-free underlease to a trust for her sons. Both the First-tier Tribunal and the Upper Tribunal considered the gift to be one with reservation since the underlease and its covenants effectively relieved the donor of the burden of the headlease covenants; therefore, the gift was not enjoyed to the entire exclusion, or virtually to the entire exclusion, of the donor and of any benefit to her by contract or otherwise and was therefore a gift with reservation within the second limb of the definition in s 102(1)(b). However, the Court of Appeal found that the second limb did not apply as the underlessees did not suffer a detriment by signing the underlease (and did not therefore benefit the donor) as they had already signed a licence with the landlord to comply with the covenants so any agreement they made with the lessee (i.e. the donor) did not affect the status of the gift.

### 14.9.1 Gifts with reservation of benefit: concession for the infirm

A house-owner who gives their house to a relative with the genuine expectation that they will not in future have any benefit from the house may, however, invoke a statutory concession if they needs to be cared for because they have become too infirm or aged to look after him- or herself. By Sch 20, para 6(1) of the Finance Act 1986, they may return to the house for that purpose without incurring IHT penalties relating to the reservation of benefit.

### 14.9.2 Gifts with reservation of benefit: incidence of tax liability

Under s 199 IHTA 1984 the donee is primarily liable for the tax payable on a gift with a reservation. If, however, the sum is not paid by the donee, HMRC may claim it from the personal representatives, who in turn may invoke s 204(9) of the IHTA 1984 to reclaim the tax from the donee.

---

26  Finance Act 1986, s 102 and Sch 20.
27  HMRC IHTM 14333 *Lifetime Transfers: Gifts with Reservation (GWRs): The Reservation: Exclusion of the Donor*, www.hmrc.gov.uk/manuals/ihtmanual/IHTM14333.htm, accessed 16 February 2015.

## 14.10 Pre-owned asset tax ('POAT')

The Finance Act 2004 introduced an income tax charge from 6 April 2005 on any benefit enjoyed where capital assets have been removed from the individual's estate for IHT purposes but they effectively still enjoy the benefits of ownership. Income Tax is chargeable on the benefit received by the continuing use of any asset that has been given away after 17 March 1986 but only to the extent that it is not already caught under the gift with reservation of benefit rules. It is a retroactive tax, but never overlaps with IHT: there is no double charge. The POAT may be charged on land, chattels or intangible property such as goodwill. The basis for the charging is the benefit the donor enjoys from the use of the property they once owned, or helped others to obtain, or their deemed power to benefit from intangible property in certain settlements in which they are is interested. The actual charges are determined by reference to detailed computational rules contained in the legislation.

## 14.11 Related property and associated operations

A further possible tax avoidance scheme is rendered inoperative by s 161 of the IHTA 1984. This rule applies mainly in respect of spouses, where, for example, a husband is making a gift to a third party and also makes a gift to his wife which she then passes to the third party. In the light of the exemption from IHT of gifts to spouses and the tax allowances existing per donor, this could give an unmerited tax advantage on what is essentially a gift from the husband to the third party. However, the rules of related property would mean that the value of the first gift should be added to the value of the related property and tax charged on the first gift as a proportion of the total value. This cannot therefore be used to avoid lifetime IHT and attempts to do so will inevitably affect the liabilities of the estate.

However, where items of property are concerned which are much more valuable as a group than they are as the total of separate items, and the property can be split up so that the value of it diminished, the rules may be avoided. For example, if the husband owned a collection of six antique chairs worth £25,000 together but £2,000 each individually, and he gave four to his wife, keeping the other two which he gave to the third party, the principle would not apply to the transfer to the third party of the second four because the husband no longer owned related property.

Associated operations arise where the transferor takes several steps which, taken separately, do not constitute a transfer of value but which, taken together, amount to the same result in terms of depleting the transferor's estate as if the property had simply been given direct. The HMRC may view these operations together, charging tax on the whole under s 268 of the IHTA 1984. Again, this may affect the liability to lifetime IHT and thus the liabilities of the estate.

## 14.12 Life assurance policies

A gift by will of the benefit of a life assurance policy will be chargeable to IHT if the donee is not the deceased's spouse or civil partner. If the donor's nil-rate band is already used up, the donor will therefore be increasing the liability of their estate to tax by 40 per cent of the value of the proceeds of the policy.

However, there is a real saving to tax if the policy proceeds go straight to a chargeable person without going into the deceased's estate by the policy having been written in trust for or assigned to that person. The premiums paid would be lifetime gifts but would probably fall within the exemption provisions relating to regular payments out of income.

Where a policy is assigned later, after being taken out, the chargeable value of the gift is the value of the policy when it is assigned. For IHT purposes that will be the higher sum of either the surrender value of the policy or the sum of the premiums paid.

# 14.13 Death

Death is the final transfer. Gratuitous intent is inferred and the estate of the deceased is treated as though the deceased had made a gift of all the property in their estate immediately before death.

## 14.13.1 What IHT is charged on at death

The liability to IHT is assessed therefore at the deceased's net wealth on the date of death. The personal representatives will need to know about any PETs made within the preceding seven years as well as any lifetime chargeable transfers before they can assess the amount of tax they need to reserve. Although donees of PETs are primarily liable to pay the tax on their gifts, for example, if they do not do so, the personal representatives may have to bear it.

Lifetime chargeable transfers will have been assessed to IHT at the lifetime rate (20 per cent) assessed by cumulating the total of all the transfers, including the one in question, over the previous seven years. Liability to IHT is then reassessed on death on all the rechargeable transfers, including PETs which have thus become chargeable, made within seven years of the date of death. The donor is primarily liable for the IHT on lifetime chargeable transfers, although the HMRC may recover from others, including the donee.

The value of the chargeable transfers made during the seven-year period will be cumulated and the total deducted from the nil-rate band on death. Credit is given for payments made but refunds are not given. Taper relief on PETs must be allowed for. Gifts under the tax threshold may, by using up the nil-rate band, increase the rate of tax payable on the deceased's estate as a whole on death.

The full percentage rate of IHT, currently 40 per cent, is chargeable on the value of all assets once any exempt gifts (to spouse or charity, for example) have been deducted and the nil-rate band at date of death has been used up.

## 14.13.2 The net estate on death

IHT is charged on the net estate on death. Where the deceased was domiciled in the UK, tax is charged on all their estate wherever it is situated; otherwise, it is charged only on property situated in the UK.

The 'estate' means all the property to which the deceased was beneficially entitled – that is, excluding property of which they were a trustee or administrator (s 5 of the IHTA 1984).

It includes:

(a)    property subject to a reservation;
(b)    non-deductible debts;
(c)    settled property of which he was a life tenant;
(d)    equitable joint tenancies;
(e)    *donationes mortis causa.*

It does not include specifically excluded property, such as foreign property owned by foreign domiciliaries and reversionary interests under a trust. Nor will it include property which does not form part of the estate, such as life policies where the benefits go straight to another person under s 11 of the Married Women's Property Act 1882 or because they are written in trust.

# 14.14 *Commorientes* and survivorship

The *commorientes* rule is contained in s 184 of the Law of Property Act 1925 and applies whether the deceased died leaving a will or intestate save for the exception below. It states that where two people die in circumstances where it is uncertain who died first, it is presumed that the elder died before the younger. The exception was set out in s 46(3) of the Administration of Estates Act 1925 and applied to intestate spouses and civil partners. This section stated that, where a couple, married or in civil partnership, die in circumstances where it was unclear who died first, *commorientes* did not apply and they were deemed to have not survived each other. If an intestate married couple, A (the older) and B (the younger), died at the same time leaving no children but each leaving a mother, A's mother would take A's free estate and B's mother would take B's free estate, but jointly-held assets would pass to B's mother. This exception was ended by ITPA 2014.

Additionally, s 46(2A) Administration of Estates Act 1925 applies when the intestate's spouse or civil partner survived the intestate but died before the end of the period of 28 days beginning with the day on which the intestate died. It is as if the spouse had not survived the intestate.

## 14.14.1 IHTA, s 4(2), ousting LPA 1925, s 184

Purely for the purposes of IHT, when a *commorientes* situation arises, death will be presumed to have occurred at the same instant. This means that the same property cannot be taxed twice because it passes out of both estates attracting tax each time. The interaction of the *commorientes* rule and the IHT rule can have IHT advantages for spouses and civil partners, but these may be lost if the effect of the *commorientes* rule is replaced by an express survivorship clause in the will.

## 14.14.2 Quick succession relief[28]

This is available where IHT is charged on a gift and the donee dies within five years, on a tapering basis of 20 per cent per year. The tax on the estate is calculated and then the appropriate percentage is deducted from the tax paid on the gift to the donee. This relief is available whether or not the donee still has the gift when they die. Rebates are available where the donee dies before the donor, who then dies within seven years of the original gift, if it was a PET.

# 14.15 Capital Gains Tax

Capital Gains Tax (CGT) was introduced by the Capital Gains Tax Act 1965, on the basis that there was no good reason why earned income should be subject to tax whereas the sums made by the sale of items of property should not. All the legislation is now consolidated in the Taxation of Chargeable Gains Act (TCGA) 1992.

## 14.15.1 Basics of assessment for Capital Gains Tax

A liability to CGT arises when a person ordinarily resident in the UK, or that person's personal representatives, effectively makes a profit on selling assets acquired at a lower price than the price at which they sell them. Assets do not include options, debts, foreign currency or property created by the owner without acquisition, for example goodwill. The tax is assessed on the

---

28  S 141 IHTA 1984.

difference between the two prices, save that acquisition is deemed to have taken place no earlier than 31 March 1982. Assets are all chargeable with a few exceptions such as sterling and motor cars, and in *Revenue and Customs Commissioners v Executors of Lord Howard of Henderskelfe (deceased)* (2014), Sir Joshua Reynolds' painting of Omai, which sold for £9.4 million, was classed as 'plant' for the purposes of s 44 of the Taxation of Chargeable Gains Act 1992. This was because it was on exhibition at the deceased's house Castle Howard, which was run as a limited company and open to the public. No CGT was payable on the sale, therefore, despite its significant gain in value.

There is an indexation allowance to deal with gains solely due to inflation, though this does not operate for periods after April 1998, and allowance for depreciation may be made in respect of wasting assets (those with a predicted useful life under 50 years).

## 14.15.2 Practical points
As with earned income, a person may make a certain amount before their profits become subject to the imposition of the tax. It is possible to incur a' 'capital gains tax loss' on one disposal and set it off against capital gains in the same year or future years.

Capital Gains Tax does not apply to the profits made from businesses trading in goods at a profit; such profits are regarded as income of their businesses and taxed under the rules for income tax or corporation tax. Transactions between connected persons are deemed not to be at open market value.[29] Individuals are connected to their spouses or civil partners and their own and their spouse's or civil partner's relatives; trustees and settlors are also connected to each other. However, husbands and wives living together may transfer between each other on a no gain, no loss basis.[30] Joint property is held in proportion to the beneficial interests in it.

## 14.15.3 CGT and personal representatives
The only liability to CGT that will arrive in the hands of the personal representatives at the beginning of the administration is any liability the deceased incurred during his or her lifetime: for example, where the deceased sold some antique furniture for a capital gain of £40,000 before their death, making a chargeable gain not covered by their allowance, and the tax had not been paid. Where they kept the furniture, thus swelling their estate by the gain of £40,000, no CGT will be payable on that gain. This is because there is an 'automatic uplift on death' for CGT in s 62 of the TCGA 1992.

## 14.15.4 Dates for calculations as to CGT liability
The result is that, when the deceased is deemed to dispose of all their property on death, the value at which they dispose of it and at which the property falls into the estate is taken to be the value at the date of death. The estate is taken to have acquired the property at the death value for Capital Gains Tax purposes, and any increase in value since the deceased obtained it is ignored. If the deceased had realised a profit from the increased value of a piece of property before death, by selling it, that realisation would have incurred a liability to CGT. If, however, the property remained unsold at death and the profit remained latent, that profit would be lost to the HMRC for CGT purposes. From the beneficiaries' point of view, this 'CGT uplift on death' can be very advantageous indeed.

---

29  S 18 TCGA 1992.
30  S 58 TCGA 1992.

## 14.16 Interaction with Inheritance Tax

Obviously, however, the item would also carry its higher valuation for Inheritance Tax purposes, so the encouragement to keep property in the estate rather than realising it, for CGT purposes, would have to be offset against the encouragement built into the inheritance tax system to dispose of the property sufficiently long before death to take advantage of the system of PETs.

## 14.17 Liability of the estate to CGT

Capital Gains Tax is chargeable to an estate when the estate disposes of the property, and is charged on the difference between the value of property at the date of death ('probate value') and the value when it is realised for the estate.

The estate incurs a liability to CGT if it sells assets at a higher price than the probate value. The expenses of sale, including any expenses of valuation attributable to the item, can be set off against the gain.[31] The difference between the probate value and the sale price after deduction of expenses will be a chargeable gain.

### 14.17.1 Allowances against CGT

Personal representatives may make a certain amount of chargeable gains in the earlier part of the administration of the estate without having to pay CGT on them. They may set off against the chargeable gains made by the estate an allowance (£11,100 from 6 April 2015), for the three years including and following the year of death.[32] This figure represents the same level of exemption as is granted to an individual.

### 14.17.2 When property is transferred in specie to a beneficiary

Where the personal representatives transfer an item of property to a beneficiary, rather than realising it by sale, the value at which the beneficiary receives it for Capital Gains Tax purposes is the probate value because they are deemed to have received the property at the date of the deceased's death. If the value of the property is rising rapidly, and the property is transferred at the end of the executor's year, the beneficiary may therefore receive an item carrying a substantial liability to CGT. If, however, the beneficiaries become entitled not as legatees but as against trustees, there is a deemed disposal for CGT purposes and tax may be chargeable.

## 14.18 Valuation of the estate

In order to arrive at the amount of Inheritance Tax payable on the estate, which must be paid in order to obtain a grant of representation, the personal representatives must first ascertain what property is in the estate and then must value each item. The value of any item of property is, essentially, what it would have fetched in the open market immediately before death. Often there is no intention of selling an item in the estate, but only of passing it on to the named beneficiary, but it must still be valued.

---

31 *Commissioners of the Inland Revenue v Richards* (1971).
32 S 3(7) Taxation of Chargeable Gains Act 1992.

## 14.18.1 Valuation is a first step in administration

Although executors can deal with property before a grant of probate is issued to them, they often will not do so, and they may in any case wish to do something for which a grant has to be produced, such as make title to property. Administrators have no power to act at all before the grant of letters of administration is issued to them.

In order to obtain the grant, the personal representatives, of whatever kind, have to submit to the probate registry some form of declaration or receipt to show that Inheritance Tax is not payable or has been paid. Where the estate is under the nil-rate band, passing to a spouse or civil partner and under £1 million, or where the estate can claim a former spouse or civil partner's full transferable nil-rate band and is under the two nil-rate bands, the personal representatives can submit an IHT205 excepted estate form (and an IHT217 if claiming the transferable nil-rate band) when they apply for the grant of representation. For estates which are not excepted, the longer IHT400 and accompanying forms must be completed and submitted to HMRC with the amount payable for Inheritance Tax before an application can be made for a grant. HMRC return a receipted probate summary schedule. This means that valuing the estate is one of the first things the personal representatives have to do.

It is also quite possible that the personal representatives' first estimate of the amount of IHT payable will turn out to be wrong, if, for example, the deceased turns out to have had property which the personal representatives discover only later. Where this happens, the personal representatives must submit a corrective account to HMRC and have the IHT adjusted accordingly.

## 14.18.2 Shares and other arguable items

The valuation of shares is incontrovertible only for listed shares, for which a system of precise valuation is prescribed. The figure is one-quarter up between the two prices given in the Stock Exchange Daily Official List.[33] The valuation of expensive individual items, such as pieces of antique furniture or jewellery, is also an art rather than a precise science.

A low valuation will be desirable if the main liability of the estate will be to IHT. However, a high valuation may be better for liability to CGT, since, in that context, any liability to tax arises from an asset passing out of the estate at a higher value than when it fell in. The valuation must be the same for both taxes.

## 14.18.3 Value altering after death (ss 178 and 190 IHTA 1984)

The valuation of some things may be altered after death. The legislation allows only the value of related property sold within three years, quoted shares sold within one year and land sold within four years to be read back into the probate valuation (ss 177, 178 and 190 of the IHTA 1984). Again, the valuation must be the same for IHT and CGT.

## 14.18.4 Deductions against tax

Reasonable funeral expenses may be deducted. If certain property is sold shortly after death (related property or land within three years, quoted shares within one year), a corrective account may be submitted to the HMRC and a refund on the IHT paid on the original probate value obtained.

Debts are deductible only if they were incurred for money or money's worth; the rules are designed to restrict avoidance of tax by the creation of artificial debts. The somewhat

---

33  S 272 Inheritance Tax Act 1984.

controversial s 176 of the Finance Act 2013 prevents the deduction of debts incurred after 6 April 2013 in order to purchase IHT-exempt assets, and of debts that the executors do not pay off after the testator's death.

### 14.18.5 Exemptions

The net estate may be fully exempt for Inheritance Tax purposes (if going to a spouse or charity for example) or fully taxable (if going to anyone else). It may, however, commonly be partly exempt and partly taxable. The distinction should be carefully drawn between a gift which is exempt and one which is taxable but on which no tax is payable because the taxable estate is worth less than the nil-rate band.

That difference is between the property not being chargeable to tax and its being chargeable, but at the nil-rate of 0 per cent. Until that basic difference is appreciated, it is not possible to see how or even whether the estate will be liable to IHT in practice or how to minimise or avoid that liability. (It should also be noted again that such individual exemptions as that allowing a testator to give away £3,000 per year free of IHT are not available on death.)

There are no exemptions for Capital Gains Tax beyond the allowances for the first three tax years of the estate and the principal private residence exemption of the deceased's residence was the main residence of at least one of the beneficiaries both immediately before and immediately after the deceased's death, and one or more of those beneficiaries are together entitled to at least 75 per cent of the proceeds of sale of the property.

## 14.19 Liability, burden and payment of IHT

It is important to know not only what IHT is payable but also who has to pay it, and when. If the recipient of a lifetime gift are to pay the IHT on it, then that fact has implications for the calculation of tax payable out of the estate.

### 14.19.1 Lifetime gifts

The donees of potentially exempt transfers are primarily liable if the donor dies within seven years of making the PETs. However, if they have not paid the requisite tax within 12 months of the date of death, the deceased's personal representatives will be liable to pay it. Of course, this leaves them open to some risk since by the time they discover the liability, they may have distributed the property in the estate. Unfortunately, that is no defence against the demands of HMRC and the personal representatives will be liable for the tax, personally if there is not enough remaining in the estate. However, in a letter to the Law Society in 1991 HMRC said that it would not normally pursue personal representatives for the 'PET' IHT if they had made appropriate efforts to ascertain whether any chargeable lifetime gifts had been made (14.7.1).

### 14.19.2 What property is considered a gift on death for IHT purposes?

Where a liability to Inheritance Tax arises on the death of the donor, there are three possible funds from which the tax may be payable:

(a)    'free estate';
(b)    donee of property subject to retention of benefit;
(c)    trustees of settled property.

The free estate is that owned absolutely by the deceased. The tax is usually paid by the personal representatives out of the free estate. Where property was included in the estate although the deceased had apparently given it away during their lifetime, because it was subject to a retention of benefit, the IHT on that gift will be payable by the donee. The ordinary personal representatives run no risks in respect of settled property, the liability for paying the tax falling on the trustees of the settlement.

### 14.19.3  Time for payment of tax

Interest is payable on tax not paid by six months from the end of the month after the deceased's death, whether or not it has actually been calculated by then.

Some property, largely businesses and property and land, attracts the possibility of paying the tax by instalments over ten years by written election (ss 227–228 of the IHTA 1984). This can be extremely useful to personal representatives who have insufficient money available to pay the IHT bill on the estate before the grant and therefore have to borrow in order to obtain the grant (see 12.20.4). The instalment provision means a much lower sum needs to be borrowed and therefore the amount incurred in interest payments is much lower. This is also an important option for non-exempt beneficiaries who reside in the property with the deceased as it means they have ten years to find all the money for the IHT and may be able to avoid selling their home.

### 14.19.4  Gifts bearing their own tax – the 'estate rate'

A testator may leave a gift specifically saying that it bears its own tax, which will then be charged at the estate rate, the remainder coming out of residue. The estate rate is the overall percentage rate of tax paid by an estate. Although the percentage at which IHT is paid is 40 per cent, this applies only to the amount of chargeable property over the nil-rate band, currently £325,000 (from 2009). If the total taxable estate is made up of a £100,000 gift bearing its own tax and £400,000 residue the total chargeable estate is £500,000. The nil-rate band is then deducted leaving £175,000 which is subject to 40 per cent IHT, giving total IHT due of £70,000. The estate rate is the amount of tax payable divided by the total value of the estate as a percentage i.e. £70,000 ÷ £500,000 × 100 = 14 per cent. Each element bearing its own tax is multiplied by 14 per cent to find out the amount of the total tax it bears. Therefore the pecuniary legacy of £100,000 bears £14,000 of the tax and the £400,000 residue bears £56,000, making the total of £70,000.

### 14.19.5  Gifts left free of tax

A testator may leave a gift free of tax; the tax it should have borne will still be payable out of the rest of the estate, sometimes leading to very awkward calculations. For example, if there is a tax-free specific gift to a non-exempt beneficiary and the residue passes to exempt beneficiaries, the gift must be grossed up at the relevant death rate in order to calculate the amount of tax to be borne by the residue. If residue is left to be shared between an exempt beneficiary and a non-exempt beneficiary, then in the absence of express provision to the contrary, the residuary estate is shared in the proportions set out in the will without regard to any IHT attributable to the non-exempt shares, and any IHT is then borne by those shared.[34]

---

34  S 41 Inheritance Tax Act 1984. See *Re Ratcliffe* (1999), in which grossing up was not allowed so the exempt and non-exempt beneficiaries received different amounts and *Re Benham's Will Trusts* (1995), in which grossing up was allowed so that the exempt and non-exempt beneficiaries received the same net amount.

# 14.20 Tax planning between spouses

The situation for a married couple in respect of liability to IHT is very special. Not only are transfers between them exempt, but they are likely (albeit not necessarily) to want to leave as much as possible to each other. Many people would like to leave all their property to their spouse should they die first, and rely on them to do what is appropriate by way of passing it on to the next generation, although the rise in multiple marriages and children from different relationships means this is not always the case. This used to be potentially a tax disaster, since it would mean that the second spouse would die owning all the matrimonial property, so often a sum substantially over the nil-rate band, which would be left to the children carrying a potentially heavy liability to IHT. To avoid this, testators would include discretionary nil-rate band trusts (see 14.6, 14.8.10) or possibly leave assets up to the nil-rate band to people other than their spouse. There were risks in doing this as the surviving spouse might need the capital given away to live on. Additionally, for most individuals their biggest asset was and is their house. If the testator left their interest in the family home to someone other than their spouse there was a chance that the survivor could lose his or her home: for example if the beneficiary divorced, went bankrupt or died or, indeed, decided they wanted to realise their interest in the property.

## 14.20.1 The transferable nil-rate band (TNRB)

The transferable nil-rate band between spouses was introduced in 2007.[35] The TNRB means that the surviving spouse acquires whatever remains of the first to die's nil-rate band. For example, Julie dies when the nil-rate band is £300,000. She leaves £150,000 to her son Fred, a non-exempt beneficiary and the remainder to her husband Bob. Julie has used 50 per cent of her nil-rate band (£150,000 ÷ £300,000 × 100). When Bob dies he will have 150 per cent of the nil-rate band available on the day he dies e.g. if he dies when the nil-rate band is £350,000 he would have a nil-rate band of £525,000.

## 14.20.2 Sometimes it is a bad idea to leave everything to your spouse

An individual can only have one extra TNRB. It may be in the above example that Julie and Bob were both widowed and so between them have four TNRBs. If they have large estates, they might leave their two nil-rate bands to someone other than their spouse – for example, their own children from a previous marriage – or use a discretionary trust so that the surviving spouse can still have use of the funds if necessary.

Alternatively, Bob and Julie might want to protect their children from previous relationships, ensuring that assets they have built up in their own right pass to their own children, but wish to allow their surviving spouse to benefit during their lifetime. In that case, they could leave a life trust in favour of their spouse, which would be exempt from IHT at that point, but which would become subject to IHT when the life tenant (the surviving spouse) died and the fund – such as the deceased's share in the matrimonial home – passed to the children. A trust of this kind can be drafted widely to allow capital to be advanced to the surviving spouse in the event they need money.

---

35 Inheritance Tax Act 1984 s 8A as inserted by the Finance Act 2008 s 10, applying to the death of the surviving spouse or civil partner on or after 9 October 2007.

### 14.20.3 Cohabitants

As with the example of the married Bob and Julie above, a cohabiting couple may wish to protect children from previous relationships or ensure that their estate passes to their own family, rather than their partner's, on death. A life interest or discretionary trust may well be appropriate. It should always be borne in mind that IHT will need to be paid on the first death as there is no spouse/civil partner exemption and, in the case of the family home, it may result in the property being sold to pay IHT if funds are not available from another source.

### 14.20.4 Discretionary trusts

The testator may not be sure enough of the future to decide where their property should be left. In that case, they might use a nil-rate band discretionary trust. The trustees can decide how the trust should be distributed depending on the beneficiaries' circumstances at the time. For example, one child might unexpectedly become a millionaire after the will is made, and another child apparently destined for greatness might become a bus driver, whilst the spouse might win the lottery. In that situation, the trustees might use the income or the capital of the fund for the bus driver, or alternatively, the spouse might need money or it might be tax-efficient to retain the nil-rate band in the spouse's estate, in which case the trustees can appoint the fund to the spouse. As long as this is done within two years of the date of death s 144 of the Inheritance Tax Act 1984 will apply and the trustees' decisions will be read back into the will for tax purposes (14.18.3).

### 14.20.5 Tax planning in context

Property can be left to a beneficiary absolutely or as life tenant, but one should bear in mind that a life tenant's estate is treated as including the capital in the trust. The overall purpose of tax planning must also be borne in mind all the time. Minimising liability to tax is not an end in itself, but a way of providing more efficiently for the testator's family and friends. The spouse's expenses must be considered whenever plans are made; they may need a sum which looks inefficient for tax in order to keep a house running, for example, in which case they will be using the money for purposes the testator will approve of and the resulting depletion of the fund should mean in any case that there is no liability to tax by the date of the surviving spouse's death.

## 14.21 Post-death tax planning

A valid will cannot be changed after the testator has died. It cannot be rewritten. However, its effects may be altered by an agreement or order for family provision (see Chapter 15), in which case the provisions will be read back into the will for IHT purposes and a reassessment of tax liability may be sought or imposed.

The original beneficiary of a gift under a will or intestacy may also choose to disclaim their interest in the estate, or alternatively to vary it even though they have obtained a benefit under the original gift. They do not have to vary their entire interest, and they can decide to whom the interest goes. A joint tenant who has inherited by survivorship (see 2.8) may choose to sever the joint tenancy by deed of variation, directing the deceased's share to a different beneficiary. Often these rearrangements are a joint effort amongst the beneficiaries to produce the best all-round tax result. Provided the variation is made within two years of the date of death and certain formalities are met, it can be written back into the will for the purposes of IHT and CGT, and this is the most common reason for the variation of wills, though it may also be important not to 'bunch' property with a wealthy beneficiary because of their future liability to IHT.[36] To be effective for tax purposes, the variation must include a statement for IHT and CGT purposes, and must be in writing (though it is usually done by deed), signed by the beneficiary making the gift. If the variation alters the amount of tax payable the personal representatives must also sign the instrument, unless they do not have sufficient funds to meet the liability. The property subject to a deed of variation can only be varied once for tax purposes.[37]

## 14.22 Income Tax

The deceased's personal representatives are liable for the Income Tax owed by him or her at the date of death, which constitutes a debt of the estate. The deceased gets their personal allowance for the year of death under s 41 of the Income Tax Act 2007, and may also have the married couple's allowance under ss 42–58, subject to election by the surviving spouse or civil partner.

## 14.23 Summary of Chapter 14

### 14.23.1 Tax and Tax Planning

A good deal of succession practice is aimed at minimising liability to tax. The structure of the tax system is generally fairly stable, although the details frequently alter.

The essence of tax planning is usually to allow the testator to retain as much control as possible over their property during their lifetime whilst still obtaining the tax advantages available from giving the property away. Care must be taken not to cross the line between tax avoidance, which is a lawful skill, and tax evasion, which is highly illegal and constitutes fraud. It is also very important not to let tax avoidance become an end in itself, forgetting that it is more important that the prospective testator has enough to live on than that tax liability is minimised.

Inheritance Tax is charged on transfers of property with gratuitous intent. It applies also to property transferred during a lifetime, when there is a more complex system of allowances, as well as to the final transfer of everything in the deceased's estate which is deemed to occur immediately before death. Gifts to a spouse or civil partner or to charity are part of the estate but exempt from IHT. The rest of the estate will be chargeable to IHT, but the first £325,000 is charged at a nil-rate of 0 per cent, some of which may, however, have been used up by chargeable lifetime transfers within seven years of the transferor's death. Transfers before that are non-chargeable as potentially exempt transfers (PETs), and a taper relief begins to operate if the donor survives three years after the gift. There are other more specific reliefs. Where IHT is chargeable, the rate is 40 per cent.

Settlements or trusts made by will are less useful a form of tax avoidance than they used to be, but discretionary trusts which will be wound up within two years of death are read as though the distribution took place at death. Although nil-rate bands are now transferable between spouses and civil partners, a nil-rate-band discretionary trust with the spouse or civil partner as a beneficiary may still be useful in balancing the surviving spouse's needs with the desire to minimise tax liability. The proceeds of a life insurance policy pass outside the estate, in trust for a third party, so are tax-efficient as the premiums paid by the deceased during their lifetime will not usually attract IHT either.

Property falls into the estate for Capital Gains Tax purposes at the value it had at the date of death. The personal representatives therefore pay CGT only on the increase in value of property whilst it is in the estate. The valuation for property must be the same for both IHT and CGT. Certain property such as land and shares may be revalued for IHT purposes if they are sold within a short time of death.

---

36 S 142(1) Inheritance Tax Act 1984, s 62(2) Taxation of Capital Gains Act 1992.
37 *Russell v IRC* (1988).

# Chapter 15

# Family Provision

Family provision is the usual term for a power a court has to alter the provision made by a testator in their will, or by the rules of intestacy, to the benefit of their family or dependants. It is never automatic – the claimant has to apply – and it does, of course, also lessen the amount available to the other relatives, friends or organisations that the deceased might have preferred to benefit. The general idea of family provision – of being able to claim against someone's estate on the basis of a personal relationship – is not apparently particularly unpopular, despite the limits it places on testamentary freedom and the rights of people to do what they want with their own property.[1] However, this may be because many people assume it is appropriate that wills can be 'challenged' and do not distinguish between challenges based on the validity of the will and challenges to the practical import of a valid will or to the effects of intestacy.

The making of family provision laws brings into play ideas about private property and distribution of wealth, about claims that family members might have on each other, the appropriateness of court interference in private family matters, and the rights of individuals to abandon their responsibilities and leave the state to take care of any particularly bad consequences. Family provision cases are difficult to decide because of the many variables in the range of family situations, and the inclusion of value-based judgements about matters which are very difficult to ascertain and evaluate. Though this is still principally an area of property law, it overlaps most with the considerations found in family law. The cases are heard in the Family Division by family judges, and the cases often read more like stories than legal problems.

## 15.1  Restrictions on testamentary freedom

Testamentary freedom may be restricted either by preventing a person from leaving their property entirely as they wish on death by having laws stating where the property should go, or by making it possible for their dispositions to be altered after death.[2] The fundamental questions about whether it should operate are complex, and much bigger than the merely legal questions about how to implement it. They are about the nature of private property and personal responsibility and how far the state should be able to curtail the former in the interests of its view of the latter. These are very basic political questions which a country's law has to address and then flesh out in its laws. To have no law of family provision is not only to uphold a strong version of private property rights, subsisting even after death, but also to admit that a wealthy testator could leave their spouse or children destitute, dependent on the state and other taxpayers for support.

---

1  Rosalind Croucher, 'How Free Is Free? Testamentary Freedom and the Battle Between Family and Property' (2012) 37 Australian Journal of Legal Philosophy 9.
2  Mary Ann Glendon, 'Fixed Rules and Discretion in Contemporary Family Law and Succession Law' (1985) 60 Tulane Law Review 1165.

## 15.1.1 Other jurisdictions

Other legal systems do not allow complete testamentary freedom but lay down that a certain part of a person's estate will go to their family regardless of the deceased's wishes. The idea is not new; it was found in Roman law.[3] It occurs now, for example, in France, where between one-third and three-quarters of an estate (depending on the size of the remaining family) goes automatically to relatives, and only the rest is available to the testator to dispose of as he or she wishes. In Scotland too, the state requires that part of an estate must go to certain relatives,[4] and in many parts of the USA, the adoption of the Uniform Probate Code (UPC) has given the spouse the right to take one-third of the estate provided he or she elects to do so within six months of the grant of probate;[5] a share may also be claimed for infant children.[6] In Ireland, during passage of the Succession Bill in the 1960s, the principle of freedom of testation was described as a peculiarly English phenomenon, foisted on the Irish with the first Statute of Distributions as a replacement for the ancient 'Custom of Ireland', under which only one-third of personalty could be disposed of by will. The differences amongst jurisdictions remain, as a matter of culture and tradition.[7]

## 15.1.2 Testamentary freedom in England

The English system does in theory allow complete freedom, although this has not always been the case (see Chapter 1). How individuals transfer ownership of property inevitably has social and political causes and consequences. The history of the devisability of land is fraught with the attempts of the Crown to retain control; the rise of primogeniture and the keeping together of estates by devolving them upon a single heir led to the phenomenon of the younger sons of the English nobility who had breeding but no money. Even the freedom to dispose of personalty, which today may seem the natural state of affairs, has little historical validity.

There were legal restrictions on testamentary freedom operating until the Mortmain and Charitable Uses Act of 1891 removed the restrictions on charitable gifts within a short period of death; married women only obtained full powers of disposition over their property after the Married Women's Property Act of 1893. There was therefore a very short period of full testamentary freedom between the last decade of the nineteenth century and the introduction of the first family provision legislation in 1938. The current law was passed in 1975 but has been substantially amended in its detail.

The essence of that legislation is that it allows individuals to claim against an estate on the basis that their share of it does not appropriately reflect their personal relationship with the deceased. Who can claim has changed to reflect changing social attitudes. The approach to families was in a state of flux even in 1975 – a few years after the Divorce Reform Act 1969 came into force, with its strong element of recognition not just of divorce but for subsequent families. Since then, there has been a strong movement to recognise the financial disadvantage, usually suffered by women, of child care, and the long-term implications of that in terms of lack of marketable skills and experience or pension contributions. In particular, the movement to the recognition of same-sex relationships has been truly rapid. The practical scope of the 1975 Act has changed greatly since its passing.

---

3  Peter Stein, *Roman Law in European History* (Cambridge University Press 1999).
4  Hilary Hiram, *The Scots Law of Succession* (Tottel 2007).
5  Uniform Probate Code, ss 2–201–207.
6  Uniform Probate Code, s 2–403.
7  Christoph Castelein, René Foqué and Alain-Laurent Verbeke (eds), *Imperative Inheritance Law in a Late-Modern Society: Five Perspectives* (Intersentia 2009).

## 15.2 Challenging the will – or intestacy

A will may be challenged under the general law because it does not satisfy the criteria necessary for it to be valid in English law. For example, it may be said that the testator lacked testamentary intention, or testamentary capacity, or that there was a failure to comply with the proper formalities. Challenges to wills on the ground that the testator lacked the mental capacity to make a will became less common since a system of challenging the effects of the will for the testator's failure to make proper provision for someone was brought in,[8] though challenges and contentious applications of all kinds have more recently increased (see Chapter 16). The decision which course to take is often a practical one, depending on which route looks most likely to succeed – or to succeed easily. Family provision cases almost always settle, and a potential claimant may be made a good offer without much argument even if their claim is not very well founded, because of the expense to the estate of dealing with even an unmeritorious claim.

## 15.3 Reasons for family provision legislation

There are various views about whether it is right to restrict testamentary freedom in any way. There are both practical and moral considerations.

### 15.3.1 Freedom or responsibility?

Some feel that people should be able to leave their property exactly as they wish, and that it is no business of the state or anyone else to permit or encourage interference in private arrangements. On the other hand, others feel that, within a family in particular, there is not necessarily any merit in where the technical ownership of property falls. The wife of a rich husband who has spent her whole life working hard to look after her husband and children may have no claim on anything as a matter of property rights. Supporters of the latter view would say that it is the business of the law to uphold and enforce obligations such as those of providing financial support for one's dependants. In the not-unheard-of situation of a husband who does leave his widow without support, there is also the consideration that she must be provided for from some resources, and if those do not come from his estate, then they may well have to come from the general taxpayer.

### 15.3.2 Interaction with other areas of law

England is unusual in that it has no system of matrimonial or family property, so that ownership of property remains with the person who acquires it under the usual rules of acquisition of property – the person who receives it as a gift or who buys it with their own money – even when they are married and the property is used for family purposes. Thus, a wife has no interest in a matrimonial home if it is in her husband's name, unless, exceptionally, she can establish one under some principle of equity. The courts have wide powers to alter the property divisions between spouses on application by either party in matrimonial proceedings (for divorce or judicial separation), but clearly these powers do not apply where a marriage is ended by death. It may be particularly important in the English jurisdiction, therefore, for a disinherited wife to be able to apply for support from the deceased's estate.

---

8 This is not to say that the process is any simpler in practice: see for example *McNulty v McNulty* (2012).

Whilst England may still have no family property regime as such, in the decades since the current Inheritance (Provision for Family and Dependants) Act 1975 was passed, there have been structural changes in the social arrangements underlying family property. Family provision has kept pace with that through gradual amendments to the 1975 Act as well as by reflecting the changes in other areas of law, but these are still in a state of flux. The family envisaged by the family provision legislation is different from that envisaged by the intestacy rules. The most obvious difference is that of the attitude to cohabitants. Cohabitants have long been able to bring a family provision claim as dependants, but dealing with financial dependency where someone dies is of the essence of family provision legislation. The difficulties of claiming dependency as a cohabitant have produced considerable case law (see 15.4.1 and 15.26) and even recent legislative change, under the Inheritance and Trustees' Powers Act 2014 (15.3.10). Standing to claim as a cohabitant, based on the existence of the relationship, is of a different order. The intestacy rules have not yet given any automatic rights to cohabitants. The property rights of cohabitants, sometimes erroneously called common law spouses, is a source of much practical misunderstanding, and the extension of family provision rights to cohabitants no doubt contributes to that. The structure of family provision law now reflects the social changes to the social definition of a family and of family responsibilities – the acceptance of cohabitation – more than does the law of intestacy. However, the advent of civil partnerships and same-sex marriage have removed the inherent gender discrimination in legal family formation in all areas of law.

### 15.3.3 Practicalities or morality?

The practical and moral bases of family provision legislation are not always easily distinguished, perhaps for political reasons. Those who would object to a form of redistribution of property on the basis of some 'moral' consideration which has nothing to do with established property rights might nevertheless be quick to see the advantage of being able to refer someone who was potentially a burden on the state to a possible claim against the estate of another private individual.

### 15.3.4 History of family provision legislation

The first statutory provision in England allowing a family provision claim was the Inheritance (Family Provision) Act 1938. Other jurisdictions were quicker to introduce legislation of this type, especially New Zealand, where the first such provision was made in 1908. This was the culmination of attempts to introduce a system of fixed shares on the Scottish model, which led to the Testators' Family Maintenance Act of 1900. The legislation was claimed to be designed to save taxpayers' money; it was, however, more usually used in situations where state expenditure was not involved, and what was altered was the arrangement of entitlements between private individuals only. Nevertheless, it is always possible that a family provision claim will make it possible for spouses and children to survive without state support after the death of a breadwinner.

### 15.3.5 Introduction of the legislation in England

The first legislation in England was introduced after pressure from various quarters, especially from women's groups. As is so often the case with property matters, legal equality between individuals almost invariably meant that, given the way legal claims and entitlements were set up, the legal ownership of property almost always rested with men. Under a system of complete testamentary freedom, those men could disinherit their wives and children as they wished. There had been considerable debate as to whether a wife should have fixed share as of right, or have to seek entitlement at the discretion of a court. The first bill presented to Parliament was one which would have awarded wives a fixed share; this bill failed. It was followed by several more bills in the next few years, which also failed, before the first Inheritance Act was passed in 1938. Spouses, infant sons, unmarried daughters or disabled adult sons or daughters could apply for maintenance or, in the case of small estates, capital payments.[9]

## 15.3.6 After the 1938 Act

The 1938 Act was, on the whole, successful. It was subject to amendment by the Matrimonial Causes Acts 1958 and 1965, which brought in the possibility of applications by ex-spouses. In 1951 the Committee on the Law of Intestate Succession (the Morton Committee) reported. Its brief was principally to look at the statutory legacy for spouses on intestacy, which it recommended should be increased from £1,000 to £5,000, but it also recommended the extension of the 1938 Act to cover cases of total intestacy. It recommended that widows should be able to be awarded the whole of the income of the net estate and that the limit for lump sums should be increased. These provisions were enacted by the Intestates' Estates Act 1952. However, a child of the deceased and surviving spouse could not claim if the surviving spouse had been left two-thirds of the estate income.[10]

The Family Provision Act 1966 extended the jurisdiction to allow more judicial discretion and to remove many restrictions on the amount and form of provision, as well as giving spouses a wider right to apply. It allowed lump sums to be given instead of periodical payments and removed the restriction mentioned above as to the child of the deceased and surviving spouse being unable to claim if the spouse had been left at least two-thirds of the income of the estate. Matters remained to be heard in the Chancery Division of the High Court however, save that the county courts were given a limited – and little used – jurisdiction.

## 15.3.7 Further need for change

By the 1960s and 1970s, a need for further change was perceived in an era of considerable social change. The Law Commission, in its Working Paper No 42 *Family Law: Family Property Law* (1971) and its Report No 61 *Family Property: Family Provision on Death* of 1974, expressed various concerns, in particular about the difference between support and property, or maintenance and capital, and the effects of divorce. When the family provision legislation was compared with that which applied on divorce, the spouse whose happy marriage was ended by death could find him- or herself in a much worse situation than the one who was divorced; there was also a suggestion that divorce should not automatically end the spouse's right to claim maintenance. Fixed shares in the property of the deceased were suggested but not emphasised.

## 15.3.8 Bases of the provisions?

There was a change during the 1970s in the views of entitlement to property, particularly where the situation of women in their traditional role was concerned. Lord Simon of Glaisdale, in the debate on the bill that became the 1975 Act, said that the 'functional division of co-operative labour ... calls in justice for the sharing of the rewards of the labour. The breadwinner is morally bound to share the loaf, he has been free to gain'. This view of matrimonial property was reflected in many court judgments during the 1970s, though the trend towards the courts regarding wives as having a share in their husband's property by virtue of their contributions to the marriage as a matter of equity has somewhat receded in more recent years. However, the

---

9  Joseph Dainow, 'Limitations on Testamentary Freedom in England' (1939) 25 Cornell Law Quarterly 337.
10  FR Crane, 'Family Provision on Death in English Law' (1960) 35 New York University Law Review 984.

rationale that a deceased husband in a traditional family, for example, should not be permitted testamentary freedom over all the property that is legally his remains, sometimes explicitly on the basis that morally he is a co-owner with his surviving wife. The changing nature of family responsibilities, especially the increasing number of women working outside the home, the spread of divorce, particularly after the Divorce Reform Act 1969, and the rise of the unmarried family all gave rise to pressure for change.[11]

### 15.3.9 Law Commission Report No 61 *Family Property: Family Provision on Death*

The Law Commission undertook a Social Survey before it made its report in 1974. It found that there was support for a spouse entitlement that was wider than maintenance. It recommended that spouses should take a just share of the estate, and that conduct should not be an issue for ex-spouses save where it would be repugnant to anyone's sense of justice to ignore it, as prescribed for ancillary relief matters by Lord Denning in the matrimonial case of *Wachtel v Wachtel* (1973). It recommended that there should be no age limit on claims by children, because certain 'special circumstances' might arise in which adult children should be able to claim. It also recommended that there should be some form of basis for claiming by dependants, mentioning the Fatal Accidents Acts 1846–1959 and their provisions for establishing those who could claim for loss of dependency consequent upon a death caused by a tort. The Law Commission cited the Ontario Law Reform Committee and the Law Reform Committee of Western Australia who were reporting along the same lines.

There was some positive antipathy towards the bill; specifically, it was said that the existence of family provision legislation encouraged disputes within families, and that the use of words such as 'fair', 'reasonable' and 'just' was unhelpful because the judge hearing a case could not know the truth of the matter and the strength of the cases would often be judged in accordance with the efficiency of the lawyers concerned (an objection which might apply to many areas!).

The essential structure of the Inheritance (Provision for Family and Dependants) Act 1975 remains, though there have been two main areas of development. The first is the general effect of the acceptance of same-sex relationships, both socially and by virtue of legal recognition, and the second is the recognition of cohabitation.

### 15.3.10 The inclusion of cohabitants: the Law Reform (Succession) Act 1995 and the Inheritance and Powers of Trustees Act 2014

By the end of the twentieth century, there was pressure for still more radical reform. Ideas about what constituted the sort of relationship that should mean a person might bring a claim had moved on further, and there was pressure for unmarried cohabitants to be given automatic legal rights in a variety of situations.[12] Much of that pressure originated from the widespread belief that they already had such rights, especially because there was a widespread myth of 'common law marriage'.[13] There was concern that unmarried cohabitants needed to show dependency on

---

11 Kate Green, The Englishwoman's Castle: Inheritance and Private Property Today' (1988) 51 Modern Law Review 187.

12 Anne Barlow, Simon Duncan, Grace James and Alison Park, *Cohabitation, Marriage and the Law: Social Change and Legal Reform in the 21st Century* (Hart 2005); Rebecca Probert, *The Changing Legal Regulation of Cohabitation: From Fornicators to Family, 1600–2010* (Cambridge University Press 2012).

13 Anne Barlow and Janet Smithson, 'Legal Assumptions, Cohabitants' Talk and the Rocky Road to Reform' (2010) 22 Child and Family Law Quarterly 328; Rebecca Probert, 'Common Law Marriage: Myths and Understandings' (2008) 20 Child and Family Law Quarterly 1. Note that 'common law marriages' do exist, but are not the same as cohabitation: they refer to marriages which are not governed by any statutory law in England or elsewhere and to which the common law rules are therefore attributed.

the deceased when their financial situation might have been co-dependent and so not meet that requirement, or that the position was otherwise unfair: 'those who have given more than they have taken (for example by devoting many years of care and possibly financial support to an ailing partner) may not be able to claim.'[14] This was a period of considerable legal concern about the position of cohabitants, producing much heat. A long-running Law Commission consultation on the property rights of home-sharers generally led to a discussion paper in 2002;[15] in 2007, the report on cohabitants' rights proposed a new statutory regime so that cohabitants and their children did not have to rely on property law, which in turn is based on financial contributions rather than family needs.[16] It proposed to give rights to couples who had been living in a joint household for a certain period – preferably two years – or who had a child together to apply for financial relief on separation, provided they had not opted out of the framework. Family provision claims would have been part of a scheme bringing the rights of cohabitants closer to those of married couples, with a provision that claims from separated parties must be brought within a year of the separation. The proposals relating to claims between living cohabitants or former cohabitants were not implemented, but s 2 of the Law Reform (Succession) Act 1995 introduced an entitlement for unmarried cohabitants to claim family provision on death. This gave standing to apply to a person who was not a spouse but who had lived in the same household as the deceased for the two years immediately before their death as their husband or wife. A court assessing such a claim was required to have regard to the age of the applicant and the length of the period during which the parties lived as spouses, and the contribution the applicant had made to the welfare of the deceased's family, including by caring or looking after the home.

In 2009 the Law Commission consulted on both intestacy and family provision together.[17] It suggested that cohabitants seeking family provision should be treated like spouses, suggesting that having a child together or living together for two to five years was the right test, with a tapering entitlement for shorter cohabitations. A wider range of eligible family members was proposed, including any child treated by the deceased as their own. The problem with valuing caring so as to exclude the necessary dependency in a relationship – see the *Bishop v Plumley* problem (15.4.1) – was removed. It reported in 2011,[18] amendments eventually being made by s 6 and Sch 2 to the Inheritance and Trustees' Powers Act 2014, which came into force in October 2014. The effects on practice will become apparent in future years.

The 2014 Act entitles all children treated as a child of the family to apply, even if the only family members were the deceased and the child who was no blood relation. The definition of dependency is also considerably broadened so its primary effect becomes the exclusion of commercial carers. The courts' powers are widened to allow for the variation of trusts and to allow assumptions to be made about the payment of taxes and liabilities. Courts are explicitly given greater flexibility in deciding what sums to award, but are also reminded to look at the maintenance of the claimant by the deceased and the deceased's assumption of responsibility for the claimant. Applications can be made before a grant of representation has been taken out (this was previously questionable), and shares of joint tenancies are to be treated as part of the deceased's estate and valued at the date of any hearing, unless the court orders otherwise.

14  Law Commission Report 307 *Cohabitation: The Financial Consequences of Relationship Breakdown* (2007) para A197.
15  Law Commission 278 *Sharing Homes, A Discussion Paper* (2002).
16  Law Commission 307 *Cohabitation: the Financial Consequences of Relationship Breakdown* (2007).
17  Law Commission 191 *Intestacy and Family Provision Claims on Death: Consultation Paper* (2009).
18  Law Commission 331 *Intestacy and Family Provision Claims on Death* (2011).

## 15.3.11 Family provision claims based on same-sex relationships

A major change to the effect of the original 1975 Act was the inclusion of civil partners as claimants in the same way as spouses; this in turn was overcome by the Marriage (Same Sex Couples) Act 2013. These changes were a radical alteration to the practical operation of the family provision rules, but came about through the inclusion of changes in other areas of law rather than directly through the rules of family provision.

Partners in same-sex relationships originally had to rely on claiming as dependants. They could not be spouses or civil partners, and cohabitants originally had no standing as such. However, in the period since the Act was originally passed, the legal landscape has changed. Arguably although the change began later than that relating to the unmarried family, it has progressed much more rapidly, so that civil partners are included in all the provisions for spouses in both family provision and intestacy, whereas cohabitants, who gained early acceptance up to a point in relation to family provision claims, still have no automatic entitlement on intestacy – the more solid, less discretionary property regime which does not require a person to make an individual claim. Although a recent bill did not succeed in its passage through Parliament it is expected that another will be presented shortly.[19]

The 1975 Act followed very shortly after the legalisation of homosexual relationships following the Wolfenden Report in 1967; the acceptance of same-sex relationships as such was a hotly contested political issue in the 1980s, which even saw legislation that prohibited 'the teaching in any maintained school of the acceptability of homosexuality as a pretended family relationship'.[20] Campaigning in the 1990s, however, led to both legislative and social change, and even progress in the case law. 2004 saw not only the notable decision of the House of Lords in *Ghaidan v Godin-Mendoza* that the right of a 'spouse' to succeed to a protected tenancy on the death of a protected tenant under the Rent Act 1977 applied to a homosexual partner of the tenant, but also the Civil Partnership Act. The 2004 Act surely marked a fundamental change to the legislation governing the definition of a family and to the scope of the regulation of family property.

Civil partners are now recognised as are spouses; since the Marriage (Same Sex Couples) Act 2013 they may convert their partnerships to marriage, or same-sex couples may marry and so be spouses. For such a fundamental change in social attitudes as reflected in legislation, it has been very rapid.

# 15.4 Who may claim now: the 1975 Act as amended

The provisions as to who may claim are in the Inheritance (Provision for Family and Dependants) Act 1975, as amended by the Law Reform (Succession) Act 1995 and the Inheritance and Trustees' Powers Act 2014. The potential claimants will therefore be the deceased's spouse or civil partner, or former such who has not formalised a new relationship; any child or person who lived with the deceased as a child of the family; cohabitants of two years' standing of those who died on or after 1 January 1996; children of the deceased; any person treated as a child of the family by the deceased; any other person whom the deceased, immediately before their death, was maintaining by a substantial contribution in money or money's worth towards their reasonable needs, other than a contribution made in the course of a commercial arrangement for full valuable consideration.

This allows claims by close family members, by persons who were financially dependent on the deceased when he or she died and by certain unmarried but quasi-marital cohabitants. The

---

19 Inheritance (Cohabitants) Bill [HL] 2012–2013.
20 S 28 Local Government Act 1988.

last category was added to the original provisions by the Law Reform (Succession) Act 1995. The rationale behind the statutory provisions appears to be a mixture of the moral and legal obligations the testator would have had had he or she lived. Certainly, ideas about moral obligations are shaped by the social mood and liable to change comparatively rapidly. The courts have taken, in reality, a wide discretion in interpreting the meaning of the Act's provisions, and the changes made by the LR(S)A 1995 and the ITPA 2014 to the classes of those who can claim under the 1975 Act were foreshadowed not only by the theories of the Law Commission but also by the practice of the courts.

## 15.4.1 The trajectory of changes to the original 1975 Act

The original provisions in the I(PFD)A 1975 allowed spouses, former spouses, children, step-children and dependants of the deceased to bring a claim against the estate. The definition of 'dependant' caused particular difficulty, especially against the background of the spread of unmarried cohabitation and changing views about that. Views changed more generally about family relationships as well, especially about gay relationships, and also about gender change.

The 1975 Act in its original form meant that an established cohabitant could not make any claim against the estate of the deceased partner unless that partner had been making contributions not merely to the joint expenses but to the remaining cohabitant's share of them – that is, if the couple had shared expenses equally, no claim could lie even if the survivor could not maintain the former joint home from their own resources. A cohabitant who had been paying their way was unable to found any claim against the deceased's estate, whereas one who had allowed the deceased to support them instead could found a claim on that basis. This was often regarded as failing to treat deserving family members appropriately, whilst encouraging 'sponging'. More broadly, there was concern to put in place legislation to protect cohabitants' financial position on separation and death similarly to the way in which spouses are protected, particularly as there was a popular misconception that that was already the legal position, so that people might easily fail to realise that they had to make specific provision for their soulmates.

The Law Commission originally rejected the idea of giving cohabitants automatic succession rights on intestacy but favoured giving them standing to make a family provision claim by virtue of the relationship itself rather than dependency.[21] A notable Court of Appeal case, Bishop v Plumley and Another (1991), stretched the definition of dependency further than some thought it could be taken – though not necessarily further than it should be taken in the particular case. The claimant had cared for the deceased with what the court described as 'exceptionally devoted care', with both of them living on welfare benefits in a house owned by the deceased. His will gave her nothing, and on her family provision claim it was at first said that the claimant's care was full valuable consideration for the rent-free accommodation he had provided for her – that is, had she not cared for him, she might have been able to establish dependency, but as she had looked after him she could not![22] However, in the Court of Appeal, Butler-Sloss LJ said the care was not to be considered in isolation from the 'mutuality of the relationship'; the deceased had provided a secure home for his partner and she had provided him with 'connubial services'. This was held to demonstrate that the deceased had made a substantial contribution towards her needs for the purposes of s 1(3) of the Act, which defined dependency for the purposes of the Act, her care being part of the relationship in its entirety. The case was remitted to the registrar to be reconsidered, amidst references to the comments by Griffiths LJ in Jelley v Iliffe (1981) (15.14) about the need to 'use common sense'. 'Common sense' was translated into legislation in this respect

---

21  Law Commission 187 *Distribution on Intestacy* (1989).
22  S 1(3) I(PFD)A 1975. Note this has been amended by Sch 2 of the ITPA 2014 in relation to deaths after September 2014.

by s 2 of the Law Reform (Succession) Act 1995, which amended s 1 of the Inheritance (Provision for Family and Dependants) Act 1975 so as to give *locus standi* under the new s 1(1)(ba) of the 1975 Act to a person who (as with dependency claims under the Fatal Accidents Act 1976) who had lived as the husband or wife of the deceased for the two years immediately preceding the death. This applies to deaths on or after 1 January 1996. It also provided special guidelines for how claims brought on the basis of cohabitation should be treated.

The changes instigated by the Law Commission and the Court of Appeal and brought into force in relation to deaths after 1995 by the Law Reform (Succession) Act 1995 went a long way towards recognising the value of caring within a relationship as something other than a commercial transaction, and something that validated that relationship as such, rather than proving it to be a commercial arrangement. During the 1990s, the structure of the family provision legislation moved away from finding that caring potentially defeated a claim by demonstrating that the potential claimant had in fact given 'full valuable consideration' for her support by the deceased, and therefore was outside the legislation, and the Inheritance and Trustees' Powers Act 2014 in effect reversed the approach by providing that a person would be treated as being maintained if the deceased was making a substantial contribution in money or money's worth towards their reasonable needs, other than on a commercial basis and for full reward.

Over the same period, attitudes to gay marriage and gay partnerships changed entirely, all over the world. Starting with jurisdictions such as Denmark and Holland, forms of 'registered partnership' akin to civil marriage, or marriage itself, began to spread. In Britain, the Civil Partnerships Act 2004 aligned gay civil partnerships with marriage for all property-related issues, and also aligned gay cohabitants with their heterosexual counterparts.[23]

## 15.5 How to claim – an overview

The I(PFD)A 1975 may be used to challenge the level of provision arising from intestacy as well as under a will. What is looked at is the entitlement the claimant has, however it arises, and whether it is reasonable.[24] As with other types of action, such claims are usually settled before they reach court, but that is on the basis that the lawyers for each party believe their client has obtained something comparable to what a court would have given. The estimate of what that would have been given has to be based on the cases decided under the Act, which judges must follow in deciding how to exercise their wide discretion as to what to award, with some assistance from the new provisions in the 2014 Act. The 1975 Act itself, though it gives certain guidelines, is remarkably short, and has allowed – or demanded – much interpretation.

## 15.6 The deceased – against whose estate can application be made?

The deceased must have died after 31 March 1976, domiciled in England and Wales. Note that being domiciled in England and Wales is not the same as living there and certainly not the same as having British nationality.[25] A person generally acquires a domicile of origin in the country in which they were born, though a child's domicile follows that of the parent with whom the child lives.[26]

---

23 Ss 1(1)(a), 1(1)(b) and 1(1B) I(PFD)A 1975, as amended by s 71 and Sch 4 para 15 Civil Partnership Act 2004.
24 A condition in a will providing a benefit on condition that no claim is made under the I(PFD)A 1975 may in fact indicate that provision is appropriate, and does not prevent the bringing of a claim: *Nathan v Leonard* (2002).
25 The unlawfulness of a person's presence also does not negate domicile: *Witkowska v Kaminski* (2006).
26 *Henderson v Henderson* (1967).

Domicile may be changed by choice thereafter: for example, a person whose established permanent home is in England and who intends to stay there indefinitely will be domiciled there, whatever their nationality. That domicile does not depend on formalities but on a state of mind makes it difficult to prove, however, especially when the person in question cannot be asked about their past intentions. The applicant under the I(PFD)A 1975, as under the legislation it replaced, has to prove the deceased's domicile.[27] Thus, where in *Mastaka v Midland Bank* (1941) the deceased appeared to have taken a Russian domicile from her husband on marriage (the rule whereby a married woman took her husband's domicile has since been abolished) and there was no evidence of her having changed it since, no claim could be made.

The nature and effect of the domicile rule in the family provision context was more recently discussed in *Agulian v Cyganik* (2006). Andreas Nathaneal had a Cypriot domicile of origin. It was originally held that before his death he had lost that and acquired a domicile of choice in England, where he lived and worked for 43 of his 63 years, before leaving an estate sworn at £6,527,362. The court reviewed the authorities on domicile of choice, especially *Re Fuld* (1965). This affirmed that the domicile of origin may reassert itself if the domicile of choice is lost, and that no domicile of choice is obtained if someone retains the long-term intention of returning to his original country. However, what intention was enough to negate acquiring a domicile of choice was unclear. Further, though the standard of proof was not 'beyond reasonable doubt', it was certainly a heavy one to satisfy. In *Agulian v Cyganik*, the contested issue was whether, having lived many years in England without changing his Cypriot domicile, Andreas later did so. He had been born in 1939 in the Greek village of Assia. Originally he left Cyprus in some fear following family troubles, but he stayed in touch and visited, and later he bought land in Cyprus. He returned, intending to stay, in 1972, but left following the Turkish invasion in 1974, settling back in London. He sent his daughter to a private school in Cyprus and visited her and his parents regularly. He continued to buy land in Cyprus and to send money there, apparently in order to start a business. Though he lived in Britain on a British passport, he kept up his Cypriot ID card and led a largely Cypriot life, though his partners were not Cypriot. The question for the court – which was characterised by the judge at para 46 in terms of how 'Soren Kierkegaard's aphorism that "Life must be lived forwards, but can only be understood backwards" resonates in the biographical data of domicile disputes' – was whether he was domiciled in England at the date of his death. The court unanimously decided that the judge below had not looked correctly at the history of Andreas' life and intentions in finding that he had changed his domicile at some late stage, and that he had remained domiciled in Cyprus. His fiancée's family provision claim therefore had to be dismissed. However, Lord Justice Longmore remarked that the notion of domicile was 'antiquated', and suggested reconsidering the family provision legislation to make the requirement one of habitual residence instead (para 58).

The Law Commission favoured removing the requirement of domicile: there is a long history of criticising the requirement.[28] It is so dependent on facts, rather than law, and on their interpretation, that it is inevitably contestable. In *Holliday v Musa* (2010), for example, the question of whether a Cypriot man who had lived in England for decades had at some point acquired a domicile of choice here was answered differently from in *Agulian v Cyganik*: despite his stated intention later in life to run for the presidency in Cyprus, the court found that he was domiciled in England. One proposed amendment to this provision was in the bill debated in Parliament that became the ITPA 2014: it was to allow any person habitually resident in England and Wales to claim, irrespective of the deceased's domicile, but this was dropped following concerns about how it would apply in Scotland as well as in relation to cross-border claims generally, especially

---

27  A domicile of choice has to be proved by the person asserting it: *Winans v IRC* (1904).
28  JHC Morris 'The Choice of Law Clause in Statutes' (1946) Law Quarterly Review 170.

whether it would mean that a person in England could claim against the foreign estate of the deceased.[29] The Law Commission originally had much broader proposals, including the suggestion of replacing the requirement as to the domicile of the deceased with one of habitual residence in England and Wales at the date of death, as proposed by Lord Justice Longmore in *Agulian v Cyganik*, but they attracted little support.[30] Nevertheless the concerns that motivated those proposals – such as the five million European Union citizens who live in countries other than that of their nationality, as well as those who own property abroad – remain valid, and further proposals may be expected in future, if not from the Law Commission then perhaps directly from the European authorities. This again, however, would involve some cultural change, making property rights more dependent on the land than the individual. However, the coming into force of the European Succession Regulation (see 6.2) may alter perspectives.

## 15.7 When to apply

If a person intends to claim against someone's estate, the application must be brought no more than six months from the date on which a grant of representation is taken out, save where the court gives leave for the period of time to be extended. Application can, however, be made before the grant, following the ITPA 2014. *Re Freeman* (1984) established that if a grant is revoked and replaced with another grant, the relevant date will be that of the second, valid, grant. In that case, a grant in common form had been revoked because it was shown later that the will had not in fact been properly attested. The court held that into the word 'representation' it would imply 'effective' or 'valid' so that time ran from the later grant.

### 15.7.1 Extension of time

The court has a general discretion under s 4 of the I(PFD)A 1975 to extend time. In *Re Salmon* (1980), the court gave some guidelines as to how its unfettered jurisdiction to extend the time limit for bringing an application ought to be exercised. It held that the discretion ought to be exercised judicially, the onus lying on the applicant to make out a substantial case for it being just and proper for the court to exercise its discretion. The court should consider how promptly, and in what circumstances, the applicant applied to the court for an extension of time and also warned the defendant of the proposed application, and the question should be addressed as to whether negotiations were commenced within the time limit. If negotiations did begin during the time limit, this will make it very likely that the court will grant the extension, unlike the comparable situation in a personal injury action where the courts, though they have a discretion to extend time, will pay comparatively little heed to the existence of negotiations before the expiration of the limit. What is more relevant is whether the estate had been distributed before a claim under the Act was notified or made. The court should also consider the effects of refusal of an extension and whether this would leave the potential applicant without redress – an unrepresented applicant who could not sue their solicitor for missing the time limit might therefore be at an advantage for that reason.

In *Stock v Brown* (1994), a widow in her nineties had delayed six years before bringing a claim against her husband's estate. The court balanced the exceptional delay against the extenuating circumstances and the widow's needs and gave her leave to claim out of time.

In *Re C (deceased) (leave to apply for provision)* (1995), the court discussed the issues arising where the applicant is a child. There is no provision under the Inheritance (Provision for Family and

---

29  HC Deb 26 March 2014, vol 578, col 423.
30  Law Commission 331 *Intestacy and Family Provision Claims on Death* (2011), para 7.25.

Dependants) Act 1975, as there is in ordinary civil litigation, that time limits run against children only once they reach the age of majority: the limit is set with reference to the date of the grant of representation. In this case, the applicant was a child aged eight years who lived with her mother. Her father had died suddenly when she was four, leaving a very large estate to trustees who distributed it in the two years allowed, without making any provision for her. Just before the distribution ended, the child's mother consulted solicitors but negotiations and litigation for various reasons proceeded very slowly, and the total delay was almost three and a half years. The court discussed the conflicting principles, on the one hand, that a father should maintain a child and, on the other, that beneficiaries should know where they stand within a reasonable period after the death. It accepted the argument that children often suffered from parents' mistakes (as here, where the mother had delayed) but 'to argue that it can happen is not to lessen the injustice of it'. In this case, no capital had been deployed. The argument that the beneficiaries' extensive and expensive negotiations as to their respective shares were now to be unreasonably upset was, the court suggested, somewhat exaggerated. Taking into account the size of the estate and his opinion that 'in none of the reported cases to which I have been referred, were the prospects of substantial success so clear', Wilson J granted leave for the child to apply out of time.

## 15.8 Who may apply

If a claimant can establish that the deceased died domiciled in England and Wales, and manages to bring their claim before a court, they will have to establish also that they are within one of the categories of persons entitled by the I(PFD)A 1975 to bring a claim. The courts will not consider anyone else and they have no power to do so, although they do have the capacity to form and revise their judgments about what the wording of the categories really mean. Showing that a person belongs in one of the categories of persons able to claim is often called establishing that person's *locus standi*. This means, literally, 'place to stand' and, in practice, that they are in a position as a matter of law to bring a claim.

There are six classes of applicant, and they are set out in s 1(1) of the Act. They are:

(a) the wife or husband of the deceased;
(b) a former wife or former husband of the deceased who has not remarried;
(ba) a cohabitant (not being the deceased's spouse, or former spouse who has not remarried) who lived as the deceased's husband or wife for the two years immediately preceding the death;
(c) a child of the deceased;
(d) any person (not being a child of the deceased) who, in the case of any marriage to which the deceased was at any time a party, was treated by the deceased as a child of the family in relation to that marriage;
(e) any person (not being a person included in the foregoing classes) who immediately before the death of the deceased was being maintained, either wholly or partly, by the deceased.

Different standards of reasonableness apply to those in s 1(1)(a) from those which apply to everyone else. Provided that there was no continuing separation under a judicial separation order, the surviving spouse must show that they not receive from the deceased's will or intestacy such financial provision as it would be reasonable in all the circumstances of the case for them to receive, whether or not that provision is required for his or her maintenance (s 1(2)(a)). Everyone else, however, must confine themselves to maintenance (s 1(2)(b)); if they receive enough for their maintenance, they will not obtain an award from the court, and maintenance sets the level of award they will receive otherwise. However, the definition of maintenance is a moot point (see 15.30).

## 15.9 Section 1(1)(a) – spouse or civil partner of the deceased

Section 1(1)(a) of the I(PFD)A 1975 gives standing to the spouse or civil partner of the deceased.

### 15.9.1 Historical claims by spouses

Historically, it was easier for a woman to claim against her husband than for a man to claim against his wife, for example, for maintenance where the couple separated. This was related to the different legal relationship of men and women to property – married women were unable fully to own or deal with their own property until the Married Women's Property Acts of the late nineteenth century; these restrictions were in turn related to the different social roles for men and women. The former were the property-owners and financial providers, and the latter performed a financially dependent domestic role.

This model is now seriously outdated, particularly given the changes in family law that now see the same-sex family formally established through civil partnerships, followed by equal rights to marriage. Yet it is only a few decades since a husband was responsible for his wife's tax returns, a practice which made perfect sense when what was hers was his, but which appeared odd in the 1980s. There remains, however, a grain of relevance – even after sex discrimination has been removed from the law, it may still remain in reality. Men still own more property than women; men are still paid more overall than women; husbands who have gone out to paid work own more property than wives who are more likely to have spent more of their earning time looked after the house and family, unpaid. In heterosexual couples, the men tend to be older than the women, and men tend to die younger. Nevertheless, the legislative structure is somewhat gender-free. The 1938 Act allowed either party to a marriage to make a claim, though the tendency for husbands to die earlier owning more property than their wives would mean that claims by husbands were comparatively unusual. However, in *Re Clayton* (1966), on an application by a disabled widower for financial relief from his wife's estate, Ungoed-Thomas J said, 'I certainly do not see in the Act a greater onus of proof on the surviving husband than on the surviving wife'. Undoubtedly, the same applies under the 1975 Act, and to civil partners as well as spouses.

### 15.9.2 Proving the marriage or civil partnership

The burden of proof of the marriage or civil partnership lies on the person alleging that they are the spouse or civil partner. In most cases this will not be a contentious point. If the marriage or partnership did not end in divorce then it will generally have subsisted until the death, even if there has been a judicial separation. A *prima facie* case can easily be made for this by production of a marriage certificate, and this will be sufficient for the court unless someone raises an objection.

For example, if it can be shown that the marriage or partnership was bigamous and therefore void, it may not be possible to base a claim on it. A court may therefore have to deal first of all with the preliminary issue of whether the marriage was valid. In *Re Watkins* (1953), the court had first of all to decide whether a widow could claim against the estate of her second husband when her marriage to her first husband had never been dissolved and it was not known whether he was dead at the time of the second marriage. The first husband had disappeared over 20 years before the second marriage, and neither his wife nor the rest of his family had heard anything further from him. The court presumed he had died before her second marriage, so that second marriage was valid. In *Re Peete* (1952), the wife produced a marriage certificate, but no death certificate for her previous husband. The evidence she had of his death was uncorroborated hearsay. Her application was dismissed on the basis that she had not proved she was the deceased's spouse. An applicant may, however, in certain limited circumstances, rely on a void marriage (see 15.9.4).

## 15.9.3 Polygamous marriages

In *Re Sehota, Kaur v Kaur* (1978), the applicant's marriage to the deceased had been a polygamous marriage. The burden of proof was on her to show that she was validly married to the deceased, just as with judicially separated spouses, but the court held that it was satisfied where the marriage had not been annulled by proceedings. The court held that the ruling in *Hyde v Hyde and Woodmansee* (1866) (the case which is usually cited as providing the definition of marriage) that the divorce legislation applied only to monogamous marriages did not apply in this case. It held that polygamous marriages were generally valid in English law, and *Hyde v Hyde* had never applied to the law of succession and had been reversed by statute in matrimonial proceedings. *Re Sehota* was applied in the polygamy and intestacy case of *Official Solicitor to the Senior Courts v Yemoh and Others* (2010) (see 9.3.1).

## 15.9.4 Void marriages

The 1975 Act itself refers to void marriages at s 25(4). Technically, a void marriage is one considered in law never to have existed, as opposed to a voidable marriage, which is considered to exist until it is annulled by a court; it is then declared never to have been valid. Thus, proceedings to annul a void marriage are technically not necessary, but may be brought because the law allows parties to both void and voidable marriages to apply to the courts for ancillary relief (orders about financial and property matters) in nullity proceedings. In the same way, there are provisions for parties to void marriages to seek relief under the 1975 Act, provided that the applicant spouse entered into the marriage in good faith and has not had the marriage dissolved or annulled by a procedure recognised under English law nor entered into a later marriage. A spouse claiming in this way will be treated as any other spouse for the purposes of the higher level of provision awarded under s 1(1)(a). It may sound odd that a marriage that has never existed at law (one that was *void ab initio*) can give rise to financial claims, but the practical situation of the parties may often be just as it would have been had the marriage been valid.

The limitations of the inclusion of void marriages have, however, been explored and developed. In *Whiston v Whiston* (1995), it was held that the wife in a void marriage could not seek ancillary relief because she was herself criminally responsible for the situation that led to the marriage being void, namely that, at the date of the marriage ceremony, she was already lawfully married to someone else, as she well knew. A similar approach was taken in the case of *J v S-T (formerly J) (Transsexual: ancillary relief)* (1997), where the marriage was void because one of the parties was transsexual.[31] *Gandhi v Patel and Others* (2001) was a case about an attempt to claim family provision as a 'spouse' after a marriage that was void because the husband was already married, and because it lacked formalities of a recognisable civil marriage (though it constituted a proper religious ceremony). The court held both that the situation was 'a non-marriage rather than a void marriage' and that the necessary good faith was lacking. However, this line of development does not constitute saying that a claim cannot be made if a marriage was void. It rather suggests that the void marriage should not be the result of the claimant's wrongdoing.

---

31 The approach to marriage and transsexuals originated with the case of *Corbett v Corbett (otherwise Ashley)* (1970), where the marriage was void but an ancillary relief claim was however allowed. Whilst the courts' approach to arrangements with an element of deception appears to have hardened, this may be because of the greater availability of regular status: civil partnership under the Civil Partnership Act 2004 and marriage for same-sex couples under the Marriage (Same Sex Couples) Act 2013, and the recognition of gender change under the Gender Recognition Act 2005.

### 15.9.5 Remarriage of spouse

A spouse who can bring him- or herself within s 1(1)(a) may pursue their claim equally if they have remarried after the deceased's death.

### 15.9.6 Judicial separation

It should be noted in respect of judicially separated spouses that, although their marriage is not dissolved, they will often have obtained, by consent or otherwise, an ancillary relief order from a matrimonial court in the course of the judicial separation proceedings. This will almost invariably include an order that, the court considering it just so to order under s 15 of the I(PFD)A 1975, the parties are no longer entitled to apply for provision from each other's estates under s 2. A judicially separated spouse does not, however, qualify for the higher level of spouse relief where the separation was continuing at the date of death.

## 15.10 Section 1(1)(b) – former spouse or civil partner who has not remarried or formed new civil partnership

Section 1(1)(b) refers to former spouses and civil partners who have not remarried or formed a new civil partnership. This subsection applies to proceedings in England and Wales, and is intended more to protect those whose ancillary relief proceedings have not been completed than to provide an avenue for fresh claims.

Notably, whilst a former spouse who has remarried may not apply under this subsection, in the case of *Grattan v McNaughton* (2001), where a husband had left his widow a right to occupy a home so long as she did not cohabit, the restriction was struck out as unreasonable and she also received other provision in a 1975 Act claim.

### 15.10.1 Powers of divorce courts

In *Re Fullard* (1982), the applicant and the deceased had been divorced. The death of Mr Fullard released substantial capital by way of insurance policies, and his former wife applied for a share in that capital. The Court of Appeal considered the powers of a divorce court to make appropriate capital adjustments between the parties in matrimonial proceedings, and in view of those powers it stated that it was likely that there would be comparatively few cases where a divorced spouse would succeed in an application under the 1975 Act. It said that where, as in *Re Fullard*, the parties had settled their financial matters by agreement or order, an application should not succeed unless there had been a material change in circumstances.

### 15.10.2 Must the agreement be overt or satisfactory?

It is not clear how far this represents a change in attitude from earlier decisions, for example, that in *Re W* (1975), where a former wife succeeded under the legislation preceding the 1975 Act in obtaining a substantial capital sum from the estate of her husband from whom she had been divorced for 26 years. In that case, the court held that he had a considerable moral obligation to her because he had failed to maintain her as he should have done, and that the capital ordered to be paid to the former wife had been accumulated by the deceased as a result of making no maintenance payments.

### 15.10.3 Unfinished ancillary relief business

Nevertheless, the claim in *Re Farrow* (1987) succeeded. On the divorce of Mr and Mrs Farrow, an order was made within the matrimonial proceedings for Mr Farrow to pay his former wife periodical payments by way of maintenance. Less than a year later, Mr Farrow died intestate. The former wife applied to the court for financial support out of his estate, and the court gave her that relief, having regard to the fact that the periodical payments order ran for such a short time. Section 14 of the I(PFD)A 1975 provides that where an application for family provision is made by a former spouse in respect of the death of the other party to the marriage within 12 months of a decree absolute of divorce (or a decree of judicial separation, if the separation is continuing), and there has been no order in ancillary relief proceedings, the court has power to look at what the spouse would have obtained from a matrimonial court had such an order been made.

### 15.10.4 Dismissal of claims in ancillary relief proceedings

As with judicial separation, it is usual for the parties to proceedings for divorce to obtain an ancillary relief order and for that to include a provision dismissing claims under the 1975 Act, pursuant to the power given to a matrimonial court to make such an order by s 15 of the 1975 Act. Similar provisions apply in relation to settlements at the dissolution of civil partnerships.

The case of *Whiting v Whiting* (1988) demonstrated how the practice of the law may operate to produce a particular result. The parties were divorced in 1975, the three children going to live with the wife and the husband paying maintenance. When the wife subsequently qualified as a teacher, the maintenance order was reduced by consent to a nominal order. In 1979, the husband remarried and, in 1983, he was made redundant. In 1986 (following the insertion into the Matrimonial Causes Act 1973 of s 25A), the husband applied to the matrimonial court for a 'clean break' – the dismissal, first, of the wife's own claim for maintenance and, second, of her potential claim against his estate under the 1975 Act. The wife was at that point in a much better financial situation, from the point of view of both income and debt liabilities, than the husband, who had since remarried. The registrar dismissed the application and the husband appealed to a judge, who upheld the dismissal. The husband then appealed to the Court of Appeal. No evidence of the new wife's situation was brought though she was known to be employed as a teacher. The Court of Appeal dismissed the appeal. It said that, though it might itself have dismissed the maintenance claim, the question was rather whether the lower court had come to an unreasonable decision. It found that the court below had been entitled to exercise its discretion as it did. The husband would have had to make out his case under s 15(1) of the 1975 Act that the dismissal of the potential I(PFD)A 1975 claim was 'just', and he had not done so.

In *Barrass v Harding* (2001), the Court of Appeal confirmed that it is only in exceptional circumstances that family provision will be awarded to a former spouse whose claims were dismissed in ancillary relief proceedings even if that dismissal was so far back that it preceded the 1975 Act.

## 15.11 Section 1(1)(ba) – unmarried cohabitant during two years preceding death (deaths after 1995)

Section 1(1)(ba) was inserted into the 1975 Act by the Law Reform (Succession) Act 1995. It gives a right to claim to a person who had lived in the deceased's household as his or her spouse or civil partner for the two years immediately preceding the death. This requirement that, for a claimant to fall within s 1(1)(ba), the qualifying cohabitation must have been 'immediately' before the death echoes not only the Fatal Accidents Act 1976 but also the requirements relating to dependency (see 15.14.6).

### 15.11.1 Meaning of cohabitation

The provision was modelled on that of the Fatal Accidents Act 1976, which gives cohabitants for the two years immediately preceding the death of the other cohabitant standing to sue the relevant tortfeasor, and accorded with the acceptance of cohabitation as creating a legally valid relationship with property consequences. The definition of cohabitant does not appear to have caused too much practical difficulty, despite its apparent vagueness. The question of whether persons are spouses is usually easily answered; without the benefit of any equivalent of the marriage ceremony, the nature of a relationship may be difficult to define – the suggestion that the appropriate test is whether one party fills out the other's tax return may be frivolous but, equally, it may be as good as any other. In *Re Watson* (1999), Neuberger J suggested that the test might be 'whether, in the opinion of a reasonable person with normal perceptions' (perhaps a variant on the views of the man on the Clapham omnibus) they were living as husband and wife, before going on to advert to 'the multifarious nature of marital relationships'.[32]

The meaning of not living together is often the emphasis where a couple has separated before the death. Although the claim was accepted as one under s 1(1)(e) (dependency), the judge in *Witkowska v Kaminski* (2006) said that a cohabitant who had been visiting family in Poland for three months before the deceased died on the day she returned to England was not only still dependent on him but also, had it been claimed, cohabiting. Three weeks in hospital did not mean separation in *Re Watson*, and in *Gully v Dix* (2004) the 'settled situation' of a 27-year-long relationship was cohabitation even though the claimant had left the deceased three months before he died because of his alcohol abuse and threats to kill her: the 'tie of that relationship ... the public and private acknowledgment of their mutual society, and the mutual protection and support that binds them together' were all continuing. What would have meant the claimant would fail would have been 'an irretrievable breakdown of their relationship': this was merely a 'transitory' interruption, 'serving as a pause for reflection about the future of a relationship going through difficult times but still recognised to be subsisting', and the joint household was 'merely suspended' but still continuing.[33] In the less dramatic situation of *Churchill v Roach* (2002), the finding that the cohabitants had not been living together immediately before the death was not based on their separate addresses. The judge found it possible that a couple could have one household in two properties, although in that case he held that they in fact had separate domestic economies. The claimant could and did, however, show that although she did not fall within s 1(1)(ba), she did qualify as a dependant under s 1(1)(e).

## 15.12 Section 1(1)(c) – child of the deceased

Section 1(1)(c) refers to the child of the deceased. It is for the child applicant to prove that they are the child of the deceased. They may, however, rely on the presumption of legitimacy if they are the child of parents who are married to each other.

### 15.12.1 Definition of children

Originally, under the 1938 Act, only unmarried or disabled daughters, or minor or disabled sons, could apply. The age at which a child ceases in English law to be dependent is in any case very variable, depending on the area of law. In the private family legislation on divorce, a child ceases childhood generally somewhere between 16 and 18 or later if they continue in full-time education.

---

32  As the parties had separate bedrooms, this case deciding they were nevertheless living as husband and wife excited some general media interest.
33  See especially paras 24 and 29.

## 15.12.2  Adult children

Section 1(1)(c) does not refer only to infant children, but to the offspring of the deceased of whatever age. Age restrictions on claims under the family provision legislation were removed in the 1975 Act, though a reading of the Law Commission's 61st Report might suggest that they did not expect large numbers of applications by adult children, and especially not by able-bodied employed children, as discussed in *Re Coventry* (1979). That case left open the idea of a 'moral claim': notwithstanding the strong English tradition of individual property rights and testamentary freedom, the idea that children in particular have a moral entitlement to a share in their parents' estate, arising from the blood relationship and more important than the right to cut a child out, persists. In *Re Hancock (Deceased)* (1998), the Court of Appeal however confirmed that claims by adult children should be treated like any other type of application under the Act. The courts nevertheless confirmed in *Robinson v Fernsby* (2003) and *Garland v Morris* (2007) that it could be reasonable for a parent to make no provision for an adult child.

The question of level of entitlement where some provision was merited was interestingly reviewed by the courts in *Ilott v Mitson* (2011), where the deceased Mrs Jackson had left her estate of almost half a million pounds to various animal charities, and nothing to her daughter, whose circumstances were modest to difficult: she had five children and her husband's wages were such that the family lived largely on welfare benefits. She was at first awarded £50,000, and appealed, with the charities resisting her claim by way of a cross-appeal. Although the High Court allowed the charities' appeal, the Court of Appeal reinstated the original decision of the district judge. 'Moral obligation' remained at most something a court might take into account in assessing whether or not the existing provision for the claimant was reasonable. In 2014, there was an unsuccessful further appeal on the basis that the claimant, who was dependent on benefits and therefore liable in effect to lose everything over £16,000 that she did not spend immediately, should have been given enough to rehouse herself. Parker J held that, though she could see the claimant's point, the judge in balancing the claims on the estate had not been manifestly wrong and so the appeal must fail.

The increasing prevalence of step-families also led the Law Commission in its 2009 exercise to consult on whether there should be some reform that would give greater recognition and strength to the perceived legitimate claims of the children of a first family over those of a second spouse, for example. The Law Commission concluded that the 'complications in a situation of that nature are so difficult that we think that such reform is impracticable', and left the hard cases to be resolved by will.[34] See also 15.18.4.

## 15.12.3  Nature of relationship

Section 1(1)(c) includes adopted children by virtue of the general law (the provisions of the Adoption Act 1976), and illegitimate children and children *en ventre sa mère* at the date of the deceased's death by virtue of s 25(1) of the 1975 Act itself. Adopted children cannot claim against the estate of their biological parent, and this remains unchanged by the ITPA 2014 despite broadening of their claims on intestacy under that Act.[35]

---

34  Law Commission 331 *Intestacy and Family Provision Claims on Death* (2011), paras 6.25–26.

35  The reluctance in the common law tradition to link blood relationships and property entitlements is noted by Nicola Peart and Andrew Borkowski, 'Provision for Adult Children on Death: The Lesson from New Zealand' (2000) 12 Child and Family Law Quarterly 333. English law has always been particularly individualistic: see Alan Macfarlane, *The Origins of English Individualism* (Wiley 1991).

### 15.12.4 Adoption and claims under the 1975 Act

The precise words of the adoption legislation may be important; they may exclude a child from claiming from the estate of its natural parent, as well as allowing them to claim against the estate of their adoptive parent. In *Re Collins (deceased)* (1990), claims were made by the two children of the deceased, Christine Anne Collins, who died intestate in 1980. Two years before her death, she had married Mr Collins, but had started divorce proceedings against him and had reached a decree nisi in the proceedings. She left an estate of £27,000 net which, under the intestacy rules, would all go to Mr Collins as he survived her. The first claimant, Bernice, was the illegitimate daughter of Mrs Collins; at the date of the hearing she was 19 years old, unemployed and living on social security with her boyfriend. The court held that although Mrs Collins had no liability to maintain the adult Bernice, the provision made for her on intestacy was not reasonable, and it awarded her a lump sum of £5,000. The other claimant, B, was the child of the Collins' marriage. He had been born in June 1979 and adopted away in 1987. Counsel for B addressed the court on the subject of the Adoption Act 1976, in particular ss 39(2) (which said that adopted children were to be treated as the children only of their adoptive parents) and 42(4), the 'saving subsection' (s 39(2) avoids prejudice to interests vested in possession before the adoption), saying that the potential to make a claim under the 1975 Act was vested before the adoption and thus covered by the 'saving subsection'.

The court held, however, that the qualifying date was that of the deceased's death. It said that the saving subsections of the Adoption Act could not affect law laid down by Act of Parliament such as the 1975 Act, which provided specifically that the application must be made by the deceased's child. As to the suggestion that B's right to apply under the 1975 Act subsisted as a chose in action, the court thought it was 'really no more than a hope'. The court commented on B's favourable position with his adoptive parents and dismissed his claim.

### 15.12.5 Relationship of blood or adoption

What is required for an applicant to have *locus standi* under this subsection is a relationship of blood or adoption; step-children cannot apply under this subsection. The relevance of earlier decisions of other courts was discussed in *Rowe v Rowe* (1980). Where there has been a finding by a court that a child is the offspring of the deceased, that will bind the child if they were a party to the proceedings by virtue of the *res judicata* (the thing has been adjudicated) rule. If, however, the child was not a party, they will not be prevented from trying to establish parenthood if the decision was not favourable to them, although if the decision was favourable to the child the estate may be prevented by that from setting up a defence on the basis that the deceased was not the child's parent. DNA testing, which has made proving parenthood much easier in the area of child maintenance, for example, is less helpful when one of the parties is dead.

## 15.13 Section 1(1)(d) – child of the family

Section 1(1)(d) refers to any person (not being a child of the deceased) who, in the case of any marriage to which the deceased was at any time a party, was treated by the deceased as a child of the family in relation to that marriage. After the coming into force of the ITPA 2014, this widens to include children whose relationship to the deceased was 'otherwise' that of a child of the family, specifically 'in relation to any family in which the deceased at any time stood in the role of a parent, was treated by the deceased as a child of the family'. This is the subsection for step-children in particular – it gives them a status that means they do not have to prove dependency. Before the 1975 Act, they could not claim at all. Before the reforms of the ITPA 2014, step-child claimants had to trace the relationship through a marriage or civil partnership. The Law

Commission considered that this was 'outdated and may operate in an arbitrary and unfair manner'.[36] Its recommendation, as embodied in the Act, in effect focuses on the child (including an adult child) rather than the parent, mirroring the approach long since taken in various aspects of family proceedings. In allowing step-child claims to run through unmarried de facto relationships and specifically including at the new s 1(2A) single-parent step-relationships, it also brings the family provision structure into line with a society that has long since accepted and normalised those relationships. Note that the applicant not only need not be an infant at the time of application but also need not have been an infant at any time during which the relationship on which they base their claim to *locus standi* subsisted.

### 15.13.1 Not an infant when the relevant family was formed

The successful applicant in *Re Callaghan* (1984) was 35 years old and living in his own home, a rented council house, with his wife when his mother married the deceased. The deceased treated the applicant as an adult child of his own by acknowledging his role as grandfather to the applicant's children, placing confidence as to his property and financial affairs in the applicant, and depending on the applicant to care for him in his last illness. He then died intestate, so that the applicant stood to inherit nothing from the £31,000 estate. Taking into account that the deceased's assets were derived from his wife, the applicant's mother, and her first husband's family, the court gave the applicant £15,000 to enable him to buy his council house.

### 15.13.2 Treated as a child of the family

Historically, there had to have been a family as such for the applicant to have been part of, fulfilling both conditions of relation by marriage – not an unmarried family – and of living together. The child therefore necessarily had to have been born, to have been 'treated' by the deceased (*A v A* (family: unborn child) (1974)). It was established in *W (RJ) v W (SJ)* (1971) that whether the deceased knew he was not the child's father is irrelevant to the question of whether the child has *locus standi* under this section, though it might be relevant to what the child can then claim. This definition became increasingly anachronistic and out of step with changing social attitudes to what constitutes a family.

### 15.13.3 How a step-child establishes 'treatment as a child of the family'

The applicant in *Re Leach* (1985) was near retirement, and had relied on her deceased step-father's stated intention to make provision for her by will, which he failed to do. The court discussed what a step-child in particular should establish in order for a claim to be entertained. The step-child should have been treated as a child of the family by the deceased, and that treatment must amount to more than a mere display of affection, kindness or hospitality. The deceased must have assumed the position of a parent towards the applicant, with all the responsibilities and privileges of that relationship. Treatment of the applicant as a child of the family after the marriage has ended by the death of the other spouse is relevant if the treatment stems from the marriage, but such treatment, if it occurs, need not continue until the deceased dies.

Though some consultees of the Law Commission thought that the expansion of the step-child category to include claims through single parents or unmarried relationships could lead to people being unwilling to sponsor children abroad or accept help from neighbours, the Law

---

36 Law Commission 331 *Intestacy and Family Provision Claims on Death* (2011), para 6.40.

Commission dismissed that as 'more hypothetical than real' and 'fanciful', pointing out that judges in particular thought the meaning of 'treated as a child of the family' was settled and clear. It also rejected the suggestion that children claiming through the new broadened definition should have had to live in the same household as the deceased, saying there was no such requirement for biological children.[37] In effect, therefore, the reforms of 2014 as to eligible family child applicants fully integrate the social change that has led to the acceptance of de facto relationships, gay relationships and single-parent families, accepting the implications of that change for the status of any children.

## 15.14  Section 1(1)(e) – dependants

Section 1(1)(e) refers to any person (not being a person included in the foregoing categories) who immediately before the death of the deceased was being maintained, either wholly or partly, by the deceased. In relation to the 1975 Act, the Law Commission recommended this particular addition to the categories of potential claimants under the previous legislation because it was concerned about the 'accidental or unintentional' or 'unfair' failure to provide for dependants. It was concerned about the increasing number of 'de facto spouses', or unmarried cohabitants, who were not catered for under the previous legislation, and cohabitants indeed proved the most fruitful source of claims. The claims of a wife under the earlier legislation had been affected by the deceased's testamentary gifts to another woman in Re Joslin (1941); where the law restricted testamentary freedom on either the moral or the practical basis, it was illogical to restrict that basis to members of the married family only.

However, the question of how a person would show they were being wholly or partly maintained was unclear. The Law Commission had originally said:

> We think that these questions can be resolved by the court on common-sense lines. The prin-
> ciple in our view is that a person should be treated as having been maintained by the
> deceased, either wholly or partly, as the case may be, if the deceased was, otherwise than for
> full consideration, making a substantial contribution in cash or kind towards that person's
> reasonable needs.[38]

### 15.14.1  Whose common sense?

Unfortunately, the Law Commission failed to say what constituted common sense, or perhaps whose sense was involved; in particular it failed to say what value should be placed on caring and how the problem of the interaction between financial dependency and caring should be resolved. If the applicant is required to have depended on the other on a value basis, then a person who has provided constant nursing care in return for something of comparatively little value has no claim, especially if the caring is valued at the market price of obtaining constant care. The valuation of caring is, however, not usually at market prices, whether the care is that of a nurse, in family provision proceedings, or a housekeeper, in divorce proceedings; it appears to be viewed as being worth very little money, as it is often done for love.

In assessing dependency for a claim under the 1975 Act the common sense of judges did not necessarily accord with the common sense of everyone: the consequences of a requirement for financial dependency often produced a result widely perceived as unfair and favouring those who

---

37  Law Commission 331, paras 6.34, 6.38; s 331 *Intestacy and Family Provision Claims on Death* (2011).
38  Law Commission 61, para 98 *Family Law: Second Report on Family Property: Family Provision on Death* (1974).

'sponged' or 'scrounged' off their providers over those whose conduct gave them a better moral claim on the estate of the deceased. This issue was however addressed by the Law Commission in their enquiries about Intestacy and Family Provision Claims on Death from 2009, and whilst most cohabitation provisions did not make it into the ensuing Inheritance and Powers of Trustees Act 2014, for deaths after September 2014, para 3 of Sch 2 amends sub-s (3). It clarifies that, where a claimant says they were being maintained by the deceased, caring for the deceased should only be regarded as being 'full valuable consideration' if it is carried out 'pursuant to an arrangement of a commercial nature'.

## 15.14.2 Other jurisdictions

Other jurisdictions or other areas of law have been looked to in the situation where a person has behaved in a particular way during their lifetime on the basis that they will be rewarded in some-one's will. In New Zealand, for example, there is testamentary promises legislation which can be appealed to; in England the doctrines of constructive trust and proprietary estoppel have been used, especially during the 1970s, to rectify the inequity perceived in such situations. In *Pascoe v Turner* (1979) (not a succession case), for example, a woman badly let down by a man who broke his promises to her was awarded the fee simple of his house. The extension of proprietary estoppel to a general equitable remedy was, however, regarded as beginning to approach a remedy for those who were unable to establish more than their reasonable expectations of reward, short of a contract. Objections were often based on the perceived disproportion between the services given to the defendant in the court proceedings and the property he or she was ordered to make over.

## 15.14.3 Moral arguments less acceptable in England?

The general approach of the English courts under the family provision legislation in the past has been to reward caring at its out-of-pocket cost, for example as in *Re Cook* (1956), unless the applicant has given up employment which they already had, when the court will find a particular detriment. The courts also regard assisting in a business as showing something more than assisting in general life by caring (*Re Brownbridge* (1942)). Their general view was perhaps expressed by Oliver J, overturning an award of £2,000 to the son of the deceased who had lived with him for many years. He said in *Re Coventry* (1979) of the 1975 Act: 'It is not the purpose of the Act to provide legacies or rewards for meritorious conduct.'

## 15.14.4 What sort of person may claim under this category?

There has always been some doubt as to who could be included in the category, and its scope continues to be interpreted by the courts. However, the breadth of scope of the category of potential applicants, so far as the type of person who might be a potential applicant is concerned, was discussed by the court in *Re Wilkinson* (1978). It found that the, category of 'dependant of the deceased' is not confined to relatives of the deceased or to members of the deceased's household, and it covers persons who during the lifetime of the deceased would have had no right to enforce a claim for maintenance against the deceased – in this case the applicant was the deceased's sister, who had been acting as a companion. The court also had to weigh up the financial circumstances of the case in order to be satisfied that the applicant was dependent on the deceased. The deceased sister had asked the applicant to live with her and she had paid all the household expenses, the two of them sharing the household tasks. The court placed a financial value on the applicant's work about the house and decided it was less than the value of the accommodation provided for her by her sister; therefore, she was financially dependent.

### 15.14.5 'Maintaining' and 'immediately'

The courts have not been entirely happy with having to interpret the detailed provisions of this subsection, which have proved much more difficult to deal with than, for example, a provision which requires the courts to say whether or not a party was validly married. The courts have comparatively little experience of defining whether a person is being maintained or not, or putting a financial value on caring in order to measure it against the value of free accommodation. The two particular areas of this subsection that caused difficulties of interpretation were, first, the requirement for the deceased to have been 'maintaining' the claimant, and, second, the requirement for the deceased to have to have been maintaining the claimant 'immediately' before their death. Much of the mischief in cases of mutual support and reliance should be dealt with by the changes made by the ITPA 2014.

### 15.14.6 'Immediately'

The court in *Kourkey v Lusher* (1982) considered the question of what 'immediately' meant. The deceased had been married for 31 years, and had a chiropodist's business in which his wife had helped him. In 1953, the wife had bought the premises in which he worked and the flats above with her savings and dowry, and in 1957 she and the deceased had bought their matrimonial home in their joint names. The applicant had married an affluent Iraqi in 1945 and had two sons from that marriage. In 1963, she had met the deceased at his surgery, and in 1969 he left his wife and went to live with the applicant, who the following year divorced her husband. The deceased remained in friendly contact with his wife, paying her wages and the outgoings on the matrimonial home. In 1977, the deceased and the applicant bought a flat in their joint names, with the applicant contributing £10,000 capital and the deceased contributing £6,350 by way of mortgage. The applicant subsequently contracted to purchase a house for £39,200 with the proceeds of sale of the flat; the deceased had agreed with that but would not agree to taking on a new mortgage. In July 1979, the deceased and his wife went away on holiday together and he told her he would return to her; in August he died of a heart attack. The applicant claimed under the 1975 Act. The court held that the deceased had been reluctant to commit himself financially to the applicant during their relationship and that she had not been maintained by the deceased immediately before his death. It was also unhappy about the claimed unreasonableness of the provision for her, where she looked to her sons and her family in Iraq for support, and where the estate was in any case very small – only £1,931 net.

### 15.14.7 Assumption of responsibility and full valuable consideration

In 1980, in the case of *Re Beaumont*, the court held that the overt assumption by the deceased of responsibility for the applicant was essential to the success of a claim. This was, however, subsequently overruled by the Court of Appeal in *Jelley v Iliffe* (1981): there would be an inference from actual maintenance of an assumption of responsibility, though as to whether 'full valuable consideration' meant 'full valuable consideration under a contract', both courts thought not.

The facts in *Jelley v Iliffe* were quite unusual. The Iliffe parents had a son and a daughter, both of whom died leaving widowed spouses. Mr Jelley, the daughter's husband, then went to live with Mrs Iliffe, the son's wife, who died eight years later leaving everything to her three children. Mr Jelley applied under the 1975 Act and the Court of Appeal considered his position on an application by the children of Mrs Iliffe to strike his claim out as showing no cause of action. It referred to the injustice done to one who has been put by a deceased person in a position of dependency being deprived of any financial support, either by accident or by design of the deceased, after the death. It held that the reference to consideration in the Act had nothing to do with the law of contract and that a broad interpretation would be put on the word 'immediately' in the subsection – the arrangement faltered before the deceased's death, where the breakdown of the arrangement was due to the deceased being too ill in her terminal illness to maintain the regular payments previously made.

The court in *Jelley* also held that a person could claim as a 'dependant of the deceased' only – and it said the word 'only' should be implied into the Act, holding that the Act should be construed as if s 1(3) (which then provided that a person should be treated as being maintained by the deceased if the deceased, otherwise than for full valuable consideration, had been making a substantial contribution in money or money's worth towards the reasonable needs of that person) qualified s 1(1)(e) and not as though it provided an alternative to it. As to whether 'full valuable consideration' meant 'full valuable consideration under a contract', the court thought not in both *Jelley* and *Beaumont*. The issue of establishing dependency nevertheless continued to cause both judicial and academic comment, of the adverse kind.[39]

## 15.14.8 Evidence and extent of assumption of responsibility

What the Court of Appeal said in *Jelley v Iliffe* about the deceased's responsibility for the applicant, as in *Re Beaumont*, was that, though some responsibility must have been assumed by the deceased while she was alive, there need be no other overt act to demonstrate the assumption of responsibility beyond actual maintenance, and it need not be shown that she had also assumed responsibility for the applicant's maintenance after her own death. This principle became established, and was further developed by confirmation in *Baynes v Hedger* (2009) that the presumption could, however, be rebutted by evidence that the deceased did not intend to assume responsibility. The high water mark of the inference of assumption of responsibility was surely *Bouette v Rose* (2000), where such an inference was made as to the intentions of a severely mentally disabled girl who had died at the age of 14. On appeal, she was taken to have assumed responsibility for her mother, who lived largely on the girl's income and in a house of which the girl owned the majority share, enabling the mother to claim against the daughter's estate.

## 15.14.9 Burden of proof of dependency

A further bone of contention was the proof of 'dependency'. This was particularly productive before the changes under the 1995 Act. For example, the applicant in *Harrington v Gill* (1983) had been living with the deceased as his wife, and would subsequently have claimed under the new s 1(1)(ba). The court held that when she was claiming under s 1(1)(e) as his 'dependant', the burden of proof lay upon her to show that he had been making a substantial contribution in money or money's worth towards her reasonable needs. She was successful and the court ordered a house comprised in the deceased's net estate to be settled on the claimant for life. The insistence on the applicant establishing financial dependency in what became known as a 'balance sheet test' echoed the decision in *Re Kirby* (1982), where the court held that the claimant, if basing the claim on having been maintained by the deceased and grounding that dependency on their having lived together and shared expenses, must establish that a substantial contribution was made to the claimant's own share of the expenses by the deceased. If the contributions were broadly equal, or the claimant's contribution was greater, the claim would not succeed.

---

39  Suman Naresh, 'Dependants' Applications Under the Inheritance (Provision for Family and Dependants) Act 1975' (1980) 96 Law Quarterly Review 534; Simon Coldham, 'Dependants' Provision on Death' (1982) 45 Modern Law Review 100; Stuart Bridge 'For Love or Money? Dependent Carers and Family Provision' (2000) 59 Cambridge Law Journal 248; Sidney Ross, 'Inheritance Act Claims by Dependants' [2010] Family Law 490; Gillian Douglas, 'Family Provision and Family Practices: The Discretionary Regime of the Inheritance Act of England and Wales' (2014) 4 Oñati Socio-Legal Series 122.

The result of this, although it is undoubtedly a reasonable reading of what the legislation says, was often felt to be completely unfair, because it meant that where both parties paid their way, neither could have a claim against the other's estate, even where in practice they could not manage alone. For instance, where they had taken on a rented flat or the mortgage on a house together and shared the expenses and the rent equally, it might well be the case that neither could afford to keep the property going alone, but still neither was dependent on the other because they did not have part of their share of the expenses paid by the other party. Conversely, someone who did not work and pay their way, but allowed the other person to support them would have a claim, even where the sole reason for their not working was laziness or a desire to depend solely on their partner.

## 15.14.10 Reform under the Inheritance and Trustees' Powers Act 2014

From October 2014, following the implementation of the ITPA 2014, s 1(3) defines being maintained by the deceased as occurring

> (either wholly or partly, as the case may be) only if the deceased was making a substantial contribution in money or money's worth towards the reasonable needs of that person, other than a contribution made for full valuable consideration pursuant to an arrangement of a commercial nature.[40]

This should mean that the family provision legislation recognises the phenomenon of mutual support, where a couple share living expenses so that neither can necessarily be said to be 'dependent' on the other, but the effect of the death of one of them on the other is much the same as if they were: they do not have enough to live on, so they need support from the deceased's estate.

## 15.14.11 Further potential categories of claimants

The Law Commission in the 2009 consultation also suggested that further categories of claimants should be introduced, with a right to claim stemming from their relationship to the deceased. There was general opposition to the inclusion of siblings, on the basis of encouraging litigation – and, from charities such as the Battersea Dogs and Cats Home, concern that their legacy income would be radically depleted should that happen.[41] There was more support for (or less opposition to) the inclusion of parents, but eventually the Law Commission recommended no change. The question of who can apply as of right because of their family relationship is involved with the issue mentioned earlier in discussing testamentary freedom: what property arrangements are enforced depends on cultural traditions. However, the lesser objection to the inclusion of parents may be a reflection of the decline of state welfare provision, which means that people must be more dependent on each other privately, and the growing insecurities of elderly people in Britain with the general decline of economic conditions. Nevertheless, parents may still apply as dependants if they were actually financially dependent on their deceased children.[42]

---

40 Inheritance and Trustees' Powers Act 2014 Sch 2, para 3.
41 Law Commission 331 *Intestacy and Family Provision Claims on Death* (2011), para 6.83.
42 Mika Oldham, 'Financial Obligations Within the Family: Aspects of Intergenerational Maintenance and Succession in England and France' (2001) 60 Cambridge Law Journal 128.

## 15.15  What the applicant may claim – matters to which the court has regard

The court has to decide first whether or not the provision for the applicant under the will or intestacy of the deceased is reasonable given the circumstances at the deceased's death. The court will look at the particular circumstances of the people involved in the case – for example, even though the intestacy rules are designed with a view to giving the beneficiaries what a reasonable testator would have given them, with the spouse having first call on the estate, the court will not assume without looking at the evidence that the spouse has necessarily obtained reasonable financial provision from the operation of the intestacy rules. The Act largely leaves the calculations to the discretion of the individual court, though there are guidelines in s 3 about what level of provision is appropriate for different types of applicant. Spouses are more favourably treated.

### 15.15.1  Showing unreasonableness

Only if the court, looking at what the deceased's will or intestacy provides for the applicant, decides that it is unreasonable will it go on to consider what provision would be reasonable for the applicant. How this should work in practice is somewhat unclear on the face of the Act, say where the applicant's circumstances change after the deceased's death. The court will take into account all facts known at the date of the hearing (s 3(5)).

### 15.15.2  Statutory directions as to unreasonableness

The court is directed by s 1(2) to the definition of reasonable provision. Reasonable provision for spouses and civil partners is not confined to their maintenance (s 1(2)(a)), but for everyone else, including cohabitants, the correct standard is that of maintenance (s 1(2)(3)), as defined in the context of family provision. For the courts' definition of maintenance, and their attitude to giving capital to spouses, see 15.23.6–8 and 15.30. A decision needs to be taken as to what is reasonable, first, in order to see whether or not a claimant's existing entitlement is unreasonable and, if it is, second, to work out what order should be made.

### 15.15.3  Standard of reasonableness for cohabitants

The Law Commission's proposals in their Report No 187 to extend the right to bring a claim – *locus standi* – to unmarried cohabitants specifically excluded any idea that they might claim the same level of provision as a spouse, leaving them to justify the level of their claim to the court on the same basis as any other applicant. The courts' treatment of spouses' apparent entitlement over and above maintenance is however, questionable (see 15.23.6).

Although the special rules as to reasonable provision for spouses in s 3(2) do not apply to cohabitants, provision was made by s 2(4) of the Law Reform (Succession) Act 1995, adding s 3(2A) to the Inheritance (Provision for Family and Dependants) Act 1975, for special rules for cohabitants which imported the same provisions as those relating to spouses, save that of the hypothetical 'divorce standard' (see, further, 15.24). In *Graham v Murphy* (1997), a long cohabitation was recognised as giving rise to a valid claim, even though during part of it the claimant had not been financially dependent on the deceased.

### 15.15.4  Time for assessment of unreasonableness

Cases before the 1975 Act showed reasonableness being based on existing and reasonably foreseeable facts at the time of the deceased's death, so that in *Re Howell* (1953) where a testator left his property to his second wife on the assumption she would care for his two children, and they returned to his first wife because of their step-mother's subsequent unexpected illness, there was no claim. Section 3(5) of the 1975 Act, which directs the court to determine what constitutes reasonable financial provision on the basis of the facts known to it at the hearing. This is however not precisely on the point, as it would cover both possibilities – assessment of unreasonableness at the time of death and at the time of the hearing.

The High Court of Australia in *Coates v National Trustees Co Ltd* (1956) also took the same view as in *Re Howell* on the question of jurisdiction to hear the case, but once having decided it had jurisdiction held that it would take account of facts as at the date of the hearing when deciding on quantum. This was followed by the Privy Council in *Dun v Dun* (1959). Later, however, the courts seemed more inclined to take account of facts at the date of the hearing in assessing whether they had jurisdiction – that is, whether the provision had not been reasonable in the first place. In *Re Clarke* (1968), account was taken of the death of the principal beneficiary under the deceased's will, and in *Re Shanahan* (1972) Lord Simon said that the value of the estate would be assessed at the date of the hearing, thus necessarily implying that assessments of reasonableness would be made at that date too.

The court in *Moody v Stephenson* (1992) stated explicitly that the assessment of unreasonableness would be based on facts known at the date of the hearing.

### 15.15.5 Objective assessment of unreasonableness

The provision in s 3(5) does, however, mean that the court is not looking at whether the deceased, knowing what he or she knew, subjectively made reasonable provision, but at whether, objectively and in the light of all the facts shown to the court, whether or not known to the deceased, the provision was reasonable. The test is the same as under the legislation which preceded the 1975 Act and which Megarry J referred to in *Re Goodwin* (1968) when he said that the question was simply whether the will or the disposition made reasonable provision, and not whether it was unreasonable on the part of the deceased to have made no provision or no larger provision for the dependant. He said that in his view the question was not subjective but objective, and was not whether the testator stood convicted of unreasonableness, but whether the provision in fact made was reasonable. Thus, the deceased in *Re Franks* (1948) could not be said to have behaved unreasonably in failing to provide for her child, as she died only two days after giving birth, but the child was still able to bring a family provision claim based on the objective unreasonableness of the lack of provision. Note that the size of the estate will be a relevant factor in assessing what provision is reasonable; in *Re Goodwin*, the court awarded the whole of the estate to the spouse, because it was not a large estate and no one else had a moral claim on it.

## 15.16 Statutory guidelines in assessing reasonableness – s 3(1)(a–g) of the I(PFD)A 1975

Guidelines as to what the court should take into account when assessing reasonable provision are laid down in s 3 of the Act. Section 3(1)(a–g) lays down seven particular points which the court is to bear in mind.

The first three provisions concern the financial situation of the applicant, other applicants and beneficiaries. Section 3(6) specifically directs that a person's financial resources in this context include their earning capacity – whether or not they are working and have any actual earnings – and their needs include their obligations – for example the maintenance of a family. There is only a finite amount of property in any estate, so there are often situations where no one can be given their full 'reasonable' entitlement without depriving someone else of theirs.

Therefore all the people who are expecting part of the estate and may be affected by whatever order the court makes have to be considered. Looking at the situations of several people and weighing it in the balance can take a great deal of work; that is why Proceedings under the 1975 Act can be lengthy and expensive.

The guidelines in s 3(1) as to assessing reasonableness are as follows:

(a)  the financial resources and financial needs which the applicant has or is likely to have in the foreseeable future;

(b)  the financial resources and financial needs which any other applicant for an order under section 2 of this Act had or is likely to have within the foreseeable future;

(c)  the financial resources and financial needs which any beneficiary of the estate of the deceased has or is likely to have in the foreseeable future;

(d)  any obligations and responsibilities which the deceased had towards any applicant for an order under the said section 2 or towards any beneficiary of the estate of the deceased;

(e)  the size and nature of the net estate of the deceased;

(f)  any physical or mental disability of any applicant for an order under the said section 2 of any beneficiary of the estate of the deceased;

(g)  any other matter, including the conduct of the applicant or any other person, which in the circumstances of the case the court may consider relevant.

## 15.17  Section 3(1)(a), (b), (c) – financial resources and needs of applicants and beneficiaries

A person's resources can include state aid. In *Re E (deceased)* (1966), the deceased left a widow, but for many years had been living with another woman, to whom he left the whole of his estate by his will. The main asset in the estate was his state death grant (the availability of these is now greatly restricted) which the court considered, holding the source of the deceased's assets to be relevant, to have been earned by him whilst he was living with the other woman. The court also held that in considering all the circumstances of any applicant for relief, including their own needs and resources, it could take into account forms of state relief, and that if the only effect of granting relief would be to relieve the state from having to pay means-tested benefits to the applicant, so the applicant was in fact financially no better off, it might be reasonable to make no provision.

The court in *Re Canderton* (1970), however, dealt with the problem by making an award which, by its careful division between income and capital, had the least possible detrimental effect on the recipient's entitlement to social security benefits.

It is questionable how far the principle of accounting for state benefits would be followed today, in a climate of different attitudes towards social security payments, when the general trend of legislation amongst other things is to avoid making or allowing people to be dependent on state resources save as a last resort, and to have them supported by other private individuals with whom they have a family relationship.

## 15.18  Section 3(1)(d) – deceased's obligations

Section 3(1)(d) refers to the obligations and responsibilities towards applicants and beneficiaries. The deceased's obligations and responsibilities under this section may be moral or legal. English law in this area does not refer to moral obligations, although in other jurisdictions such as New Zealand it does. In *Re Allardice* (1910), the court referred to a 'moral duty' test independent of actual dependence.

### 15.18.1  English courts define relevant obligations

The English courts have thus been given a fairly free hand to define what obligations and respons-ibilities are relevant. The court in *Re Haig* (1979) explicitly said that its decision was based on the morally reasonable thing to have done. The court in *Re Fullard* (1982) (15.10.1) considered the question of actual dependency very relevant, and moral obligations to cohabitants are clearly recognised, as they were in *Re E* (1966) (15.17) and in *Re Joslin* (1941). Both these cases involved gifts by will to cohabitants of the deceased; because they predate the 1975 Act, those persons could not themselves have claimed under the family provision legislation, because until the law was amended by the 1975 Act, it did not include any provision allowing cohabitants *locus standi*. Nevertheless, although the courts particularly in 1941 might have regarded unmarried relation-ships as inappropriate or even improper, in these cases they recognised not just the existence of the gift by will – which the law obliges them to – but also the deceased's moral obligation to his cohabitant.

### 15.18.2  Moral obligations to spouses

Moral obligations between spouses are usually clear, but where the spouses have been separated for a long time, a court may find on the facts of the case that no moral obligation existed. The case of *Re Gregory* (1971) may be contrasted with that of *Re W* (1975). In the former case, the husband deserted the wife a year after their marriage and lived with another woman for over 20 years before asking his wife to return to him on the other woman's death. She refused to do so and emigrated a few years later. After ten years of unsuccessful appeals to her, by letter, to return to him, the husband died, leaving her nothing in his will. The Court of Appeal held that, on the facts of such a lengthy separation and the wife's independence from the husband, he owed her no moral obligation and her claim under the relevant family provision legislation failed. In *Re W*, the parties had been married for 12 years when they were divorced, and the husband failed to maintain the wife thereafter. After 26 years of divorce, the husband died and the wife success-fully claimed a capital sum from his estate. The court held that the husband's capital effectively represented the maintenance payments to which his wife had been entitled but which he had not made.

### 15.18.3  Competing moral claims – spouse and beneficiaries

An example of competing moral claims between a spouse and another party may be seen in *Re Parkinson* (1969). The deceased left his house and contents to his widow for life, with remainder to the RSPCA. At first instance, the court refused to interfere with the deceased's testamentary freedom on the basis that the widow, who at that point wished to continue to live in the house, would be no better off. The Court of Appeal, hearing that the house would have to be sold to pay the costs of the appeal and that in any event the wife no longer wished to continue living there, held that she should receive the whole estate outright. It may be noted, however, that the strong-est support in this court for the decision to give the whole estate to the wife came from Lord Denning, who at that time appeared to regard a matrimonial home very much as family property, with the wife having an enforceable moral claim to it in any event. This view gave comparatively little regard to the conception of property rights which would support the view that it was for the deceased to dispose of the house entirely as he wished. There was, however, dissent in the court from another judge, who felt that the widow, though she should obtain the whole estate, should do so only because the body with whom she was competing had no moral claim on the testator.

### 15.18.4 Obligations

The moral obligation of parents to their children as such, however, appeared originally to change considerably, and perhaps to end, once the child had grown up. This did not mean the child could not bring a claim, but just that the court would probably not find any support for it in this particular subsection. The case of *Re Andrews* (1955) showed a court deciding that a woman who had left her father's home to live for some decades with a man who was married to someone else had ceased to be dependent on her father and become dependent on the other man. It is questionable how far a court would follow such reasoning today, since the attitude to women's dependency on men has changed, but it may be that the changes in terms of legal practice will turn out to be as much a matter of form as of substance; the courts may well come to the same decision in effect, but phrase it differently.

The Court of Appeal held in *Re Jennings (Deceased); Harlow v National Westminster Bank and Others* (1994), that the failure of a father to make proper provision for his son whilst still an infant child was not a basis on which to ground a finding of obligation, under this subsection, to provide for him in adulthood on death. Claims by adult children may now, however, be treated like any other claim under the Act (*Re Hancock* (2008)).

## 15.19 Section 3(1)(e) – size and nature of estate

Section 3(1)(e) refers to the size and nature of the net estate. The courts are unhappy about applications which claim from a small estate. Where the estate is not substantial, the costs of bringing a case, particularly one which goes all the way to trial, are likely to exceed the amount the applicant is claiming. This makes such a claim self-defeating, and the courts are conscious of the inappropriateness of expensive legal actions over small estates. On the other hand, what to the Court of Appeal appears to be a small matter may to the applicant be somewhat larger, and where the courts tend not to regard a point of principle as being a valid reason for bringing a claim, applicants may not agree. The court in *Re Gregory* (1971) (15.18.2) specifically stated that it would be unwilling to interfere with a testator's dispositions where, as here, the estate amounted to less than £3,000. In *Kourkey v Lusher* (1982) (15.14.6) the court also criticised the bringing of a claim against an estate worth less than £2,000. The point has been returned to frequently, including more recently in *O'Brien v Seagrave and Another* (2007).

## 15.20 Section 3(1)(f) – disability

Section 3(1)(f) refers to any physical or mental disability of any applicant or beneficiary The factual situation to be taken account of under this subsection could, of course, be referred to under other headings. Any disability of an applicant or beneficiary would be very likely to affect the deceased's moral obligation to them, as well as probably their financial needs and possibly their financial resources, such as their earning capacity. However, there might be situations in which having the ground spelled out was useful: for example, it might be argued that the deceased had no extra moral obligation because they were unaware of the disability or its effects, or it might be difficult to prove to the court that the disability had materially affected the applicant or beneficiary's financial situation. Putting the factor of disability in a separate category not only ensures that the courts will take account of it, but also demonstrates the importance of it to the legislature. The statutory requirement for the court to have regard to an applicant or beneficiary's disability is something to which they can draw the court's attention in support of their case.

### 15.20.1 Disabled applicant to rely on state support?

A disabled applicant or beneficiary may be being cared for under the National Health Service. The question of whether this would excuse the failure by a deceased to provide for such a person was answered differently in different cases. In *Re Watkins* (1949), the court thought it would be reasonable for the deceased to take into account the applicant's secure position and accordingly to make no provision. In other cases, however, the court has come to a different conclusion. For example, in *Re Pringle* (1956), the testatrix's mentally incapable son was resident in hospital and maintained by the state; he obtained £10 per week from the estate of his mother, who had left her property to two friends. In *Millward v Shenton* (1972), the Court of Appeal held that provision should have been made for the testatrix's son, who was totally incapacitated, married to a disabled wife and reliant on state benefits, even though he was in his fifties when she died. He obtained eleven-twelfths of the estate, which his mother had left to charity. Changes to NHS care, and any prospect of future changes, are likely to affect the operation of this principle.

## 15.21 Section 3(1)(g) – any other matter

Section 3(1)(g) refers to any other matter including conduct. The scope of this catch-all provision is clearly potentially very wide, but the courts have so far used it only for certain particular areas. They have looked at the provenance of the assets in the estate and the deceased's own stated wishes, as well as the behaviour of an applicant or beneficiary towards the deceased.

### 15.21.1 Provenance of assets

The provenance of the assets in the estate may be a particularly important consideration. This was referred to in *Jelley v Iliffe* (1981), where the court said it might be material that most of the deceased's assets had been inherited by her from the father of the claimants, as well as in *Re Callaghan* (1984) (15.3.1). In *Re Canderton* (1970) (15.17), much of the deceased's estate had been inherited by him from a woman with whom he had lived instead of with his wife. She had provided in her will that if he predeceased her, her estate should go to a niece and a friend. The court, considering an application by the estranged wife, avoided substantial reduction of the gifts the deceased then made by will to the other woman's niece and friend.

### 15.21.2 Conduct of the applicant

In *Williams v Johns* (1988), the applicant had been adopted by the deceased and her husband at the age of six weeks, when their natural son was 17 years old. She had had a stormy childhood and continued into adulthood as an offender. Her adoptive parents had supported her both financially and morally. The son, on the other hand, was found to have been a 'model son'. In 1985, the mother died, leaving her entire estate by will to her son and appending to the will a statement that she had provided for her daughter during her lifetime beyond any reasonable expectation and had no response or affection from her. The applicant was very hurt by that statement and claimed the will had been made after a quarrel between them, following which they had reconciled. She based her claim on, first, her own impecuniosity, second, the fact alleged by her that the deceased had held her in continuing affection and, third, that the disposition of the estate was not reasonable. At the time of the claim, she was 43 years old, unemployed, impecunious, divorced and without capital save for the houseboat in which she lived. Her claim failed, because the court held she had not established any obligation by the deceased to maintain her beyond the mere fact of the adoptive relationship. She was physically fit and capable and had been independent for many years. The court said she had taken no care of her mother but had caused her shame and distress.

### 15.21.3 Statements left by deceased

The court in *Williams v Johns* did not, however, say how much, if any, importance it attached to the statement left by the testatrix. It is not clear from the judgment whether the evidence on which it was making findings of fact about the applicant's behaviour included the statement or not. The deceased's statement is admissible as part of that evidence even though clearly the deceased cannot be called to be cross-examined on it, under the provisions of s 21 of the I(PFD)A 1975 and s 2 of the Civil Evidence Act 1968. However, there is no separate direction to the court to take account of it as there is of the factor of disability, for example, or indeed as there was under the original Inheritance (Family Provision) Act 1938 (s 1(7)). This leaves the court a very free hand to consider what the deceased says and ignore it or take account of it as it will, and perhaps in context that strikes a balance.

Where the deceased has left any sort of statement about their testamentary gifts, that statement is likely to explain the gifts they have made in terms of their motivation and feelings. In that sense it may be regarded as simply duplicating the terms of the deceased's will, for example, where the deceased has failed to leave anything to one child and has expanded in a separate statement, or one in the will itself, as to the reasons.

It may however, simply show that the deceased had put what the court thought was an inappropriate interpretation on his or her moral obligations to the applicant, or ignored them completely, whereas in considering a claim the court certainly will take account of such obligations, under s 3(1)(d) above. In such a situation, the deceased's statement will, by explaining their reasons for making the provision, have the opposite effect from that intended, since it will clarify for the court the deceased's failure to take all the necessary factors into account and show that the provision, in the court's terms, is not reasonable. In *Re Clarke* (1968), the testator, who had been aged 49 on his marriage to a woman in her thirties, stated that he had made no provision for his wife because she had deserted him; the court found as a matter of fact that her behaviour had been quite reasonable, and the deceased had rather deserted her by refusing to leave his mother's house. The deceased's statement may thus address the court's mind to, or make it aware of, facts which otherwise might have been lost, such as the applicant's treatment of the deceased, and will provide evidence to support a court's finding of fact in that area.

More recent cases in which the claimant's conduct towards the deceased has been relevant include *Garland v Morris* (2007), where the claimant adult daughter failed despite her own relative poverty. Part of the reason was her own conduct, including that she had not been in touch with her father for many years before his death. However, generally the rule is that the court will look at all the factors and weigh them up: thus in *Espinosa v Bourke* (1999), the claimant daughter had behaved badly but, against that, she was poor and the estate was large, her father had promised to pass on to her some of her mother's and grandmother's property and, though she had received benefits from the deceased during his lifetime, she had also cared for him over many years. Her appeal was allowed partly because in the court below too much weight had indeed been placed on her poor conduct.

### 15.21.4 Agreement not to claim

The court in *Re Fullard* (1982) also said that an agreement between a couple on separation that they would not claim against each other's estate should not be ignored simply because it was not embodied in a court order.

### 15.21.5 Related case failed – concealment from deceased

In *Re Goodchild (deceased)* (1997), the applicant for family provision had originally sought to have his parents' wills declared as mutual wills (see 6.9.5). When that failed, he sought provision out of the estate of his father, to whom his mother's estate had passed and who had left much of it to his second wife. At first instance, the mutual wills case failed but the court gave Gary a substantial sum, talking about how part of the father's property had come from the mother. On appeal, the second wife claimed the court had been improperly implementing the provisions of the father's revoked will as though it were a valid mutual will. She also claimed that Gary could not cite, as a relevant consideration in seeking family provision, his own indebtedness from which he would have been able to release himself had he inherited as he expected, because he had unconscionably concealed that indebtedness from his father during his lifetime when seeking loans from him. The Court of Appeal held, however, that the existence of Gary's indebtedness did not relieve Dennis of his moral obligation towards his son, and the second wife's appeal was dismissed. It also confirmed that the agreement between the parties to an order arranged in such a way as to minimise liability to tax was valid, provided the order arrived at was one which was within the court's power to make under the Act.

### 15.21.6 Effect of scope of court's discretion

Because the court has a wide discretion, if it makes what a party thinks is an unfair or unreasonable order, what they will have to show if they wish to appeal is that the court exercised that discretion unreasonably. If the court is not entirely clear about its reasons, for example, if the applicant believes that a statement about his or her behaviour was given undue weight – the applicant will have to show not that another view of strength of the statement would have been better but that the view the court did take was unreasonable. It is not sufficient for the court hearing the appeal merely to feel that it would have taken a different view. Where there is a wide-ranging provision such as that allowing the court to take account of 'any other matter', this also inevitably gives scope for uncertainty as to the likely outcome of a case at first instance and a lesser chance of establishing unreasonableness in that decision on appeal. Note that appeals in relation to small estates are deprecated by the courts, because of the excessive effect of the costs.

## 15.22 Applying s 3(1) to the claimant s 3(2)–(4)

The court is required by the terms of the 1975 Act to apply the results of its assessment of the individual applicant's position and the nature of the deceased's estate differently, depending on the basis on which the applicant claims. The special rules or guidelines for each category are set out in s 3(2) for spouses and former spouses who have not remarried, s 3(2A) for cohabitants, s 3(3) for children of the deceased and his or her family and s 3(4) for those claiming on the basis of financial dependency on the deceased. Spouses and former spouses are treated alike; the guidelines for cohabitants are very similar. The provisions relating to those claiming as children include aspects of the parental role such as education, and those relating to dependents require an evaluation of the extent of the dependency.

## 15.23 Section 3(2) – spouse and former spouse

Spouses and former spouses who have not remarried are more favourably treated in that they may reasonably expect more than others. Thus what is reasonable provision for others may not be reasonable for them. They therefore have a greater chance of establishing that provision for them was not reasonable as well as the expectation of a larger award.

### 15.23.1 Who these guidelines apply to

Applications in the first two categories from s 1(1) are governed not only by the guidelines in s 3(1)(a–g) above, as are all applications, but also by the specific guidelines for spouses set out in s 3(2). The cases tend to be about claims by widows against the estates of their late husbands. The same provisions apply to both spouses and former spouses.

### 15.23.2 Substance of the extra guidelines

The court is directed to take into account the applicant's age, the duration of the marriage and the contribution made by the applicant to the welfare of the deceased's family – this specifically includes caring for the family and the family home. Where the parties were not judicially separated and still living apart at the date of the deceased's death, the court is also directed by s 14 of the I(PFD)A 1975 to take account of what the applicant would have received from a matrimonial court had the marriage been ended by divorce rather than by death (but at the same date). There were long-standing difficulties with this, including that English law does not properly prescribe any method of calculation for how property will be divided on divorce. The traditional 'one-third rule' was often criticised and also stated never to have been a rule; the discretion of the court – or the practice in one's local court – was often felt to be of great importance to the result in a contested case. Obviously the legislation must cover not only the spouse who has the means or capacity to support him- or herself, but the spouse – often the wife – who has been divorced by her husband when she is too old and unqualified or inexperienced in paid work to support herself; such a person may be reliant on maintenance payments from her husband to survive, which will come to an end on his death. It was said in the case of Eyre v Eyre (1967) that a court could not guarantee a first wife equality with a widow, but that if all other things were equal they would be treated the same.

### 15.23.3 Conduct of the spouses

A particular point to note in this respect is that the principle which operates in matrimonial proceedings which says that a spouse's conduct within a marriage is unlikely to influence the award the court makes to her also applies in the context of proceedings by spouses under the 1975 Act. The irrelevance of conduct to financial applications between spouses, save where it is particularly gross, has been firmly established in matrimonial law since Wachtel v Wachtel (1973). In Re Bunning (1984), the court assessed the provision for the applicant widow on the basis of what she would have received had financial arrangements been made on a divorce at the date of the husband's death. The court took the view that, in the situation where the marriage had broken down at the date of death, it was even less relevant than it would have been on an application for financial relief within divorce to consider whose conduct might have led to the breakdown of the marriage.

### 15.23.4 Former spouse of wealthy testator

In Re Besterman (1984), Mr Besterman left an estate of over £1,400,000, most of it to the University of Oxford. To his wife he gave his personal chattels and a yearly income of £3,500 for life. The University acknowledged that this provision was inadequate for a millionaire's widow, accustomed to a high standard of living, and who after 18 years of dutiful marriage at the age of 66 years had as her only other source of income a widow's pension of £400 per year. What the court was asked was therefore to set the amount she should receive. The trial judge awarded Mrs Besterman £238,000, calculating it by reference to what was sufficient for her to buy an annuity giving her a reasonable level of maintenance. Mrs Besterman appealed to the Court of Appeal for an increase in the lump sum, and on appeal received £378,000 instead.

### 15.23.5 The divorce standard?

The Court of Appeal disagreed that the basis used previously had been correct – what should have been looked at was the appropriate sum for a surviving spouse, not the level of maintenance the wife might have received had there been a divorce. On divorce, after all, the calculations take into account the continued living expenses of the spouse who in a family provision claim no longer has any such expenses. In any case it felt Mrs Besterman might have expected to receive £350,000 on divorce.

The hypothetical divorce standard was discussed in Re Krubert (deceased) (1996), where a widow aged 87 sought family provision from her late husband's estate. There had been a long marriage without children. The matrimonial home had been the husband's, and he gave her a licence to remain in it as long as she wished to do so, a legacy of £10,000 and the income of the residue after payment out of some specific gifts. The deceased's brother and sister, also elderly, were to take the house subject to the wife's interest. The court gave the wife the house absolutely at first instance, as well as the residue subject to the specific gifts and legacies of £7,000 each to the brother and sister. The brother and sister appealed and the Court of Appeal replaced the original order, giving widow a life interest in the house and an absolute interest in the remainder of estate. The reasoning of Nourse LJ was: 'she needs the house to live in and, if she has to move, she will need the additional income generated by the reinvested proceeds. But no financial need for an absolute interest in the house has been made out.' Cazalet J discussed the 'divorce standard':

> One unsatisfactory aspect of placing too much emphasis on the award which would have been made on the hypothetical divorce is that ... such an approach may well, in what may be described as small asset cases produce financial provision below reasonable financial provision ... because the funds available cannot provide satisfactorily for two homes ... the court in claims under the Act is concerned with one spouse and not two.

It might be noted particularly that the legal costs in this case amounted to about £23,000 out of an estate worth about £78,000.

When the legislation referring to what an applicant might have got on divorce was drafted, the intention was to ensure that an applicant got at least their 'reasonable needs', which was the ceiling for divorce awards. Values in matrimonial proceedings changed considerably after that, though – true to its pervasively individualist character – English law remained unusual in having no matrimonial property regime as such; and the landscape was changed particularly by the case of White v White (2000), where the House of Lords spoke instead of a 'yardstick of equality'. Although that case was a 'big money case, the idea had influence in both divorce and family provision cases. However, the Court of Appeal in Cunliffe v Fielden (2005) denied that White v White gave rise to any presumption of equal division in the context of family provision. The widow, who had originally been the deceased's housekeeper and had been dependent on him then and later as his wife, was given £800,000 from an estate of £1,400,000. million.

However, it has been sensibly noted in a variety of cases that there is a very substantial practical difference between divorce and family provision. It was pointed out in Re Besterman (1984) that a court dealing with property on divorce is directed to put the parties in the position they would have been in had the marriage not broken down, but that under the 1975 Act that is only a consideration, and the overriding requirement is that of reasonableness. Still more to the point, the court in Re Krubert (1996) pointed out that: 'on a divorce there are two parties to be provided for, whereas on an application under the 1975 Act there is only one.' The point was reiterated by the Court of Appeal in Cunliffe v Fielden (2005):

> Divorce involves two living spouses.... In cases under the 1975 Act a deceased spouse who leaves a widow is entitled to bequeath his estate to whomsoever he pleases: his only

statutory obligation is to make reasonable financial provision for his widow. In such a case, depending on the value of the estate, the concept of equality may bear little relation to such provision.[43]

In P v G (2004), another 'big money' case, the widow was awarded £2,000,000, including the matrimonial home, and an annuity, out of an estate with £5,000,000 in relatively ready assets and more than that in pension funds and nominated to an earlier family. Black J in the High Court described the divorce standard as the 'minimum' she should receive, adverting to how different the situation is on death rather than divorce in any event. An alternative approach was, however, that of the judge in Aston v Aston (2007), who found the lack of provision for the widow to be reasonable. However, she had left the deceased to live with another man somewhat before he died, so the marriage was really already over, and she had substantial assets in any event.

In smaller money cases, there are often pressing practical considerations which mean that debates about divorce standards are less relevant. In Iqbal v Ahmed (2011), a widow with no likely earning capacity after a long marriage, who had been left a right to occupy the matrimonial home rent free and £8,000 was instead given a right to occupy it for her life and half of any proceeds of sale, as well as the residuary estate. The other beneficiary was the deceased's son from an earlier marriage, who agreed to assist with the costs of house repairs and insurance.

The statutory direction to the court to take into account the same factors in respect of married and divorced spouses was, however, a source of two principal specific problems which the Law Commission considered to be in need of reform. The first was that the courts tended to regard the 'deemed divorce' test as 'setting a ceiling or cap on the amount of family provision that a surviving spouse maybe awarded',[44] and the other was that the recently bereaved found the reference to divorce offensive. The Law Commission thought the cap was a 'widespread misconception', thought, interestingly, it did not point out that the situation on death is always different from that on divorce in that account of the ongoing personal financial needs of the deceased need not be taken into account. The ITPA 2014 specified that the analogy with divorce entailed no upper limit on awards.[45] However, as well as the reference to divorce, the possibility of a lower limit was specifically retained, for fear that courts would otherwise attempt a 'slavish and wholly artificial comprehensive enactment of the ancillary relief process'.[46] The Law Commission identified the use in family provision cases of forms intended for use in divorce proceedings as a direct source of the distress to the bereaved, since for example they asked for the date of separation, and suggested strongly to practitioners that they adapt the forms to deal appropriately with family provision cases.[47]

## 15.23.6 Maintenance or capital?

There are also other indications that the courts may be influenced by the idea of giving the widow maintenance, rather than capital, even where what they award is a lump sum. In Re W (1975), the registrar who originally heard the application awarded the elderly divorced wife £14,000, but this was reduced on appeal to the judge to £11,000 on the basis that, as she was aged 75, she could buy an annuity that would give her a reasonable income at a comparatively low price, and this figure would still give her some capital left over. In this situation, the spouse's

---

43  Wall LJ at Para 21. See also G Miller, 'Provision for a Surviving Spouse' [2007] Private Client Business 144; Sidney Ross 'The Implications of White v White for Inheritance Act Claims' (2001) Family Law 547 and 619.
44  Law Commission 331 *Intestacy and Family Provision Claims on Death* (2011) para 2.141.
45  Law Commission 331 *Intestacy and Family Provision Claims on Death* (2011), para 2.144; Inheritance and Trustees' Powers Act 2014 Sch 2, para 5(2).
46  Law Commission 331 *Intestacy and Family Provision Claims on Death* (2011), paras 2.146–148; P v G (2004), per Black J at 67.
47  Law Commission 331 *Intestacy and Family Provision Claims on Death* (2011), para 2.150.

age meant she received less than had she been younger, although the effect of taking into account the a spouse's age might be at least as likely to increase the potential award by drawing the court's attention to her inability, at an advanced age, to change tack and obtain employment outside the home.

The method of calculation of the wife's claim in Re W clearly looked at the wife's reasonable entitlement principally from the point of view of satisfying her claim to be maintained, rather than regarding her as having a claim to the capital represented by the property in the estate as such; it did not allow her much by way of freedom to control such spare capital as there might be after considerations of maintenance were dealt with. That approach leaves that spare capital, however much of it there is, in the control of the testator to will away as he wishes. In such a scheme, the wife will, on the other hand, be left with no capital over which she has control and therefore nothing to will away as she wishes on her death. That this conflict was exemplified in Davis v Davis (1993), where the applicant was the deceased's widow. He also left a 16-year-old son from a previous marriage. He had given his wife £15,000 just before his death, and left her most of his chattels and a life interest in a trust fund of £177,000, expected to increase to £267,000. The widow's claim for the house worth £70,000 which the trustees had bought for her to live in to be transferred to her absolutely was rejected by the judge. She appealed to the Court of Appeal, which agreed with the judge. He had said:

> can it be said that the disposition by will is not such as to make reasonable financial provision for the plaintiff, by which is meant such financial provision as would be reasonable in all the circumstances for her to receive whether or not the provision is required for her mainte-nance? I am bound to say, for my part, I regard the proposition as startling.... In terms of what he deployed for his surviving widow, he could not have done more.... If in this case it can be said that the provision of a life interest in the entire residuary estate is not reasonable provision then I think that could be asserted in almost any case in which the testator elects to make provision for his surviving spouse by that means.

Though the court was concerned, on an appeal, not with what it would have decided itself but with whether the judge's decision was properly made, the tenor of the judgment is that it is not inappropriate to dismiss any claim that a wife may have by virtue of her marriage to the capital value of her husband's property and to regard her right as only that of maintenance.

### 15.23.7 A different view from the bench?

One might compare this with the decision in the ancillary relief proceedings in the matrimonial case of Vicary v Vicary (1992). The judge rejected the husband's contention that the wife had no claim to capital, saying:

> In the instant case should not the wife have the opportunity to feel as much independence as her husband? The opportunity to spend the remaining years she has in the knowledge that she has substantial capital which she can leave to her children or to a dogs' home as she pleases.

The Court of Appeal also refused to overturn that judgment. If matrimonial courts were to follow the spirit of Vicary and family provision courts that of Davis, that again would give rise to the spec-tacle of divorcing wives having a greater entitlement to property than widows of a successful marriage, despite the dicta in Moody v Stephenson (1992) as to the aim of the 1975 Act.

## 15.23.8 Entitlement to capital recognised by family provision courts

However, a different approach to where the claims to the capital owned within a family lie may be perceptible in the case of *Re Shanahan* (1972). In that case, the court awarded half the capital to each of the testator's current and former wives. Both had reached retirement age, but the latter was better off financially in her own right. The court may, however, have considered there was some 'fairness' in dividing the estate equally between them.

## 15.24 Section 3(2A) – cohabitants

The Law Reform (Succession) Act 1995 amended the 1975 Act to allow a cohabitant who had been living in the deceased's household as her or his husband or wife for the two years immediately preceding the death to claim on that basis. Such a person would claim under s 1(1)(ba) of the amended 1975 Act. That person might also be a dependant within the meaning of s 1(1)(e), but it is likely that the treatment of dependants under s 3 will be seen to be less favourable than that of cohabitants.

Where a cohabitant is concerned, the court is directed by guidelines inserted as s 3(2A) by the 1995 Act to take account of the applicant's age, the duration of the relationship and the contribution of the applicant to the welfare of the deceased's family. These guidelines are the same as those for spouses and former spouses in s 3(2) but, as is logical, without the further direction as to a hypothetical order on divorce.

## 15.25 Section 3(3) – child of the deceased and child of the family

A person applying under the categories in s 1(1)(c) and (d) does not have to be a child in the sense of being young, but if they are then the court is directed by s 3(3) to take account of the manner in which they were being educated or trained, or the manner in which they might be expected to be educated or trained. It will also be relevant to whether an adult child ought to succeed if the deceased was supporting the child in the process of acquiring some educational or occupational qualification, and relevant to the question of provision for an adult applicant generally if that adult gave up work in order to care for the deceased during illness or old age. For those in the category of children of the family, s 3(3) also directs the court to consider whether the deceased made any assumption of responsibility by the deceased for the child, for how long and on what basis, whether they knew the child was not their own child, and the liability of any other person to maintain the child.

## 15.26 Section 3(4) – dependants

In considering an application by a claimant under s 1(1)(e), the court is directed by s 3(4) to have regard to the extent to which, and the basis upon which, the deceased assumed responsibility for the maintenance of the applicant, and how long they discharged that responsibility for. It is submitted that the general attitude suggested by the wording of s 3(4), with its emphasis on the deceased's personal relationship with the applicant, offers some support for the attitude taken by Butler-Sloss LJ in *Bishop v Plumley and Another* (15.4.1) that what is important in considering an application by a dependant under s 1(1)(e) is the 'mutuality of the relationship'.

## 15.27 Any impediments to bringing a claim?

An applicant is not precluded from bringing a claim under the 1975 Act, and a court is not precluded from hearing it, by assurances given by the beneficiaries of the estate that they will not enforce their rights. In *Rajabally v Rajabally* (1987), the beneficiaries under the will had assured the applicant widow that they would not insist on their rights. Their assurances were not, however, legally enforceable by the widow, and the court held that they did not defeat the application.

### 15.27.1 Right to claim under the 1975 Act does not survive the applicant

The right to bring an action under the 1975 Act does not survive the applicant and cannot be carried on by their estate. It is, therefore, like an action for defamation in tort in that it is not covered by the usual rule under the Law Reform (Miscellaneous Provisions) Act 1934, which allows most actions by or against a deceased person to be carried on by their personal representatives, with particular rules relating to limitation. It is more akin to the rules in matrimonial proceedings, where actions do not subsist after death. This fits in with the nature of applications in family matters, where what the court is looking at is the situation of the parties and their respective needs and resources, rather than the enforcement of contracts and strict property rights.

### 15.27.2 *Whyte v Ticehurst* (1986)

Both these points were made in the decision in *Whyte v Ticehurst and Another* (1986). The couple were married in 1953, and the husband died in February 1984 after executing a will in 1982 leaving his house to charity subject to his wife's right to live there during her lifetime. The wife commenced proceedings under s 1(1) but then, in December 1984, before the final hearing, she too died. Her personal representatives applied to the registrar of the court for leave to carry on the proceedings on behalf of her estate but he dismissed the application saying there was no cause of action. The personal representatives appealed to the Family Division saying first that the Matrimonial Causes Act 1973 had been extended by the 1975 Act and second, relying on the Law Reform (Miscellaneous Provisions) Act 1934, that the rights of a surviving spouse were not extinguished on death. It was accepted by counsel for both sides at the hearing that an ancillary relief claim does not subsist against the estate of a deceased spouse and that a claim for maintenance dies with an applicant.

The court dismissed the appeal, saying that the whole claim under the 1975 Act died with the applicant. The court also looked at the true effect of the claim; since the personal representatives' claim could not benefit the deceased wife herself, it was essentially a contest between the beneficiaries under the husband's will and those who would take under the wife's. The court commented on the inappropriateness in any event of considering such a claim, especially given the statutory direction to the court as to the factors to be taken into account in deciding any award to be made. Those factors did not fit in at all with the situation which arose once the original claimant had died.

### 15.27.3 Personal nature of claim confirmed

This decision was followed in *Re Bramwell, Campbell v Tobin* (1988), which concerned a potential claim by a widow against the estate of her late husband. They had married in 1975 when the wife was 65 and the husband 71; they separated four years later, and in 1986 the husband died. The wife instructed her solicitor to act in a family provision claim against her husband's estate, but no proceedings had been issued when the wife died, having survived her husband by only six months. The solicitor was then instructed by the widow's personal representative. The plaintiff in the action was the personal representative of the wife. It was argued on her behalf that the judgment in *Whyte v Ticehurst* (1986) was correct but confined to its context of a matrimonial cause. The court, however, held that the right to claim under the 1975 Act was not and did not give rise to a 'cause of action' under the Law Reform (Miscellaneous Provisions) Act 1934 unless an order was made before the death of the person entitled by virtue of the provisions of the Act to make the application. Sheldon J said, 'Until then it remains no more than a hope or contingency of no surviving value to a deceased claimant's estate.' The same phrase – 'no more than a hope' – was used in the case of *Re Collins* (1990) (15.12.4) though *Re Bramwell* was not referred to in that case.

# 15.28  If no claim lies under the 1975 Act

It may be possible for a person to establish that they have ownership of some of what appeared to be the deceased's property as a matter of law, so that they do not have to seek a court order for it to be given to them out of the estate.

This might be particularly important for unmarried cohabitants if they do not fall within s 1(1)(ba) – for example, if the cohabitation lasted less than two years or had ceased before the death. For example, where a person owned a property jointly with the deceased, if it could be established that they owned it as joint tenants in equity as well as at law, the deceased's share would pass to them automatically on his or her death in accordance with the right of survivorship (*jus accrescendi*). Even if the property was in the deceased's sole name, the potential claimant might be able to establish ownership of some or all of the property under a constructive trust or the doctrine of proprietary estoppel. There might also have been the possibility of establishing that there was a valid and enforceable contract for the property to be left to the potential claimant by the deceased.

## 15.28.1  Constructive trust, proprietary estoppel and contract?

In *Layton v Martin* (1986), the court was asked to consider the applicant's claim on several bases. She had first formed a relationship with the deceased in 1967, when she was 29 and single and the deceased was 50. In 1975 he asked her in a letter to live with him, offering her emotional security and financial security during his life and after his death. His wife was ill and the implication was that on her death he would marry the applicant. He paid the applicant £100 a month plus £30 a week housekeeping, but when his wife did die in 1977 he did not marry her. (She appears to have been little bothered by this.) In 1979 he made a will providing for the applicant, but in June 1980 he rescinded that provision when the couple parted, albeit on friendly terms.

In April 1982 he died and the applicant claimed under the 1975 Act. She also claimed, first, that she had relied on the representations in his letter that he would provide for her, and alleged a constructive trust in her favour. Second, she alleged proprietary estoppel, saying that equity should subject the estate to such beneficial rights in her favour as would give effect to the representation on which she relied. Third, she said there had been a contract between herself and the deceased resulting from her acceptance of his offer – the courts are unwilling to find a contract in these circumstances. The court dismissed the application, holding that she had not been living with him until his death and did not fall within the meaning of dependant under the Act.

## 15.29 Orders which the court can make

Section 2 of the Act sets out the orders the court may make. The range is wide, and is increased by the court's power to attach conditions to its orders. The court may specifically order any one or more of the following, which are set out in s 2:

- maintenance;
- a lump sum;
- transfer of property to the applicant;
- settlement of property for the benefit of the applicant;
- acquisition of property and its transfer to or settlement on the applicant;
- variation of any relevant marriage settlement.

Where orders for maintenance are concerned, the court is permitted by s 2(2) to relate the order to the whole income of the estate or some smaller amount, expressing the order in terms of a fixed sum or of a proportion of the income of the estate. Alternatively, it may order the appropriation of a sum of capital within the estate for the production of the income to meet the periodical payments (s 2(3)). Maintenance is the traditional order under the family provision legislation for any dependant. There is a noticeable difference between orders for maintenance made to spouses and those made to former spouses; in the case of spouses, the order is not bound to cease if the spouse remarries, whereas in the case of former spouses, it must do so.

### 15.29.1 How the court applies the provisions of the law in practice

There is nothing in the 1975 Act which sets out exactly how its provisions should be applied, and in particular the definition of 'maintenance' has been unclear. The courts have laid down principles in the course of their decisions, but these have also conflicted.

The underlying justifications for family provision legislation may be influenced by cultural or political assumptions. For example, under the New Zealand jurisdiction, Salmond J in *Allen v Manchester* (1922) had said that a man should provide proper and adequate support for his wife and children and that, if he did not do so, the court would imply the provisions which a just and wise father would make. The words 'wise and just' were repeated in the Australian case of *Bosch v Perpetual Trustee Co Ltd* (1938). But courts in England have arguably had a stronger eye to the testamentary freedom of the deceased and have tended to interfere with it as little as possible, only in so far as the legislation requires it rather than in so far as it might allow it, albeit with some exceptions. The growing acceptance in the family provision legislation of a broadening definition of the family, bringing in cohabitants and a much wider definition of dependants and children of the family, means that many more people may bring challenges to a person's testamentary dispositions, or the results of their intestacy. As yet, much of that broadening does not apply to intestacy itself: cohabitants have no automatic entitlement on intestacy. The broadening of the definition of the family and the strengthening of family rights means a lessening of testators' powers and certainties that they can reliably leave their property as they wish. Whether this is considered a good idea depends, still, on the moral approach to property, families and obligations.

## 15.30 Defining 'maintenance'

The definition of 'maintenance' has been particularly contentious. It is accepted that it is not the same as keeping someone on or even off the breadline and cannot be equated with subsistence – that was established in *Re E* (1966) (15.17) and *Millward v Shenton* (1972) (15.20.1). The court in *Re Borthwick* (1949) disagreed with a suggestion that the standard of living to which a wife has become accustomed during her marriage would necessarily dictate the level of provision she might expect from her husband's estate. 'In other words it is said that the worse a man treats his wife in his lifetime the less he need leave when he is dead', said the judge. He was unimpressed by the argument: 'I cannot accept such a cynical conclusion.' He thus confirmed the court's comments in the appeal in the New Zealand case of *Allen v Manchester* (1922), where the standard of maintenance appropriate to a widow was defined as the standard required for her 'to live with comfort and without pecuniary anxiety at such a standard as she was accustomed to in her husband's lifetime, or would have been accustomed to if her husband had then done his duty to her'. The Court of Appeal in *Bahouse v Negus* (2008) confirmed this, saying:

> It cuts both ways. The applicant who lived with the deceased in a hovel will not be able to look to maintenance at the same level as the applicant who lived together with the deceased in a palace.... If the lifestyle was indeed lavish and extravagant then it is entirely acceptable, and a proper application of established principle, for a judge to reflect that.

## 15.30.1 *Re Christie* (1979) – maintenance and well-being

The testatrix in *Re Christie* (1979) left an estate of £13,000. Under her will, she made gifts of a share of a house in London to her adult daughter and of a house in Essex to her adult son, with the residue divided equally between them. By the time of her death, the half-share of the house in London had been made over to the daughter by deed of gift and the house in Essex referred to in the will had been sold and replaced with another. The son claimed the new Essex house worth £9,000 from her estate to replace the one which had been adeemed. The court discussed what was meant by 'reasonable financial provision' and 'maintenance'. It held that, although maintenance is not restricted to subsistence level, 'on the other hand, it does not mean anything which may be regarded as reasonably desirable for his general benefit or welfare'. Maintenance, said the court, 'refers to no more and no less than the applicant's way of life and well-being, his health, financial security and allied matters such as the well-being, health and financial security of his immediate family for whom he is responsible'. In his conclusion, however, the deputy judge appeared to rely heavily on the admission by the daughter that she had probably benefited more than her brother and stated that he would 'redress the balance' by giving the son the new Essex house.

## 15.30.2 Criticisms of *Re Christie*

This case has been much cited and also heavily criticised for several reasons. In particular, though the son was not very well-off and had two young children to support, he already owned a house and was in no particular need. The court did not apply an objective test of whether the provision made for him was reasonable for his maintenance; indeed it appears to have regarded the 1975 Act as indeed giving it carte blanche – an invitation to recast the provisions of the deceased's will entirely rather than to adjust them in accordance with the claim for 'maintenance'. Moreover, the court took oral evidence of the deceased's intentions and implemented them in order to avoid the effects of the ademption of the old house in Essex, thus – given that this was not really a claim for 'maintenance' – using the provisions of the 1975 Act to bypass the requirements for the formalities laid down by the Wills Act 1837.

## 15.30.3 *Re Coventry* (1979)

The breadth of interpretation of 'maintenance' in *Re Christie* was criticised by both the High Court and the Court of Appeal in *Re Coventry* (1979). It approved instead the Canadian case of *Re Duranceau* (1952), in which the court said that reasonable maintenance was what was sufficient to enable the dependant to live neither luxuriously nor miserably, but decently and comfortably according to his or her station in life. The deceased in *Re Coventry* had died intestate, leaving a net estate of about £7,000 consisting largely of his house. The sole beneficiary under the intestacy rules was his estranged wife, who was then 74 years old and who had lived apart from him without any maintenance for the previous 19 years. The applicant was the deceased's son, then 46 years of age, who had been living rent free with his father for many years. It appeared that he and his father had driven out the mother many years earlier. The son had, in return for his free accommodation, provided his father's food and contributed to the household outgoings. His salary did not, however, allow him sufficient income for anything but the necessities of life, particularly once the son was faced with having to pay for his accommodation when his mother started possession proceedings against him.

The master gave the plaintiff £2,000; he appealed to a judge for more, but Oliver J considered that requests for 'maintenance' from a young, healthy man in employment should be regarded with circumspection and, after considering whether there were any particular reasons why the plaintiff should receive anything from the estate, discharged the master's award altogether. The plaintiff appealed to the Court of Appeal, who agreed with Oliver J. It concurred in particular with his test of maintenance and his analysis of the relevant question, which was not whether the applicant needed maintenance but whether he could show that it was unreasonable that the intestacy provisions that were applicable did not provide for him. The decision was 'a qualitative decision, or what is sometimes called a 'value judgment' ... particularly difficult to disturb on appeal'. It concurred also with Oliver J's statement that the court did not have carte blanche to reform either the deceased's dispositions or those provided for him by the intestacy rules (it found there was no difference in the two cases, as the deceased might have taken a conscious decision to remain intestate, save where he left a statement explaining that he specifically desired, for example, to exclude someone). The court must decide on the basis of the facts known to it at the date of the hearing. Oliver J had been entitled to conclude that the intestacy provisions were not unreasonable to the son.

## 15.30.4 Courts not designed to assess what is just?

The difficulties inherent in this approach were, however, identified by Ormrod J in *Re Fullard* (1982) (15.10.1), when he said that it was impossible to consider what was 'reasonable' without considering what 'ought' to have been done, and 'ought' brought with it considerations of what was just as between the deceased and the applicant.

## 15.30.5 Payment of debts can be maintenance

In considering further what may constitute maintenance, the court in *Re Dennis* (1981) held that 'maintenance' connotes provision which, directly or indirectly, enables the applicant 'to discharge the cost of his daily living at whatever standard of living is appropriate to him'. The court held that although payment of an applicant's debts to enable him to carry on a profit-making profession or business could be maintenance, in this case that did not apply; the debt concerned was the tax liability consequent on the deceased's death within six years of a substantial gift to the applicant. However, as well as maintenance by periodical payments, an applicant may also be maintained by a lump sum or the provision of accommodation or the wherewithal to buy it, or even by money to pay off debts to enable the applicant to re-establish a functioning financial life. This principle has been followed in several cases.[48] In *Espinosa v Bourke* (1999), discharge of the claimant's debts would enable her to make an income from her business.

---

48  *Re Hancock* (1998); *Bahouse v Negus* (2008); *Re Watson* (1999); *Graham v Murphy* (1997); *Baynes v Hedger* (2008) and (2009); *Espinosa v Bourke* (1999).

## 15.31 How the court may carry out calculations – example

The way that a court proceeds to calculate the amount to be awarded in a fairly large estate can be seen from the example of *Malone v Harrison and Another* (1979). Albeit this case is now dated on the figures, it remains a useful illustration.

The deceased and his wife Agnes had been separated in 1939 but never divorced; he paid her maintenance voluntarily. In 1958, one Christina Milne moved in with the deceased, and she subsequently took the surname Harrison. In 1965, he met the applicant, Mavis Cynthia Malone, who at his request gave up her job, albeit it was not well paid. He gave her assurances about her future security but told her he would not be providing for her in his will; however, he sent her a newspaper clipping about the passage through Parliament of the 1975 Act.

By the time of his death in 1977, the deceased had given the applicant shares to the value of £15,000, the flat in Sutton Coldfield in which she lived and a flat in Malta valued at £10,000. The deceased had been giving Miss Malone about £4,000 a year, but had continued to live with Christina Milne. He had told Christina Milne that he no longer had any relationship with the applicant; he had told the applicant that Christina Milne was no more than his housekeeper, but very possessive of him. The deceased left a substantial estate. Provision was made in the will for the deceased's wife, for Christina Milne and her son and for the deceased's brother Mr Harrison. The applicant was earning £23 per week and had no greater earning capacity; her shares less her overdraft were worth about £13,000. She was 38 years old, with an actuarial life expectancy of 38 years.

It was agreed that she should get, if anything at all, a lump sum. The court (commenting that 'the deceased worked hard and for long hours, but he also allowed himself considerable relaxation') held:

(a)     The deceased had maintained the applicant on the basis of a promise that she would be provided for by him after his death; if the provision in his will was not reasonable, the court would alter it.

(b)     The court would balance the plaintiff's needs with the deceased's obligations to the beneficiaries. The plaintiff would have to resort to capital during her lifetime but the value of her home was not expendable.

(c)     The plaintiff reasonably needed £4,000 a year, to which figure the court would apply a multiplier of 11 (a multiplier represents the number of years for which a person will be compensated for a loss which is expected to continue; it is invariably considerably less than the number of years they are expected to live, because they obtain the capital early and can invest it). She was already earning £2,000 so she would get £22,000 by way of capitalised maintenance. She should get capital of £4,000 with a multiplier of five. From the total of £42,000 they court deducted her free capital of £13,000 and the value of the flat in Malta, so she got £19,000, which the court directed to be paid from the deceased's brother's share of the estate. It is perhaps interesting that the court rejected the argument that the applicant's award should be put in trust so that it reverted to the brother after her death. It allowed her to take the capital and the independence and control it represented, saying the brother had already had enough.

## 15.32 Property available for provision

All of the deceased's net estate is available to satisfy any order the court may make. The net estate is all the property the deceased had power to dispose of by will (other than by virtue of special power of appointment), less funeral, testamentary and administration expenses, debts, liabilities and Inheritance Tax. It includes property in respect of which the deceased held a general power of appointment not exercisable by will and not exercised, money or property passing by statutory nomination or *donatio mortis causa* (less the Inheritance Tax referable to it (s 8)), the value of the deceased's severable share of property held on joint tenancy and money made available by the court exercising anti-avoidance powers in relation to family provision.

The scope of s 8 of the 1975 Act and what is available for a family provision claim was discussed recently in *Goenka v Goenka and Others* (2014). It was asserted that money from life assurance policies should not be taken into account because the quantum was to be worked out on the basis of what the claimant might have got on divorce (see 15.23.2 and 15.23.5); life assurance comes into play on death, not divorce. However, the court confirmed that the divorce standard was only one factor, and if there were life assurance monies in the estate, they would be taken account of in the family provision claim. There was also a 'death in service payment' from the deceased's employer, and the court confirmed that that was also part of the estate for the purposes of family provision.

### 15.32.1 Joint tenancies

Section 9 of the I(PFD)A 1975 states that the deceased's share of a severable joint tenancy may be ordered to be included in the net estate provided that an application under s 2 of the Act is taken out within six months of the grant of representation to the estate, with a provision that anyone who does anything before such an order is made is not rendered liable by the section for anything they did prior to the making of the order. Thus, a bank paying out the proceeds of a joint account or a survivor of joint tenants dissipating assets may be rendered not liable by this provision. The section is not restricted to holdings of land; it specifically states that a chose in action may be held on a joint tenancy. In *Re Crawford* (1983), the court was considering a claim by the deceased's first wife against money held in building society and bank accounts held jointly by the deceased and his second wife. It held that the net estate of the deceased against which the first wife could claim included his share of that money. The ITPA 2014 provides that the value of the deceased's severable share will be that at the date of the hearing had the share been severed immediately before death, subject to the court ordering otherwise, so the six-month time limit for bringing property held on a joint tenancy into a family provision claim has in effect for most purposes been removed, with practical provisions about valuation, as that may change over time.

In *Dingmar v Dingmar* (2007), the question was how to deal with a valuation problem that arose when the value of the property had more than doubled during the seven years between the death and the claim under the 1975 Act, when the deceased's son obtained a possession order against the widow. The trial judge held he could award only the value of the deceased's half-share at his death, not the half-share itself, but the Court of Appeal, by a majority, held that on a proper construction, s 9 meant the property rather than its value.

More complex questions of joint property relating to insurance policies have also been explored.

In *Powell v Osbourne* (1993), there was a joint life policy designed to pay off a mortgage should one of the parties die during its currency. After a decree nisi of divorce, the husband died and the widow claimed the proceeds of the policy under s 9 of the Act. The trial judge said the deceased's interest in the policy was nothing, as before his death it had no surrender value, but the Court of Appeal held that it should be valued with regard to his imminent death. The previous analysis was described by Dillon LJ as 'slightly startling and anomalous'. In *Murphy v Holland* (2004), the policy additionally had a terminal illness benefit (also held jointly), and the question was whether the deceased and the claimant had joint or separate rights. It was held that the death benefit was not intended to be severable by notice of severance, but was intended to go to the survivor, with

Chadwick LJ however dissenting on the basis that the rights were joint rights until the death of the first to die. In *Lim v Walia* (2014), the deceased and the claimant held a life policy which included a provision that the benefit would be brought forward and paid out were one of the insured to show they were suffering from a terminal illness. The deceased died abroad, in the process of divorce from her husband, leaving a young son from a new relationship. The husband was entitled to a grant and, because of the size of it, to the estate on intestacy. The question for the trial judge was one preliminary to an Inheritance Act claim by the deceased's infant son: whether, immediately before her death, the deceased had been beneficially entitled to a joint tenancy of the terminal illness benefit. He found that she was. The husband appealed, and the Court of Appeal, by a majority, held that the deceased had had a severable interest in the terminal illness benefit but that, as an acceleration of the death payment, it should be valued (unlike in *Powell* and *Dingmar*) taking into account that it was contingent on a successful claim and ceased to have a value if it was not claimed before she died. McCombe LJ dissented, arguing from *Dingmar* that it was the existence of the severable share before death that mattered, not its value at any particular time.

## 15.32.2 Insurance policies

It has long appeared that the proceeds of insurance policies written in trust were not available, the report of the Law Commission having apparently assumed that the act of creating a trust of a policy did not amount to a disposition of property. Given the breadth of the categories of property which are included in the net estate, this was surprising. In *Re Cairnes* (1983), the court considered whether occupational pension benefits formed part of the net estate for the purposes of family provision orders, and held that they were an example of property which is not included in the net estate of the deceased, if they were payable direct to a beneficiary and not to the deceased's estate.

Especially with the retreat of state provision, many people hold a great deal of their wealth in their private pension. Whilst they cannot obtain the money for their own use except on the terms of the pension fund agreement, they can nominate someone to receive benefits from the fund after their death. Nominating such a beneficiary is therefore somewhat like leaving them something by will. The Law Commission consulted in 2009 on including pension benefits in the family provision system, but decided against recommending it for reasons including administrative efficiency.[49]

## 15.33 Burden of orders

Once the nature of the net estate has been established, the court may order where the burden of its provisions should fall, under its powers in s 2(4). It may, for example, order one particular beneficiary under the will to transfer part of their property to the successful applicant, rather than dividing the burden amongst all the beneficiaries, if it sees fit. If any trust is created or affected by the order the court makes on an application under the 1975 Act, it may confer on the trustees such powers as appear to it to be necessary or expedient.

---

49  Law Commission 331 *Intestacy and Family Provision Claims on Death* (2011), paras 7.111–112.

## 15.34 Anti-avoidance

Avoidance of the family provision legislation was a particular problem under the 1938 Act. A person who wished to ensure that some particular person benefited from their estate, to the detriment of a potential applicant with a valid claim under the Act, could avoid the consequences of the act by selling at an undervalue or giving away the property before their death. Where the recipient provides full consideration for the property, it is not regarded as falling within the anti-avoidance provisions and cannot be recalled into the deceased's estate by the hopeful applicant under the Act.

Anti-avoidance is dealt with in ss 10–13 of the I(PFD)A 1975. Section 10 relates to dispositions (the giving away or selling of property) less than six years before death and s 11 to contracts to leave property by will. In either case, the transaction must have been at an undervalue; where the property has been effectively sold for its full market value, it will not be available to be pulled back into the estate under these provisions so as to be used to satisfy a claim under the 1975 Act.[50]

### 15.34.1 Powers and guidelines

Section 10 sets out the court's powers in relation to avoidance. It provides that it is for the applicant for financial provision to show that the disposition was made less than six years before the date of the deceased's death, with the intention of defeating an application under the 1975 Act, that full valuable consideration was not given and that the exercise of the court's powers under s 10 would allow the court to make financial provision for the applicant, or allow it to be made more easily than otherwise. In considering whether and how it will exercise its powers under this section, the court is directed to have regard to the circumstances in which any disposition was made and any valuable consideration that was given for it, as well as any relationship between the donee and the deceased and his or her conduct and financial resources. The court is also directed to have regard to 'all the other circumstances of the case'. This means that the court may well find a situation in which the deceased undoubtedly made a transaction at an undervalue, or a gift, within six years of their death, intending to put the property beyond the reach of a potential applicant for family provision – but that it was reasonable for the testator to do so in the circumstances, because of their relationship to the donee, and that it is not a disposition that should be disturbed by the court.

Section 11 refers to contracts made by the deceased to leave property by will. This is essentially the same provision as in s 10, but referable to cases where the deceased has held on to the property until death rather than disposing of it beforehand. Again, an intention to defeat the operation of the 1975 Act must be shown, as well as a lack of full valuable consideration. There is no time limit on when the contract may have been made save the commencement of the 1975 Act.

Section 12 provides for how the court will decide whether or not the relevant disposition was made by the deceased with the intention of defeating an application for family provision. It allows the court to base its decision on the opinion on the balance of probabilities that this was, in whole or in part, the deceased's intention. This may be presumed where a contract is alleged but no valuable consideration was given for it. The court is also empowered to make directions so as to obtain property for the applicant whilst treating the lifetime recipient of the property fairly

---

50  Croucher 'Contracts to Leave Property by Will and Family Provision after Barns v Barns [2003] HCA 9' (2005) 27 Sydney Law Review 263.

Section 13 deals with applications made about property given to persons as trustees; the court may not order the trustee to provide more than the trustee has in their hands at the date of the order in respect of the property involved in the claim.

## 15.34.2 Joining the lifetime recipient

If an applicant wishes to ask the court to make an order against a donee under these sections, then procedurally that person has to be joined in the proceedings. This means making them a party to the court proceedings by issuing an application against them and making them one of the named people against whom the applicant is making his or her claim under the 1975 Act.

## 15.34.3 Disposition cannot be set aside as such

The court does not have the power to set aside dispositions and contracts directly, but to order a person who has benefited to help to provide the resources from which a family provision claim can be satisfied. This is different from the powers a bankruptcy court has to set aside transactions at an undervalue within certain periods of the bankruptcy – those powers have caused grave problems particularly where land is concerned, because they mean that a court may come back at a later date and effectively wipe out retrospectively the good title to property obtained by a third party with no connection with the bankrupt, who bought for full consideration from the bankrupt's donee. The provisions under the 1975 Act allow the court to order the donee, or recipient at an undervalue, to provide a sum of money representing the property given to them by the deceased. Section 10 provides that it may order a donee to provide money representing no more than the value of the property given to him or her, after deducting any inheritance tax they had to pay on it as a result of the deceased's death. Section 11 makes the same provision in relation to the money paid under a contract, but additionally provides that, if the contract has not been carried out, the court can order it not to be fulfilled.

## 15.34.4 Order to provide funds

In the case of *Re Dawkins (deceased)* (1986), the deceased's estate was insolvent. Fifteen months before he died, he had sold his house, worth £27,000, to his daughter for £100 with the intention of defeating an application under the family provision legislation. His second wife applied under the 1975 Act. The court was satisfied that an anti-evasion order was appropriate and it ordered the daughter to provide £10,000 for the purpose of providing the applicant with a lump sum.

# 15.35 Family provision and contracts to leave by will

A person may make a valid contract to leave property by will (see *Hammersley v De Biel* (1845) and *Synge v Synge* (1894)) (see 2.5). If the deceased concluded a valid contract to leave their property by will in respect of which the applicant cannot show that there was an intention to defeat family provision claims and that there was a lack of full consideration, the property or the value it represents will not be available to the court to satisfy claims under the 1975 Act.

### 15.35.1  A valid contract to leave by will

The most helpful case may be one under the relevant Australian legislation, *Schaefer v Schuhmann* (1972), which came to the Privy Council from New South Wales. The deceased had made a will in 1962 leaving his four daughters $2,000 each, the residue to be divided between his three sons. In 1966 he bought a house and engaged a housekeeper at $12 a week. In May of that year, he made a codicil, which he asked the housekeeper to read to him, giving his house and its contents to her if she should 'still be employed by me as a housekeeper at the date of my death'. He then told her she would have no more wages because of the provision in the codicil. In November 1966, when the testator died, she was still his housekeeper. The estate was valued at $68,700 net, of which the house and content were valued at $14,500. The daughters applied under the relevant New South Wales legislation for extra provision.

### 15.35.2  Valid contract but could the family provision court overrule it?

The court of first instance found that the testator and his housekeeper had a contract but that the court had jurisdiction to throw the burden of the daughters' additional provision onto the housekeeper's part of the estate, putting a charge on the house except as to $2,300, thereafter the burden to fall on the residue of the estate. The housekeeper appealed saying the court had no power to make such an order and that all the extra provision should come from residue.

The court allowed the housekeeper's appeal, upholding the contractual arrangements as genuine and declaring that there was no basis for the contention that the rights of a party to a contract became simply the rights of a legatee. Property over which someone had rights of ownership under a contract did not form part of the net estate available for distribution.

### 15.35.3  Would that case be followed in England today?

If a case were brought in England today on the same facts, the housekeeper might have greater difficulty in establishing her right to the house, because of the effects of s 2 of the Law Reform (Miscellaneous Provisions) Act 1989. The enforceability of her contract with the deceased was based on the doctrine of part performance, which is no longer applicable. Someone in a similar position might instead seek to rely on establishing a constructive trust or might base her claim on proprietary estoppel.

### 15.35.4  Should that case be followed in principle?

Lord Simon of Glaisdale was cited by the Law Commission in its 61st Report as having made a particular objection to the exclusion of property passing under a contract to leave by will from being available for family provision. He suggested the situation in which a widower with two infant children proposes marriage to another woman, promising her all his estate if she will accept his proposal. She does accept him on those terms. He then dies, leaving the court powerless to award any provision for the infant children. Although the Law Commission suggested only contracts for which full valuable consideration was not given or promised by the proposed donee (marriage not being valuable consideration for these purposes) should be upheld, there is no specific reference to marriage consideration in s 11 of the I(PFD)A 1975, which deals with contracts to leave property by will. Moreover, the courts are not quick to find that a contract is invalid for being designed to defeat a claim (*Midland Bank v Green* (1981) is a case in point).

## 15.36  How to apply – jurisdiction and procedure

Applications for orders under the 1975 Act can be made in the county court, or in the Chancery or Family Divisions of the High Court. The county courts' jurisdiction is now unlimited, but some cases will still be suitable for transfer to the High Court, for example where there is a great deal of money or property involved or the action is particularly important or raises any questions of general public interest. Where there is a problem of construing the will, the Chancery Division may be thought more appropriate than the Family Division, although the Law Commission had proposed that all cases under the 1975 Act should be heard in the Family Division. Where there has already been an order in matrimonial proceedings, the Family Division will be the appropriate choice. Persons under a disability may be parties in the usual way and proceedings may be compromised (settled between the parties rather than decided by a judge), although the Act does not provide specifically for this. Costs can be awarded out of the estate and usually are. Procedure in the county court is essentially the same as in the High Court, though every defendant, not just the personal representatives, must file an answer to the action.

## 15.37  Costs

The question of costs, whilst essentially one of practice, does impinge on the substantive law, especially in the area of family provision. The courts have comments to make on the subject of costs in many of their judgments, and they are very ready to condemn the bringing of cases about small estates, since the legal costs will exhaust the estate and the net effect is often simply to deprive anyone, save perhaps the lawyers involved, of any benefit at all. One might bear in mind, however, that what a judge considers to be a small estate is not always seen as such by the aggrieved claimant, and that a prohibition on 'small' cases being brought to a court might mean that a good claim, to which any reasonable beneficiary would accede by agreement, could be defeated by any unreasonable beneficiary without fear of the consequences.

The rules about the payment of other parties' costs are based on the person whose case is better not suffering, and on the prevention of unreasonableness by deterrence; in family provision claims, however, costs usually come out of the estate, on the basis that the deceased was responsible for not having made proper provision. That is no comfort to the person who succeeds in a very reasonable claim against an estate that has been totally depleted by legal fees.

The operation of costs can have a very material effect on a case and has to be borne in mind by practitioners at all times. In *Re a firm of Solicitors* (1982), the court heavily criticised the solicitors acting for the widow of the deceased Mr Coventry for incurring the costs of Queen's Counsel. Even though the legal aid authorities had authorised the instruction of a leader, and the case was one of great public interest, the expense of using such a senior barrister meant that the widow gained no benefit from the action, even though she had been reasonable throughout the case, willing to accept the original order of the master giving the son provision, and indeed had become involved in further litigation only when the son appealed, disastrously, to Oliver J and the Court of Appeal.

In *Powell v Osbourne* (1993) (15.32.1), both parties had obtained legal aid, and the court made an order for costs so that the losing cohabitant should have paid the costs of the winning widow. However, the order was not to be enforced without leave (as is usual against a legally aided party), so the widow would have had to bear her own legal costs of the case, including a hearing before the Court of Appeal, out of her award of £15,000.

The details of legal aid provision may have a substantial effect on the course or outcome of a case. In *Moody v Stephenson* (1992), for example, the effect of the court's careful consideration of the appropriate order was thrown into some disarray by the revelations about the plaintiff's legal aid contribution of £3,700 and the revocation of his certificate during the case. Legal aid provision has continued to be restricted, but family provision may be one of the areas where the spread of litigants in person causes less disruption and difficulty: much of it is about the story, and the legal rules are awkward to implement and unclear principally because the cases involve so many important non-legal considerations.

## 15.38  Summary of Chapter 15

### 15.38.1 Family Provision

Although testamentary freedom as such has a comparatively short history, the possibility of bringing an action against a person's estate after their death on the basis that they have failed to make reasonable and proper provision is very recent in succession terms, and is entirely a creature of statute. The first legislation was passed in 1938. The current Act is the Inheritance (Provision for Family and Dependants) Act 1975.

Section 1(1) of the 1975 Act as amended gives six categories of persons who have the right to apply:

- the wife or husband of the deceased;
- a former wife or husband who has not remarried;
- a cohabitant for the two years preceding death;
- a child of the deceased;
- a person treated as child of the family by the deceased;
- a person not in the above categories who was being maintained by the deceased immediately before the deceased's death.

The applicant must first show that they falls within one of the above categories before they can bring a claim. They must then show that what they receive under the deceased's will or intestacy is not reasonable. The court will then assess what award to make. The assessment of both unreasonableness and what would be a reasonable order is made on the basis of the facts known to the court at the date of the hearing, thus taking into account changes in people's situations since the date of death as well as earlier facts unknown to the deceased.

The statutory guidelines to assessing reasonableness under s 3(1) have a very wide scope and allow the court to consider anything it wishes, though it is specifically directed to look at the financial situation of anyone who might benefit from the estate, the size of the estate, the obligations the deceased had towards them and any disability of any beneficiaries.

Actions should be brought within six months of a grant of representation to an estate, but the courts are fairly liberal with leave to apply out of time. They discourage applications about small estates, which can be rendered useless by the legal costs involved. However, cases are often settled out of court, sometimes by an offer made largely to forestall proceedings.

The court may order maintenance, a lump sum, transfer, acquisition or settlement of property or the variation of a marriage settlement. This is much wider than the original provisions under the 1938 legislation, which allowed maintenance only. It has sometimes been suggested that the courts, in particular cases, have used the provisions of the 1975 Act to provide for a general distribution of property for which it was not intended.

#  15.39  Further reading

## Book

Rebecca Probert, *The Changing Legal Regulation of Cohabitation: From Fornicators to Family, 1600–2010* (Cambridge University Press 2012).

## Journal articles

Anne Barlow and Janet Smithson, 'Legal Assumptions, Cohabitants' Talk and the Rocky Road to Reform' (2010) 22 Child and Family Law Quarterly 328.

Rosalind Croucher, 'How Free Is Free? Testamentary Freedom and the Battle Between Family and Property' (2012) 37 Australian Journal of Legal Philosophy 9.

Gillian Douglas, 'Family Provision and Family Practices: The Discretionary Regime of the Inheritance Act of England and Wales' (2014) 4 *Oñati* Socio-Legal Series 122.

Mary Ann Glendon, 'Fixed Rules and Discretion in Contemporary Family Law and Succession Law' (1985) 60 Tulane Law Review 1165.

Rebecca Probert, 'Common Law Marriage: Myths and Understandings' (2008) 20 Child and Family Law Quarterly 1.

Sidney Ross, 'The Implications of White v White for Inheritance Act Claims' [2001] Family Law 547 and 619.

# Chapter 16

# Problem-Solving and Contentious Issues

In the past two decades, the numbers of reported contentious probate cases has increased substantially. This does not indicate a change in succession law so much as a change in the public attitude to contesting wills, or perhaps other background factors. The biggest relevant social change recently must be the change in the legal structure of the family. The gradual change wrought by the growing acceptance of informal cohabitation as founding claims to family provision was overshadowed by the speedy change in the legal view of same-sex relationships. Often criminal until the late 1960s, they were legitimised and accepted by the Civil Partnership Act 2004; that legal change was consolidated by the Marriage (Same Sex Couples) Act 2013. These developments both reflect and alter the landscape of succession law, even if formally they change principally the operation of intestacy and family provision, given that English law still allows a broad testamentary freedom. In intestacy, however, cohabitation is still not recognised. There has been little legal change that fundamentally affects succession law: even the growth of European and human rights law, whilst of interest, has not particularly affected the English succession jurisdiction.

## 16.1 Practical and contentious issues

Whilst succession is essentially part of the fundamentally non-contentious subject of property law, some aspects of the topic were always defined by events that might lead to litigation – testamentary capacity and the scope of mistake have always been important basic topics (see Chapter 4, especially 4.11), for example, and the powers of those administering the estate have always been defined by limits that could easily be breached (see 13.19 and 13.20). The reason for the increase in contentious actions may be a rising culture of litigation, perhaps lagging behind the formerly more general availability of legal aid; or people may have a stronger sense of entitlement than before or be more willing to pursue it openly. It may be that substantial property ownership has spread and so more estates are more worth disputing, perhaps especially in a time of rising social inequality or spreading economic gloom; or it may be that the fact that people are living longer and the phenomena of dementia and mental incapacity are more readily acknowledged that has opened the way by provoking more frequent assertions that a will does not embody the testator's true testamentary intentions.

Claims against lawyers for error have also increased. What was once a relatively quiet area of practice has become more obviously a worrying maze of potential traps and pitfalls, apparently just like other fields of practice. However, succession remains an essentially non-contentious area. Discussion of what can go wrong should be focused on how to avoid letting that happen, as well as what to do if it does. This book aims to lay the foundations of the landscape for the student and general lawyer, and to explain how to cross the field without falling off the path rather than how to fight battles as one goes. The practical aspects of succession law generally fall within the scope of the Non-Contentious Probate Rules, and these deal with ordering property rather than resolving disputes. Nevertheless there are some more obvious pitfalls that do illuminate the true path, and some rescue remedies that may comfort the traveller.

## 16.1.1 The absence of a body: presuming death

In dealing with succession law and practice one generally assumes that either a will is being made by someone who is still alive to do that, or that someone has died and their estate needs to be administered according to law. Succession law is principally about how a property owner ensures the last property rights are exercised as they wish, after their death, and how the legal system enables that to happen; a small – and legally quite unclear – part of succession practice is about the disposal of the deceased's body (see 12.1). But occasionally a property owner may disappear without physical trace: for example, a skier on holiday may disappear under an avalanche and their body may not be recoverable. This means that the person is no longer managing their own property, paying their mortgage and doing their house repairs – but there is no death certificate to start off the process of administration either.

If there is no body and no death certificate, an application for death to be presumed may be made. There has long been a general presumption that seven years of absence indicates death, but that has always been rebuttable and often difficult to establish. Some areas of law have long provided specific procedures for establishing death as a matter of law in the absence of a death certificate. For example, death of a spouse could be presumed under s 10 of the Matrimonial Causes Act 1973 so that the other spouse could remarry, or on the report of a coroner and at the ensuing direction of the Secretary of State, an inquest could be established under s 15 of the Coroners Act 1988 if the death was in the vicinity of the coroner's court: this could lead to the issuing of a death certificate. A person could also apply under r 53 of the Non-Contentious Probate Rules 1987 to swear death when taking out a grant. This required the applicant to swear to the reason for the application and to supply details of any life insurance policies and any other information the registrar might require.

The new Presumption of Death Act 2013, however, establishes a new procedure for obtaining a High Court declaration that the missing person is deemed dead, which can be used for general purposes. Such a declaration will be made if the High Court is satisfied that the person has died, as for example where they were present at a disaster, or that they have been missing for seven years, and such declarations will be entered on a Register. Their property will pass as though they were dead. A certified copy of the declaration will operate as does a death certificate. The declaration is conclusive and there is no appeal.

However, should the declaration require revocation or amendment (for example should the deceased appear alive, as in the case of *Re Napier* (1809)), application for that can be made to the High Court, which can then also consider what orders to make about the person's former property. It is foreseen that the rate of orders will run at 30 to 40 per year and that there will be 'very few' variations.

## 16.1.2 Disputes about the estate: common form and contentious probate

Most grants of probate are obtained in 'common form'. That is, they are considered and granted in an administrative manner, and there are no court proceedings as such. There is rarely a dispute about who should take a grant, though it is important to remember that in relation to some actions – particularly claims for family provision under the Inheritance (Provision for Family and Dependants) Act 1975 – there are time limits within which proceedings must be issued. Failure to adhere to those time limits could lead to serious loss, or at least to the need to seek an extension that one might not get, so those issues should be addressed at the outset of any administration.

There are around half a million deaths, wills and grants in England and Wales each year, and even though only a small proportion of them are disputed, that is still more than a few overall. Where something falls to be decided within the court process, the matter becomes one of contentious probate. It then becomes a court process like any other, and is governed by the Civil Procedure Rules. Part 57 refers to contentious probate and it states that contentious probate matters will be heard in the Chancery Division or the Family Division of the High Court. The court may issue relevant Practice Directions in the same way as with other forms of court process and Practice Direction 57, which supplements Part 57 of the CPR, is very practical and informative about how to begin and pursue a contentious probate claim.

Contentious probate matters arise from a variety of causes, and include challenges to the will or grant on the basis that the testator lacked mental capacity, or that the will was not duly executed, or even that it was forged; or a combination of these (see 16.1.4). Note, however, that anyone seeking to contest a will must have the necessary standing: that is, they need to have some potential interest in the estate, whether as personal representative or beneficiary. In *Randall v Randall* (2014), the would-be claimant was the divorced husband of the executrix, who was herself the daughter of the deceased. His case was that, in the divorce proceedings, it had been agreed that she would take the first £100,000 of any future legacy from her mother and then any excess would be shared between them. The deceased mother left her exactly £100,000; he claimed he was sufficiently interested in the estate because, if the last will and also an earlier one were both found to be invalid, the daughter – his ex-wife – would inherit the whole estate, worth about £250,000, so giving him a claim to £75,000 from the ex-wife. Deputy Master Collaço Moraes said that being a creditor of a beneficiary might mean he was interested in the estate but it was not a sufficient interest to give him standing to bring contentious probate proceedings.

### 16.1.3 Disputes about solicitors' handling of the will or estate

Claims that a solicitor has failed to deal properly with a will or estate and that the solicitor is liable may clearly be linked to a claim about the estate itself, but are of a different order. A claim against a solicitor must be based on the breach of some obligation by the solicitor. The potential for such claims is considered below in outline. It is important for any solicitor to consider the likely sources of potential action in order to be able to guard against likely errors, to the benefit of all. Something to bear in mind is that things can and do go wrong, that no one should make a mistake but anyone can, and that is why lawyers are insured. Junior lawyers who think they have made an error should first of all report it to a senior colleague. It is up to the firm to report potential claims to their insurer, who will no doubt have a right under the terms of the policy to take over the process of dealing with the complaint. Solicitors also have a professional duty to report any negligence to the client concerned and to invite them to pursue it.

A solicitor is clearly liable in contract to the client. However, where there is an error in drafting a will, the person who has lost out is usually someone who claims the deceased meant to make them a beneficiary but who receives little or nothing under the will. In this case the would-be beneficiary is a third party to the contract and would have to claim in tort.[1]

There are some solutions to problems that are built into the probate system, such as rectification (see 4.11 and 16.4.2) and the variation of wills by a deed that can be read back into the will (see 14.20 and 16.4.4). These avenues are well developed and should be explored wherever they may assist. Would-be claimants are expected to seek rectification where it is possible. It is also advisable for solicitors to consider the possibility of rectification themselves should they find themselves to have made a rectifiable error. The point that it is cheaper to spot a problem and rectify it than to await the consequences of error was made in *Corbett v Bond Pearce* (2001), where the insurers paid the full claim of the disappointed beneficiaries as well as their legal costs.

---

1 Kit Barker, 'Are We Up to Expectations? Solicitors, Beneficiaries and the Tort/Contract Divide' (1994) 14 Oxford Journal of Legal Studies 137.

## 16.1.4 Multiple claims

Disappointed beneficiaries are not uncommon, but most do not pursue their disappointment into court, or even as far as a solicitor's office. Some, however, do. And some are justified and others less so.

On any particular set of facts, there may be various avenues of potential dispute. These cases can lead to convoluted and expensive proceedings. Claims may be based on proprietary estoppel (see 2.5), where the point alleged is not a dispute about the will as such, but about whether the testator was really entitled to leave their property as they did because it is asserted that they had effectively already parted with it in equity. The testator's knowledge and approval of the will may be disputed on the basis of facts that might also show a lack of testamentary capacity; these issues are often considered together in the same case. Where a disappointed beneficiary thinks the testator was generally competent but really meant to leave them more than apparently they did, the dispute may be framed as one in which the testator was tricked and the will itself was not validly made, or as one where the testator was subject to undue influence (a term lay persons often expect to cover much lesser forms of pressure than it does), or the will may be accepted but its disposition challenged in a family provision dispute. Re Sherrington (2005) was such a case, where the assertion that the will drafted by the step-daughter of a successful solicitor was not properly made failed for want of sufficient evidence to rebut the presumption of due attestation, especially given the testator's professional knowledge, and the wife and first family, who had been disinherited in favour of the second wife went on to make a family provision claim.

Sometimes claimants base their claims on an understanding that the testator had moral obligations he or she would have wished to fulfil: their understanding of those obligations, or of the testator, may be different from the testator's own viewpoint. Others may be pinning their hopes on obtaining money or property they feel they have a moral claim to through need. The facts are likely to include both issues of personal relationships and awkward property and tax considerations which perhaps do require outside adjudication, as for example in Bahouse v Negus (2008). But proceedings may often become more burdensome than the original dispute, being both expensive and stressful – sometimes. Collins J in Re Loftus, Green and Others v Gaul and Others (2005), before suggesting that the court proceedings formed part of the weaponry of this particular dispute, characterised the case saying:

> Although it was famously said that every unhappy family is unhappy in its own way, in my experience there is a depressing similarity between unhappy families when it comes to disputes over the assets of deceased parents. This is a particularly bitter dispute, where the sums of money are modest by modern standards, and which has been going on ever since the death in 1990 of Ivor Loftus.... As is usual, the dispute is not really about the money, but about long-running sores within the family.

An attempt to make such cases simpler by separating the issues and holding a split trial was however found to be ultimately unhelpful in Fox and Pettigrew v Jewell (2013). Issues in the case included proprietary estoppel, lack of knowledge and approval, lack of testamentary capacity, rectification for the will not reflecting the wishes of the testator, and mutual wills. But a split trial, it was found, would be likely to produce a prolonged process as the same facts would have to be covered, requiring repeat attendance of witnesses and taking of evidence, and so was not appropriate.

## 16.2 Liability of lawyers in tort

It used to appear unlikely that solicitors would accrue liability in tort in the area of wills, and that the only duty was that owed in contract to the client and future testator. Moreover, probate practice is a generally non-contentious area that is, or should be, characterised by a lack of the haste and stress that classically lie behind mistakes. Nevertheless, in recent decades the field of probate has produced some leading cases on solicitors' liability, especially the classic early case of *Ross v Caunters* (1979), which concerned the rule in s 15 Wills Act 1837 that a witness or their spouse (and now civil partner) may not take a benefit under the will.

The testator had instructed a solicitor to draw up a will which included gifts to a Mrs Ross. The solicitor drew up the will and at the testator's request sent it to him for signing. At the time, the testator was staying at the Rosses' house, where the solicitor addressed the will to him. A covering letter was sent about how to execute the will, but it did not mention the provisions of s 15. The will was witnessed by Mr Ross. After the testator's death, the mistake came to light. Mrs Ross lost her benefit and sued. The solicitor argued that he owed a duty only to the testator, and could not be liable to Mrs Ross as a third party. He also argued that there were reasons of public policy against holding him liable. It was held, however, that the solicitor owed a duty of care to the third party intended to benefit under the will.

### 16.2.1 Liability in tort to a prospective beneficiary

The decision in *Ross v Caunters* held that a solicitor owes a duty of care to a beneficiary under a will, a person the solicitor may never have met. It also held that the relationship between the solicitor and the beneficiary is sufficiently proximate for the purposes of a claim for economic loss, which is what a claim relating to the loss of a benefit under a will amounts to. On the one hand, it meant that beneficiaries who were disappointed as a result of a solicitor's error had a means to seek compensation. On the other, it meant that solicitors were liable for a form of economic loss sustained by people who were not clients, when they had no duty to those people and those people had no claim on the solicitor's client either for the gift they had 'lost'. Moreover, the estate, to which the solicitor would be responsible after their client's death, has not suffered any loss in these cases.

### 16.2.2 Limits of a solicitor's liability to a beneficiary

Once *Ross v Caunters* had established that a solicitor owed a duty to the prospective beneficiaries under a will which he or she was instructed to prepare, it was inevitable that there would be further claims by disappointed beneficiaries. The case of *Clark v Bruce Lance* (1988), however, established that there are limits on this duty In that case, the solicitor drew up a will for the testator under which he made a gift of a petrol station. Subsequently he assisted the testator in his grant of an option to purchase the petrol station. The option was exercisable after the death of the testator and his wife. When the option was exercised, the beneficiary was deprived of his benefit and he sued the solicitor, alleging that in acting for the testator in the grant of the option he had breached his duty to the beneficiary who would lose his benefit if the option were exercised. The court held that the solicitor owed the beneficiary no duty of care in the later transaction, because to impose such a duty would entail 'a liability in an indeterminate amount for an indeterminate time to an indeterminate class'.

Such a line of argument would also have other implications. A will has no effect until death, and the testator's freedom to deal with their property is unaffected by the making of the will. There seems no good reason at all why a person's solicitor should be precluded from advising that person further on dealing with their property just because a will has already been made; that would preclude the altering of the will as well. A solicitor's duty cannot logically be to protect the beneficiaries' interests against a change of mind or heart by the testator, since the testator is fully entitled to change their will if they wish. The situation may require careful explanation by the solicitor of the consequences where the testator, rather than merely revoking gifts, is in breach of contract in doing so (see 2.5), or where, for example, the anomalous rule in *Lawes v Bennett* (1795) may produce an effect the testator did not expect when granting an option (see 10.7.6).

### 16.2.3  Why tort liability to beneficiaries?

A solicitor's negligence, if there is any, usually comes to light only once the testator has died and it is too late for anything practical to be done about the error. The testator's estate will probably not have lost anything, so the personal representatives will be unable to show the loss necessary to bring an action against the solicitor. Applying the usual basic rules for bringing an action in negligence, they will be able to establish that the solicitor owed the testator a duty of care which he or she breached, but unable to establish any loss arising from the breach. Therefore, they would have no action. Before *Ross v Caunters*, it would have been thought that the beneficiary who does have a loss arising from the breach of duty of the solicitor could not establish that the solicitor owed them a duty of care, so they would not have had an action either.[2]

### 16.2.4  Scope of solicitors' liability

The area of solicitors' liability to beneficiaries developed considerably and remains likely to continue to do so. The plaintiffs in the case of *White v Jones* (1995) were the daughters of the testator, who had intended them to benefit under a new will. He had already instructed his solicitors, but they had not yet drawn up the new will when he died. At first instance, the court held that the liability of solicitors in negligence did not apply to an omission to draw up a will, as opposed to the *Ross v Caunters* situation, where the will was drawn up, but negligently. However, in the Court of Appeal the claimant daughters won on the basis that they were identifiable to the negligent legal executive who had failed to deal with the new will during the several weeks between the testator's instructions and his death.

The solicitors appealed to the House of Lords, who upheld their liability on a majority, but on different principles. Instead of applying *Ross v Caunters*, they applied the negligent misrepresentation case of *Hedley Byrne & Co Ltd v Heller & Partners Ltd* (1964). This appears to continue the Court of Appeal's point that the claimant daughters were identifiable to the solicitors, but to do so by different means. The basis of *Hedley Byrne* liability is that a person has taken on a responsibility and knows that someone specific is relying on their carrying it out. The House of Lords was, however, unclear about how a potential beneficiary comes into the necessary relationship with the solicitor to have a right to sue if the solicitor fails to fulfil their responsibilities. In *White v Jones*, one of the plaintiff daughters had been in personal contact with the solicitors' firm, but it appears that the class of beneficiaries who can sue may be much wider, potentially including anyone whom the testator intends to benefit.[3]

---

2  CG Veljanovski and CJ Whelan, 'Professional Negligence and the Quality of Legal Services: An Economic Perspective' (1983) 46 Modern Law Review 700; Harold Luntz, 'Solicitors' Liability to Third Parties' (1983) 3 Oxford Journal of Legal Studies 284.

3  Sebastian Allen, 'White v Jones: What if the Claimant Was Not the Client?' (2012) 18 Trusts & Trustees 401.

## 16.2.5 Costs claims

Costs are a highly relevant consideration where there are disputes about wills or estates. The court in *Servoz-Gavin* (2009) ordered all costs to come out of the estate because of the inevitability of challenge and the moderate way in which it was pursued. In *Rowe v Clarke (Costs)* (2006), similarly the litigation was attributed largely to the disarray in which the testator had kept his papers, so again costs were ordered out of the estate. But courts are able and perhaps increasingly willing to order costs against parties who they feel have been unreasonable. In *Varmer v Mason* (2011), a contested case on domicile, the court confirmed that, as to costs, it ultimately had complete discretion. The scope and limits of this area are being explored.[4]

There have been various cases recently in which claims have been made against solicitors for damages where a will has been found to be invalid, the claim being for the costs of the proceedings occasioned by contesting the will. In *Worby v Rosser* (1999), the beneficiaries under a will executed in 1983 succeeded in contesting a later will, made in 1989, which appointed the drafting solicitor as executor and left the residue elsewhere. The successful beneficiaries sought the costs of those proceedings against the solicitor, claiming he had breached his duty to them to ensure that the later will was not invalid, as it had been, for undue influence by one of the beneficiaries and for want of the testator's testamentary capacity and knowledge and approval. The Court of Appeal held that the solicitor drafting the later will was not liable to the beneficiaries under the earlier, valid, will. He would, however, have owed a duty to the estate. In *Corbett v Bond Pearce* (2001), a later will was invalidly executed. The solicitor was liable to the estate in negligence for the costs of the resulting probate action, and the insurers paid the disappointed beneficiaries the interest they had lost without deducting the costs of the action. The personal representative under the earlier, valid, will then sought the costs of the action against the same solicitor, but were unsuccessful, as the Court of Appeal viewed this not as the negligent solicitors paying the actual costs of the litigation but as a form of double recovery.

In *Sifri v Clough & Willis* (2007), the claimant had successfully disputed two wills made by her father, but had not obtained any order as to costs. She has also not taken out any grant of administration: she sued in her personal capacity. She then brought an action for the costs of the successful claims. The court held that she could recover the costs that were reasonably foreseeable as a result of the solicitor taking instructions from a third party instead of the testator, but not those resulting from claims which did not relate to the solicitor's actions. Moreover, the solicitor was not responsible for delay in the administration of the estate or the losses resulting from that.

In the case of *Feltham v Bouskell* (2013) (16.3.2), a solicitor was sued for his slowness in drafting a will after the client died before he finalised it. The intended beneficiary had been left the estate by a will which she had drafted herself, at her aunt's request; she sued for the costs of contested proceedings over that will.

These cases remain difficult to reconcile. The area of solicitors' liability for damages for legal costs in contested probate actions resulting from negligence in preparing wills will no doubt develop further.

## 16.3 The likely sources of trouble

Whilst no one can foresee the full range of potential problems that may crop up across the range of solicitors' files, certain areas are more predictably a source of disaster.

---

4 James Weale, 'Probate Litigation: The Incidence of Costs' (2014) Trusts & Trustees, http://tandt.oxfordjournals.org/content/early/2014/07/06/tandt.ttu117.abstract, accessed 17 February 2015.

Some of these relate to a breakdown in the solicitor's own vigilance in their interactions with the client and basic processes; such as failing to ensure that instructions are clearly and correctly identified, recorded and translated into the written draft; being slow in responding to instructions; and not having proper storage and retrieval systems so that documents are in effect lost. Others may arise from not being careful enough with matters that require more directly legal skill and judgement, such as checking the client's domicile and any potential issues of conflicts of laws if there is a cross-border element, ensuring that joint tenancies are efficiently severed where appropriate; ascertaining and recording the client's sufficient mental capacity, including obtaining third-party medical evidence where necessary; or making errors in tax calculations or advice. Mistake in the will, simple or otherwise, has long been appreciated as a source of error and systems of rectification are well established.

Most real problems for lawyers arise from their own error (difficult questions from clients being merely opportunities rather than problems), but deliberate conduct should also be watched out for, especially by being vigilant in checking that the client is who he or she says they are and is entitled to whatever he or she is claiming; and even bearing in mind that on occasion there is fraud and forgery. Errors may be compounded by ignoring them: it is always best to confront them as soon as they come to light, as there may be a relatively easy, inexpensive and unembarrassing solution if one acts quickly enough.[5]

## 16.3.1 Misunderstanding instructions

Taking clear and accurate instructions is obviously central to the work of a solicitor. There is some dispute as to whether misunderstanding instructions means that a solicitor is necessarily negligent. The solicitor in *Gibbons v Nelsons* (2000) was not held liable where one of two widowed sisters left her half-share of their house to charity, since it was found that, although it was not clear that she understood the effect of the will, it was also not clear that she would have made a different disposition in any event: this case seems to push the boundaries, however.

In *Walter v Medlicott* (1999), a misunderstanding was found to be rectifiable and not negligent, but the decision in that case was disputed in *Horsfall v Haywards* (1999), where it was held that a failure to understanding instructions, which was the ground for rectification, was always negligent. For more on rectification, see 16.4.2. If there is a dispute, the beneficiary should sue on both bases: it had not been feasible in *Horsfall v Haywards*, but the claimant in *Grattan v McNaughton* (2001) was criticised for failing to do so.

## 16.3.2 Slowness in responding to instructions

In the field of will-making, a failure to act promptly or to keep an appointment may be particularly fatal, as it were, should the client then die before the will can be executed. A particularly sad example, but not an isolated one, is that of *Hooper v Fynmores* (2001), where a solicitor prepared a will but had not taken it to the client for signature when the client was taken into hospital. A friend of the client passed on the message, saying they would be in touch again when the client was back home, and an appointment was made, but later the solicitor himself was taken into hospital and failed to keep the appointment. The client died before any alternative arrangements were made, and the Court of Appeal held the solicitor to have been negligent in that last failure.

In the recent case of *Feltham v Bouskell* (2013), a solicitor was found liable for failing to chase up a medical report. He had accepted instructions to draft a new will by which the 90-year-old

---

5 Eoin O'Dell, 'Restitution, Rectification, and Mitigation: Negligent Solicitors and Wills, Again' (2002) 65 Modern Law Review 360.

testatrix would give the bulk of the estate to a niece on whom she appeared to be reliant. He needed to be satisfied that he had a client who was mentally capable both of giving him instructions and of changing her will, and arranged to instruct the testatrix's doctor directly to prepare a medical report. When the client died before the solicitor could act on the report, he was found liable because he had taken on the responsibility for satisfying himself of the capacity issue but did not chase up the report, which took five weeks. The case has, however, been criticised because, though the solicitor's concerns about the testatrix's mental state were reasonably grounded given her age, and it was appropriate to seek a medical report, the testatrix was 'a feisty old lady with a strong personality', who, when her solicitor did not turn up, arranged for the proposed new residuary beneficiary, the niece, to prepare the will and arrange for its execution. Notably, though the claimant in the action was the niece, the claim was therefore not that she had lost out under the will, but that the challenge to the will by the beneficiaries under the previous will would not have happened had the solicitor been more prompt. The niece succeeded in her claim about costs, but it has been suggested alternatively that the testatrix could have been regarded as having terminated the solicitor's retainer, as surely would have been the case had the new will been prepared, in the same terms, by another solicitor.

### 16.3.3 Domicile and conflict of laws

Questions related to domicile are increasingly causing difficulty, as cross-border living becomes more accepted, perhaps as a result of easier travel as well as the ability of European citizens to work anywhere across the Union. As previously discussed (see 15.6), domicile is not a matter of paperwork but is more a state of mind, and so some careful consideration may need to be given to establishing what a person's domicile is. It could make all the difference to how their will should be drafted.

A person's domicile can of course change, although this does not happen easily. In *Perdoni v Curati* (2011), the testator, whose wife had predeceased him, had made a will in the 1980s leaving all his English property to the wife's niece and nephew. In 1994 he made a holographic (handwritten) will in Italian making his wife his sole heir. If the later will revoked the earlier one, then his English property would go on intestacy to his sister in Italy. The first question to be considered was where he was domiciled, because that would dictate which laws applied. If he was domiciled in England, the English will was not revoked, but it would be if he had been domiciled in Italy. In the end the court found that he was domiciled in England but that in any case the Italian will did not wholly revoke the English one.

There has been particular focus on the issue of domicile domestically in the area of family provision claims (see 15.6), and this may be where changes will be seen in the near future.

### 16.3.4 Severance of joint tenancies

The difference between holding a house on a joint tenancy and holding it on a tenancy in common is one to which lawyers are introduced early, in their compulsory land law courses. Students can find it difficult to grasp, and the general public rarely does so at all, particularly because tenancies in common of land at law have not been possible for almost a century, so the issue arises in equity only and is not even immediately obvious in ownership documentation. Clearly the point at which the difference becomes vital is when one of the parties dies, and it is also clearly then too late to rectify the situation if a joint tenancy should have been severed so that the client's wishes would take proper effect. A joint tenancy cannot be severed by will.

Severance is easy to effect, and effecting it when it is unnecessary is a risk worth running if the alternative risk is leaving the property on an inappropriate joint tenancy. The failure to ensure that a beneficial joint tenancy was severed was the substance of the claim in *Carr-Glynn v Frearson*

(1998), where property passed by survivorship (under a joint tenancy) to a nephew, instead of to a niece as the testator had intended. The niece sued and the Court of Appeal held the solicitor negligent, saying that, whether or not the solicitor had checked the deeds, a notice of severance could have been served immediately to ensure that the joint tenancy was definitely severed. This would have ensured that the gift of an interest in the property would be effective.

## 16.3.5 Ascertaining and recording testamentary capacity

Many wills are contested on the basis that the testator lacked the mental capacity to make a will. Such claims are often accompanied by assertions that the testator did not know and approve of what was in the will, or of undue influence.

Claims of undue influence and lack of knowledge and approval can be headed off by the professional using and recording their use of good practice. Where instructions appear to come from a third party, or someone seems to be pressurising or even hurrying the person who is giving instructions and signing the will, clearly enquiries should be made and the outcome recorded.

Testamentary capacity (see Chapter 3) can be more difficult. The Law Society has produced jointly with the British Medical Association a booklet of guidance, *Assessment of Mental Capacity*, which may assist. The will drafter should do all that is reasonably possible to prevent the will being challenged on the grounds of lack of capacity. If there is any doubt, the testator should be encouraged to obtain a medical report. If the testator refuses, the will drafter should protect their own position (as well as possibly confirming the testator's strength of mind) by making a detailed file note, and – as always when advice is not being accepted – the advice should be repeated in writing, including the risks being run as to future challenges to the will, and a copy of that advice should preferably be signed by the testator as well. Refusals are not uncommon; the testator may reasonably feel insulted by the suggestion that they may be mentally incapable, and medical reports can cause delay as well as expense. However, any future litigation would no doubt be even more expensive.

Even where there is no medical report, there is a strong presumption that, if the proper procedures can be shown to have been followed, the will will stand. In *Gill v Woodall* (2010), the court cited Lord Hatherley in *Fulton v Andrew* (1875) saying:

> When you are once satisfied that a testator of a competent mind has had his will read over to him, and has thereupon executed it,... those circumstances afford very grave and strong presumption that the will has been duly and properly executed by the testator.

Lord Neuberger MR said (at para 16) that 'a court should be very cautious about accepting a contention that a will executed in such circumstances is open to challenge'. He pointed out the practical effects of being too ready to accept such challenges:

> Wills frequently give rise to feelings of disappointment or worse on the part of relatives and other would-be beneficiaries. Human nature being what it is, such people will often be able to find evidence, or to persuade themselves that evidence exists, which shows that the will did not, could not, or was unlikely to, represent the intention of the testatrix, or that the testatrix was in some way mentally affected so as to cast doubt on the will. If judges were too ready to accept such contentions, it would risk undermining what may be regarded as a fundamental principle of English law, namely that people should in general be free to leave their property as they choose, and it would run the danger of encouraging people to contest wills, which could result in many estates being diminished by substantial legal costs.

As already mentioned (16.1.5), often multiple grounds are produced to challenge wills, and this is particularly the case where it is asserted that there was some gap between what the testator wanted and what the will appears to say. In *Singellos v Singellos* (2010), the judge, Andrew Simmonds QC, discussed the interrelationship of knowledge and approval, testamentary capacity and due execution. He confirmed that the phrase 'knowledge and approval' refers to a test of whether the will truly represents the testator's testamentary intentions, and that 'In normal circumstances, knowledge and approval is established by proof of testamentary capacity ... coupled with due execution of the Will'. Knowledge and approval will then be inferred by the court unless there are circumstances that arouse suspicion. He emphasised that what constitutes such circumstances depends on the facts of the case. Thus merely asserting a lack of testamentary capacity and in effect trying to put the propounder of the will to proof is unlikely to work: if there is a proper-looking will, something substantial and relevant must be asserted if it is to be questioned.

## 16.3.6 Bankrupt beneficiaries

The status of beneficiaries is also a potentially important issue. When a person is made bankrupt, a trustee in bankruptcy is appointed for them and all their property vests in the trustee in bankruptcy.[6] This includes choses in action (intangible forms of property) such as their interest in an unadministered estate (see 13.11). If a personal representative pays out monies to an undischarged bankrupt beneficiary he or she may be liable to the trustee in bankruptcy.

In *Re Bertha Hemming Deceased; Raymond Saul & Co v Holden* (2008), it was also confirmed that when a person goes bankrupt during the administration but is discharged from the bankruptcy before the administration is completed, nevertheless the right to have the estate administered has already passed to the trustee in bankruptcy, and the trustee in bankruptcy will also have the right to receive the assets on distribution. Richard Snowden QC held that the composite right had already passed to the trustee in bankruptcy:

> Because the entitlement to receive such assets as may comprise the residue in the future is the very foundation for the legatee's right to compel due administration of the estate, it seems to me that there is no sensible basis upon which the two can be separated.

A personal representative who paid out to the discharged bankrupt in error would therefore potentially be liable to the trustee in bankruptcy.

There is a searchable register of bankrupts on the Internet, but it will not necessarily show the information needed if the bankruptcy has been discharged. As well as asking a beneficiary whether they have been made bankrupt in the previous five years, it is prudent and usual to make a 'bankruptcy search' in the Land Charges Register against the person's name. If the person's name is found there, written evidence should be obtained that it refers to a different person, or the bankruptcy search entries should be removed before it is safe for the personal representatives to make a payment to the beneficiary. As always, in cases of uncertainty the personal representatives can seek directions from the court.

A person who is unable to meet their debts immediately may make an Individual Voluntary Arrangement with their creditors by which they formally agree a schedule of repayment over time.[7] There is a searchable register of Individual Voluntary Arrangements on the Internet. If a beneficiary is found to be on the IVA register, the personal representative should look at the terms of the arrangement so as to find out who the correct person to pay is. However, a beneficiary who has made an IVA will generally still have a right to receive payment and give a good receipt.

---

6  S 436 Insolvency Act 1986.
7  Ss 252–263G Insolvency Act 1986.

### 16.3.7 Criminal offences

Occasionally there is fraud or forgery in the field of succession. A particular issue to which solicitors must be particularly alive, and in relation to which they are now heavily regulated, is money-laundering, a process by which money arising from illegal transactions is transferred amongst assets and accounts so as to appear 'clean' when it comes out again at the other end.

Ongoing monitoring of business relationships and care in transactions that might be used for money-laundering or furthering terrorism is required by the Money Laundering Regulations 2007, and the Proceeds of Crime Act 2002 requires the reporting of suspicious transactions. Solicitors may be particularly vulnerable because their client accounts may be used as a means of laundering money. The risk in administration of estates is regarded by the Law Society as low, but still extant. It suggests being particularly alert to the definition of criminal conduct in the 2002 Act where the estate assets have been earned overseas, and making particular checks on the sources of any funds earned or located in a 'suspect territory'. Note however that money acquired through benefit fraud or tax evasion is also covered. A solicitor who discloses suspicions may continue to work on the matter so long as no funds are transferred or any irrevocable steps taken.[8]

Suspicions that beneficiaries are not disclosing gifts from the deceased made within seven years before death (and so liable to IHT) are not of the same order, but the position in such a case should be considered in the light of the solicitors' conduct rules. Similarly, where dealing with overseas assets, particular care should be taken to establish any tax liability in the foreign jurisdiction.

## 16.4 Where the will seems to be wrong: an outline of practical approaches

Where the will itself seems to be wrong, and the testator has died and so is in no position to put it right, the court may have power to alter the words. There are three such powers to alter the words in a will:

(a)   omission for want of knowledge and approval by a court of probate;
(b)   rectification in equity under s 20 of the Administration of Justice Act 1982 (where the testator died after 1982);
(c)   rectification by a court of construction where the will on the face of it can be construed as containing an error and showing what the true intention was (rare in practice).

### 16.4.1 Omission of words in probate for want of knowledge and approval

Words can be omitted in probate if the testator did not know and approve of them. The court had no power to add words to a will if the testator died before 1983, because that would have contravened the Wills Act 1837. A court of probate could only omit, and then only if it did not alter the sense of the rest of the will. This was the reasoning, set out by Latey J, behind the decision in *Re Morris* (1971); the method of all those available which produced the result the nearest to the testatrix's true intention. This should be compared to the situation in *Marley v Rawlings* (2014) (see 4.11.12), where although the will purported in its opening words to be the will of

---

8   *Bowman v Fels* (2005).

Mr Rawlings' wife, it clearly could not be her will as she had not signed it. Mr Rawlings had signed it, and in the proceedings it was successfully claimed that he was the testator for the purposes of s 9. It was found from the evidence that it had been Mr Rawlings' intention at the time he signed the will that it should have effect. Therefore, although the contents of the unrectified will did not satisfy the requirement of full knowledge and approval, and even if the will did not satisfy the requirements of s 9, it was open to Mr Marley to invoke s 20 of the 1982 Act.[9]

### 16.4.2 Applications for rectification

Speculation as to a person's true intention is not sufficient grounds on which to rectify their will in which, in a formal way, that person was presumed to have set out their testamentary intentions.[10] Lord Neuberger noted in *Marley v Rawlings* (2014) that there was no limit to the extent of the courts' power to rectify wills. In that case, rectification amounted to 'transposing the whole text of the wife's will into [the husband's] will … the greater the extent of the correction sought, the steeper the task for a claimant who is seeking rectification'.

An application for rectification must be made within six months of a grant of representation unless the court gives leave for an extension of time. The application should be supported by an affidavit setting out the details of the application including the grounds on which it is based and evidence of the testator's mistake and true intention.

Applications for rectification may be made in effect by solicitors seeking to mitigate the effects of error: in this situation, it is particularly useful that, as Hodge J pointed out in *Re Ryan, Gerling v Gerling* (2010), the six-month time limit for applying for an order can be extended indefinitely by the court. The scope of applications relating to solicitors' error was interestingly considered by Behrens J in *Clarke v Brothwood and Others* (2006), where the will as drafted appeared to include the substitution of 1/20 for 20 per cent and left the testator partially intestate. The court therefore held that the will could and would be rectified, commenting, however, that the case put by the other side, which was not incompatible with the wording of the Act, would mean that a mistake in typing the will could be rectified, and a mistake in recording the client's instructions could be rectified but a mistake in recording that was faithfully typed out by a solicitor without thinking about it could not be rectified. As the judge said, it would be 'difficult to see why Parliament should have intended such a consequence'.

### 16.4.3 Construction

A court of construction can construe the will as if certain words were inserted, omitted or changed, if it is clear from the will itself first that an error has been made in the wording and, second, what the substance of the intended wording was. This is difficult to show in practice.

### 16.4.4 Deeds of variation and the rise and fall of the *Hastings-Bass* rule

As discussed (see 14.20) it is common for disclaimers and variations to wills to be made by agreement amongst beneficiaries for tax reasons. They have in effect two years to rearrange the provisions in the will so as to minimise the tax burden by making the appropriate documents. In a similar spirit, where trustees have made errors that have led to tax disadvantage, they have applied to the courts to have matters rearranged so as to minimise both tax and the potential

---

9 *Marley v Rawlings* (2014), para 809.
10 *Bell v Georgiou and Another* (2002).

attribution of fault to the trustees. This practice itself arguably went wrong though: over some years a further practice, described by Robin Mathew QC of New Square Chambers as 'a heresy ... the earnest application of principle without the benefit of perspective'.[11] The heresy amounted to a practice of courts habitually excusing trustees' errors in the use of their discretion, and it was ended by the Supreme Court in 2013.

The practice was established particularly in the case whose name it bore: *Hastings-Bass*. The practice grew of allowing trustees to have their decisions invalidated where the error consisted only of lack of sufficient careful thought or an unforeseen tax implication. Trustees would assert that this meant they had failed in their duty as trustees and that the court should therefore invalidate whatever decision they had taken that had led to the extra tax. For a couple of decades, the courts allowed this practice, but in *Futter v Futter* in the Court of Appeal (where tax liability arose because the trustees' advisers gave advice that was out of date), Longmore J described the application of the rule as having taken a 'seriously wrong turn'; and that analysis was upheld by the Supreme Court in *Pitt v Holt; Futter v Futter* (2013).

The rule now is that trustees' actions or lack of them must be sufficiently serious to amount to a breach of fiduciary duty before the court will intervene. Mistake as to tax effects is not sufficient, but where trustees have conscientiously obtained and followed professional advice, this is still available as a defence. Otherwise, the question is whether the trustees' decision is voidable or void: if it was truly outside their powers, in which case it would be void. The circumscribing of the *Hastings-Bass* rule means that the process, or heresy, can no longer be used routinely to avoid problems in the administration of estates, that it is less likely to attract applications not least because it cannot be used to excuse trustees' defaults, and that the issue is returned to being one of trustees' liability rather than a way of arranging the tax affairs of estates.

## 16.4.5 Removing personal representatives: s 50 Administration of Justice Act 1985

There was nothing in the inherent jurisdiction of the High Court that allowed the removal of a personal representative.[12] An administration action could be commenced, but, as the Law Commission said in its 23rd Report, this was 'an extremely clumsy, costly and time consuming procedure' and to be recommended only in exceptional cases, though things were different once the personal representative had become a trustee as there were always means within the court's power to control trusts.[13] The power introduced under the Judicial Trustees Act 1896 was also difficult to use, and in 1985 a significant change was made under the Administration of Justice Act of that year. It became relatively easy to remove an executor or administrator, although one still had to move into the contentious probate arena to do it. This power is reserved to the High Court, which may in its discretion remove existing personal representatives, though it may not remove all of them; or it may appoint someone to act in their place. Substitute representatives could always be authorised by the court to charge for their services.

In *Goodman v Goodman* (2013), the court considered whether s 50 could be applied to a person before they had actually taken out the grant of probate. The family members had fallen out amongst themselves and, presenting a more difficult issue, there was an earlier case that appeared to say that, until a person had taken out a grant and thus had the status of personal representative, there was nothing relevant to s 50 from which they could be removed by the court. However, Newey J, after considering the history of s 50 AJA 1985 and its intended use, managed to

11  Robin Mathew, 'A Heresy Extinguished: *Hastings-Bass* Reformed', New Square Chambers Legal Update, June 2013, art 1, www. newsquarechambers.co.uk/files/Newsletters/Legal%20Update%20-%20June%202013.pdf.
12  *Re Ratcliff* (1898).
13  *Re Smith* (1880).

distinguish the point and to find that s 50 AJA 1985 could be used. The application was by an executor and beneficiary, seeking that an independent professional be appointed because of the familial disputes. The judge pointed out that, had the objection to the use of s 50 AJA 1985 succeeded, it would have generated even more expense and delay than the unsuccessful objection had, and he considered that the use of the process was itself 'symptomatic of the breakdown in relations between the parties'. Nevertheless, the removal or replacement of personal representatives may often, as here, be the way to resolve intractable difficulties related not to the will itself, or the solicitor who drafted it, but to the personalities of and relationships amongst the executors or administrators, or perhaps especially the beneficiaries.

Note that where the situation is one of mutual wills, Lewison J in *The Thomas and Agnes Carvel Foundation v Carvel and Carvel Foundation, Inc* (2007) thought that s 50 AJA 1985 did not apply. Instead, a person wanting to remove a personal representative should apply under s 1 Judicial Trustees Act 1896 or, if not, then he analysed the situation of the personal representative administering the estate of the second to die as a trustee for the purposes of s 1(2) of the 1896 Act and the situation of the person claiming to be entitled as that of a beneficiary under the same Act.

So far as mutual wills in general are concerned, this is an area mined with potential for negligence actions against solicitors. In *Charles v Fraser* (2010), the court found *per curiam* that it was the plain duty of a solicitor, then as now, faced with two people wishing to make reciprocal wills, to ascertain their intentions as to revocation, to advise as to the effect of making mutual wills and to ensure that any agreement the testatrixes wished to make was clearly and accurately recorded. Many lawyers explicitly include a statement in mirror wills that the will is not intended to be a mutual will. As an alternative, clients are likely to be encouraged to include a life interest trust with the power to advance capital to the life tenant instead of making a mutual will, particularly if the life tenant is the deceased's spouse. If however wills are indeed intended to be mutual, all the terms of mutual wills should be made clear in the wills, since the court will not be able to imply terms where there are express provisions. This would also concentrate the minds of the potential mutual testators on the possible consequences of their actions.[14]

## 16.5 Human rights claims: delay, discrimination and disposal of the dead

Claims relating to the will itself are considered above, but a new field of dispute has emerged in recent years that focuses not on errors in the will itself so much as the law and legal process surrounding wills. It has not proved possible to harmonise wills and succession at the regional level, though see 6.2, but the European Convention on Human Rights has occasionally been brought to bear on their content and process.

The two principal areas of claims are delay and discrimination. As the UK has fared reasonably well in this area, these will be considered here only in brief. Both academics and practising solicitors will want to bear in mind, however, that – as recent approaches to the rights of the dead may suggest – the potential for new approaches to vindicating rights on the basis of the ECHR is probably yet relatively untapped in the field of succession.

### 16.5.1 Delay

Excessive delays in proceedings are a contravention of Article 6, the right to a fair trial in the determination of one's civil rights, including a hearing 'within a reasonable time'. There have

---

14  Mark Pawlowski and James Brown, 'Problems with Mutual Wills: A Study of Probate Practice' (2012) 76 Conveyancer and Property Lawyer 467.

been many cases brought on this basis, including a considerable number related to succession cases.

The cases brought tend to contain one or both of two elements that make them unsustainable. The first is that they are often cases of considerable complexity, where the delay cannot necessarily be attributed to any deficiency on the part of the country's processes. The other is that the applicant has often contributed substantially to the delay by failing to issue proceedings on time or pursue matters promptly.

The basis on which the European Court of Human Rights (ECtHR) will consider such cases was set out *Frydlender v France* (2000). This was not a succession case, but an employment case. However, the test was adopted explicitly by the court in the succession case of *Träxler v Germany* (2010), where it said:

> The Court reiterates that the reasonableness of the length of proceedings must be assessed in the light of the circumstances of the case and with reference to the following criteria: the complexity of the case, the conduct of the applicant and the relevant authorities and what was at stake for the applicant in the dispute.

The applicant in *Träxler* was, however, ultimately successful. The original proceedings whose delay was complained of had been started in 1996 and concerned an action by the children of the deceased against his wife and heiress. Delays were caused by, amongst other things, illness amongst the judges, a settlement proposal that did not go through, changes of counsel and approaches to the process, delays caused by legal aid applications and postponement by the court pending informative decisions elsewhere. The ECtHR found that the length of the proceedings was excessive, and that the government of Germany had been unable to persuade it that there had been no breach of the Convention. It found breaches of Article 6, the right to a hearing within a reasonable time, and of Article 13, the right to an effective remedy, and awarded Ms Träxler €10,000 plus about half that in costs.

## 16.5.2 Discrimination

The case of *Burden and Burden v UK* (2007) was perhaps somewhat tangentially a succession case. Two elderly sisters who had inherited a great deal of property and money from their father objected to the liability to Inheritance Tax that would arise on the death of the first, to the detriment of the sister left behind. The sisters had always lived together and, hypothetically, the remaining sister might have had to sell their home in order to pay the IHT on the death of the first – though in fact these particular sisters had enough money to cover the eventuality. Their case was that UK law discriminated against them in not allowing them, as being within the prohibited degrees of affinity, from marrying or forming a civil partnership, and so gaining the benefit of the spouse exemption from IHT. The European court found that the UK was entitled to set its marriage, civil partnership and tax systems in this way and that there was no actionable discrimination. Had they not done so, they would have run against those elements of the IHT and general tax systems that aims to have people distribute their assets more widely rather than keeping them narrowly within the family.

More commonly, discrimination disputes have concerned the entitlements of non-marital children. This taps into a related vein to that of *Burden*, since historically succession law was designed to keep property within the formal marital family, and it is only in recent decades that the definition of the family has changed radically. The focus on women's and children's rights is still developing. In Britain, most automatic discrimination against non-marital children has already been taken out of the law (see 11.17). However, it does remain an area in which public policy touches on what people may feel is purely private law. The scope of the legal process in this area was dealt with in the leading case in this area, *Marckx v Belgium* (1979), where the ECtHR said that the court

> cannot remain passive where a national court's interpretation of a legal act, be it a testamentary disposition, a private contract, a public document, a statutory provision or an administrative practice appears unreasonable, arbitrary or, as in the present case, blatantly inconsistent with the prohibition on discrimination established by Article 14 and more broadly with the principles underlying the Convention.

In the leading case of *Camp and Bourimi v Netherlands* (2002), Mr Bourimi died without formally recognising the child Ms Camp was then pregnant with, and he was not recognised as Mr Bourimi's child until two years later. Mr Bourimi's parents did not believe that the child was his, or that the relationship with Ms Camp was significant. They believed that they and their other children were the heirs of the deceased, and moved into his house, ejecting Ms Camp. The local court refused to oust the parents, and because the formal recognition of the child, Sofian, did not refer back to the time of Mr Bourimi's death, Sofian was not entitled to the house under Netherlands law. The ECtHR held that there was no interference with Sofian's Article 8 rights to respect for his family life. However, there was discrimination against him, contrary to Article 14, because his exclusion from his father's estate on the basis of his non-recognition at the time of his father's death was an unlawful discrimination against him on the grounds of birth. Sofian was therefore awarded damages.

Most cases are less obviously satisfying to the applicants. A related case, *Hout v UK* (2007), concerned a Dutch national living in Australia. Her father, who was from Guernsey, died in 2004 leaving no other children. His estate passed to his siblings, but the applicant contended that he had intended it to pass to her. Guernsey had passed human rights law dealing with the recognition of non-marital children in 2006, but it did not have retroactive effect that would give the applicant what she wanted. Where changes to the treatment of illegitimacy are concerned, the timescale is often significant, as countries have gradually removed the discrimination;[15] the Guernsey case has not yet been decided on the questions of whether there was a breach of Articles 14 and whether the facts disclosed a breach of Article 13 (the right to an effective remedy). The case of *Pla and Puncernau v Andorra* (2004), a complex dispute based on a will requiring that 'the future heir to the estate must leave it to a son or grandson of a lawful and canonical marriage', required consideration of religious as well as national and civil law, but confirmed that adopted children were included in the definition of children. In *Haas v Netherlands* (2004), the non-marital child's claim to entitlement in the estate was based on a claim that his notary father had visited him and paid for his upkeep, and that the child called him Daddy. The court found, however, that Articles 8 and 14 did not apply. It held that there was no relevant 'family life' which the law was not respecting and that the case was not equivalent to *Camp and Bourimi* (2002): it was open to the child or his mother to seek a declaration of paternity.

### 16.5.3 Disposal of the dead

Human rights laws have been most influential on British succession law in the interesting new area of the rights of the deceased over their bodies. This is perhaps the logical next step from the issue of end-of-life decisions over health care, since both areas were historically usually dealt with by the relevant authorities – doctors, or funeral directors – dealing with the close

---

15  See for example *Vermeire v Belgium* (1993), *Mazurek v France* (2000); *Fabris v France* (2013).

family. Whilst this would mean the wishes of the family could be substituted for those of the deceased, it also meant that it was particularly unlikely anyone would contest what had been done. It was confirmed in *Buchanan v Milton* (1999) (see 12.1) that the primary duty of proper burial lies with the personal representatives, but a rights-based approach has a different emphasis.

In *Hartshorne v Gardner* (2008), the deceased was the son of the parties. He had died intestate in a road accident leaving no instructions as to burial, and his parents each had different ideas as to where he should be buried. The court considered that the place where the deceased had made his life was an important matter: he worked and had lived in Kington, and that was where his brother, his fiancée and all of his friends were based. Though his father supported burial in Kington, his mother wanted him to be buried in Worcester, where she could more practically visit the grave. However, the other factors outweighed her views, especially as they had not been close in recent years.[16] But in *Burrows v HM Coroner for Preston & Joan McManus* (2008), the deceased had died in a Young Offenders Institution. The right of burial was claimed by his paternal uncle, with whom he had previously lived, and his mother. On the basis of case law,[17] Cranston J found two Articles of the ECHR relevant: Article 9, freedom of religion, and Article 8, the right to respect for one's private and family life, and that the deceased's views must be taken into account, and that they were liable to displace the rights of those entitled to a grant under the NCPR. In *Ibuna and Tanoco v Arroyo and Dignity Funerals Ltd* (2012) (see 12.1), though, Peter Smith LJ said he had 'some difficulty in a post-mortem application of human rights in relation to a body as if it has some independent right to be heard', and confirmed the view in *Buchanan v Milton* (1999) that the executor had the primary duty of disposal and was entitled to have regard to the deceased's expressed wishes but was not bound by them.

## 16.6 Conclusion

Succession is an established area of study and practice, ripe for more academic and professional development.

Changes in technology give rise to opportunities for debate as to the effect of non-traditional property transactions, as where it now appears probable that *donationes mortis causa* of registered land will never come into being because one cannot pass dominion over a dematerialised title. It also invites discussion of the possibility of new forms of wills, made electronically as is almost everything else now, or even new forms of property that may present particular issues when the 'owner' dies.[18]

The development of human rights has begun to influence succession law, which also now produces ever more nuanced case law not only on the substance of the topic but on its practice – especially contentious practice. The scope of lawyers' duties where their most obvious client is dead is being explored, and the growth of cross-border issues gives rise not only to issues of law and practice but also to new regional and international laws. Beyond these practical matters lie the big questions of life and law – What constitutes property? When should the state control an individual's right to dispose of their property as they wish? How far will the rights of private property be attenuated for the benefit of those who might otherwise be a burden on the state,

---

16  Conway 'Dead, but Not Buried: Bodies, Burial and Family Conflicts' (2003) 23 Legal Studies 423; Thomas L Muinzer, 'The Law of the Dead: A Critical Review of Burial Law, with a View to Its Development' (2014) Oxford Journal of Legal Studies, http://ojls.oxfordjournals.org/content/early/2014/04/17/ojls.gqu009, accessed 17 February 2015.

17  *X v The Federal Republic of Germany*, application number 8741/79, 10 March 1981, DR 24, 137; *Dödsbo v Sweden*, ECHR 2006 No 5.

18  Lilian Edwards and Edina Harbinja. '"What Happens to My Facebook Profile When I Die?": Legal Issues Around Transmission of Digital Assets on Death', in by Cristiano Maciel and Vinícius Carvalho Pereira (eds), *Digital Legacy and Interaction* (Springer International Publishing 2013) 115.

whether as regards general taxation or claims against a relative's estate, especially where the 'owner' of the property rights is dead?

Students should enjoy the disputes and conflicts in the legislation and case law, against the background of the breadth and depth of succession law, which concerns everyone, since we are all going to die.

## 16.7 Further reading

### Book chapter

Lilian Edwards and Edina Harbinja "What Happens to My Facebook Profile When I Die?": Legal Issues Around Transmission of Digital Assets on Death', in by Cristiano Maciel and Vinícius Carvalho Pereira (eds), *Digital Legacy and Interaction* (Springer International Publishing 2013) 115.

### Journal articles

Sebastian Allen, 'White v Jones: What if the Claimant Was Not the Client?' (2012) 18 Trusts & Trustees 401.

Kit Barker, 'Are We Up to Expectations? Solicitors, Beneficiaries and the Tort/Contract Divide' (1994) 14 Oxford Journal of Legal Studies 137.

Harold Luntz, 'Solicitors' Liability to Third Parties' (1983) 3 Oxford Journal of Legal Studies 284.

Thomas L Muinzer, 'The Law of the Dead: A Critical Review of Burial Law, with a View to Its Development' (2014) Oxford Journal of Legal Studies, http://ojls.oxfordjournals.org/content/early/2014/04/17/ojls.gqu009, accessed 17 February 2015.

Eoin O'Dell, 'Restitution, Rectification, and Mitigation: Negligent Solicitors and Wills, Again' (2002) 65 Modern Law Review 360.

CG Veljanovski and CJ Whelan, 'Professional Negligence and the Quality of Legal Services: An Economic Perspective' (1983) 46 Modern Law Review 700.

James Weale, 'Probate Litigation: The Incidence of Costs' (2014) Trusts & Trustees, http://tandt.oxfordjournals.org/content/early/2014/07/06/tandt.ttu117.abstract, accessed 17 February 2015.

# Index